W9-BKP-829

International Handbook on Local Government Reorganization

CONTEMPORARY DEVELOPMENTS

edited by
Donald C. Rowat

GREENWOOD PRESS
WESTPORT, CONNECTICUT

Library of Congress Cataloging in Publication Data
Main Entry under title:

International handbook on local government
   reorganization.

   Bibliography: p.
   Includes index.
   1.   Local government—Addresses, essays, lectures.
I.   Rowat, Donald Cameron.
JS67.I57   352'.0009'047   79-54063
ISBN 0-313-21269-4

Library of Congress Catalog Card Number: 79-54063
ISBN: 0-313-21269-4

First published in 1980

Greenwood Press
A division of Congressional Information Service, Inc.
88 Post Road West, Westport, Connecticut 06881

Printed in the United States of America

10 9 8 7 6 5 4 3 2 1

Contents

III. THE BASIC UNITS IN DEVELOPED COUNTRIES

Introduction   209

North America and Japan

Western Europe

Eastern Europe

IV. THE BASIC UNITS IN DEVELOPING COUNTRIES

V. CONCLUSION: TRENDS AND PROBLEMS

Tables

Figures

Introduction

In recent years, local governments around the world have undergone structural reorganization to a remarkable extent. Even many of the older Western democracies, where local self-government has been well established since the turn of the century, have reorganized their systems of local government. In some cases this reorganizations has involved mainly metropolitan areas, where serious problems had been created by rapid urban growth, as in Canada, Switzerland, and the United States. In others, however, the reorganization has been more far-reaching, and has involved either creating or restructuring a second tier of regional government, as in Belgium, France, Italy, and Norway, or reorganizing the basic units of local government, as in Sweden and West Germany, or both, as in Great Britain. Similarly, most of the countries of Eastern Europe and many of the developing countries have been reorganizing their basic units of local government in recent years.

This remarkable phenomenon indicates that there must be common causes for these reorganizations and that countries can learn much from each other about their experiences with reorganization. Written with this aim by experts on the countries or areas concerned, this book is a compendium of forty-eight essays on recent reorganizations of local government around the world.

Perhaps the most significant recent development in the structure of local government has been the creation in several Western democracies of a second tier of local government either for metropolitan areas or for a whole country or province. Therefore, the book begins, in Part 1, with essays on countries in which there has been a recent restructuring of government in metropolitan areas, while Part 2 deals with recent cases of a second level of local government for a whole country or province being created or officially proposed. This second level is usually referred to as regional or county government but may also be called district government (British Columbia) or provincial government (Finland). This type of reorganization has taken place mainly in the developed Western countries, even in federal countries that are divided into provinces or states and already have a tier of government between the central and local governments. Thus, Canada's two most populous provinces, Ontario and Quebec, have established a second level of local government for all of their large metropolitan areas, while British Columbia has created a second level for the entire province, including its two large metropolitan areas, Vancouver and Victoria. Except for British Columbia, however, the states or provinces in most federal countries have not thought it necessary to create a regional level of local government.

Parts 3 and 4 discuss the recent restructuring of the basic units at the lowest level of local government in developed and developing countries, respectively. For easy reference, each part of the book is divided into geographical regions of the world, and under each geographical heading the essays are arranged alphabetically by country. However, in Part 2 countries in which official proposals have not yet been adopted have been placed at the end of each section in order to distinguish them from countries where regional reorganization already has been implemented.

In a few cases of restructuring metropolitan or regional government in conjunction with that of some or all of the basic units in a country, there are separate essays on these developments in different parts. Thus, a country's name may appear more than once as the title of an essay. For example, in the case of the United States there is an essay in Part 1 on metropolitan areas and another in Part 3 on the general system of local government. Similarly, there is an essay in Part 1 on metropolitan areas in West Germany as well as essays in Part 3 on the reorganization of the basic units of local government in North-Rhine Westphalia and in the rest of West Germany. In the cases of Finland and Sweden, proposals for restructuring provincial government are dealt with in Part 2, while the reform of the basic units of local government is discussed in Part 3. Otherwise, where there has been a restructuring of metropolitan and/or county or regional government as well as the basic units this has been dealt with in in Parts 3 and 4, as, for instance, in the cases of Great Britain and the fertile crescent countries of the Middle East. In order to indicate the nature of the reorganizations undertaken or proposed, I have provided a brief introductory comment to each part.

Since so many countries have reorganized their system of local government in recent years, a book that tries to deal with the whole world is bound to be long. I have struggled with the problem of excessive length in two ways. The first was by insisting that the authors write short essays or, if they did not, by exercising the editor's prerogative of eliminating nonessential material. The second was to concentrate on the developed Western countries, which have provided the main models of local government for the rest of the world. To cover Eastern Europe and the developing countries, I tried to include for each region or continent two important countries in which a recent reorganization had taken place and then searched for an area specialist who could write an essay for all of the remainder of the region. This approach had the added advantage of providing a number of genuinely comparative essays.

Hoping to draw some general conclusions from these recent experiences with reorganization, I tracked down a specialist on each part of the book to write a comprehensive analysis of all the essays in that part. Although this procedure delayed the book's completion by many months, readers will find the insights revealed well worth the delay. I then added some concluding comments of my own on general trends and problems.

This book deals more with structures and institutions than with politics and the political process. The comparative study of local government and politics is at such a rudimentary stage that one must start with the basic structural information, which itself is extremely difficult to gather and compare on a worldwide basis. Moreover, although the study of politics rather than institutions is currently popular with political scientists, attempts at studying local politics on a comparative basis have not been notably successful because we do not yet have a deep enough understanding of the varying political cultures involved. At the same time, the governments of the world are very much concerned with finding viable structural arrangements for local government. If we wish to make a significant contribution to solving the current problems of local government, then, we must devote more attention to its structural aspects.

Unless one has actually been engaged in preparing or contributing to a book requiring such widespread international collaboration—in this case, fifty-two scholars from around the world—it is difficult to imagine all of the problems of search, uncertainty, delay, translation, and editing involved. I am happy to be able to say that I received an enthusiastic response to this project from scholars around the world. Those who could not write an essay themselves advised me on others who could and on which countries were worthy of inclusion. Almost inevitably in such a wide-ranging project, it proved impossible to include all recent reorganizations. For instance, Denmark consolidated its basic units of local government some years ago, but I failed to find a Danish author willing to write up this experience. Although considerable time has passed since the essays were written, at my request the authors have been kind enough to update them to the end of 1978.

The state of scholarly publishing being what it is, the authors undertook their essays without any assurance of payment or even publication and cheerfully endured the editor's whip under these conditions. I should like to thank all of them for doing so and for making valuable contributions to the English-language literature on this subject. I should also like to thank Janice Tyrwhitt for helping me put some of the translated essays into more readable English.

D. C. R.
June 1979

PART I

The Government of Metropolitan Areas

Introduction

One of the most puzzling structural problems of local government is how metropolitan areas should be governed. Since the end of World War II, the rapid growth of metropolitan areas has been a worldwide phenomenon. Populations of large cities have spilled over their boundaries into surrounding municipalities that are usually too small and ill-equipped to handle the problems of large-scale urban migration. The postwar metropolitan area is in many ways a social and economic unit, yet usually local government is fragmented within it. Many political problems are of area-wide concern, and many services can be supplied most cheaply and efficiently on a metropolitan basis. Yet, usually the metropolitan area has no corresponding unit of area-wide government to handle these problems and services.

The earliest device used for meeting the problem of urban expansion was to expand the boundaries of the central city, but this device failed because the city's annexation of territory was opposed by the surrounding municipalities. As a result, annexations were too little and too late to control the expansion and to solve the ensuing problems of urban sprawl. Indefinitely extending the boundaries of a large city as it grew meant that eventually its local government was no longer really "local." The government of a city with a million or more inhabitants could be as far away from its citizens as a state or national government.

In recent years the developed Western countries in particular have been experimenting with various structural arrangements designed to deal with the problem of governing metropolitan areas. One of the most interesting of these has been the creation of a two-tier form of local government for metropolitan areas in the Canadian provinces of Ontario and Quebec. Involving a division of powers between the local governments and a new metropolitan government, the two-tier form of local government is commonly referred to as a metropolitan federation. In his essay on Ontario, Professor Plunkett describes how this form was first installed by the Ontario government in the Toronto metropolitan area in 1953, and eventually in all of the large metropolitan areas in that province. The Toronto plan was so successful that it was discussed widely in Canada and the United States. Professor Quesnel-Ouellet's essay explains how this two-tier plan later was adopted by the province of Quebec for its two largest metropolitan areas, those surrounding the cities of Montreal and Quebec, and for the part of the National Capital Region that lies within the province of Quebec and surrounds the city of Hull, the Outaouais region. The province of British Columbia also established a two-tier plan for Vancouver and Victoria when it set up a second tier of regional government for the whole province. This means that all of the large metropolitan areas in Canada except Calgary, Edmonton, and Winnipeg now have a second tier of government covering the whole metropolitan area.

An essay on Winnipeg has been included because it is a particularly interesting case. Winnipeg's metropolitan area was the second in Canada to be provided with a metropolitan government modelled on the Toronto plan, in 1960. However, it was considered unsatisfactory, for reasons explained by Professor Axworthy in his essay, and in 1970 a new government in Manitoba under the New Democratic Party decided to consolidate the whole metropolitan area into a single city, popularly called "unicity," with a single city government. The problem of the remoteness of such a government from the citizens was to be met by elected district and neighborhood advisory councils. This scheme may be regarded as an alternative to the two-tier plan—as perhaps a more effective way of combining efficiency and citizen participation in large metropolitan areas. For this reason it has attracted much attention recently in Canada and the United States. Since

Professor Axworthy has been a close observer of its operation for several years, readers will be interested in his conclusions regarding its success.

Professor Zimmerman's essay reveals how much experimentation has taken place in the United States in an attempt to solve the problem of metropolitan government. He explains why, despite a number of interesting experiments with various metropolitan arrangements and the availability of the county in many cases as the basis for a metropolitan government, the idea of a general purpose metropolitan government has not been popular in the United States.

Since there has been considerable restructuring of local government in the metropolitan areas of France, Switzerland, and West Germany, essays have also been included in Part 1 on these countries. West Germany in particular, as Professor Siedentopf explains, has done much experimenting with various governmental arrangements for metropolitan areas.

Many countries have a second level of regional or county government, some units of which may cover metropolitan areas and serve as their metropolitan governments. Thus, the district governments for Vancouver and Victoria in British Columbia have been granted special powers to deal with metropolitan problems. Such cases are dealt with in Part 2 or, where the restructuring of the second level occurred as part of the reorganization of the whole system of local government, in Parts 3 or 4.

Part 1 makes no claim to include all metropolitan restructuring that has occurred apart from the general reorganization of local government. Most of the world's largest metropolitan areas, such as London and Paris, have had a long history of special arrangements for their government, which are quite different from their country's general system of local government. For instance, metropolitan London's unique two-tier form of government, with metropolitan and borough councils, was reorganized some years before the general reform of local government in Britain and is not dealt with in this book. Since it would have been impossible to include in a single volume a discussion of recent reorganizations in all large metropolitan areas, Part 1 includes only countries where a considerable amount of metropolitan reorganization has occurred. Readers interested in the government of a particular one of the world's large metropolitan areas may consult the two-volume work by Robson and Regan, *Great Cities of the World*.

NORTH AMERICA

CANADA
UNITED STATES

Canada: Ontario

T. J. Plunkett* **1**

The first and undoubtedly most widely publicized attempt at metropolitan reorganization in Canada was the establishment of the Municipality of Metropolitan Toronto in 1954, which provided for a multipurpose metropolitan structure superimposed on the traditional municipal framework. While local municipalities yielded many of their responsibilities to this new creation, some of their elected representatives were members of its decision-making body, the metropolitan council. The Municipality of Metropolitan Toronto is, in fact, a federation of municipalities within the Toronto metropolitan area.[1]

In the 1960s the province of Ontario embarked on a comprehensive program of regional government reform. By 1974 ten regional governments and one district government had been established. With few variations in detail these new regional structures are based on the Metro Toronto principle of federation.

The purpose of this paper is twofold: to set out the principal elements of what has come to be known as Ontario's regional municipal reform program and to provide an assessment of the general acceptability of the regional governments established under it. However, any such assessment would quickly become an exercise in sterile organizational mechanics without considering the current dichotomy in Canada, and particularly in the province of Ontario, between the traditional view of the purpose of local government and what now appears to be an emerging, but not yet adequately defined, conception of its role in the political structure. As this dichotomy evolves from the impact of urbanization on the institutional framework of local government, it is essential to note its implications for local government in Canada and, more specifically, the province of Ontario.

*Director, School of Public Administration, Queen's University, and author of *Urban Canada and Its Government* (Toronto: Macmillan, 1968).

URBANIZATION

From the Canadian perspective the expansion of cities and the ever-increasing concentration of urban growth in metropolitan or regional urban and urbanizing areas is a relatively recent phenomenon. It should be emphasized that it is really only since the end of World War II—just three decades ago—that Canada became a predominantly urban nation. And Ontario became the most urbanized of the country's ten provinces. In 1941, for example, there were ninety local municipalities in all of Canada with populations exceeding 10,000, and these accounted for approximately 42 percent of the total Canadian population. However, thirty-nine of these municipalities, or about 43 percent, were located in the Province of Ontario. By 1971 the number of local municipalities in Canada in this category had increased to 246, and these accounted for about two-thirds of the total Canadian population. Eighty-three of these were located in Ontario, representing almost 74 percent of the total population of the province and 42 percent of the total Canadian population in 1971. Of the twenty-five municipalities in Canada with populations exceeding 100,000 in 1971, fourteen were located in the Province of Ontario and accounted for nearly 47 percent of the province's population. Thus, while Canada as a whole has felt the pressures of urban expansion in the post-World War II period, they clearly have been strongest in Ontario.

Despite the continuing concentration of population in relatively few urban centers, more than 4,300 general purpose local government units have been established throughout the country—more than 800 in Ontario alone. While some of these serve relatively small populations (often less than 500 persons) in isolated communities, many others exist within the orbit of major urban centers and are little more than bedroom communities. Others, originally established to serve rural communities, are now becoming urbanized.

The Traditional Role of Local Government

Canada's local government structure was developed to meet the needs of its largely pre-urban history. The traditional role of local government was confined mainly to the provision of a limited range of what might be termed essential community housekeeping services. The principal concern of municipal councils was to ensure the prudent administration of these activities without placing what was considered an undue burden on the property tax. This concept of local government predominated until almost the end of the first half of this century, and it was a role suited to a period characterized by both a limited view of the responsibilities considered appropriate for governments and relatively little use of the automobile in comparison to the post-World War II period.

From this kind of society there emerged a concept of local government as a local service delivery agency exercising responsibilities that were viewed largely in nonpolitical terms. In keeping with this view there evolved a strong belief in the virtues of the nonpartisan tradition. It was believed that supposedly independent-minded members of council could make the necessary decisions on the delivery of local services in the "best interests of the community." These decisions were not considered to have any political content; it was assumed that controversial issues involving conflicting values or policy choices simply would not arise in the realm of local government. Technical and financial criteria were considered to be the main determinants of local decision making.

A New Dimension in Local Decision Making

As a result of the urban expansion of the post-World War II period, the principal concerns of the residents of Canada's growing cities and expanding metropolitan and regional urban areas were extended beyond the provision of essential community services. There is little real argument over their continued quantitative and qualitative extension. The new concerns now involve such matters as the social dislocation caused by urban redevelopment, the provision and location of public housing, the effective control of skyrocketing urban land prices, the protection of city neighborhoods with a particular life style, and the resolution of the conflict in urban transportation between the movement of people (urban transit systems) and the movement of vehicles (expressways)—to name but a few.

The old tools of technical and financial criteria alone are totally inadequate for these new issues, for example the determination of a city's transportation requirements. If decision makers choose to emphasize vehicular passage to and through the city, more expressways or freeways will be the likely result. But such a proposition is almost certain to be challenged by those increasing numbers of citizens who are alarmed by the effects of such facilities on the city's social and economic life, as well as its physical appearance. In the past such a decision would have been regarded within the service delivery framework of extending the roadway network, with technical and financial considerations the primary criteria and the social consequences largely ignored. The omission of the latter from the local decision-making process is no longer tolerable.

From the illustration regarding transportation it must be concluded that the elevation of a decision that had long been regarded as falling within the traditional framework of a roadways delivery system to a consideration of transportation requirements widens the whole spectrum of concerns. Not the least of these is the question of community choice between modes of transportation—the movement of people or vehicles—and their respective effects. In any city there will be advocates of a range of choices who apply differing value systems and varying perspectives of the consequences of the choices they advocate. All of this involves conflict and controversy that can be

resolved only through a representative and responsive political system, elements that have not been particularly emphasized in the present structure of
local government.

It is demonstrably clear from this assessment that the traditional local
government structure is not geared to deal with the rapid expansion of municipal services and responsibilities, particularly in metropolitan and regional
urban areas. It is even less capable of furnishing the essential political dimension required to resolve or even respond to the controversial issues generated
by aroused citizen concern for the quality of life in cities. The scale and kind of
metropolitan and regional structural reform that has been attempted in Ontario
has to be viewed against this background of the traditional role that has been
assigned to a local government in the political life of the country.

REGIONAL MUNICIPAL REORGANIZATION IN ONTARIO

While all metropolitan areas in Canada experienced the problems associated
with rapid urban growth and expansion immediately after World War II, the
most critical of these was metropolitan Toronto, where the pace of urban
expansion was the most dramatic in the country. Virtually all growth in this
area was concentrated in suburban municipalities, particularly in the large,
formerly rural townships. It soon became evident that the suburban municipalities were finding it difficult to furnish a minimum level of such essential
services as water, sewerage, and roads, to say nothing of meeting expanding
educational needs. Some form of orderly planning, not only for growth and
development but also for the pooling of limited municipal fiscal resources on a
metropolitan basis, became mandatory. The structure developed to meet these
needs was the Municipality of Metropolitan Toronto. A municipal federation
was created through the establishment of a second-tier government, which
would be responsible for certain assigned functions on a metropolitan basis.
The thirteen municipalities retained responsibility for specific local functions
and were represented on the council of the new metropolitan municipality.

The Toronto achievement attracted much external interest, particularly in
the United States. It came to be regarded as a sort of breakthrough in metropolitan reform. In retrospect, however, it can be considered as only a step—albeit
an important one—in the process of achieving a form of government for a
metropolitan area. Its establishment in 1954 had important results. It provided
the area with means to deal with the financing and constructing of essential
facilities. Further structural revisions, made in 1967, reduced the number of
municipalities from the original thirteen to six by a series of amalgamations.
But, the scheme also postponed the demand for a more genuinely responsive
political structure which would provide a decision-making mechanism capable
of resolving metropolitan issues involving conflicts in ideology or social goals
and objectives. The political and administrative machinery that proved so

effective in dealing with concrete services, such as the construction of major collector sewers, water production plants, and sewage treatment plants, did not, in the first ten years of its existence at least, have to deal with genuine political controversy. Moreover, there was widespread public acceptance of both the need and the desirability of such facilities. Thus the kind of accommodation and compromise necessary put a minimum of strain on the decision-making mechanism that had been established.

By the latter part of the 1960s there was growing evidence that the Toronto federation was experiencing difficulty in resolving or clarifying the metropolitan populace's new concerns, including such controversial issues as public housing, downtown redevelopment, the effects of freeway route choices on the social and economic life of particular neighborhoods, the allocation of resources between freeway construction and the extension of public transit, and new concerns in public welfare. The emergence of these issues has brought into question the metropolitan structure's ability to give genuine political expression to the conficts that inevitably emerge and to provide the kind of political accommodation that results in decisions that have reasonably wide support. As a consequence, the Province of Ontario established a royal commission to examine the structure of metro Toronto. This commission, headed by a former premier of the province, reported in June 1977, but the provincial government has not been inclined to act on any of its recommendations.[2]

The Regional Municipal Program

During the 1960s Ontario turned its attention to other major urban areas within the province, urban or urbanizing regions characterized by social and economic interdependence but fragmented politically in terms of the number of local governments that had been established. Initially, the province launched a series of local government reviews in a number of designated regions. Each review was carried out by an independent review commission. With the exception of the Lakehead, where there was an amalgamation of the former cities of Fort William and Port Arthur, all of the new regional governments involved the establishment of a second-tier regional municipality based on the metropolitan Toronto model (see Table 1.1). Reports of review commissions recommending other structures were given scant attention.

The objectives of the Ontario government's approach to regional government were stated by a former premier in the following terms:

The basic aim of the Government in arriving at the policy of establishing regional governments is to make local government as strong and meaningful as possible. As our society becomes more complex, the people of Ontario to whom governments are responsible must be able to participate in the decisions and directives of their government. If our municipal partners are unable to cope with the problems they face because of their small size, limited financial resources and inability to provide the services which all residents of Ontario should expect, participation becomes meaningless.[3]

The main focus of this regional municipal reform program has seemed to be on the creation of regions large enough to deal more efficiently with specific problems and to deliver particular services. It was recognized that many small local governments could not deal adequately with certain services. This was reflected in a statement by a cabinet minister responsible for municipal affairs in the province who observed:

Municipal governments—over 900 of them—cannot be expected to deal effectively with problems that are common to the residents of wider local areas . . .there are too many special purpose boards and commissions. They obscure the accountability of councils, and impede comprehensive priority setting.[4]

Despite these statements of objectives, the structures established were based on the much more limited objective of grouping municipalities into larger units to deal with specific problems. In the main, regional municipalities were given certain responsibilities to direct the orderly development of such services as water, sewerage, and roads. However, the local or area municipalities retained responsibility for purely local aspects. Similarly, parks were distinguished as being regional or local in nature with responsibility divided accordingly. Planning was divided similarly, but it was intended that local plans would fit into regional plans. With one or two exceptions responsibility for the police was transferred completely to the regional government. However, responsibility for fire protection generally remained local, as did recreation. Public health services, except in metropolitan Toronto, were generally transferred to the regional government, as was responsibility for social welfare services.

The financing arrangements in all of the new regional governments followed the pattern already established in metropolitan Toronto under which the regional municipalities do not act as tax collectors. This task still rests with the local or lower tier municipalities. However, the regional government determines the regional levy, the annual funds that must be raised to support regional responsibilities in addition to the support provided through grants and subsidies from the province. The regional levy, a uniform percentage of the local property tax, is based on the equalized property assessment of all municipalities in the region, so that each municipality is required to raise an amount proportionate to its share of the regional property tax assessment within that region. Regional governments, like the Municipality of Metropolitan Toronto, also undertake and control long-term borrowing, whether for regional or local purposes.

Table 1.1 provides some basic data on the twelve metropolitan, regional, and district governments established to date. It will be noted that these twelve governments serve a total population of over 5 million people representing more than 60 percent of the province's total population. Two of these, however, have relatively small populations but relatively large areas. One is actually a resort area of scattered small communities, while the other is an urbanizing area of small towns that has become the location of a couple of large

Table 1.1
CANADA: METROPOLITAN AND REGIONAL GOVERNMENTS IN ONTARIO, 1979

Name	Date Established	Area (Square miles)	1976 Regional Population	Population of Largest Municipality and (Percent of Regional Population)	Size of Metro or Regional Council[b]	No. of Area or Lower-Tier Municipalities Currently	No. of Area or Lower-Tier Municipalities Previously
Municipality of Metropolitan Toronto	January 1, 1954[a]	243	2,154,279	678,103 (31)	38	6	13
Regional Municipality of Ottawa-Carleton	January 1, 1969	1,100	521,418	305,975 (58)	31	11	16
Regional Municipality of Niagara	January 1, 1970	720	362,388	122,773 (36)	29	12	26
Regional Municipality of York	January 1, 1971	645	202,232	56,333 (28)	17	9	14
District Municipality of Muskoka	January 1, 1971	1,688	34,622	10,553 (30)	23	6	25
Regional Municipality of Sudbury	January 1, 1972	1,088	166,767	97,618 (58)	21	7	15
Regional Municipality of Waterloo	January 1, 1973	519	291,164	131,801 (45)	25	7	15
Regional Municipality of Peel	January 1, 1974	484	377,013	250,399 (66)	22	3	10
Regional Municipality of Halton	January 1, 1974	405	266,145	103,728 (41)	25	4	7
Regional Municipality of Durham	January 1, 1974	875	243,839	105,663 (43)	31	8	21
Regional Municipality of Hamilton-Wentworth	January 1, 1974	432	409,331	312,162 (76)	28	6	11
Regional Municipality of Haldimand-Norfolk	April 1, 1974	1,117	86,841	18,928 (22)	20	6	28
Total		9,316	5,076,039		310	85	201

[a]Dates indicated are the effective dates of incorporation, that is, the date the new municipality came into legal existence. In most instances the actual date of incorporation was up to six months earlier to allow for an organizational period.
[b]Includes chairman.

industrial developments. When these two municipalities and metropolitan Toronto are excluded, it will be observed that none of the other regional governments is unusually large in terms of population, ranging in 1976 from 166,767 in the Regional Municipality of Sudbury, to 521,418 in the Regional Municipality of Ottawa-Carleton. It will be noted, too, that the establishment of regional governments was, in most instances, accompanied by a reduction in the number of area or lower-tier municipalities.

Regional council membership is based on an allocation of a specific number of representatives from each of the lower-tier municipalities within the region, as set out in the legislation establishing the regional municipality. Thus, some members of local councils serve in a dual capacity, on the regional as well as the local council. However, the voter does not make a direct choice at election time of the representatives on the regional council; rather its composition is determined on an indirect basis.

Regional Criteria

In explaining the rationale for establishing regional governments the province accepted the two prime values of *access* and *service* that had already been elaborated in the report of the Ontario Committee on Taxation (the Smith Committee). The committee defined these values as follows:

By *access* we mean the most widespread participation possible on the part of all or virtually all individual citizens. Access to governments in terms of capacity to influence public policy decisions and to enhance responsive and responsible administration is, of course, fundamental to any democratic government. But that local government is peculiarly conducive to the realization of the access value has been recognized by political philosophers since the time of Plato. The central reason is that the capacity of government to provide access is in part an inverse function of size. The local government that is sufficiently small to enable all citizens to participate directly in public affairs—in short, the town meeting government—is that local government which is capable of realizing the access value most fully.

By *service* we mean not only the economic discharge of public functions, but the achievement of technical adequacy in due alignment with public needs and desires.[5]

From the interplay of these two values the province derived certain criteria about the size of the regional governments. Thus, in a policy statement entitled *Design for Development: Phase Two* issued in 1968, the province emphasized that its objective was "a set of regional governments with a population of at least 150,000 to 200,000" and supported this objective on the following grounds:

On the service side the major determinant of size is the population base needed to carry out effective local government programs. Our experience and discussions with other departments and with municipalities suggest conclusively that a minimum regional population of from 150,000 to 200,000 is required for the efficient provision of most local services.

It is interesting to note that *Design for Development: Phase Two* was issued in 1968, just before any regional governments, other than Metropolitan Toronto, had been established. The statement implied that the proposed regional governments might reflect a variety of both one and two-tier approaches and direct and indirect methods of election. In reality, however, those established are all two-tier governments and all but one have the regional councils selected by indirect election, the single exception representing a combination of both direct and indirect election.

In the five-year period, 1969-74, the Province of Ontario established one district and ten regional governments. In 1972 it served notice that it would pursue a more aggressive approach. With the release of *Design for Development: Phase Three* in June 1972, the minister responsible for municipal affairs described the approach to that point as "very slow and selective." He emphasized that the province would assume responsibility for "what is ultimately and properly provincial policy—the design of the structure and organization of local government and the definition of responsibilities that should be carried out within that structure." *Design for Development: Phase Three* also set out a timetable for action, which indicated that proposals for municipal reform affecting virtually all of southern Ontario would be presented by 1975. But this timetable was never kept. In fact, by 1973 opposition to the regional government reform program was evident, and the province abandoned its aggressive approach. It remains, therefore, to indicate some of the grounds for this discontent and to assess the regional government program in Ontario.

REGIONAL GOVERNMENT IN ONTARIO: AN ASSESSMENT

Given the province's impressive record of legislative action in the establishment of regional governments as well as a timetable for further reorganization of local government, the question arises as to why little further action was taken after 1973. It is unlikely that any single factor caused the province to abandon its regional government reform program, but a number of developments may have played a part.

By the early 1970s the effects of the establishment of the first regional governments began to be felt by citizens living within their jurisdictions. One of the basic objectives underlying the establishment of regional governments was the improvement in the delivery of services on a regional basis. However, it was inevitable that the accompanying upgrading of certain services would result in increased expenditures. As a consequence, in some regions certain residents, particularly those in formerly rural areas, were now required to pay an increased tax levy for urban services provided by the new regional governments. Moreover, some of these residents could not perceive that these services would have any immediate benefit to them. These citizens were joined by others who believed that the two-level approach to government only increased the size of the total bureaucracy and resulted in unnecessary duplication of effort. These effects combined to produce a vocal expression of discontent in some regions.

At the political level, mayors and councillors found that the new regional government made their role much more demanding, at least in the case of those who had to serve not only on the local council but as members of the regional council as well. Elected representatives in this position found themselves with conflicting loyalties—to the regional government and to the local municipality to which they were elected and which provided their political constituency.

In the implementation of the regional government reform program the province made little effort to explain its purpose to the public. As one observer has noted, "It [the province] has not seen its role as one whereby there was an obligation to go out to the public at large in an attempt to explain, or to educate the citizens as to what was happening and why."[6] For the most part the province confined its explanations to meetings with local politicians, administrative officials, and associations of municipalities. A more aggressive public education program might have helped the public better understand the purpose of the reorganization undertaken.

While these factors undoubtedly contributed to public unease about the new regional governments, the concept of the two-tier structure also played a part. It helped, for example, to make government less intelligible, and it diminished rather than enhanced citizen access to government.

The province's tendency to favor the two-tier regional structure was undoubtedly based on the initial success of Metropolitan Toronto. Moreover, while the stated objectives of the reorganization emphasized both access and service it was the latter that became the prime focus. Thus, the two-tier structure seemed to be a relatively safe way to secure larger units for more efficient service delivery:

Functions were allocated between upper (or second tier)—the regional governments, and area municipalities (or lower tier). In short, "mini-metros" all over the province. Politically, this was a safe way to reallocate services and functions as there would be a minor consolidation of the smaller municipalities, but essentially most local government units would remain governmentally intact. At the lower tier, most often they were rendered functionally impotent.[7]

The retention of the smaller area or lower-tier municipalities was apparently for the purpose of providing greater citizen access while the establishment of the upper-tier or regional government was to provide a more effective area for the delivery of major urban services. However, access to "functionally impotent" units means little when the major decisions are made elsewhere by a more remote regional government over which the citizen has little, if any, direct influence.

Accompanying the process of regional municipal reform in Ontario has been a tendency for the province to play a more direct role in determining the acceptable level of service delivery in such areas as public health, welfare, roads, and planning through the extensive use of a system of conditional grants and subsidies and regulatory controls. This development tends to reduce further the scope of local decision making. If this trend continues there is a real possibility that "a profound alteration of the role of local government will occur, as it will be expected and required more and more to conform to broad policy guidelines established by the Province."[8] Moreover, this suggests a movement in a direction at odds with the goal announced in the 1973 provincial budget, "to enhance the autonomy of municipalities and broaden the scope for decision making at the local level."

In a very real sense the regional governments established in Ontario reflect the difficulty of balancing the requirements of access and service. The latter seems to have been given major emphasis. But the apparent lack of concern with access may simply reflect adherence to the traditional view of local government in Ontario as primarily concerned with service delivery through an institutional structure that emphasizes a nonpartisan and nonpolitical approach. Under the two-tier structure it is difficult to ensure that controversial issues receive a thorough hearing, particularly if the decision-making responsibility is located at the regional level where the representatives are not directly accountable to the electorate.

Since 1973 the province has virtually abandoned the regional municipal reform program. In addition to the establishment of a commission to review metropolitan Toronto, study commissions were established to review the structure and operation of government in three other regions.[9] All have now reported but no action has been taken on any of their recommendations. With one exception the reports of these commissions all accepted the two-tier system; their recommendations were aimed mainly at modifications. The exception was the commission reviewing the Hamilton-Wentworth region, which proposed a consolidated single city government for the region. This alternative has not found favor with the provincial government.

If, as has been suggested here, the two-tier approach to regional government as developed in Ontario does not appear to be the most appropriate means of governing urban areas, what would constitute an alternative approach? The most likely would appear to be the consolidation of all units in a region into a single city. This would seem to be feasible in those regions where a central city is now dominant. In other regions the approach might be a single-tier county with responsibility for all local functions within the region.

It has to be noted that in terms of population only one regional government, other than metropolitan Toronto, exceeds 500,000 persons. Thus, if served solely by a single-tier government, none would be excessively large in terms of population. While there undoubtedly is some justification for the maintenance of a two-tier system in metropolitan Toronto, where the population served exceeds 2 million persons, there hardly seems any real need to perpetuate this arrangement in regions where the population is less than 500,000.

But if a single-tier government is to serve effectively in place of the existing regional governments in Ontario, at least two important conditions would have to be met. First, such governments should be designed to improve representation and accountability. This would undoubtedly mean establishing larger councils than are generally the case in Canada. Representation would have to be on a ward or district basis, and electoral units should represent identifiable communities or neighborhoods where possible. Ideally, electoral units should not exceed a population range of 9,000 to 12,000 persons. In a region with a population of 300,000, this would mean a council of approximately thirty members.

As the council of a single-tier municipality, whether an enlarged city or a county, would now be dealing with all issues, both local and regional, citizens would have direct access to the decision makers involved and would be able to hold them accountable. Under regional governments as presently constituted the citizen votes only for members of the local councils and does not know at the time of voting just who will be serving on the regional council where the major decisions are made. At best the citizen has only indirect access to or influence on this body. A directly elected representative council of a single-tier government offers the possibility of enhancing citizen access to government.

The second element required in this proposed approach to regional government is recognition of the need for an identifiable political executive. In most Canadian municipalities this role is supposed to be undertaken by the mayor, who is generally elected at large. However, the incumbent of this office is rarely given any real power and is usually dependent on his powers of persuasion. In regional government the role of the political executive usually accrues to the council chairman who, like the mayor, does not possess much formal executive power.

In establishing a political executive for regional government, the parliamentary model—familiar to most Canadians through its operation at the provincial and federal levels of government—might serve as a basis. Under this arrangement the council would select a small committee from among its members to serve as an executive body and to whom executive powers could be assigned. Such a body could provide the bridge between the legislative body and the administration and provide a focus for policy initiation.

While other elements obviously deserve consideration, the foregoing has been suggested in broad outline as an alternative to the present structure of regional government in Ontario. At the very least it suggests a structure and process through which controversial urban issues might receive an appropriate airing and through which citizens might be able to achieve greater influence on decision making than they have presently under the two-tier arrangement. The alternative proposed is also based on the notion that government involves more than service delivery, that an important part of its role is to deal with issues with an important bearing on the quality of life in urban centers. *Design for*

Development: Phase Three revealed an awareness of the need to develop this broader role for local government:

As a general observation about local government, I think it is fair to say that over the years there has been a preoccupation with something called "service delivery". A vast array of municipalities and special purpose bodies, boards and commissions have grown up to deliver services. Surely, however, government is more than an instrument through which to deliver services. Its central role must be to deal with issues. One of the major and insistent issues of our time is the quality of life and conservation and preservation of our environment. Taken as a whole our "system" of local government is unsuited to providing the broad policies and priorities to tackle this issue.

Subsequent developments, however, have given little indication that the institutional means will be established to undertake this role.

NOTES

1. For a complete review of the establishment and subsequent development of the Municipality of Metropolitan Toronto, see Albert Rose, *Governing Metropolitan Toronto: A Social and Political Analysis, 1953-1971* (Berkeley: University of California Press, 1972).

2. *Report of the Royal Commission on Metropolitan Toronto*, June 1977 (Toronto: Queen's Printer, 1977).

3. From a statement by Hon. John Robarts, former premier of Ontario, in *Design for Development: Phase Two*, 28 November 1968 (Toronto: Queen's Printer, 1968).

4. From a statement by Hon. W. Darcy McKeough, included in *Design for Development: Phase Three*, 19 January 1972.

5. *Report of the Ontario Committee on Taxation* vol. 2 (Toronto: Queen's Printer, 1967), p. 503.

6. Lionel D. Feldman, *Ontario 1945-1973: The Municipal Dynamic* (Toronto: Ontario Economic Council, January 1974), p. 27.

7. Ibid., p. 15.

8. Ibid., p. 41.

9. See *Report of the Ottawa-Carleton Review Commission*, October 1976; the *Report of the Hamilton-Wentworth Review Commissioner*, May 1978; and the *Report of the Regional Niagara Study Commission*, June 1977.

Canada: Quebec

*Louise Quesnel-Ouellet** 2

Quebec has twice as many local governments as Ontario, and ten times more than British Columbia.[1] This local government system has been marked not only by the French regime but also has been subjected to American ideologies. Quebec has inherited from the French regime its large number of local governments. The only local organizational unit during French occupation was the parish. Communities developed in the surroundings of the church. Following Lord Durham's recommendations in 1839, local governments were created based on the territorial boundaries of the parishes, and these boundaries became the basis for local government until the middle of the twentieth century.

American local government ideologies have been adopted rapidly by Quebec municipalities. For example, Quebec has the most city managers of any province in Canada. The first Canadian city to adopt this new form of local government was in the Province of Quebec. The "good government" movement, which accompanied this new form, reflected such values as effectiveness, democracy, economies of scale, and opposition to political parties at the local level.[2]

The proliferation of local governments and their relative ineffectiveness were the main reasons for the local reform undertaken by the provincial government in the 1960s. Although the reorganization took the form of amalgamations, annexations, and the creation of regional governments in metropolitan areas, this study will focus on the regional governments, touching only incidentally upon amalgamation and annexation problems. The subject will be covered in three parts: the general and the immediate causes of regional reform, the structures and functions of the new governments, and the actual working as well as the current problems of the new governments.

Our analysis is based on newspaper coverage of the issues, mainly by *Le Droit* in the case of the Outaouais Regional Community, *Le Devoir* for the

*Professor, Department of Political Science, Laval University, Quebec.

Montreal Urban Community, and *Le Soleil* for the Quebec Urban Community. Interviews and discussions with leaders (both elected and nonelected) helped identify some informal aspects of the reform, while direct observation of the experience, especially in the case of the Quebec Urban Community, completed the data gathering.[3]

CAUSES OF REGIONAL REFORM

Regional reform in Quebec was brought about by two major tendencies of the late 1950s: urban growth and fiscal difficulties. Urban growth transformed the province's configuration. While 61 percent of the population was rural and 39 percent urban in 1901, the proportion had been reversed by 1961, with 26 percent rural and 74 percent urban.[4] Montreal and Quebec increased their importance as economic and social poles, attracting more and more population. This growth was accompanied by a need for additional services at the local level and by an increase in the cost of the already existing services. Hence a financial crisis occurred, with a high tax rate at the local level and municipalities almost buried under the burden of their debts. Reform was necessary to avoid a duplication of services. One objective of the provincial government was to facilitate economies of scale.[5] Urban growth also required the initiation of planning at the regional level through regional units within which the municipalities could be consulted.[6]

Regional government in the three major urban poles of the province appeared to be the solution. While assuring the maintenance of the local level with its autonomy towards the provincial government, this form of government meant a compromise between amalgamation and Balkanization and was intended to diminish the existing "futile rivalries" between municipalities. These objectives were accepted in principle by the local governments.

Each regional unit was created within a particular context. Though public protection was the key issue in the Montreal region, other problems, such as urban transportation, garbage disposal, sewage, public health, and urban development, were crucial. The Quebec Urban Community (QUC), which encompassed Quebec City, the provincial capital, had different objectives. Serving only 400,000 inhabitants, compared with the 2 million in the Montreal Urban Community (MUC), the QUC was intended primarily to promote the economic development of the region. Among the major issues were public transportation, the financial disparity between local governments and the central city, which paid the entire cost of certain services used by the whole area, the lack of control of urban development in the region, and the need for more cooperation among municipalities within the region.

The Outaouais Regional Community (ORC) was also created in a particular context. Its core city is Hull, directly across a river from the federal capital, Ottawa. In 1968 a report on the administration of the region had mentioned that the area's problem was not so much the presence of the federal government as the absence of the Quebec provincial government. The ORC was designed to give Quebec an authority that could negotiate on equal terms with two bodies on the Ontario side of the river: the federal government's National Capital Commission and the Ottawa-Carleton regional government. The Outaouais region wanted to receive as many grants from the federal government as the municipalities on the Ontario side received. The ORC also was intended to solve the public transportation problem in the area, stimulate the economic development of the region, and help the municipalities coordinate their commercial and tourist activities, the region being the first access to Quebec for all tourists coming from Ontario and the western part of Canada.

Thus, the main reasons for the creation of regional governments in Quebec in 1969 were urban growth and financial problems. The three regions had similar concerns, such as public transportation, urban development and planning, and public security, but each region needed its own solutions to its own particular problems. These were the short-term objectives of regional government as seen by the provincial authorities and the local governments. The abolition of rivalries between municipalities and the development of a regional political consciousness were intermediate objectives. The provincial government's long-term objective, although not openly stated, was to reduce the number of municipalities and eventually transform the two-tier form of government into an enlarged one-level regional government.

STRUCTURES AND FUNCTIONS OF REGIONAL GOVERNMENTS

The three regional units created by the provincial government as an intermediary level between the municipalities and the province were called "supramunicipal" governments because of their close link with the municipal level. This link was assured by a representation of the municipalities on the regional council and by a limitation of the functions transferred to the regional unit. Hence the structures, power relationships, and functions of the new entities must be examined in order to understand the significance of the reform. A comparative approach will be used, since the three regional units have both similarities and peculiarities.

All three regional governments are public corporations with powers similar to those of the municipal governments. They are decentralized units like the municipalities because their officials are elected (though indirectly) and because of their power to decide on specific questions and to levy taxes.

The Regional Council

The three regional governments are headed by a regional council. In the MUC, the regional council has remained the same since 1969. Each municipality is represented by one member, usually the mayor, and Montreal is represented by all members of the city council, that is, fifty-two councilmen and the mayor. The ORC and the QUC regional councils have been changed drastically since 1969. At the beginning, their composition followed the same model as the MUC, but recent amalgamations and annexations as well as legislative modifications in the regional structures have transformed the regional governments. Hence, in the Hull area, the number of municipalities was reduced from thirty-two to eight in 1974, and regional members have decreased from thirty to fourteen (including the chairman, seven members representing the two major cities, and one member for each of the remaining municipalities).

In the Quebec region, the number of municipalities is now thirteen, and the regional council has thirty-one members (see Table 2.1), each municipality being represented by one member per 15,000 habitants. This gives eleven members to Quebec City, another eleven members to the other three large cities, and one member to each of the remaining nine suburban municipalities.

Table 2.1
QUEBEC: NUMBER OF MUNICIPALITIES AND MEMBERS ON REGIONAL COUNCIL, 1969-78

	Municipalities		Members on Council	
	1969	*1978*	*1969*	*1978*
Montreal Urban Community (MUC)	29	29	81	81
Quebec Urban Community (QUC)	26	13	26	31
Outaouais Regional Community (ORC)	32	8	32	14

In the ORC as well as the QUC each member of the regional council has one vote, while in the MUC votes are weighted according to population, each member having at least one vote. For Montreal, the fifty-three representatives (mayor and councilmen) share the city's total votes.

The Executive Committee and Other Committees

The composition of the executive committee differs depending on the number of muncipalities and the importance of the central city.

Table 2.2 shows the predominance of the central city within the MUC executive committee. In fact, all members of Montreal's executive committee also sit on the MUC executive committee. Clearly, Montreal holds a strong position on the regional council, with a majority of seats on both the regional council and its executive committee. Although members from the noncentral cities are more numerous in the QUC executive, the predominance of the central city had also been felt. From the formation of the committee until 1978, the two heads of the regional unit (regional council chairman and executive chairman) were from Quebec City.

Recent amendments have put an end to the bicephal leadership that was a target for general discontent from the municipalities except Quebec City. The QUC now has only one chairman who is head of the executive committee (now called the administrative committee) and chairman of the regional council. Actually, the chairman is the mayor of one of the smallest municipalities within the QUC. The ORC executive committee was abolished by the provincial legislature in 1975 when the size of the regional council, which facilitated the direct participation of its members in the decision-making process at this level, was reduced. The most important responsibilities of the executive committees are the general supervision of the administration, the preparation of the annual budget and the hiring of the regional government's employees. This role can be extended depending upon the existence of other committees.

Table 2.2
QUEBEC: MEMBERS OF EACH REGIONAL GOVERNMENT'S EXECUTIVE COMMITTEE

	Members from the central city		Members from other cities		Other members		Total members	
	1969	1978	1969	1978	1969	1978	1969	1978
Montreal Urban Community (MUC)	7	7	5	5	0	0	12	12
Quebec Urban Community (QUC)	3	1	4	6	0	0	7	7
Outaouais Regional Community (ORC)[a]	3	—	4	—	1[b]	—	8	—

[a] *The executive committee was abolished in 1975.*
[b] *The chairman of the committee was nominated by the provincial government. In the case of MUC, one chairman was exceptionally a provincial nomination.*

While committees have been formed in the ORC, no such means for participation have been opened in the QUC and the MUC except for the executive committee. Local representatives who are not on this committee participate only in the regional council meetings. This lack of general participation through committee work appears to be one of the reasons for the general dissatisfaction with these two regional governments. Committees thus seem important to the success of the two-tier type of government.

Functions and Services

In 1969, the regional governments were given two types of function: those to be handled immediately or within a few years by the regional authority, and those that eventually could be handed over to the regional government by the municipalities if they so wished. The first type included public transportation, property assessment, regional planning, data processing, uniform construction standards and traffic regulations, and public protection in the case of the MUC. The second type included water works, garbage disposal, regional libraries, low-cost housing, regional recreation facilities, and coordination of public security services.

The many services to be created and operated needed human and financial resources. The top personnel of the regional units generally came from the central city or the provincial government. If the regional unit took over a service already existing in a municipality, the personnel of the service was integrated. For example, the QUC integrated all employees working on property assessment.

Regional governments have been funded principally by property taxes and subsidies. Taxes are levied by the municipalities, which add this item to their own annual budget. Governmental subsidies come from the federal and provincial levels (federal contributions to the planning activities of the QUC and the ORC, and provincial contributions to meet the annual deficit of the regional governments). Although regional governments received per capita grants during their first years, financial support now has to be negotiated every year.

IMPLEMENTATION PROBLEMS

The Montreal Urban Community

To analyze MUC implementation problems, let us consider two phases: before 1974, when the opposition within the regional council came from the suburban municipalities, and after 1974, when the opposition of the "Rassemblement des citoyens de Montréal" (RCM) partly offset that of the suburbs.

The city of Montreal dominated numerically both the executive and the regional council although the suburbs have a veto power in the council. In the first years, the suburbs seldom intervened except to oppose many executive-prepared projects on the grounds of high cost. Discussions were complicated by the fact that some local representatives on the regional council spoke only one language, English or French. However, each member agreed to speak his own language, while documents would be published in both languages.

The fact that the MUC had always been considered as the core city's idea did not help suburban officials develop a regional political consciousness.[7] The suburbs' opposition to the budget was condemned by Montreal leaders, who argued that the suburban members should not be allowed to veto the budget as they represented only a few hundred thousand people of medium or high socioeconomic status compared to the more than a million less affluent people in the core city.

This situation changed somewhat from 1974 to 1978, when the RCM representatives on the regional council succeeded in breaking the consensus among the delegates of the central city. RCM councillors have occasionally sided with the suburbs, making it more difficult for the Montreal Civic Party leaders to control the regional government.

Nevertheless, the aims of the RCM and of the suburbs were very different ideologically. In the case of public transit, for example, the suburbs blocked the budget because of the rising costs, whereas the RCM held out for free transit services for old people. Again, when the regional plan was presented to the regional council in 1973 and discussed in 1974, the executive committee proposed that the project should be returned to it without adoption so that the executive and its planners could prepare the implementation part of the plan. The council refused this proposition because the suburbs feared they would lose their autonomy in the field of planning, while the RCM did not want to leave such an important issue to the executive.

These two cases reveal the current configuration of interests and ideologies. First, the Montreal Civic Party leaders had increasing difficulty in passing whatever they wished at the regional council, although they held a majority of seats on the executive committee. Their strategy therefore was to transfer more powers to the executive committee. Conversely, the RCM defended social policies, community involvement in policymaking, and more participation of the elected officials in the discussion of regional policies and planning. Suburban representatives wanted to protect their local autonomy and maintain existing quality of services without raising property taxes. While the suburbs' position has been reinforced with the nomination of a suburban mayor as chairman of the regional council in 1978, the core city's point of view has come back to more homogeneity since the November 1978 defeat of all but one RCM representative in the Montreal civic election.

An overall evaluation of the MUC's activities since 1969 shows some success in its implementation of major departments and services[8] but indicates major structural and political problems. The failure of the few amalgamation movements (such as the Westmount project in 1971 and the West Island plan for amalgamation in 1973) has maintained Montreal's dominance and prevented the suburbs from becoming more influential in policy making. Also, the regional government is in an ambiguous position midway between the municipality and the provincial government. It imposes an additional tax burden on local ratepayers who already complain about their ever-increasing tax bill. The use of governmental subsidies to ease this burden is regrettable; it increases the dependence of local governments on the provincial government, renders almost impossible any kind of local long-range policymaking because spending is controlled by the conditions of the subsidies, and opens the door to patronage and political intervention.

These structural problems have engendered many political difficulties. The most serious is the power imbalance that has characterized the decision-making process since the MUC's creation. This situation has been made worse by the presence of Montreal's very authoritative leaders. One of the instruments of this power is the control of information. For example, the MUC has no information service for local officials and residents. Important decisions are usually made at the executive level, under the control of the city of Montreal. Because local representatives have no effective means of participating at the regional level, journalists have commented on the MUC's false parliamentarism:

Meanwhile, in the absence of committees like those of the [provincial] Assemblée Nationale, or of regular communications, the councillors of the Community will have no choice other than to revolt against their useless role, as did members of the House of Commons or of the Legislatures a long time ago.[9]

The revolt predicted in *Le Devoir* took the form of a refusal by some suburban municipalities to pay their share of the regional budget. This gesture was strictly symbolic since the municipalities were compelled by the law to pay their contribution, but they succeeded in stimulating public discussion of their problems: lack of influence at the regional level and the intervention of the provincial government through subsidies. The dissatisfaction also prompted the Hanigan report in 1973 (issued by the MUC's executive committee and named after its chairman), which proposed changes in MUC functions and financing. The proposed solutions were not satisfactory to all parties, and in 1975 the provincial government formed a committee to study the same question. Presided over by the minister of municipal affairs, this committee included representatives from the central city and the suburbs and prepared another report on regional services and finances.

The Quebec Urban Community

Within two or three years, the new Quebec Urban Community had a well-organized structure, with its own staff (finance, information, personnel) and technical services (assessment, industrial and tourist promotion, data processing). Regional planning and urban transportation were under the control of commissions that were relatively independent of the regional council. Was this new organization effective and widely supported? In fact, the QUC has been constantly criticized. Complaints have focused on two points: the financial burden of the QUC and the municipalities' inability to play an active role in the decision-making process.

The financial problems started with the provincial government's assessment reform based on uniform norms. In some municipalities, local assessments rose as much as 70 percent. The tax rate was not proportionately lowered by local authorities and the regional data processing service, which sent the tax bills, consequently associated the QUC with the tax increase. Also, the QUC staff, like that of the other regional governments, was hired with salaries equal to or higher than those of the central city. In the view of most municipalities, this treatment was unusual and unnecessary for the well-being of the regional unit. However, the salary advantage of the QUC did not prevent a high turnover of personnel, which seriously handicapped regional government operations. The vicinity of the provincial departments is one reason for this turnover, but the inside working atmosphere and the hostile attitude of local representatives probably did not encourage a stay in the regional organization.

The municipalities' lack of power in decision making aggravated the situation. Like the ORC and the MUC, the regional council did not have the right to stop or even significantly modify the annual budget presented by the executive. If the council refuses to adopt the budget, as it did in one instance (the transportation commission's budget), the budget is nevertheless adopted automatically if the provincial municipal commission approves it.

The attitudes of regional council members were also significant in the decision-making process. The mayors sitting on the regional council were trapped between two choices: acceptance of the regional government because of provincial party pressure or because of the importance of the regional council and the influence of the other members of the council or a rejection of the QUC and a 'defense of the local municipality's interests. In fact, on the regional council a mayor is, above all, the delegate of his local council, and his initiative is very narrow.

Finally, the QUC's legitimacy was conditioned by its performance in the areas of planning and municipal reorganization. The QUC planning commission was mandated to draw up a regional plan and made amalgamation and annexation proposals in the fall of 1975, but it did not have the power to implement a regional plan. Following the 1978 amendments, the QUC received the mandate to present a regional plan that will be compulsory for the area municipalities. This reform has put an end to municipalities' periodical manifestations of discontent. While critics were encouraged by the provincial government's uncertainty in recent years, the reform will probably reinforce the regional unit by increasing its legitimacy.

The Outaouais Regional Community

The ORC was created to solve political and economic problems in the Hull region. It differed from the two other regional governments because of the rural character of many of its municipalities. The word "regional" instead of "urban" community was used for this reason. Although the ORC was the smallest regional government in terms of the population involved,[10] it was the most important politically because of the growing power of the federally controlled National Capital Commission (NCC), which owns about 30 percent of the territory in Hull. The Quebec side, therefore, needed a strong authority to deal with its federal partner.

The implementation of the regional services was achieved with some difficulties: refusal to accept the transportation commission's budget, rejection by the central city of a proposal to integrate police forces, problems in finding service staff, and a reappraisal of the ORC's planning role. This important function was confirmed to the ORC in 1975 by the provincial legislature. The control of all construction permits and zoning changes was then given to the ORC, hence giving it a power that the two other regional governments did not have. The ORC is certainly in a strategic position, but it nevertheless has a budget of only a few million dollars, while the NCC budget is more than a hundred million. ORC leaders see this as an indication of NCC dominance and expect an eventual takeover of the ORC by the NCC.

The attitudes of local governments toward the ORC were framed by their role in the decision-making process. The municipalities were permitted to participate in this process through their membership in commissions and committees. Their voting power in the regional council was first determined by the population represented by each member. This voting procedure produced an imbalance similar to that of the two other regional communities. It was, however, eliminated by the amalgamation of the thirty-two municipalities into eight local governments in 1974 and a reform of the voting procedures in 1975.

The ORC has been favorably accepted by most municipalities, except for a few with a mainly English-speaking population. The ORC is similar to the MUC with its two ethnic groups. While discussions can be carried on in both languages on committees and council meetings, only the French language is now used in written exchanges and publications of the regional government. This unilingual character has provoked dissatisfaction in some municipalities of the area. Although most municipalities were satisfied with the regional service, some movements similar to those seen in the other metropolitan areas appeared. Some municipalities adopted a resolution demanding that they be excluded from the ORC. English newspapers of the area even wrote that "the CRCRO (regional transportation commission) is so bad that it can't help but improve."

While the Hull region was struggling with these internal problems, the federally sponsored Fullerton Report of 1974 recommended the formation of a national capital district with authority over the Hull region. Leaders of the ORC were not informed of the conclusions of the former NCC chairman's report until the moment it was formally transmitted to the federal authorities. Such a recommendation would eventually necessitate major adjustments in, if not the abolition of, the ORC. Thus, the existence of the ORC is even more precarious than that of the MUC or the QUC, but for external reasons. The region's problem is no longer the absence of the provincial government, but the presence of the federal government.

CONCLUSION

The three regional governments created in Quebec in 1969 share many characteristics. Creatures of the provincial government, they must strive for survival while threatened from inside and out. Also, they have tackled the same problems, mainly public transportation and planning. It seems clear that they were created chiefly for economic and political reasons and not to solve social problems. The effectiveness of the new governments was the main concern, as measured by the quality and the cost of the services they provided.

Economies of scale were not realized. The regional budgets have increased considerably under the pressure of the general trend of the economy (for example, the MUC budget increased from $17.4 million in 1970 to $229 million in 1975, including public transportation and police protection.[11] Although it has not been proved that the services would have cost less had the functions remained local, it is certain that in some cases the quality of the services improved. During the first years, the problems encountered by the regional governments were mainly structural and political. Intended to provide coordination among the municipalities, the regional governments have turned out to be a fourth level of government. Could it have been otherwise, with new entities that were better organized than the largest city in the area and were given the active responsibility for certain services previously controlled by the municipalities?

The decision-making structure was problematic at the very beginning: the ambiguity of dual leadership, lack of participation opportunities for all members of the regional council, and the strong hold of the central city. Opposition appeared outside the regional structures, especially in the municipalities, where it had a bandwagon effect on the local population. The degree of acceptance of the new level of government by local officials has been conditioned by their role in its decision-making process. Perhaps the existence of political parties at the regional level could have allowed local officials to become more involved through discussions with party leaders and members. However, the general feeling is that party politics are not for the local or regional levels, where the problems are thought to be "mainly administrative." The effect of this early twentieth-century ideology is now evident in the dissatisfaction with the decision-making process and the difficulty of creating a region-oriented political consciousness. Some observers have suggested that local officials who sit on the regional council are in a situation of conflict of interest, having to defend their community's interests while taking part in decisions concerning the whole region. The direct election of the regional council members seems a doubtful solution to this serious problem. Unless the regional authority becomes the only local authority, direct elections would mean only a proliferation of elections and confusion for the electorate.[12] Reflection on the nature of the "conflict of interest" between local and regional levels might be more stimulating.

Political problems of regional community building have been encountered in the Montreal and Quebec regions. Although more than half the local officials of 1969 have been replaced, the present local decision makers have not learned to think "regionally" and to accept the role of the regional body. The ORC has been generally "better integrated," no doubt helped by the strengthening of solidarity that a common "enemy" often produces. The English municipalities in the Hull region, which did not feel threatened by the ambitions of the federal government, were dissatisfied with the ORC because they did not feel the pressing need of regional consciousness. These considerations emphasize the importance of integration in a political system. One factor that has directly influenced the degree of integration of the regional populations is their social status. The municipalities that have opposed the new regional governments most radically in all three cases were those with high-income residents and no evident dependence on other municipalities or the regional government.

In fact, do any of the three urban communities actually constitute a political system? According to H. Kaplan's analysis of urban political systems, it may be said that a regional government is a political system if its parts reflect either a normative or a non-normative integration.[13] It seems that none of the three regional units has attained either type of integration. No consensus on the goals and values of the system has emerged (normative integration), and no sense of instrumentality or usefulness of the regional government has been felt (non-normative integration).

What will become of the new regional governments? Will they survive even if, as systems, their parts are not integrated? Kaplan states that integration is not necessary to the survival of urban systems because the latter are stabilized by the legitimacy of the global system (provincial in this case).[14] In fact, the important reforms brought to the ORC in 1974-75 and to the QUC in 1978 by the Quebec National Assembly certainly have strengthened the regional government and favored a general acceptance of the two-tier form of government in these regions. But one should not underestimate the pressure put on the global system by its various subsystems. It is our contention that the subsystems have a network of influence strong enough to compromise the legitimacy of the global system itself. Hence the major problem of the regional governments, their need for financial resources, still has not been solved because of the pressure of competing subsystems (municipal and educational) and of the anticipated dreadful political impact of controversial changes. Since the main purpose of the global system, as of all systems, is to maintain itself, it will respond to the various and unequal pressures of the subsystems. While the pressure of the regional governments' leadership is in favor of its maintenance, the municipal officials are divided on this point.[15] Local populations are also divided if they have an opinion.[16] Other attitudes have been less identified, such as those of provincial parties and various interest and professional groups.

Further research will reveal the relative influence of these forces on the outcome, which is still uncertain. Meanwhile, one may suggest as a working hypothesis that the maintenance of the regional governments, with structures and functions substantially similar to those existing now, will be determined jointly by the legitimacy of the global system and by the power play of the various subsystems.

NOTES

1. N. H. Lithwick and G. Paquet, eds., *Urban Studies: A Canadian Perspective* (Toronto: Methuen, 1968), p. 249.

2. Syed Anward, *The Political Theory of American Local Government* (New York: Random House, 1966).

3. I am grateful to Mr. Roland Cousineau (MUC) and Mr. Jacques Forgues (QUC), who commented extensively on a first draft of this paper.

4. Jean Meynaud and Jacques Léveillée, *La régionalisation municipale au Québec* (Montréal: Editions Nouvelle Frontière, 1973).

5. Ministre Robert Lussier, *Journal des Débats* (8 December 1969).

6. Meynaud and Léveillée, *La régionalisation*, pp. 70-71.

7. Centre de recherche en droit public, *Les communautés urbaines de Montréal et de Québec*, premier bilan (Montréal: Presses de l'Université de Montréal, 1975).

8. Gérard Divay and Jean-Pierre Collin, *La communauté urbaine de Montréal: de la ville centrale à l'île centrale*, Rapports de recherche, no. 4 (Montréal: INRS-Urbanisation, 1977).

9. Jean-Claude Leclerc, "Bloc Note," *Le Devoir*, 20 June 1970. Translation by the author.

10. The population of the three regions in 1969 was: MUC 2,214,999; QUC 420,678; ORC 156,017. *Analyse budgétaire, Municipalités du Québec, année financière 1971-72* (Quebec: Bureau de la statistique du Quebec, 1971).

11. Divay and Collin, *La communauté urbaine de Montréal*, p. 100.

12. The Bureau of Municipal Research examined the possibility of the direct election of the chairman of Metro Toronto in its *Comment*, no. 152 (January 1975).

13. H. Kaplan, *Urban Political Systems* (New York: Columbia University Press, 1967), pp. 25-26.

14. Kaplan, *Urban Political Systems*, p. 19.

15. Louise Quesnel-Ouellet, "Régionalisation et conscience politique régionale: la Communauté urbaine de Québec," *Revue canadienne de science politique* 4, no. 2 (June 1971); 191-205.

16. Louise Quesnel-Ouellet, "Situations et attitudes face au changement dans les structures municipales," *Revue canadienne de science politique* 6, no. 2 (June 1973); 195-218.

Canada: Winnipeg

Lloyd Axworthy*

3

In 1972 a new, amalgamated form of local government was established in the Winnipeg region, replacing the two-tier style of government that had been operating for over a decade. This new scheme included several new institutional ideas designed to achieve wider citizen involvement and a decentralization of political control. At the time, the Winnipeg "Unicity" scheme, as it came to be called, was viewed as one of the most innovative forms of local government. Its innovative features, however, have been whittled away by successive changes made by the provincial government to the City of Winnipeg Act and by decisions of the city council. Political realities have intruded upon the visions of the Unicity architects.

The Winnipeg experiment presents an interesting case of how major institutional reform is brought about and how effective it ultimately is in altering a city's political process.[1]

BACKGROUND

Winnipeg is a city of just over half a million people constituting approximately half the population of the Province of Manitoba. The greater part of all the goods and services produced in the province are generated in the Winnipeg area, which in turn provides most of the jobs and most of the tax revenues needed to run the province.[2]

For generations there has been an underlying sociopolitical consensus shaping the city's political environment. The business-oriented Anglo-Saxons, who originally dominated city government, were firm believers in "good government," "efficiency" and "business principles." They had strong

*Minister of Employment and Immigration; formerly Director of the Institute of Urban Studies, University of Winnipeg, and a member of the provincial legislature in Manitoba. He has co-authored a study of the first two years of Winnipeg's experiment in local government, called "Unicity: The Transition."

feelings about keeping politics out of local government and operating local government according to sound, no-nonsense administrative procedures. Representatives of ethnic groups, primarily Ukrainian, German, and Jewish, who have increasingly taken over municipal political posts seem to hold an even stronger belief in these principles of nonpartisanship, efficiency, and conservatism.

Winnipeg has grown slowly. The population increase from 1966 to 1970 was only 5 percent, as compared with 16 percent in Toronto, 15 percent in Vancouver, 16 percent in Edmonton, and 21 percent in Calgary.[3] Thus, while Winnipeg's heterogeneity of population would seem to indicate the development of a more divergent set of political values, its slow growth has promoted the continuation of a more stable, traditional outlook. The small property owners who make up a good part of the Winnipeg population are concerned about the provision of basic services at low cost. As a result, local government has been characterized by its lack of involvement in programs of social reform, the support of civic good works, and an overriding concern with keeping taxes low.[4]

Beginning in the 1970s, however, Winnipeg began to feel the same kind of pressure for change experienced by cities elsewhere in the country. Downtown renewal, transportation systems, suburban land development, and low-income housing have emerged as major issues. In addition, there is the particularly striking problem of substantial in-migration of native people from rural areas. An estimated 30,000 urban native people reside in the core of the city, most of them on the lowest income level.[5]

Thus, just at the time when a new organization of local government was introduced, the city's political, social, and economic environment was changing, and new political forces were coming into play. The degree to which new institutions affected the new political climate raises important questions. Have these new institutions opened channels for the expression of new political forces, or have they consolidated the hold of the conservative, business-oriented political groups? Is the city able to plan and initiate innovative programs in response to changing conditions in its downtown core or to meet problems posed by urban growth? These are some of the real tests for measuring the impact of Winnipeg's new form of government.

The Metro System

Winnipeg's new system is a successor to a form of local government that in its own time was considered a reform. In 1960 the provincial government introduced a two-tier metropolitan form of government for Winnipeg.[6] The division of powers between the separate municipalities and the Metropolitan Corporation was similar to the metro scheme of Toronto, with powers divided between the separate municipalities and a central metro council.

Unlike Toronto, the political representation on Winnepeg's metro council was not drawn from elected representatives of the respective municipalities. Instead, the city was divided into ten pie-wedge constituencies, each electing a separate councillor. This division created a critical separation between the individual political jurisdictions and the metro level and enabled politicians in the municipalities to evade all responsibility for the metro operation.

While there were certain major achievements in public works and tranportation under the metro system, its ten-year history of operation is one of unending disagreement between the City of Winnipeg led by Mayor Stephen Juba and the Metro Corporation. Many unfriendly words were exhanged, and, more seriously, many needed programs were forestalled, particularly in sensitive areas such as downtown planning and new transportation programs. Metro became a convenient political whipping boy for the City of Winnipeg and the municipalities. It became clear to provincial leaders that major changes were necessary, and a blue ribbon commission led by a former Conservative cabinet member was set up in 1966 to review the organization of local government.

Before the commission could report, however, a provincial election was held and the New Democratic Party under Edward Schreyer took over. During the campaign Schreyer had pledged to set up a form of regional government, but he was not going to trust a Tory-appointed commission to give him advice. Instead, a group of Toronto consultants were hired, and in a short time—a matter of about one year—a different kind of local government was proposed for Winnipeg.

Unicity Proposals

In December 1970, the provincial government produced a White Paper outlining its plans for the reorganization of Winnipeg, a concept that quickly became labelled Unicity.[7]

The report proposed the complete amalgamation of all the municipalities. A council would be elected from forty-eight single-member wards, based on an electoral base of 10,000 population. The mayor was to be elected by a majority of council members, a departure from the longstanding practice of direct election by the populace at large and a move interpreted as an effort to create a parliamentary-style government.

The model of a parliamentary-cabinet structure was also seen in the organization of the council and the administration. There were to be committees for finance, public works, and environment, but over the committees was to be a central executive policy committee composed of the mayor and other committee chairmen and exercising the functions of central policymaking coordination. The administrative arrangements paralleled this cabinet executive structure. Three commissioners, one for each committee, and a chief commissioner would gather together in their own executive group or as a board of commissioners to act as the staff arm to the executive policy committee. The political link in this executive policymaking apparatus was the mayor, who would have to hold the confidence of a majority of council.

In company with this centralizing, amalgamative arrangement was a series of proposals designed to decentralize the political system and give the citizen greater access to government. The White Paper proposed that the new city be divided into thirteen community committee areas composed of between three and four wards. These wards fell approximately within the boundaries of the old suburban municipalities and within traditional neighborhood designations of the old City of Winnipeg.

The community committees were to supervise local administrative functions, such as the running of local parks, playgrounds, and libraries, to consider applications for zoning variances or development plans, and to advise the central council on the needs of the local area. Tied in with the community committees was another innovation called Resident Advisory Groups (RAGs). Resident advisors were to be elected each year by private citizens in each of the community committee areas and were to meet at least once a month with the community committee on issues of interest and importance to the local area.

The Winnipeg system sought, in effect, to combine two very different goals. While some urban areas have had regional forms of government and others have experimented with techniques for decentralizing the political system, Winnipeg attempted to achieve both these goals with one integrated system. This is what makes the Winnipeg experience somewhat unique.

Bill 36: A Hybrid System

After a six-month period of public hearings and legislative debate, the basic outline presented in the White Paper was adopted by the provincial legislature, but only after a significant change—a return to direct election of the mayor. Undoubtedly many Winnipeg citizens were in favor of this move,[8] but the influence of Steve Juba, the incumbent mayor who wanted to maintain the old method, cannot be discounted. This change in the form of mayoralty election disrupted the neatly devised formula for strong executive leadership under the parliamentary model and resulted in a hybrid system of executive organization on council. Other modifications included a change from a forty-eight-member to a fifty-member council, changes in the number of members on the council committees, and an increase in members' base salary.

The provincial government selected 6 October 1971 as election day for the new council, and the new system was to begin officially on 1 January 1972. This hasty introduction of a new system was certainly ill-advised compared with other local government reform procedures that seem to extend to a lengthier transition period in order for administrators and politicians to ease into their jobs.[9]

UNICITY: ITS PERFORMANCE, 1972-76

Rule by the Suburbs

What was the effect of reorganization on Winnipeg? First, there were important political consequences. In the November election, a group named the Independent Civic Election Committee gained thirty-seven of the fifty seats. The ICEC is a nonsocialist, normally nonpartisan group of political people who in provincial or federal politics would be Conservatives or Liberals. The election for Unicity council, following closely on the surprise victory of the NDP provincially in 1969, was treated with deadly seriousness by the anti-socialist business groups in the city and resulted in a strong organizational effort and a well-funded campaign by the ICEC. The NDP, which had made a strong showing in Winnipeg during the provincial election, managed to elect only seven members. Independents won in five wards, the Communists in one.

The reorganization of government was a major factor in giving the ICEC its strong hold on council and reinforcing the position and power of the suburban property-owning constituency represented by the ICEC. There are those who contend that the real source of power in city politics is the property development industry.[10] But the importance of the property-owning taxpayer who regards his single-family home as his castle and who supports the political group that will serve his interests should not be overlooked, especially in a city like Winnipeg, where property owners make up the majority of electors.

Subsequent elections in 1974 and 1977 have only confirmed the ICEC hold on council and the domination of suburban interests.[11] In fact, two inner-city councillors elected under the ICEC banner in 1974 resigned from the caucus over the issue of suburban domination. As one city hall reporter noted:

Suburban councillors generally want new residential development in their areas, major commercial development in the downtown area and an efficient transportation system, private or public, connecting the two centers of activity. Their interests are in direct conflict to Inner City Councillors who see protection of established neighbourhoods and redevelopment of deteriorated areas as prime concerns.[12]

The reorganization, then, has had its influence on the priorities of the city and the policies it has adopted. In contrast to other Canadian cities, which are showing signs of some concern over the environmental damage caused by major development projects, the Winnipeg city council has provided support and subsidization of large-scale development, premised on the need for generating further tax revenue. There has also been a noticeable lack of attention paid to matters of low-cost housing and a disregard for economic or social development policies that would meet the needs of native people who have migrated to the central city.

Fiscal and Administrative Results

The results of the reorganization on the financial and administrative side of city government have been mixed. On the plus side, the equalizaton of mill rates immediately brought greater equity to the fiscal system. Formerly, wealthy suburbs had relatively low mill rates because they could utilize services provided by the central city. In 1972 this came to an end and the mill rates, for example, in the suburb of Tuxedo, a very high-income area, went up by 40 percent, compared to only a minor increase for the central city.

In other areas the results are less clear. The general assessment by politicians, administrators and citizens alike is that the delivery of basic services has remained the same, although there are some complaints from residents of former suburban areas that some services such as road repair or snow clearance are not as efficient.[13] There has also been some concern that raising service standards to a common level has added to costs, but the evidence on this point is scarce.[14]

Centralized Planning and Control

The more serious question arising from a centralization of authority is whether it has led to an improved system of planning and development control. A major complaint under the old system was the confusion and delay caused by having several jurisdictions responsible for matters of subdivision approval, zoning control, and the supply of new land services. In some ways the new arrangement made the old system look like a veritable model of efficiency.

The most serious trouble has occurred in housing.[15] Bill 36 introduced a series of new requirements that were to provide a greater degree of public protection on subdivision plans and zoning variations through public hearings and administrative control. The end result was a process requiring ninety different procedural acts and doubling the time for approval. According to housebuilders this made the housing shortage more serious after 1972.[16]

In the area of downtown development, however, the bill did achieve its goal of more effective decision making, albeit with questionable results. Prior to 1971 both the City of Winnipeg and the Metro Corporation had plans for revitalizing the downtown core. Both the city and the corporation plans were predicated on major commercial high-rise development, but, because of the political differences, neither plan was implemented. Under the new unified system the pro-development forces from the old metro council, city council, and suburban councils work together and have made a series of decisions that support major downtown development projects. Many of these have been passed with little scrutiny. One 100 million-dollar project involving a complicated land transfer from the city was approved in four days from the time it was proposed by the developer.[17]

To counter this unfettered development, some citizen groups tried to impose the requirement of environmental impact studies on major public works, a little-noticed provision of Bill 36. For the first few years of operation under the new act, city administrators didn't apply the environmental impact requirement. Pressured by citizens' groups, the city was forced to begin enforcing environmental impact provisions, thus prompting the Executive Policy Committee efforts to have the provincial government rescind the environmental impact requirement under the act.[18]

In the matter of regional land use and transportation, the unified system has not yet had a chance to demonstrate its full worth. In 1974 city council did pass two major proposals, one of them involving plans for major shopping center locations in the suburban areas. This proposal occasioned a sharp conflict between suburban councillors, who supported the plan, and the commissioner of environment, who originally tried to limit such development. In the second case, the council has passed some control on land use in the additional zone around Winnipeg, utilizing the technique of large-lot zoning. Without commenting on the worth of each decision, they would appear to have been achieved more readily under the unified system than under the old metro system. In transportation planning, the network of expressway systems adopted by the old metro council (WATS) has, after increasing public opposition, been rejected by the new council. Nothing new has been offered in its stead. Signs of positive initiatives—the introduction of experimental Dial-a-Bus, a free downtown shuttle bus service, and the planning of a high-speed transit route using a railway corridor—have been obliterated by recent budget restrictions.

An underlying concern that has emerged during the operation of Unicity has been the problem of administrative accountability. Any governmental agency that takes the issue of accountability seriously must demonstrate that it informs its citizens of an open procedure for receiving citizen complaints and that the agency makes its choices based on citizen preference. These requirements have not been met in the Winnipeg system, particularly because of the erosion or disappearance of local community office employees and an increasing concentration and centralization of staff downtown. A prime example of this occurred when the board of commissioners proposed and council accepted a plan for establishing a system that divided the city into six districts for the purpose of administering city services. Such an arrangement was a direct contradiction of the community committee formula and clearly indicated that the chief administrators of the city disregarded the intentions of the act, which sought to provide some degree of local control and supervision over the delivery of services. It thus raised the question of just how well the goal of greater citizen contact and access to city government had been achieved.

Electoral Involvement

The new system was designed to encourage citizen participation in two ways. First was to increase the electoral involvement of citizens and add to minority representation through the small ward system. In this it has been no more successful than other local governments.[19] It appeared from the 60 percent turnout in the first election that progress had been made. In the second election, turnout fell to 35 percent, about the level under former municipal schemes. People vote when there is competition of people or issues.[20] The reorganization of local government, at least in Winnipeg, has had limited effect in inducing such competition. In fact the 1974 election saw ten council seats filled by acclamation.

Community Involvement

The second way of improving citizen involvement and perhaps the most heralded aspect of the new government system in Winnipeg was the community committee-resident advisory system, designed to give local citizens close contact and access to city decision makers. This was to be a continuing institutional framework whereby private citizens could advise councillors on matters affecting the local neighborhood.

The resident advisory groups began well. Over four hundred people were active in the initial thirteen resident advisory groups, with membership ranging in each from about twenty to over two hundred. They organized themselves usually into committees corresponding to the committees on council, works and operations, environment and finance, and several undertook special tasks, such as neighborhood planning projects. Most of the resident advisors were people who had been community activists previously and who now saw in RAGs a new vehicle to pursue their concerns.[21] The work of the resident advisors, however, was seriously constrained by a lack of resources and support from either the city administration or the provincial government. Technical documents were referred to RAGs as were many tasks of neighborhood contact and communication, all without any significant staff or financial help. This reflected the generally unenthusiastic attitude of most city councillors and administrators towards RAGs. In a survey conducted among councillors, when asked if RAGs should be given additional support, 50 percent said no, 34 percent yes.[22] The council has never seriously discussed the role of RAGs or citizen involvement generally. It appears that they were viewed as apart from the normal governing process.

In part, this view was deserved. RAG members themselves admitted that they had not been particularly successful in communicating with their respective communities or in involving many citizens. Because of strong dominance of citizen activists, RAGs often found themselves talking about matters of little interest to the general population. As a result, they became marked as a forum for the "troublemakers."[23] This is not to suggest that RAGs were irrelevant. On several important issues affecting the city, such as rail relocation, zoning, and changes in the civil services, RAGs were influential. These signs of vitality in the new neighborhood structures were limited, however, to a few areas of the city. In general RAGs are slowly declining in citizen influence and involvement. In fact, some councillors publicly called for an abolition of the system, and many councillors and civic administrators privately see little use for it.[24] Many citizens are unaware of the existence of RAGs and have made little use of the institutions.

1977 Amendments

Under the City of Winnipeg Act a review of Unicity was required after five years. To fulfill this requirement the provincial government established a three-man commission headed by Judge Peter Taraska. Hearings before the commission commenced in 1976.

The criticisms of Unicity centered primarily on the confusion in City Hall and the duplication of work between the community committees and council. The major complaint was that decisions were not being made due to the large number of councillors. This was the view of civic administrators and influential civic politicians, many of whom had been tutored under the old metro scheme in which there were only ten councillors and decisions were made by a small elite. The commission report echoed these views and recommended a substantial reduction in the size of the council and a limitation on the role of the community committees.

The provincial government went even further than the commission recommended in restructuring Unicity. The 1977 amendments reduced the number of councillors to twenty-nine and the community committees to six. Considering that the population base for the community committees was now well over 100,000, the concept of small units of government designed to ensure political accountability was eroded. The legislation also eliminated other innovative features of the original Unicity scheme. Requirements for environmental impact assessment were eliminated and the right of the province to override city bylaws and procedures in cases of provincial public works was restored because of the constant warfare between the province and city over provincial public housing programs, an issue that engendered much bitterness on the part of the socialist provincial politicians, who were constantly frustrated by city officials in the development of housing projects.

The most unusual and confusing change, however, was born out of provincial antagonism to Winnipeg's mayor, Steve Juba, who frequently embarrassed and tormented provincial cabinet members. In a move to silence Mr. Juba, the amendments eliminated the mayor as a member of the executive policy committee and as ex-officio on the standing committees. The council would choose the chairman of the executive policy committee, the new position of power. Winnipeg would now have a two-headed executive, a mayor chosen by popular election and a chairman of the executive policy committee chosen by council.

Juba then decided not to run in the civic election held in 1977, leaving an emasculated mayor's office. The new mayor's only official, legal function was to chair council meetings. A further sequel was that in 1977 the NDP provincial government was defeated by the very right-wing Conservative party, which has very close ties to the business community of Winnipeg. This new administration has talked about even further changes to Winnipeg's city government, but at this writing nothing of consequence has happened.

CONCLUSION

What the major legislative changes in 1977 demonstrate is the reassertion of older, traditional political patterns and processes in Winnipeg. The 1972 Unicity Act attempted to redirect priorities and policy in Winnipeg by developing new structures through which different political influences could flow. But these structures—the small wards, RAGs, and the community committees—were not strong enough, nor did they have a sufficiently strong constituency of support to allow them to evolve into effective new institutions. Thus the pattern of highly centralized bureaucracy and conservative politics on city council has reemerged in Winnipeg as the dominant style of city government.

What lessons can be learned from the Winnipeg experience? First, it is obvious that too much is expected of institutional reform. There has been a tendency, particularly in Canadian provincial governments, to use local government reform as the placebo for urban ills. The old belief that reorganizing local government will solve problems of ineffective decision making, inefficient administration, and apathy among the populace, has been adopted by provincial governments in New Brunswick, Quebec, Ontario, and Manitoba and has led to major efforts at government reorganization. This provincial tinkering with the machinery of local government seems to be thought preferable to undertaking major political action on land use, transportation, tax reform, and planning.

This is not to suggest that institutional change should be ignored, as it has played a major role in influencing the division of political power. While the basic social and political forces are not changed by the institutional system, their form of expression is channeled differently by new institutional frameworks, and this has a strong impact on the city's policy choices. In Winnipeg, reorganization brought about a political system highly oriented toward the concerns of suburban residents, an outcome quite the reverse of the intentions of the original Unicity proposal.

Another area in which institutional arrangements can be important but little attention is paid to them is in the design of structures for dealing with the city's intergovernmental arrangements. Few cities, Winnipeg included, have structures specifically designed to deal with senior levels of government, to relate to rural municipalities on the borders, or to undertake many of the myriad functions that a city must perform in a complex intergovernmental system. On the other end of the scale, institutional reorganization plays an important role in overcoming the growing estrangement between individual citizens and government. Traditional political activity is often seen by private citizens as meaningless. Government administration and planning is not responsive or accountable. In Winnipeg, innovative steps were taken to overcome these problems. But, unfortunately, these good intentions were never carried through. The resident advisory groups were not given any real assistance in their crucial first stage of operation. Civic administrators, hostile to the idea of decentralization or any form of citizen control, were allowed to establish administrative districts that ran counter to the community committee and resident advisory systems. City politicians and the provincial government only half-heartedly set forth the goals of citizen involvement and have never established an action program for developing a meaningful form of public participation. Many innovative techniques were open to them—neighborhood development corporations, community information systems, urban resource centers—but they were never tried.

The Winnipeg reorganization was old-fashioned reform. It was designed primarily to overcome problems of fragmentation and of little governmental unity in planning and administration. In these endeavors it met with some success; however, the reform did little to meet problems of intergovernmental relations, citizen activism, social and economic development, decentralizing authority and power, and the need for new managerial techniques and reorganization. While lip service was paid to such concerns in the original White Paper, the actual design of the new system fell short of the mark.

NOTES

1. The material is drawn from a more extensive study undertaken by the Institute of Urban Studies at the University of Winnipeg, published in the spring of 1974, although some new data have been added. See Lloyd Axworthy and James Cassidy, *Unicity: The Transition* (Winnipeg: Institute of Urban Studies, University of Winnipeg, 1974).

2. Government of Manitoba, "Proposals for Urban Reorganization in the Greater Winnipeg Area," December 1970, p. 2.

3. See the *Globe and Mail* (Toronto), 9 November 1971.

4. Winnipeg has a rate of 60 percent single-family homeownership. For a discussion of how population characteristics, including property ownership, influence political behavior and policy outcomes, see Edmund P. Fowler and Robert Lineberry, "The Comparative Analysis of Urban Policy: Canada and the United States," in *People and Politics in Urban Society*, ed. Harlan Hahn (Beverly Hills, Calif.: Sage, 1972).

5. Don McCaskill, "Migration, Adjustment and Integration of the Indian into the Urban Environment" (Masters thesis, Carleton University, 1970).

6. Before 1960 the urban region of Winnipeg had been divided between a central City of Winnipeg and a group of surrounding municipalities, along with a number of regional boards and commissions looking after water supply and public transit. For discussion of this period and an expanded history of the metro years, see George Rich, "Metropolitan Winnipeg: The First Ten Years," in *Urban Problems*, ed. Ralph Krueger and Charles Bryfogle (Toronto: Holt, Rinehart and Winston, 1971), p. 359.

7. For a collection of views on the meaning of the White Paper proposals, see Lloyd Axworthy, ed., *The Future City* (Winnipeg: The Institute of Urban Studies, The University of Winnipeg, 1971).

8. For an amplification of survey results, see Axworthy and Cassidy, *Unicity*.

9. For example, in Britain orientation periods of two to three years were set aside for councillors and administrators to develop an understanding of reform structure and organize traditional techniques. See Joyce Land and Alan Norton, *Setting Up New Authorities* (London: Charles Night and Co., 1972).

10. See James Lorimer, *The Real World of City Politics* (Toronto: James Lewis and Samuel, 1972).

11. Eight out of ten members of the Executive Policy Committee were from the suburbs.

12. Robert Matas, "Ghost of Metro Lingers on Council," Winnipeg *Tribune*, 9 November 1974.

13. This is based on a series of interviews with public officials and a survey of the populace. A more comprehensive assessment of administrative performance of the new

system is difficult to achieve at such an early stage, although work has now begun by the author in analyzing budget changes. See Axworthy and Cassidy, *Unicity*, pp. 38, 39.

14. In the Winnipeg *Free Press*, 18 October 1974, Chief Stewart stated that the cost for unifying the police force would be an additional $400,000.

15. See "Building Sites: A Prime Component of Housing" (Report prepared by Underwood McLellan for the Winnipeg Housebuilders' Association, 1973), p. 29.

16. Ibid., pp. 22-25.

17. "City's Trizec Study Takes a Beating," Winnipeg *Free Press*, 20 December 1974.

18. See Lloyd Axworthy and Don Epstein, "Urban Populism" (Paper presented to Canadian Studies Conference, Toronto, June 1974).

19. Some individual instances of minority representation did occur. In the first election the director of the Indian-Metis Friendship Center was elected in a downtown ward. He declined to run for a second term, but his seat was won by a representative of the Chinese community.

20. Sydney Verba and Norman H. Nie, *Participation in America* (New York: Harper & Row, 1972).

21. Axworthy and Cassidy, *Unicity*, p. 117.

22. Ibid., p. 117.

23. For a discussion of the issue differences between citizen activists and the general range of citizens see Verba and Nie, *Participation in America*, ch. 5.

24. See Robert Matas, "Citizen Role in Big City Government to be Scrapped," Winnipeg *Tribune*, 16 November 1972.

United States

Joseph F. Zimmerman*

4

The maze of local governments and single-purpose regional governmental entities has made the governance system of the typical U.S. metropolitan area exceedingly complex. The multiplicity of governments, according to some reformers, is responsible for conflicts of authority, duplication of services, inadequate service levels, financial inequities, a long ballot, lack of area-wide programming, and other problems. These reformers are convinced that a metropolitan area possesses adequate resources to solve its problems provided the resources can be mobilized on an area-wide basis. Numerous structural and nonstructural changes in metropolitan governance systems have been implemented or proposed to facilitate the solution of area-wide problems. This chapter examines proposals for increasing the ability of the local government system to cope with metropolitan problems—the one-government, two-tier, and ecumenical approaches—and the role of the state and federal government in solving metropolitan problems.

THE LOCAL GOVERNMENT ROLE

Early reformers favored the creation of a single local government for each metropolitan area by authorizing the central city to annex contiguous land as it became urbanized or by consolidating all local governments. Other reformers, recognizing the seriousness of area-wide problems and the practical political obstacles to the formation of a single local government for an area, have recommended the development of a two-tier system, with the county, a multifunctional metropolitan council, or a metropolitan special district occupying the upper tier. Supporters of the ecumenical approach reject the contention that

*Professor of Political Science, Graduate School of Public Affairs, State University of New York at Albany, and author of *The Federated City: Community Control in Large Cities*.

the polynucleated system is incapable of solving area-wide problems. Ecumenicists maintain that these problems can be solved by inter-local cooperation.

The One-Government Approach

The failure of central city boundary extensions to keep pace with urbanization in the twentieth century has been identified by some as a root cause of the metropolitan problem. Annexation can have several advantages. Service levels in the annexed area may be raised, responsibility consolidated, economies of scale in service provision achieved, orderly growth promoted, benefits of the city's services better correlated with its taxing jurisdiction as benefit spillovers are reduced, the tax base of the city expanded significantly, and the governmental structure simplied as fewer units result and new incorporations are frustrated. Motives for annexation also have included a desire to increase the population and land area of the city to make it larger and more prestigious and to block annexation of land to another city.

Annexation was little used by central cities in the period 1900-45, as suburban and fringe area residents were successful in having state laws amended to make annexation more difficult. New laws often prohibited the annexation of incorporated territory and required the consent of the residents of the proposed annexation area before the city's boundaries could be extended. Annexation remains a procedure encumbered by restrictive requirements in a number of states, particularly in the Northeast. Although annexation is the method most commonly employed for changing boundary lines, the typical annexation in recent years has involved a small area and population.

Enactment of the Voting Rights Act of 1965 (79 STAT. 439, 42 U.S.C.A. 1973c) has added a federal dimension to annexation proceedings in several states since in 1971 the United States Supreme Court held (*Perkins* v. *Matthews*, 400 U.S. 379 [1971]) that annexation comes under the act's mandate. A United States district court ruled in 1971 in favor of a group of black voters who contended that the annexation of a twenty-three-square-mile area by Richmond, Virginia, was designed to dilute black voting strength in the city, thereby violating their rights under section 5 of the Voting Rights Act. The reversal of the decision by the Circuit Court of Appeals was upheld by the United States Supreme Court (*Holt* v. *Richmond*, 408 U.S. 931 [1972]). In a related case, *City of Petersburg* v. *United States*, 410 U.S. 962 (1973), the Supreme Court affirmed a decision of a district court denying Petersburg, Virginia, the right to annex fourteen miles of land because the boundary extension would increase the white population from forty-five to fifty-four percent in a city which elects its councilmen at large, thereby discriminating against black voters. The Court added that annexation would be approved if the city adopted the single-member district system as a replacement for the at-large election of the council. Some cities have decided that they do not wish to change their election system as the price for permission to annex land.

In the nineteenth century, city-county consolidations without referenda occurred in Boston, New Orleans, New York City, Philadelphia, and San Francisco. Motivations for the consolidations varied, and in the case of the consolidation of all local governments in a five-county area to form the City of New York the chief motivation appears to have been a desire by the Republican Party to perpetuate Republican control of the city. City-county consolidation may be either complete or partial. In a complete consolidation, a new government is formed by the amalgamation of the county and municipal governments. Partial consolidation may involve the merger of most county functions with the city to form a new consolidated government, with the county continuing to exist for the performance of the few functions required by the state constitution. A second form of partial consolidation involves the merger of several but not all municipalities with the county. Relatively few proposals for city-county consolidation were advanced in the twentieth century prior to 1947. Voters did approve the merger of Denver and Denver County in 1904, and the Hawaiian Territorial Legislature amalgamated the City and County of Honolulu in 1907 without providing for a referendum. Three proposals for mergers in other areas were rejected by the voters.

Prospects for voter approval of consolidation proposals are slim. Only eighteen of sixty-six proposals, or 27 percent, were approved between 1947 and mid-1979. Seven mergers receiving voter approbation occurred under special conditions prevailing in Virginia, and three other consolidations—Carson City-Ormsby County, Juneau-Greater Juneau Borough, and Sitka-Greater Sitka Borough—occurred in nonmetropolitan areas. The Virginia consolidations must be placed in a special category because of the commonwealth's practice of separating a city from a county when the city reaches the population of 5,000 and allowing it to perform city-county functions. Consequently, the Virginia mergers typically involved the amalgamation of a city-county with a county.

All post-World War II mergers, with the exceptions of the Indianapolis-Marion County, Las Vegas-Clark County, and Lexington-Fayette County mergers, and a major semiconsolidation, Dade County, occurred in the South. The first two were partial consolidations ordered by the state legislature without a referendum. The Las Vegas-Clark County amalgamation was declared unconstitutional by the Nevada Supreme Court in 1976 on the grounds that it violated the state constitutional prohibition of special legislation and the "one-man, one-vote" dictum of the United States Supreme Court (*County of Clark* v. *City of Las Vegas*, 92 Nev. 104. [1976]). An analysis of the Southern consolidations reveals that their metropolitan areas possess a number of similarities as well as dissimilarities from the typical non-Southern metropolitan area.

Prior to consolidation, there were relatively few local governments in each area, and each government had a small population with the exception of the central city and the county. The small municipalities in the Nashville and

Jacksonville areas were given the option, by referendum, to remain out of the consolidation, and all chose to do so. The Baton Rouge consolidation was partial in that the city, the parish, and two small municipalities were retained. The Dade County reorganization provided only for functional consolidation, and no units were merged. The reorganization in each area utilized an existing government, the county, upon which to build a new metropolitan government. This strategy improves the prospects of creating an area-wide unit with sufficient powers to cope with major problems since it is easier, under state-enabling legislation, to restructure the county government than to create a new metropolitan unit.

In many Southern areas, city-county consolidation was not a new concept to the voters; partial consolidation had occurred incrementally over the years, and citizens were accustomed to look to the county for solutions to area-wide problems. Each Southern consolidation relied upon special service districts. A separate tax rate was established for each district based on the number and level of services provided. The use of the districts has made mergers more appealing to residents of unincorporated territory, and all proposed Southern mergers have provided for the use of service and tax districts. The fact that the political system in Southern metropolitan areas is, in general, not highly competitive has facilitated the securing of voter sanction for the amalgamation of governments. Where the party system is strong, a proposal for the amalgamation of governments usually becomes a partisan issue.

The existence of scandals in Nashville and Jacksonville prior to the consolidation referendum worked in favor of reformers. There were charges of police scandals in Nashville, and Jacksonville was plagued by a high crime rate and insurance and police scandals. Several months prior to the Jacksonville referendum, a grand jury indicted two city commissioners, four councilmen, the recreation director, and the city auditor. Shortly before the referendum, the tax assessor resigned and the city's fifteen senior high schools were disaccredited. Racial overtones were attached to the Nashville and Jacksonville referenda campaigns. Charges were advanced in each area that the mergers were designed to dilute the growing black voting strength in the central city. Blacks and whites have tended to oppose consolidation proposals for different reasons. The increasing political power of blacks in central cities may predispose some whites to favor amalgamation of governments, yet one must not overlook the fact that the deep and growing fiscal crisis of many central cities has convinced many voters that consolidation is essential if the fiscal health of the cities is to be restored.

The use of district elections by the consolidated governments in Nashville, Jacksonville, and Lexington is chiefly responsible for increased black representation on their councils. Prior to consolidation there were two blacks serving on the thirty-one-member Nashville city council and none on the fifty-five-member county court or in any other local office. Currently, seven of the forty members of the metropolitan council are black. Two blacks were elected to the nine-member Jacksonville city council shortly before the merger of governments, the first time a black had been elected to local office. Fourteen of the nineteen members of the new Jacksonville city council are elected by districts, whereas the old council was elected at large. In 1968, three blacks were elected to the new council by districts and one was elected at large. The at-large councilman and two of the district councilmen were reelected in 1971. In addition, a black has been elected to the seven-member school board, and a second black has been elected to the seven-member civil service board. No blacks served on the former twelve-member Lexington city council or former five-member Fayette county commission; members of both bodies were elected at large. Two of the twelve district councillors currently are black, but the three at-large councillors are white.

Southern metropolitan areas generally have less industry than Northern areas, and evidence indicates that manufacturing interest groups play a lesser role in Southern areas' politics. It is possible that Northern industrial firms, which have fled central cities for suburbia, may be opposed to consolidation of the city and the county if it appears that their taxes will be increased substantially to help solve central city problems. The threat of further use of annexation has been a factor influencing voters outside a central city to approve the merger of the city and the county. Nashville, Tennessee and Columbus, Georgia, each annexed a sizable amount of land prior to the consolidation referenda and threatened to annex additional territory. A court-ordered annexation of contiguous urban land to Lexington helped to persuade voters outside the city to approve the merger of the city and the county.

The limitations of available statistical data must be taken into consideration in any discussion of the effectiveness of city-county consolidation. The absence of cost accounting systems in most local government before the mergers makes it impossible to measure the achievements of economies with any precision. The use of raw tax rate data prior to and subsequent to a merger to measure its effectiveness should be considered suspect. A decline in the total property tax rate may be attributable to the raising of assessments, federal revenue sharing, larger federal and state grants, and levying of new service charges as well as the attainment of economies in service provision. Furthermore, a high per capita direct tax does not necessarily suggest that the administration is inefficient, as high per capita costs may be the product of more and higher quality services.

John M. DeGrove writes, concerning the Jacksonville-Duval County merger,

Costs did in fact go up after consolidation, but the quality and quantity of services to the public *was* increased. . . . The Consolidated Government seems to be moving on many fronts to launch new and upgrade old services, with tangible and substantial benefits to the central city and suburb; black and white; and to the region as a whole.[1]

York Willbern writes that the Indianapolis-Marion County amalgamation

may have permitted some economies of scale. Purchasing for City and County agencies, which was previously done separately, has now been centralized. Improved accounting and data processing equipment and procedures have been instituted. The combined Unigov agencies employ significantly fewer total personnel than did their predecessor agencies in the City and County governments.[2]

The Two-Tier Approach

Three varieties of a two-layer system—the county, federation, and special district—have been employed in North America. Since responsibility for certain functions is consolidated at the upper-tier level, each variety may be viewed as a type of semi-consolidation. A new unit of government is formed on the upper-tier level when a decision is made to establish a federation or a special district whereas the metropolitan county model provides for the modernization of an existing unit to enable it to serve as the area-wide government. Every metropolitan reorganization in the United States approved by the voters since 1947 has involved the county, and it is evident that there is less political opposition to the modernization of county government than to a proposal for the creation of a new multifunctional upper-tier unit. The county obviously has the most potential as a metropolitan government in the ninety-nine single-county metropolitan areas.

A county government with sufficient powers and resources to serve as an effective area-wide government can be established either by assigning additional powers to it incrementally or by adopting a home rule charter converting the county into a metropolitan government. Los Angeles is the outstanding example of the incremental approach, and Dade County, Florida, is the only example of the second.

Los Angeles County has provided contract services to municipalities since 1907, and its provision of urban-type services to unincorporated areas obviated the need for incorporation to obtain such services in a local area. Only one small municipality was incorporated in the county between 1930 and 1950. The county had entered into more than 400 service contracts with the existing 45 municipalities by 1954, when fears of being annexed by the City of Long Beach and the availability of contract services led the residents of the unincorporated Lakewood area to form a municipality. Lakewood immediately contracted to have all municipal-type services provided by the county, and the thirty-two cities incorporated since 1954 have followed Lakewood's lead by contracting initially with the county for the provision of all services. A newly incorporated city finds the Lakewood Plan attractive as it obviates the need for a large investment in capital facilities and permits the city to share in the economies of scale resulting from the production of certain services by the county. Seventy-seven cities currently have contracts with the county for the receipt of services.

Most observers have concluded that the two-tier system in the county has worked well and enables citizens to obtain many high-quality services at a lower cost. Robert O. Warren writes,

Evidence supports the conclusion that the level of information available to contract cities concerning the service inputs they receive from the County, access to County decision makers, and the ability to induce favorable responses to localized values have all increased over what these same areas could command as unincorporated communities directly served by the County.[3]

The Lakewood Plan is opposed by individuals who charge it encourages governmental fragmentation via defensive incorporations, as residents of unincorporated areas seeking to avoid being annexed to an adjoining city know that they can obtain needed services on a contract basis from the county upon incorporation. The Lakewood Plan, according to Richard M. Cion, works against the creation of a true metropolitan government. He writes that

by creating new and more aggressive enclaves of particularism in the County, each one protected by the home rule provisions of the state constitution, by strengthening the desire for status quo on the part of county officials, and by making the Regional Planning Commission totally ineffective, the Plan builds the first line of resistance against metropolitan approaches to metropolitan problems.[4]

The plan undoubtedly has inhibited the creation of an upper-tier unit with strong powers, yet we believe the plan has met the service delivery needs of the county and represents a unique metropolitan governance system in which the administration of many services is centralized on the county level and policy-making is decentralized on the municipal level.

The incremental strengthening of county governments in a number of states during the past two decades is a significant development. Although the granting of home rule to counties in fifteen states facilitates the modernization of county governments, there has not been a rush to adopt home-rule charters authorizing counties to provide urban services. The increase in the number and magnitude of metropolitan problems and the failure of voters to approve the formation of an area-wide government with strong powers, however, have generated interest in several states in shifting responsibility for certain functions up to the county and state levels.

Constitutional and statutory provisions dealing with the voluntary transfer of functions fall into two main groups, those requiring voter approval—in Florida, New York, Ohio, Pennsylvania, and Vermont—and those that do not—Alaska, California, Illinois, Michigan, and Virginia. The requirement of voter approval hinders transfers to the county level. The New York State Constitution, for example, requires the separate approval of voters of cities as a unit and voters of towns as a second unit within a county before a function can be transferred by a city or town to the county.[5] The transfer of a village function to the county is more difficult to achieve since a triple concurrent majority—separate affirmative votes in referenda by city, town, and village voters—is required.

Functional transfers from the municipal to the county level are occurring with increasing frequency in charter and non-charter counties. In a number of instances, the transfer is state-wide, for instance, in Florida where property tax administration was shifted to the county level and in New York where welfare was shifted to the county level.[6] More commonly, a function is shifted voluntarily by one or more municipalities to the county.

Three Florida counties have adopted home-rule charters partially preempting responsibility for functions. The 1957 Dade County Charter authorizes the board of county commissioners to ''set reasonable minimum standards for all governmental units in the County for the performance of any service or function.''[7] If a municipality fails to comply with the standards, the county ''may take over and perform, regulate, or grant franchises to operate any such service.'' The county has yet to exercise this power.

The Volusia County charter, approved by the voters in 1970, grants the county the power of preemption with respect to the protection of the environment.[8] The power has been exercised once to regulate the location, construction, repair, and abandonment of wells and the installation and repair of pumps and pumping equipment.[9] The Broward County charter, adopted in 1974, authorizes the Broward County planning council to prepare a county land-use plan and to approve or reject any land-use plan submitted by any governmental unit within the county.[10] If a submitted plan is found to be in substantial conformity with the county land-use plan, it is certified and becomes the effective plan for the unit submitting the plan. If a plan is rejected or a unit fails to submit a plan for certification, the county land-use plan becomes effective within the unit.

A twelve-year attempt to restructure the governmental system in Dade County preceded the creation of a metropolitan government in 1957. Voter approval of the home rule charter is attributable to several *sui generis* factors in the county, including the lack of a strong political organization, organized labor groups, or organized ethnic groups. Although described as a two-layer system, the Dade County system is a one-government system in the unincorporated areas where the county is the only local government.

The early years of the new county government were plagued by conflict in the form of lawsuits affecting the operation of the government and attempts to weaken the government through charter amendments. Although many municipalities have opposed the county government, there has been a considerable amount of city-county cooperation, and the county provides a number of services to various cities on a contract basis. Cities also have turned responsibility for functions over to the county voluntarily. By providing a high level of services to unincorporated areas, Dade County has abated pressures for the incorporation of municipalities and thereby has prevented further political fragmentation. DeGrove concludes, "It is safe to say that all residents have benefited to some degree as a result of the metropolitan approach."[11]

Interstate metropolitan problems and the lack of voter approval for comprehensive metropolitan reorganization plans have promoted the organization of numerous metropolitan special districts. Their organization can also be explained by a variety of other reasons, including the need to solve an acute problem and avoidance of constitutional debt and tax limits, civil service requirements, and the annual legislative appropriation process. A district has a number of advantages when assessed in terms of its ability to solve a specific area-wide problem. The principal advantage of a district is its relative ease of formation, since a proposal to create a district typically does not generate the strenuous political opposition that develops when a proposal is advanced for the creation of a multipurpose regional government. The single function usually assigned to a district may not be perceived as a threat by municipal officials who either have not been responsible for the function or have experienced problems with it. And, of course, the district may be established to perform a wholesaling function—supply of water, for example—with the municipalities performing the retailing function—water distribution.

The ease of creating a district is enhanced by the fact that a constitutional amendment and popular referenda usually are not required. Since districts often rely upon user charges for revenue, they are not restricted by constitutional and statutory tax limits. The absence of the power to tax makes the proposal for a district more acceptable to some taxpayers, and revenue bonds, exempt from debt limits, can be issued without a popular referendum. Since these are "moral commitment" rather than "full faith and credit" bonds of a general purpose government, an authority may be forced to pay a higher rate of interest in order to market its bonds.

A district often is able to take advantage of economies of scale and specialization by concentrating on the provision of one service in a relatively large geographical area. The district, unless it is multifunctional, does not have to consider competing functional interests which might reduce its ability to achieve economies of scale and specialization.

Metropolitan reformers object to the creation of unifunctional special districts for two major reasons. First, a new district further fragments an already fragmented political system, thereby making the government of the metropolis more complex. Second, it may be more difficult to achieve a comprehensive approach to area-wide development since the activities of an autonomous special district may adversely affect other governmental programs. Bridge and tunnel authorities in metropolitan areas have injured public transportation programs by facilitating the movement of the private automobile.

The Ecumenical Approach

Proponents of the cooperative approach are convinced that area-wide problems can be solved by local governments acting on the basis of comity and support their position by pointing out that the fragmented metropolitan governance system has averted collapse by adaptive responses to the pressures of urbanization.

Ecumenicists are convinced that metropolitan planning commissions and councils of governments (COGs), voluntary associations of local governments, can develop plans to deal with area-wide problems that will be implemented by the cooperative action of local governments. The federal government has stimulated the formation of commissions and COGs by requiring all applications for 155 federal grants-in-aid to be channelled for review through a commission or COG composed primarily of locally elected officials.

The advantages of COGs are several, including their relative ease of organization, provision of a forum for the discussion of metropolitan problems, and provision of a coordinating mechanism for local governments. Unfortunately, the COG suffers all the disadvantages of the United Nations. The voluntary nature of a COG is viewed by its supporters as one of its major advantages, yet this advantage is also its greatest weakness. No COG has solved a major problem in any metropolitan area, and many have become inactive. COGs have concentrated on the solution of relatively minor problems, and certainly they will continue to do so. Since COGS are controlled by elected officials generally dedicated to preserving the organizational status quo, it is highly improbable that COGs will be converted into general purpose metropolitan governments, and to the extent COGs succeed in solving area-wide problems, prospects for forming metropolitan governments will diminish.

THE STATE ROLE

The states have played one or more of three roles—inhibitor, facilitator, and initiator—in the formation of general purpose metropolitan governments. In several states, the formation of such governments is impeded by constitutional restrictions. State legislatures have facilitated the creation of general purpose metropolitan governments by establishing or authorizing the establishment of study commissions and by enacting enabling legislation for the creation of such governments. Forty-two states also have attempted to facilitate the resolution of metropolitan problems by enacting statutes authorizing, and in some cases encouraging, intergovernmental agreements and cooperation. To facilitate the solution of particular metropolitan problems, state legislatures have authorized voters to decide in a referendum whether to form a single or a multipurpose metropolitan special district. Currently, there are 1,028 such districts in the United States.

States have sought to solve environmental problems by totally or partially preempting responsibility for a regulatory function. Rhode Island has forbidden cities and towns to enact air pollution control ordinances and bylaws, whereas Delaware allows local governments to establish standards higher than those established by the state air pollution control agency.[12]

In the nineteenth century, Massachusetts and New York directly initiated the establishment of metropolitan governments as numerous towns were annexed to Boston by mandate of the general court, and New York City was formed in 1898 by a legislatively directed merger of all governments within a five-county area. Despite the precedent of direct state action, no other major consolidation of local governments was ordered by a state legislature without provision for a referendum until the Indiana legislature in 1969 enacted a law merging Indianapolis and Marion County.[13] This must be viewed as an isolated merger resulting from special circumstances in a state lacking a home-rule tradition.

The establishment by the 1967 Minnesota legislature of the metropolitan council for the seven-county Twin Cities area is the most important state-initiated organizational response to area-wide problems of the past decade.[14] The governor with the advice and consent of the senate appoints the chairman, who serves at the pleasure of the governor, and sixteen other members for overlapping six-year terms. The council was assigned responsibility for the functions of the Metropolitan Planning Commission, which was abolished, and was granted authority to review and suspend indefinitely plans of each metropolitan special district in conflict with the council's development guide. The suspension may be appealed to the legislature. The council also may review and suspend for up to one year proposed projects of local governments, act as a housing authority, and appoint members of the Metropolitan Transit Commission and the Waste Control Commission. The 1969 legislature created a Metropolitan Park Reserve Board to operate a park system and provided for the board's appointment by the council. The board's role as an operating service body was terminated in 1970 by a Minnesota Supreme Court ruling, *Knapp* v. *O'Brien*, 179 N.W. 2d 88 (1970), invalidating laws passed on the 121st day (one day past the constitutional limit) of the 1969 legislative session. The inter-county council and the Hennipin County Park Reserve District have blocked reenactment of the original park reserve bill, and the Metropolitan Council has retained the board—renamed the Metropolitan Parks and Open Spaces Commission—as an advisory body. The major distinguishing characteristic of the metropolitan council is the separation of policy execution from policymaking, with the council determining policies to be executed by the service boards. In theory, the council can devote its full attention to broad policymaking for the region and leave routine administrative problems to the boards.

The Twin Cities model of metropolitan governance is innovative and still evolving. The governance system, however, remains fragmented, suffering from three weaknesses. First, the most important problems generally are being attacked on a piecemeal basis, and the legislature plays a major referee role between competing metropolitan groups. A second and related weakness is the possibility of deadlocks resulting from the failure of various regional entities to cooperate with each other. To cite only one example, the council has twice exercised its power to veto indefinitely a new jetport site proposed by the Metropolitan Airport Commission, yet the council lacks the power to order the commission to construct the jetport at a council-selected site. The 1974 legislature strengthened the powers of the council by authorizing it to appoint members other than the chairman of each regional commission with the exception of the airport commission.[15] Chairmen of commissions, with the exception of the Metropolitan Parks and Open Spaces Commission, are selected by the governor. A third and inherent weakness of the model is the possibility of disputes between the council and the service boards it appoints. The council and the sewer board, now the Waste Control Commission, engaged in a major dispute relative to the board's 1971 construction program. Dennis Farney reports,

Some members of the Minnesota Legislature, which created the Council, now mutter it has grown too big for its britches. Some other units of area government with which the Council must deal now charge it with high-handedness. Meanwhile, even Council supporters agree that it remains rather remote to the lives of the 1.9 million people it is trying to serve.[16]

A different approach to regional problem solving was taken in the 1960s by New York, which established both state-wide and regional public authorities, under state control, for special purposes: Urban Development Corporation (UDC), Environmental Facilities Corporation (EFC), Job Development Authority (JDA), five regional transportation authorities, and twenty-three others.

The ad hoc creation of state-controlled authorities has resulted in a division of responsibility on the regional level and a nearly total neglect of essential coordination of authorities' activities with those of regional planning commissions and local governments. New York has utilized the corporate device of the interlocking directorate in the New York City area since 1968 to coordinate transportation authorities. The board of the newly created Metropolitan Transportation Authority was made the ex officio board of the Long Island Rail Road, New York City Transit Authority, Manhattan and Bronx Surface Transit Operating Authority, and Triborough Bridge and Tunnel Authority.[17] It is the ex officio board of the more recently created Staten Island Rapid Transit Operating Authority, Metropolitan Suburban Bus Authority, and Stewart Airport Land Authority. The interlocking directorate model is somewhat similar to the Twin Cities model but differs in that the metropolitan council has no direct operating responsibilities.

THE FEDERAL ROLE

State governments since 1965 have been playing a more important role in the metropolitan governance system as the result of partial federal preemption of responsibility for solving environmental problems. The federal government first began to play an important role in helping to solve metropolitan problems in 1962, when Congress enacted the Federal Aid Highway Act mandating a continuing, comprehensive planning process in each urban area as a condition for the receipt for federal grants-in-aid for highways. Commencing in 1965, the federal government placed heavy emphasis upon metropolitan planning as a mechanism for promoting interlocal cooperation as an approach for solving area-wide problems. A more important federal development is the increased use of preemptive powers since 1965.

Preemption

Congress in the mid-1960s concluded that many regional problems—particularly environmental ones—could not be eliminated by reliance upon state and local governmental action encouraged by the "carrots" of federal grants-in-aid. Enactment of the Water Quality Act of 1965[18] and other preemptive acts has had great significance for metropolitan United States. The Water Quality Act required each state to adopt "water quality standards applicable to inter-state waters or portions thereof within such state" as well as an implementation and enforcement plan. The administrator of the Environmental Protection Agency (EPA) was authorized to promulgate water quality standards that became effective at the end of six months in the event a state failed to establish adequate standards. The federal role has since been strengthened by other enactments, particularly the Federal Water Pollution Control Act Amendments of 1972.

Partial federal preemption of responsibility for air pollution abatement is beginning to have a major impact upon metropolitan United States. In 1967, Congress enacted the Air Quality Act and completely preempted the right to establish automobile exhaust emission standards for 1968 and subsequent model vehicles.[19] The act also partially preempts other air pollution abatement activities of state and local governments by following the general procedure embodied in the Water Quality Act of 1965. The Clean Air Amendments of 1970 established as a national policy direct federal action to protect public health and set explicit dates for the adoption of standards and abatement plans by states. In contrast to earlier ones, the new standards were mandated without considering the economic or technical feasibility of pollution control systems.

Of particular importance to metropolitan areas is the provision directing the adminstrator to publish in the *Federal Register* within ninety days of the effective date of the amendments a list of categories of stationary sources of air pollution subject to the performance standards to be established under the amendments. Each state was authorized to submit to the administrator a procedure for implementing and enforcing standards of performance for new sources located in the state, and the administrator was empowered to delegate authority to each state to implement and enforce the standards for sources that are not federally owned. On 24 February 1974, the adminstrator published final regulations for reviewing the air quality impact prior to construction of new facilities—labeled indirect sources—which may generate significant amounts of automobile traffic.[20] The regulations were scheduled to become effective on 1 January 1975, but were postponed until 30 June 1975.

The 1975 automotive emission standards and the regulation of new major indirect sources of air pollution—electric power generating plants, factories, and shopping centers, for example—have major land-use implications. If stationary source controls combined with new motor vehicle emission controls cannot ensure the attainment of statutory ambient air quality standards within an air quality control region, transportation controls must be adopted. Such controls will force significant changes in the life style of residents of the region.

A decision portending important consequences for metropolitan America is the four-to-four decision of the United States Supreme Court on 11 June 1973 to let stand a district court decision forbidding states to permit significant deterioration of existing air quality.[21] Since the Supreme Court's decision was without opinion and the district court did not elaborate upon its ruling, the EPA has been forced to execute a nondegradation policy without judicial guidelines.

To implement the courts' decisons, the EPA proposed four steps to be taken, including the establishment of clean-air and polluted-air zones. Although pollution levels would not be allowed to exceed federal standards in either zone, only minor increases in the degree of pollution would be allowed in the former zones, whereas larger increases would be allowed in the latter. Any further growth of the so-called Spread City will be ruled out if this proposal is implemented, since development would not be allowed in fringe areas if it would degrade the area's existing air quality.

CONCLUSIONS

Evidence to date suggests that the local governmental system will not be reorganized comprehensively in most metropolitan areas within the foreseeable future for three reasons. Nonstructural changes will prevent the collapse of the metropolitan governance system, and the creation of either a single government or an upper-tier unit with substantial powers is perceived as a threat by strong political interests, who are convinced that a metropolitan government would control sensitive functions, such as housing, land use, and police, and redistribute resources to their disadvantage. Also, the United States Supreme Court on 11 January 1977 applied to housing and school desegregation cases its June 1976 ruling in *Washington* v. *Davis*, which involved a written examination for applicants for the Washington, D.C. Police Department, that an action was not unconstitutional simply because a "substantially disproportionate" burden is placed on blacks.[22] An action would be unconstitutional only if there was proof the action had a "racially discriminatory purpose." Consequently, school and housing desegregation can be ordered on a metropolitan-wide basis only if there is direct evidence that actions were taken deliberately by suburban governments to prevent housing and school integration in the past. Complete consolidation of all local governments within a metropolitan area could lead to court-ordered integration of housing and schools in the former suburban municipalities. Furthermore, there will be strong resistance to creation of a single-county school district for the same reason.

Critical problems in the typical metropolitan area during the next decade will be alleviated or solved by intergovernmental tinkering. COGs will promote interlocal cooperation but will not play an important role in the governance system because they lack the power to control land use and reallocate resources. Service provision agreements, often arragned on a trade-off basis, will be entered into frequently by municipalities with other governmental units, and responsibility for a troublesome function occasionally will be shifted upwards to the county or state level or to a newly created, unifunctional, regional special district. The county will be converted incrementally into a metropolitan government by the upward shift of functional responsibility in many of the ninety-nine single-county metropolitan areas. Public works functions are the ones most likely to be shifted upwards to the county level, as it is reasonable to assume that lower-tier units will seek to retain responsibility for the most politically sensitive functions.

The urbanized states undoubtedly will become more deeply involved in solving area-wide problems through direct state action and standard setting. The enlarged state role will the attributable in part to prodding by the federal government as it continues to rely upon the states to develop and implement programs meeting minimum federal environmental standards. Increasing metropolitan scale and the development of megalopolises, however, will generate additional pressure for the transfer of complete functional responsibility to the federal government.

NOTES

1. John M. DeGrove, "Southern Regionalism," in *The Regionalist Papers*, ed. Kent Matthewson (Detroit: Metropolitan Fund, 1974), pp. 184-85.

2. York Willbern, "Unigov: Local Government Reorganization in Indianapolis," in Matthewson,ed., *The Regionalist Papers*, p. 225.

3. Robert O. Warren, *Government in Metropolitan Regions* (Davis: Institute of Governmental Affairs, University of California, Davis, 1966), p. 260.

4. Richard M. Cion, "Accommodation Par Excellence: The Lakewood Plan," in *Metropolitan Politics*, ed. Michael N. Danielson (Boston: Little Brown and Company, 1966), p. 280.

5. State of New York, *Constitution of the State of New York*, art. 9, sec. 1 (h).

6. State of Florida, *Florida Laws of 1970*, ch. 70, p. 243; State of New York, *New York Laws of 1972*, ch. 28 (McKinney 1972).

7. Dade County, *Metropolitan Dade County Charter*, art. 1, sec. 1.01 A 18 (b).

8. Volusia County, *Volusia County Charter*, sec. 1305.

9. Volusia County, *Volusia County Ordinance Number 72-6*.

10. Broward County, *Broward County Charter*, art. VI, secs. 6.01, 6.05.

11. DeGrove, ''Southern Regionalism,'' p. 195.

12. State of Rhode Island, *Rhode Island General Laws Annotated*, sec. 23-25-19 (1968); State of Delaware, *Delaware Code Annotated*, tit. 7, sec. 6207 (1968).

13. State of Indiana, *Indiana Acts of 1969*, ch. 173.

14. State of Minnesota, *Minnesota Statutes*, ch. 473B (1971).

15. State of Minnesota, *Minnesota Laws of 1974*, ch. 422. The act has been codified as *Minnesota Statutes*, ch. 473B (1971).

16. Dennis Farney, ''The Twin City Experiment,'' *Wall Street Journal*, 21 March 1974, p. 1.

17. State of New York, *New York Laws of 1967*, ch. 717 (McKinney 1967).

18. U.S., *Water Quality Act of 1965*, 79 Stat. 903, 33 U.S.C.A. 1151 *et seq.* (1969).

19. U.S., *Air Quality Act of 1967*, 82 Stat. 485, 42 U.S.C.A. 1857 *et seq.* (1969).

20. U.S., 39 *Federal Register* 7271 *et seq.*

21. Fri *v*. Sierra Club, 41 U.S.L.W. 4825 (1973).

22. Washington *v*. Davis, 426 U.S. 229 (1976); Village of Arlington Heights, et al., v. Metropolitan Housing Development Corporation, et al. (United States Supreme Court case number 75-616); Metropolitan School District of Perry Township v. Buckley (United States Supreme Court case number 76-212). See also the related case numbers 76-458, 76-468, 76-515, 76-520, and 76-522.

WESTERN EUROPE

FRANCE
SWITZERLAND
WEST GERMANY

France

*François d'Arcy** *Professor of Political Science, University of Grenoble.

5

For a long time urbanization was a slower process in France than in other industrialized countries. Until the beginning of the 1950s the rural population remained large. Since then a series of factors have combined to make cities grow with brutal speed: ever swifter rural depopulation, overall population growth, the rise in living standards, and the transformation of the productive apparatus.[1]

In the phase of advanced capitalism, it is less and less necessary to set up units of production in proximity to raw materials or to natural communication channels. On the other hand, these units are dependent on large urban centers where they can obtain both an abundant and skilled labor force and a market where new consumer models are present. Paris, with its surrounding built-up area, was for a long time the only French city on the same scale as the great urban centers of the other industrialized countries. One fundamental objective of urban policy in the 1960s was the creation of new urban centers capable of meeting the needs of advanced capitalism. It was in this context that the government defined the *métropoles d'équilibres* (Lille, Metz, Nancy, Strasbourg, Marseilles, Lyon, Toulouse, Bordeaux), which were to benefit from a special effort in terms of public investment, in order to counterbalance the growth of Paris.

Over the last ten years, however, there has been a certain diversification in urban development policy. Whereas formerly the emphasis was put on large towns of about one million inhabitants, it would now seem that the smaller towns (*les villes moyennes*) also have a part to play. This is a reflection of the change in strategy of the national and multinational firms that no longer systematically seek out the large urban centers but rather diversify their location procedures.

This change in the overall urban landscape has been accompanied by profound social changes: the withering of a traditional urban petty bourgeoisie, new living and working conditions for the working class as it struggles against capital which in turn is increasingly difficult to locate, and the development of new middle classes, well equipped intellectually and with more and more control over the local political apparatus. In order to adapt local government to these changes, a number of reforms or attempts at reform have come into existence since the beginning of the Fifth Republic by President de Gaulle in 1958. To understand these reforms, it is necessary to review the characteristic features of the preceding period.

THE PRE-REFORM PERIOD

The Fragmented Administration of Cities

This period takes in the whole of the Fourth Republic, set up in 1945, and goes back as far as the end of the Third Republic. Social regulation inside the urban framework was progressively taken over by state public services. Education, police services, cultural and sports activities, postwar reconstruction, and, later, state housing, roadways, and public transport all were taken over directly or placed under strict technical supervision by a state department. Each one of these state departments intervened according to its own criteria and its own norms and without any coordination with the others.

During this period there was a decline in local administration. On the one hand, the more complex and diversified services called into play by new tasks became the almost exclusive domain of state departments. The growth of these services reinforced, in particular, the influence of the upper echelons of the state administration. At the same time, the people's elected representatives had less and less control over these activities. Their role tended to become limited to that of intermediary between their electors and the various state departments.[2] The fragmentation of the town framework into a large number of commmunes was an extra factor reinforcing this tendency.

The limits and inconveniences of this fragmentation of services became apparent particularly when a rapid change in land use necessitated the simultaneous intervention of a great number of services (large zones of construction of new houses or of implantation of factories on the outskirts of towns, restructuring of old quarters). However, neither the state departments directly involved nor the local authorities assumed responsibility for working them out and coordinating them. In a great number of cases this role was taken over, de facto, by a body which grew up on the periphery of state administration: the *Société Centrale pour l'Equipement du Territoire.*[3]

Rediscovering the City through Planning: the 1960s

A new phase began in 1960. The inconveniences of overly fragmented services were no longer restricted to large but localized operations but rather encompassed all regulative operations within the urban framework. In other words, after being eclipsed momentarily the town as such reappears, a specific area within which a number of social antagonisms arise, antagonisms which can be acted upon only if the political authorities take into account the totality of social interactions at play within this framework. But the other distinctive feature of this period was that this regulation remained essentially in the hands of the central state machinery. The reforms affecting the central state machinery were as follows: setting up the "district" in the Paris region, followed by the appointment of a district commissioner collaborating directly with the prime minister; creating in 1963 the *Délégation à l'Aménagement du Territoire et à l'Action Régionale* (DATAR), which at first was also to work under the direct authority of the prime minister (it is now under the Home Office); and, finally, in 1966, bringing together the Ministries of Public Works and Housing to form a new ministry (*Ministère de l'Equipement*) whose first minister, E. Pisani, claimed to be in effect the minister in charge of towns.

Setting up these new administration structures gave rise to a thorough transformation in town planning, which henceforth attempted to view urban growth synthetically and with foresight. In the Paris region, the district commissioner, helped by an important new research unit, published a master plan for the whole Paris *région*. In the main urban centers in the provinces, the DATAR, working closely with the *Ministère de l'Equipement*, had a number of plans elaborated by local research units. The new head of the *Ministère de l'Equipement* prepared a reform of town planning, which was passed as a new land use act in Parliament in 1967.[4]

At the same time, the Plan Office (*Commissariat Général du Plan*) attempted to integrate the programming of those facilities linked to urban growth into the economic plan. The objective was for each town of more than 50,000 inhabitants to elaborate a medium-term program of public works that would correspond to the period of the national plan and be compatible with it. But it rapidly became evident that the needs expressed by the towns were greatly in excess of the plan's provisions, and all attempts at achieving some coherence in the programming of public works at the national, regional, and town levels failed.

This enormous effort in the sphere of planning and programming came up against serious limitations for both technical and political reasons, the latter being more important. In many cases the town councils have not been allowed or have refused to participate in the formulation of the plan. Given the town councils' influence in actually putting urban policy into practice this deprives the documents of much of their effectiveness. But, much nearer to the point, it is debatable whether the discussions that take place during the formulation of urban development plans can really bring out the complexity of the social antagonisms at play or which will come into play in a given urban setting. The resultant political tensions probably would be insurmountable. Given these conditions, the documents either reiterate decisions taken elsewhere or are no more than one phase in the complex strategies of the state departments involved. Either that, or they are able to obtain agreement over narrowly limited conflicts of interest, most notably those between different factions of the bourgeoisie. These different plan functions are not mutually exclusive.[5]

Provisions for the long-term spatial development of the large urban centers also face the demands of blow-by-blow negotiations with the large finance groups which, because of the implantation of large units of production or the realization of vast housing schemes, have a crucial influence on urban growth. The procedure of "concerted development zones" was an attempt to reconcile opposing demands through the institutionalization of negotiations between authorities and large investors.

Although it has been more or less impossible, as we have seen, to make forecasts concerning the activities of the authorities in urban development, it is nonetheless true that there has developed a new understanding of urban problems, characterized by the capacity to integrate particular decisions into a much large context. This was also the orientation set out by the Towns Commission of the Sixth Plan.

FROM TERRITORIAL DISPERSION TO POLITICAL UNITY

Town planning on the scale of the urban center (agglomeration) was possible only if the agglomeration existed as a political and administrative entity. However, unlike what happened in other European countries, in France administrative boundaries of villages taken over by towns did not change. Those villages that had become the suburbs of towns maintained their status as communes, and the central commune of the town maintained the same boundaries as before industrialization. This can be explained perhaps by the fact that French communes have comparatively less responsibility in the direct management of public services, the state administration playing the major role in this sphere.

Since the end of the nineteenth century, those problems that necessitated a certain coordination between communes gave rise to limited and fairly unrestrictive forms of cooperation. On the other hand, the maintenance of the old administrative divisions allowed social groups to have a differentiated representation given their unequal distribution within the urban framework. This phenomenon undoubtedly facilitated the local authorities' function of social integration. Since 1958, more and more attempts have been made to bring together the communes of the same agglomeration. These attempts usually have been resisted vigorously by the local elected representatives. Inasmuch as these attempts gave no extra power to the local councillors, they were probably correct in believing that their main role of defending their electors with regard to the state administration would be better fulfilled if those electors kept their specific representation and were not lost in the mass of inhabitants of a whole agglomeration. Thus, local elected representatives have always rejected any solution involving the idea of amalgamating the communes. It is even doubtful that the government itself wishes some form of amalgamation. For although the administrative fragmentation is a barrier to administrative rationalization, the breaking up of political power within the agglomeration often gives the state the opportunity to play the part of referee.

The various solutions that have been devised—multipurpose intercommunal syndicates (*syndicats intercommunaux à vocation multiple*), districts, and urban communities (*communatués urbaines*)—are, then, all based on the same principle of a two-tiered administration. Existing communes continue to exist, and elections are held at this level. A federal body is set up at an agglomeration level; its council is composed of representatives from the communes. The nature of these bodies—obligatory or not—varies, as does the way in which the number of representatives for each commune is calculated, the area of their competence, or their financial power.

The Urban Community

The solution the central authorities have opted for is the urban community, an idea first formulated in the act passed on 31 December 1966, which made them obligatory in the four urban centers where the problem was most acute (Lille, 88 communes; Lyon, 60 communes; Strasbourg, and Bordeaux). But there were only five more of these urban communities in existence in 1974. The suburban communes are in fact extremely hesitant to accept the setting up of an urban community. The principle is that the communes are represented in the community council proportionally according to their population, unless another form can be agreed upon. This gives the central town commune a determining influence. What is more, the urban communities have all come up against considerable financial difficulties, especially since the way of apportioning the financial resources and costs among the community and the member communes is far from satisfactory. More recently, an act passed on 16 July 1971, attempted to speed up the process of bringing the communes together. But by leaving the final responsibility for the decisions in the hands of the prefect, who is normally more influenced by local pressures than the central administration, the government that put through the act showed quite clearly that it did not intend to force confrontation with the local elected representatives.

To sum up, then, these regroupings or attempts at regrouping illustrate the necessity, set out explicitly in the Sixth Plan, to create an administrative unit at the level of the agglomeration in order to be able to set into motion the urban development policy of the central authorities. Certain local councillors are now also beginning to realize that political action is feasible only at this level. But, more generally, and sometimes for opposing reasons, there has been up to the present a large consensus opposing the setting up of full-fledged political authorities at an agglomeration level who would be independent of the existing communes.

State or Local Technicians

A framework for political negotiations, the agglomeration is also a sphere in which local public services, both technical and administrative, can be developed. Until quite recently, local authorities were obliged to make use mainly of the technical services supplied by the state. This situation was not improved by the fact that the regulations imposed by the state on the communes concerning the recruitment and pay of administrative staff were a hindrance to hiring highly qualified staff unless the commune went about the matter indirectly by setting up a private association or corporation. After much discussion, an act passed in 1972 has tended to improve the professional prospects and training of the communes' administrative staff. But the solutions adopted still are not up to the mayors' expectations.

Without a doubt, the political weight of local elected representatives in their negotiations with the state administration is largely dependent on the quality of the public services they dispense in order to justify technically their positions. For example, the Land Use Act of 1967 stated that town planning documents would be worked out jointly by the local authorities concerned and the state administrative services. For this purpose, there were to be set up public research units controlled by the local authorities and under the auspices of the Ministry of Public Works and Housing. But the texts concerning the application of this act never saw the light of day, and in most agglomerations the role of the ministry remains preponderant in the preparation of the documents. In a certain number of agglomerations, however, agglomeration-level town planning agencies with differing legal status have been created. Thus, Grenoble has been able to develop a relatively original town planning policy since 1965, simply because the town council elected at that time rapidly set up a town planning agency that was largely under its control, even though the director of the agency was a state civil servant from the *Direction Départmentale de l'Equipement*. In other words, the political power of the local authorities is tied to their "specialist power," and this expertise is derived essentially from the quality of those services which they directly control.

THE SERIOUS PROBLEM OF LOCAL FINANCES

The most delicate problem concerning the government of the large towns remains that of finance. The financial situation of the communes began to be alarming at the beginning of the 1960s, when their need to spend more and more money on public facilities plunged them dangerously into debt. It was not until this period that a serious statistical analysis of commune finances was made by the Ministry of Finance.

With the Fifth Plan in view (it began in 1965) a committee was given the responsibility of finding out whether the communes were capable of financing their public works themselves (this meant between one-fourth and one-third of total public investment). The report brought out by this committee was rather pessimistic, and the government decided that its publication would be politically ill-advised. For the Sixth Plan a similar study was undertaken and another question added: Was it possible to prevent the communes from financing public works that were not part of the national plan? In the meantime, national planners had learned to distinguish between those public works which were of direct use to production and those which were tied to consumption. Whereas the Sixth Plan quite clearly gave priority to the former, the attitude of the communes revealed their marked preference for the latter. As long as there was no unified plan at different levels, national, regional and town, the best way to prevent the communes from investing in projects outside the plan was to delay as long as possible the reform of commune finances, which nonetheless was generally considered indispensable.

French local fiscal policy is, it is true, archaic. As soon as local councils are obliged to step up fiscal pressure they create inequalities that quickly become unbearable politically. The communes, then, meet three-fourths of their expenditures in the sphere of public works with outside help: state subsidies and, more particularly, loans. A large though decreasing part of these loans comes out of public funds at low interest rates but on the condition that a state subsidy has already been granted. Thus the state effectively controls all of the communes' investment expenditure. Until recently, however, these controls were extremely bureaucratic and only rarely made use of economic criteria.

Two distinct pressure groups, then, are pushing for a reform of local finances: the national planners, so that these finances may be more compatible with the objectives of the plan; and the communes, which hope to obtain more freedom of action. A reform of local taxes was undertaken and effected in June 1975 with the passing of an act reforming the *patente* (local tax paid in order to exercise a trade or profession). Although the bases for taxation were modernized, the total structure of local fiscal policy was left intact. As this structure stands it is incapable of allowing the towns to increase their fiscal resources without creating serious social tensions.

THE FUTURE

Perhaps a new phase has opened up recently, aiming at giving local authorities more exclusive responsibility for at least part of local policies. This may become more evident particularly in those activities aimed at better social integration.

It is now quite banal to say that the institutions formerly assuring social integration by diffusing common values are in a state of crisis: the school, the family, the church. The problem of social integration is becoming acute particularly in the large, new, housing schemes. Until the present, the authorities have attempted to resolve this problem by creating a certain number of public facilities, sometimes called "sociocultural" (youth centers, community centers, and so on), whose structures and functioning are determined by national norms. In practice, this policy defined in terms of public facilities has often been disappointing, for it results in a fragmentation of activities and the identification of a certain number of "needs" to be met by the authorities—be they in the sphere of education, health, activities among old people, socio-cultural action, or the prevention of juvenile delinquency—to which should be added what can properly be termed repressive, action. In fact, what is important is not so much each one of these functions taken individually but their total effect within a given social area.

Local situations are too fluid for such policies to be implemented on the basis of norms established in a rigid manner by state departments. At the same time, the failures of the Fifth and Sixth plans in the sphere of regional and town programming have also shown that urban policy cannot be defined through a vast planning and programming process taking in the totality of public activities through a series of perfectly articulated plans. The Seventh Plan is thus directed towards a less ambitious system of contracts: the state agrees and commits itself to supplying subsidies over the period of the plan on the basis of precise programs bringing together a sum of coordinated actions worked out by the
local authorities. Their responsibility is, therefore, more direct.

On the other hand, it seems likely that the state will maintain its responsibility for those activities directly affecting the economy. The greater latitude that may be left to the communes will in certain areas of activity be limited by financial mechanisms, which will prevent the total volume of local expenditure from growing as rapidly as the local authorities would wish. Such an evolution will necessitate a redefinition of the levels of decision making in the urban framework. The agglomeration level most notably should be more than simply a level at which local authorities meet.

The resistance encountered so far concerning all formulas aimed at regrouping the communes often results from a certain social specificity in the various communes within an agglomeration, which itself arises from the social segregation within the urban framework. Such resistance, which goes far beyond the simple wish of the mayor to maintain his political mandate, will subsist as long as there is no specific form of policial expression at the level of socially homogeneous areas. But little thinking has yet been done in this sphere. One thing is certain: the local political landscape in France has been significantly modified. The 1971 and 1977 local elections, in comparison with the 1965 local elections have accentuated certain tendencies.[6] In the first place, the attitude of the political parties concerning local politics has changed. Local political mandates are no longer sought as a means of obtaining political mandates at a national level, and the political parties are beginning to have real local political programs. Second, the polarization that has been a feature of national politics over the last ten years has now become visible at local elections. Third, the elections have provoked a significant turnover of local politicians, calling much more on candidates from the technical and executive level and from the teaching profession and much less on the traditional petit bourgeoisie of shopkeepers and liberal professions. The changeover has often been accompanied by a political landslide to the benefit of the Left, particularly in 1977.

The forward thrust of the Left in municipal elections, however, has not prevented the government from going ahead with its plans for decentralization. These were first prepared by the Guichard Commission for the Development of Local Responsibility, which published an important report in 1976.[7] The government then proposed a bill on the reform of local bodies that was put to Parliament in 1979. If this law is actually brought into application there could follow some rather drastic changes in the interaction between the state administration and local authorities.

NOTES

1. The urban population, which had in a century (1846-1946) slowly climbed from 24 percent to 53 percent of the total population, went up over a period of fourteen years (1954-68) from 57 percent to 70 percent, bringing France close to most other industrialized countries. At present the urban population rises at a rate of 2.7 percent per year, while the total population rises at a rate of 1.1 percent. It is estimated that by the year 2000 the urban population will have almost doubled and the total surface covered by urban areas quadrupled.

2. P. Gremion, "Introduction à une étude du système politico-administratif local," *Sociologie du Travail*, no. 1, (1970).

3. F. D'Arcy, *Structures administratives et urbanisaton, la S.C.E.T.* (Paris: Berger-Levrault, 1968).

4. Each urban center of more than 50,000 inhabitants must elaborate a master plan (*schéma directeur d'aménagement et d'urbanisme*, SDAU), setting out in advance the long-term changes (thirty years) in the urban layout and the main public works to be realized. These plans, which are not legally binding on individuals, are made complete by land occupation plans ("*plans d'occupation des sols*," POS) which determine zoning and land rights over a shorter period (ten years).

5. For the application of this analysis to the SDAU, see H. Coing's contribution to the Uriage Planning Conference, in *Planification et Société* (Grenoble: Presses Universitaires de Grenoble, 1974).

6. See special issue on local elections of 1971 of *Revue Française de Science Politique* (April 1972).

7. *Vivre Ensemble* (*Living Together*), Report of the Commission for the Development of Local Responsibility, 2 vols. (Paris: La Documentation Française, 1976).

Switzerland

Jean Meylan*

6

It is often a difficult task to describe the political institutions and their mutation in a federal state. In the case of Switzerland such a description is particularly complex; for, although the country is modest in size, it has a rich diversity of local and regional peculiarities that may have little in common except the national ground on which they stand. In this chapter we shall first outline the characteristics of Swiss communes and then describe the methods used for the reorganization of local authorities. Finally, we shall deal with the reorganization of local government in the five main metropolitan centers of Switzerland, particularly Lausanne.

MAIN CHARACTERISTICS OF SWISS COMMUNES

The Swiss Confederation, in spite of its official name, is a federal state consisting of twenty-six cantons that among them contain some 3,000 communes. Switzerland does not have a uniform communal system: it leaves the task of determining the limits of municipal activity to the twenty-six cantonal systems of law. The result is a great diversity in the types of communes, tasks, responsibilities, land, population, and means—especially the available personnel, real estate, and finance—by which tasks and responsibilities, either direct or delegated, are executed.

Types of Communes

All the cantons contain political communes, which are granted general powers of jurisdiction. About twenty cantons also maintain concurrently bourgeois communes (*communes bourgeoises*, about 2,000)[1] and parishes; half a dozen retain school communes, and two even contain welfare communes. There are still other bodies of public law (notably consumer associa-

*Head of the Office for Socioeconomic Studies, City of Lausanne. Translated from the French by Miss Alison Martin, assistant at the University of Lausanne.

tions), which are relics of the old communal system. In certain Catholic and less developed cantons in the German part of Switzerland, up to six different types of communes may coexist. On the other hand, three cantons in western, French-speaking Switzerland—Geneva, Neuchâtel, and Vaud—rather more under the influence of their neighbor, France, contain only political communes. This chapter deals only with the political commune, although the bourgeois commune especially—traditionally more conservative and often endowed with valuable estates—may act as a brake in the reorganization of local government, for example by holding up progess or putting obstacles in the way of communal fusion.

Communal Tasks and Responsibilities

These may vary from canton to canton, especially if there are other communes with particular functions. However, Swiss communes generally assume the following tasks and responsibilites: internal organization (appointment of authorities, personnel); administration of privately owned estates; finance (financial system—above all the settlement of local tax rates—and financial administration); granting of citizenship; public education (primary and secondary); social welfare (public assistance, but mainly administration of the national system of social security); local policing in the wide sense (public order, use of public land, traffic control, hygiene, regulation of business, population control, fire protection, civil defense, approval of construction); land planning; public works (mainly roads); technical equipment (water supply, purification of used water, waste disposal); industrial services (distribution of water, gas and electricity); public transport (in the large towns); and sport and cultural activities.

Number, Land, and Population of Communes

Of the more than 3,000 communes (3,034 in 1979) half (53 percent) are found in only five cantons, which also contain most of the small communes. The Swiss commune is distinguished by the relative smallness of its average land area (1,361 hectares) and population (2,085 inhabitants in 1977). There is, however, a considerable range between extremes (from 30 to 28,230 hectares, and from fewer than 20 to nearly 400,000 inhabitants).

Today, the distribution of population in the communes is the result of a development marked by two principal phenomena: an increase in number of very small and very large communes at the expense of those of medium size, and a concentration of population in the urban communes. Thus, in 1970, 213 communes of more than 5,000 inhabitants (7 percent of all communes) contained 69 percent of the population, while 2,859 communes of less than 5,000 inhabitants (93 percent of all communes) contained 31 percent of the population.

This movement has been accompanied by an increasingly marked socioeconomic specialization, particularly around towns that are metropolitan centers. In this way, the makeup of the active population and the daily commuting of workers establish types of communes (large metropolitan centers, suburban residential or industrial communes, semi-industrial or service towns, or rural communes), to which correspond specific types of financial resources and municipal policies.[2]

Communal Means of Fulfilling Responsibilities

PERSONNEL AND REAL ESTATE. In 1965 the communes employed a total of 94,800 people—more than that of the cantons (83,900) and less than that of the confederation (118,300). This work force was unequally distributed, since 275 communes had no employees, 396 only one, and, at the opposite pole, twelve had 500 or more.

The Swiss communes are important property owners. In 1965 they privately owned 7.3 percent of the national territory. The towns are particularly well off; for example Zürich, as a private freeholder, owns a third of its own area and Lausanne more than half. Moreover, the towns often have a policy of systematic acquisition.

FINANCE. Of the total public expenditure—which represents about a quarter (27 percent) of the gross national product—the communes are responsible for about 34 percent, with an expenditure of 13,950 million francs in 1977. The heaviest expenses are for schools (25 percent of the total expenditure), protection of the environment (11 percent), interest on loans (10 percent), general administration (9 percent), social welfare (9 percent), roads (9 percent), public health (7 percent), culture, leisure, and sport (5 percent), and police (3 percent).

In order to cover expenditures the communes have recourse to various sources of income. In 1976 these were, in order of importance: personal taxes on wealth and income (55 percent), fees and service charges (22 percent), subsidies (15 percent), revenues from estates and/or industrial services (7 percent), and shares in cantonal revenues (1 percent).

Communal expenditures and revenues vary according to the canton, and also the population and socioeconomic specialization of the commune. The communal expenditure per head averaged 2,200 francs in 1977. The divergence among cantons is represented by the ratio 1:3 (from less than 1,150 francs to more than 3,500). These disparities result from the unequal distribution of wealth among the population and the unequal division of tasks and responsibilities between cantons and communes. The rate of expenditure per head also varies in proportion to the size of the communes: towns of more than 100,000 inhabitants spend nearly twice as much as the communes of less than 5,000 inhabitants. These differences are due mainly to the number of services offered. Lastly, expenditure per head varies according to the socioeconomic specialization of the communes. Thus, the greater the proportion of resident population active in industry and, more particularly, in services the higher the rate of receipts and expenses.[3]

METHODS OF REORGANIZATION

The cantons have adopted two principal ways of attempting to reorganize their communal system: integration (by the absorption and fusion of communes) and cooperation (particularly by means of intercommunal association and convention).

Fusion of Communes

Switzerland has shown herself less inclined than other European countries to reduce the number of her communes. Until 1972 there had been a reduction of only 148 (4 percent) in about one hundred years, the net result of 176 fusions or absorptions and 28 creations. Regarding size, 112 of the 176 communes that had gone out of existence had fewer than 500 inhabitants, 44 (one-quarter) had a population of fewer than 100. Most of these small communes were entirely rural and situated outside zones of urban attraction. On the other hand, 32 of the abolished communes had more than 2,000 inhabitants, and nine had a population of more than 10,000. All were suburban communes and were annexed by their respective central cities. Of the twenty-six cantons, six—among the smallest, most traditionalist, and least developed—have not recorded any abolition of communes. On the other hand, certain large cantons have strikingly reduced their number (for example Zürich, which has reduced its number by twenty-eight, or 14 percent). Finally, almost half the abolished communes have been absorbed by towns. This has been done mainly in the canton of Zürich, where the capital has annexed nineteen communes, and Winterthur five.

Since 1960 the movement toward fusion has accelerated: fifty communes went out of existence between 1961 and 1972; eighteen between 1972 and 1979. There is a new factor involved here: this phenomenon is affecting cantons that were little or not at all concerned in the past; in addition, it is favored by several cantonal governments that are trying to promote or facilitate the concentration of their communes. However, this fusion phenomenon especially affects those communes situated outside metropolitan areas. In contrast to prewar events (in Zürich, for example), urban areas are affected very little. The local authorities, particularly those of suburban communes near large towns, are taking advantage of their local population growth and the strengthening of their economic potential—a result of overflow from the central cities—in order to affirm their autonomous existence. Fusion having become very difficult, other methods of collaboration have been developed.

Intercommunal Collaboration

Apart from direct relations—often on the personal level—between the different administrations and local authorities, or private law agreements, which are the primary methods of settling common problems, regional organization is really based on cooperation under public law, essentially by means of intercommunal conventions and associations of communes. The intercommunal convention limits the means of collaboration to one, or sometimes several, determined aims, theoretically without supracommunal authority. The communes do not transfer any of their powers of jurisdiction because the decisions taken by the intercommunal institutions must be ratified by each member commune. The main areas of application foreseen by the cantonal laws are public education, protection of the environment, and land planning.

The association of communes is a public corporation designed to carry out one or more responsibilities of public interest but with no general jurisdiction. Although the association of communes existed in the nineteenth century, it has only recently gained explicit recognition in almost all cantonal legislation. Most often, it is formed by voluntary adherence by the communes, and for its activities commands resources obtained mainly from subscriptions of member communes, possibly from state subsidies, from revenues from some services, or from borrowings.

Intercommunal collaboration extended considerably in the 1960s. Today, half the communes are connected by agreements on waste disposal, land planning, water supplies, and water purification, and one-third by agreements on education. The rate of collaboration has been particularly high in urban agglomerations; it has been much lower between rural communes that find it less necessary. In 1970, an inquiry gathered information on the methods favored by the communal authorities to solve intercommunal problems. Centralized solutions (state intervention, strengthening of the prefect's role) were strongly contested, while communal fusion collected almost 20 percent of the votes in favor (mainly from the towns), the institution of regional authorities about 25 percent (mainly from the suburban communes), and intercommunal associations more than 60 percent.[4] Thus, the great majority of communes agree with intercommunal collaboration; but the communes remain wary of supracommunal involvement since the majority accept only measures that represent a simplification in administration and allow them to keep their right of veto. This general attitude shows the difficulty of promoting the necessary restructuring of the local authorities.

THE LAUSANNE AGGLOMERATION

Lausanne, with 227,000 inhabitants in 1977 in an area of 12,565 hectares, is the fifth largest population center in Switzerland. Its population increased by 63 percent between 1950 and 1977. We shall briefly decribe the main problems of the central city and then outline the various stages of regional organization.

Problems of the Central City

In all important agglomerations, urban growth and its disparities cause the central city certain problems. In the case of Lausanne these are principally:

1. Increasing scarcity of available space (lack and high cost of land), which is driving out industry and requiring the installation of some public services outside communal land
2. Urban congestion, due to the considerable increase of cars (in 1977, one car per three inhabitants)
3. Its specialization in tertiary activites (77 percent of all workers in 1975), which makes the local economy more dependent on neighbors and also on general economic fluctuations
4. The increasing load of central functions, aggravated by a relative stagnation in fiscal revenue due to competition—especially undertaxing—on the part of certain suburban communes
5. Finally, the number of decision-making bodies within the agglomeration (twenty-four local authorities, the prefects of four districts, the cantonal government, and the numerous decentralized cantonal services, administered in different sections and areas)

To solve these problems the executive authority (*Municipalité*)[5] of Lausanne has undertaken a series of activities representing stages in the constitution of a regional authority.

Steps toward Regional Organization

The city's first step was to supply neighboring communes with services, acquire land, and move some public works and institutions outside the territory of Lausanne. Then, parallel with internal measures (restructuring of the administration, creation of institutions of liaison with the private local economy), the city's executive authority launched a series of attempts at intercommunal relations (attempts to fuse, meetings with the municipal corporations of neighboring communes, constitution of an intercommunal regional planning commission).

SUPPLYING OF SERVICES. Lausanne holds an important trump card in its attempt to realize its true territorial and political dimensions: the whole group of installations and services it has been developing since the end of the nineteenth century. Acting as entrepreneur toward its clients it has, in return for remuneration, put its installations at the service of neighboring communes. Thus, in 1974 it was supplying:

1. Forty-one communes with gas, four wholesale (one from the agglomeration) and thirty-seven retail (fourteen from the agglomeration);
2. Eighteen communes with electricity, twelve wholesale (eight from the agglomeration) and six retail (six from the agglomeration);
3. Sixty communes with water, forty-six wholesale (six from the agglomeration) and fourteen retail (ten from the agglomeration).

Moreover, twelve communes (ten belonging to the agglomeration) use the abattoirs of Lausanne, thirty-five (five in the agglomeration) use the Lausanne incinerator for waste disposal, and nine (all part of the agglomeration) have their water purified by the installation of the central city. Apart from this, Lausanne provides the neighboring communes with a number of other services, most of which come under bilateral conventions. In 1972, 132 such conventions were operating between Lausanne and the sixteen communes of its agglomeration.

The importance of these supplied services goes beyond the technical level; it allows the central city to intervene in the development of the adjoining communes. This is particularly evident in the strategic field of water supplies, where certain suburban communes confronted with great demographic expansion have been forced to ask Lausanne for supplementary water, abandon their own network of distribution, and also give up their power to establish an autonomous investment policy.

Here the central city possesses a lever for pressure toward regional integration. Some of the communes that have had to give up their supply network have, therefore, asked Lausanne to include them in decisions, notably by the expedient of intercommunal association. This solution has been refused by Lausanne out of fear of loss of control and of profit from businesses for which it has taken risks. However, in 1966 the Lausanne authority set up an intercommunal commission of industrial services, a consulting body of thirteen members of which nine are representatives of the partner communes. The next step will be the regionalization of industrial services. This will probably occur within the framework of a more extensive regional organization, of which the Intercommunal Regional Planning Commission is the initial stage.

LAND ACQUISITION AND TRANSFER OF PUBLIC WORKS. To meet the need for public services, Lausanne has been practicing a systematic policy of real estate acquisition since 1953. By 1973 it had increased its own property by 445 hectares. Until the 1960s it carried out the essential part of the buying on its own territory first, and since then on the territory of the adjoining communes (three-quarters of the area bought in the period 1970-73), to which the central city transfers public services that it cannot—and sometimes does not wish to—keep on home ground. Lausanne thus determines the layout of the periphery.

Until World War II Lausanne's communal territory was sufficient for the development of the town. Only a few industrial installations were moved outside (gasworks, abattoirs, and a pumping station). Since the war, and especially since the 1960s, Lausanne has had to transfer other public works and institutions that are impossible to expand on their original sites. The first such attempt, proposed in the 1940s, was the plan to convert the local airport into a suburban commune. Opposition from residents, who were just as concerned about the disturbance of their community as they were about the "imperialism" of the central city, has delayed the approval of this scheme for twenty years and probably forever. On the other hand, the suburban communes have accepted other public installations fairly willingly, such as the relocation of the shooting range in 1959, the new university under construction since 1968, and a second pumping station built in 1970.

Other projects are ready to be carried into effect. These include moving the federal polytechnical college to a site near the new university and moving a professional school, barracks, and duty-free port. The construction of two secondary schools outside the city will, for the first time, transfer some responsibility for teaching at this level from the city to the suburbs. Lastly, the construction of a bypass motorway, completed in 1974, has charged the peripheral communes with the load (with all the opposition that this suggests) of building the network of roads connecting the motorway with the center. This belt of main roads, like the medieval city walls, defines the boundaries of the modern urban area within which an adaptation of the political structures has become necessary.

INTERCOMMUNAL RELATIONS. Apart from bilateral relations with neighboring communes concerning particular services, the government of Lausanne did not attempt to introduce a policy of regional collaboration until World War II. From then on, until the mid-1950s, Lausanne tried to absorb some of the suburban communes. Due to negative reactions and the 1956 revision of the cantonal law on communes, which offers new opportunities for institutionalized relations (intercommunal conventions and associations), the local government has favored meetings with the executives of other communes since 1962. Since 1964 it has been developing a multilateral collaboration in a regional compass in order to set up a guiding plan of urbanization. This latter step foreshadows the construction of a supracommunal organization.

Of all the large towns in Switzerland, Lausanne is the only one that has not absorbed a single adjoining commune, even though after the war Lausanne's executive body had advocated this solution as "the only one that would allow harmony in urban development." Although opposition from the neighboring communes frustrated this policy, fusion was very nearly achieved in one case. The problems encountered by the city when it tried to absorb one or more suburban communes are typical, although both parties had more to gain than lose by fusion. The suburban commune had an opportunity to enjoy the many services offered by the city; Lausanne wanted more space. Moreover, there were practically no differences in tax rates between the two communes. But, the suburban commune rejected fusion chiefly from fear of being reduced to a mere sector drowned in a great urban center, with no opportunity for the residents to settle local affairs. A policy of absorption would have met with greater success if it had been accompanied by a scheme for the decentralization of the city's municipal power to a district level. From failures such as this Lausanne's government has learned to rely on means of intercommunal collaboration that have less impact on local susceptibilities and interests.

In 1962, Lausanne's executive body introduced a policy of meetings with the executive bodies of neighboring communes. From 1962 to 1974, there were twenty-eight sessions (twenty-five with suburban communes) concerning thirteen communes (eight of which were suburban). These meetings generally dealt with affairs directly concerning Lausanne and the partner commune, allowing an exchange of viewpoints and the clarification of misunderstandings, but they failed to reach a satisfactory solution to the problem of regional organization.

THE INTERCOMMUNAL REGIONAL PLANNING COMMISSION OF THE LAUSANNE AREA (IRPCLA). The IRPCLA is the first multilateral intercommunal institution that foreshadows the future constitution of a supracommunal body.[6] It was created by an intercommunal agreement signed on 29 September 1967 by representatives of twenty-seven communes of the area. This agreement marked the formal result of a series of acts that, since 1959, had progressively established the nature, powers, structure, and geographical extent of the grouping. Since then eight communes have joined, bringing the membership figure up to thirty-five in 1974.

The aim of the IRPCLA is limited to setting up a guiding plan for the regional layout. In practice, however, the commission is concerned with the principal communal activities, since land planning affects the basic data of local demography and economic activity. To carry out its mission the IRPCLA has two main bodies: a consulting committee of delegates from the communal executives and an executive council of eleven members designated by the consulting committee. Finances are provided by the member communes in proportion to population. The IRPCLA makes its decisions by a majority vote, but these decisions must be approved by the member communes before they can be put into effect. Moreover, the communes are not obliged to follow the guiding regional plan, which thus has only an indicative value. These limitations stemmed from the suburban communes' distrust of the city's initial proposal to set up a regional association (with powers delegated by the local authorities) with an intercommunal council, consisting of representatives elected by the consulting bodies of each member commune, and a steering committee designed to act as a supra-local council. Although most communes were suffering from the effects of urban expansion, they were not yet prepared to renounce even a small part of their autonomy.

After six years of work, a guiding regional plan was adopted on 26 June 1973. The communes agreed to limit urban development to established zones; to relieve the city of traffic congestion and to favor public transport; to protect green spaces; to create secondary centers; to develop the area in accordance with the guiding plan; and to coordinate communal and intercommunal projects. The communes had agreed to follow the established directives; however, they retained their full power to make decisions. Several incidents have indicated the limits of their commitment. The future of regional organization will depend on investments to realize its objectives and on the financing of joint operations. Moreover, to induce certain communes to accept the role assigned to them (in particular the restrictions on construction), it will be necessary to give them compensation, particularly by means of a system of intercommunal equalization. In the last analysis, only measures seeking to eliminate inequalities—above all financial inequalities—can make this scheme work. But, first, the opposition of the most priviliged communes must be overcome.

An attempt made in 1973 (mainly by the central city) to achieve a more extensive plan of integration did not succeed. This failure shows the difficulties of persuading certain local authorities to renounce a part of their powers for the good of a regional institution.

OTHER AGGLOMERATIONS

Having given a detailed account of the situation in Lausanne, aimed at showing the methods and problems of regional organization in the urban zones of Switzerland, we shall now briefly outline the situation in the four other large agglomerations (those with more than 250,000 inhabitants).[7] These are, in order of importance: Zürich (fifty-one communes, 718,000 inhabitants), Basle (twenty-four communes, 367,000 inhabitants), Geneva (28 communes, 323,000 inhabitants) and Bern (nineteen communes, 284,000 inhabitants).

In Bern and Zürich the process of regionalization resembles that of Lausanne, while Geneva and Basle have differences stemming mainly from their geographical situation, which gives their regional plans a transnational dimension. None of these agglomerations has progressed further than Lausanne in regional organization. Noteworthy, however, is the fact that before World War II all of these towns, except Lausanne, succeeded in enlarging their territory by the absorption of suburban communes.

Bern and Zürich

Bern's position is similar to that of Lausanne. As in Lausanne, intercommunal collaboration in the Bern region enjoyed an upswing in the 1960s; in the same way, the effort towards intercommunal grouping comes essentially from the central city. Moreover, the principal structure of cooperation effected in the field of regional planning resembles the IRPCLA.

Created in 1963, the Regional Planning Association of the town of Bern and its adjacent communes consists of twenty-one communes (with a total of 283,000 inhabitants in 1970) covering an area of 30,114 hectares. Its aim is the establishment of a regional plan. Its instruments are a general assembly (four delegates per commune) and a direction committee (one delegate per commune and three for Bern). It enjoys legal status but has no real powers of jurisdiction; its powers are limited to recommendations based on studies and research. As in Lausanne, the Bern Association has encountered difficulties because of the absence of any institutional means of strengthening intercommunal collaboration, in establishing common objectives of planning and in financing proposed projects. Thus a different approach to regional organization seems essential, but it will depend on putting into effect a new cantonal law on construction and on revising the law on communes.

In Zürich, efforts toward regionalization and intercommunal collaboration initiated by individual areas have been attempted for about twenty years. Since 1957 planning groups (of seven to fourteen communes each) have been formed, four of which worked in association with private law and two with public law. In 1958 they united their efforts in the Regional Planning Association of Zürich and District (RZD), which consisted of the six groups mentioned above (sixty-nine communes with a total of 792,000 inhabitants covering an area of 69,417 hectares) as well as the town and canton of Zürich. The RZD possesses a general assembly (representatives from the communes, the town and the state of Zürich) and an executive committee. Its aim is to establish a general regional plan.

Basle and Geneva

The cities of Basle and Geneva, both situated close to national frontiers, are participating in new schemes for collaboration with the communes of other countries (France and Germany in the case of Basle, France in the case of Geneva). Both Swiss cities have a strong influence on the foreign communes because they attract workers, many of whom commute daily from France and Germany.

The Basle region extends over Germany, France, and Switzerland and in 1972 contained 1,080 communes (210 in Switzerland, 570 in France and 300 in Germany), with a total of 1,975,000 inhabitants covering an area of 8,880 square kilometers. In 1963 a suprafrontier work group, the Regio Basiliensis, was formed, the result of private initiative that aimed to plan and encourage the economic, political, and cultural development of the defined region. This group is financed 60 percent by business concerns and 40 percent by public authorities. In France an equivalent body, the Work Group of the Haut-Rhine Area, was formed in 1965, while in Germany coordination is ensured by the District Authority of South Baden (*Regierungspräsidium Südbaden*) in Freiburg. Since 1970 the three work groups have been collaborating by means of an International Bureau of Coordination. Since 1971 a Standing Tripartite Conference of Regional Coordination, consisting of representatives from the regional political authorities of the three countries, has headed the three national bodies for the purpose of defining the general options of the Basle international region.

In Geneva intercommunal cooperation is restricted by the weak autonomy of the local authorities and the strong role of the canton. Since the 1960s, however, there has been some collaboration among the communes, as well as between the canton and the communes, within the framework of land planning. The communes work together to elaborate the sectorial guiding projects for planning undertaken by the Cantonal Commission of Urbanization. The

Geneva region, which includes the zones adjacent to the canton of Vaud and neighboring French departments (Ain and Haute Savoie), had no organization until the recent creation of the Commission for Regional Coordination, which hopes to establish exchanges of information between regional governments and coordination on particular problems.

EVALUATION AND PERSPECTIVES

If the desired aim is to give urban agglomerations an adequate political organization, the results of the Lausanne experience and of the other large towns of Switzerland may seem rather scanty. In the end, any description of the reorganization of local authorities in Switzerland comes back to drawing up an inventory of the obstacles and difficulties rather than presenting exemplary results. In a federal state the central authority cannot, as in unitary states, impose a ready-made institutional solution on its internal entities; the procedure is slower than that. But the movement has begun. It is to be hoped that from now on the authorities concerned will reach a suitable agreement before urban problems have expanded so much and grown so acute that metropolitan areas are ungovernable.

The most appropriate solution is the integration by fusion of the different communes that form the agglomeration. Other measures are incomplete, ineffective, or even contrary to the desired aim. At the same time, integration must be accompanied by a decentralization of local power from the government of the enlarged city to the district level. Thus, the agglomeration can reap the advantages of the greater rationality of global decisions, for example, investments concerning the urban community as a whole. At the level of the smaller divisions—perhaps absorbed communes—the advantages of decision making by local bodies for purely local affairs can be retained.

This solution would probably meet with the consent of the population. Most inhabitants of urban zones, especially those directly faced with the problems raised by an irrational political and administrative division, would probably welcome better organization. It is only a privileged minority that benefits from keeping the existing state of affairs by conceding minor reforms. The reorganization of local authorities is thus only one aspect of the general problem of social reform.

NOTES

1. In Switzerland, the bourgeois commune is formed by families that have their place of origin there.

2. See the study by Jean Meyland, Martial Gottraux, and Philippe Dahinden, *Communes suisses et autonomie communale* (Lausanne: Group d'étude de l'autonomie communale en Suisse, 1972).

3. See note 2 above.

4. Since some communes may have favored more than one type of reorganization, the total is more than 100 percent.

5. In the communes of Vaud, the executive body (*Municipalité*) consists of three to nine members elected directly by the people in the small communes and by the consulting committee (called the Communal Council) in the large communes such as Lausanne. It is chaired by a trustee (the equivalent of the French mayor).

6. The Intercommunal Regional Planning Commission of the Lausanne Area (*Commission intercommunale d'urbanisme de la région lausannoise*) includes the seventeen communes of the Lausanne agglomeration and about the same number of peripheral communes situated for the most part to the northwest, where urban expansion is foreseen.

7. Miss Nicole Chollet, sociologist, has done the basic research for this part of the text.

West Germany

Heinrich Siedentopf*

7

Owing to the nature of its historical development, West Germany now has a substantial number of metropolitan areas. Most of these can be regarded as instances of a decentralized economic, cultural, and social development. Outstanding examples are Berlin, the Ruhr area, Frankfurt, Stuttgart, Hamburg, and Munich. Much the same problem of reorganization arose in all other cities with a large surrounding urban area. It, therefore, was reasonable to discuss and develop organizational plans for these areas without consideration of their size or population. Later, when considering the details, the particular area was then taken into account.

The special problems related to the execution of public functions and to the political and administrative organization in metropolitan areas of West Germany have been known for many years, and effective organizations were developed in some areas at the beginning of the twentieth century that have been widely recognized at the international level, such as Greater Berlin and the *Siedlungsverband Ruhrkohlenbezirk* (SVR) (land settlement association of the Ruhr coal district). In addition, schemes of organization and procedure for cooperation among local authorities were also developed and were usually successful in enabling several territorial bodies to fulfill common functions.

However effective these examples have been, the industrial and economic development in West Germany has led to a considerable extenson of the same problems and to a variety of other problems in metropolitan areas in city-suburb relationships. In modern, industrialized society, public functions are no longer dependent upon boundaries set on the basis of local politics. Nor is it possible to depend on voluntary cooperation among several politically and administratively independent territorial bodies.

*Professor, Post-Graduate School for Administrative Sciences, Speyer, Federal Republic of Germany.

METROPOLITAN AREAS AND OVERALL REORGANIZATION

Reform in metropolitan areas is closely related to the reform of all local administration in West Germany. Though in all of the states they are dealt with as a special field, they are affected by general territorial reform and the reform of functions. It is therefore necessary to explain briefly the objectives and results of these two aspects of reform.

Territorial Reform

Since 1964 there has been a territorial reform of the administrative units in all states. This reform was largely completed by 1977 (its objective being to create units based on catchment areas) at all administrative levels (basic communal unit, municipal federation, county, and state administrative district) to provide modern administration of planning and services while simultaneously ensuring the political integration and participation of the citizen. In the course of reorganization the goal of creating larger and more efficient administrative units became predominant in order to promote the economic, social, and cultural life of the population in accordance with the requirements of our modern industrial and efficiency-oriented society. Yet the success of the territorial reform can be evaluated only by considering both the administrative and technical criteria, on the one hand, and the sociopolitical criteria on the other.

The results of the territorial reform show a substantial reduction in the number of administrative units at the various levels. Accordingly, the units have been enlarged. Many towns and cities in metropolitan areas have been enlarged by amalgamating them or including surrounding communities within them.

The accompanying table shows that the state administrative districts have undergone the least change in their number and area. The decrease in the number of non-county towns is comparatively small, whereas the number of counties has been cut almost in half. The decrease in the number of communities has been great, from 24,438 (1965) to 10,828 (1975). In some states, moreover, surrounding communities have been forced into municipal federations or administrative communities. They fulfill the majority of local functions. If we regard them as real communities, we obtain an overall number of only 6,526 communities, slightly more than a quarter of the number of communities that existed in 1965.

Reform of Functions

The far-reaching territorial reform has been supplemented by a reform of functions which assigns the administrative functions to the new administrative units according to their new area, the number of inhabitants, and the degree of efficiency. This redistribution of functions and responsibilities was completed in all federal states by 1978. However, it will remain a continuing task in the future because administrative requirements are constantly changing.

Table 7.1
WEST GERMANY: DIVISIONS OF THE FEDERAL TERRITORY FOLLOWING TEN YEARS OF TERRITORIAL AND ADMINISTRATIVE REFORM

State	Communities		Non-County towns		Counties		State Administrative districts	
	December 31, 1965	July 1, 1975	December 31, 1965	July 1, 1975	December 31, 1965	July 1, 1975	December 31, 1965	July 1, 1975
Bad-Wurttemberg	3381	1098[a]	9	9	63	35	4	4
Baryen (Proposal of 1/7/75)	7097	4178[b] 1925[c]	48	25	143	71	7	7
Berlin (West)	1	1	—	—	—	—	—	—
Bremen	2	2	2	2	—	—	—	—
Hamburg	1	1	—	—	—	—	—	—
Hesse (January 1, 1977)	2693	591	9	6	39	24 (20)	3	2
Niedersachsen (Proposal January 1975)	4245	1017[d]	15	10 (6)	60	24 (31)	8	8
North-Rhine Westphalia	2362	370	38	23	57	31	6	5
Rhineland-Pfalz	2920	2354[e]	12	12	39	24	5	3
Saarland	347	50	1	—	7	6	—	—
Schleswig-Holstein	1389	1166[f]	4	4	17	11	—	—
Totals	24438	10828	138	91	425	250	33	29
Provisional Final Result:		8401		87		229		25

a 178 unitary communities and 271 administrative communities (with 920 communities).
b 4123 unitary communities and 13 administrative communities (with 55 communities).
c 768 unitary communities and 352 administrative communities (with 1157 communities).
d 271 unitary communities and 143 collective communities (with 746 communities).
e 34 unitary communities and 165 municipal federations (with 2320 basic communal units).
f 100 unitary communities and 122 offices (with 1066 communities).
g Including the city association of Saarbrucken.
h If the districts of Muenster and Detmold are amalgamated as is being considered, the number of state administrative districts in North-Rhine Westphalia will be reduced to four.

The redistribution of functions has, of course, been determined by the average size and efficiency of the new administrative units. Like territorial reform, the reform of functions is based on aims that are partly contradictory. According to the specialized context of a particular task, administrative responsibilities should be combined at one administrative level; be assumed as efficiently as possible in a simple and well-defined administrative structure, with clearly drawn fields of competences, avoiding coordination shortcomings and duplication of work; improve the cost-benefit relationship; promote coordination with the appropriate local authority; and take into account the interests of the citizens, thus contributing to political integration. The reform of functions has led to a considerable shift of tasks to the lower administrative levels and to the concentration of parts of functions belonging together at one level. Compared with territorial reform, which takes place over long periods of time, the reform of functions is a constant process.

The reorganization of the metropolitan areas in West Germany contains elements of the territorial reform and the reform of functions. Administrative boundaries have been partly renewed and certain administrative functions have been newly assigned. Above all, the reorganization constitutes an organizational reform because new models of administration have been developed and realized for these areas.

Models for Metropolitan Areas

For several years intensive discussion has led to differing models of administrative organization for different metropolitan areas. Before individual examples are presented, the nature of these models should be explained.

The extreme positions are, on the one hand, voluntary, nonbinding cooperation among local authorities unchanged in territory, tasks, and finances, and on the other, the integration of the whole metropolitan area as a single city. Within this city the previously independent local authorities would be legally and actually dependent but would be retained as administrative subdivisions with limited rights of consultation and codetermination. Neither extreme represents a realistic solution to the specific problems of a metropolitan area. The first method would not integrate the area's service and planning functions. The second would eliminate self-governing political bodies in many fields despite their efficiency.

Between these extremes, reorganization must take account of the experience already gained from cooperation among local authorities and from the functions to be fulfilled by a metropolitan area. The new organizational form must depend not only on the good will and willingness to cooperate of the cities, towns, and communities involved; it must be binding and at the same time flexible and easy to develop. The powers and responsibilities of the continuing cities, towns, and communities, on the one hand, and the new organizational level of the metropolitan area, on the other, must be divided according to considerations of both administrative efficiency and local politics. It has to be ensured that the cities, towns, and communities can continue to fulfill tasks that enable them to integrate their citizens politically. The new body for the whole metropolitan area has to be entrusted with the tasks that determine the long-term development and provide the supralocal services in the area. To carry out these tasks, the new body must be given the power not only to plan but also to coordinate and implement services. As well as administrative control, there must be political control, achieved by having the decision-making bodies elected directly by the population or indirectly by the elected bodies of the cities, towns, and communities of the area.

As far as possible, each reorganization must take into account these partially contradictory objectives. It must also be accepted by the cities or towns concerned and by the state legislature. These requirements are difficult to meet. For instance, for sixteen cities and towns in the Ruhr area, the state government of North-Rhine Westphalia suggested in 1972 that four city associations be set up. With the aid of a legislature elected indirectly, each city association was to control the building activities of its member towns and was asked to draw up a development program for the whole area. It was also intended to supply services of regional importance, such as central markets, recreation centers, hospitals, refuse disposal, and slaughterhouses. This model failed because all the Ruhr area cities and towns concerned refused to accept it. In their view such an organization was not practicable because the two administrative levels overlapped and the responsibility for some tasks was not clearly defined. As a result, instead of implementing this model, the legislature adopted a considerably more drastic form of reorganization in this area by amalgamating towns to cities.

RECENT METROPOLITAN REORGANIZATIONS

It is still too early for a final assessment of the new organizational forms implemented since 1972. These forms vary widely. We shall not report on the organizatons in the metropolitan areas of the Ruhr and Hanover because they are no longer recent examples, except that the functions of the association of Greater Hanover were considerably extended by the law of 11 February 1974. We shall concentrate mainly on a comparison of the organizational structures, the setting of functions, and the provision of funds.

City Association of Saarbrucken

In the state of Saarland, the City Association of Saarbrucken was formed by the law of 19 December 1973. The metropolitan area of Saarbrucken was to be reorganized so that the state capital would be in a position to execute the growing number of tasks it has to fulfill as the economic, administrative, and cultural center of the state. Some towns and communities of the surrounding area therefore were integrated with the city to form a city association covering an area of 423.5 km^2 and comprising more than 400,000 inhabitants. Within this association, the city covers an area of 183.6 km² with about 221,000 inhabitants. The city association fulfills the supralocal public tasks for the entire area. By law, the city association is a transitional organization designed to create the preconditions for the future integration of the whole area into one city. For this purpose, voluntary cooperation of the cities, towns, and communities is not sufficient. The stage of common planning and common execution of administrative tasks preceding the formation of a uniform city requires constant and reliable cooperation in all administrative fields.

All tasks conferred by federal law upon the counties and non-county towns (which are independent of the counties) are assigned to the city association; the member towns and communities are left with functions that are, in general, conferred upon the county communities. Also, the state capital of Saarbrucken has lost its previous non-county position. The city association is a "circle" along the lines of the systematic approach usually applied in the federal republic. This means that the tasks of the city association can be extended, to the disadvantage of member towns and member communities, by decisions taken by the council of the city association. The council has its own legitimacy independent of the member towns because it is elected by the citizens by direct universal suffrage and by secret ballot. This confirms the predominant position of the city of Saarbrucken in the association and its council. On the other hand, the number of functions and the advancement of the city association can be justified only by this direct democratic legitimacy of the highest decision-making body. Moreover, the city association is entitled by law to levy taxes, fees, and so forth upon the members. The state grants the remaining funds required to execute its functions.

In a decision of 18 December 1974, the Constitutional Court of the Saarland declared that the city association of Saarbrucken was in accordance with the constitution. The court considered such a limitation of communal autonomy admissible because the supralocal interests of the general public required such a restriction. A longer period of administrative practice will be necessary to prove whether the planning of the development of the area by the city association and by the administrative authorities in the member towns and communities can be harmonized effectively, and whether the area can be integrated into a single city.

Surrounding Area Association of Frankfurt

By the law of 5 February 1974, the Surrounding Area Association of Frankfurt was formed as a corporation under public law. It comprises sixty-six towns and communities belonging to counties, two non-county towns, two entire counties, and parts of five other counties. The association includes about 1.5 million inhabitants and an area of 1,400 km². The surrounding area association is a multipurpose association that settles matters by statutes on its own responsibility. As opposed to the City Association of Saarbrucken, the Surrounding Area Association of Frankfurt is not a territorial body along the lines of a county but a communal, multipurpose association of a special kind.

Its task is to support and secure a proper development of the association area. To enable it to do so, its powers have been listed individually. Unlike the City Association of Saarbrucken, it is not authorized to withdraw tasks from member towns and communities. The fact that it has planning jurisdiction to influence the development of the area is its strongest feature.

The council of the association is made up of representatives of the towns and communities belonging to the association. However, in 1977 it was laid down in the law that the members of the council would be elected directly by the voters. The federal structural element would be a community chamber in which the member communities are represented. Thus there is no plan for an organizational amalgamation of the member towns and communities in the Frankfurt area.

Cities with District Councils

The current examples of reorganization in metropolitan areas are solutions involving associations—in the case of the city association, in a transitional form. These organizations maintain the territorial bodies of the area and their principal autonomy. After the city association system was rejected in North-Rhine Westphalia, the reorganization was carried out so that new cities were formed by amalgamating towns and communities. Within these cities the towns and communities continue to exist as legally dependent districts with a very limited right of codetermination.

The community area of such new cities is divided into districts following the original geographical boundaries. On one hand, these districts are administrative subdivisions of the central city administrations. On the other, they are first approaches to meet the local need for codetermination. The representative councils at the district level are not decision-making bodies but act as channels for information between the citizens and the central administration, exchanging views on the appropriate initiatives and activities of the central administration.

As with the organizational models already discussed, only a relatively long period of experience will show whether the district councils can develop a politically integrating force or whether the new central administration will eliminate the remaining possibilities of citizen participation provided by the district councils. Thus, a report on recent reorganizations in the metropolitan areas of West Germany can be only an inventory, not a final appraisal.

PART II

Regional or County Government

Introduction

Many countries with a unitary form of government have a second level of elected government between the municipalities and the central government. But often this level of government is weak. It may consist of only administrative areas for the central government, with elected councils who are only advisory to appointed governors and other officials. Or it may consist of federations of municipalities that send representatives to regional councils with only minimal powers and functions. At the same time, the basic units of local government are usually small in area and population. Because of the modern need for units of government with larger areas and populations and because a consolidation of the basic units would make them too remote from the citizens they serve, in several countries regional governments have been created or strengthened in recent years as an alternative to consolidation of the basic units. Examples of such countries, on which essays have been included in this part, are Belgium, France, Italy, and Norway. Also included are essays on proposals for regional reorganization in Finland, Ireland, the Netherlands, and Sweden.

The conflicting needs for keeping local government close to the citizens and for larger units of government have even persuaded some provincial or state governments in federal countries that they ought to have a regional level of government. Thus, the government of British Columbia has created a regional level of elected district government for the whole province. This development is described in the essay by Professor Tennant. Ontario and Quebec already have counties as a second level of local government, with county councils made up of members from the councils of the municipalities that the counties contain. But the counties exclude all cities, and in Ontario the largest towns, and the county governments are weak. A few years ago the government of Ontario announced its intention of installing province-wide regional government in place of county government, the chief differences being that the regions would be larger and would include the cities and towns. But then the government abandoned the plan in favor of regional governments for only the metropolitan areas, as explained in Professor Plunkett's essay on metropolitan government in Ontario. The essay by Professors Wettenhall and Power reveals that regional government has also been considered for the largest states in Australia.

The essays in Part 3 on Britain and West Germany reveal that these countries, which formerly had a large number of second-tier governments, have recently restructured or consolidated these governments along with the basic units of local government at the lowest level. Thus, in England and Wales, many of the county boroughs were placed under the jurisdiction of the counties, and county boundaries were redrawn to produce six metropolitan and forty-seven nonmetropolitan counties, while in Scotland the thirty-three counties were replaced by nine regions. In West Germany the number of counties has been drastically reduced by the state governments, from 425 in 1965 to 250 in 1975. In Northern Ireland, on the other hand, the two-tier county system, based on six counties and sixty-seven first-tier authorities, was abolished in favor of twenty-six unitary districts based on towns. The Carrolls argue in their essay that the results were unfortunate because the enlargement of the basic units created new religious minorities that felt threatened. The old two-tier system seemed better able to satisfy the conflicting needs of efficiency and participation.

WESTERN EUROPE

BELGIUM

FRANCE

ITALY

NORWAY

FINLAND

IRELAND

NETHERLANDS

SWEDEN

Belgium

Jacques Stassen [*]

8

Although they have been highly stable since the country became independent in 1830, Belgian institutions have, during the last few years, undergone thorough changes as a result of the 1967-70 constitutional amendments.

The changes became necessary because of certain problems present in most countries that are undergoing governmental changes. These include the increased intervention of public authorities in the economic and social fields, the need to ensure coordination of work and efforts in those fields, the need—for the sake of effectiveness—to bring the centers where decisions are made closer to the places where they are carried out, and the inability—for lack of means—of small local bodies to carry out the many tasks and provide the many services required by modern life. But, to understand Belgium's specific situation and the solutions put forward, a series of factors peculiar to the country should also be kept in mind.

First, with an area of less than 12,000 square miles, Belgium is a small but densely populated country, with an average of 830 inhabitants per square mile. It is also highly industrialized.

Second, Belgium is a country that, before attaining independence in 1830, was always under the domination of a major power—Austria, Spain, or France. The result has been a feeling of mistrust toward central authority in general. Popular feeling has reacted by attaching particular importance to the autonomy of local authorities. Today, Belgium has nine provinces and more than two thousand communes. The contrast with its northern neighbor, the Netherlands, is striking, since that country, with roughly the same population and originally as many communes, today has less than a thousand communes.

Third, Belgium is, moreover, a country comprising three cultural communities and three languages: French, Dutch, and German. The north of the

[*]Professor of Law, University of Liège, and former Secretary General, International Institute of Administrative Sciences, Brussels.

country, that is, the provinces of West Flanders, East Flanders, Antwerp, and Limburg, is predominantly Dutch-speaking. The south is French-speaking and comprises the provinces of Hainaut, Namur, Liège, and Luxembourg. As to the province of Brabant, it comprises a Dutch-speaking part, a French-speaking part, and Brussels, the capital, which is considered to be bilingual. The German-speaking region is in the east of the province of Liège, along the German border.

Until the beginning of the century, the north of Belgium was chiefly looked upon as an agricultural region and the south as an industrial region. However, since the end of World War II, the north has become highly industrialized. The south, where economic activity was centered primarily on coal mining and steel production, is suffering the consequences of recession in its various activities. Politically speaking, there are also differences between the two regions. The *Christelijke Volkspartei* (CVP) holds a large majority in the north, while the *Parti Socialiste Belge* (PSB) has a majority in the south. Psychologically, too, there are differences between the two regions. The Belgian state long had French as its one official language. Only after long exertion did the Dutch speakers manage to get their legitimate aspirations regarding language and culture recognized. They have remained sensitive to this issue and, therefore, agreement is sometimes difficult when the interests of the regions differ.

The 1967-71 revision of the Constitution established the notion of "region" in Belgian public law. But the notion varies in that the Constitution itself distinguishes several kinds of regions, namely, language, cultural, and socio-economic regions. The idea of region, before appearing in the Constitution, had already been used in special statutes, such as the Town and Development Planning Act of 15 March 1962, the Economic Expansion Act of 18 July 1959, and the Planning and Economic Decentralization (Organization) Act of 15 July 1970. In the first of them, the term *region* was nowhere defined. In the second, the region was equivalent to a portion of the national territory that was essentially variable in area and had to be specially aided by the public authorities due to its economic position. In pursuance of the third statute, the territory of Belgium was divided into three regions, Wallonia, Flanders, and Brabant, subject to certain districts of Brabant also belonging to either the Walloon or the Flemish region.

This study will examine the regions as they have been established by the constitutional amendments and the Planning and Economic Decentralization Act, under four main headings:

1. Language regions
2. Cultural communities
3. Socioeconomic regions
4. Regional economic decentralization

LANGUAGE REGIONS

Out of Belgium's population of some ten million inhabitants, about three-fifths are considered to be Dutch-speaking and two-fifths French-speaking. About 60,000 are German-speaking. The drafters of the most recent constitutional amendment intended to recognize officially the existence of these languages that form the basis of the cultural communities whose autonomy was provided for later in the Constitution. They also intended to determine the regions in which the languages would be used. They were, however, faced with a difficulty in Brussels, the capital of the kingdom, since among the million or so inhabitants in its area some are French-speaking and others Dutch-speaking. This is why Belgium today is divided into four language regions, French, Flemish, German, and bilingual.

Each of the kingdom's communes must belong to a given language region, which determines the language used within its boundary. The regions have been mapped by statute. The bilingual region of Brussels thus only comprises the nineteen communes of the Brussels urban area. As a result, Brussels is surrounded by the Dutch-speaking region. The boundaries of the language regions may be altered by Parliament, but only when a special majority has been secured. The bill to that effect has to be voted by majorities of the French-speaking and Dutch-speaking groups in each of the Houses, subject to majorities of both groups being present and to the number of votes in favor in the two language groups being at least two-thirds of the votes cast. In other words, the amendment was formulated so that, as far as possible, the language boundaries would not be brought back into question.

CULTURAL COMMUNITIES

After the country had been divided into four language regions, the existence of three cultural communities—French-speaking, Dutch-speaking, and German-speaking—was incorporated in the Constitution. The provision is important because it has introduced the entirely new notion of "cultural community" into Belgian public law. Until then, the Belgian State had only taken cognizance of Belgian citizens, as individuals, and, beyond them, of the official organs of the state. [1]

The communities have organs of their own called cultural councils. But the Constitution left to Parliament the task of settling the powers and membership of the German-speaking community's cultural council, though it had decided both points for the other two cultural councils. The difference in treatment was justified because the German-speaking population accounts for only some 60,000 of the country's population and is established in a small area having specific problems. The majority at the time believed that a sui generis solution ought to be found for that community.

Membership of the Cultural Councils

The French-speaking cultural council is comprised of the French-speaking deputies and senators of the national Parliament, while the Dutch-speaking cultural council is comprised of the Dutch-speaking deputies and senators. The language group to which a deputy or senator belongs has been determined by an act of 3 July 1971, according to the region in which he was elected. Deputies and senators elected in the French-speaking and German-speaking language regions belong to the French-speaking group. Those elected in the Dutch-speaking region belong to the Dutch-speaking group. Deputies and senators elected in the Brussels region and the senators elected by the Provincial Council of Brabant as well as the senators elected by the Senate, belong to the group in whose language they took the constitutional oath or, should they have taken it in both languages, to the group of whichever language they used first. The French-speaking cultural council now has 172 members and the Dutch-speaking cultural council 215 deputies and senators.

The membership of the German-speaking cultural council has been determined by an act of 10 July 1973. It is comprised of twenty-five members elected directly by the electors of the communes forming part of the German-speaking region, which is a language region for administrative purposes. Moreover, members of Parliament considered to belong to the German-speaking region and certain provincial councillors, because they reside in a commune of the region and have taken the constitutional oath in German, may, if they are not already members through direct election, attend the meetings with the right to speak but not vote.

Powers of the Cultural Councils

The councils of the French-speaking and Dutch-speaking cultural communities are empowered by the Constitution to issue decrees in the matters specified further on. The notion of ''decree'' is new in Belgian public law, and it may unquestionably be inferred from all the discussions preparatory to the constitutional revision that the intention was to assign to the cultural councils ''a norm-making power with the force of law in any matters attributed to them and within the limits assigned to them,'' particularly concerning territorial competence. The cultural councils are not qualified to deal with any matters which the Constitution has expressly reserved to legislation, that is, to the legislature. As to their subject matter, the decrees may be looked upon as ''regional'' norms having the force of law. Accordingly, they do not come under the control exercised, in pursuance of article 107 of the Constitution, by the judiciary over the acts of the executive.

The question arises of possible conflicts either between a law and a decree or between two decrees. The Constitution made the legislature responsible for organizing a procedure whereby such conflicts might be forestalled and settled. That was one of the purposes of the act of 3 July 1971, under which a third section, the Conflicts of Competence Section, was added to the two existing sections, the Legislation Section and the Administration Section, of the Council of State.

Two kinds of remedies are provided for, a direct appeal and a pre-judicial appeal. A direct appeal may be made by the Council of Ministers only. A pre-judicial appeal may be made, except by the Court of Cassation, by any court of law, judicial or administrative, which has before it a question relating to a contradiction either between a law and a decree or between decrees of different cultural councils and is of the opinion that the question needs to be solved for it to deliver its decision. The Conflicts of Competence Section issues its decisions in rulings that become enforceable unless they have been annulled by the Houses of Parliament within ninety days of the presidents of both Houses having been notified of them by the clerk of the Council of State. Opinions about the procedure have varied very widely. The fact remains that, by the beginning of 1979, no appeal had been placed before the section which, to our knowledge, in any case, had not yet been formed.

As to the German-speaking cultural council, its powers are different (act of 10 July 1975). In some cases, it is empowered to express an opinion, which it does either *sua sponte* or at the request of the presidents of the Houses or of one or more ministers. It also has rule-making power. Certain of its rules, for instance those concerning the languages used in education, only come into force after they have been ratified by the Houses of Parliament. One of the reasons put forward for refusing this council the power to issue decrees was that, unlike the other two councils, it is not solely composed of members of Parliament.

Competence of the Cultural Councils

SUBJECT MATTER. In some matters, the cultural councils' competence is conferred directly by the Constitution, while in others it is defined by the legislature. Competence in the following matters is conferred by the Constitution:

1. Education, excluding everything related to the Schools Pact (*paix scolaire*), the organizational structure of education, academic awards, grants, salaries, and pupil-number standards, which are reserved to Parliament
2. Use of languages for public administration, for teaching in establishments provided, assisted, or recognized by public authorities, for labor relations between employers and employees, and for the formal and other documents required of enterprises by legislation and regulations

Before competence may be exercised in certain other matters, it has to be defined by the legislature by a special majority. This applies to cultural matters and to cooperation between the cultural communities and to international cultural cooperation.

An act of 21 July 1971 has determined what should be understood by "cultural matters":

1. The defense and progress of the language
2. The promotion of training for research workers
3. The arts, including the stage and the film
4. The cultural inheritance, museums, and other cultural scientific institutions
5. Book and record libraries and similar facilities
6. Radio and television, except for government broadcasts and advertising
7. Youth policy
8. Continuing education and cultural stimulation
9. Physical training, sport and open-air life
10. Leisure and tourism

As will have been observed, the list is detailed. Moreover, the act specifies that "the Council's competence to regulate cultural matters shall include the power to adopt decrees concerning the infrastructure," thus leaving plenty of scope for interpretation and action.

TERRITORIAL COMPETENCE. The territorial competence of the French-speaking and Dutch-speaking cultural councils varies according to the subject matter. First, there are language matters, which are those connected with the use of languages in public administration, teaching, labor relations, and the documents of enterprises. Decrees relating to such matters are normally enforceable in the council's language region only. Then, there are cultural matters, teaching, cooperation between the cultural communities, and international cultural cooperation. In this area many problems had to be dealt with differently because of the existence of the Brussels region, where members of two language communities are found together and where each consequently has special interests to defend. Decrees relating to such matters have the force of law in the language region of the cultural council concerned. They also apply to any institutions that, on account of their activities, have to be regarded as belonging exclusively to one cultural community or the other in the bilingual area of Brussels Capital.

The preceding distinctions do not exist for the council of the German-speaking cultural community. The council's territorial competence only covers the German-language region as delimited by the Use of Languages for Public Administration Act.

Enforcement of the Decrees

Since the cultural decrees are, in fact, "regional laws," their enforcement is beyond the powers of the councils that have adopted them. Rather, the responsibility devolves on the executive as specified in the Constitution, that is, on the king, but, in fact, on the government. It is part of the latter's functions to make the necessary regulations and orders for the purpose without being entitled to rescind the decrees or decide against enforcing them.

Financial Means

The revisers of the Constitution decided against providing the cultural councils with their own financial means and, more particularly, empowering them to levy rates, which would have helped to entrust them with an autonomy they sometimes claimed. The Belgium hoped for by the majority was a regionalized Belgium, not a federalized Belgium.

The system that was adopted is as follows. For the French-speaking and Dutch-speaking cultural councils, the national Parliament, on the government's proposal, fixes the appropriations placed at the disposal of each cultural council. The amounts are worked out in two parts. One is based on objective criteria, such as the number of inhabitants and projects to be carried out. The other, for purposes such as radio and television, for which no objective criteria can be found, is calculated on the basis of equal grants. The total appropriations for each council are voted by Parliament. It then rests with the councils, according to their own policies, to settle by decree the purposes for which the amounts will be assigned. The German-speaking cultural council, instead, receives a grant for financing its activities which appears each year in the cultural grants budget, to which its operating expenses are also chargeable.

Cooperation between the Cultural Communities

Though it was desired that the Constitution should ensure the cultural communities a measure of autonomy, it was not intended that the result should be to sever all bonds between them. To avoid such a danger, it was provided that each cultural council should include a committee for promoting cooperation between the two communities. During each session of the councils, the committees are to hold at least two joint meetings as combined committees for cooperation.

Conclusion

This reform of the Belgian institutions has established, beside the national Parliament, two new parliamentary assemblies, which are, at the same time, of a regional nature and limited competence. As a result, some feel that Belgium has entered into a period of pre-federalism. The time has not yet come to appraise the reform. One can only note that the cultural councils have availed themselves sparingly of their power to issue decrees and that their influence has chiefly been felt in the financial field, through the use of the block allocations appropriated in the national budget.

Neither may it be overlooked that the cultural regionalization that has been sketched in this chapter has gone hand in hand with an economic and social regionalization. The latter has perhaps been devised from a different approach, which may, in the the future, produce effects whose significance are difficult to assess today.

THE SOCIOECONOMIC REGIONS

Like most countries, Belgium has been faced with the need for what has sometimes been called decentralization, sometimes regionalization, and sometimes other names, but whose purpose, in any case, is to bring the economic, social, and administrative decision-making centers closer to those they affect so that they may be better suited to their objectives and rendered more effective.

Parliament had certainly made some efforts in that direction, especially by voting various acts, the latest of which was passed on 15 July 1970 and will be discussed further on, but it was widely thought that advantage should be taken of the constitutional revision in progress to establish the existence of the regions, lay down the basis of their organization, and determine their competence. Unfortunately, although almost unanimous agreement could easily be reached on the first of these points, no agreement was reached on the other two. Finally, the following article 107D of the Constitution was adopted:

Belgium shall comprise three regions: the Walloon region, the Flemish region, and the Brussels region.

A law shall assign to the regional organs, which it shall set up and whose members shall be elected representatives, competence to regulate, in the territories and in the manner it shall establish, such matters, except for those referred to in articles 23 and 59B, as it shall determine.

The law must be passed by a majority of votes in each language group of each of the Houses, provided that the majority of the members of each group are present and that the number of affirmative votes in the two language groups amounts to two-thirds of the votes cast.

The division of Belgium into three regions has thus become a constitutional reality. There will definitely be regional organs with elected representatives, but the regions' boundaries have not been fixed. No explanation is given of the nature of these regions. All that is known is that they should not be mistaken for the language regions or the cultural regions, since those matters have been expressly placed outside their competence. This has been done by articles 23 and 59B, mentioned in the new article, which deal with the use of languages and cultural matters, respectively. It seems, however, to follow from a study of the parliamentary proceedings that these regions will be of an economic and social nature. The division of Belgium into regions appears to be the consequence of a series of political and human factors, such as community problems, the development of a regional consciousness, and the quest for a better way to manage the state.

From the various proceedings prior to the adoption of the text quoted above, it may be deduced that the following matters might be within the competence of the regions: town and development planning and land policy, regional economic expansion policy and employment policy, certain aspects of industrial legislation and energy policy, housing policy, family and population policy, public health and sanitation, tourism and the welfare of immigrants, and fishing, hunting and shooting, and forestry.

It should be observed, however, that the lack of agreement among political parties has so far prevented a law from being passed, since the special majorities referred to above could not be assembled. The Tindemans government, nevertheless, persuaded Parliament to vote a preparatory and experimental law on the subject. It was passed on 1 August 1974, and may, at the most, provide some indication about future regionalization. It is therefore examined in the following pages.

The act provisionally delimits the three regions. Their boundaries coincide with those of the regional economic councils set up by the Economic Decentralization Act of 15 July 1970, which will be returned to later. The three regions are placed on an equal footing in organs and attributions. The membership of the organs of the Brussels region is, however, adjusted to its special position.

As has been stated very aptly, the institutional structure is a prefiguration of the final organization. Regional councils cooperate with specialized departmental committees to prepare policies and draft legislation applicable to their regions. They are only able to present proposals which, to be carried out, need to be examined and adopted by the organs of national sovereignty in compliance with the ordinary procedure.[2]

The Regional Organs

The act instituted two regional organs in each region: one a deliberative assembly, the Regional Council, and the other an executive body, the Ministerial Committee on Regional Affairs.

MEMBERSHIP. Some people would have liked the regional councils to be elected directly, but others were afraid that this would form a kind of second parliament. They considered that the regional councillors should be drawn from among the members of the existing elected assemblies, either Parliament or the local assemblies, or both.

The latter opinion prevailed. The seats were distributed on the basis of two criteria: place of residence and language group. Thus, the Flemish Regional Council was comprised of the senators who resided in the Flemish region and belonged to the Dutch-language group. It was an assembly of ninety-seven members. The Walloon Regional Council was comprised of the senators who resided in the Walloon region and belonged to the French-language group. They formed an assembly of sixty-two members. The Brussels Regional Council was comprised of the senators who resided in the Brussels region and belonged to the French-speaking or Dutch-speaking language group, and also forty-two members of the Brussels Urban Area Council, distributed proportionally to the number of members of each language group. An assembly of fifty French-speaking and fourteen Dutch-speaking members was thus formed.

The regional councils were abolished by an Act of 1977, since the government and the political parties together were looking into the possibility of moving on to a final regionalization, as provided for in article 107D of the Constitution. The negotiations led to the Egmont and Stuyvenberg Agreements, named after the mansions in which they were signed. Then, everything was suddenly brought back into question. New elections were held on 17 December 1978, and no final solution to the regional problems has since been found. Only the ministerial committees remain. These ministerial committees on regional affairs, the regional executive bodies, are comprised of members of the government appointed by Royal Order in the Council of Ministers.

In this connection, it should be explained that for some years already, apart from the fields of national education and of culture where, as already pointed out, ministers' competence is specialized, regional powers have been allocated to certain members of the government. This was particularly the case in the 1973-74 Leburton government, which included several secretaries of state with regional competence in certain sectors, as well as a minister of Brussels affairs, a minister of Flemish affairs and a minister of Walloon affairs.

In June 1974, Mr. Tindemans, the new prime minister, went further on those lines: the first three ministerial committees on regional affairs, set up by the Royal Order of 8 October 1974, are quite naturally composed of the ministers and the secretaries of state whose powers are limited to one of the three regions.

COMPETENCE. The competence of the regional organs is strictly limited to the matters, specified by the act, ''in which wholly or partly different regional policies are justified'': town and development planning, including land policy, the regrouping of rural holdings, urban renovation and the clearing of derelict industrial sites; economic expansion policy and employment policy; housing policy; family and population policy; public health and sanitation policy; the welfare of immigrants; water policy; hunting and shooting, fishing and forestry; industrial and energy policy; and commune organization. It will be observed that the matters selected are, with slight changes, those listed during the discussions preparatory to the vote on article 107D.

POWERS. The regional councils were consultative organs. They stated their opinions but took no decisions. During the preparation of legislation or regulations, the regional councils had the right to state an opinion in some cases and had to be asked for their opinion in others. The opinion was optional when the provisions concerned were of a regional nature and their subject matter was within the competence of the councils. Such opinions were given in the form of reasoned proposals addressed to the prime minister, the minister responsible for the region's affairs, and, if draft legislation was involved, the presidents of the Houses. The council's opinion, however, had to be requested before introducing any bill whose field of application was limited to the whole or to a part of the council's region or to an institution established there, and by which legal provisions concerning any of the matters listed above as within its competence would be made, amended, or rescinded.

In cases where the council's opinions must be requested, the legal obligation went no further. Should the council fail to make known its opinion after having been so requested, there was no stalemate, and the national legislature, which remained sovereign, might proceed to the examination of the bill. In addition, the council had a duty to volunteer opinions, particularly about anything affecting regional policy in the matters listed and about the budget appropriations for covering the regional policy expenditure.

As to the ministerial committees on regional affairs, the act specifies that their terms of reference are:

To examine any reasoned proposals presented by the council

To discuss any bills about which the council's opinion must be requested

To discuss any draft royal orders concerning any matters within the council's competence, which are intended to apply only in the territory of the region, and which have been presented to it either by one of its members or by the prime minister

To prepare and coordinate the region's policy in the fields in which that policy may be carried out

To propose the budget estimates for covering the regional policy expenditure

To discuss any proposals for the establishment, decentralization, or deconcentration of public services, agencies, or institutions entrusted with the implementation of the regional policy

Generally speaking, the committees express their opinions concerning the policies. It may be added that the operation of the committees is regulated by the Royal Orders of 19 November 1974 and 20 November 1974.

FINANCE. Like the cultural councils, the regional institutions do not have any resources of their own. They are only able to use those funds which the national Parliament has consented to place at their disposal.

Each year, the government sets apart a lump sum in the general budget to cover regional policy expenditure in the three regions. The amount is distributed on the basis of statutory criteria, one-third proportionately to the number of inhabitants, one-third proportionately to the area of the region, and one-third proportionately to the yield of income tax. The data required for the calculations have to be fixed yearly by an order in the Council of Ministers. After the distribution, each ministerial committee on regional affairs proposes how the appropriations for covering the regional policy expenditure in its region should be allocated. Finally, after the regional council concerned has given a reasoned opinion, separate regional budget estimates for each region are presented to the Houses of Parliament.

Conclusion

It may be asked what the outcome of the experimental act will be. It is difficult to judge at this stage of initial application and it may, perhaps, be regretted that, from the outset, the act has met with difficulties. Some of these are due to the negative attitude of certain political parties, including the Belgian Socialist party, the largest in the opposition, and others are due to the possible danger of conflicts of competence with organs set up in the framework of economic decentralization a little more than four years ago by the Act of 15 July 1970, which will be discussed below.

ECONOMIC DECENTRALIZATION

As stated above, a measure of economic decentralization has been achieved in Belgium since 1970, under the Act of 15 July 1970. It was in that year that three regional economic councils were established: the Regional Economic Council for Wallonia, the Regional Economic Council for Flanders, and the Regional Economic Council for Brabant.

Each of the first two councils comprises, first, thirty members, of whom eighteen are nominated by the Houses of Parliament and twelve by the provincial councils, and, second, thirty members, of whom fifteen are nominated by organizations representative of industry, large nonindustrial enterprises, small enterprises and self-employed persons, and agriculture, and fifteen are nominated by organizations representative of the workers. These members are appointed by the king on two lists, and together they designate from six to ten members chosen as authorities in the fields of economics. The governors of the country's nine provinces each attend the meetings of the economic council of their province's region with the right to speak but not vote.

As to the Regional Economic Council for Brabant, the fact that the Brussels urban area is in its territory and also the language chart have to be taken into account. Following the same principles of representativeness, it comprises an equal number of representatives of the Brussels urban area and the remainder of the province, nominated by the other two economic councils, respectively.

The three councils are competent to express opinions and, generally, to make recommendations. Their terms of reference are to study problems; to state opinions previous to decisions concerning the appointment of the members of the regional directorate of the Planning Office, the geographical areas covered by the regional development companies, the distribution of the principal budget appropriations and their allocation to purposes such as the companies' infrastructure and equipment, bills or draft general regulations about regional development and the determination of development areas, and either voluntarily or at the government's request, any problems affecting economic development; to collect all data and suggestions supplied by the regional development companies, coordinate them, and reconcile divergent interests, if any; to adopt the drafts of the regional plan; to transmit those drafts to the planning office; and to collect all information or reports relating to the implementation of the part of the plan that concerns them.

The act also provides that the king may, by order of the Council of Ministers, extend the advisory competence of the regional economic councils and determine in which cases they must be consulted by the government. It is, moreover, specified by the act that the regional economic councils' opinions and proposals must be formulated in reports in which any minority views expressed during their discussions are recorded. This provision is important, since the various opinions are reproduced in the document transmitted to the higher authorities and an opportunity is given to state them in the debate.

The Regional Development Companies

The Act of 15 July 1970 also provided for the institution of regional development companies, which are public corporations endowed with personality at civil law. Their establishment is, however, a matter for the provinces. So far, seven regional development companies have been formed and, together, cover the whole country. There are five of them in the Dutch-speaking region. In the French-speaking region, however, the provinces preferred to establish only one regional development company for the whole area, since in that part of the country the communes had already formed a number of associations that had established companies for regional development. What was needed was to coordinate hitherto dispersed efforts, a task which a single regional development company could perform. A regional development company has also been established in the administrative district of Brussels Capital.

Under the Act of 1970, the objectives of the regional development companies are: the general study, the policy and the promotion of economic development in their area; and listing the requirements of their region, making progress reports, and providing the regional economic council with the necessary data for drafting and implementing the regional plan. It should be added that, if the private sector shows indifference, the regional development companies have received authority to take up the implementation of industrial projects, particularly those suggested by the Industrial Promotion Office, with the technical and financial assistance of the National Investment Company or of any regional investment company concerned. The necessary powers to enable them to do so are defined by royal order after the competent regional economic council has been consulted.

Though these development companies have only been in existence for a short time, one observation may already be made. In the Flemish region and the Province of Brabant, the regional development companies seem to have made a good start, but the same cannot be said of the Walloon Regional Development Company. Its articles were approved by a Royal Order at the end of 1973, and, since then, most of its time seems to have been taken up by political discussions.

CONCLUSION

From this rapid survey it can be realized that Belgium has, for some years, been undergoing a thorough institutional change. As stated in the introduction, the change is due not only to causes common to all countries at a certain stage of development and based on the requirements of modern life, but also to causes peculiar to Belgium, such as the language question, the special position of the City of Brussels, and the sociological and political differences between the language communities.

The establishment of the cultural councils has tended to give the country a new look. It is no longer altogether a unitary state and is not yet a federal state. The competence of the councils is, of course, limited to cultural matters, but it also includes ''the power to adopt decrees concerning the infrastructure related to such matters.'' This provision might extend their sphere of action. However, it should be stated that, during their three years of existence, they have shown comparatively little activity.

As to regionalization, it will have been observed that the Constitution simply contains a few brief provisions proclaiming the existence of three regions and declaring that the regional organs will comprise elected representatives and may have no powers in matters of a linguistic or cultural nature. Its application comes up against various kinds of difficulties, particularly owing to the grudging support of certain political parties, including an important party now in the opposition.

Even if the legislature contrives to carry out the task devolved to it by the Constitution, the problems will not be solved. A controversy has already arisen over the legal nature of the regional organs' decisions and whether they will be rule-making acts or regional laws like the cultural decrees. Another problem is that raised by the relations among the three regional councils established by the Act of 1 August 1974, and the regional economic councils and development companies established by the Act of 15 July 1970, which is still in force. The competence of the former is certainly wider than that of the latter. At all events, if they wish to be effective, it is essential that they coordinate their methods of action and intervention.

There is also a final problem that will require solution, namely the distribution of powers between the regional and provincial organs. Some people have maintained that in a country like Belgium, which covers only a fairly small area, the existence of provinces will no longer be justified, especially when large urban areas and federations of communes have been formed. There certainly will be problems of competence to solve, but the provinces have many tasks of a general as well as provincial nature that it appears difficult to take out of their hands. Besides, from a sociological point of view, the provinces unquestionably meet very definite needs.

We conclude with a general impression. A comprehensive view of the new regional institutions already set up, combined with those which, though legally provided for, remain to be established, inevitably gives rise to the thought that the resulting governmental machinery is quite cumbersome and certainly will be difficult to operate.

NOTES

1. Robert Senelle, *The Belgian Constitution—Commentary*, Memo from Belgium *Views and Surveys*, no. 166 (Brussels: Ministry of Foreign Affairs, 1974). p. 17.
2. P. Wigny, *Journal des Tribunaux* (1974), p. 633.

France

Fred C. Bruhns

9

It is probably no exaggeration to state that the need for an effective partnership between national and local governments constitutes the main reason for the development of regional levels of governance. With the worldwide demand for more "grass-roots" democracy and a greater devolution of power to local levels, national governments, whatever tradition and political ideology they represent, have had to respond and to pay at least lip service to the cause of local self-government. New legal government structures have sprung up and proliferated almost everywhere. The result has been that the articulation of local interest became so diverse, fragmented, and conflict-laden that national governments today find it increasingly impossible to deal with it without assistance. They are looking for this assistance to come from intermediary governmental levels, which are expected to consolidate, coordinate, and reconcile conflicting local interests and then negotiate and integrate these with national interests.

The French case with which we are concerned here furnishes a particularly instructive illustration for the high fragmentation of local interests and the urgent need for their consolidation and integration with national aims. While France in 1971 had 37,650 communities (communes) with local government structures and elected officials, only .1 percent (37 communities) of these had more than 100,000 inhabitants. Sixty-one percent had less than 500 inhabitants, and 93 percent less than 2,000.[1]

The integrative task of regional management is highly difficult and exacting. It must deal, simultaneously, with pressures for consolidation and centralization (due to local government fragmentation), decentralization and devolution of power (due to the need for local participation), and deconcentra-

*Associate Professor of Public Administration at the Graduate School of Public and International Affairs, University of Pittsburgh, and author of a related article entitled: "Recent Regional Approaches to Local Government Reforms: A Comparison Between France and the United States," in *Polish Round Table*, Seventh Yearbook of the Polish Association of Political Sciences (Warsaw: Ossolineum, 1977), pp. 283-306.

tion (due to the national government's responsibility to direct national development). Regional governance must properly balance these task ingredients. In addition, it must skillfully handle acute political and economic sensitivities in its area, be obedient to but also critical of national directives, and devise effective channels of communication and administrative procedures for its middle-man functions, which fit in the area of negotiation rather than executive implementation. From many points of view, regional governance must play the role of an "honest broker."

There is, however, one redeeming factor to alleviate the difficulties of regional governance. This is its limited visibility when compared with national or local government. The average citizen is keenly aware that local and national government decisions will affect him directly and immediately; he therefore will press his right to vote and to be heard on these levels. Regional governance, however, is often new and much less clear to him. Since his total capacity to be concerned with government is limited, he frequently pays little attention to that level. Regional governance may thus be able to work in a "twilight" conducive to the sensitive nature of its negotiational functions.

France, when coping with its regional task, had two basic alternatives. She could recognize the region as a separate human collectivity distinct from local and national collectivities and provide it with a full-fledged level of government subject to all rules of the nation's political system, such as election by direct, popular vote and a proportionally representative political assembly or parliament. This was the alternative of establishing a genuine regional government.

The other alternative was regional governance, a system of management for regional affairs which stops short of claiming to be, and of being perceived by the citizenry, as an official subnational level of government. It is a complex administrative arrangement that emphasizes technical rather than political tasks. It furnishes to national government the opportunity of experimenting with a much larger variety of formulas for governmental organization than are at its disposal at the national and local levels, which are in the limelight of citizen attention. To some extent, it permits them to keep regional issues and conflicts involving political power in the background, at least camouflaging if not fully hiding them, and to direct public attention to the more neutral problems of planning and public investment technology, which the average citizen is neither inclined nor competent to scrutinize. While the political tasks of regional management, that is, the negotiation, conflict mitigation, and integration of local and national interests, still have to be tackled, they can, under this option, be performed under rules less strict than those applicable to an official level of government and in the "twilight" that shields regional authorities from excess public glare. Regional governance, as a formula, thus seems to offer more flexibility, discretion, and protection to its executives than does formal regional government to its officials. France, after weighing the implications of both alternatives, decided to choose regional governance as the formula best suited to her particular conditions.

While the French region appeared first as a sort of spatial thinking device for various administrative and planning purposes, it was formally legitimized only on 5 July 1972, when Law No. 72-619, the so-called Regional Reform Law, was promulgated. In accordance with the policy decision to create regional governance in preference to a new intermediary level of regional government, President Pompidou's government proposed, and the National Assembly accepted, giving each French region the status of a "public establishment" (*établissement public*). They thus created a kind of public corporation rather than an additional territorial or local human collectivity that would have required a constitutional amendment.

There were other reasons for France to embark on the venture of regionalism by giving, at least initially, its new regional units the legal framework of a public establishment. It seemed to permit a tighter steering and control of the nation's regional development without limiting unduly the articulation of regional interests and the representativeness of regional decision makers, even if the latter were not elected for this function by direct popular vote.

DEVELOPMENT OF THE DESIGN

Essentially, France developed her modern regionalism only after World War II, under the Fourth and Fifth Republic, though there had been a good deal of theorizing about regions since the latter half of the nineteenth century and also some short-lived practical experiments in the 1930s and during World War II. Three governmental decrees issued between December 1954 and November 1956 constituted a major milestone. The first recognized as official bodies representing regional interests a number of privately organized "regional expansion committees," which had sprung up here and there; the second established the principle of "regional action programs," and the third divided all of metropolitan France into twenty-two "circumscriptions of regional action," or program regions. Each program region simply grouped together as entities several of France's approximately ninety departments, without splitting any of them. Thus, the department was left intact not only as a territorial unit but also as a juridical collectivity entitled to local government, a status for which the program region did not qualify.

The so-called regional reform of 1964 constitutes the second major milestone on the road to modern French regionalism. While this reform did not solve the regions' identity problem but continued to refer to them vaguely as "circumscriptions" for regional planning and action, it defined some basic premises for the new regionalism and conferred to the regions important attributes. It established the post of regional prefect as a *primus inter pares* among the prefects of the component departments of a region and defined their role and decision-making powers in regional constrictions to national planning. It also set up new regional institutions, such as Regional Economic Development Commissions (CODER) and Regional Administrative Conferences (CAR) with which each regional prefect had to consult, and provided each regional prefecture with a staff of highly trained administrative and technical specialists, the regional mission (*mission régionale*), which was given overall responsibility for regional planning and development.

While the 1964 reform, modified only slightly through a few refinements in 1968, resulted in rather limited participative features for the region part way between deconcentration and decentralization, the most recent 1972 reform, though it gives no guarantees, creates far greater potential for regional autonomy. This, in the main, is due to the flexibility of the 1972 reform law which expresses many of its prescriptions for regional action in the form of choices between alternatives and between minimum and maximum financial constraints. The extent of decentralization and autonomy a region can obtain thus depends to a substantial degree on its will and capability to participate in governance as a partner of national and local levels of government. To facilitate this partnership the reform created the following legal premises applicable to all regions.

For the first time, the region is endowed with a legal personality. The name "region" now replaces what was called a "circumscription for regional action." Two assemblies, each representing certain regional interests, are constituted as bodies separate and distinct from the national administration to formulate plans and policies for the region's economic and social development. The first, the regional council, has decision-making powers concerning the raising and expenditure of funds for regional development projects. The regional prefect, as representative of the national government, is responsible to the regional council for having its decisions implemented. While he guides and advises both regional assemblies and may attempt to influence their deliberations, he cannot veto the regional council's final decisions as long as these stay within the limits defined by the law. He also is obliged, de jure, to report to both assemblies in detail the status of implementation, within the region, of current national plans, in order to facilitate assembly deliberations. The second assembly, the economic and social committee, which replaces the former regional economic development commission (CODER) has advisory powers only and makes no financial decisions except for its own housekeeping and study or research functions. It must, however, be consulted by the regional council before the latter can finalize decisions legally.

The reform law also determines for both assemblies the approximate representation of interests. The regional council, as the political body, must include all representatives directly elected within the region to be members of either the National Assembly or the Senate. It must also include representatives from departmental, municipal, and communal councils within the region whose total number must equal that of regionally elected parliamentarians and senators. In the economic and social committee, which reflects professional interests, at least 50 percent of the members must represent industry, agriculture, commerce, labor unions, independent professions, and so on; at least 25 percent represent regional activities in health, education, scientific and cultural affairs, social affairs, and sports; at least 10 percent represent economic activities that are a specific attribute of the region concerned, such as tourism or wine growing. Finally, a maximum of 10 percent of the members are nominated by the national government on the basis of special qualifications for a contribution to regional development.

The financial resources the reform makes available to the new regions will be discussed in the next section, which observes regional governance at work. The principal features this reform retains from the previous regional reform of 1964 are the important roles that the regional prefect and his general staff, the regional mission, play as mediators in the continuing dialogue between national and subnational levels on the charting of France's economic and social future. But the reform of 1972 established the region as a more equal and vital partner in this dialogue.

THE NEW REGIONAL GOVERNANCE AT WORK

Some Field Research Findings

Since the Regional Reform Law of July 1972 itself provided for a fifteen-month preparatory period, determining the date of its applicability as 1 October 1973, in 1974 few data were as yet available with which to evaluate France's actual experience with her new system of regional governance. We will summarize, in this section, data and impressions gathered in September 1974 during three weeks of intensive field research in three of France's twenty-two continental regions, with one week allotted to each region.

In each regional capital, we interviewed as many key members as we could of the three regional institutions which, as partners, are mainly responsible for stimulating and orienting regional development: the regional council, the economic and social committee, and the prefecture's regional mission. Most of these interviews were held in private. We also attended as an observer plenary sessions or meetings of specialized committees of the regional council and the economic and social committee, and internal staff meetings of the prefectoral regional missions. Through these meetings and interviews, to which various informal social gatherings must be added, we had the opportunity of discussing the problems of French regionalism with participants in regional efforts from many walks of life. They represented a diversity of interests, including national, regional, departmental, and municipal administration; industry and commerce (for example, the staff of the local chamber of commerce); higher education (university professors); labor unions; social welfare; environmental concerns; and tourism.

Finally, we were permitted to study many highly instructive documents concerning regional problems and actions. These included detailed minutes of past policy deliberations held by the two regional assemblies, planning and budgetary proposals prepared by the regional mission, implementation reports rendered by the regional prefect to the regional assemblies, and even internal correspondence and critical evaluations of regional problems and processes, which had limited distribution and originated from various sources within the administration. The fact that we were permitted to keep the larger part of these documents, as well as the relative ease with which private interviews and attendance at meetings could be arranged, speaks for the hospitable attitude and high degree of cooperation the French regional authorities extended to a foreign scholar.

We therefore feel that we ought to keep the sources of the following information in strict confidence. Though we were not expressly asked to do so, we will identify neither persons nor documents from which our information is drawn. Nor will we identify the regions we visited by name; it will be sufficient for our purpose to indicate that two of them are located in the South of France, and we will call them S(1) and S(2). The third region, located in the Northwest, will be referred to as the NW region.

All three are among France's less developed regions. While all of them possess a considerable agricultural potential, its exploitation is in great need of modernization and diversification. These regions have serious problems also with the development of their industrial potential; while two of them have little industry at all, the third needs a more balanced and diversified industrial productivity. Sound planning for regional development, therefore, is of real importance to all of them, and regional governance is being perceived as a potentially large contributor to a solution for regional dilemmas. Thus, each of these regions can serve as a good testing ground for the ideas and intentions underlying the new French regionalism.

We will summarize our research findings in the form of two general, tentative conclusions reached and through the identification of five major problem areas in which we feel more effective solutions than those now available will have to be found to make French regional governance work satisfactorily. At this time, any predictions concerning the ultimate success or failure of the French formula for regionalism would, we believe, be premature. We must stress, of course, the severe limitations to our research: its short duration, the smallness of the sample, the impossibility of applying proper sampling techniques, the limited structure that could be given to the open-ended (though systematic) interview questions, and many other deficiencies. But when we consider what was done as a systematic first step to inquire into a subject about which, as yet, little is known, we feel that the effort was worthwhile. It yielded much needed preliminary information from which we may be able to derive promising approaches to be tested in future and scientifically more rigorous research.

The first of the two tentative conclusions we reached, not without surprise, was that motivation *within* the region to make the reform an outstanding success seems to be very strong indeed. The diverse interests located within the region, including the many local community and departmental interests, take the reform and the concomitant new arrangements for regional governance quite seriously, making a considerable and purposeful effort to give life, shape, and meaning to the new regionalism. This fact would have been less surprising to us had we not been subject to countless expressions of skepticism, even cynicism, concerning the reform's success potential. A national reform law could be aborted effectively through the passive resistance of the local forces concerned. We had read previously published research reports sponsored by the reputable French National Center for Scientific Research, which had found considerable reluctance on the part of local society to accept regional governance and institutions.[2] But what we found in the regions we visited as well as in what we heard and read about other regions was that the very persons who declared themselves pessimists as to the region's ultimate success were often also those who worked hardest to make their regional governance an effective going concern. The constant expression of doubt and skepticism is perhaps a cultural trait of France's intellectual elite which may mislead when taken too seriously.

Whatever the reasons for this negativity, one only has to listen to or read the carefully kept stenographic minutes of the discussions held by the regional council, the economic and social committee, or their many working committees to become convinced of the seriousness, energy, and even enthusiasm with which these bodies pursue their goal of decentralizing the monolithic French bureaucracy and increasing regional autonomy. As one high civil servant (a *chef de service* in a regional mission) summarized, in spite of his skeptical remarks on certain aspects of the reform, "Regionalization and, with it, genuine decentralization will come about because social forces impel it to become a reality. It has gotten off to a start and we cannot turn back the wheel of history." Thus, our overall impression was that the region, with its autonomy and representative participation, that had been born and baptized through the reform law of 1972, was now "kicking" vigorously in most of France and in no need of being placed into an incubator.

Our second tentative conclusion, more subject to substantiation on the basis of available "hard" data, was that regionalism wears a different face in each French region. What had happened was what the fathers of the reform law had predicted and President Pompidou expressed in a speech made in Brest on 22 October 1971. "[The regional reform] . . .will be what the people in charge of implementing it will want to make of it."[3] The great flexibility and, in part perhaps, intended ambiguity of the reform law itself, especially in its financial provisions, lie behind this variety, a variety far greater than that which usually results when a less flexible law is subject to different human interpretations. From our description of the French regional reform legislation in the preceding section, it becomes clear that the reform law of 1972 might well be called a "framework" law. It unambiguously prescribes, without allowing the possibility of regional choices, a relatively limited amount of administrative behavior; on the other hand, it establishes a good deal of potentialities and limitations in respect to which each region has relatively large discretionary choice.

What the law does unambiguously and uniformly prescribe for each region is the delineation of its geographical boundaries (which, however, can be changed under certain conditions) and its character as a "public establishment." It also establishes in each region two representative assemblies and defines their general functions, decision-making power, and composition. In addition, the law provides through a revenue-sharing formula (the transfer to the region of revenues derived from fees for drivers' licenses issued in the region) sufficient funds for the regional assemblies to function and keep house. Finally, it defines the limited authority and responsibility of the regional prefect, but only in his capacity as the representative of the national government to the two regional assemblies. These are the main features of the new French regionalism that will look alike in each of France's regions.

The features that give each region a specific face stem from those provisions of the law establishing either broad objectives intentionally left without detailed definitions or well-defined ranges of regional activities in respect to which the regional institutions are permitted to choose between a legal minimum and maximum. An example of the former is the function of the regional prefect, not as the representative of the national government (which is clearly defined) but as the region's promoter and advocate of its interests. While the reform law clearly recognizes this dual role for the regional prefect, it also takes the position that the nature of this role must be negotiated between the prefect himself and regional interest or pressure groups. The outcome of this negotiation is considered neither predictable nor as a desirable object of national legislation. That this is the case, we believe, is a truly significant and even "revolutionary" aspect of the French regional reform. What can be observed here is the metamorphosis of the French prefect's traditional role as a "deconcentrated" official of the national government. While he has not been replaced by a locally elected official, as a fully decentralized system of power would require, and while the importance of his position has been enhanced rather than diminished, there can be no doubt that his role has changed profoundly from one of merely supervising a territorial unit for purposes of implementing the national government's objectives to one that includes pushing subnational objectives before the national government. A large step toward genuine decentralization has thus become a possibility, and the degree to which each region's prefect makes use of it for his region in Paris must be a part of any inquiry into how France's new regionalism actually works.

Most of the differences between regions stemming from the range of choices the law permits are expressed in the fiscal and budgetary decisions the region makes. Each regional council has at its disposal a significant number of different taxes or fees it may collect as a supplement to already existing taxes in order to finance regional programs. In addition, it can apply for loans to various financial institutions, governmental or private, and may be entrusted with funds by lower as well as by the national level of government for agreeing to perform special functions in projects in which the region has interests and capabilities. Here, the flexibility of the law results in a great variety of ways in which each region uses its fund-raising potentials and spends its funds.

While we had the opportunity of reading minutes of budgetary debates in the three regions we visited, our research was too limited to come to definite conclusions concerning expenditure patterns, except to state that these patterns indeed appeared to be different in each region. We will discuss some of the more important factors bearing on regional expenditures later when we point out major problem areas. We did succeed, though, in collecting complete data concerning the methods which each of the twenty-one regions (the Paris region is not covered by the reform law) used in 1974 to exercise its legal fund-raising authority.[4]

The reform law prescribes a limit of 15 francs for 1974 (and 25 francs for subsequent years) as the maximum average amount per inhabitant that a regional council can levy through taxes. In 1974, that amount varied among regions from 0.9 francs to the full legal limit of 15 francs. In each case, these amounts included the revenues derived from fees for drivers' licenses issued in each region, an item that amounts on the average to 1.25 francs per inhabitant and accrues to each region automatically, without the need for a regional decision to tax, as a national revenue-sharing item. The 0.9 francs minimum taxation reported, therefore, means that the region concerned (Corsica) levied no regional taxes at all; it was the only French region to make this decision. On the other hand, the maximum taxation of 15 francs was adopted by a total of seven regions, among them one we visited. The median region shows a taxation of 12.1 francs per inhabitant; the arithmetic mean for all twenty-one regions amounts to 11.8 francs. The taxation decided upon by the other two regions we visited was a little lower than either the median or the arithmetic mean.

In regard to the loans the law permits, only six of the twenty-one regions decided in favor of borrowing funds in 1974, among them one we visited. Amounts applied for, again calculated per inhabitant of the region, involved a range from 4.2 francs to 45.5 francs; total amounts per region range from 5 million to 150 million francs. The statistics on regional tax levies and loan applications in the regions that used both methods of fund raising do not reveal a meaningful relation between the two methods (that one method was used more to compensate for the lesser use of the other). However, in the region we visited using both methods, we noticed that a vigorous and sometimes acrimonious debate took place between the regional council and the economic and social committee concerning the relative benefits and costs of either method. Imposing taxation, even if sound from an economic viewpoint, is likely to be less popular politically than borrowing funds for interest; thus, the debate reflected different political and economic pressures in the two regional assemblies.

The facts and illustrations reported above support our contention that it was the reform law itself—with its ambiguity resulting from its failure to define functions and responsibilities, and with its flexibility in offering broad ranges of choice—that caused regionalism to be implemented differently in each region. And it is highly significant that the lawmakers had intended it to be that way. One department's secretary general (who served de facto as the department's prefect) told us that the reform law and its underlying philosophy, which holds that "the law would be what the people make of it," was by itself quite "a new little French revolution," especially against the spirit of traditional French legislation which views a law as close to immutable, prescribing the same procedures and behavior for all citizens. He went on to say that he considered it "great progress" that pragmatic evolution and change had been built into the reform law. But he also pointed out that this flexibility, as promising as it was for obtaining increased decentralization and popular participation in government, caused problems of adjustment, especially to certain administrations in Paris that were still accustomed to the tradition of a highly centralized bureaucracy. This last remark leads us to what the French perceive to be major current problems or impediments in the implementation of their regional reform.

Specific Problem Areas

That the application of the reform law has its problematic aspects and must cope with numerous obstacles was stressed by almost every person we interviewed. We sifted, condensed, and classified these difficulties and thus identified five major problem areas.

THE DEEP-ROOTED TRADITION OF CENTRALISM. This, we feel, is probably the single most serious problem. Among the modern industrialized nations of the West, France has had, and probably still has, the most centralized government machinery. Can a national administration steeped in this tradition for several hundreds of years suddenly change and muster the honest will to decentralize and accept participation in national policymaking by a variety of subnational interest groups? Can this be expected in a country reputed to be, as a nation, basically conservative and skeptical of the social change ideas advocated by its fragmented political and intellectual elites?

It was this nagging doubt most of all that seemed to plague those who were pessimistic concerning the success of the regional reform. There is substantial evidence, communicated to us orally by high civil servants and substantiated in written reports and official correspondence, that certain ministries in Paris consistently attempt to exercise a degree of centralized control over regional affairs, which is perceived by the region as violating the spirit and even the letter of the reform law. Several regional officials explained how this had come about. The lawmakers had intended to pave the way for a large degree of genuine decentralization and sharing of decision-making power with the regions. In general, the regional institutions, including the regional prefects and their staff, supported this intent fully and were quite ready to assume their new responsibilities. However, before a law can be implemented, it must first go through successive stages of official interpretation in the form of decrees, executive orders, and procedural rules, most of which are issued by the national administration. This process of setting details provided the opportunity for some national administrators, and especially the Ministry of Finance, to counteract the decentralizing intentions of the law and maintain tight reins of centralized control in Paris.

An example of how such countervailing tendencies, reflecting traditional centralist attitudes, have "slipped," as one administrator expressed it, into executive orders is furnished by the decrees issued 5 September 1973, which regulate the basic application of the law. Article No. 17 of Decree No. 73-856, which established basic budgetary controls and accounting procedures for regional funds, stipulated at that time that expenditures from regional budgets were subject to prior approvals from the regional treasurer and disbursements officer (*trésorier-payeur général*), who represents and acts as a watchdog for the Finance Ministry in Paris, though he is stationed in the region.[5] It should be noted here that expenditures from departmental or local community budgets did not have to undergo this pre-audit; only national and regional funds, qualifying as "funds of the state," were subject to this condition.

The overwhelming majority of regional actors, including the highest ranks in the regional prefectures, rebelled openly against this manifestation of centralized control by the Finance Ministry. They saw no reason why regional funds should not be subject to the same system of more liberal controls as are public funds raised on other subnational levels, such as the department, municipality, or rural community. They felt that the lawmakers conceptualized the region as a mechanism to articulate and present local interests to the national administration rather than national interests to local administrations. They all pointed out that the existing system of controlling regional expenditures through deconcentrated finance officials who were responsible to Paris constituted a "heavy bureaucratic burden" for regional officials which slowed down the implementation of the reform law.

In a report written by the chief of a regional mission (de facto the number two person in rank at the regional prefecture in regard to regional development) to his supervisor, the regional prefect, the former illustrated the excessive bureaucratic delays caused by having to satisfy the Finance Ministry's pre-audit requirements. He stated that for approving expenditures for a simple regional assistance project, duly voted on and approved by the regional council, the treasurer had demanded supporting documents which constituted an as yet incomplete dossier weighing, so far, 1 kilo 530 grams (about 3.35 English pounds).

The Finance Ministry's official, however, is not the only "villain" for the regional authorities. Other ministries are also the source of frustrating bureaucratic bottlenecks, and for the same reason. In a different region we were shown a letter from the Ministry of Public Health which on its first page approved—but on the second page de facto disapproved—a small regional health project which all regional authorities had approved long before. But the region had been obliged to change its location, due to unavoidable circumstances. Since the ministry insisted on its "right" to approve expenditures as well as locations for all regional health projects and had approved the "wrong" location on the second page, the compilation of another regional dossier became necessary.

The attitudinal evidence we could collect in the three regions visited, however, indicated a spirit of resistance on the part of most regional actors and a vigorous effort to overcome the impediments of a centralist tradition still alive in parts of the national administration. We always asked and were given assurances—and at times concrete examples—that regional prefects do push regional interests in Paris and protest against bureaucratic impediments. We also have evidence that the same is being done by the higher officials of the regional mission, whose travels to Paris are frequent, and by leading members of the two regional assemblies who often have influential connections there. Finally, the regional prefect may be strongly pushed to favor his regional rather than his national administrative role in Paris by his own closest staff, the members of his regional mission.

Reading the above-mentioned report from the chief of the regional mission to the prefect, we were surprised at the candor, vigor, and thoroughness with which the dominant position and veto power of the regional treasurers was denounced as being "absurd" and not only contradictory to the law but as making a "caricature" of it. The same document pictures regional prefects who, according to the law, should be accountable to both the national government and the regional assemblies, as servants in "bondage" ("*tutelle*") to the regional treasurer, an official who has no such legal responsibilities. In a section entitled "The Falisified Decentralization," the document states that the regional prefect not only lacks "any real negotiating power deriving from his legal functions as representative of the national government" but also "appears as a minor actor and a servant in the exercise of his strictly regional responsibilities."

This report was no diatribe but a well-documented though highly critical study which called a spade a spade. We had the occasion to study it at leisure. While it is applicable to prefectoral positions all over France, it could well have offended the particular prefect, to whom it was sent by his subordinate, and harmed their working relationships. That this did not happen in this instance indicates, perhaps, that regional prefects, in spite of the split loyalty inherent in their functions, are becoming increasingly aware of their regional responsibilities and are ready to defend these to the national administration, especially when pushed and supported by their own administrative staff in the region.

REGIONAL CONSCIOUSNESS AS A PRECONDITION FOR REGIONAL POLICIES. This, we feel, constitutes the second most serious problem for successful regionalization in France, though it was seen as the most important uncertainty by some of our interviewees. To develop and then fight for a regional policy that is separate and distinct from a national as well as from departmental and local community policies is no minor task for the regional institutions. An example was the budget debate concerning the commitment of regional funds to road building that was ablaze in one of the regions we visited. The national administration had provided funds for a superhighway linking Paris with the regional capital. Among the departments in the region, two, as well as many mayors of communities located therein, advocated a regional expenditure for several feeder roads which would link the superhighway with the region's tourist beach resorts. The regional administration, on the other hand, advocated building a medium highway linking the regional capital with the capital of the neighboring region, since this would produce the greatest overall economic benefit for the region as a whole.

We do not know the final decision. But we listened to or read in minutes about many similar debates in which intra-regional interests came into conflict. We often heard the accusation that the limited regional credits were subject to *saupoudrement*, to being spread far too thin to be effective in order to placate politically the communities and departments which have their own local funds but are represented in the regional council. This tendency, we believe, may become a real danger to effective regional governance. However, we also found substantial evidence that this political temptation is being resisted. There is proof that regional bodies, especially members of the regional prefectures and the consultative economic and social committees, are working hard to develop a regional policy that distinguishes between the interests of the region as a whole and those of its local components, viewing the former not as a simple addition of the latter but as eclectic, integrative, and responsible for providing direction. An important factor here is the availability of regional leaders able to select from local demands those significant for clienteles which are wider than local clienteles and of interest to one or several regions or even to the nation. The leadership then must be able to educate and convince the region's local components to abandon some of their more parochial views. While we could reach no conclusion concerning the availability of such leadership in French regionalism in general, we thought that we found some truly remarkable examples of it in two of the three regions we visited.

THE REQUIREMENT OF EXPERTISE. Regional policymaking, with its focus on area planning and the integration of diverse but intricately interwoven and interdependent economic and social interests, requires educational and technical qualifications, which are frequently in short supply. This is true especially for the decision-making regional council, which is composed of politicians. The consultative economic and social committee, representing a range of professional interests, can provide specialized but perhaps somewhat narrow expertise, while the regional prefecture with its considerable staff of highly trained administrators is the largest and a supposedly neutral source of comprehensive expertise. It is, therefore, the regional prefect who, according to the reform law, "instructs" the two regional assemblies concerning their agenda of business and the decisions they must debate; however, he then must implement the decisions made, having not even the right to veto them.

The prefect's right to "instruct" the assemblies and thus to "control" the information they must process is a favorite argument of those who accuse the national administration of denying the new regions a sufficient measure of genuine decentralized autonomy. It makes the regional prefecture an easy target of political criticism in the region, especially by members of leftist parties which oppose the present national government coalition. This criticism, however, seems to be largely unfounded since the reform law provides both assemblies with sufficient funds to engage outside expertise independent from the administration to undertake in-depth research on regional economic and social problems. Study groups involving qualified experts from chambers of commerce, labor unions, universities, or private research organizations are being hired to provide regional councils and economic and social committees with independent expert advice and evaluations which are used to counter-check regional policy positions presented by the administration. It is our impression that the problem of deficient education and expertise on the part of regional policymakers—a problem which plagues most policymakers every-where—is not insoluble, especially where regional leadership is dynamic and takes initiatives in this respect.

INSUFFICIENT REGIONAL FUND ALLOCATIONS. While an insufficiency of regional credits was frequently given as "proof" of the national government's unwillingness to tolerate real decentralization and as a reason to predict the ultimate failure of French regionalism, we must state that we found this argument quite unconvincing. Certainly, the per capita limit for regional taxation of 15 francs (about $3.30) for 1974, and 25 francs (about $5.55) for subsequent years, does not yield huge funds for regional expenditure. Among the seven regions that adopted maximum taxation in 1974, the median total of taxes raised by a region was 34,050,000 francs (less than $7.6 million), which happened to be in the Lorraine region which has about 2.3 million inhabitants. However, tax-raising potentials expressed in absolute figures are quite mean-ingless if the following is kept in mind.

Regional credits are intended by the reform law to perform the function of "pump priming" that is, of stimulating, matching, and steering into desirable regional channels the separate local funds raised and allocated for expenditure by the departments, cities, and local communities of a region. On a per capita basis, these local funds are, in general, far more substantial than funds available to regional governance. Local taxation also is a heavier financial burden for the individual than regional taxation; this was one important reason why in 1974 only seven out of twenty-one regions dared apply the maximum regional taxation permitted by law. This may change in the future as regional governance comes to feel more secure in the performance of its task.

Other points to be kept in mind are that regional assemblies can increase their financial resources by contracting loans under tolerable terms and that local as well as national funds may be assigned to them in trust if they can gain recognition for sound regional planning and leadership. We also heard that the legal regional taxation limit was expected to be raised to more than 25 francs after 1975, to account for general inflationary pressures. All in all, we gained the impression that the present system of funding regional governance presents no major problems since it is sufficiently flexible and geared to actual performance.

RELATIONSHIPS BETWEEN THE TWO REGIONAL ASSEMBLIES. This is the last problem that was brought to our attention in each region we visited. However, the tensions and difficulties that do exist between the regional council and the economic and social committee were often viewed as being characteristic and expected of the initial stages of French regionalism—and also resolvable. A certain amount of rivalry and conflict over recognition and prestige is perhaps unavoidable. The economic and social committee with its considerable professional expertise has only consultative functions, while the regional council with its elected but technically less qualified politicians has budgetary decision-making powers.

The conflict is likely to be sharper in regions where the majority of elected politicians who may also be regional council members belongs to parties that are in opposition to the incumbent national government. Many economic and social committee members, however, since they represent various and often conservative business interests, are more likely to support than to oppose national government policies and are, therefore, hostile to a regional council dominated by opposition politicians. We thus heard many more complaints about noncooperation, resentment, and even bickering about trivia such as office and parking space between the two assemblies in regions S(1) and S(2), where the opposition dominated, than in the NW Region, where Gaullists and allied parties formed the majority. In all three regions, however, and especially in S(1) and S(2), we also heard urgent calls for more common work between the two assemblies, specifically for joint sessions of each assembly's specialized working committees as well as for joint plenary sessions. If these calls are heeded, there is hope that present patterns of mutual distrust, where they exist, can largely be overcome and that a more fruitful and cooperative relationship between the assemblies will develop over time.

CONCLUSION

What sort of conclusions, concerning regional governance in general, does our limited study permit? As stated before, conclusions concerning the ultimate success or failure of the French effort would be premature. Nevertheless, when we limit the applicability of potential lessons to be learned to nations with a unitary system of government, the French experience appears to be sufficiently rich to reflect on a number of hypotheses. These may yield new approaches to the problem of how to make central-local relationships more fruitful and increase participation and integration of local interests in the national design.

France furnishes an excellent example of a unitary nation with the tradition of a highly centralized government machinery making a serious—and also highly sophisticated—effort to decentralize its ancient bureaucratic apparatus and devolve power to local levels because it needs their active participation in economic and social development. At the same time, France needs to prevent, consolidate, and integrate excessive local fragmentation. As we noted in the first section, many other unitary countries, those with a large private sector as well as socialist-communist nations, highly developed as well as less developed nations, are facing the same urgent task under similar traditional constraints. Could they learn from the lessons of the French regional reform?

We think that the French effort at least merits serious study and a close and continuous observation of outcomes. The formula of creating, at intermediary levels, a "public establishment" and thus governance, which is more flexible but less formal and visible than a new level of "official" government, may be attractive for various types of political systems, especially those which prefer to devolve power to local levels more gradually and through negotiating a quid pro quo. The French reform law that created this formula may itself be less acceptable as a model to nations still deeply entrenched in administrative centralism, though its framework character, flexibility, and stipulation of ranges of choice rather than precise codes of behavior may attract the reform-minded and those who believe change to be inevitable.

Few would deny, however, that as models for regional arrangements both the law and the public establishment formula have one salient attribute: they contitute an approach to handling central-local relationships that is essentially pragmatic, relies on negotiation rather than edicts, permits learning by trial and error, and thus has a flexibility based on experience. This built-in change orientation in the pragmatic approach is often in conflict with other approaches to government which view political ideology, doctrine, and law as basically stable, even immutable. Since, in our experience, a worldwide rebellion against this view seems to be on the increase, the French pragmatic approach to regionalism will not fail to attract much international attention. There are now many nations besides France that are wrestling with the problem of reforming their central-local relationships. The current debate between Eastern European countries on how "democratic centralism," a tenet of Marxist doctrine, can be implemented more pragmatically reflects an issue for which the French experience might well be relevant.

Finally, if the French experiment succeeds, it may stimulate a rethinking of past theories concerning deconcentration and decentralization. In the past France frequently has been cited as the prime example for countries that use deconcentrated officials effectively to prevent genuine decentralization. If on the basis of her present regional reform she can prove that these two concepts are not necessarily opposites but can be contiguous and sequential and that deconcentration may be used as a preparatory stage for a more gradual but also more educated and effective decentralization and devolution of power, the French experience may have theoretical significance as well.

NOTES

1. Céline Wiener, "Les transformations actuelles du pouvoir local dans le monde contemporain" (Paper presented at the conference on Current Trends in Local Power and Authority in the Contemporary World in Warsaw, Poland, 24-28 September 1974), p. 10, is the source of the statistics.

2. Pierre Gremion, *La mise en place des institutions régionales* (Paris: C.S.O., 1966); and Pierre Gremion and Jean-Pierre Worms, *Les institutions régionales et la société locale* (Paris: C.S.O., 1968).

3. La Documentation Française [French Government Printing Office], *Cahiers Français* 158-59 (January-April 1973), p. 22 (translation by this writer).

4. Statistics taken from *Bilan comparatif des budgets régionaux—1974*, compiled by one of the regional prefectures we visited.

5. On 3 February 1975, after completion of our research, a new Decree (No. 75-61) fundamentally changed the provisions of Article No. 17 of Decree No. 73-856, substituting a post-audit control of regional budget expenditures by the treasurer and disbursements officer for the former pre-audit control. In matters of financial control, regional authorities are thus somewhat less dependent on the power of central authorities in Paris today than at the time the research was conducted. Nevertheless, the generally "rebellious" attitudes of some of the regional actors against Paris which we describe hereafter are thought to be still applicable and highly relevant to present-day problems of French regionalism.

Bibliographical Note:

Few publications concerning the French regional reform of 1972 have appeared in English. For the many publications that have appeared in French, the best source is the French Government Printing Office, especially the double-number issue of the *Cahiers* referred to in note 3, which offers an excellent and comprehensive description of the reform, its historical antecedents, and its significance.

Italy

Robert H. Evans [*]

10

In 1946 the Constituent Assembly of the Italian Republic envisaged a state based on regional units endowed with limited political and administrative powers as a safeguard against authoritarianism and a means to develop democratic values. In accordance with transitory provisions 8 and 9 of the Constitution of 1 January 1948, Italians were to elect regional councils to represent them within a year, while "within three years . . .the Republic [would] adjust laws according to the requirements of local autonomy and the legislative competence attributed to the regions." Only on 1 April 1972, twenty-four years later, did the regions become reality. The bold regional experiment came into existence after twenty years of acrimonious discussions and resentments that had made it a stale political problem.

Since 1972 center and periphery have had only a limited amount of time to grasp their changing relationships. The formative process is still in its experimental stage. Thus, the present situation calls for an examination of these factors that delayed the implementation of the reform, the organs of regional government and their powers, the problems the new order has created, and the consequences it will have. Can the regions instill some vigor in the faltering Italian democracy?

THE ORIGINS OF THE REGIONAL PROBLEM

In 1861 Italian unification corresponded to the wishes of a minority of the population, notably the northern upper bourgeoisie and the southern landowners. The Savoy monarchy held it essential to impose its principles and ideas upon the ex-sovereign states that constituted the new kingdom. Political and administrative centralization were necessary to ensure survival and were equated with national integrity, while proposals for any form of political devolution were taxed with subversion[1] and considered harmful to the political

[*]Associate Professor of Government, University of Virginia.

and moral fiber of the nation. On 20 March 1865 (Law 2248), Italy was administratively unified on the French pattern adopted by the Piedmontese.

Necessities of the moment led to centralization and spelled defeat for regional projects, such as those sponsored by Cavour, the major artisan of unification, Farini, and Minghetti who, in 1860-61, envisaged the region as an organ of bureaucratic and institutional decentralization under government control. Though never very strong, two schools of regional thought developed in Italy. The pure federalists (Carlo Cattaneo, Giuseppe Ferrari, Gaetano Salvemini) remained a minority while most exponents of regionalism envisaged the new units as decentralizing bodies that would cope with the southern problem (Napoleone Colojanni) and provide the best defense against the parliamentary degeneration (Stefano Jacini) that menaced the integrity of the young state. In 1919 varying degrees of regionalism were adopted in the platforms of the radical, socialist, republican, and popular parties.

Swept away by fascism, regionalism was reborn more vigorous in 1945, and espoused by all the political parties in the Constituent Assembly, particularly the Republicans and the Christian Democrats. A functional approach to regional problems—the product of Catholic thought in the nineteenth and early twentieth centuries, but traceable to the projects of the 1860s—called for the division of Italy into nineteen regions (Article 131). The new regional organization, providing extensive legislative power to the units under rigorous government control, corresponded to no preexisting model of federative or unitary state, creating on paper a regional state that was very much part of the Italian heritage.

However, as in 1865, events as much as ideals determined the structure of the republic and the partial implementation of its Constitution. Separatist movements in Sardinia and Sicily, international difficulties on the borders (Valle d'Aosta, Trentino-Alto Adige, and Friuli-Venezia Giulia) led to the creation of the five special regions (Article 116). For practical purposes these (with the exception of Friuli-Venezia Giulia), received statutes recognizing their existence as entities within the state, two years prior to the approval of the 1948 Constitution. They were formally recognized and adopted into constitutional law by the assembly one month after the ratification of the Constitution, the government admitting it had been unable to examine the texts pertinent to Sardinia and the Valle d'Aosta. The special regions corresponded to an effective need and to constitutional provisos but were hardly the product of governmental initiative.

The country's search for a new political and social equilibrium was brought to an end by the Cold War, which polarized Left and Right, leading the latter to abandon its regional policies (which might not have been very deep) only to see them adopted by the former (where they may remain shallow). Valid reasons and artificial pretexts were invoked by the government parties to slow down regional implementation. Patriotism and anti-communism (the creation of a Red Belt), the cost of fifteen regional governments, a danger of increased bureaucratization, and the poor performance of the special regions (Sicily in particular) were cited by politicians as an indication of what could be expected. More seriously, jurists noted that the Constituent Assembly had not clarified the "regional knot," that compromises and ambiguities were the cause of the delay in setting up the ordinary regions.[2] At heart, by 1960, the Christian Democratic party was only marginally interested in regionalism. By 1962 the Socialist party made regional reform part of the price it requested to enter a center left government, proclaimed that the creation of the ordinary regions would determine its continued presence in government and thus forced all parties to jump on the bandwagon. Tepid regionalists now saw an opportunity to increase their share in the spoils of the *sottogoverno*. The Christian Democrats, however, still viewed the issue of regional autonomies more as an institutional and administrative problem than a political one.

The fifteen ordinary regions (Abruzzo and Molise were separated in 1963) effectively came into existence in 1969-72. A tottering government, weakened by the student uprisings of 1968 and the worker strikes of 1969, confronted a surge of regional feelings shared not only by the parties at the center but also by provincial and local leaders at the periphery. Frustrated by twenty years of government inactivity, they argued that the perspective of the 1946 constituents was no longer applicable and that the regional provisos of the Constitution, particularly Article 117, had to be interpreted in an evolutionary manner corresponding to the needs of the country in the 1970s and 1980s. The regions wanted more power.

The issue was political: the regional elections of 7 June 1970 became the test of the moribund center left.[3] The regions with their new expanded powers were put in the broader perspective of revamping, though hardly rethinking, the tax system, bureaucratic reform, and planning mechanisms, elements on which they felt entitled to a definitive say.

THE INSTITUTIONAL FRAMEWORK

On 1 April 1972, the twenty regions listed in the Constitution (Article 131 modified by Constitutional Law No. 1, 31-12-1963) became operational. They are: Piedmont, Lombardy, Venice, Liguria, Emilia Romagna, Tuscany, Umbria, Marche, Lazio, Abruzzo, Molise, Campania, Puglia, Basilicata, Calabria, and the five special regions of Valle d'Aosta, Trentino-Alto Adige, Friuli-Venezia Giulia, Sicily, and Sardinia. The latter, in accordance with Article 116, were granted "particular forms and conditions of autonomy." The diversity of the regions is reflected in the size of their populations and incomes that, among the ordinary regions, vary between 8.2 million inhabitants and 15.2 percent of all regional income for Lombardy and 336,000 and 1.1 percent for Molise.

The revolutionary step of creating a regional state rests in the Constitution, and in the laws and decrees of the Italian Republic. Article 5 declares that "the

Republic, one and indivisible, recognizes and promotes local autonomies; . . . and adjusts the principles and methods of its legislation to the requirements of autonomy and decentralization.'' Article 117 grants the regions powers to legislate on specific matters and also foresees the extension of their legislative competence to "matters indicated by constitutional laws.'' Article 118 regulates the administrative functions of the regions and their relationships with the provinces, communes, and other local bodies. Constitutional laws recognized the statutes of the special regions. In May-July 1971, Parliament endorsed the statutes drafted by the ordinary regions in consultation with the regional commission of the Senate. These statutes were presented by the government, symbol of the unitary state. This, and the parliamentary endorsement that ensued, implicitly recognized their constitutional validity, though all claimed powers far more extensive than those granted in Article 117.[4] The regional bodies were established by Law No. 62 (10-2-1953) modified by Law No. 1084 (23-12-1970). Presidential decrees on 14 January 1972 delegated powers of the state to the region in matters covered by Article 117. The administrative mechanisms were outlined by Law No. 382 (22-7-1975), and enabling decrees of 23 July 1977 started the dismantling of the state bureaucracy and the effective transfer of powers to the regions. However, until the state establishes framework laws the regions must "legislate within the limits of the fundamental principles established by the laws of the state," and this restriction considerably decreases their autonomy. In brief, the foundations of regional order in Italy provide a prime example of piecemeal legislation, reflective, as we shall see, of the reluctance on the part of the government and the Christian Democratic party to divest itself of powers of state and transfer them to the regions.

The Structure of Regional Government

Minor variations notwithstanding, the institutions of the special and ordinary regions can be considered together. Their structures are similar, regional entities are now the rule and no longer the exception, and the exercise of regional functions is determined in a uniform manner with regard to the ordinary regions.[5] The institutions consist of a council, a junta, and a president of the region (Article 121).

The council (consiglio regionale) is a politically autonomous, yet not sovereign, unicameral legislative body. It is elected for five years by direct universal suffrage. The number of councillors is proportional to the size of the population and varies between thirty for regions with less than 1 million inhabitants and eighty for those with more than 6 million (Lombardy being the only one). Elections are held under a list system of proportional representation $Q = V/(s + 1)$, and constituency boundaries coincide with those of the provinces. Candidates may run in three constituencies that elect the number of representatives proportional to the size of their population. The final selection is based on list votes received by the parties and, within these lists, on preferential votes received by the candidates. Leftovers are tabulated at the regional level. Elected councillors represent the region and not the province in which they were elected. Studies indicate that the councillors are predominantly recruited from the middle class.[6] The council elects its president by secret vote, preferably by an absolute majority, thus implying previous agreement among the major groups in the assembly.

Some regional statutes call for a general debate on policies to be followed before council elects the junta, the size of which is variable: for example, Campania, Article 38, states that the junta should be neither less than one-tenth nor greater than one-fifth of the council. The statutes of Sardinia (Article 37) and Valle d'Aosta (Article 33) call for selection of the junta, the executive branch of the council, by the regional president, thus creating a form of government by assembly. As Gizzi notes, the regional council not only participates in determining regional policies but also in implementing them, accentuating the subordinate role of the junta, which does not hold even administrative power.[7] The members of the junta (*assessori*) are held responsible for specific departments in the five special regions, while responsibility is collective in the ordinary ones. The council elects the president of the junta who is also president of the region. He represents the regional political interest and is empowered to bring cases against the state to the constitutional court.

The Powers of Regional Government

The regions dispose of three forms of legislative power: exclusive, complementary, and integrative. Only the special regions hold all three because the ordinary regions are not granted exclusive legislative power. In this category, and within constitutional norms, the special regions may legislate unhindered and to the exclusion of national legislation. Complementary legislation requires the council to comply with the principles underlying national legislation as established by framework laws or as deduced by the regional legislator from the existing body of national law. It refers exclusively to matters outlined in Article 117. Integrative legislation (not recognized in the Sicilian statute) adapts the details of national laws to the specific requirements of the region.[8]

Thus special regions have a broader area of legislative competence than the ordinary ones, though there are wide variations among them, for instance, in agriculture and forestry. Special regions also have greater powers with regard to economic matters (industry, commerce, credit, mining), education (elementary and secondary), and finance (levying taxes). All regions have complementary powers within the areas specified by Article 117, namely,

organization of the offices and the administrative bodies dependent on the region; communal boundaries; urban and rural police; fairs and markets; public charities and health and hospital assistance; vocational training, training of artisans and scholastic assistance; museums and libraries of local bodies; town planning; tourist trade and hotel industry; tram and motor coach services of regional interest; roads, aqueducts and public works of regional interest; lake navigation and ports; mineral and thermal waters; quarries and peat bogs; hunting; fishing in lake and river waters; agriculture and forestry; artisanship.

The broad interpretation by the regional statutes of Article 117, ratified by Parliament, gives the ordinary regions greater de facto, if not de jure, powers than those granted to the special ones.

As a legislative body the regional council approves the budget, deliberates on matters of taxation, organizes the administration of regional offices, initiates proposals for popular referenda to repeal national laws (Article 75), and participates in the election of the president of the republic (Article 83). The junta, in its executive function, adopts the necessary measures for the application of the laws deliberated by the council, administers the regional patrimony, supervises the regional offices, prepares the budget, and reports to the council, whose confidence it must enjoy. The regional president promulgates the laws and regulations and nominates the members of the provincial and communal control committee.

Regional power is tied to financial autonomy and to the size of income of each region. Article 119 explicitly recognizes the regional right to financial autonomy; it is, however, limited by the provisions of Law No. 281, 16-5-1970, pending the implementation of tax reforms that will allow the regions to levy a 2 percent income tax. Regional taxes on public property, regional concessions, road traffic, and rents on public property provide the regions with 10 percent of their global income. The remainder comes from a state common compensation fund in which—until exact per capita regional income can be determined—regional population, area, emigration, and unemployment rates determine the quota received by each region. Thus Lombardy disposes of 23.5 percent of all direct regional income (versus 0.4 percent for Molise) but only 15.2 percent of the total income available to the regions (versus 1.1 percent for Molise). In addition, the state provides the regions with funds earmarked for specific purposes: development of mountain areas, hospitals, and so forth. Regions can contract loans up to 20 percent of their direct income as well as issue bonds. Regional development programs may be financed through special state funds administered by a national planning body. In 1973, the total amount available to the regions, some 2,600 billion lire, was equivalent to one-fifth of all state expenditures.[9] It is undeniable that the regions dispose of considerable sums; however the small percentage of the total amount generated through regional taxes considerably reduces their financial autonomy. These limitations are further compounded by rigid government controls.

Regional Controls

Italy is a unitary state (Article 5). Since its creation, control of local government through the institution of the prefect has become an ingrained habit and a convenient tool in government hands. Changes have been brought about with the enforcement of the regional provisions of the 1948 Constitution; however, five of its twenty articles on regional government deal with state controls.

Exceptional limitations on regional power can be imposed for reasons of national security, dissolution of regional councils (Article 126) and international obligations (Article 93 EEC treaty, aids granted by states). More significant are those limitations imposed on the grounds of administrative competence, legitimacy, and merit of regional legislation.

Constitutional and administrative supervision of all regional acts is exercised by the government (Articles 124, 125) acting through a commissioner (*commissario del governo*) and a control commission heavily weighted in favor of the central authorities over which he presides. The commissioner, usually a prefect, resides in the regional capital. He can dissolve the regional council (Article 126) in the case of "acts contrary to the constitution, serious violation of laws or, when by reasons of resignation or through the impossibility of forming a majority, it is no longer in a position to fulfill its functions." A decree of the president of the republic, following consultation with a regional commission of twenty senators and twenty deputies, makes the dissolution effective. New elections must be called within three months by a committee of three citizens eligible to the regional council who administer the region pro tempore. Considering the past use of similar powers by the prefect on the communal level, one is entitled to doubt that deadlines will be respected; yet, regions carry more political weight than municipalities, and the government will only use such a power in cases that are clearly justified.

Article 127 gives the government the right to reject a regional law on the grounds of legitimacy and of merit. Laws approved by the regional council are submitted to the government by the commissioner with a reasoned opinion. They must be approved by the commissioner, except in cases of governmental opposition, within thirty days. When confronted with an urgent request on the part of the regions, the government is under no obligation to shorten the thirty-day period. All rejections must be motivated. The regional council may modify the law, drop it, or approve it again by an absolute majority, in which case the government may take the case to the constitutional court on the grounds of the illegitimacy of the law, or to Parliament on the grounds of its merit if there are conflicting interests. Once promulgated, regional laws may still be challenged on grounds of unconstitutionality (Article 23, Law No. 87, 11-3-1953) as they are also state laws. The government appears to have exercised its right of veto without anti-regionalist feelings and on technical grounds due to regional errors, with the highest rate of vetoes applying to the south (30 percent, 1970-75).

The Constitution grants the regions autonomy, but they remain closely controlled by the state and dispose of none of the limited forms of sovereignty granted to members of federal or confederal states. The broad interpretation the regions have sought to give to Article 117 has not been upheld by the court.

Furthermore, government financial control imposes definite limits on the regions' freedom of choice. In this formative stage, regions and the state are faced with numerous problems, the solution of which will determine the success or failure of regionalism as a form of government in Italy.

PROBLEMS OF IMPLEMENTATION

The political and juridical consequences of regional government call for a reconsideration of the relationship between the state and its component parts. The state needed twenty years to grant regional claims and sought to decrease its responsibility by invoking bureaucratic impediments; the regions, animated by a vigorous Jacobinic spirit, have attempted to transform their relationships with the state in a radical manner, exploiting the normative framework of the 1948 Constitution, which the actions of the political class, of the unions, and the praxis of the institutions have obscured. However, "the frequent conflicts between the regions and the central government over their respective powers should not be misinterpreted. They do not constitute proof that regional government is unworkable. . . .Such conflicts are to be expected."[10]

Juridical Problems

Three sources of difficulties are to be considered: the regional statutes, the ambiguities deriving from the Constitution and the law; and the jurisprudence of the constitutional court.

The regional statutes diverge considerably from a strict interpretation of the Constitution. The regions define themselves as "autonomous on the bases of the principles and within the limits of the Constitution" but omit any reference to the laws of the republic as required by Article 123. All statutes attribute to the region a directing and coordinating power over local bodies, public economic bodies, and public economic corporations (*enti a partecipazione statale*). However, regions have neither competence in terms of ordering communal and provincial units, nor in matters related to commerce and industry where public economic corporations explicate their functions. The regional claims of legislative and administrative power to deal with matters such as full employment, workers rights, education in general, and the use of television clearly go beyond the limits set by Articles 117 and 118. The same is true with regard to financial autonomy, which many statutes consider as a matter of regional competence, ignoring Article 119 that only recognizes it "within the forms and limits established by the law." While Parliament voted the regional statutes and provided them with a certain degree of constitutionality, regional legislation still has to stand up to the test of the constitutional court.

Difficulties stemming from the constitutional text and the government decrees of 14 January 1972 delegating specific powers to the regions are numerous. In certain cases Article 117 is clearly restrictive and out of step with the times: it would appear impossible to establish a coherent regional transport policy on the basis of regional control of "tramways and local motor coaches." The theory of implicit powers nevertheless has been set aside by the constitutional court, which has rejected all teleological interpretations. Without judging on the merits of a strict interpretation of Article 117, it is undeniable that the transfer decrees either have failed to provide clear definitions of matters involved (for instance, artisanship or town planning) or have been overly precise in other cases, leaving the regions with nominal power only. Under health and hospital assistance, twenty-three specific sectors are reserved to the central administration, and the decree only falls short of providing detailed blueprints for hospitals to be built by the regions.[11] Basically, the transfer of power has taken place in a fragmentary way, creating serious difficulties for the regional legislator who, until the publication of framework laws (which have been frequently solicited) must depend on his own interpretation of constitutional norms, the national body of laws, and more specifically the jurisprudence of the constitutional court.

Since it became operational in 1956, the court has ruled in an overwhelming majority of cases in favor of the unitary state. No consideration has been given to regional power in a functional perspective: regional legislation can only adapt and integrate national legislation. National interest, as defined by the government, appears to have been the court's guide for restrictive interpretation, in spite of numerous solicitations from parliamentary groups. In fact, it has reduced regional power to administrative autonomy and, notwithstanding a few timid efforts in 1971, does not appear prepared to reverse itself. As the eminent jurist Paolo Barile notes, in the absence of framework laws and in the midst of many ambiguities, the court must ascertain the limits of competence and national interest, and it often confuses the latter with the principles and laws of the state. In this way its arbitration function becomes a power of unlimited discretion.[12] The failure of the body politic may well force the court to become the exclusive holder of all power to establish the regional order. The juridical problem is an indication of the political ones.

Political Problems

Two conflicting views of regional order compete for preeminence. The Left, notably the PCI (Italian Communist party), envisages the regions as political-legislative bodies that will offer a "dynamic, modern and open interpretation"[13] of Italian society; the Right, particularly the DC (Christian Democats), sees the regions as simple administrative bodies. Local and regional politicians from all parties espouse the more progressive view granting the regional assemblies greater powers than those outlined by the Constitution and the governmental decrees on transfer of powers. The regions are seen as the active element of the state, the protagonists of national economic planning, the critical element in the reorganization of local government, the focal point of all the public social services required in an advanced industrial democracy. In brief, the regions want to transform their relationship with the state and upgrade their position, exploiting governmental weakness and the juridical ambiguities of the regional statutes and the constitutional provisions.

The regional question has become politicized and the testing ground for the *rottura degli equilibri*, "the breaking of equilibria," and a search for "more advanced ones." Following the local and regional elections of 15 June 1975, the PCI is the largest group in all major Italian cities. It is the major governing partner in four regions (Emilia-Romagna, Tuscany, Umbria, and Liguria), while it is associated with the PSI in the governance of three other regional governments. The Christian Democrats still govern Venetia single-handedly but must rely on faltering majorities in twelve others. Nevertheless, the Christian Democrats insist that regional political alignments must reflect those at the national level; the Socialists believe that regional policies can be dissociated from national ones; the Communists insist that the regions must establish coalitions reflecting local conditions and providing for the most functional regional governments. The Left pursues a somewhat inconsistent line, making the region a testing ground for the strength of national formulas of government but in the same breath arguing that regional government should be depoliticized. Guido Fanti, the Communist president of Emilia Romagna, declares that the regions should bring about "a rupture of centralism, . . .of provincialism, a pluralistic state, articulated in spheres of separate powers, coordinated and guaranteed by reciprocal autonomy."[14] The government is hardly more consistent in viewing regions as administrative units that should respect national political alignments. The regional issue is political: regional elections in 1970 and 1975 were a test of the center left and of Mr. Fanfani's policies; regional politicians debated national rather than regional issues; the selection of the regional capitals of Calabria and Abruzzo were the product of political settlements worked out in Rome rather than by regional councils.

The state's reluctance to provide the regions with sufficient personnel to fulfill their task has forced them to politicize issues. The transfer of state powers in matters relating to Article 117, along with certain residual powers (Law No. 281, 16-5-1970) was accompanied by a token transfer of personnel from the central administration (14,443 or 0.08 percent). This effectively prevented the regions from spending a good share of the special funds they had been assigned, forcing them to assume their own personnel, thus providing additional sources of patronage and increasing the size of the bureaucracy, but hardly increasing their problem-solving capacity.

The dangers of a broad interpretation of Article 117 are evident from the Christian Democratic point of view. In the name of freedom of information the regions refuse to participate in state-run television programs until they obtain a voice in the administration of the DC-controlled national television network and a de facto predominance in the distribution of cable television. Similarly they have claimed a major role in national planning—though "it is clear that in any development and planning in the regions that can even begin to be considered comprehensive, the role of the state is bound to be primordial"[15]—and have ignored the constitutional court's Decision 92, 1968, giving all planning powers to the state even in matters covered by Article 117.

The government's overly narrow interpretation of Article 117 has unnecessarily politicized matters that could have been dealt with administratively. Thus the constitutional court (Decision 139, 1972) has clearly distinguished public charity (Article 117) from social assistance (Article 38) and entrusted the latter to "bodies and institutes predisposed or integrated by the state."[16] Such limitations, clearly out of step with the times, have led the regions to claim extremely broad powers (for example, all measures dealing with problems connected with old age). These same limitations apply to the question of hospital assistance where, in the government project (V. Colombo, 12-8-1974) regional functions, organs, autonomy, and controls are directly disciplined, outlined, and described by state law, which imposes a single model, defined and specified in all its dimensions.[17]

The regional state is searching for "equilibrium." The Constituent Assembly hardly could have foreseen the host of problems susceptible to a regional solution that would come with Italy's transformation into an industrial society. The Christian Democratic party during its uninterrupted tenure of government has refused, under the pressure of international events or by deliberate choice, to allow a progressive interpretation of the Constitution. Faced with a multitude of juridical and political problems, the regions have taken more advanced positions than most probably wished. In turn, their constitutionally recognized autonomy has been thwarted. The impact of this process on the state, the parties, and society at large cannot be overestimated.

THE EFFECTS OF REGIONALISM

It is too early to assess accurately the impact of regional reorganization upon the Italian state. The regions only became operative in April 1972, and have had to labor against obstacles that are not yet fully removed; they must define their personality and role in a way acceptable to the state. The regional problem has become part of the broader issue of state credibility. Regional reform is tied to bureaucratic and financial reforms and to the creation of an effective planning body. The very existence of the regions has accentuated these problems and forced the state to take action, albeit insufficient, in matters of taxation and medical care. Acting as a constant prodding body, they must force the government to produce framework laws that will define clearly their mutual relationship. Presenting a united front—for instance, they offered a joint project on animal husbandry[18]—the regions can pressure the state and prevent it from engaging in dilatory tactics. The creation of a new class of competent regional politicians and administrators can lighten the burden of the central government and may lead to a more pluralistic state.

The government, and those factions of the Christian Democratic party that control the bureaucracy, have been reluctant to abide by the regional commitments they have formally endorsed. The state has often sought to regain with one hand what it gave with the other. Thus the regional committees that control the legitimacy of the acts of the provinces, communes, and local bodies (Article 130) considerably decreased the effectiveness of the prefect, who previously held this power of control. The government presented a project of law (8 June 1974) attempting to create a uniform and homogeneous local order "which [would] replace what was lost by the ending of prefectoral controls."[19] The state and the regions remain as antagonistic as the center and the periphery have been since Italian unification.

The state is dominated by parties, and regionalism has provided them with a new power base to modify the existing one, as well as with new sources of patronage.[20] All parties changed their structures to match the regional structures. The new order has, however, heavily taxed the parties' organizational capacities, as some 2,600 militants were directed to new tasks in regional councils. The parties no longer can devote as much attention to local government and organization as in the past. This is particularly visible in the case of the PCI. An increase in power of regional politicians has become evident in all parties except the Socialist (seven regional secretaries and one regional president have become members of the PCI *direzione*). Factions that are strong regionally but weak nationally have become more autonomous, and regional politics less ideological (for example, *Sinistra di Base* in Lombardy, and *Dorotei* in Emilia). A new breed of politicians, less paternalistic and intellectualistic, is being formed. But old habits die hard. Parties define themselves in a national perspective, and electors at the regional level still cast their votes in function of this identification, and of national rather than regional programs. A good or poor record of regional administration may not carry considerable weight, which in turn, does not force regional parties to act responsibly.[21] Since June 1975, however, regional government has been in the process of wresting effective power from Rome. Regionalism thus may have an enduring effect on the power structure of the national parties; at the level of national government, the periphery is modifying the center and may lead to radically changed political alliances and governmental formulae. The crisis at the end of the 1970s may well find an outcome in the regional elections of 1980.

The impact of the regions on citizens is difficult to assess. All regional statutes grant them an important participatory role. The right of information, consultation, inquiry, and petition are recognized, and some regions have instituted the equivalent of an ombudsman (*difensore civico*). Abrogative referenda can be held, except on budgetary and fiscal matters, as well as consultative referenda on communal and regional reorganization. Projects of law can be presented by electors (2,000 in Basilicata, 15,000 in Puglie), municipal councils, and trade unions. These procedures must be rendered effective and imply an increase in civism which is not particularly developed in Italy. In all probability, the greater role open to citizens will allow the parties to manipulate them more effectively.

The Italian state has been reluctant to surrender any of its powers to the regional bodies foreseen by the Constitution. A restrictive interpretation has prevented adapting the constitutional document to the realities of a developed industrial society, making the solution of political problems more complex. The regions have an effective role to play in the Italian system short of becoming an instrument of patronage or another bureaucratic hurdle. In time, acting in concert, the regions may be able to pressure the government and force it to relinquish some of its powers.

Presently, judgment on the outcome of the regional experiment must be suspended. The northern regions, Emilia Romagna in particular, have an acceptable record of accomplishments, while the performance of the southern regions could be best termed abysmal. The national political forces must provide the regions with more autonomy, financial and administrative, if they are to develop into the politico-administrative bodies called for by a regional state. The responsibility for the development of regionalism in Italy still remains with the national political class.

NOTES

1. P. A. Allum and G. Amyot, "Regionalism in Italy: Old Wine in New Bottles?" *Parliamentary Affairs* 24 (Winter 1970-71): 54.

2. Elio Gizzi, *Manuale di diritto regionale* (Milan: Giuffré, 1972), p. 13.

3. George Woodcock, "Regional Government: The Italian Example," *Public Administration* 45 (Winter 1972): 403.

4. Giovanni Miele, ed., "Introduzione," *Le regioni: politica o amministrazione?* (Milan: Comunità, 1973), p. 19.

5. Livio Palladin, "Problemi e prospettive dell'autonomia normativa regionale," in *Le regioni*, ed. Miele, pp. 28-31.

6. P. A. Allum, *Italy, Republic without Government?* (New York: Norton, 1973), p. 227.

7. Gizzi, *Manuale di diritto regionale*, p. 143.

8. Ibid., pp. 28-35.

9. Ibid., p. 328.

10. Woodcock, "Regional Government," p. 412.

11. Franco Bassani, "Per una politica regionale dei servizi sociali," in *Regioni e servizi sociali*, ed. Angela Zucconi (Milan: Comunità, 1974), pp. 142-46.

12. Paolo Barile, "Corte costituzionale e regioni a statuto ordinario," in *Le regioni*, ed. Miele, p. 93.

13. Enzo Modica, "Struttura istituzionale delle regioni," *A che punto siamo con le regioni*, *Quaderni di Ulisse* 13 (September 1974): 26.

14. Guido Fanti, "L'esperienza emiliana," in *Quaderni di Ulisse* 13 (September 1974): 78.

15. M. M. Watson, *Regional Development Policy and Administration in Italy* (London: Longmans, 1970), p. 72.

16. Umberto Pototschnig, "Il ruolo della Regione nell'organizzazione dell' assistenza," *Rivista di documentazione e giurisprudenza* 2 (November-December 1974): 941.

17. Marco Cammelli, "Le Regioni nelle proposte statali di riforma sanitaria," in *Rivista di documentazione e giurisprudenza* 2 (November-December 1974): 991.

18. Sergio Bartole, "Le provvidenze regionali per la zootecnia," *Rivista di documentazione e giurisprudenza* 2 (November-December 1974): 873.

19. Giorgio Berti, "Commento. Schema di disegno di legge 8 giugno 1974," in *Rivista di documentazione e giurisprudenza* 2 (November-December 1974): 974.

20. Norman Kogan, "Impact of the New Italian Regional Governments on the Structure of Power within Parties," *Comparative Politics* 7 (April 1975): 388-404.

21. Alberto Romano, "Rappresentanza politica e democrazia diretta nell' ordinamento regionale," in *Le regioni*, ed. Miele, pp. 235-38.

Norway

Jan Fridthjof Bernt*

11

Norway is divided into nineteen counties (*fylker*) and 454 municipal corporations (*kommuner*). Local self-government, though not mandated by the Constitution, is generally considered an important element of the democratic structure. The independence of the municipal corporations in local matters rests not only on the legal framework of the Local Government Act of 1954, but also on a strong political tradition. The municipalities have been given their own economic basis (primarily an income tax presently running between 12 and 14 percent and a property tax of between 0.4 and 1.0 percent), and they are considered to hold a general governmental competency as long as they do not impinge on the rights or freedom of individual citizens without the required statutory basis.

Still, in many respects, time has been working against the local municipal corporation as an independent political decision-making unit in Norway, as in other countries. There is the problem of inadequate economic resources and, above all, the problem of the increasing importance of economic planning and administrative and political decisions, which have to be made on a larger scale than local municipalities with their average population of only about 10,000 inhabitants (5,000 for the rural municipalities, which are by far the most numerous).

Of the two problems, the issue of economic resources, though tricky to handle, clearly can find its solution within the framework of an existing administrative structure, essentially by rechannelling state funds presently applied to state-administered local projects or to specialized grant programs supporting various municipal undertakings.

Far more fundamental is the conflict between local self-government and efficient and rational planning and administration. To a certain degree these two ideals are incompatible. Modern society and government, as we know

*Assistant Professor, Institute of Public Law, University of Bergen.

them, seem to imply more macro-planning and highly specialized administrative decision making, which, by implication or practical necessity, must take place on a region-wide or nation-wide basis. A major concern, however, is to limit this "upward drift" of decision-making power so that it does not comprise more decisions and does not bring the decision-making authority to a level higher than is absolutely necessary. In this situation interest has been renewed in the role of the counties as units of intermediate-level, local self-government and has revived discussion of some fundamental issues concerning the structure of local and regional self-government and the relationship between the state and these levels of government.

STRUCTURE OF COUNTY SELF-GOVERNMENT

The Norwegian counties were originally mere administrative divisions of state government. The local government acts of 1837, which created the urban and rural municipal corporations, made no change in this, and the county administrative staff was still a local branch of the state administration. The head (*fylkesmannen*) was a state civil servant subject to instructions only from the central government in Oslo.

County-wide local government was not really contemplated in the 1837 acts. However, the Rural Local Government Act of 1837 laid the foundation for popular participation in county government by providing that the mayors of the rural municipalities in each county should convene once a year to control and give their consent to expenditures that were to be apportioned between these municipalities. A refusal to give such consent could be overruled by the central government.

From this modest start the counties more or less stumbled into a process of developing a county self-government based upon statutory provisions differing from that of the local municipalities only in a few, important points. One may say that the dissimilarities reflected the fact that the "county municipality" was not a premeditated "missing link" between central and municipal government and did not spring out of any well-defined philosophy about the roles of local, county, and national administration and government.

The main popular body, the county council (*fylkestinget*), until autumn 1975 was a body of politicians representing the individual municipalities of the county and not the electorate as a whole. They were elected by and among the members of the municipal assemblies in the county, and municipality representation was proportional only to a limited degree.

County councilmen generally did not consider themselves obliged to the county electorate as a whole, and the incentive to initiate new and important county-wide projects was rather small, particularly since the counties had no economic resources of their own. The county council levied its taxes on the municipalities as such; so an expansion of the county budget necessitated corresponding cuts in the local municipal budgets. Thus, county councilmen, who subsequently had to go back to face their brethren in the local municipal councils, hardly encouraged overspending.

On the other hand, the "county muncipality" had no adminstrative staff of its own to speak of. The head of the state regional administration in the county was also in charge of preparing and executing the decisions of the county council and its committees, and therefore he, and through him the central government, exerted a considerable influence on them. Besides giving the central government considerable control over what went on in the counties, this relationship also tended to hamper the initiative of the county politicians, as it was uncertain whether a reform could be prepared and carried through when the deciding body lacked control of its own administration.

In sum, county municipal government, in spite of its general competency and power to levy whatever taxes it found appropriate on the local municipalities (subject to state approval), confined itself largely to the tasks which it had a statutory duty to undertake, mainly planning, building, and maintaining regional highways, hospitals and high schools. In 1971 the net expenses of these levels of government were in billions of Norwegian kroner: state 21,200, local municipalities 8,100, and county municipalities 1,800. [1]

On this background, three major reforms were proposed by an expert committee [2] and enacted by the Norwegian Parliament in 1974-75: direct county-wide election of the county council, the establishment of a completely separate "county municipal" administration organized in the same way as that of the local municipalities, and the introduction of a system whereby the counties levy their taxes directly on the citizens instead of proportioning their expenses among the local municipalities in the county. I will give a brief outline of some aspects of these reforms and discuss some of their intended and probable consequences. Subsequently, I will present and discuss some of the proposals and points of view on the division of functions among national, regional, and local government from which these reforms spring.

THE REFORMS AND THEIR CONSEQUENCES

Direct Election of the Councils

The first major step in the process of restructuring the county government was the 1974 enactment of statutory provisions introducing direct and county-wide elections to the county councils. The first election under the new rules was held in the autumn of 1975.

By enacting these provisions, the Norwegian Parliament expressed its adherence to the idea that the county municipalities should be given a new and independent role as bodies for regional self-government on a county-wide basis and not merely act as "secondary municipalities" for intermunicipal cooperation. The reform also created the necessary political conditions for a living county-wide democratic political structure. Until the 1975 election most of the members of the county councils also occupied leading positions in their local municipalities. This had obvious consequences for their loyalties and priorities as well as for their work capacity. Besides, the absence of election campaigns and specialized county politicians generally tended to make public opinion rather indifferent to what went on in county government.

The introduction of direct elections to the county council was intended to create favorable conditions for the development of a new breed of politicians in the leading positions of county government. By making county politics a separate career it was hoped to make the interests of the county as a whole the dominating factor in the decision-making process and to stimulate the interest of political parties, politicians, and public opinion in county affairs.

Although the reform had broad, general support, some of the political parties had misgivings that the reform might tend to act as a centralizing factor in the counties, depriving the minor local municipalities of their influence and representation in the deciding bodies of the county municipality. These objections mirror to a considerable degree, however, a major concern behind the reform: to abolish the system of loose "county-wide federalism" and make the counties viable units for regional political decision-making authority, thus, by implication, reducing local control and influence over the county municipality.

A kind of compromise was worked out, however. A complicated system was introduced wherein one-fifth of the seats in the county council were designated as "equalizing seats," to be distributed among the local municipalities not represented or least represented in the county council. The system has no influence on the proportional representation of the political parties in the county council, but only on *who* on the ballot should represent the party. The candidates given an "equalizing seat" are taken from the ballot of the party, which is in turn to have a seat according to the rules for proportional representation. The prospects that a representative given such a seat should consider himself a representative for his local district rather than for the county-wide electorate of his party are rather bleak, and it is likely that this system, now that it has fulfilled its mission of neutralizing opposition against the electoral reform, eventually will be abolished as a superfluous complication.

The County's New Administrative Structure

The County Municipality Act of 1961 was nearly identical to the Local Government Act of 1954, which applies to the local municipalities. There were, however, some rather important differences, most of them reflecting the absence of a separate and independent county municipal administrative staff. Wishing to create an effective system of democratic government on a county-wide basis, the Standing Committee on Reforms of Local Government proposed to give the county municipality control of its own administration by creating separate administrative staffs for the county municipalities. Provisions to this effect were enacted in the spring of 1975, the reorganization started subsequent to the election in the autumn of the same year, and, after one year of accommodation, the new administrative structure was implemented on 1 January 1977. This legislation will leave the county municipalities with a legal framework for their administrative structure similar to that of the local municipalities. For one thing, the county mayor, who is one of the county aldermen, possesses responsibility for having cases adequately prepared by the staff before they are put before the county council, the county committee (which consists of the county aldermen), or any other deciding body. This, in turn, means a considerably stronger political influence on the preparatory work done by the administrative staff than when the regional head of the state administration had the sole responsibility for this aspect of the decision-making process.

Second, the new system implies a general political control of the county municipal staff by the county committee. Like his colleagues in the local municipalities, the head of this staff, though subject to some instructions, will have considerable independence once he has been engaged. A proposal to introduce a parliamentary system in the county municipalities appears to have gone to its final rest in the standing committee. Still, the relationship between the popularly elected bodies of the county and the administrative staff will be fundamentally changed from a staff headed by a state official, who was completely removed from any county municipal control, to a staff integrated in the administration.

The creation of a separate county municipal administration is expected to have beneficial effects on the ability and motivation of the county politicians to initiate new projects and tighten political control over existing ones. In addition, it is likely that tasks presently allocated to regional state administrative bodies will tend to gravitate towards a politically potent and administratively integrated county municipal administration. Presently the lack of coordination among various sectors of specialized governmental functions on a regional basis presents a serious problem. The lines of command and communication today often go directly from specialized regional bodies to various state departments that find it very hard to coordinate their efforts without creating administrative bottlenecks. Earlier attempts to obtain coordination on the county level through the state county administration have not been very successful, but it is possible that the new interest in regional government may lead to a reexamination of these questions and, ultimately, a "new deal" in the division of functions between the state departments and their regional offices, the state county administration, and the county municipality. This is, at least, what the Standing Committee on Reforms of Local Government is recommending and working for.

THE FUTURE ROLE OF THE COUNTY MUNICIPALITIES

The Present Situation

Except for an article providing that the country should not be divided, the Norwegian constitution contains no provisions of direct relevance to the question of local self-government. This issue is left largely in the hands of the legislature, which has the power and responsibility to define the legal framework for local and regional self-government as well as to create its economic and administrative conditions.

In the present legal situation the county and local municipalities have a general competency in regional and local matters, and the prevailing opinion is that there are no special limitations on the authority of these administrative units compared with state agencies and departments. Like these latter, the municipalities need statutory authorization for decisions that deprive an individual of a right or make him subject to a duty, and the system of procedural safeguards laid down in the Norwegian Administrative Procedure Act and by the courts applies also to the municipalities. The division of functions among national, regional, and local government consequently depends partly on provisions in special legislation and partly on economic resources.

The present role of the county municipalities in Norwegian government is rather modest. It is estimated that county municipalities administer about 6 percent of public expenditures, compared with 68 and 26 percent for the state and local municipalities respectively. Of this, about 90 percent is spent on schools, health institutions, and construction, mainly roads. In addition, the county municipalities are engaged in various kinds of business enterprises, especially electric power supply companies.

The reforms of the county municipal administration and the introduction of direct elections to the county council and of direct taxes to the county municipalities are not intended to have any considerable immediate consequences for the role and the tasks of the county municipality. Obviously, the idea behind these reforms is to revitalize county self-government and create political and administrative units with the political and economic resources for playing an independent and far more active role in the government of the county. A long-term expansion of the role of the county municipality is programmed into the reform, and a major issue is what form this expansion should take and how to make sure that it takes place as intended and is limited to the areas where it is considered desirable. Thus, the enactment of the provisions restructuring county municipal administration is, in a sense, more the beginning than the end of the discussion about the relationship between the three levels of government.

The Relationship to the National Government

The desire to decentralize decision-making authority from the central state administration to a regional level is motivated chiefly by three considerations:

efficiency, a simplification of the decision-making process; a closer relationship between the citizens and the administration, that is, decisions by lower and decentralized governmental bodies, where direct personal contact between the private parties and the officials handling the case is possible; and democracy, using the county council and its committees as a means of popular control over the administration of regional matters.

There appears to be a broad political consensus behind the drive for decentralization of state governmental authority, but it is obvious that the breaking up of established decision-making routines that this implies, is a painful process. It also appears that the various departments and agencies in the central administration are reluctant to give up any part of their authority. The general experience seems to be that they have far from overstretched their present competency to delegate decision-making power to regional administrative bodies. Commonly the authority of central government bodies to give general instructions to the regional administration (for example, concerning the organization of schools or hospitals) has been used to issue extremely detailed provisions regulating in the most minute detail matters that should have been decided on location.

It seems that the success of the attempt to decentralize authority to the counties will depend greatly on whether it is possible to work out reasonably clear-cut divisions between matters of a general character requiring expert competency, which should still be decided by the central government, and administrative and practical matters or issues pertaining to individual cases, which should be for the regional agency to decide. The years to come should give us valuable information about the character and strength of the forces that drive or counteract such a decentralization.

The Relationship to Local Government

A touchy issue is the consequences for the local municipalities of the reform of county government. Though the county municipality no longer can be described as ''secondary,'' it is still a much heeded maxim that it in no way should be a ''superior commune'' in relation to the local municipalities. Thus, to the extent that the decisions by the latter are subject to control or approval, this authority is a state matter and exercised by the central or regional state administration.

It is doubtful to what extent the principle of complete mutual parity between the two types of municipalities will survive in the years to come. To the extent that the central government delegates decision-making authority to the county municipalities, the county municipalities will make a number of decisions of direct consequence to the local municipalities, often also necessitating action by the latter or at least setting certain limits to their freedom of choice.

The best example of this is the planning sector. In 1973 an amendment was made in the Planning and Construction Act of 1965 introducing a ''county plan.'' The county plan does not regulate in detail the use of land in the

individual local municipalities, but it does have concrete and direct consequences for local planning and land use. What is more, it may force a local
municipality to revise its land-use plans. There has been some discussion about
the extent to which the county municipality itself should have the final say in
situations that conflict with local plans. It has been argued that the regional and
central state planning authorities should produce a compromise when county
and local municipal plans conflict. This may uphold the illusion that the local
municipalities are in no way subject to county municipal control, but it is
obviously not very realistic to expect the priorities of the individual local
municipality to prevail in such a conflict.

The concept of coordinated planning necessarily implies superiority for a
higher level in a conflict with units on the lower level, and this fact will be
important, not only in the sector of land-use planning. As long as we do not
abandon our efforts to have a coordinated and integrated use of resources in
various sectors of government control and services, the idea of complete local
independence in such matters is a fiction. The Norwegian reform of county
government represents no such abandonment of the concept of coordinated
planning. Rather it is an effort to reduce the harmful consequences of this
development by restructuring an intermediate level of government to enable it
to perform tasks that would otherwise have to be taken care of by the central
administration. It cannot, and is not intended to, alter the fact that decisions
made on the primary level, in the local municipalities, to a great extent will be
ruled by priorities laid down by higher authorities. If it is successful, however,
it may create the basis for a new kind of effective local self-government based
upon a hierarchical system whereby no decision is made on a level higher than
necessary and democratic control is an active element on all levels, an administrative structure which we may describe as a kind of "democratic feudalism."

NOTES

1. NOU 1974, 53, "Mål og retningslinjer for reformer i lokalforvaltningen" (Aims
and Principles for Reforms of Local Government), Report to Parliament, no. 31,
1974-75, p. 22.

2. "Hovedkomiteen for reformer i kommunalforvaltningen" (the Standing Committee on Reforms of Local Government); see NOU 1974, 53.

Proposals for Finland

R. Harisalo and P. Rönkko*

12

A survey of the proposed reorganization of provincial administration comes at an appropriate time in Finland. It is already possible to see the consequences of changes in Finland's economic structure and to assess the efforts to accommodate administrative machinery to emerging conditions. Compared with other industrialized countries, Finland has been relatively late in its economic restructuring and urbanization. Geographically the change has proceeded from the south into the eastern and northern parts of the country.

During the decades 1950-70, the proportion of the working population employed in agriculture and forestry fell from about 46 to 20 percent. The labor force thus released transferred primarily to the service sector. The percentage distribution of the working population over the respective sectors has developed as follows:

	1950	1960	1970	1980*	1985*
Agriculture and forestry	46	36	20	21	15
Industry	28	32	35	35	36
Services	26	32	45	44	49

*Forecast

These changes in the Finnish economy have brought with them a wave of migration draining the population of the east and north into the conurbations of the south. The concentration of population is reflected in the growth in the proportion of the population in the ten largest cities from 24 to 31 percent between 1960 and 1970 due to migration. The proportion of the urban population in the country as a whole increased from 56 to 64 percent in the same

*Risto Harisalo is Assistant in Municipal Politics and Economics, and Pentti Rönkko is Lecturer in Municipal Politics, Institute of Municipal Sciences, University of Tampere.

decade. At the same time, there are marked differences within the urban population. In the province of Uusimaa, containing the capital Helsinki, the urban population in 1970 comprised 86 percent, whereas in some of the provinces in the east and north the corresponding figure is about 40. The total number of work situations has increased since 1960 in only two of the twelve provinces in the country. This increase is concentrated in the capital and its environs.

These changes in the structure of the Finnish community have meant changed demands upon the functions of society. Up to the 1950s the status and functions of the administration were regarded as passive; the authorities existed to secure conditions necessary to the activities of society but by no means should interfere directly in them. Since the 1960s this state of affairs has been the subject of wide debate. The function of the administration has come to be seen as the safeguarding of welfare, a change of attitude particularly manifest in social legislation reforms over recent years. Restructuring is in fact currently under way in the health services and education, and a reform of the welfare system is being planned.

Until now the work of renewal can be said to have concentrated on the development of certain services. The next step must be a reorganization of the administration at all levels: in central, provincial, and local government. The 1970s have already brought proposals for a revision of the Constitution and the system of provincial administration and of the laws governing the structure and activities of authorities in the communes as well as preliminary proposals for a change in state government at the local level. Changes in the system of provincial administration have in fact been on the way since the turn of the century, the chief concern being the establishment of autonomy at this level.

ADMINISTRATIVE ORGANIZATION IN FINLAND

The Finnish administrative system falls into two spheres, state and municipal government. State administration embraces all levels, central, provincial, and local government. Municipal administration, again, functions primarily at the local level, but in the case of hospitals and vocational training establishments, for example, it also extends to the intermediary sphere. The structure of the administration may be set out as follows:

Central administration	Parliament
	The government and the president
	The ministries
	The central boards
Intermediary administration	The provincial governments
	Regional state authorities
	Federations of communes
Local administration	Communes (municipalities)
	Local state administration

The central governing system of the state comprises Parliament and the government together with the ministries and affiliated central bureaus responsible for the most important spheres of administration. Within the ministries the ultimate authority lies with the minister, who is a member of the government and politically accountable. A central board is by nature executive.

At the provincial level, state administration is somewhat inchoate—the result of long historical development. General administration is the responsibility of the provincial governments, alongside which a number of separate authorities have been set up to administer such spheres as taxation, employment, and road construction. The provincial government is the general administrative authority in the province, supervising the activities of the communes and acting as the instance of appeal in matters of administrative justice and as the intermediary authority in welfare, health and hospital services, and education.

At the intermediary level, there has evolved since the 1930s a basically autonomous administrative organization in the form of federations of communes contracted to implement the kind of municipal schemes that require more considerable population backing. No such system seems to have developed on the same scale in other countries. The federations are formed ad hoc, so that a given commune may simultaneously belong to as many as six or even eight such bodies. The organization has gradually come to compensate for the higher level of self-government otherwise lacking in Finland.

At the third level, communes and the local level of state administration function concomitantly. Municipal government traditionally has held a position of great significance in Finnish society. In the course of its history it has come to form the basis of a democratic system of administration, being founded upon the principle of representativeness. Thus the municipal councils, which are governing authorities at this level, are elected every four years.

REFORM OF PROVINCIAL GOVERNMENT

Current Problems

The central problems in government at the intermediary provincial level are seen to lie in the absence of possibilities for direct citizen participation, deficiencies in social policy, and coordination and integration with various levels of the administration. Likewise the lack of centralized organizations, the coordination of their functions, and certain inconsistencies in regional divisions have proved problematic for administrative activity.

Democratic principles applied at the provincial level logically would imply a system whereby the inhabitants of the region in question had the power of deciding on matters pertaining to that region. At present, however, neither provincial government nor the system of regional state administration allows this. In both cases administration is in the hands of civil servants, with elected boards occupying only an advisory position.

The planning of social policy at the provincial level is at present very loosely organized, being the responsibility of a variety of bodies, such as the planning department of the provincial government, the regional planning associations, various regional state authorities, and the federations of communes formed for the provision of health services. All of these bodies are relatively independent of each other, so that coordination is difficult, while none has of itself sufficient resources to act as an effective center for the implementation of social policies.

The scattered nature of this system has meant a drain on both state and municipal finances in that, for example, each federation of communes concentrates on fulfilling its own functions as well as possible without the support of a central body that understands the overall activity in question and is capable of bearing its overall costs. Different administrative units may make considerable investments simultaneously without mutual planning, for example, as to the timing of their transaction. There has, however, been some increase in recent years in the amount of systematic planning and cooperation in provincial administration.

The territorial divisions in intermediary administration are inconsistent in many respects, for the provinces do not always represent natural economic or regional entities. Since their borders are not in keeping with natural spheres of influence, the functions of their administration and other functions of society cannot appropriately serve the needs of the population and the balanced development of various fields of activity. Other regional divisions of intermediary government are also not always in keeping with the demarcation of the provinces.

Reform Objectives

The aims envisaged in the reform of provincial government are a reduction in the degree of inequality among the various regions and an increased level of welfare in them. The former implies in particular that basic services be made available to all citizens regardless of their income, property, schooling, or place of residence. Welfare is the promotion of a satisfactory level of living for all members of the community.

The regional development policy emerges as a central factor in the reform objective, that is the channelling of development in the various parts of the country in a direction favorable to the overall goals of development and involves components from all sectors of social policy.

The point of departure in regional development must be the potential of each region involved, its needs, and special objectives according to which the pattern of national policies must be molded and applied. Here, one prime consideration must be the equality of the regional population in economic, social, and cultural senses. The appropriate structuring of the regional communities entails an active influence upon the location of population groups, production, and various services. Development policies should allow supervision by society of the direction and speed of change in regional structure.

The ends and means of regional policymaking are defined at the central administrative level, while its implementation is primarily the task of administrative bodies functioning at the provincial level. The organization and demarcation of the regions and the specification of their centers of administration will be of the utmost significance in the pursuit of regional development goals.

The promotion of democratic principles in administration is the chief objective in the current reform plan. Efforts also will be made to shift control of administration from the separate district state authorities to general administrative bodies; in particular, the maintenance of hospital services by the federations of communes will be transferred, as far as possible, to one authority, and cooperation and coordination among the various units will be promoted. The commencement of regional development along these lines will entail organizing and coordinating social planning with other functions at the intermediary level.

In revising the regional divisions of intermediary administration the main objective is the greatest possible equality of accessibility for administrative units throughout the country. Most important at this level is the provincial division. The provinces should be constituted as integral and natural economic, agricultural, and administrative entities, in which facilities can serve the needs of the population appropriately and promote the development of conditions within the area. The basis envisaged for the provincial system comprises the so-called functional regions or economic divisions, of which there are seventeen to nineteen in this country. A province would constitute one or more such areas. However, such a revision in many cases will be a difficult task, as not all of these areas coincide in the spheres of influence of their centers, nor are they sufficiently self-contained to function independently. In planning the provincial system an effort should be made to combine areas whose mutual intercourse is by reason of their present administration, communications, population grouping, language, tradition, and economic interdependence. The capitals of the new provinces should be established in the most influential conurbation in each province, or, where there are several potential capitals, in the one offering greatest ease of access for the inhabitants of the province. Also, an aim of this planning should be to preserve the integrity of smaller centers. These, together with their respective spheres of influence, should, wherever possible, be accommodated intact within the same provincial entity.

The size of provinces cannot be defined sharply. In order to afford a reasonably economical level of administrative services, population should range between 200,000 and 300,000.[1] The separate district state authorities should be adapted to the economic pattern of provincial government. It is difficult to estimate the costs involved in this revision of the intermediary administration. However, overall taxation burdens should not increase in consequence of the reform.

Reform Proposals

The matter of administrative reform in the provinces has been under consideration in a series of committees ever since the latter years of the last century. The object throughout has been the creation of an autonomous regional government separate from the state administration. All proposals have so far, however, fallen through. The present plan for intermediary administration is based on proposals by a committee set up during the 1970s, with the object of outlining the main alternatives upon which a reform might be based. Four possibilities have emerged:

1. Province and communal federation model
2. Province and regional autonomy model
3. Combined intermediary administration model
4. Provincial government model

The following is a consideration of the chief characteristics of each of these alternative modes of administration, with detailed analysis confined to the first and fourth, between which the final decision will probably be reached.

In the province and federation model there would be a provincial government functioning as the general state administrative authority at the intermediary level, alongside which the various district state authorities would continue as separate units. The activity of the extensive federations of communes would be integrated by the formation of hospital service federations in which the various specialized service federations would be combined into regional entities. The provincial government would be rendered democratic by the introduction of an elected provincial council. Executive authority would be transferred from the state to the provincial authorities, and, similarly, certain functions of the state district authorities would pass to the province. The costs of both state intermediary administration and the federations of communes would be met in principle on the present basis, and the expenses of provincial government and state district administration would come under the state budget. The health services of the federations would be financed with revenues from the member communes, subsidized by state grants.

The committee's own proposal was the provincial government model, in which the present state provincial administration and the extended federations of communes would be combined into one body, by nature a state authority. This body would assume executive functions at present fulfilled by the state and its district authorities, as well as responsibility for special health services, general vocational training, and certain other activities of the present federations. Costs would be met entirely by the state in its annual budget. The transfer of functions from the federations to the province would free the communes of expenditure on special health services.

There are numerous similarities between the models proposed. For example, there is considerable agreement on regional divisions, but there are, in some cases, considerable differences about their tasks. One feature common to them all is the development of provincial administration. Furthermore, the organization of provincial administration planned in the various models is similar to the present pattern. All of them envisage a basic system of a council elected by proportional, secret, and direct ballot, a governing board elected by the council, a provincial governor, and a provincial center of administration with divisions, bureaus, and various boards. In the combined intermediary administration model the council and governing board would be shared between provincial and regional administration. The most marked differences between the models are in the way the functions of the present federations of communes would be executed.

The most significant factor from the standpoint of costs is whether the respective models would afford possibilities for more effective economic and other functional planning. The transfer of special health services from the federations to the provincial level should lower the municipal taxation burden by some 10 to 15 percent. On the other hand, the transfer of functions from the federations to the state might increase overall taxation, because municipal taxation could not be reduced correspondingly in the prevailing conditions of financial strain on the communes.

The committee was not unanimous in its choice of an alternative for reform. The majority supported the provincial government model, but there were also some in favor of the provincial and federation model. There must be more detailed discussion of regional divisions and of the transfer of authority from the central state administration to the provinces before any decisions are taken on reform.

In addition to the arrangement of special health services the organization of social policy planning at the provincial level has proved difficult. The committee proposes concentration of this planning in the reformed provincial government as a planning department under the jurisdiction of the provincial council. The council would have the power, within the framework defined by the central government, to set the goals and draw up plans for population and economic policies at the regional level, as well as for regional structure and the use and exploitation of resources.

At present the planning taking place at the intermediary level is concerned mainly with land use and with pertinent functional aspects. Here, the responsible authority is the regional planning federation constituted by the communes in each province. Land use planning at the moment is under the jurisdiction of the communes. It has, however, been remote from decision making, that is, from the central administration. The problem now is whether to leave planning in the hands of the communes or transfer it to the state, as the committee's proposal envisages. According to another view, common social policy planning should be concentrated in the federations of communes, the scope of the present federations being appropriately altered to a common social policy planning system at the intermediary administrative level.

Regardless of the ultimate form the revision of provincial administration takes, the regional demarcations presumably will be modified in the near future to conform to the natural economic, population, and functional pattern. Provincial boundaries will follow the economic divisions defined for the whole country in a number of studies. The basis of division is the system of centers and areas of influence hierarchically defined. The plan eventually must consider whether a structure of twelve to fourteen provinces or a denser seventeen to nineteen division should be implemented. Of the two the latter would comply more closely with the functional economic distribution. The drawback here would be the small size of the units formed, which would be apt to raise the costs of administration.

NOTES

1. Under the present system provincial populations range from 200,000 to 400,000, with the exception of Uusimaa (1 million, or a quarter of the total population of Finland) and the archipelago of Ahvenanmaa (20,000 inhabitants).

Proposals for Ireland

Joseph F. Zimmerman*

13

The origin of local government in the Republic of Ireland can be traced to judicial counties formed in the Middle Ages.[1] With the passage of time, the grand jury—composed primarily of landlords—became fiscally responsible in whole or in part for a number of local government functions, including public works, district asylums, fever hospitals, infirmaries, industrial schools, and courthouses.

The current local government system is primarily a product of the nineteenth century. Although most borough corporations were created by royal charter prior to the nineteenth century, they were reconstituted in 1840 by the Municipal Corporations (Ireland) Act. Poor Law Guardians were created in 1838, and in 1878 became the rural sanitary authorities. Most town commissions were created under provisions of the Town Improvement (Ireland) Act 1854, but some were created under provisions of an 1828 act and private acts. Rural and urban sanitary districts were organized by an 1878 act and were reorganized as rural district councils and urban district councils by the Local Government Act 1898. Under provisions of this act, the boards of guardians lost their role as rural sanitary authorities.

Representative county government dates only from 1898, when elected councils were created and assumed the local government functions of grand juries. A major trend since 1898 has been the gradual strengthening of county government.

*Professor of Political Science, Graduate School of Public Affairs, State University of New York at Albany, and author of *The Federated City: Community Control in Large Cities*. Desmond Roche of the Irish Institute of Public Administration kindly read the manuscript and offered valuable suggestions for improvement.

POST-INDEPENDENCE REORGANIZATION

The first action taken to reorganize the local government system following the establishment of the Irish Free State was the Local Government (Temporary Provisions) Act 1923, which abolished boards of guardians and assigned their functions to the county councils. Two years later, rural district councils were abolished, and their functions—chiefly road maintenance and sanitation—were transferred to the county councils.

The 1923 act also authorized the minister for local government and public health to order an inquiry into the performance of the duties of any local government and order its dissolution for failure to discharge effectively its duties or for deliberately neglecting "to comply with any lawful order, direction, or regulation of the Minister." In 1924, the minister dissolved several councils, including the Cork and Dublin city councils, and appointed commissioners in each city to exercise the powers of the corporation. The minister also appointed the Greater Dublin Commission of Inquiry following the dissolution of the Dublin city council. The commission's 1926 report recommended annexing contiguous urbanized areas to the city and appointing a professional city manager.[2] Cork, however, became the first local authority to have a manager with the enactment of the Cork City Management Act 1929, and the election of a new council. Special legislation extended the management system to Dublin and Dun Láoghaire Borough in 1930, Limerick in 1934, and Waterford in 1939. The County Management Act 1940 extended the system to the remaining local authorities, effective in 1942.

The 1940 act provided for the pairing of small adjoining counties for management purposes. Initially, a manager was appointed for each of six pairs of counties. Subsequently, an individual manager was appointed for each of four of the paired counties, and today there are only four pairs of counties for management purposes.

With the exceptions of three county boroughs—Cork, Limerick, and Waterford—which have their own managers, and the Dublin area, the county manager is the manager of all other local authorities—boroughs, urban district councils, town commissions, and joint bodies—in the county. In other words, executive integration exists even though there are several local governing bodies in each county. The 1940 act specified that the Dublin city manager would also hold office as the Dublin county manager, the Dun Láoghaire Borough manager, and the Balbriggan town manager.[3]

Although several national laws relating to the local government system have been enacted since 1940, the only function affected in a significant manner was health. Urban district councils lost their health administration responsibilities under provisions of the 1947 Health Act which made county councils and county borough corporations the health authorities. In 1960, joint health authorities were established in Cork, Dublin, Limerick, and Waterford areas. The 1970 Health Act transferred responsibility for the administration of health services to eight newly established regional health boards, effective 1 April 1971.

THE 1971 REORGANIZATION PROPOSALS

The Irish local government system currently consists of 110 elected authorities: 27 county councils, 4 county borough corporations (the cities of Cork, Dublin, Limerick, and Waterford), 7 borough corporations, 49 urban district councils, and 23 town commissions. In addition, there are five towns in which the commissions have been dissolved and their functions are performed by the county council. The counties and county boroughs are the principal local units.

The system has five distinguishing characteristics: the universality of the council-manager plan of administration; a sharp legal distinction between the powers possessed by the council and those possessed by the manager; tight control by the national government; nomination of higher-level personnel after open competitive examinations by the Local Appointments Commission, a national body; and the sharing of a common manager by all local authorities in each county with the exceptions of Cork, Limerick, and Waterford. In each of these counties the county manager serves as manager of all local authorities with the exception of the county borough, which has a city manager.

In February 1971, the government laid before each house of the Oireachtas (Parliament) a White Paper—*Local Government Reorganisation*—proposing the first comprehensive reorganization of the local government system since 1898. Although labelled a White Paper, the document actually is similar to an English Green Paper in that proposals were presented for public discussion in contrast to a White Paper, which reports policy decisions made by the government. The minister had considered establishing a special commission on local government but decided to have the review conducted by the Department of Local Government because of the belief that a special commission would need several years to prepare recommendations. No formal studies were conducted by the department, and the White Paper's proposals for change originated with various officials in the department and published reports.

Unfortunately the White Paper confined itself to functions falling under the jurisdiction of the Minister for Local Government. Consequently, it contained no proposals relating to economic planning and development, education, or social welfare service. A second limitation was its failure to discuss finance, a subject of crucial importance in view of the fact that local authorities receive more funds from national grants than they raise from rates based on antiquated valuations. In December 1972, the government laid a second White Paper—*Local Finance and Taxation*—before each house of the Oireachtas.

The Proposals

Proposals contained in the White Paper may be viewed as evolutionary rather than revolutionary in that no change in the council-manager plan of administration and no new units of local governments, such as regional authorities, were proposed. Many local elected officials, however, viewed the proposals as revolutionary since they proposed the abolition of many urban district councils and all town commissions; their functions would be transferred to the county councils.

Under the proposals, the county would become the principal unit of local government with the exceptions of the county boroughs of Cork, Limerick, and Waterford, and the Dublin area. While admitting that county boundaries often are arbitrary and split natural communities, the paper did not propose a modification of county boundaries other than in cases where major towns are situated at the boundaries. The paper suggested that in small contiguous counties administrative offices in addition to the office of manager should be amalgamated and added that a case could be made for establishing one council for some pairs of counties. The government announced its willingness to consider the establishment of special machinery to determine those urban district councils to be abolished and retained. The management consultant firm of McKinsey & Company, Incorporated, was retained to study and make recommendations for a new staff structure and management methods for the new system of local authorities. The firm concluded that a system of county governments "alone would be the most economical and effective."[4] In view of the fact the government had announced its intention to retain some urban authorities, the consulting firm recommended that only authorities with a population in excess of 12,000 be retained. The White Paper proposed extending the boundaries of retained urban district councils to include areas in which development was projected to occur during the next twenty years.

The four county boroughs would be variously affected by the White Paper proposals. Limerick would be basically unaffected, but the offices of Waterford city manager and Waterford county manager would be merged "when an opportunity arises." The government rejected the merger of Cork City and Cork County but stated that steps would be initiated to ensure that the plans and activities of the two authorities are harmonized.

The most drastic proposal affecting a county borough were those pertaining to Dublin. The bulk of the population growth is occurring in the Greater Dublin area, and the government reached the conclusion that integration at the level of the chief executive alone would be inadequate to cope with projected problems in the area. The White Paper's proposal calling for the amalgamation of the four existing local authorities was similar to the proposal advanced by the Greater Dublin Commission on Inquiry in 1926 and the recommendation of the Local Government (Dublin) Tribunal in 1938 that the existing local governments be amalgamated to form a metropolitan government.[5]

In 1930 the Pembroke, Rathgar, and Rathmines urban districts were merged with the city along with other contiguous urbanized areas by the Local Government (Dublin) Act 1930. No territory has been annexed to the city since 1953, and annexation was rejected by the White Paper. The government recognized that the creation of an authority with a population of approximately 800,000 would increase the distance, for communication purposes, between citizens and the local authority. In consequence, the paper suggested that committees responsible for "local services" might be provided with offices and staff. Smaller local electoral areas also were suggested as a means of ensuring that citizens would be able to keep in close contact with their councillors.

In a report to the minister for local government, the Irish Institute of Public Administration rejected the government's proposal for an amalgamated government and recommended retaining existing local authorities and creating a regional authority—covering the city and the counties of Dublin, Kildare, Meath, and Wicklow—responsible for strategic planning, new town development, pollution control, sewage disposal, and water supply.[6]

A cursory reading of the White Paper leads one to conclude that the government proposed a single local government for each county with a few exceptions. Upon closer examination, it is evident that the government proposed an unusual two-tier system, unusual in that the lower tier would not be composed of statutory authorities.

The paper suggests that an area committee be appointed for each county electoral area. Most counties have four or five electoral areas with populations generally ranging from 10,000 to 20,000. Each committee "could consist of the councillors for the area together with representatives of local development associations and other bodies concerned with the economic, social, and cultural development of the area." The principal functions of an area committee would be to present recommendations to the county council to promote the development of the area and comment on proposed bylaws. These committees would be somewhat similar to "neighborhood" or "little" city halls in large U.S. cities but would differ in that the "little" city halls are under the direct control of the mayor rather than the councillors and representatives of local development associations. The government announced its intention to encourage county councils to establish offices, under the control of area committees, in each of the larger towns and to administer certain services—such as local planning applications, water supply, repair of houses, and local road maintenance—on an area basis.

In a supplemental memorandum, the Department of Local Government indicated that each area committee would be composed of five to seven councillors and representatives of local voluntary bodies and might be allocated funds annually by the county council for "amenities such as parks, public walks, and recreational facilities."[7]

The final major proposal was for a substantial revision of the *ultra vires* rule by means of a broad restatement of the permissive powers of local authorities, possibly including "a general provision empowering local authorities to spend money on the betterment of their areas or in the interests of the inhabitants of their areas."

THE CURRENT STATUS

The February 1973 general election witnessed the defeat of the Fianna Fáil Government; local government reorganization was not a major issue in the election campaign. In December 1973 the Department of Local Government issued a discussion document—*Local Government Reorganisation*—containing the views of the new Fine Gael-Labour government. The minister for local government conceded the system needed improvement but rejected the abolition of a large number of small local authorities. With the possible exception of the larger urban district councils, planning and development, most housing functions, and sanitary functions would be shifted to the county councils. The formation of a large authority for the Dublin area was rejected by the minister, who announced that the need for boundary adjustments and methods of improving coordination of local authorities would be studied.

In May 1974, Fine Gael and Labour released a joint document—*The National Coalition at Work*—reiterating that the government had "rejected the plans by the previous administration to abolish small local authorities and further centralise the local government system." The document added that "urban areas presently without a statutory local authority have been invited to consider establishing one." To date, no new local authority has been created.

In June 1977, the coalition government was defeated in a general election by Fianna Fáil; campaign issues were primarily economic and included Fianna Fáil's promise to abolish rates. The new Fianna Fáil government has been silent to date about plans to reorganize the local government system.

CONCLUSIONS

One can conclude with certainty that the manager system of administration is firmly entrenched and is unlikely to be changed significantly in the foreseeable future. John Collins wrote in 1953 that "at the end of another half century another transformation may have taken place and the county may have followed the parish, the barony, the rural district, and the poor law union into the limbo of discarded administrative areas."[8] As of mid-1979, there is no evidence indicating that by the turn of the century the county will no longer be an important unit of local government. The major political parties are in agreement that the county should be the principal local unit.

The most major change affecting county government may occur in the Greater Dublin area, where pressure probably will continue to build for the creation of a two-tier system with the existing local authorities serving as the upper tier and councils or committees, responsible for services of a personal or neighborhood nature, serving as the lower tier. A coordinating committee for the Dublin metropolitan area also is under consideration.

NOTES

1. For the most complete information on the origin of the Irish local government system, see the second edition of John Collins's *Local Government*, ed. Desmond Roche (Dublin: Institute of Public Administration, 1963), pp. 1-35.

2. Greater Dublin Commission of Inquiry, *Report* (Dublin: The Stationery Office, 1926).

3. For further details, see Joseph F. Zimmerman, "Council-Manager Government in Ireland," *Studies in Comparative Local Government* 6 (Summer 1972): 61-69; and Joseph F. Zimmerman, "The County Manager System in Ireland," *The American County* 37 (July 1972): 15-18.

4. McKinsey & Company, Incorporated, *Strengthening the Local Government Service* (Dublin: The Stationery Office, 1972), p. 4.

5. *Report of the Local Government (Dublin) Tribunal* (Dublin: The Stationery Office, 1938), pp. 123-33.

6. "More Local Government—A Programme for Development," *Administration* 19 (Summer 1971): 172.

7. *Local Government Reorganisation*, Mimeographed (Dublin: Department of Local Government, 25 May 1971), pp. 3-4.

8. J. Collins, "Notes on Local Government: II. The Evolution of County Government," *Administration* 1 (Summer 1953): 88.

Proposals for the Netherlands

*A. Bours**

14

The Dutch government system has three tiers: the national level; the provincial level, consisting of 11 units, and the local level, formed by 833 municipalities.[1] The Netherlands is a small country, less than 34,000 square kilometers of land, with a population of almost 13.9 million. Distances are short; the maximum for the whole country is only 340 kilometers, or 210 miles, and the population density is high (400 per km²). About half of the population is concentrated in the western part of the country, called "Randstad Holland" (density 750 per km²). These are key preliminary facts from a geo-administrative point of view.

The roots of the local government system trace back to medieval times. Even before any form of management of common affairs existed, another system of communal cooperation resulted from the need for joint defense against river floods and the sea.[2] Without dikes, even today about half of the Netherlands, the most densely populated part, would be flooded. This need gave rise to the establishment of water control boards composed of all the landowners in the area concerned. Such boards still exist apart from the municipalities and even exceed them in number, although they have been reduced drastically: from over 2,500 in 1953 to 678 on 1 January 1978.[3] This process is still continuing; water boards are being adjusted to the enlargement of the technological and organizational scale.

The Netherlands became independent in the course of the Eighty Years War with Spain (1568-1648), when a Dutch republic was established. The state became a confederation of provinces within which the many merchant cities

*Senior Lecturer and Doctor of Research, Institute of Public Administration, University of Amsterdam, and author of several publications on urban development and public administration.

held a strong position. The state's influence grew gradually during the seventeenth and eighteenth centuries until 1789, when the country was annexed by France. At that time the French pattern of a strongly centralized government was established.[4] After independence in 1813, Thorbecke, the greatest Dutch statesman of the last century, initiated a body of legislation—constitutional as well as provincial and municipal—that forms the basis of the state today. The Local Government Act of 1851 is still in force, as is the Act on Provincial Government.

The government system as a whole can be characterized as a decentralized unitary state. It is decentralized in that the central authority is not vested in a single central government body but rests with authorities at various levels. The term unitary indicates that the policies adopted by the provinces and municipalities must be in line with those pursued by the central government.[5] Legislative power at the central level is vested in a parliament (*Staten-Generaal*) consisting of two houses. The members of the lower house (*Tweede Kamer*) are elected by the people on the basis of proportional representation and those of the upper house (*Eerste Kamer*) by the provincial councils on the same basis. The members of the provincial as well as local councils are elected by the citizens of the unit concerned. Executive power at the central level rests either with the Crown (the Queen; however, she herself is not responsible to the legislature) together with one or more ministers (who are responsible) or with the lower central government authorities, who may be a single minister. The provincial and local levels are governed by executives elected by and from among the council members and are presided over by the Queen's provincial commissioner or, in the case of the municipalities, by the burgomaster. Both officials are appointed by the Crown (that is, the central government). So, in the Netherlands a mayor is not elected but is instead a full-time civil servant, independent of the council. Appointments are prepared by the Home Office, valid for six years, and are politically influenced by the main parties on the national level as well as the concerns of the municipality.

DEFECTS IN THE GOVERNMENTAL MACHINERY

Many governments in Western Europe suffer from a certain degree of organizational deterioration. In the Netherlands, more than a century after the reformer Thorbecke, the call for a new Thorbecke is rising. There have been continuing tensions between the capacity of government at each level and a great variety of problems to be solved. These tensions are intrinsic tensions of scale determined by a growing incongruency between the scale of societal needs and the scale of governmental organization and operation.[6] The number of municipalities has been reduced (from 999 in 1956 to 833 in 1978) in a continuous attempt to adjust local territories to the scale on which societal demands operate. This adaptation, however, has proved insufficient because the number and complexity of tasks to be carried out by local government have increased. The span of control has failed to extend as the catchment areas have extended, covering larger areas than the territories of the existing municipalities (and provinces). Futher irritating this problem is the insufficient number of inhabitants to support the specialists needed for carrying out local tasks.

Another problem arises from the lack of coordination in policymaking by the local, provincial, and central governments. At all levels the functional bifurcation of governmental organization into departments and separated field services creates an additional coordination problem. Attempts to solve this problem have given rise to a large number of coordinative and advisory boards. Nevertheless, the effectiveness of government and the democratic control of procedures and processes have become more and more questionable.[7] More complexity has been added by the rise of a large number of ad hoc authorities. At the central level in the Netherlands, twelve departments operate 101 services in 158 different kinds of districts, partitioning the country into 2,743 different units.[8] At the local level, at least another 1,500 units of cooperating municipalities are operated, based on the Joint Regulations Act. Direct democratic control of these functional organizations by councillors has proved to be ineffective at both the central and local levels. The number of directly controlled bodies (municipalities and provinces) related to the number of indirectly controlled ad hoc authorities and field administrations is now 1:6 (leaving out the water control boards, which in a way are democratically controlled).

INADEQUATE POSTWAR DEVELOPMENTS

After World War II, adjusting local government to the enlargement of scale in society did lead to amalgamation of municipalities at a rate of about four a year, with some exceptions of ten to fifteen a year, until 1970. Then the number increased to about twenty or more a year, as territorial reorganization was carried out in one region after another. Recently, amalgamation has slowed down because of a significant change in policy. The central government has proposed an entirely new approach.

What efforts have the municipalities themselves made to meet the problem of scale enlargement? Since 1957 local governments have effected a process of voluntary cooperation designed to establish and develop a kind of "regional government at the local level." Local authorities regard cooperation not only as a vehicle for new developments but also as a means by which to escape amalgamation, especially in metropolitan areas.[9] The fear of annexation perhaps has been the main motive for voluntary regionalization, using the Act on Joint Regulations. Smaller municipalities in particular hoped that regional cooperation would help them to avoid annexation. Larger municipalities also favored this form of collaboration because it avoided the administrative unrest and the emotions aroused by annexation as well as its long procedures, which frustrate the settling of important policy issues. Regionalization by intermunicipal cooperation was also pushed forward strongly by physical planning. Long-term policymaking in this field was an important incentive toward local collaboration.

The official gazette (*Staatsblad*) has published the following figures on the number of collaborative regions formed between 1957 and 1975.[10]

1957: 1	1966: 7	1970: 7	1974: 3
1960: 1	1967: 5	1971: 6	Total 52
1964: 1	1968: 5	1972: 4	
1965: 3	1969: 3	1973: 6	

By 1978 the number of regions had reached fifty-eight. The number of inhabitants of these regions varied from 50,000 to over 700,000. The regions now cover about 75 percent of the total population.

These "preliminary" regions (*pré-gewesten*) possess hardly any executive or legislative powers; in most cases they are just a forum where the municipalities of a region can meet and policies can be coordinated. There is only one exception: the Rhine Delta Authority, or Rijnmond Public Authority, in the Rotterdam area. This multipurpose experimental regional government is based on a special law on the Rijnmond Authority and now covers twenty-three municipalities and over one million inhabitants (not included in the above figures). It has a few, but still insufficient, legislative and executive powers. The same development for "greater Amsterdam" is still in preparation, but seems to be at a standstill.

UNSUCCESSFUL POLICYMAKING

The developments previously described are, with the exception of the Rijnmond Authority, based on a figurative use of the Joint Regulations Act (1950). This act was originally designed for a single purpose: mono-functional cooperation among municipalities. The purpose of the law was to prevent multifunctional collective cooperation and general policymaking that could lead to the origin of a fourth tier of government. A leading principle of central governmental policymaking on administrative reform is to avoid such a fourth tier. In other attempts, too, the central government was not successful in meeting societal demands for scale enlargement in administration, nor citizen demands for scale diminution in client-oriented administration. Three series of documents are indispensable for any appraisal of the present state of affairs in policymaking concerning reorganization.

First is the Memoranda of Administrative Organization submitted to Parliament by the Minister of Home Affairs during the 1969-70 session,[11] in which guidelines were formulated regarding the reorganization of local government. Provincial government's defects were hardly mentioned; in a few places it was suggested that the provinces could be combined into larger units, for instance a reduction from eleven to five or six. But time and again in the memoranda the provinces proved to be "sacrosanct." This series of documents was followed by a draft bill (1970-71 session of Parliament).[12] The concept contained in the bill was criticized and rejected by a committee of the Parliament, and the bill was withdrawn. It was to become a law designed to extend the Joint Regulations Act: cooperation was still to be voluntary and regional government would still be a powerless administration. The parliamentarians asked for powerful regional authorities and for the central government to enforce the development of regional government if the local authorities should fail to do so.

A study of these two series gives the impression that administrative reform in the Netherlands wavers between two poles. First is a functionally effective administrative centralization, which not only would help create a greater uniformity in welfare and living standards but also benefit from scale enlargements. Second is territorial decentralization, which would be under the influence of the best local traditions and democratizing trends.

NEW PROPOSALS FOR THE PROVINCIAL LEVEL

Recently, the Ministry of Home Affairs, now working with the Ministry of Urban Planning, started a third series of publications, initiating the concept of a structural scheme for administrative partition of the country (*Struktuurschets 1974*).[13] This series proposed a division of the Netherlands into forty-four regions. The scheme was based on the already existing organs of intermunicipal cooperation, the catchment areas of market and industrial towns and cities, as adjusted for carrying out primary governmental tasks, a minimum regional population of 75,000, and further regional development. In presenting this scheme to Parliament, however, the Minister of Home Affairs withdrew the essence of the proposal for small regions by stating that, if desired, the number of regions could be brought down.

Within six months a fundamental change in the proposal had been prepared. In July 1975 a draft for a reform bill was published, which abandoned the concept of cooperative local government.[14] Instead of regionalization through the cooperation of municipalities in forty-four adminstrative units, the formerly sacrosanct provinces now became the object of reorganization. The new scheme was announced to be a system of decentralization with optimal chances for more democratic government and policymaking because it would promote a diminution of scale at the provincial level: the system of eleven provinces would be altered into a system of twenty-six "mini-provinces." These "new-style provinces" would still be based on the existing traditional Provincial Government Act but would be strengthened by transferred local powers, mainly in the fields of physical planning, welfare, and economic development.

In fact, however, the new scheme represented a system of centralization, because there would be a shift of power from the local to the provincial level. The proposals for centralization of local powers at the provincial level exceeded the proposals for decentralization of state powers to the proposed provinces of a regional character. The decentralization proposals concerned only minor aspects of education (including school planning and building, thresholds of pupils, and the provision of infant schools), dwelling permits, the preservation of monuments, and the care of archives. Powers not shifting from the local to the new provincial level would all be of a restricted nature: management of local roads, sewerage, parks, playing fields and accommodations, and so on. The main legislative and executive powers, however, would be transferred: public transport, sea harbors, industrial estates and development, urban and regional planning, social and economic planning, health and welfare, larger social and cultural services and institutions, protection of the environment, exploitation of land, legislative powers concerning nature and landscape, fire protection, a certain taxation autonomy, and so forth. The new regional governments also would have to prepare regional overall plans of the middle range (four years), to be adjusted annually, including the related budget. Thus regional planning, programming, and budgeting would be developed. At the local level, reorganization would continue through the amalgamation of municipalities into units with a minimum of 10,000 inhabitants and by the deconcentration of city government. The existing municipalities of Amsterdam and Rotterdam, for instance, would be split up and in each case replaced by five or six smaller municipalities, each with a population of about 100,000. Reorganization of municipal territories would be continued region by region.

The proposed increase of powers at the new provincial level, by hollowing out the local authorities, has naturally caused a lot of resistance, especially in view of the weak decentralization of powers from the central government. People seem to be disgusted with the wearisome process of policy formulation without implementation. So the call for a new Thorbecke continues.

EVALUATION

Political science has failed to guide governments because it lacks adequate theories, such as a theory of organizational change.[15] At the theoretical level, a helpful suggestion is that government should operate under three main principles: to be goal-directed, effective, and democratic. Also, Dr. A. F. Leemans has stated that a decentralized system can be used as an instrument for nation building, democratization, local autonomy, efficiency of administration, and social and economic development.[16]

Two central concepts that must be taken into account in any structural reorganization are efficiency norms and democratic norms. Efficiency norms concern the number of population within an area that will enable responsible exploitation of all kinds of services, the catchment area of social phenomena, and the delimitation of an adequate administrative area on the basis of both of these factors. Democratic norms are related to the citizen's feelings of involvement in local government, the proximity of local government to the citizen, the possibilities of participation, and direct electon of the representative bodies.[17] In elaborating these norms, eight criteria can be formulated:[18]

1. The zonal concept or criterion of homogeneity (in economic, social, and/or cultural terms)
2. The nodal or communication concept (catchment areas and contact patterns)
3. The hierarchical concept or criterion of competence (in legislative and executive powers and jurisdictions)
4. The servicing concept (public duties and services rendered by government)
5. The concept of decision making and planning (the capacity of problem-solving and long-term policymaking)
6. The concept of coordination or integrated policymaking (horizontally as well as vertically)
7. The concepts of perception and participation (involving territory, proximity of government, and democratic policymaking and control)
8. The concept of financial capacity (in the Netherlands mainly based on the number of inhabitants; over 90 percent of the local finances come from central government funds)

Basically, these criteria refer to scale and tensions of scale in operation capacity, territory, and societal needs. The most important problem, however, is how these criteria can be turned into adequate theory and then operationalized. Here political science and public administraton still fail, despite continuing scholarly research, further development of research agencies by the government, and recent scholarly emphasis on the construction of operational theories.

Clearly, administrative reform at the local and regional levels in the Netherlands is necessary to meet new conditions and demands. Nevertheless, so far every proposal has failed to reach the critical threshold of political consent necessary to pass a reform bill through Parliament. This has not been caused by improper policymaking procedures within the administrative system but by the evident lack of explicit adminstrative reform megapolicies. According to Dror, such megapolicies must deal with such issues as overall goals of administrative reform, the boundaries of administrative reform, time priorities, risk acceptability, and choice between more incremental or more innovative reform.[19] The absence of a full consideration of these elements, which should constitute the necessary guidelines for more detailed policies, is evident.

Relatively vague concepts, such as administrative effectiveness and democracy, cannot be transformed successfully into policy proposals without an elaborate plan on the megapolicy level. Such a plan is the result of a decisonmaking process in which choices have crystallized, based on an overall administrative philosophy, that is, a coherent whole of sometimes conflicting, sometimes reinforcing, administrative norms.[20] Without such a plan, reform proposals shift from one solution to another, completely different, one. Thus, the mainstream of ideas concerning regionalization has suddenly changed from cooperation at the local level to decentralizing state jurisdictions to the provincial level. Meanwhile, the confusion over the scale of territorial integration continues, and decisions are postponed.

If we try to underline some elements of a megapolicy, we must first turn to the setting of goals, since megapolicy goals are still diffuse. One element may be adjustment of the citizen preferences. A theory has to be prepared and a policy developed regarding citizen participation and the significance of territory in relation to participation. Thus the scale of the territorial framework of admininstrative organization may be able to further democracy as well as the effectiveness of governmental operation. At the same time, we must keep in mind the spatial hierarchy of the decision-making process,[21] as well as the areal span of control on the executive level.

Megapolicy goal setting means the development of master plans that can serve as guidelines for the adjustment of government operating capacity (in terms of the territorial framework) to the societal and spatial problems to be solved. As a consequence, megapolicy analyses have to be directed to an inventory of the long-term structural problems of social and economic development to be solved by the government. Subsequently, the priority ordering of the problems, as well as the operational demands, must be decided and listed. Unless a megapolicy is formulated, administrative reform in the Netherlands will be no more than "muddling through." It will not exceed the level of incremental policy proposals where the political feasiblity in terms of the degree of consensus among the relevant political actors is valued more highly than the quality of a proposal's substantive contents. Proof of this is given by developments since 1975. The proposal for twenty-six new provinces was reduced to twenty-four in 1977 and to seventeen in 1978.[22] In 1979 another revision of the concept is expected, leading to a further reduction, without solving the problems of scale at either the local or regional level.

NOTES

1. Netherlands Central Bureau for Statistics, *Population of the Municipalities of the Netherlands* ('s Gravenhage: Staatsdrukkerij, 1978).

2. W. J. Alberts, *De geboorte en groei van de Nederlandse Gemeente* (Alphen ad Rijn: Samson, 1966); and A. F. Leemans, "The Dutch Decentralisation System in Transformation," *Planning and Development in the Netherlands* (Assen: van Gorcum) 6, no. 2 (1972).

3. Instituut voor Bestuurswetenschappen, *Onderzoek naar de Bestuurlijke Organisatie*, part 1 (Rijswijk Z. H.: Stichting IBW, 1972); and a white paper on water boards in the Netherlands (*Tweede Kamer*, zitting 1976-77—14480).

4. Leemans, "Dutch Decentralisation," p. 94.

5. A. Bours and L. E. M. Klinkers, "Regionalisation in the Netherlands" (Paper prepared for the XVI International Congress of Administrative Sciences, Mexico City,

July 1974) (subject 1: "The administrative aspects of regionalisation within countries").

6. A. Bours, "Towards a Geography of Public Administration and Policymaking," *International Geography 76* vol. 6 (Moscow: International Geographical Union, 1976), pp. 88-93.

7. Voorlopige Wetenschappelijke Raad voor het Regeringsbeleid, *De Organisatie van het Openbaar Bestuur* ('s Gravenhage: Staatsdrukkerij, 1975).

8. Ibid., annex 7.

9. A. Bours, "Dynamics in Local and Regional Government," *Planning and Development in the Netherlands* (Assen: van Gorcum) 6, no. 2 (1972).

10. Instituut voor Bestuurswetenschappen, *Onderzoek naar de Bestuurlijke Organisatie*, part 2 (Rijswijk Z. H.: Stichting IBW, 1972).

11. Ministerie van Binnenlandse Zaken, *Bestuurlijke Organisatie*, nos. 1, 2, 3, zitting 1969-70—10310 (Den Haag: Staatsdrukkerij).

12. *Voorschriften met betrekking tot de gewesten: Ontwerp van Wet* [Regional Government, draft bill 1971], zitting 1970-71—11246.

13. *Concept Stuktuurschets voor de Bestuurlijke indeling* ('s Gravnhage: Staatsdrukkerij, 1974).

14. *Concept-ontwerp van de Wet Reorganisatie Binnenlands Bestuur* [Reorganisation of Government, draft bill] ('s Gravenhage: Staatsuitgeverij, 1975).

15. The author thanks Ron Verhoef for his help with this section.

16. A. F. Leemans, *Changing Patterns of Local Government* (The Hague: International Union of Local Authorities, 1970).

17. R. Verhoef and A. Reinders, "Current Trends in Local Power and Authority in the Netherlands" (Paper given at Warsaw conference sponsored by Polish Academy of Sciences, 1974).

18. Bours and Klinkers, "Regionalisation in the Netherlands," pp. 19-23.

19. Yehezkel Dror, *Ventures in Policy Sciences: Concepts and Applications* (New York: American Elsevier, 1971).

20. Verhoef and Reinders, "Current Trends in Local Power."

21. A. F. Leemans, "The Spatial Hierarchy of Decision-making," *Development and Change*, 1, no. 3 (1969-70).

22. *Wet reorganisatie Bennenlands Bestuur* [Reorganization of government, draft bill], nos. 1-4, 6, 14322/3 ('s Gravenhage: Staatsdrukkerij, 1976-77).

Proposals for Sweden

Gunnar Wallin *

15

During the last decades the controversy concerning the structure and content of communal self-government in Sweden has been based on the same postulates as in a number of other countries. Implementation of the ''welfare state'' has involved a tremendous expansion of the public sector, which, in turn, has given rise to the question of how the administration of social services can best be divided between state and communal bodies on both local and regional levels. This deliberation has brought about several organization reforms in acknowledgment of the fact that strict efficiency demands must be met if a complicated social apparatus is to function acceptably. The second important factor—which in itself has been a partial prerequisite for the development of the welfare system and increased public commitment—has been a large-scale population migration, chiefly characterized by rapid urbanization.

In Sweden, however, the reform of communal self-government has been coupled with the task of providing the country with a new constitution in such a way as to strongly influence both the exchange of public opinion and reforms. This relationship was particularly noticeable in the debate on whether to have a uni- or bicameral parliament and the method by which this parliament was to be elected. Hitherto the First (upper) House had been chosen by members of the county councils, which are the self-government bodies on the regional level. Undoubtedly, this link also led to the ensuing and uncommonly intensive examination of work and competence distribution between state and commune. It also contributed to increasing the understanding that one of the most intricate and pressing tasks during continued reform would be to find an administrative organization on the regional level that could satisfy contemporary needs.

*Assistant Professor and Chairman, Department of Political Science, University of Stockholm.

The new Constitution, which was finally ratified in 1974, has had remarkably few consequences for the structure and function of communal self-government. In looking back on recent reforms, one is struck by the absence of any comprehensive grasp of the problems of society that these reforms were to have rectified. The decision in 1962 to carry out a sweeping amalgamation reform at the local level was made without relating it in any way to the constitutional problems it could occasion on the national level and, even more surprisingly, without regard to boundary apportionment and organization on the regional level. The problems for the communes and especially for regional self-government were reserved for future consideration when the Constitution was decided upon. When interest was subsequently shifted to the regional level, this earlier reform work on the national and local level served as a barrier to more radical reforms. The limited reforms of regional administration that have been carried out or merely proposed are interesting in themselves and will be dealt with in the following section.

ADMINISTRATION ON THE REGIONAL LEVEL

The structure and tasks of Sweden's basic units of local government will be discussed later in this volume. Therefore, only the most important features of regional organization will be described here.

The geographical base for state administration on the regional level is the county (*län*). There are at present twenty-four counties. The state regional administration consists of several types of bodies. The county administrative board (*länsstyrelse*), which is headed by the county governor (*landshövding*) and is directly subordinate to the government, is the central administrative organ on the regional level. During the past few decades an increasing number of new county authorities has grown up alongside of the county administration board as more tasks have been brought to the state regional administration.

The regional commune (*landstingskommun*) normally has a county as its territorial base, that is, it has the same geographical area as the state regional institutions. Certain exceptions will be described further on. There are twenty-five regional communes. The county council (*landsting*), which is selected by general election, is the regional commune's decision-making organ. There are approximately 1,500 county councillors in the entire country, the smallest council having 33 members, and the largest 149. The administrative committee (*forvaltningsutskott*) handles the preparation and execution of communal affairs. Also included in the adminstrative apparatus is a large number of authorities (*nämnder*) with special administrative duties.

The activities of the county councils have increased enormously during the past decades. This increase has been mostly within the field of health care and medical services, which now account for approximately 80 percent of council expenditures. The rest of the outlay goes to items such as special education, welfare programs, and communications. This development corresponds to a general desire to place all related areas of social services under the same authority. The county councils have at present total responsibility for all health care, a sector that recently has undergone an especially sharp cost rise for a number of reasons.

The previously outlined organization for the management of regional-level public administration makes it clear that a sweeping reform can scarcely be confined to either the state or communal activities; it must encompass both areas. Therefore, the following questions, though dealing primarily with regional communes, are also related to those problems of regional administration that are the state's concern. The issues that have awakened the most interest in the reform work of the 1960s and 1970s can be placed under four headings:

1. *County Apportionment*. Assuming that the county will continue to serve as the territorial base for both the state and communal administration, how can these counties best be reapportioned?
2. *Primacy*. Which matters involving decision making on the regional level should be handled by the commune's county council and which by the state's regional organs? What is the most suitable balance between regional-communal and local-communal primacy?
3. *Democracy*. Through which reforms can the regional administration achieve a higher degree of citizen participation?
4. *Metropolitan Regions*. Should the special relations existing in large metropolitan areas necessitate special construction of their communal organization?

DEBATE AND REFORMS

County Apportionment

An age-old issue was brought to the fore when an overhaul of county boundary apportionment was undertaken. Apart from small adjustments, the apportionment decided upon in 1810 was still in force. In fact, the county boundaries in large parts of the country were identical to those drawn up in the early part of the seventeenth century. In 1967 the county apportionment commission gave a report in which it was stated that a conflict between tradition and expediency was unavoidable when considering a revision. The commission felt that expediency should be favored.

The enormous changes that industrialization had brought about in society's economic, technical, and social structures, as well as the large population migrations that had taken place, had resulted in a marked deviation between the administrative areas that the county administration encompassed and the important geo-economic areas. A restructuring of the counties was to aim at balancing both the geo-economic and population aspects, thus meeting the various demands for comprehensive planning in a modern society. Regional planning organs under the supervision of the county administrative boards could make better assessments and thereby promote a sound and balanced regional development. An alteration in county apportionment also would give the county council increased opportunities to run its activities more efficiently, particularly in dealing with the rising expenditures for health care. The population base in a county was not to be under 300,000 residents. As it stands now, there are only a few counties that do not come up to that figure. The principal motive for an extensive county reapportionment must be to create, therefore, a suitable geographical work area for the different social developments undertaken on the regional level.

Using these criteria as a point of departure, the commission proposed a drastic restructuring of the counties. The suggestion was to reduce the number of counties from twenty-four to fifteen. This proposal was widely criticized. It was claimed that the resulting counties would be too large, which would have detrimental consequences for service to both the public and the communes. Objections of just the opposite type were lodged from other quarters: the suggested counties would be too small to meet demands, especially those for comprehensive social planning. The government postponed consideration of the issue until a later date.

In 1970, however, this issue, along with other unsolved problems concerning regional administration, was taken up by a public commission, the Regional Government Commission (*länsberedningen*). Its report, *State and Commune in Co-operation*, submitted at the end of 1974, confronted the criticism directed against the previously suggested apportionment reform. Within the already existing county boundaries, established regional patterns have developed comprising ingrained channels of communication, which should not be disrupted without good reason. However, the commission did find grounds for questioning the new and highly varied apportionment patterns that had grown up gradually alongside the county apportionment and as a result of which caused the county to no longer stand as a naturally demarcated area with internal cohesion. The apportionment issue was to be attacked in two phases. First, the existing counties would be examined to see if they comprised appropriate geo-economic areas, the assumption being that county administration would be located in the already existing county seats. Second, it should be determined what demands the different branches of county administration placed on the geographical activity areas. It was clear from previous investigation that only regional social planning called for an activity area larger than what the already existing counties could provide. The problem was to decide whether it was appropriate to bring the counties together in groups in order to solve certain overlapping planning issues.

The commission's investigation of the first phase resulted in only a few minor adjustments. The analysis of the second goal resulted in a suggestion that the country should be divided up into eight cooperative areas, each comprising two or more counties. The county administrative boards within those areas would work together continuously on regionally important planning policy. Correspondingly, collaboration on the county council's activities would simplify common issues, such as health care and maintenance of the transportation system. Area apportionment also would partially solve coordination problems that had arisen due to many central administrative departments with regional activity bases larger than the counties. It would also be instructive for similar apportionment in the future. The commission emphasized that the formation of cooperative areas should not be regarded as a measure in preparation for a future general county apportionment reform but rather as an alternative to such, which could make it possible to limit future boundary adjustments to a minimum.

In a bill to the 1976 Parliament, the government rejected the proposal for adjustment of county apportionment based on the objections raised by the county councils and primary communes concerned. The bill did not support the proposal for cooperative areas either. According to the government, it was meaningless to predetermine these areas since the need for cooperation has such varying aims and directions. The Parliament adopted the bill.

Primacy

The expansion of public affairs on the regional and local levels has made current a number of questions regarding the division of responsibility and organizational forms. On the regional level, the reform debate has been based on several different observations and assessments. First, the county councils' health care commitments have risen sharply, whereas other regional tasks have only been designated to them to a minor degree. The result has been the molding of the regional governments into special communes for the management of health care. Second, the regional state administration has undertaken a number of new tasks without following a central plan and without following consistent organizational principles. Third, the need for coordinated social planning on the regional level has become even more important: the desires and efforts of the state public administration, the regional communes, and the local communes must be attuned to one another.

Different solutions have been presented over the years. Differences of opinion have centered upon whether the national government's regional organ (the county administrative board) or the self-government organ (the county council) should have the leading role in the counties' administrative construction. The conflict has been concentrated increasingly on the question of primacy in social planning. The argument for giving the county councils chief responsibility is based on the assumption that this would give citizens the possibility to control the administration of the counties through elections. "County democracy—not county bureaucracy" has been the slogan of this viewpoint. Its opponents have claimed that only by giving the central government primacy could both effective interregional coordination and equalization between the regions be guaranteed.

On 1 July 1971, a reform of the state regional administration was effected whereby the county administrative boards were given partially altered duties and a new organizational form. The reform's principal aim was to cope with the split structure of the county administration and to give the county administrative boards the rank of central coordinating organs for the state county administration. The reform did not represent any final decision as to the question of primary allocation on the regional level. The year before, the Parliament had set up a commission which was to make a comprehensive assessment of the regional administration's tasks and organization. This commission, the above-mentioned Regional Government Commission, using several fundamental assumptions, tried to test whether the division of tasks between state and commune was well balanced. On the whole the answer was affirmative, and the commission therefore proposed only minor changes in the existing structure.

The commission was of the opinion that the state should have primacy as regards coordinated regional planning and that this responsibility should lie with the county administrative boards. The regional and local communes would, through a series of different arrangements, be provided with access to comprehensive information and thereby could convey their viewpoints on different regional policies to the county administrative boards.

The representatives of the nonsocialist political parties who sat on the commission supported this proposal but emphasized in a special statement that they regarded the proposal merely as a first step toward extending county democracy. The reform work should continue with the predetermined goal of letting regional communes take over primacy in coordinating and planning regional tasks.

The Social Democratic government brought a bill to the 1976 Parliament that closely approximated the commission's recommendation. The voting outcome, however, was in favor of the nonsocialist parties. The Parliament passed the bill as only a provisional arrangement and made a statement that the reform work towards an extended county democracy should continue. A new commission was appointed and presented its proposal in 1978. After the resignation of the Social Democratic government in 1976, the commission had a nonsocialist majority. It suggested that the final decision on the regional level concerning the planning tasks should be made by the county council. The Social Democratic minority opposed this suggestion in a formal reservation. The proposal has not yet been subject to parliamentary consideration.

The Regional Government Commission also took up the problem of the division of tasks between the regional communes and the local communes. The apportionment reform at the local level had been aimed at bettering the opportunities for the local communes to assume new and expanded social tasks. According to the commission, although the trend is toward transferring additional tasks to the communal sector, the primacy of the local communes should be weighed carefully. Even after the apportionment reform, issues could arise that could be poorly managed by the local communes. On the other hand, it could happen that certain regional issues might be better dealt with on the local level. The commission therefore proposed an arrangement whereby it would be possible in certain situations for the local and regional communes to decide among themselves which should have primacy. However, the 1976 Parliament bill rejected this part of the commission's proposal.

County Democracy

The differences of opinion described in the preceding section can be seen as a conflict over what form citizen control of regional decision making should take. Those who claim that the county councils should function as a type of "county parliament" with wide-reaching authority have as a basis for their argument the belief that a democratic society is realized to the extent that one creates an organization fostering insight, cooperation, control, and political responsibility. This goal is fulfilled by giving a popularly elected body, in this case the county council, great decision-making powers. Opponents have contradicted this standpoint on various grounds. The risk of a collision between governmental and parliamentary guidelines and regional opinion has been cited, as well as administrative reasons which argue for giving the central government chief responsibility for regional issues. It is contended that these differences of opinion are not centered on whether or not there should be citizen influence on decision making but rather what form this influence should take.

The county administrative reform in 1971 brought about an important reorganization of the county administrative boards. Previously they had given sole decision-making powers to the county governor, but these powers were now transformed to layman boards, with decision-making powers distributed among the county governor and ten citizen representatives, half of whom were appointed by the county councils and half by the government. This reform has had good results, and there is reason to question whether the top-steered county councils could really provide more room for popular influence than these new county administrative boards.

The Regional Government Commission was unanimous that the layman element in the county administrative boards should be further strengthened. The Social Democratic majority wanted the government to have the right to make these appointments, whereas the political opposition felt that county councils should have appointment powers. The government proposed in the 1976 bill that the number of laymen on the boards be further increased and that certain arrangements be made to guarantee that these laymen would provide representation for the different political parties. The government,' however, maintained for itself the right of appointment on the grounds that it is a question of selecting members for a state organ. The outcome was that the Parliament accepted the government's proposal. However, as soon as possible the non-socialist parties, after winning the 1976 parliamentary elections, forced a bill through the Parliament to the effect that the county councils themselves should choose their representatives in the county administrative boards.

The foregoing debate was based on certain conceptions about what weight should be given to the county council in its function as a body for citizen influence or county democracy. There seems to be a general notion that the county councils do not at the present meet the demands placed on them. The nonsocialist parties do not regard self-government on the regional level as successful when they suggest that the county councils should be expanded into "county parliaments" and equipped with additional authority so as to become a cornerstone of the Swedish democratic system.

In the mid-1960s a series of organizational reforms was carried out aimed at strengthening the county council's position. A central criticism against the councils had been that the administrative committee had been given far too strong a position. The administrative committees, which generally had ten to fifteen members, based their power on the fact that they served as general deputies for the county councils when the councils were not in session. The importance of this is clear in that the county councils as a rule meet only once a year and then only for a week. A number of reforms attempted to increase the possibilities of the county councillors to follow the management of county council business and to form independent opinions of at least the more pressing issues. The time for meetings was extended, and the county councillors' participation in these meetings was made easier by such changes as generous economic compensation, improvement of the preparation procedure, and extension of the right to put forth questions. Furthermore, the county councils have themselves taken the initiative in spreading information about their activities to the populace.

The new Communal Government Act of 1977 completed the reform work designed to strengthen the position of the county councils. The function of the administrative committee as a general deputy for the county council was repealed. It was also decided that the county council should hold at least four meetings per year.

Metropolitan Areas

The larger cities—six cities representing nearly half of all city dwellers and approximately one-fifth of the land's inhabitants—were not included in the regional communes originally. These six cities handled local communal tasks as well as those matters pertaining to the county councils. This constituted a rather significant exception to the principle of two coexisting communal levels. However, a later amendment made it possible for these cities to join in the county council system. At present only two cities, Gothenburg and Malmö, Sweden's second and third largest cities, remain outside the county council system. An effort has been made to overcome the particular problems this has caused by emphasizing comprehensive cooperation with nearby primary communes as well as the county council in the region.

Before the development in the Stockholm area is commented upon, it should be noted that in comparison with international standards, Sweden has few truly large city regions or metropolises. Stockholm county has about 1.5 million residents, of whom fewer than 700,000 live within Stockholm city limits. However, the special "big city" problems, even if of a more benign type than elsewhere, have also appeared in Stockholm. It was not until long into the 1960s that drastic countermeasures were undertaken to attack the root of these problems, that is, to slow down population expansion. As part of the "balanced regional development" policy, measures have been taken which have contributed to slowing down to a large degree further urbanization of metropolitan areas. The relocation of state authorities from Stockholm to different parts of the country is one such measure which has gained much attention.

The problem of communal coordination for the Stockholm region has occasioned a succession of reforms during the past fifty years. The expansions of both population and communal action has changed the prerequisites for the existing communal organizational structure and led to new solutions designed to fit new situations. It should be noted here parenthetically that for a long time Stockholm had its own regional state administration. It was not until 1968 that Stockholm was incorporated into a county.

The need for communal coordination was first felt in Stockholm and its suburbs. In several cases the solution was to incorporate the suburban communes with the city. Incorporation, however, awakened criticism that the measures were too far-reaching since the community of interest was often limited to only a few activity areas. It was thought that a better solution for such coordination problems might be intercommunal cooperation. Different forms of intercommunal cooperation then became the most frequently chosen expedient. Increasing contact grew up between Stockholm and its suburban communes, then between Stockholm and a gradually growing circle of communes in the county, and between Stockholm and the county council. In time a close net of intercommunal contacts and organs was formed. The apportionment reform on the primary commune level, which reduced the number of communal units to one-fourth the original number, thereby reduced the need for cooperation. Even so, increasingly strong criticism was raised against the cooperation principle. It was thought to render it difficult to get an overall picture of communal affairs and also to diminish the citizens' possibilities for demanding responsibility from the political decision makers. Therefore, the row of ad hoc solutions must be replaced by more sweeping organizational reforms which could satisfy the need for assessment and planning for the entire region.

Various solutions have been suggested. One proposal was to create a third communal level endowed with specific planning functions, but this was rejected. Also turned down was a suggestion for a united commune, whereby Stockholm commune and the other primary communes within the county plus the county council would be integrated into a single unit which would deal with all communal issues within the county. The solution finally chosen was an enlarged county council (*storlandsting*), which began functioning in 1971. This reorganization meant that Stockholm's regional communal tasks were separated from Stockholm's primary communal tasks and, along with the old county council functions, constitute the activity area for the enlarged county council. The council was given the same competence as other county councils in Sweden, with the exception that this enlarged council can also handle certain primary communal tasks if there is a great need for cooperation. This structure can be considered a forerunner to the recommendation that the Regional Government Commission submitted in 1974 that led to a weakening of the distinction between local communal and regional communal primacy. By utilizing the scope that the general competence regulations have given it, the enlarged county council now has more extensive and simultaneously less one-sided powers than those of the other county councils.

CONCLUSION

The preceding account has shown that the past decade's discussion of regional public administration has resulted in fairly limited reforms:

1. No reorganization of the regional boundaries has occurred.
2. The division of tasks on the regional level between state and communal bodies on the whole has been maintained, though the issue will be further investigated.
3. No comprehensive reform of the county council's organization has been carried out.
4. The current regional communal organization has been extended to include several larger cities, but the reform is still not completed.

Opinion in Sweden is fairly unanimous that the regional communal self-government does not function well. While some feel that the solution lies in equipping the county councils with new important duties, other speak out for partial reforms of the county council's organization combined with an effective state steering of regional development. There is, however, general agreement that regional administration should have an increased element of citizen participation.

ELSEWHERE

CANADA
AUSTRALIA

Canada:
British Columbia

Paul Tennant*

16

Until 1965 the structure of local government in British Columbia was typical of Canada's western provinces. Cities, towns, and larger villages, as well as the more heavily populated rural districts, had fully developed local governments in the form of municipalities with elective councils. Although 80 percent of the province's 1965 population of approximately 2 million lived in these munici-palities, the municipalities themselves occuped less than 1 percent of the province's 366,000 square miles.

Commencing in 1965, regional governmental units were created throughout the province. The process of creating this new level of government was distinctive in several ways. First, the existing municipalities were left intact in both structure and authority within the new regional units. Second, the effect of the new level of government varied according to population density and number of municipalities. In highly urbanized regions containing contiguous municipalities (as was the case in greater Vancouver), the new level amounted to metropolitan government; while, at the other extreme, in rural regions having no municipal organization, the new level became the only level and thus approximated a new municipal government. In between these two ex-tremes the new level brought municipal and nonmunicipal areas together under one government. Third, the process of forming the new governments was sequential, with structures established before activities were undertaken, and with activities assumed one by one over a period of years rather than all at once. Fourth, individual regional units were allowed some voice in deciding which particular activities they would assume; thus each unit came to have a different complement of activities. Finally, the formation of the new level was carried out, if not in secret, at least out of the public view. Royal commissions

*Associate Professor of Political Science, University of British Columbia.

of inquiry, consultants, and policy study groups, so frequently used in other Canadian provinces to advertise and legitimize regional reform, were entirely absent. The initiative and impetus for regional government in British Columbia came entirely from a few senior officials in the provincial Department of Municipal Affairs.

LOCAL GOVERNMENT BEFORE 1965

In 1964 there were 123 municipalities in British Columbia. With the exception of those in the contiguous clusters centered on the cities of Vancouver and Victoria in the southwest coastal area of the province, municipalities normally were separated by considerable distances, with each municipality serving as the commercial hub of the unorganized (nonmunicipal) territory around it. The mountainous terrain of the province as well as the distances involved had, for most of the province's history, isolated the interior municipalities from one another and from the large urban municipalities in the coastal area. Not until the early 1960s did the province have a system of high-speed, all-weather highways and regularly scheduled air services connecting the various parts of the province. These improvements stimulated greater exchange of information among municipalities, eroding the traditional parochialism, and allowing greater communication between municipalities and officials of the Department of Municipal Affairs. An important organizational link between municipalities had existed for decades, however, in the form of the Union of British Columbia Municipalities, an organization to which most municipalities belonged.

In addition to municipalities there were three quite separate types of local authority. The province was divided into large school districts formed just after World War II through the consolidation of numerous small school districts. Each school district had an elected board of trustees. It is noteworthy that school districts have remained completely apart from and quite unaffected by the creation of regional government in the province. At no time was there even serious discussion that regional government should include education. Two circumstances would seem to explain the exclusion of education. First, there are strong local sentiments that education is not "political" and so should remain separate from other local government. Proposals to meld school districts into the new regional units undoubtedly would have produced strenuous opposition from trustees, teachers, and parents at the local level. Second, the provincial ministry overseeing school districts, the Department of Education, would have acted strongly to protect its charges from any incursion by the Department of Municipal Affairs.

Another type of local authority consisted of small, single-purpose authorities in unorganized territory. These were called "improvement districts" or "specified service areas." They provided, under direction of locally chosen boards, one or two services, such as fire protection and flood control, financed by local rates. The third type of local authority consisted of single-purpose regional authorities, such as those serving the urban municipalities in the Vancouver area. The authorities performed such functions as supplying water, disposing of sewage, planning regional land use, acquiring park land, and providing some health services. These authorities, in most cases, had been established by the municipalities but received their authority through provincial legislation. Each authority had a board of directors composed of one member from and chosen by the council of each participating muncipality. As the new regional level of government was formed these authorities were used as the structural model for the new governments. In contrast to the school districts, the single-purpose authorities in unorganized territory and at the regional level were absorbed into the new regional units.

At the provincial level in British Columbia the Department of Municipal Affairs (DMA) exerts continuous influence and control over the municipalities. The provisions of the basic statute dealing with local government, the Municipal Act, derive almost entirely from DMA recommendations. The act grants authority to municipalities and sets out in great detail the organization and procedures required of municipalities. The DMA is given delegated legislative authority and ensures, by regular inspection, that the municipalities are conforming to the act and regulations. The DMA is one of the smaller provincial departments (its staff has never exceeded a few dozen persons); it receives little public attention; and the post of minister of municipal affairs is not regarded among politicians as any great prize.

A further institutional facet of British Columbia local government manifests itself in what is, in effect, a corps of administrative officers. The Municipal Act authorizes the training, examination, and certification of persons as municipal administrative officers. Senior administrative positions (excluding those involving technical specialization) in all but the few large municipalities are normally held by such officers. Although hiring and payment of particular officers rests entirely with the municipality concerned, the career pattern of individual officers rests upon transferring among municipalities. The profession of municipal administrator thus contributes to the creation and maintenance of rather uniform values among muncipal officials throughout the province. These values, which are accepted by elected officials as well, fall within the Canadian and American nonpartisan tradition with its emphasis upon economy and efficiency rather than popular participation and influence.

More specifically, it is generally believed that local government is a matter of ''administration'' rather than ''politics,'' and thus it is accepted that local and provincial appointed administrators should play a dominant role. Second, it is generally maintained that the elected councillor should, in the tradition identified with the philosophy of Edmund Burke, follow his own judgment and his own conscience rather than either the whims of public opinion or the dictates of party policy. This belief, which is strongly held, tends to isolate the elected councillor from the public (thus leaving him more reliant than would otherwise be the case upon local administrators and provincial officials) and to remove the public from the municipal decision-making process. As for beliefs about local autonomy, there are several elements. While there is great pride in and attachment to the particular municipality, this is indicative almost entirely of a sentimental attachment to locale and scarcely at all of resentment towards external authority. That the province determines municipal structures, procedures, and powers and imposes these in a uniform way across the province is entirely accepted. It is believed, however, that only local officials have the knowledge and incentive to deal with local policy problems. All of these values and beliefs were considered by the DMA officials as they created a regional government for British Columbia.

In general, local government in British Columbia before 1965 seemed to present few problems. The late 1950s and early 1960s were a time of economic boom and rapid population growth in the province; as a result, land subdivision and housing development began to occur more rapidly than previously in unorganized territory—for the most part as spillover from municipalities but also in recreational areas (as on coastal islands) and at the sites of resource extraction industries. There was no suggestion, however, that anything more consequential than the traditional response of extending municipal boundaries and creating new municipalities was required to deal with the situation. Intermunicipal coordination was required only among the contiguous urban municipalities in the Vancouver and Victoria areas; there was no suggestion that the existing single-purpose regional authorities were inadequate for this task. As far as local government in the province was concerned, then, there were no demands for reform. Metropolitan government had been discussed for the Vancouver area in the late 1950s (the idea had come from local academics and citizen reformers; it was opposed by municipal officials), but by 1964 the idea had been forgotten. That a new level of regional government would be required was a notion utterly absent among the public, among academics, among municipal officials, and among provincial politicians. This is a point all too easily overlooked as one considers the rapid emergence of regional government that began in 1965.

PROVINCIAL STRATEGY FOR REGIONAL GOVERNMENT

The senior officials of the DMA did not believe that the existing local government structures were capable of taking care of the myriad problems that would come with future population growth and urbanization. Extending the scope of central control by the DMA to meet the problems was rejected as undesirable and unfeasible. Extending the scope of local government to the regional level over the entire province was seen as a simple but radical solution—however desirable, it appeared quite unfeasible, especially in the absence of demand for reform. Then, fortuitously, in early 1964, the Honourable Dan Campbell was appointed minister of municipal affairs. He accepted the idea of regional government and with his officials, chief among them Mr. J.

E. Brown, the deputy minister, immediately began the substantial task of implementing the idea. The major elements in the policy and strategy of the DMA may be summarized as follows:

1. Every portion of the province, except for the uninhabited portion adjacent to Alaska, would be included within a regional unit called a "regional district." The number of units was originally envisioned as between twenty and twenty-five.
2. The policy and motive force would come from the DMA itself. Municipal officials and the Union of B. C. Municipalities would be consulted, however, since these were the very persons who could easily feel threatened by the new level.
3. The process of creation would take place in stages, over a period of several years, to some extent by trial and error. Legislation could be easily amended as the DMA saw fit.
4. The new entities, while being created from above by the DMA, would not impair existing municipalities. To do otherwise would be to court local hostility. Moreover, there was no existing local leadership structure other than that provided by the municipal officials. The same group would have to provide the leadership in the new units. For these reasons the potential of the new units would be downplayed, and they would be presented as mere coordinating committees.
5. A new leadership structure would have to be created in unorganized territory. Dividing the territory within a regional unit into constituencies and providing for direct popular election was accepted as the method.
6. Individual regional units would be allowed to decide which functions they would undertake. There would be no provincial dictate requiring uniformity of functions. The DMA officials, however, intended to use their powers of persuasion, especially to encourage the adoption of the functions of land-use planning and control.
7. Existing single-purpose authorities would be absorbed into the new entities. Strong resistance was (quite accurately, it turned out) expected on behalf of the single-purpose regional authorities, and so the Minister took every opportunity to criticize the single-purpose boards as leading to functional fragmentation.
8. It would not be stated or admitted that a new level of government was being created. When challenged on this point the Minister and his officials would obfuscate. (Not until 1970 did the DMA officials publicly refer to the new entities as "governments.")
9. The structure and financing of the new entities was to be patterned upon those of the single-purpose regional authorities. So too was the terminology, hence the term "board of directors" rather than "council," and also the redundant and meaningless term "regional district." Both the words "region" and "district" were commonly and vaguely used in connection with the single-purpose authorities and carried no threatening connotation.

THE REGIONAL LEGISLATION OF 1965

During 1964 the DMA officials discussed the major outlines of their proposals with the Union of B.C. Municipalities and set up, for a short period, a simulated or trial-run regional board of directors composed of representatives of municipalities and unorganized territory in the Victoria area. The simulated board was an informal creation having no powers, but its members were able to provide the DMA officials with otherwise unobtainable advice and insights. The regional legislation, in the form of a series of amendments to the Municipal Act, was presented by the minister to the spring 1965 session of the legislature. During consideration of the bill an important provision, which had been suggested by the Union of B.C. Municipalities, was added to allow a municipality or unorganized territory to "opt out" of a particular function within a region. In practice this meant that a member unit could not be compelled to contribute to the cost of a particular function. The legislation received little publicity in the province and obtained the unanimous support of all parties in the legislature. The major details of the legislation were as follows:

1. The provincial cabinet, upon recommendation of the minister, was empowered to establish regional districts, name them, set their boundaries, set the boundaries of electoral areas within unorganized territory, and assign functions to each district. Member units could "opt out" of a function provided that a rate-payer referendum endorsed the opting out.
2. For each regional district the cabinet would specify a "voting unit." This unit, when divided into the population of a municipality or electoral area, would determine (with any fractional remainder counting as one) the number of votes on the board. For example, if the voting unit were set at 2,000, a municipality with a population of 12,000 would have 6 votes, and one with more than 12,000 but less than 14,000 would have 7 votes. The number of votes, however, would not necessarily be the same as the number of delegates or representatives. The number of delegates would be determined by dividing the number of votes by five (with any remainder counted as one). Thus, municipalities with from 1 to 5 votes would have one delegate; those with from 6 to 10 votes would have two. It will be seen that each municipality and electoral area was guaranteed at least one vote and one delegate. Votes would be divided as evenly as possible among a member unit's delegates, and a delegate could not split his votes. Ordinary board decisions would require a majority of the votes.
3. The general provisions of the Municipal Act relating to rules, requirements, and procedures of municipal councils were made applicable to regional boards.
4. Regional revenues would be provided by member units proportionate to assessed value of property. Municipalities would have no choice but to pay the amount owing; the provincial government (which collects property taxes in unorganized territory) would pay the amount owing from electoral areas.
5. All districts were empowered to hire staff, borrow money, and expropriate private property.
6. All districts were empowered, but not compelled, to regulate zoning, subdivision, and building standards in electoral areas.
7. All districts were empowered, but not compelled, to prepare and adopt a plan "of the projected uses of land with the region by major categories of use." Once "a majority of all the Directors, having among them a majority of all the votes" had adopted the plan, no land use in conflict with the plan could be undertaken. Thus, a district could voluntarily adopt the function of regional planning.

8. A district could undertake additional functions with the consent of all member units which would be participating in the function. A regional function could apply to some member units and not to others.

9. Each regional board was to select annually from among its members a person to act as chairman. The chairman would have no special powers. No other mention was made of executive structures.

10. A municipality or electoral area could appeal to the DMA against any decision of the regional board. The DMA could, if it saw fit, order an inquiry; the recommendations arising from such an inquiry would, upon cabinet approval, be binding upon the member unit and the district. [1]

THE FORMATION AND FUNCTIONING OF REGIONAL GOVERNMENTS

From 1965 until 1969 the major part of DMA time and effort was given over to formation of regional districts. The senior staff (privately dubbing themselves "the travelling road show") journeyed about the province, holding countless meetings with local officials to explain the new legislation. The first district was established in August 1965, in the area of the Minister's own legislative constituency. Four more districts were formed in 1965; six in 1966; fourteen in 1967; and the final three in 1968. Twenty-eight districts were formed in all—a number slightly greater than originally intended because of the hesitancy of some local leaders in adjacent areas to have their areas combined. The most basic and frequent difficulties faced by the DMA officials were those arising from local ignorance of the legislation, indifference over its implementation, sloth in responding to suggestion from the DMA, and, especially in unorganized territory, suspicion about DMA motives and intent. In a very few cases the DMA officials met with outright hostility but never in forms more serious than stormy meetings and irate letters to the Minister.

In all cases the officials proceeded circumspectly. In each proposed district informal ad hoc steering committees were formed composed of municipal officials and coopted prominent and interested residents of unorganized territory. The committees were encouraged to suggest electoral area boundaries and discuss the functions the district might undertake. Meetings of the committees were attended and guided by DMA officials for the purpose of giving information to the local people, identifying bases of misunderstanding and hostility, and identifying and encouraging persons in electoral areas who might stand for election to the new regional board. In all cases the officials stressed that the leaders in the region would determine which functions would be undertaken and that the opting-out mechanism would protect local interests. In no cases were functions imposed against local wishes as districts were formed. Indeed, in a number of cases districts were formally established and the boards set up before any functions at all were granted or assumed. In some cases the first function assigned by the Minister was that of inquiring into functions that the district might assume. The methods pursued by the DMA officials in forming the districts engendered little hostility and left the officials themselves intimately familiar with each regional district. Thus, with the formative stage completed, the DMA officials were well prepared to monitor and mold the regional districts' early growth.

The size of the regional districts ranges from 282 to 80,542 square miles, with the average size somewhat greater than 11,000 square miles. In 1971 the populations of districts ranged from 3,693 (in an isolated coastal district) to 204,000 in Victoria, and 1,027,000 in Vancouver. Aside from these last two, however, the largest population was about 80,000, with an average, excepting these two, of 35,000. Fewer than 3,000 persons in the province, those living in the "non-district" area adjacent to Alaska, were not subject to regional government. The average number of municipalities in a district is about four, with only Vancouver (with fourteen) having more than nine municipalities; the average number of electoral areas is also about four. Although there is no typical district, Table 16.1 illustrates the structure of one district as it was in 1974.[2]

Table 16.1
BRITISH COLUMBIA: DEWDNEY–ALOUETTE REGIONAL DISTRICT
(voting unit=2,500)

Member Units	Population (1971)	Delegates on Board	Votes on Board
Municipalities			
Maple Ridge	24,476	2	10
Mission	10,220	1	5
Pitt Meadows	2,771	1	2
Electoral Areas			
A	113	1	1
B	790	1	1
C	715	1	1
D	168	1	1
E	668	1	1
Totals	39,941	9	22

In the years immediately following 1968, several fundamental changes were made affecting the regional districts. First, the DMA departed from its earlier permissive stance and compelled all districts to adopt certain functions, the most notable being regional planning. Second, the opting-out provision was eliminated; provided that two-thirds of the members of a regional board, having among them two-thirds of the votes, were in favor, and that two-thirds of the member units expressed agreement, recalcitrant member units would have no choice but to participate.[3] The third change occurred in 1973, after Mr. Campbell's Social Credit Party had been defeated (the defeat was not caused by the issue of regional government), and replaced by the New Democratic Party. The new government amended the act to require that municipal delegates on regional boards be directly elected by the electorate. The potential of this change was nullified, however, by requiring that a board candidate would have to seek simultaneous election to his municipal council in order to qualify as a candidate and that he would have to be elected to the municipal council to qualify as a regional board member. The change was a highly confusing one that, in effect, merely allowed the electorate rather than the council to choose which councillors would also sit on the regional board.[4] After the Social Credit Party returned to office in 1975, it repealed the NDP amendment.

By the end of the first decade of regional government in British Columbia, several conclusions could be made about the functioning of the new level of government. The term "regional government" had come into general usage, and each regional government had adopted a set of functions and hired a group of permanent officials. The function of regional planning, despite the legislative and persuasive pressures from the DMA, had become a meaningful activity in only a few regions. In almost all regions the strength of parochial interests remained sufficient to preclude the possiblity of the regional board devising anything more than the blandest of plans. Had Mr. Campbell and his Social Credit government remained in power it is possible that the DMA would have redoubled its efforts to ensure that regional planning became an effective function, but under the new government no such effort was made. Indeed, in a step not initially presented as relating to regional government or to DMA concerns, the new government established a provincial land commission with broad powers to preserve farm land and establish agricultural land reserves. This step had the effect of decreasing the freedom of regional districts in carrying out regional planning and of decreasing the political incentive of the new Minister to compel the districts to plan effectively.

Almost all of the regional governments had undertaken the function of borrowing on behalf of member units; this function was welcomed by the municipalities since the credit base of the districts led to lower interest rates. Yet this was not a policymaking function since the districts merely acted as agents for the member units. Most districts, however, were making policy by the end of the decade for the electoral areas within them. The districts were controlling zoning, subdivision, and building standards in the electoral areas and were providing, in the more populous portions, such services as street lighting, fire protection, water supply, refuse disposal, and recreation facilities. This extension of local government into the hitherto unorganized portions of the province was the most notable effect of regional government in the early years. Despite the absence of regional planning, planning was taking place in the nonmunicipal areas, and these were the areas most in need of rational guidance.

By the end of the first decade only a few districts had adopted functions that could be considered important to the municipalities within them. The Greater Vancouver Regional District was one of these, having acquired, with much prodding from the DMA, the functions of each of the former single-purpose regional authorities as well as the functions of air pollution control, public housing, and labor relations for member municipalities. In general, though, it remained true that municipal government in the province had not yet been seriously affected by the emergence of regional government. Councillors who were also regional board members continued to regard their municipal role as more important, and by all evidence the public continued to be much more aware of municipal than regional government. No major functions had been transferred from municipalities to the regional districts, and regional government had generally not impinged upon the operation of the municipalities. Nevertheless, by the end of the first decade criticisms of regional districts were being heard—notably from residents of nonmunicipal areas (who resented the intrusion of government) and from the leaders of smaller municipalities (who resented regional district control of use of adjacent land). Opposition to regional government was especially evident among the rank and file of the Social Credit Party. In September 1977, in response to the criticism, the Social Credit government established the Regional District Review Committee, consisting of five persons who had been active in municipal government. Contrary to what might have been expected, the committee produced a comprehensive report strongly endorsing regional districts and recommending the further strengthening of regional government in British Columbia.[5]

NOTES

1. British Columbia, *Municipal Act* (R.S.B.C. 1965, chap. 28), secs. 765-98.

2. A full description of each regional district is contained in the annual publication *Statistics Relating to Regional and Municipal Governments in British Columbia*, prepared by the Department of Municipal Affairs and published by the Queen's Printer, Victoria.

3. *Municipal Act* (R.S.B.C. 1970, chap. 29), sec. 766.

4. *Municipal Act* (R.S.B.C. 1973, chap. 59), sec. 57A.

5. British Columbia, Department of Municipal Affairs, Regional District Review Committee, *Report of the Committee* (Victoria: Queen's Printer, 31 October 1978).

Proposals for Australia

R. L. Wettenhall and J. M. Power*

17

Local government reform is often viewed in relation to amalgamations and boundary changes, but in fact it involves much more. This essay begins with a brief review of the total reform situation in Australia and then explores the regionalizing tendencies discernible in the country's public administrative system as a whole. The goal of a unitary Australian state has long had adherents within the Labor Party, and under the Labor governments of the 1940s a much greater commitment to planning also emerged. A series of Premiers' Conferences and related agreements produced a new map dividing the country into almost one hundred regions and a scheme for the creation of regional development committees to function in each. However, although many of the regional committees continued to exist and a few were even to perform useful if limited functions, for the most part little was achieved. The regionalizing impetus was lost after the defeat of the federal Labor government at the end of 1949, and interest did not reawaken until the 1960s.

LOCAL GOVERNMENT REFORM IN AUSTRALIA

Levels and Units: A Static System

The years around the turn of the century saw the establishment in all its essentials of the present structure of government in Australia. The six state governments were well established, and, during the nineteenth century, somewhat haphazard local government systems of each were consolidated as compulsory and normally state-wide networks containing, in all, about 1,000 separate units of local government. Though new, the commonwealth government (the outcome of a compact among the states) was soon firmly established,

*Head of School, School of Administrative Studies, Canberra College of Advanced Education, and Professor of Political Science, University of Melbourne, respectively.

and both the upper levels of government (state and commonwealth) were already beginning to make great use of the device of the statutory corporation. The final component, the federal territory, was added almost as an afterthought in 1911.

There has been little significant development since that time. There has, of course, been growth and development *within* some of the elements (especially the federal government and the two statutory corporation sectors), but the basic structure has not changed. Moreover, if the local government sector has become notably adept at anything over the ensuing years, it is at resisting the proposition that it might undergo change to modernize and accommodate it to the realities of the middle—and now later—twentieth century.

This lack of movement in the local government systems is all the more surprising when we consider demography's message: the 1971 census results classified 85.56 percent of the Australian population as urban, indicating that Australia has become one of the world's most urbanized countries.[1] The main cities have spilled their suburbs far outside the local government boundaries they were given at the turn of the century (so that, for example, Sydney and Melbourne are today each collections of about forty to fifty cities and municipalities), while many of the rural shires, districts, and municipalities have watched their own populations dwindle as migration to the city continues. State governments have commissioned inquiry after inquiry into their local government systems, and almost invariably it is concluded that the number of individual units should be reduced to strengthen the systems as a whole—for, it is argued, fewer local authorities would be stronger and more viable. But local authorities are strongly entrenched in the state legislatures (many legislators begin their political careers as local councillors), and in some states they have become masters in the techniques of judicial challenge.

There have been a few exceptions to the generalized picture presented above. The most spectacular have involved the acceptance of ''greater city'' plans for Brisbane, the capital of Queensland, in 1925, and for Newcastle, the second city of New South Wales (NSW), in 1937. In each case many previously separate local authorities amalgamated to form a single and powerful integrated authority whose jurisdiction extended to a total metropolitan area. The redrawn Brisbane boundaries were bold enough to allow the bulk of growth through to the present day to take place within them; the Newcastle reform was not so bold. Less dramatic but significant was the 1948 reduction of the local authorities in metropolitan Sydney from sixty-six to thirty-nine and the present-day joining together—on the strength-through-unity argument—of three sets of towns assembled along common-interest strips of coastline or mountain highway, to produce the Cities of the Gold Coast (Queensland), Greater Wollongong (NSW) and the Blue Mountains (NSW). However, such substantial reforms have been few and far between. All the capital cities have had their greater city movements, but only Brisbane's succeeded. Metropolitan Sydney's intramural boundary reorganization in 1967 actually *reduced* the size of the central city, a move seen by many as part of a state-inspired gerrymander to break the municipal power or the Labor Party.

Nevertheless, as we move into the last quarter of the twentieth century, there are fresh auguries of municipal reform, at least in the largest states. The Local Government Boundaries Commission in NSW has in the past few years succeeded in reducing the number of nonmetropolitan authorities by about 10 percent and is attempting to gain momentum for a thorough restructuring of local government in Sydney. In 1978, the Victorian government established a Board of Review of the Role, Structure and Administration of Local Government in that state. The board enjoys unprecedentedly wide terms of reference and is expected to make recommendations which, if implemented, would lead to a significant restructuring of the Victorian system.

We have previously suggested that the basic structure of Australian government has become ossified since World War I.[2] The achievements of the boundary review process have not allayed that charge, although the decade of the 1970s has made a substantial impact on the local government sector in a number of ways.

Federal Money for Local Government

A common cry from the councillors, and sometimes the officers of Australian local governments, has been for more money for the councils. Until December 1972, a sequence of mainly Liberal-Country Party federal governments had insisted that local government remain a state responsibility under the federal constitution; the states saw themselves as hard pressed financially in their own dealings with the commonwealth and in turn handed out parsimonious treatment to their local authorities.

All this changed with the formation of the Whitlam Labor government in December 1972. Disenchanted with the states, the government sought to find a place in the constitution for local governments: they were given representation at a new constitutional convention and, for the first time, access to the Commonwealth's expanded Grants Commission, whose responsibility hitherto had been to recommend scales of equalization grants to the smaller states. Even though the electorate turned down a referendum proposal that would have authorized the commonwealth to make payments *directly* to local authorities (so that federal moneys still had to flow through state treasuries), in two years commonwealth grants for local government purposes had become twenty times greater, from $4.2 million in 1972-73 to $97.5 million in 1974-75.[3]

New Conceptions of Management

This trend has not continued since the passing of the Whitlam administration in late 1975. Nonetheless, management in local government has been irrevocably altered by the experience of the Whitlam years. Grantsmanship skills became all-important, and for the first time in Australian history significant connections were forged between federal and local bureaucrats.

Local administrators had been stirring, however, even before the advent of the Whitlam government. They had been one of the most professionally depressed groups within Australian management, and the qualifying certificates for service as council clerks were falling increasingly into disrepute. The typical clerk saw his role as secretarial rather than managerial—and yet found himself having to cope more and more with professional officers around him educated to tertiary level. Under an enlightened leadership, the Institute of Municipal Administration began in about 1970 to seek out tertiary institutions prepared to assist in the professional upgrading of management in local government; the senior management program at the Canberra College of Advanced Education and the substitution of tertiary courses in at least two states for the old certificating system, pay tribute to its efforts. The combination of developments such as these with the new functional challenges facing Australian local governments is producing a long overdue transformation in the style and quality of management.

Participation and Politics

The other area of change that deserves notice concerns the role of the local politician. He, too, is now coming to be provided with formal educational opportunities to increase his understanding of the administrative work of the officers responsible to his council and of the policy process in general. He, himself, is also confronted, especially in the suburbs of the large cities, with new residents' organizations strong enough to endanger his own place in the pattern of community leadership. In the last half-decade or so, such associations have become sufficiently prominent to attract the notice of Australian political scientists;[4] they have also contributed to a transformation of political styles in numerous local councils previously held captive by urban political "machines." Where this has happened, a distinct change has been observed from the ad hoc "survive and prosper a little" approach to a deliberate and consistent concern with the development and application of public policy.

In all these ways (and doubtless others too) Australian local government has been changing in recent years. Clearly it also has been affected by the growing interest, discernible at many levels, in finding regional solutions to administrative problems. To what extent has local government itself initiated these developing regional arrangements? Or, if it has been merely a passive witness, how far has it been affected and even restricted by them?[5]

PRE-1960 REGIONAL ARRANGEMENTS

The States as Regions?

Reviewing the record to date, the administrative historian could well be tempted to regard the states themselves as Australia's most lasting achievement in regional organization. It has been suggested that they do, in fact, constitute viable city regions.[6] But the gross inequalities of size among the states create serious administrative problems, some so vast as to demand differential regional action. Moreover, their heavy overload of historical traditions and their entrenched constitutonal position now appear to hinder rather than help the development of regional policies and institutions along national and rational lines.

One result has been the emergence from time to time of "new state" movements seeking to create as separate states parts of New South Wales and Queensland remote from the state capitals. But the play of politics around those capitals has so far defeated such movements.

Existing Patterns of Regional Administrative Action

Within the commonwealth-state-local framework, however, several forms of regional administrative action have been employed over the years. These may be divided into two main groups, those stemming from initiatives taken in the regions themselves and those stemming from initiatives taken at the center (either at the state or commonwealth government level). These movements may be described as "upwards to region" and "downwards to region," respectively, and it would seem that grass-roots participation is unlikely to be realized unless the first is prominently in evidence.

A few of the local authority amalgamations demonstrate "upwards to region" characteristics. Australian local authorities do collaborate from time to time in joint endeavors that fall short of amalgamation. There are, however, numerous well-known cases of failure to cooperate among neighboring authorities, so here, too, it would appear that parochialism carries the day. New South Wales has established a set of "county councils" to serve as joint committees
of neighboring local authorities in the undertaking of some specific function, such as electricity or water supply, noxious weed control, or airport management. They are not, however, second-tier authorities as in Britain, and, although in a few cases they have resulted from local initiatives, more often their creation has been forced on local authorities by the state.

As the emerging municipal arrangements increasingly fragmented the growing cities, Australian governments showed themselves ready to create statutory boards to administer services the technological needs of which could be met by a single unit of organization covering a whole contiguous built-up area. Vast areas of urban administration were thus removed from municipal jurisdiction, one of the gains being the recognition for particular purposes of the administrative unity of the "metropolitan area." When the Greater Brisbane Council was formed in 1925, most of Brisbane's ad hoc boards were absorbed by the municipal authority. Elsewhere they grew apace, composed mainly of commissioners appointed by central government (with perhaps a few municipal representatives) and presenting all those familiar problems associated with the murkiness of public corporation accountability and with the difficulty of coordinating the work of separate technical/specialist authorities all operating in one urban area.

The device of the statutory corporation has occasionally been used to reflect regional administrative needs in areas away from the state capital. In one notable case, TVA-style ''grass-roots'' linkages were apparent until the region passed its development threshold and adjusted to the more usual pattern of Australian district administration.[7] More significant, however, has been the extension of the state departments into ''the provinces,'' a development that has been particularly apparent during the twentieth century. Whereas the earlier construction of the local government systems had, in the language of administrative decentralization,[8] followed the process of *statutory devolution*, this twentieth century trend has been ever more strongly towards *administrative deconcentration*.

Regions Crowded but Uncoordinated

The development of the field-office networks of central departments is clearly a product of the rapid technological advances especially evident in transport and communications, leading to the shrinkage of administrative space and to the possibility of organizing over much larger areas than those offered by the local government pattern. Accordingly, state departments and corporations providing services, such as agriculture, forestry, irrigation, grain storage, transport, public works, education, and civil defense, have all been engaged in this process of establishing field offices. Much more so than in some other federations, so too have commonwealth agencies: the post office is widely represented, and most towns of any size have field offices of services such as social security, taxation, employment, public banking, and public broadcasting.

Consequently, any single provincial area is now likely to possess an administrative apparatus comprising numerous, small, multipurpose local governments, possibly an ad hoc authority or two, and a dozen or so field offices of state and commonwealth agencies. Past Australian experience suggests (though the new advocacy of regionalism is trying to break this down) that there will be little or no coordination either within or among the various groups. Moreover, each of the central agencies will have drawn its own regional boundaries so that very few of these administrative areas will coincide. Until recently field offices have been staffed by people fairly low in the respective functional hierarchies, reinforcing the tendency for all important matters to be referred along those hierarchies for decision at the capital.

TOWARDS REGIONALISM: UPWARDS OR DOWNWARDS?

Downwards from the State Level

After the mid-1960s Australian governments began to place more senior departmental officers in the field and to give them greater discretionary powers. The trend, however, has been far from uniform, and there has rarely been a serious attempt to establish mechanisms that would enable these field officers to exercise their discretions so as to promote distinctively regional interests. There admittedly have been attempts by town planning authorities in all states to set up various regional planning and advisory councils and committees, but these seem to have had relatively little effect on the activities of the other state and commonwealth departments. It may well be that the significant influence of town planners on the regionalizing movement has been indirect and somewhat diffuse, heightening the area awareness of other administrators and thus shaping the culture of contemporary administration.

By the early 1970s three states large in area—New South Wales, Queensland, and Western Australia—were ready to take further steps in the direction of regional planning. In the first state, the lead was taken by the Department of Decentralization and Development, a small new organization that had come into existence shortly after the 1965 election of a Liberal-Country Party coalition government. The system of regional organization that emerged was weak and permissive. The regional advisory councils were advisory in fact as well as title and had no power to compel government bodies within their region to conform to their decisions and plans. The traditionally powerful departments in the regions evidently considered it important to be represented on most of the councils.[9]

In Queensland, by contrast, the sponsor of the regionalizing program was probably the most powerful department of all—the co-ordinator-general's—which has extensive responsibilities in the area of works and other programming for all state government bodies and, increasingly, for local authorities as well. Further, each regional co-ordination council was chaired by one of the department's most senior officers. Even so, few observers expected much of this development: the chairman's position was still far from that of a prefect, and the co-ordinator-general, one of Australia's most influential state public servants, specifically declared at the outset that there was "no prospect that the Regional Co-ordination Council structure will become a 'Regional Government' in the classic sense," that "the major principle" of the scheme was that "the existing functional organizations are best suited to contribute to the formulation of regional policies and to the implementation of these policies."[10] The system was destined to enjoy a short life, and was dissolved by the state government in 1977.

In the Western Australian case, special mechanisms have developed for administering the remote northwestern region, and their operation is gradually being extended throughout the state. The other three states have allowed their regional programs to be developed by single departments, with the inevitable proliferation of regions and confusion of boundaries. Nowhere has a state government seen these regionalizing activities as ways of enhancing the status and responsibilities of local government.

The Awakening of Federal Concern: Downwards Again

The awakening of federal concern had much to do with the rise of Gough Whitlam as leader of the federal Labor Party in the late 1960s. For Whitlam, a reformer with a keen interest in the structure of government, Labor's formal antipathy towards the federal system had strong appeal. Before coming to government, he sketched a concise blueprint for a system he considered more suitable than his generation had inherited:

If we were devising anew a structure of representative government for our continent, we would have neither so few State governments nor so many local government units. We would not have a federal system of overlapping parliaments, and a delegated but supervised system of local government. We would have a House of Representatives for international matters and national matters, an assembly for the affairs of each of our dozen largest cities and a few score regional assemblies for the areas of rural production and resource development outside those cities. Vested interests and legal complexities should not discourage or deter us from attempts to modernise and rationalise our inherited structure. [11]

Under Whitlam, however, traditional Labor attitudes towards government also had been modified and wedded to newer (or revived) concerns, such as a populistic impulse toward greater public participation in governmental decision making, often accompanied by a distrust of established administrative structures. These themes had wide appeal among professional urban and social planners who had lacked influence under the postwar, non-Labor governments. Accordingly, with the advent of a Labor government at the end of 1972 came the creation of new organizations, such as the Department of Urban and Regional Development (DURD) and the Social Welfare Commission, within which these professionals found an opportunity to introduce a range of programs capable of delivery at regional level. Partly because of their unfamiliarity with the existing structures of regional and local government, they were able to engage in rather adventurous organizational planning.

The most comprehensive scheme was unveiled by DURD late in 1973. It divided the entire country into sixty-eight regions (subsequently increased to seventy-six) and established a regional assembly representative of local authorities in the area in each. The primary function of these assemblies, which came to be known as Regional Organizations of Councils (ROCs), was the formulation of proposals for financial assistance from the federal government. Almost simultaneously, the Social Welfare Commission announced its "Australian Assistance Plan," which called for the establishment of Regional Councils for Social Development (RCSDs) comprising representatives of commonwealth, state, and local governments, trade unions, employer groups, welfare consumer groups, and nongovernment bodies concerned with social welfare, and serviced by quite senior professional social planners. Other commonwealth departments—Health, Education, Tourism and Recreation, Attorney-General's—were not far behind, although they did not publish details of similarly comprehensive schemes. [12]

The development of the several regionalizing programs by various governments in Australia inevitably posed grave problems of coordination. The commonwealth government established an interdepartmental committee on its regional programs and boundaries, which had some success in gaining agreement on common regional boundaries, but severe political and administrative problems were still ahead as its various field programs gained momentum. Many participants saw the new programs as exercises in grantsmanship, while one of the major funding bodies, the reconstructed Grants Commission, seemed much more interested in promoting fiscal equalization among local authorities, whatever their geographical location, than in promoting regionalism. Moreover, it was never clear that the departments and commissions embarking upon regional programs had any commitment to the prime minister's cause of regional government.

The internal inconsistencies were nowhere better revealed than in the case of the two federal territories, the Australian Capital Territory and the Northern Territory. While the government as a whole was theoretically committed to advancing them towards some form of self-government, many of its functional departments competed to establish separate presences in them. For proponents of regional government who had been encouraged by Whitlam's statements in opposition, the territories presented a magnificent opportunity for demonstrating how to reform Australia's presently ossified system of government. But Whitlam's functionaries wanted them as laboratories in which to develop new educational programs, health programs, recreation programs, and so on, all firmly orchestrated from commonwealth headquarters.[13]

The ambivalence of the Whitlam government thus seemed to demonstrate that a commitment to regional government is antipathetic to a commitment to a range of regional programs identified and defined centrally and primarily in terms of their functional characteristics. If this is indeed so, then it would appear that the whole notion of regionalism may be confused whenever a central government has positive ideas about what regions should do.

Upwards to Region? Unresolved Political Problems

The Fraser Liberal-National Country Party government replaced the Whitlam administration at the end of 1975. The Fraser government's "New Federalism" policy and its commitment to prune federal expenditures and programs speedily led to a significant return of powers and functions to the states and a winding down of most federal regional programs.

Nevertheless, it remained inconceivable that commonwealth-local relations could return to the status quo of the pre-Whitlam days. To begin with, the Fraser government accepted the responsibility for providing local government with a guaranteed share of personal income tax collections. At present this share stands at 1.52 percent, but the federal government is pledged to increase it to 2.00 percent before the end of 1980. Furthermore, local government interests are now firmly represented at the national level. Since 1973 the Australian Council of Local Government Association has been served by a permanent secretariat in Canberra, and municipal representatives have figured prominently in the membership of the new Advisory Council for Inter-government Relations (ACIR).[14]

The 1970s have seen a steady increase in pressures for greater community access to public decision making and, correspondingly, strong pressures for change in the structure of Australian government. The architects of "downwards to region" decentralization are scarcely likely to seek remedies that limit their own prerogatives and may be expected to try to accommodate demands for greater participation through the elaboration and development of their own field networks in the regions. They are thus attempting to find administrative solutions to problems that are at base political.

This tendency already can be seen in the work of a task force set up by the Royal Commission on Australian (Commonwealth) Government Administration (RCAGA) which was appointed in 1974 and which submitted its main report in 1976. Enjoined to design a flexible basis for administration at regional and local levels, the task force confronted the problems caused by the hardening of our governmental system and made a number of valuable recommendations that would widen the delegations made to Australian government field officers, more effectively coordinate their activities and those of state and local government administrators, and provide greater access to Canberra-based policymakers, both for field officers and regional and local interests.[15] The task force's limited terms of reference (which of course derived from the limited terms of reference of its parent commission) did not, however, allow it to consider the political and constitutional dimensions of the problem it was confronting. Unwittingly or not, its findings lent support to the common view that administrative solutions can be found to problems that are ultimately political.

In a system of representative democracy, there are severe limitations to the effectiveness of programs of organizational development. A system grown notably unresponsive stands in need of new institutions of representation at those points exhibiting the most pathological symptoms. New directly elected assemblies will be needed at those points to make authoritative resource allocation decisions sensitive to the needs of their constitutents, a function that administrators from other levels of government can never be expected to perform.

Perhaps the dominant forces within Australian state and local government have learned from the experiences of the last decade and are capable now of taking genuine, concerted, "upwards to region" initiatives. State governments may have found the political resolve to restructure their municipal systems in order to ensure the emergence of stronger, viable local authorities. Australia may yet find acceptable political answers to the problems that have given rise to the regional movement. For, as the former director of the NSW Department of Decentralization and Development has recently observed, regionalism is a problem that won't go away.[16]

NOTES

1. *Official Year Book of Australia* (Canberra: Australian Bureau of Statistics, 1973), p. 135.

2. J. M. Power and R. L. Wettenhall, "Regional Government versus Regional Programs," *Australian Journal of Public Administration* 35 (June 1976).

3. From estimates provided by the Australian Government Bureau of Statistics.

4. See especially J. M. Power, "The New Politics in the Old Suburbs," in *Public Policy and Administration In Australia: A Reader*, ed. R. N. Spann and G. R. Curnow (Sydney: Wiley, 1975); and R. F. I. Smith, "Collingwood, Wren Left-overs and Political Change," *Labour History* (Canberra) 30 (May 1976).

5. The following sections summarize a number of themes we have developed in a variety of papers over the last seven years. Most of these papers are listed in R. L. Wettenhall, "Trends in Regional Administration," *Local Government Administration* (Melbourne) 18 (June-September 1978): 33.

6. Geoffrey Sawer, "Managing the Cities: An Evaluation" (Comment, Annual Conference of Australian Institute of Urban Studies, Canberra, 1 November 1973), p. 7.

7. Joan Tully, "The Murrumbidgee Irrigation Area Experiment in Agricultural Extension," in *Decisions: Case Studies in Australian Administration*, ed. B. B. Schaffer and D. C. Corbett (Melbourne: Cheshire, 1965).

8. See, for example, A. W. Macmahon, *Delegation and Autonomy* (Bombay: Asia, 1961), ch. 2.

9. For an early study of the NSW system, see John Power and Helen Nelson, eds., *The Regional Administrator in the Riverina: A Set of Working Papers* (Canberra: Canberra College of Advanced Education, 1976).

10. Sir Charles Barton, *Regional Planning and Regional Co-ordination* (Brisbane: Co-ordinator-General's Department, 1973), p. 27.

11. E. G. Whitlam, *An Urban Nation*, First Annual Leslie Wilkinson Lecture (Sydney: University of Sydney, 1969), p. 10. Repeated (with a few stylistic alterations) in Whitlam's "A New Federalism," *Australian Quarterly* 43 (September 1971): 11.

12. Australia, Department of Urban and Regional Development, *Regions: Suggested Delimitation of Regions for the Purposes of Section 17, Grants Commission Act, 1973* (Canberra: AGPS, 1973); and Australia, Social Welfare Commission, *Australian Assistance Plan: Progress Report 30 August-31 December 1973* (Canberra: AGPS, 1974).

13. The position of the territories is considered more fully in Power and Wettenhall, "Regional Government." Since that paper was published, the Northern Territory has in fact been granted its own government.

14. The ACIR's first major research project has been a comprehensive and searching inquiry into the local government systems of Australia and the ways in which all three spheres of government may develop policies that will benefit these systems. The findings of this project will be reported in the latter part of 1979, in J. M. Power, R. L. Wettenhall, and J. A. Halligan, eds., *The Local Government Systems of Australia* (forthcoming for the ACIR from the Australian Government Publishing Service).

15. The relevant documents are: *Regionalising Government Administration*, RCAGA Discussion Paper, no. 1 (Canberra: RCAGA, 1975); and RCAGA, *A Regional*

Basis for Australian Government Administration: Task Force Report, vols. 1 and 2 (Canberra: AGPS, 1975).

16. P. D. Day, "The Regional Mirage," *Royal Australian Planning Institute Journal* 5 (May 1977).

PART III

The Basic Units in Developed Countries

Introduction

A fundamental problem of local government in the developed countries has been the small size and financial weakness of the basic units of local government. Created at a time when communities were small, they are unable to provide the skills and services demanded of modern municipal government or to benefit from the savings and efficiency of large-scale operation. Also, due to modern means of communication and transportation, much larger areas of administration have become feasible. It is mainly for these reasons that many developed countries have decided that their local governments must be consolidated and enlarged.

It is curious that very little reorganization of this kind has taken place in North America. In Canada, only in New Brunswick has there been a restructuring of the basic units. In this case, the reorganization was drastic: in 1966 the rural units were abolished entirely and the provincial government took over from the urban units all services that would benefit from large-scale operation. In the first essay in this part, Professor Higgins gives an account of this reform and compares it with proposals made for reorganization in New Brunswick's sister province, Nova Scotia. Professor Bowen's essay on the United States reveals that even though there have been significant changes in the nature and powers of local government in that country there has been little structural consolidation. Indeed, the number of basic units actually increased between 1962 and 1979 (from about 35,200 to about 35,700). In Canada, the number of basic units similarly has remained relatively stable in recent years, at about 4,000. A main reason why consolidation has not been considered necessary in the United States and Canada may be the feeling that, if the average population of the basic units is greatly increased, local government may become remote from the citizens and participation may decline. Another reason may be that these federal countries already have a state or provincial level of government to handle wider-than-local problems, and also a county level in the most populous states and provinces. On the other hand, West Germany, which is also a federal country with state and county levels of government, has drastically reduced the number of not only counties but also local communities. Professor Siedentopf's table reveals that the latter were reduced by more than half—from nearly 25,000 in 1965 to under 11,000 in 1975. The process and nature of this massive reorganization in the largest state, North-Rhine Westphalia, are analyzed in Professor Doeker's essay, while Professor Wagener's essay presents a survey of the reorganization of the basic units in the whole of West Germany.

Another federal country in which large-scale reorganizations have taken place is Austria, discussed in Dr. Rossmann's essay. The essays by Professor Norton on England and Wales, Professor Page on Scotland, and the Carrolls on Northern Ireland describe the far-reaching reorganization that has taken place in Britain, where not only the second-tier counties have been restructured but the lower-level units have been consolidated and their numbers drastically reduced. In Scotland's case, the number of first-tier units was reduced from nearly 400 to 53. In Northern Ireland, as mentioned in the introduction to part 2, the two-tier system was abolished entirely and replaced by twenty-six unitary local governments. Other countries of Western Europe in which considerable restructuring has occurred are Finland and Sweden, dealt with in the essays by Drs. Harisalo and Ronkko, and Dr. Stromberg, respectively. Part 3 also includes an essay on Japan by Professor Ukai which reveals that, though there has been some restructuring, there has been no fundamental reorganization of the basic units in Japan.

The section on Eastern Europe has an essay on cities in the Soviet Union by Professor Hough, one on Yugoslavia by Professor Pavić, and an essay on the socialist countries of Central and Southeastern Europe by Professors B. Zawadzka and S. Zawadski, two experts on local government with the Polish Academy of Sciences. These essays show that the socialist countries of Eastern Europe have had much the same problems as other developed countries resulting from the small size of local governments at the lowest level and that there has been a similar reorganization, consolidation, and reduction in the number of these governments in recent years, as well as other changes designed to integrate central policies and local activities more effectively. Professor Hough's essay also indicates that in the Soviet Union, even though there has been little formal reorganization, the power of political officials in city soviets, as shown by such indicators as their educational level and their role in providing housing and related city services, seems to be increasing.

NORTH AMERICA
AND JAPAN

CANADA
UNITED STATES
JAPAN

Canada: New Brunswick and Nova Scotia

Donald J. H. Higgins*

18

Of Canada's three maritime provinces, by 1979 only Prince Edward Island had not embarked upon a review or reorganization of its basic units of local government.[1] This essay concerns the remaining two maritime provinces— New Brunswick, which began its province-wide reorganization of municipal government in 1967, and Nova Scotia, where a Royal Commission established in 1971 reported in 1974.[2] Any substantial implementation of that commission's recommendations was deferred pending completion of the work of a special committee of the provincial legislature, the report of which was tabled in 1975.[3]

A full, comparative analysis of the two provinces is not a simple task, for there have been several royal commissions in New Brunswick dealing with municipal reorganization. Only one of them (the Byrne Report) involved the large-scale reorganization of basic units.[4] and it is with that report that this article is concerned, in company with the report of Nova Scotia's royal commission (the Graham Report). The second problem for comparative analysis is the wide scope (and the actual size) of the two reports. The Byrne Report was a relatively modest 500 pages; the Graham Report a massive 7,000. Finally, reorganization actually has occured in New Brunswick but is not far advanced in Nova Scotia. The analysis that follows is, therefore, highly selective, focusing on the functions of the new or proposed units of local government in the two provinces, the nature and size of those units, and the nature of provincial-municipal relations. The premises upon which reorganization was recommended are also described, and a comparison and assessment of the two systems constitutes the last section of this essay.

*Associate Professor of Political Science, Saint Mary's University in Halifax, Nova Scotia, and author of *Urban Canada: Its Government and Politics* (Toronto: Macmillan of Canada, 1977).

BACKGROUND

New Brunswick and Nova Scotia share more than a common border. The areas of the two provinces are comparable (New Brunswick having 73,437 square kilometers and Nova Scotia 55,491) as are the populations (New Brunswick with an estimated 697,600 in 1978, Nova Scotia with 843,900). In 1976 about 52 percent of New Brunswick's population was classified as urban, as was about 56 percent of Nova Scotia's.

The provinces' units of local government are shown below. For New Brunswick the situations both before and after the reorganization of 1967 are shown; for Nova Scotia the 1974 and proposed situations are given.

Table 18.1

**NEW BRUNSWICK AND NOVA SCOTIA: UNITS OF MUNICIPAL
AND NONMUNICIPAL LOCAL GOVERNMENT**

	New Brunswick		Nova Scotia	
Unit	*1961*	*1978*	*1974*	*proposed*
Counties	15	0	24	11
Villages	1	85	(25)	(25+)
Towns	20	21	38	(28)
Cities	6	6	3	0
School boards	(562)	(33)	(71)	(11)

Note: Figures in parentheses indicate nonmunicipalities.

NEW BRUNSWICK: THE PROGRAM FOR EQUAL OPPORTUNITY

New Brunswick's Byrne Commission, created in 1962 and reporting in 1963, proposed what is described as a set of "revolutionary" recommendations. As one commentator noted, "More surprising than the revolutionary proposals of the Byrne Commission was the fact that the New Brunswick government implemented most of the recommendations."[5] They took effect January 1967. The Byrne Commission's report offered a more elaborate rationale for the reorganization than did the provincial government's White Paper embodying the proposals or the legislation itself.[6]

Functions of the Local Units

The overall effect of the reorganization of 1967 was to completely remove from the municipalities responsibility for providing and financing a number of services by making those services the responsibility of the provincial government. This move was recommended on the basis of a distinction between local and general services:

The wide variety of services currently [1962] provided by New Brunswick municipalities can be divided roughly according to whether they are of a local or of a general nature; that is, according to whether the benefits from them accrue only to the inhabitants of the municipalities or whether they are spread throughout the province or the nation. . . .

The distinction between local and general services is of value because it divides functions of government into those which are more or less clearly the preserve of the local government and those for which the province might appropriately share or assume responsibility . . .that is, in education, health and hospitals, social welfare, administration of justice, and the provision of court houses and gaols.[7]

After analyzing data on per capita expenditure by function and type of municipality in 1961, the commission concluded that levels of services varied considerably—highest in cities, lower in towns, and lowest in the counties. It was implicitly assumed that there is a direct connection between per capita expenditure and the level of service provided. It followed that the rural residents, who then comprised more than half the province's population, were disadvantaged.

The commission considered two alternative courses of action: first, retain the existing division of responsibilities but add a system of equalizing conditional grants paid by the province to municipalities to enable provision of defined levels of general services with equal tax burdens, and, second, reallocate responsibility for services by having the province assume responsibility for the general services as well as such support services as property assessment and tax collection, leaving the provision of local services to the municipalities. The commission also noted and rejected a third option—to enlarge the counties and reduce their number. The first and third options were rejected because they would necessitate even greater degrees of provincial influence over services provided by municipalities than were already present. Also, these two options would be less "efficient" and they "would do nothing to adjust the structure of government to the fundamental economic and social change of the last half century."[8]

Adopting the second option, as recommended by the Byrne Commission, the provincial government assumed responsibility for the general services that had previously been partly the responsibility of the municipalities (education, justice, public health, and welfare) as well as property assessment and tax billing and collection. The administration by the province of some of these functions remained decentralized, however, and the municipalities continued to play a minor role regarding some of the general services.

The general effect of the reallocation of responsibilities was to strip all municipalities of a number of important functions (particularly the most expensive ones), leaving them with responsibility for such local services as fire and police protection; streets, sidewalks, and related public works; sewage and garbage removal, water supply, and recreation. Since 1973 there is no distinction among categories of municipalities in terms of their service responsibilities.

Nature and Size of the Local Units

The most obvious aspect of the reorganized basic units emanating from the Byrne Report was the abolition of the counties and the creation of numerous villages. Prior to implementation of the commission's recommendations in 1967, there were fifteen counties, the earliest created in 1852. By 1875 the entire province had been divided into the fifteen counties, which were the basic units of municipal government. New Brunswick provided for city and town representation on county councils, thereby attempting to integrate urban and rural units of municipal government. However, while members of county councils from cities and towns were free to participate, debate, and vote on almost all matters, the county councils were virtually powerless in matters respecting the urban municipalities. This situation persisted without any substantial change until 1967, and the governmental significance of the counties declined. Between 1901 and 1961 the urban proportion of the province's population, concentrated in the towns and cities, rose from about 20 to 46 percent. The commission found that the mechanism intended to integrate urban and rural residents municipally was unable to reflect the growing interdependence of town and country. Further, the rural population in many counties was comparatively small in 1961, and the capacity of counties to provide adequate levels of service to rural residents was low. Having both small populations and financial bases, counties were unable to afford the desired expertise and equipment. As a consequence, the provincial government was compelled to intervene to greater degrees in county affairs, thereby reducing the counties' autonomy and significance.

While these points constituted grounds upon which the abolition of counties was proposed and implemented, the commission's main reason related to functions:

We wish to emphasize that the termination of county government is not arrived at as a result of a direct policy decision on our part. It is, rather, an inevitable outcome of our findings that those functions presently being performed by the county governments can be satisfactorily performed only under provincial administration.[9]

Counties have become mainly tax collecting agencies—a function which they are singularly ill-equipped to perform. There is no important function or field of government responsibility for which they are empowered to formulate policy. . . . They possess vestigial administrative powers which cannot properly be exercised on their present fragmented basis.[10]

The creation of villages and local service districts was recommended to ensure that some of the rural residents would not be left without any form of representative local government. Until 1967 only four villages had been incorporated, and three of them had disappeared by acquiring town status. By 1969 ninety-three villages were incorporated, several were amalgamated to cities and towns, and several more have been created since then. Villages have elected councils and possess responsibilities which make them units of municipal government, but the rural local service districts created first in 1967 do not have elected councils. In 1978 there were 219 such districts providing a limited range of local services and collecting the required taxes. Districts were intended for situations where small scattered populations were unsuitable for incorporation either because the population was too small or because the residents did not desire village status.

However, by 1975 it was apparent that the 1967 decision to abandon local self-government in rural New Brunswick was not an unqualified success. Recognizing the shortcomings of the local service districts, the provincial government created a task force, chaired by the deputy minister of municipal affairs, to examine the nonincorporated areas of the province. The Allen Task Force reported in 1976 and identified a number of general problems, such as the facts that over 35 percent of the province's total population (and 96 percent of the total land area) were without local self-government, that the structure of local service districts did not provide for effective citizen participation in such local affairs as planning, that local services were inequitably financed in New Brunswick because rural residents paid no property taxes but residents in incorporated areas did, and that effective implementation of community planning could not be achieved at the centralized provincial level. [11]

Basically, the task force recommended something of a return to the pre-1967 structure of the basic units. All local service districts would be abolished, and eleven rural municipalities created in their place. Together, the new rural municipalities would cover virtually all the rural areas and would have the same powers and responsibilities that the existing municipalities possessed. Thus, the proposed rural municipalities would be considerably stronger than the pre-1967 county form of rural local government. The task force's recommendations were not accepted by the provincial government. A committee was set up to rework the report, and some legislation may be enacted in 1979.

Nature of Provincial-Municipal Relations

One of the reasons for proposing the particular form of municipal reorganization that was implemented in 1967 was that the other two options would have necessitated even greater degrees of provincial influence over municipalities' services. Clearly what both the commission and the provincial government wanted was as clear and sharp a division of responsibilities as possible to simplify provincial-municipal relations and to increase municipal autonomy over services for which they were to be responsible.

The commission showed how complex the then existing legal lines of responsibility for services were as well as nonservice relationships. In terms of legislation there were numerous special charters and amendments to them, by which municipalities were incorporated. There was a multitude of special purpose boards and commissions throughout the province, some municipal, some provincial, and some joint. In consequence the citizenry could not be sure who had responsibility for what, particularly regarding the "general" services. The commission pointed out that prior to 1967 the municipalities had held responsibility for raising revenue to support general services but often had a minimum of discretion in policy making regarding them:

Local autonomy with respect to the general services is already minimal. The rural municipalities, the counties, are now in the position where four-fifths of their expenditures are out of their direct control. The funds they must raise for education account for three-fifths of their over-all total expenditures, and these as a rule are requisitioned from the councils by school boards . . .Although the school boards have some budgetary and administrative discretion, even they are bound by a network of provincial regulations.[12]

An indication of the financial relationships can be seen by looking at the municipalitites' revenue sources prior to the reorganization. For later reference, figures for Nova Scotia are given as well. (See Table 18.2.)

Table 18.2
NEW BRUNSWICK AND NOVA SCOTIA: MUNICIPAL
REVENUE BY SOURCE[13] (% OF TOTAL REVENUE)

Source	New Brunswick (1961)		Nova Scotia (1971)	
Total taxation revenue	66.1		67.0	
Licenses, permits, rents, fines	1.3		1.6	
Interest, penalties, service charges	1.0		2.1	
Total of municipalities' own sources		68.4		70.7
Grants from federal government	5.8		5.3	
Grants from provincial government	19.4		21.3	
Grants from other municipalities	4.6		1.8	
Grants from other sources	1.0		0.3	
Total of grants and subsidies		30.8		28.7
Miscellaneous revenue		0.9		0.7
Total revenue, all sources		100.1		100.1

Almost a third of the 1961 revenue for all municipalities in New Brunswick was in the form of grants, subsidies, or contributions from other governments. The bulk of these grants was conditional (tied to specific purposes) and therefore largely outside municipal discretion.

The changes in functions designed to simplify lines of accountability and responsibility have been described above. They had the effect of substantially reducing municipal revenue requirements, and were reflected in diminished sources of revenue being made available to the municipalities.[14] The outcome was exemption of all personal property from taxation, abolition of poll taxes, abolition of exemption on some previously exempt commercial and industrial real estate, payment of grants in lieu of taxes by the province on private property used for educational, charitable, and religious purposes (as well as on provincial property), setting a uniform province-wide rate of real property taxes, and instituting a system of equalizing unconditional grants paid to municipalities by the province. Therefore, the four basic sources of municipal revenue after 1967 were the property tax, the equalization and unconditional payments from the province, grants in lieu of taxes from the federal and provincial governments and their public corporations, and nominal revenue from licenses, fees, and utilities. The maximum total of unconditional grants that a municipality could receive in any one year was set at 70 percent of the estimated expenditures for that year. The proportion of the total net municipal budgets accounted for by unconditional grants in 1978 was 46.0 percent.[15] A limited range of conditional "stimulation grants" was recommended and implemented particularly to encourage municipalities to embark upon sewage treatment projects. These grants were intended to make up only a small fraction of municipal revenues, but their scope was extended in 1974 to include water supply and road construction projects. Since then, the scope of stimulation grants has been broadened progressively to include roadwork, fire protection, sewage treatment, garbage dumps, and arenas, for example. Thus the desired simplicity of provincial-municipal financial relations in 1967 has since regressed to a more complex situation involving increased provincial action in local finance.

Regarding the nonfinancial relations between the province and municipalities (that is, provincial agencies that supervise, direct, and control municipalities), the commission recommended the creation of four provincial, semi-autonomous administrative commissions for public schools, hospitals, social welfare, and municipal affairs. The Municipal Affairs Commission was to be a nonpolitical body to replace the existing Department of Municipal Affairs. This was recommended "in view of the greatly expanded responsibilites to be assumed by the provincial government in the areas of property assessment and appeals, tax collection, municipal debt management, administration of local services in the new local service districts, and supervision of municipal administration."[16] It is difficult to reconcile the Byrne Report's desire to buttress municipal autonomy with its statement that the Municipal Affairs Commission should generally "tighten up the supervision and control over the activities of the municipalities."[17] The Municipal Affairs Commission was to perform a long list of duties, including deciding whether to authorize forming new villages, defining and revising municipal boundaries, overseeing municipal elections, auditing municipal accounts, exercising "close" supervision over villages, administering local service districts, approving municipal capital projects, and providing "systematic" surveillance of municipal administration.

The provincial government rejected the proposed Municipal Affairs Commission (and the other three too) on the grounds that it would wield considerable power without being responsible to the public and therefore would not be in harmony with the principles of responsible government. Instead, the Department of Municipal Affairs, which had already been performing some of those tasks, was to continue to perform them as well as the others. The department administers the local service districts, for example, through a decentralized system of eleven regional offices, each with a municipal services representative who also advises and aassists municipalities.

The elections branch of the department is responsible for municipal by-elections and determines election regulations. The community planning branch prepares regional and municipal plans and advises and guides municipalities in planning matters. There is also a municipal capital borrowing board which authorizes municipal borrowing for capital projects. The assessment branch of the department assesses all real estate property. The stimulation grant program is administered by the engineering and technical services branch, which is also responsible for some water and sewer services and for providing engineering and technical assistance to municipalities. In general it now seems clear that while New Brunswick's municipalities are still subject in many ways to provincial supervision and control, the relationships are still less complex than they were before 1967, despite the changes made from year to year since then that have complicated matters somewhat. The nature of supervision and control exercised by the province remains less heavy-handed than the Byrne Report proposed.

Summary

Since 1967 New Brunswick's Program for Equal Opportunity has wrought considerable changes in municipal structures, responsibilities, and operations in the province. Its main features were abolition of the counties, creation of numerous villages, reallocation of functions, equalization of municipal finance, and new (and usually higher) minimum standards of service. However, the fact remains that a significant proportion of the province's population has no form of municipal government. The province has not been reluctant to make adjustments to the new municipal system (particularly in 1973-74, when a series of recommendations of the provincial Task Force on Municipal Structure and Finance was implemented), such as giving villages the same responsibilities as cities and towns for local services, altering the granting formula, and expanding the system of stimulation grants. It is significant, though, that changes in provincial-municipal financial relations and the proposed new rural municipalities represent something of a reversal of the 1967 "revolution" in New Brunswick's municipal system.

NOVA SCOTIA: THE GRAHAM ROYAL COMMISSION

The government and people of Nova Scotia have been digesting the Graham Report since its presentation in June 1974. That some people acquired indigestion is evident from the criticism many of the commission's recommendations received. The scope of the report was so broad that there was something for everyone to fault, and the provincial government has taken an extremely cautious stance. The first few pieces of legislation related to the report were introduced in the House of Assembly in June 1975, but in introducing that legislation the minister of municipal affairs stated that the Graham Report "is not going to be adopted in total" but would be a "useful guide in developing policies of municipal reform.''[18] Since then, the report has faded into relative oblivion.

Functions of the Local Units

In designing its proposed municipal structure the commission began by deciding which services should be provided by municipalities and which by the province. After distinguishing general from local services, it recommended that the province remove responsibility for providing and financing several important and expensive services from the municipalities.

> The essence of our recommendations is that the general services should be provided and financed entirely by the provincial government and that the local services should remain the responsibility of the municipalities, who would finance them largely from their own resources but with some provincial assistance.[19] The provincial government should provide those public services that are primarily of province-wide concern because all Nova Scotians are significantly affected, directly or indirectly, by their quality and effectiveness; and...the municipalities should provide all those other public services that are primarily of local concern.[20]

Services identified as "general" were education, health, social welfare, housing, administration of justice, and some aspects of transportation (limited-access highways and all roads in rural areas). In addition the commission recommended that the province take over responsibility for certain support services: property assessment, property tax billing and collection, municipal capital borrowing, billing and collection of local improvement charges and utility user charges, and administration of pensions for municipal employees. The province would decentralize its administration of the general services and the municipalities would have a minor role to play with regard to some of those services.

Local services for which municipalities would be responsible include general government ("housekeeping" matters), protection (police, fire, safety inspection, and emergency measures), the water supply, sewage, garbage, physical planning and zoning, transportation (such as streets and roads, parking and public transit), beautification, business and tourist promotion, and recreation and culture. Since all the general and support services are presently the sole or partial responsibility of municipalities, and since the list of local services contains nothing that the municipalities do not already have, the commission's proposals would constitute a significant reduction in the municipalities' role.

Nature and Size of the Local Units

The recommendations regarding reorganization of the basic units met with particularly widespread criticism. The existing three cities, thirty-eight towns and twenty-four rural municipalities would disappear as municipal units, being replaced by eleven unitary counties that would cover both urban and rural areas and together would cover the whole province. Twenty-eight of the towns would become administrative-consultative units within the new counties.

The municipal system dates from Halifax's incorporation in 1841. The Counties Incorporation Act of 1879 established rural municipal government, and the system was completed in 1888 with the Towns Incorporation Act. Villages are not full-fledged municipalities. While there have been changes over time in boundaries and while some towns have lost their status or become cities, one analyst noted, "Perhaps the principal lesson that emerges from the history of municipal government since 1888 is that the basic units are highly impervious to change."[21]

The commission identified four problems of the existing municipal system (besides that of functions):

(1) Existing municipal government areas no longer fit the pattern of life and work in modern Nova Scotia.

(2) The fragmentation of responsibilities for municipal services in the province among three cities, thirty-eight towns and twenty-four rural municipalities splits urban communities, divides town from country, and makes proper planning for the provision of services impossible.

(3) The present division of responsibilities for services between urban and rural governments . . . means that services that should be in the hands of one municipality are the responsibility of several. Often the city and town boundaries are no longer relevant.

(4) These structural faults are one of the reasons why municipalities have been responding less and less adequately to the needs of their citizens.[22]

However, provision of services was what worried the commission most and remained the main reason for restructuring the municipal system: "The first task is to determine what functions municipal governments ought to perform and then to examine the type, geographic area, population size, organization and revenue sources of municipalities and the relations between the provincial government and the municipalities *that would be best suited to those functions.*"[23] It was in light of the proposed division of functions that the commission recommended replacing the existing municipal units with the eleven counties. The Graham Commission did consider alternative forms of municipal reorganization. It rejected two-tier government because the province's population was considered too small to afford two-tier municipal government, because it would result in a multiplicity of municipal authorities with overlapping responsibilities, and because it would not be conducive to effective and economical provision of services to both urban and rural citizens.[24]

The structure proposed was not to be quite as simple as eleven unitary counties. In the eight new nonmetropolitan counties the twenty-eight existing towns and twenty-five villages (plus possible additional ones) would continue in existence with elected councils but with no powers independent of their county. Basically they would be channels of communication to represent local opinion to the county council and would have the right to negotiate with the county for permission to provide certain local services under a contractual arrangement.

In the three metropolitan counties there would be no cities and only a single town. However, village councils could be created outside the more heavily urbanized areas if the citizens wished. Residents in the urban cores and in the surrounding rural areas would have the right to establish community associations to communicate local views and concerns to their county council, especially on planning matters. The associations would perform no other functions.

Nature of Provincial-Municipal Relations

In proposing a new division of responsibilities between the province and the municipalities the commission seems to have been much more concerned with improving the level and quality of services than with simplifying provincial-municipal relations. The question of municipal autonomy seems to have been of peripheral concern. Financial relations were of concern to the commission, and the reallocation of responsibility for services was viewed as simplifying provincial-municipal financial relations. By enabling municipalities to finance the provision of local services largely from their own resources the level of municipal autonomy would presumably be raised:

Municipalities are to a very large degree making mandatory financial contributions to mandatory programs prescribed by the provincial government. Yet in most municipal units the municipal financial contribution to these four general services is larger than the total municipal expenditure on all local services. In consequence, municipalities find that they can exercise very little effective control over the general services to which they contribute most of their revenues. . . .A very large part of the municipal budget, and therefore of the levy on the municipal property tax base, is outside of municipal control. The municipalities are not free to allocate this large part of their property tax revenue in accordance with their own priorities. [25]

As the data presented earlier show, more than a quarter of the revenue of municipalities in Nova Scotia in 1971 came from other governments. The bulk of this revenue was in the form of conditional grants, which diminish municipal autonomy. The commission recommended that "since conditional grants seriously infringe municipal independence, they should not be used unless a very strong case can be made for them."[26] The proposed division of responsibility for services would result in much reduced municipal revenue requirements. This is reflected in the proposals for provincial-municipal finance: eliminate all grants presently paid to municipalities by the province, eliminate personal property taxation and occupancy taxation by municipalities, and all nonresidential property taxation would be taken over by the province. The municipalities would then rely on (1) residential real property taxation, including a county-wide rate, area rates, and local improvement charges; (2) user charges for utilities; (3) unconditional grants from the province related to the value of nonresidential real property in each municipality; (4) unconditional equalization grants paid by the province; (5) part of the province's motor fuel tax; and (6) a limited range of conditional grants to upgrade urban roads, public transit, and water supply and sewerage systems.

As well as financial relations the commission was concerned with provincial agencies that supervise, direct, and control municipalities. There are presently three such agencies; the Department of Municipal Affairs, the Board of Commissioners of Public Utilities, and the Planning Appeals Board. The Department of Municipal Affairs was created in 1935 primarily to ensure that the financial position of municipalities remained sound. The department thus functioned somewhat as a financial policeman, and the report expressed concern that the department had not moved far enough beyond that role. The report was generally highly critical of the department:

Nowhere at the provincial government level is the need for reorganization and almost complete change in past and present approaches more apparent than in the Department of Municipal Affairs. . . .

In the nearly forty years that have passed since its establishment, the Department of Municipal Affairs and the municipalities have been confronted with challenges of increasing magnitude to which the Department has rarely responded in any fundamental way, and to which, in consequence, the municipalities have been unable to respond effectively.[27]

The Board of Commissioners of Public Utilities has a formidable array of responsibilities that go far beyond what its name would suggest. It is responsible not only for regulating such public utilities as electricity and determining the price of gasoline, fluid milk, and bridge tolls, but for municipal amalgamations and annexations, municipal boundary changes, and incorporating and dissolving municipalities. The Planning Appeals Board has authority to hear appeals from individual citizens or other interested parties against various kinds of municipal planning decisions and to overturn or amend the decisions.

What the Graham Commission proposed regarding supervision of municipalities was to retain the Planning Appeals Board much as it is, to remove from the Public Utilities Board responsibility for municipal boundaries, municipal incorporation, and changes in municipal status, and to reorganize the Department of Municipal Affairs and change its role from that of a financial policeman to that of a leader, advisor, and coordinator. Responsiblity for property assessment would be transferred from the department to a new Provincial Assessment Service. The department would continue to oversee the financial health of municipalities but would put greater emphasis on assisting and advising municipalities through eleven regional offices (one for each of the eleven new counties). It would also function as the focal point for all provincial-municipal relations by coordinating activities of other departments and by being the channel of communication between municipalities and all departments. It was also recommended that a semi-autonomous Municipal Board be created by the province to determine municipal boundaries (both internal and external); to establish and dissolve towns and villages; to set maximum permitted expenses of candidates for election to county councils; and to perform several other more minor functions.

The overall intent of the recommendations seems to have been to reduce the extent to which the municipalities are under the tutelage of the provincial government and shift the emphasis on providing guidance and assistance to the municipalities.

Summary

The recommendations of the Graham Commission would, if implemented, fundamentally alter the municipal system in Nova Scotia. The number of municipalities would be drastically reduced; their functions would be substantially reduced by a provincial takeover of all general services; and, while municipalities would lose a major portion of their tax base, municipal finance would be equalized. Finally, the nature of nonfinancial provincial-municipal relations would be less one of tutelage than historically has been the case.

NEW BRUNSWICK AND NOVA SCOTIA: A COMPARISON AND ASSESSMENT

It should be apparent from the above sketches of developments in New Brunswick and proposals for Nova Scotia that there are several parallels as well as several major differences. Both the Byrne and Graham reports were extremely wide ranging because their terms of reference were broad (particularly Professor Graham's). The terms of reference for both commissions were specifically financial. In the author's view this is important in explaining the thrust of the two commissions' recommendations and the premises upon which the recommendations were based. Reading the two reports gives the impression that their authors were specialists in finance and law rather than local government theory. Mr. Byrne's background was in law, and Professor Graham's in economics, specializing in provincial-municipal fiscal relations. None of their fellow commissioners were political scientists. It is worth noting that Professor Graham was not only chairman of the Nova Scotia commission but also had been a consultant to the Byrne Commission in New Brunswick.

Neither report approached the subject of municipal reorganization from a systematic theoretical perspective of the democratic purposes and value of local government. Both commissions approached the subject from the perspective of provision of services, with a shared concern that the services be provided in the most economic and efficient manner possible. In a sense their terms of reference required this approach. Hence both commissions' proposals for municipal reorganization commenced with a consideration of service functions, and only after that did they take up questions of municipal organization and structures.

Not only did both commissions first settle upon a division of responsibility for services but they did so in almost exactly the same way—distinguishing "general" from "local" services, using virtually the same definitions, and arriving at the same conclusion that the province should take over responsibility for education, health, social assistance, justice, and certain support services.

There are also strong parallels to be seen in the two commissions' recommendations regarding municipal finance, their concern with financial inequities among municipalities, and with variations in levels of service. Equalization payments to municipalities were recommended for both provinces and, by extension, there was to be provincial takeover of property assessment. The sources of municipal revenue were to be similar in the two provinces. Regarding nonfinancial provincial-municipal relations there are again similarities in the two reports. While the Byrne Commission envisaged a more powerful and perhaps more forceful Municipal Affairs Commission than the Graham Commission had in mind for its Nova Scotia Municipal Board, the semi-autonomous agencies were to have a number of functions in common.

Although there are close parallels in the two reports, the Graham Commission's proposals were far from a carbon copy of the New Brunswick report. The most fundamental difference was in the nature of reorganization of the basic units of municipal government. Here the two reports went in opposite directions. In New Brunswick the (large) counties were abolished and replaced to some extent by a larger number of small municipalities, but a large portion of the province was left without any form of representative local government. In contrast, the Graham Commission proposed a smaller number of larger counties so that the entire province of Nova Scotia would be included in one or another of only eleven municipal governments. Small municipalities would cease to exist. It is also interesting to note that both commissions presented their respective recommendations as packages, insisting that the whole package needed to be implemented if the reforms were to work properly. While the Byrne Commission's package came surprisingly close to being implemented in its entirety, the Graham Commission's package for Nova Scotia has not fared as well. Many of its recommendations have met with heavy criticism, and it is apparent that large segments of the report will not be implemented at all.

It is no more possible to summarize here all the reactions to the Graham Report than it was to summarize all the recommendations it made. The select committee of the Nova Scotia legislature established to consider the report conducted a series of public hearings in 1975. The committee's report, tabled in June that year, refrained from making recommendations, but it did summarize arguments made in the 162 written presentations it received. Regarding the Graham Commission's key recommendation that Nova Scotia be divided into eleven unitary counties, the committee wrote, "This particular recommendation was almost without exception unacceptable to all parties."[28]

Another aspect of the Graham Report that received criticism was the recommendation that each of the eleven county councils have twelve members. For the whole province this would mean a change from 616 municipal councillors, each representing an average of 1,300 persons in 1975, to 132 councillors, each representing 6,000. In the proposed metropolitan county of Halifax, each *municipal* councillor would represent an average of over 20,000 persons at a time when each member of the *provincial legislature* represented an average of only 17,000 persons. Even taking into account the proposed community associations and town and village councils, the claim that there would be a crisis of representation seems particularly valid.

The future of the Graham Report is far from bright, even though bits of it have been enacted. For example, in the past few years the provincial government has taken over responsibility for property assessment, progressively removed the costs of education from residential property tax payers, assumed responsibility for regional planning (leaving the municipalities with responsibility only for local planning), strengthened the Halifax area's metropolitan authority, and is about to revamp provincial-municipal financial relations and municipal election procedures. However, none of these measures entails the kind of fundamental restructuring of the basic units of local government recommended by the Graham Commission. The basic units remain, as noted earlier, ''highly impervious to change.''

In 1975, one member of the governing party in the Nova Scotia legislature and also a member of the select committee on the Graham Report indicated that the report is ''dead,'' that ''there is definitely no intention of thinking any more about the arithmetic in the Graham report, the boundary recommendations and most everything else in there.''[29] It is therefore likely that the Graham Report will remain on the shelf where it will have the honorable company of the only other study that proposed fundamental municipal reorganization for Nova Scotia. That earlier report was written by the editor of this book.[30] Nova Scotia's governments have not been noted for an enthusiasm to undertake such fundamental reform (although it might be argued that the municipal system in the province has not deteriorated so far as to require such reorganization). If there is ever to be a Nova Scotia equivalent of New Brunswick's municipal ''revolution,'' that day is not imminent.

NOTES

1. In Newfoundland, Canada's fourth Atlantic province, the Whalen Royal Commission Report on municipal government was made public in late 1975. Generally, the commission recommended the gradual creation of an unspecified number (perhaps as many as twenty) of regional governments to be created over a period of some thirty years. They would be two-tiered, with councillors at both levels being directly elected, and designed to greatly increase municipal self-reliance, especially with regard to finance, relative to the provincial government. A year after the Whalen Report was made public, another commission presented its final report on the St. John's metropolitan area and also recommended two-tier government for that region. By early 1979, the two commissions' recommendations still had not been put into effect. However, with

regard to St. John's, legislation has been introduced twice but then abandoned. A third attempt to create two-tier regional government for the capital city area is expected in 1979. Some tentative moves have been made to give legislative force to some recommendations of the Whalen Commission, but regional government (supported by the Federation of Municipalities) is still only a future possibility. See Newfoundland, *Report of the Royal Commission on Municipal Government in Newfoundland and Labrador* (St. John's, 18 September 1974); Newfoundland, *Third and Final Report of the Commission of Inquiry into the St. John's Urban Regional Study* (St. John's, 30 October 1976); and Peter Boswell, "St. John's: Strike Two for Regional Government," *City Magazine* 3, no. 8 (October 1978).

2. Nova Scotia, *Report of the Royal Commission on Education, Public Services and Provincial-Municipal Relations*, 4 vols. (Halifax: Queen's Printer, 1974).

3. Nova Scotia, *Report of the Select Committee of the House of Assembly on Education, Public Services and Provincial-Municipal Relations* (Halifax: Queen's Printer, 1975).

4. New Brunswick, *Report of the Royal Commission on Finance and Municipal Taxation* (Fredericton: Queen's Printer, 1963).

5. Ralph R. Krueger, "The Provincial-Municipal Government Revolution in New Brunswick," *Canadian Public Administration* 13 (Spring 1970): 51.

6. New Brunswick, *White Paper on the Responsibilities of Government* (Fredericton: Queen's Printer, 1965).

7. *Report of the Royal Commission on Finance and Municipal Taxation*, pp. 70-71.

8. Ibid., p. 116.

9. Ibid., p. 117.

10. Ibid., p. 170.

11. New Brunswick, *Report of the Task Force on Non-Incorporated Areas in New Brunswick* (Fredericton: Queen's Printer, 1976), pp. 7-9.

12. *Report of the Royal Commission on Finance and Municipal Taxation*, p. 113.

13. Ibid., appendix 01; and *Report of the Royal Commission on Education, Public Services and Provincial-Municipal Relatons*, 2: 88.

14. It is of interest to note that total municipal net budgets for 1973 (after reorganization) were still less than total municipal expenditures in 1961, the figures being $41.85 million and $45.54 million, respectively. (*Report of the Royal Commission on Finance and Municipal Taxation*, appendix 07a; and *Government and the Community: 1974 Annual Report of the Province of New Brunswick Department of Municipal Affairs* [Fredericton: Queen's Printer, 1975], p. 34.) Municipal expenditures in 1978 were more than twice the 1961 level, though.

15. New Brunswick, *1978 Annual Report of Municipal Statistics*, vol. 1 (Fredericton: Queen's Printer, 1978), pp. xiv-xvi.

16. *Report of the Royal Commission on Finance and Municipal Taxation* p. 121.

17. Ibid., p. 171.

18. Mr. F. Mooney, quoted in *The Mail-Star* (Halifax), 12 June 1975.

19. *Report of the Royal Commission on Education, Public Services and Provincial-Municipal Relations*, 2:21.

20. Ibid., 2: 64-65.

21. J. Murray Beck, *The Evolution of Municipal Government in Nova Scotia 1749-1973* (Halifax: Queen's Printer, 1973), p. 39. This was a study prepared for the Graham Commission.

22. *Report of the Royal Commission on Education, Public Services and Provincial-Municipal Relations*, 2: 15-17.

23. Ibid., 2: 19-20 (emphasis mine).

24. Ibid., 2: 22.

25. Ibid., 1: 3. The report noted that expenditure for general services by all municipalities in Nova Scotia in 1971 was 57.6 percent of total municipal spending.

26. Ibid., 2: 5.

27. Ibid., 2: 278-79.

28. *Report of the Select Committee of the House of Assembly on Education, Public Services and Provincial-Municipal Relations*, p. 10.

29. Mr. Glenn Ells, quoted in *The Mail-Star* (Halifax), 19 June 1975.

30. Donald C. Rowat, *The Reorganization of Provincial-Municipal Relations in Nova Scotia* (Halifax: Institute of Public Affairs of Dalhousie University, 1949).

United States

Elinor R. Bowen *

19

This essay concerns the patterns of municipal governance in the United States, particularly in the nation's larger cities, during a period of approximately fifteen years when the federal government has paid much attention to alleviating the problems of the poor and disadvantaged residents of central cities. It begins with an account of the legal status of municipalities, counties, and special districts and of the several legal formats for municipal government and then reports that legal structures do not accurately predict the actualities of local political patterns and that the sources of change for local political patterns tend to be extra-legal and extra-local. The second section is about the major source of recent change in municipal governance in the United States—an increased federal financial role—and its effects on local politics. A third section treats the interesting, albeit limited, movement toward neighborhood government in the larger cities of the United States. Finally, several interpretive models that attempt to account for political patterns in large cities are presented, and some predictions about future patterns of municipal governance are hazarded.

U.S. cities traditionally enjoyed considerable autonomy; political ideology has emphasized the value of viable general-purpose government at the local level. Nonetheless, the size of the federal contribution to municipal coffers, the preconditions for receipt of some federal grants, and, in one extreme instance, a federal requirement for state supervision of a municipality's expenditures, have threatened the continued vitality of general-purpose government in cities. Community control of neighborhood governments, should it come about, would extend the principle of ''grass-roots'' representation to the point where no viable government would exist at the municipal level. For these reasons, this essay also discusses the present and future of general-purpose government in municipalities.

*Associate Professor of Political Science, University of Illinois, Chicago Circle.

LEGAL STRUCTURE OF LOCAL GOVERNMENT

In the United States the major units of general-purpose government at the local level are counties, municipalities, and townships.[1] There are also many special districts, such as school districts and fire protection districts, that provide a single service to areas whose boundaries need not coincide with those of general-purpose jurisdictions.

County Governments

Counties are administrative subdivisions of the various state governments, which could, at least in principle, create or abolish them at will. Nonetheless, abolition and creation of counties is an option that is rarely exercised. Between 1962 and 1977 the number of counties in the United States remained virtually unchanged. In most states, counties are the building blocks of political parties, the normal basis of representation in state legislatures and Congress, and the channel for a large number of patronage appointments. County government generally has a large budget, reflecting receipt of substantial state monies, notably for highway construction and maintenance, and receipt of federal grants-in-aid, notably for welfare programs.

Municipalities and Townships

Municipalities and townships are in a different position. They are corporations that, like private corporations, derive their powers from charters granted by the states. But, even when the city charters call for ''home rule,'' a common grant of power to municipal corporations to frame, amend, and adopt their own charters and to exercise all powers of local self-government subject to the constitution and laws of a state, municipal and state officials confront each other regularly over how municipal governance should proceed. Questions such as cities' rights to levy new taxes, extend debt ceilings, regulate such mundane matters as roller skating on sidewalks and placement of billboards have all found their way to state legislatures and state courts. In these confrontations, municipal officials generally lose. This control by state government of local government, however, generally is done on a piecemeal basis as issues arise. Just as there is no federal equivalent to a Ministry of the Interior with overall control over state and local government, there are few states with agencies charged with general control of local governments.

Special Districts

Special districts are jurisdictions created to provide a single service, or occasionally a larger but still limited range of services, to citizens. The manner in which special districts are structured and the purposes they are intended to serve vary widely. Special districts may be governed by a state-appointed body or by a body appointed by local officials. In some instances, though not frequently, governing bodies for special districts are elected. In general, political scientists interested in implementing the democratic principle at the local level fault special districts because they are not directly responsible to a local electorate either in law or in practice. A further disadvantage stems from fragmentation of control over policy and the difficulties citizens encounter in locating responsible persons who can resolve their difficulties with respect to services provided. The advantage of special districts lies in their ability to provide a service to a population that requires it, to charge only the affected population for the service, and to do this when other governmental boundaries are inappropriate and consolidation of governmental units unfeasible.

While the number of general-purpose governments in the United States has not changed appreciably in the recent past, two patterns of change are present in special districts. First, a marked consolidation of school districts has occurred, especially in rural areas where small districts have been merged. At the same time, the number of special districts of other kinds has increased. Some of these new special districts encompass areas larger than those encompassed by the boundaries of existing general-purpose governments, such as water pollution control districts; others, such as urban renewal districts, encompass areas smaller than those of existing municipal governments. Many of the former are, in effect, a functional substitute for consolidation of general-purpose governments (see Table 19.1).

Table 19.1
UNITED STATES: CONSOLIDATION OF LOCAL GOVERNMENTS

Type of Government	Units in 1962	Units in 1979
Counties	3,043	3,042
Municipalities	18,000	18,856
Townships	17,192	16,822
School districts	34,678	15,260
Other special districts	18,323	26,140
Total	91,186	80,120

Source: U.S., Bureau of the Census, *U.S. Census of Governments, 1962,* and *Preliminary Report no. 1, U.S. Census of Governments, 1977* (Washington, D.C.: Government Printing Office).

Legal Formats for Municipal Government

Not only has the number of general-purpose governments at the local level in the United States remained essentially unchanged in recent years, their legal position with respect to state and federal government remains unchanged as well, as do the legal provisions for their internal structure. The usual form of government for U.S. municipalities remains the council-mayor form, especially in larger cities; the major alternative structure remains the manager-council form.

In the council-mayor form, authority is divided between an elected mayor and a separately elected city council. Councils may be elected from as many as fifty wards, as in Chicago, or at large, as in Detroit. Elections are generally partisan but may be nonpartisan. There is a "strong mayor" form, in which mayors, typically, prepare an executive budget, have substantial staff, appoint and remove department heads, and can veto legislation. There is also a "weak mayor" form, in which city department heads submit separate budgets to the council, the mayor lacks support staff, heads of city departments are elected to office or appointed by council, and the mayor lacks power to veto legislation. At one time, city councils were stronger than mayors, an arrangement fostered by traditional U.S. distrust of executive authority. But in recent years, most councils in the larger cities have become relatively weak "veto groups," capable of blocking mayoral action but generally incapable of initiating policy. Conflict between mayors and councils is not uncommon.

Where the manager-council form exists, elected councils hire a city manager who serves at their pleasure. The position of mayor is weak and frequently rotates among council members. In theory the manager is a professional administrator carrying out a legislative mandate, not a political leader with his own program. While there are no fixed criteria for the selection of managers, most managers have degrees in business administration, public administration, or civil engineering. They may be "promoted" from smaller to larger cities, and they are members of the International City Managers Association, which promotes professional standards and ethics. The manager form of government is the result of a movement to increase the efficiency of local government through depoliticization. But the extent of the difference in the behavior of mayors and managers remains an unanswered question, as does that of the relative efficiency of the two forms.[2]

Sources of Change

The theme for general-purpose government in the United States in the recent past has been legal and structural constancy. Nonetheless, changes of considerable magnitude have taken place in de facto patterns of governance. That political process can vary in spite of constancy in formal governmental structure has long been a characteristic, perhaps a hallmark, of the U.S. political system. To cite one popular illustration of such variation, the late Mayor Daley of Chicago was probably the strongest mayor of a large U.S. city in recent years. Yet the formal structure of government within which he operated was not significantly different from and in fact may have given him less legal authority than that in numerous other cities where mayors were in de facto terms less powerful. The explanation of Daley's strength lay not in the law but in the existence of an unusually strong Democratic party in Chicago, which ensured that the city council would approve his programs, and in a large and unified Democratic delegation from Cook County to the state legislature, which ensured that he would not be thwarted at that level either. As this case suggests, one can't understand municipal governance in the United States without reference to extra-legal and extra-municipal factors.

THE NEW FEDERAL ROLES AND THEIR IMPACTS

In the past fifteen years, the major source of change in municipal governance in the United States has been exogenous, involving both an increase in the amount of federal funds provided to local governments and the development of new mechanisms for allocating these funds. Municipal governments in the United States are political rather than simply administrative entities. Municipal officials traditionally have had greater discretion than local officials in many other nations; and the major constraints on the behavior of municipal officials have been placed there by state rather than federal agents. However, some of the mechanisms for allocating federal revenues among subnational governments have severely limited the exercise of power by local officials, especially those who are political generalists rather than functional area specialists, such that the continued vitality of general-purpose government at the local level has been threatened.

While the federal government remains, as it has been since the 1930s, the major collector of revenue, and while growth in state government expenditure has been at a greater rate than growth in expenditure by other levels of government, in recent years local governments have become the greatest spenders of revenue. By 1975-76 intergovernmental transfers constituted almost half of the revenue expended by the governments of cities with populations of half a million or more, and at least a third of the expenditure in other cities. Of these transferred payments, 1-2 percent originated at the state level, and the remainder at the federal level.[3]

Categorical Grants-in-Aid

Categorical grants-in-aid, intended as a mechanism for employing federal funds to achieve national purposes without weakening local government as much as direct federal intervention would, have long been part of intergovernmental relations in the United States. During the 1960s, as part of the domestic "War on Poverty," categorical grants became the major vehicle for transferring federal funds to subnational governments and were given to private, nonprofit groups as well.[4] Categorical grants are given for purposes mandated by Congress and monitored by the federal bureaucracy. While the rigidity of these mandates can be exaggerated and federal officials sometimes complain that recipients do not use the money as intended by federal agencies, the grants nonetheless represent a restriction on local officials' freedom of action.

To begin, the designation of the purposes for which monies can be used prevents local officials from establishing their own priorities in terms of expenditure. It is undoubtedly the case that some local officials who receive monies for public housing would rather have had monies to spend on expanding police forces and possibly that some who receive monies to augment police forces would rather have spent monies on, let us say, fire departments. As a general rule, local officials apply for and accept the maximum federal revenue

Table 19.2

UNITED STATES: TOTAL INTERGOVERNMENTAL AIDS TO CITY GOVERNMENTS, 1961-76

City Size	1964-65		1971-72		1975-76		11-Year Change
	Per Capita	Proportion of City Revenue	Per Capita	Proportion of City Revenue	Per Capita	Proportion of City Revenue	
1 million or more	$65.66	23.4%	$256.73	41.4%	$469.33	46.1%	+23%
500,000-999,999	52.11	27.2%	141.73	36.6%	270.21	45.5%	+18%
300,000-499,999	30.31	21.8%	92.53	31.3%	184.75	39.0%	+17%
200,000-299,999	22.25	17.4%	97.28	34.1%	176.06	40.7%	+23%
100,000-199,999	29.60	20.9%	74.44	29.6%	148.52	37.9%	+17%
50,000-99,999	25.58	19.5%	50.14	24.8%	100.74	32.9%	+13%
49,999 or less	15.88	20.6%	31.03	22.5%	72.21	33.5%	+13%

Source: U.S. Bureau of the Census, *Compendium of City Government Finances in 1964-65* (and *1971-72*), and *Preliminary Report no. 3, U.S. Census of Governments, 1977* (Washington, D.C.: Government Printing Office).

possible in all categories, but the pattern of expenditure would be different if local officials had control over expenditures; which is one hallmark of a general-purpose government.

In addition, federal law almost always mandates that a single, specified agency is to receive and administer a grant. Thus Oregon was prevented by the federal Department of Health, Education and Welfare from combining separate administrative units to constitute a state equivalent of the Department of Health, Education and Welfare, and another state was prevented from transferring its Bureau of Sight Conservation from the Division of Vocational Rehabilitation to the Department of Social Services because federal regulations specified that monies received be given to "a state agency primarily concerned with vocational rehabilitation."[5] Recipients' ability to reorganize administrative structure is further restricted in that some federal grant-in-aid programs call for the creation of new agencies with specified characteristics. The Equal Opportunity Act of 1964, for example, called for creation of community action agencies in cities, and the Model Cities legislation called for the creation of local model city agencies in affected neighborhoods. In both cases federal law mandated a composition that included representatives of neighborhood residents and responsibilities that cut across normal departmental boundaries.

The manner in which categorical grants are allocated among potential recipients has also led to a marked change in local political processes. Rather than allocating monies for a specified purpose in specified amounts to specified states, municipalities, or private organizations, grant-in-aid programs have called for a competition for funds among potential recipients which is resolved in the federal bureaucracy. Congress passes programs and appropriates monetary totals, and federal departments develop guidelines. Prospective recipients then must develop their own programs within these guidelines and apply for funds. Awards are made on the basis of the quality and appropriateness of the local programs described in the applications. Since the domestic War on Poverty was waged simultaneously with the war in Southeast Asia and a skirmish directed against inflation, programs were consistently underfinanced, and scarcity of funds heightened the competition among potential recipients. In order to produce the right kind of grant applications, many mayors relied on local bureaucrats who had the same training as their federal counterparts, may have known them personally, and specialized in the ways of "grantsmanship." Local directors of community development departments, in particular, became virtually autonomous figures; they were granted "hunting licenses" by mayors to seek maximal funding and were more dependent upon their bureaucratic counterparts in federal agencies than upon local officials for the success and nature of programs. Where the other aspects of federal grant-in-aid programs limit a mayor's ability to act as chief executive of a general-purpose government, competition under conditions of uncertainty created by federal programs further strengthens the role of specialists in local, state, and national bureaucracies and their allies on congressional committee staffs and in private foundations. Together they constitute what have been termed the "new machines" or "professional guilds," which are increasingly important in the United States.[6] Their increasing strength means by definition that policies will be carried out in separate functional areas with minimal generalist oversight.

Formula Grants

The alternative to categorical grants-in-aid are formula grants, which distribute monies to subnational governments on the basis of relatively fixed criteria, such as population size, and indicators of need for specific programs, such as unemployment rates or proportion of disadvantaged schoolchildren. Formula grants may be either block grants, which allocate funds for specified functional areas such as community development, comprehensive health care, employment and training programs, social services, law enforcement, or education, or they may be general revenue-sharing grants, carrying virtually no restrictions on their use. Block grants represent the imposing of national policy priorities on local government in much the same manner as categorical grants, but unlike categorical aid programs they leave the choice of programs within policy areas to local officials. General revenue sharing differs from both categoric and block grants in that it provides federal support for locally determined priorities. In terms of legal provisions for local autonomy, then, we have a continuum from categorical grants-in-aid to general revenue sharing, with block grants occupying an intermediate position in terms of national versus local control.

But there is a dichotomy between these forms of aid programs in the way that funds are allocated among subnational government units. The competition for scarce resources under conditions of uncertainty associated with categorical grants has already been described, as has the important role thus created for policy specialists in the bureaucracy. Block grants and general revenue sharing are allocated on the basis of formulas worked out in the national Congress, using criteria which in the main cannot be changed at will by local grantsmen. Thus there is no need for local officials to complete lengthy applications and rely upon local bureaucrats with training similar to that of their federal counterparts to write applications. The more important alliance here is among mayors, governors, and congressmen, not among the members of "professional guilds." As the figures in Table 19.3 indicate, the proportion of intergovernmental transfers of revenue that come in the form of formula grants has increased markedly during the 1970s, and the threat to general-purpose government in municipalities has been lessened.

Preventing Bankruptcy

While the increased use of formula grants has strengthened subnational general-purpose governments, the mechanisms developed to stave off bankruptcy in the nation's largest city have not. In 1975, the City of New York

Table 19.3

UNITED STATES: FEDERAL AIDS TO STATE AND LOCAL
GOVERNMENTS, BY TYPE (PERCENTAGE OF TOTAL GRANTS-IN-AID)

Type of Grant	Fiscal Year			
	1972	1974	1976	1978*
General purpose	1.5	15.6	11.9	11.4
Block	2.8	2.6	11.9	34.5
Categorical	95.7	81.8	76.2	54.1
Total	100.0	100.0	100.0	100.0

Source: U.S., Office of Management and Budget, *Special Analyses, Budget of the United States Government: Fiscal Year 1978* (Washington, D.C.: Government Printing Office, 1977).

*Tentative figures as proposed in the Ford administration FY 1978 budget.

confronted bankruptcy as it was unable to sell a new bond issue to private investors and therefore was unable to meet payments due on outstanding bond issues. The sale of bonds by municipalities and other local governments, including special districts, is an important source of revenue for capital improvements. The federal government has long given indirect support to this arrangement by not taxing the interest paid to bondholders. New York City was on the verge of default on bonds throughout 1975, and default was averted only by the intervention of the state and federal governments. First, the State of New York created the Municipal Assistance Corporation to issue bonds, which, it was hoped, would be more attractive to investors than city bonds. Second, the state created the Emergency Control Board, dominated by the governor and his appointees, to receive all city revenues and approve all expenditures. Third, the state passed a Moratorium Act which converted much of the city's short-term debt to long-term debt. These steps taken by the state government coupled with the advance of state revenues to the city, the purchase of bonds by municipal public employee pension plans, and some purchases by private investors could not end the danger of bankruptcy for the city. At this juncture the federal government, previously reluctant to become involved in the city's financial crisis, extended short-term loans due in 1978.[7] At this writing, the structures created by the state to oversee the city's finances remain in place, public employee pension funds remain important purchasers of bond issues, and the federal short-term loan has been renewed.

New York is not the only city in the United States to confront fiscal strain and possible default on bonds.[8] In 1978 Cleveland was unable to sell a new bond issue to private investors, and its mayor and councilmen are presently quarreling about whether to improve the city's attractiveness to investors by raising the city's income tax or by selling the municipality's electrical generating plant to the area's major private electric utility corporation. Numerous other municipalities, especially the older cities of the Northeast, are experiencing the same growth of short-term indebtedness, rising interest rates, and increasing expenditures that have been so troublesome for New York and Cleveland.

AN ATTEMPT AT DECENTRALIZATION WITHIN CITIES

Another area of change potentially as far-reaching as that associated with intergovernmental fiscal relations involves attempts to replace city-wide governance with neighborhood governance. Political ideology in the United States emphasizes the importance of general-purpose government at the local level on the grounds that such units of government can be open to citizen participation, achieve accurate representation of citizen interests, and be especially capable of responding to varied local conditions. These have been important premises in U.S. political thought. Although rates of voter turnout in municipal elections are generally lower than those for national elections, local politics are usually dominated by a single political party, and the initiative and resources for programs to ameliorate urban and other problems comes increasingly from the national government. Implicit in this emphasis on the value of local government is the assumption that local territorial units encompassed by local governmental jurisdictions constitute communities. During the 1960s this assumption was challenged by representatives of the poor and members of minority groups who asked for a decentralization of power that would substitute neighborhood government for municipal government, but they gained only a modest increase in neighborhood representation.

The Community Control Concept

"Community" is a word that has often been used loosely. In the literature on community power structures, for example, it is simply a synonym for municipality. But more careful attention to this concept would limit the term to collectivities characterized by significant interpersonal interaction, normative consensus, and possibly demographic homogeneity sufficient to support that normative consensus. In U.S. cities, patterns of residential segregation by race, religion, ethnicity, and social class are marked. Political attitudes generally are correlated with demographic characteristics, especially, and increasingly, with race. Thus the normative consensus and, of course, the numbers of persons who might be engaged in significant interpersonal interaction are more likely to be found in neighborhoods than in municipalities. In one recent book on the subject, neighborhoods were conceptualized as political communities and municipalities were viewed as analogous to empires.[9] The rhetoric of the community organizations formed in the United States during the last decade and also the thrust of some recent federal legislation, such as the Community Action Programs, locates political communities at the neighborhood level as well.

Decentralization can mean a number of things. The vesting of important powers in municipalities and states rather than in the national government is a form of decentralization. Delegation of increased responsibility to bureaucratic subdivisions is another form of decentralization. But it is a third form of decentralization, generally termed community control, that is of primary interest to those who see neighborhoods as communities and municipalities as empires. This mode of decentralization would involve a complete political process and general-purpose government at the neighborhood level. In its most radical form, this position calls for government only at the level of demographically homogeneous neighborhoods and at the level of units large enough to provide an adequate resource base for programs, normally the national level.

Such radical proposals have not been implemented, and municipal government is in no immediate danger from such ideology, but there have been some attempts at decentralization to the neighborhood level, notably the Community Action Programs.

Community Action Agencies

As part of the Economic Opportunity Act of 1965, which launched the War on Poverty, funds were to come directly from a new Office of Economic Opportunity in the White House to new community action agencies in municipalities. The architects of this legislation apparently intended to provide for adjustment of programs to local conditions without allowing unsympathetic state and local governments, especially in the South, to divert funds from members of minority groups. Local community action agencies were to include representatives of public agencies (including local government), representatives of private groups (including business, labor, and civil rights organizations), and representatives of the areas affected. CAAs were to consult with an advisory panel of community representatives. In this form, community representation was a minimal element in the CAAs, and community control was nonexistent. Since programs had to be approved by the federal Office of Economic Opportunity, the extent of delegation of authority was limited as well. However, phraseology calling for "maximum feasible participation of residents of the areas and members of the groups served," which appeared in the bill, led some, especially liberal anti-poverty workers, to heed what they interpreted as a call for community control. In San Francisco, the legitimacy of a CAA appointed by the mayor was challenged by an ad hoc citizens group, and the legitimacy of that group was challenged by several other citizens groups representing, or claiming to represent, various ethnic and racial factions.[10] But this kind of political free-for-all was not typical. In two cities where elections for community representatives were held, Philadelphia and Cleveland, the voting turnout was under 10 percent of the eligible electorate. In most cities, members were appointed, and CAAs were dominated by professional bureaucrats and other members of the professional guilds.[11]

Community Control in the New York Schools

Decentralization of schools in New York City,[12] as originally conceptualized by a panel appointed by the mayor and headed by the president of the Ford Foundation, involved dividing the school system into thirty to sixty community districts, each with 12,000 to 40,000 students. The districts were to correspond to relatively homogeneous residential areas. Each community school district was to be headed by a board of education chosen in part by parents and in part by the mayor from a list of eligibles maintained by the central school administration. Community boards were to have broad personnel powers, including the right to appoint a district superintendent, and control over teaching and other professional employees, provided that tenure rights of existing staff were protected. Community boards were to receive annual operating funds from the state and city and were to determine their own priorities for expenditure, within the limitations of city and state educational standards and union contract requirements. The central education agency, a pared down version of the existing board of education, was to set educational standards and policies, provide centralized services to communities upon request (it was anticipated that some community boards would decide to continue with existing curricula), and had operating responsibility for special educational functions such as education of the handicapped and vocational education. The period of transition to the new decentralized system was to be supervised by the state commissioner of education.

This became an extremely controversial proposal, strongly opposed by the teachers' union because of the transfer of personnel powers to the community superintendents. Where proponents had hoped for state enabling legislation, which would mandate decentralization, the legislation passed in 1968 by the state legislature permitted decentralization, at the discretion of the mayor and board of education, and permitted the mayor to appoint additional members to the board. The mayor, who favored decentralization, appointed new members and filled the vacancies on the board in order to create a pro-decentralization majority. But various developments, among them a lengthy teachers' strike, led to lesser action. Three demonstration districts were created, each in predominantly minority group districts, and the rest of the system continued to operate, as it had, under the auspices of the city-wide board of education. After another year of considerable controversy between local administrators and the teachers' union, the state legislature passed a bill in 1969 that divided the school system into thirty to thirty-three districts, each larger than the demonstration districts and with a minimum size requirement that prevented them from corresponding to homogeneous neighborhoods; provided for district boards of education which appointed district superintendents; and preserved the powers of the city-wide board of education in all respects. In effect, the result of this legislation was a limited delegation of responsibility to district school boards and district superintendents.

THE FUTURE OF LOCAL GOVERNMENT

Several themes that help to forecast the future of local government in the United States have been discussed in this essay. First, the legal boundaries and legal structure of local governments have been highly stable. Second, de jure structure is not necessarily descriptive of de facto practice. Third, the transfer of federal revenue to local units, especially when competition for categorical grants-in-aid is the mechanism and when federal aid requires external supervision, as it did in the case of the Emergency Control Board in New York, has had a dramatic effect on local political practice. Finally, a degree of decentralization of power to neighborhoods is possible. Several interpretive sketches, or models, presented by social scientists interested in city politics are useful in integrating these points and in identifying those factors which seem to be preconditions for the existence of various political patterns at the local level.

Past Political Configurations

At one time, cities could be seen as governed by political machines in which party "bosses," sometimes serving as mayors and sometimes not, acted as brokers arranging a mutually advantageous exchange among not only citizens, who offered votes in return for jobs and social support, but also legitimate businessmen, who offered financial support and sought municipal services, and illegitimate businesmen, who offered financial support and sought protection from strict enforcement of the law.[13] This type of political machine declined after the 1930s with the advent of national social security and welfare programs, the attainment of middle-class status by formerly impoverished immigrant families, regularization in the provision of municipal services to legitimate businessmen, and state and federal regulation of business, which transferred businessmen's interests to those governmental levels. Only illegitimate businessmen, since law enforcement remains primarily a local governmental function, legitimate businessmen involved in real estate and retail businesses, which depend on local land-use policy, and city employees continued to be interested in exchanges with the local boss.

The replacement for this classic version of the political machine is alleged to have been a "machine of the incumbents," in which voters who were loyal and in some sense "captive" Democratic voters because of their attachment to the policies of the national Democratic party provided votes for incumbent Democratic office holders at the local level without getting anything in return from local politicians.[14] Whatever electoral competition existed was decided in party primary elections, where low turnout guaranteed the dominance of voters who were public employees. Local politicians were also linked in reciprocal exchange with national politicians through their roles in political parties since parties in the United States are organizationally stronger at the local level than at the state or national levels and the support of local party officials is needed to gain nomination as a candidate for higher office and to stimulate voter turnout for state and national elections.

A More Recent Political Configuration

More recently a "new machine" with access to the resources to be gained from intergovernmental transfers of revenue seemed to be in the offing. These new machines, or "professional guilds," center on the functional specialists who hold professional positions in national, state, and local administrative agencies and their colleagues on the staffs of congressional committees and private foundations.[15] The functional areas of housing, urban renewal, welfare, and education are most often mentioned as those in which such new machines or professional guilds have developed. Looked at in transaction model terms, the new machine involves a mayor who offers federal dollars to voters and gains these dollars from professionals employed at the national level by supporting professionals at the local level. Allocation decisions by professional guild members, as in the case of categorical aid programs, is one prerequisite for the existence of this political configuration.

A Future for Decentralization

The machine of the incumbents and the new machine share a common central role for public employees, albeit different kinds of public employees who have gained their positions in different ways, through patronage appointments in the case of the machine of the incumbents and through membership in professional guilds in the case of the new machine. Community control and the categorical grants which have sometimes encouraged community control have never been preferred by patronage appointees. As the case studies of the community action agencies and school decentralization indicate, professional guild members have sometimes supported decentralization to the neighborhood level as a planning or consultative mechanism but have strongly opposed community control when it threatened their professional networks. Neighborhoods can be conceptualized as an instance of the special district and, like other special districts, their future is more likely to be as administrative units largely immune to popular control than as units controlled by communities. Current proposals to use neighborhoods in large cities as aggregates for the reporting of statistical data in the 1980 census point to such usage.

The Future for General-Purpose Government

The classic political machine and the machine of the incumbents, whatever their other shortcomings, are instances of general-purpose government in municipalities. The new machine is not. While it is unlikely that the preconditions for the classic machine will exist in U.S. cities again, both the machine of the incumbents and the new machine are possible. There is no reason to anticipate that federal financial grants to subnational governments will diminish. It is also clear that the use of categorical grants makes the new machine a likelihood and that formula grants are compatible with the machine of the incumbents. The choice between these alternatives, in spite of local repercussions, will be made at the national level on the basis of national political concerns. National decisions about the magnitude of appropriations for domestic programs also will have important effects on the viability of general-purpose government below the national level. Federal assumption of full fiscal responsibility for expensive functions, an increase in general revenue sharing, more block grants to support essential municipal services, and even categorical aid programs if they specify support for essential local services could all relieve fiscal strain in cities without a duplication of the scenario in New York with its external veto over all municipal expenditures.

NOTES

1. Nomenclature for units of local government in the United States varies among the states. Following the practice of the Bureau of the Census in its publications, the term "county" is used here to refer to similar units with other names, such as parishes in Louisiana; municipality refers to the lowest level of general-purpose government for an incorporated area, whether that jurisdiction is officially known as a municipality, a town, or a village. Townships encompass smaller jurisdictions, incorporated or unincorporated, and are contained within counties. In some areas, particularly where the constituent units are unincorporated, townships are an important unit of local government; in other areas they are unimportant as functions are performed by municipalities or counties. Counties and municipalities exist in all states; townships do not.

2. For examples of research findings on this question, see Lloyd M. Wells, "Social Values and Political Orientations of City Managers," *Social Science Quarterly* 48 (December 1967): 443-50; Charles R. Adrian, "Leadership and Decision-Making in Manager Cities," *Public Administration Review* 18 (Summer 1958): 208-13; Robert L. Lineberry and Edmund P. Fowler, "Reformism and Public Policies in American Cities," *American Political Science Review* 61 (September 1967): 701-16.

3. Distinguishing federal from state monies in intergovernmental transfers to local government is difficult because most federal funds intended for local government are channelled through state governments. Official reports of state transfers to local government exaggerate the role of state government in that these figures include monies levied by federal government, and official figures on direct federal grants to localities are a gross underestimate because funds channelled through states are excluded.

4. For a more extended discussion of the differences between post-1960 federal programs and earlier ones, see James L. Sundquist with the collaboration of David W. Davis, *Making Federalism Work* (Washington, D.C.: Brookings Institution, 1970), pp. 1-6.

5. For additional examples of federal restrictions on restructuring state and local government, see Harold Seidman, *Politics, Position and Power* (New York: Oxford University Press, 1970), pp. 30-31.

6. Theodore J. Lowi, "Machine Politics: Old and New," *The Public Interest* 9 (Fall 1967): 83-92.

7. This account follows that in Donald H. Haider, "Fiscal Scarcity: A New Urban Perspective," in *The New Urban Politics*, eds. Louis H. Masotti and Robert L. Lineberry (Cambridge, Mass.: Ballinger, 1976).

8. For data on fiscal strain and its correlates, see Terry Nichols Clark, et al., "How Many New Yorks?" Mimeograph (Chicago: University of Chicago, April 1976).

9. Milton Kotler, *Neighborhood Government* (Indianapolis, Ind.: Bobbs-Merrill, 1970). Kotler emphasizes that neighborhoods have historically been political communities, not communities in a sociological sense. His examples are primarily drawn from the Eastern United States.

10. This account of events in San Francisco follows that of Richard Kraemer, *Participation of the Poor* (Englewood Cliffs, N.J.: Prentice-Hall, 1968), pp. 25-67.

11. A synopsis of several studies of community action programs is available in Robert L. Lineberry and Ira Sharkansky, *Urban Politics and Public Policy* (New York: Harper & Row, 1971), pp. 278-303.

12. For extended discussion of the decentralization of schools in New York with an emphasis on political and ethnic factors, and from an advocate's perspective, see Mario Fantini, Marilyn Gittell, and Richard Magat, *Community Control and the Urban School* (New York: Praeger, 1970).

13. The classic analysis of such machines is Robert K. Merton, *Social Theory and Social Structure* (New York: Free Press, 1968), pp. 125-36.

14. Scott Greer, *Governing the Metropolis* (New York: John Wiley, 1962), pp. 65-74.

15. See Lowi, "Machine Politics," and Seidman, *Politics, Position and Power*, on these points.

Japan

Nobushige Ukai*

20

When comparing the Constitution of 1890 with the postwar Constitution of 1947, several differences become evident. These differences indicate the progress of constitutional ideas and institutions during this sixty-year period of social and political development in Japan. This progress is particularly evident when viewing the issue of local autonomy. In the old constitution there was no article on this subject, whereas in the new constitution an entire chapter, Chapter 8, is devoted to guaranteeing the basic principle of local self-government. However, the mere declaration of this basic principle does not guarantee its realization either in the form of law or in its political and administrative implementation.

The purpose of this short article is to explain to Western readers how far the Japanese have come in achieving the goal of local self-government during the thirty-year period since 1947. By extracting a few basic questions from among the many that could be asked, this article will attempt to explain the nature of local autonomy in the particular social and political context of contemporary legal and administrative development in Japan.

IMPACT OF CITIZEN PARTICIPATION

First, the impact of the citizen's participation in local administration should be clarified. It cannot be denied that the basic principle of democracy requires direct citizen participation in various areas of governmental functions. Title 2, Chapter 2 of the Local Autonomy Law stipulates, among other things, two important provisions of popular participation. One (Article 12) deals with the right of initiative in legislation and the right of popular control of local government affairs. The other (Article 13) is concerned with the popular power of dissolution of the local assembly and the dismissal of not only its members from office but also members from various other administrative offices and boards.

*Professor of Constitutional and Administrative Law, Senshu University.

Local autonomy, as stipulated in Chapter 8 of the Japanese Constitution as well as in the Local Autonomy Law of 1947, implies that citizen participation in as wide an area of the local government as possible is necessary. In Title 2, Chapter 5 of the Local Autonomy Law, the requisites, procedures, and validity of citizen participation are stated in greater detail. The first section of Chapter 5 provides for two cases of popular control: control of legislation and control of other government activities. One-fiftieth or more of the voters of a particular public entity have a right to initiate a petition demanding enactment, amendment, or abolition of a bylaw. However, bylaws relating to the levy or collection of local taxes or to the collection of assessments, charges, or fees are exempted from the control by popular initiative. One-fiftieth or more of the electors may also present a petition to the inspection commissioners demanding that the performance of services in the locality or services within the powers of the chief executive, administrative commissions, or commissioners be inspected.

The second section provides for, first, the dissolution of the local assembly. One-third or more of the total voters may present a petition demanding dissolution, whereupon the election commission shall put such a petition to a vote. The local assembly shall be dissolved if a majority vote so demands it. A similar procedure is applied for the recall of the chief executive, members of the assembly, and administrative boards and commissions. Several of these initiatives have taken place in the past, showing the awakening of the people's political consciousness in local self-government.

As far as the election of the chief executive of a local public entity is concerned, the present constitution provides for his direct election by the citizens of that particular community. This practice is based on the idea that by providing the people with more chances of participating directly in the election of officials, their political consciousness will be strengthened. Although it cannot be asserted definitely that the direct election of the chief executive is more democratic than his election by the assembly, as far as the nomination of the local chief executive is concerned, the 1947 Constitution adopted the former as the more proper practice in postwar Japanese local government.[1]

In 1952, the Diet passed a law providing for revisions of the Local Autonomy Law. These revisions abolished the system of directly electing the heads of special wards in the Tokyo metropolitan government and replaced it with a system of elections by ward assemblies along with the consent of the governor. The new system of electing the chief executive of wards in the Tokyo metropolis did not fulfill its expectations because of the difficulties in obtaining a working majority from among the conflicting sects of the various political parties. In the early 1970s, confronted with the multiplicity of environmental dysfunctions and other urgent affairs, citizens of the wards demanded efficient and responsible ward officials headed by the chief executive whom they themselves nominated. This materialized in the ward bylaws in which the nomination of the chief executive was to be conducted by popular vote and then confirmed by the ward assembly. Following the enactment of this type of bylaw by the wards, the National Diet passed a revision of the Local Autonomy Law (enacted on 1 April 1975), abolishing Article 281-3, Clause 1, which provided for the election of the chief executive by the assembly. The same revisional law reallocated services between the metropolitan government and the ward offices, with the former managing those services which need to be handled uniformly, while the latter administers those services connected with the daily life of the people.

The assumption that more direct participation of the people in the business of local government will better serve the principle of local autonomy will have to be verified by future experience.

STRUCTURAL PROBLEMS

Japan is composed of forty-seven prefectures, which are subdivided into cities, towns, and villages, all of which are guaranteed local autonomous government under the provisions of the Constitution of 1947.

Many small towns and villages faced financial difficulties because of the newly entrusted administrative duties, such as compulsory education and a local police force. Therefore, an amalgamation of towns and villages took place throughout the country. Professor Shoup's commission advised in its *Report on Japanese Taxation*, submitted in 1948, that cities, towns, and villages be encouraged to amalgamate if they found it too difficult to maintain schools, police, and other like activities independently. In 1953 a bill for Encouragement of Amalgamation of Towns and Villages was submitted to the Diet and was enacted in October of the same year. By the end of June 1961, the number of cities, towns, and villages had decreased from 9,895 to 3,472. At the same time, the amalgamated towns became cities, thus increasing the number of cities from 285 to 556. It is generally believed that the amalgamation strengthened local communities as units of central government rather than as units of local autonomous government. Even now there is a basic problem of how to make local government truly autonomous.

During the 1950s, a new demand arose for the amalgamation of the prefectures. This demand grew stronger after the amalgamation of cities, towns, and villages was completed. The boundaries of the forty-seven prefectures had been formed during the period of political modernization in Japan in the late ninetenth century and were based on the feudal territories then existing, but their boundaries were drastically altered, changing the territories into larger prefectural areas as local units of the central government. After 1947 they were reorganized into full-fledged local autonomous government units that were comprised of thousands of communities on the city, town, and village levels.

When the amalgamation of the cities, towns, and villages was nearly completed in the late 1950s, the demand for the amalgamation of the prefectures was not far behind. There are presently two variations of this demand. One favors a simple expanson of the prefectural area without changing the nature of the prefecture as the unit of local autonomy. The other contends that through amalgamation a prefecture should change to a new organization which has as its intrinsic duty the local administration of the central government. The new organization would be called either *Dō* or *Shū*. Therefore, this new plan is commonly called "The Institution of the *Dō Shū* Plan."

In 1957 the Local Government Research Committee submitted its official report on *The Reform of Local Government*. Its majority opinion proposed abolishing the prefecture as the local autonomous unit and establishing a new local entity between the cities, towns, and villages on the one hand and the central government on the other. This unit was called *chihō* (district). The chief executive of the *chihō* would be appointed by the prime minister, with the consent of that district's assembly. The minority opinion opposed the establishment of a new local agency and instead advocated the preservation of the prefecture as the local autonomous entity, with the condition that several of the prefectures should be unified in order to meet the need for rapidly extended local administration. This difference of opinion has continued, with no practical solution yet emerging. However, in 1969 the Kansoi Economic Federation proposed a new *Dō Shū* plan, which was followed by the Japan Chamber of Commerce and Industry's tentative plan for a new local autonomous agency.

According to the existing laws, the merger of prefectures is to be executed by national law. In order to avoid any criticism that the merger was initiated by the national government rather than the local autonomous agencies, a bill was submitted to the Diet whereby the merger of prefectures could be conducted not only by national law, but also by the autonomous decision of the prefectures themselves. This plan was suggested originally by the Local Government Research Committee in 1965. However, the bill did not receive the consent of the National Diet. Therefore, at the present time, the plan is still pending, without any consensus as to whether the merger of the prefectures is desired or not.

THE LOCAL AUTONOMY ISSUE

As mentioned above, in today's social and political context the daily problems of public administration on issues of environmental dysfunctions and other urgent affairs give rise to a need for even greater participation by the people. Therefore, the citizens of local communities are requested to solve their own daily problems, such as air and water pollution, traffic congestion, and the like, through direct participation in government.

Several questons have arisen regarding the local autonomy issue. How valid are the local bylaws when they come into conflict with existing national acts? According to Article 94 of the Constitution, local public entities have the right to enact their own regulations (which are called bylaws) only "within law." If there is a conflict between the bylaws of a community and national law, bylaws are invalidated. For example, there are cases where antipollution bylaws set stricter regulations than those of the national law. Unless national law has a provision to permit a bylaw to stipulate stricter provisions (for instance, Article 4 of the Air Pollution Prevention Act), it may prove difficult to assert whether or not the bylaw is valid. But judging from the importance of local autonomy in the fight against pollution, bylaws may be permitted to stipulate stricter regulations in this area.

Second, citizen participation may result in the inclusion of agreements between industry and the local autonomous entity, whereby control of the sources of pollution within the industrial compound is stipulated. But is it permissible for private persons to obligate the public entity to perform public functions such as control of pollution solicited merely by private contract and not by law? If this is interpreted as a valid contract, it can only be so because citizen participation is indispensable in solving the whole environmental question.

Finally, what procedures should be adhered to in order to invite citizen participation in the local government, for instance, if an administrative decision is needed for the selection of a site for a garbage incinerator? Does the chief executive of the local government need the consent of the citizens of the community to reach a decision? Should consent come from the citizens of the whole community or a part of the whole, that is, just those from the area where the site is to be located? If the chief executive tries to listen to the whole community, he may be able to arrive at some definite decision benefiting the community as a whole, but he may have strong dissent from those who reside near the incinerator site. In Article 8 of the National Land Use Planning Law of 1974, there is a provision stating that a public hearing is necessary when the heads of towns, cities, and villages plan the use of local land. But this is only a guarantee for a hearing. The decision-making process itself still rests in the hands of the executive, with the consent of the local assembly.

The Local Autonomy Law has been going through a period of trial and error in the political development of postwar Japan. The people's consciousness of self-government appears weak in the face of the long-established strength of the hierarchical power structure of the central government bureaucracy. However, I feel it to be not only important but indispensable to democracy to strengthen the autonomy of the local public entities in the whole power structure of present-day Japan.

NOTES

1. Article 93 of the Constitution says, "The chief executive officers of all local public entities . . .shall be elected by direct popular vote within their several communities."

WESTERN EUROPE

AUSTRIA

ENGLAND AND WALES

SCOTLAND

NORTHERN IRELAND

FINLAND

SWEDEN

WEST GERMANY

Austria

*Harald Rossmann**

21

In 1962 an amendment to the Austrian Federal Constitution was designed to make the system of local administration more coherent. It established communal self-government and decentralized administrative functions according to the fundamental rules of democracy. It also confirmed the right of municipal authorities to administer local matters, which were to be expressly specified by federal or state legislation. Federal or state authorities may also delegate other administrative functions to the municipalities, which then act as agents of these authorities. Moreover, the municipalities may operate economic enterprises, and they have the right to manage their budgets independently within the framework of the constitutional, federal, and state laws.

The representative organ of each municipality is the "communal assembly" (*Gemeinderat*). Its members are democratically elected by the community and are not bound by any instructions (principle of the free mandate). The communal assembly is entrusted with significant powers concerning financial administration and, as a rule, deals with appeals against decisions of the mayor or other organs of local administration within its own sphere of competence. For specific matters, subcommittees may be established to prepare proposed decisions of the communal assembly. These subcommittees also may be delegated decision-making powers by the assembly.

Similar functions are carried out by the "communal board" (*Gemeindevorstand*), composed of the mayor, his deputies, and additional members elected by the communal assembly. The mayor (*Bürgermeister*) represents the community externally and is also the chief executive of the municipality for matters of self-administration as well as of allocated powers. In the latter case, he may

*Assistant in the Faculty of Law, University of Vienna, and Secretary to Dr. Franz Bauer, one of the three Ombudsmen for the Republic of Austria. This essay is based on a paper by E. Melichar and H. Rossmann, "Current Trends in Local Power and Authorities in Austria," prepared for an international conference on local government sponsored by the Polish Academy of Sciences in Warsaw in 1974.

be bound by the instructions of federal or state authorities. The administrative arm of the communal executive is the "municipal office" (*Gemeindeamt*), subordinate to the mayor. It serves chiefly as an auxiliary institution for the communal organs but may also be set up as a separate municipal organ with decision-making powers.

PROBLEMS OF URBANIZATION

Population growth in urban areas has seriously increased the housing problem in the cities. Considering that in 1975 nearly 4.8 million Austrians were living in urban areas (4.3 million in 1961), it is imperative to overcome the shortage by long-term planning and building and to improve public transport.

The problems of urban planning can be solved only by coordinated measures at the regional level. Unsatisfactory industrial accommodation and bad working conditions in urban areas concern not only the urban planning authorities. Successful provision for industrial development can be achieved only by coordinated planning schemes of local, federal, and state authorities and private enterprise, taking into consideration the general economic development, suitability of possible locations, special demands of industrial units, and effects of development on the environment. The final goal of such activities will be the separation of housing and working districts to improve their accommodation to the environment.

Nevertheless, the renewal and expansion of city regions has certain limits. One barrier is the image of a city, and especially its center, as a product of historical development and, like Vienna or Salzburg, as conglomerations of architecturally valuable buildings and other amenities. The preservation of the city's image is often incongruent with the modern needs and functions of urban centers. This problem presently is the source of citizen initiatives and public discussions in favor of the preservation of amenities.

Another barrier is the rapid expansion of cities leading to a closer relationship with the surrounding rural areas. Citizens of adjacent rural communities work in the cities and use urban shops and entertainment facilities. At the same time, some city dwellers choose the more agreeable countryside for second homes. This overlapping of rural and urban interests and regions forces the communal authorities to coordinate their development schemes and budgeting and to create common planning associations or find other forms of "peaceful coexistence."

In spite of the tendencies mentioned above, the present organizational structures of urban management have been able to cope with the problems arising from urbanization. In contrast to the rural communities, cities governed under their own charter not only perform local tasks and certain delegated matters, but, as the first level of federal and state administration (see Figure 21.1), also discharge the functions of district administration. This gives them considerable regional influence. The creation of such administrative

Figure 21.1
THE ADMINISTRATIVE SYSTEM IN AUSTRIA

Federal Administration   **State Administration**

Direct federal administration   *Indirect federal administration*
by special federal authorities   by state authorities
e.g. financial administration

LEVELS

III. Federal minister of   III. Competent federal
      finances   minister, if administrative
                                       appeal is extended to him
                                       by federal law

II. State department for   II. Governor of a state   II. State government
     financial administration

I. District finance authorities I. Political district adminis- I. Political district ad-
                                      tration (or cities governed   ministration (or cities
                                      under their own charter)   governed under their
                                                                        own charter)

Local Government
(matters of predominantly local interest)

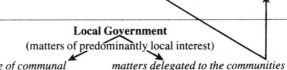

autonomous sphere of communal   *matters delegated to the communities*
competences   *by the federation or the states*

no appeal to the state authorities;   appeal extends to the federal or state
certain supervisory competences of   authorities;
the federal or state authorities;
regularly two levels;

II. Local communal assembly

I. Mayor   I. Mayor

units by state law requires the approval of the federal government and is
feasible only if the urban district has a population of at least 20,000. The
federal capital, Vienna, is an exception as it combines municipal self-government, district administration, and state government. For this reason, the
communal assembly also functions as the state legislature, the city board
functions as the state executive, and the mayor is also the governor of the state
of Vienna.

Some minor improvements in urban administration have been achieved in recent years. The administrative staff of city departments now have to meet certain educational standards (high school, university degree) and have to pass special examinations on administrative management, law, and economics to qualify for tenure of employment. This selection system in the civil service provides a skilled staff of specialists.

In some of the bigger cities attempts have been made to keep data relevant to public administration permanently accessible by means of electronic data processing. For the time being, this has proved practicable for administrative tasks that can be computer-programmed easily and cheaply, such as financial administration, public health service, and election lists.

STRUCTURAL REFORMS OF RURAL COMMUNITIES

The functions of rural governments have increased, especially regarding the development of housing, industry, and holiday resorts for the growing non-farm population. The problems of most rural areas stem from their poor agricultural organization, lack of dynamic industrial centers and efficient central communities, underdeveloped tourist trade, and inadequate communication systems, energy and water supplies, and provisions for health, education, and housing, as well as the natural barriers resulting from the mountainous character of the country. To overcome these problems a regional development policy is required for each state territory and its individual sections in order to plan development and set priorities for reform. Administrative matters within the competence of the federation enable the federal authorities to carry out a nationwide development policy which is mainly concerned with the improvement of infrastructures: railways, shipping and aviation, highways, postal, telephone and telegraph systems, electrical plants, and the control and conservation of lakes and rivers. The regional development programs issued by the state governments prescribe measures for development within the state territories in accordance with the nationwide federal planning. Local planning is confined to the municipal area and is bound to the regional programs.

Every society based on the division of labor creates "central places" that provide public and private institutions, goods, and services for the population of the surrounding area. Central places differ in the number and capacities of their institutions and services and in the size of their catchment areas. The framework of central places is one of the most important structural principles of spatial development and for the administrative reform of territorial divisions.

The services of the capitals of the Austrian states (except Eisenstadt) are now so good that their catchment areas are identical with the state territories. On the district level, the situation is not as good. In 1965, of eighty-one central places that are the seats of district administration, only forty supplied their catchment areas with adequate institutions and services; sixteen of the remaining forty-one communities did not even satisfy minimum standards. On the communal level, centers are often underdeveloped as a result of population loss and poor economic conditions. Many of the smaller local units could not keep abreast of the socio-economic development of the past twenty years. The underdeveloped condition of rural centers called for structural reforms designed to increase their administrative capacity.

A program based on central places created the legal prerequisites for the various planning authorities to work together on the coordination of public institutions (offices, law courts, schools, and so on); local planning for central institutions within the community; economic development and working places; residential and commercial building, if aided by public funds; traffic arrangements, road building, and public transport; health services, providing at least one doctor for each local center and hospitals for some district centers and all regional centers; and schools to provide adequate education in rural areas.

In accordance with this program, the competent authorities decided that certain services should be planned and administered over a wider area than that of the existing local communities. Each community should have a town center with at least a medical doctor, an elementary school, a post office, a parish church with regular services, entertainment facilities, a bank, an office of the agricultural association, a municipal office, shops, and private services. Research had shown that most small communities had none of these essential services. The chief aim of local reform therefore was to enlarge the communal area and raise the average municipal population to at least 1,500, thus making public and private services economically feasible and management more effective.

THE AMALGAMATION OF LOCAL COMMUNITIES

Amalgamations of communities in Austria take two forms. Annexation means the extension of a town or city to incorporate all or part of neighboring communities; merger is the creation of a new local entity covering the territory of two or more existing communities. These patterns of amalgamation, analyzed by Professor Arne Lemans, may be achieved by different legal methods and lead to different results. In Austria, merged or annexed communities cease to exist as independent corporate bodies, and their administrative functions, civil rights, and property are shifted to the new local unit. Voluntary amalgamation, arranged by communities themselves, requires their agreement on the financial and civil relations of the new administrative unit and presupposes the approval of the appropriate state government. If communities whose amalgamation is advantageous from the viewpoint of regional planning cannot agree on the terms, compulsory amalgamation may be carried out by state law or administrative measures. Amalgamation is feasible only if this change is necessary for the satisfactory performance of local administration. The economic and cultural interests of the communities concerned must also be taken into consideration.

SUBREGIONAL AND REGIONAL ENTITIES

Some state laws enable the municipalities to form "administrative unions" (*Verwaltungsgemeinschaften*) composed of two or more local communities which assign certain administrative functions to the subregional level. This allocation of municipal duties does not create legally independent bodies, since the unions have only auxiliary functions and act only as agents of the municipalities. These unions generally carry out the common administration of such matters as accounting, collection of land taxes, fire protection, and water and electric supplies.

"Communal associations" (*Gemeindeverbande*) for specific purposes of administration can be formed under the appropriate legislation. These are territorial corporate bodies at the subregional level which have decision-making powers delegated to them by the participating communities. The latter thus relinquish their authority to perform the services concerned. Such administrative units can be instituted either by an act of state legislation or by administrative measures of the competent authorities. Communal associations have been established for such purposes as district welfare, hospital administration, social services for invalids and accident victims, sanitary districts, school districts, water supply, and an index of Austrian citizens.

Finally, the combination of public and private planning entities that exist in Austria should be mentioned. Public and private planners may cooperate on projects by discussion with one another and with the people or institutions concerned. This informal coordination may be institutionalized by the creation of private planning associations composed of representatives of the competent authorities, private enterprises, the communities, and citizens concerned. The organization of such bodies is determined by private association law and provides only an instrument of informal coordination, since each member of the association remains responsible for carrying out its own part of the project. Nevertheless, the experience with an association of this kind in Styria (the regional development project of Aichfeld-Murboden) and in Vorarlberg (the regional planning association of Bregenzer Wald) has been successful enough to justify the conclusion that in future this organizational pattern for development planning will be used more frequently.

Britain: England and Wales

Alan Norton *

22

The reorganization of local government provided for in the Local Government Act 1972 and completed in 1974 was remarkable for its speed and comprehensiveness. Only London, where new authorities had replaced the old under the London Government Act of 1963, was excluded from this major reconstruction. Elsewhere in the country the former county, county borough, non-county borough, and rural and urban district councils vanished into history on 31 March 1974, succeeded by new county and district authorities with new sets of powers and functions.

Simultaneously, certain functions were shifted from local authorities to new central government agencies. Such personal health functions as had remained with local government after the establishment of the postwar National Health Services were transferred to a new system of local health authorities, and new regional water authorities took over from local authorities the statutory responsibilities for water supply, drainage, and sewage disposal. It might be expected that such extensive reforms would have been the result of long and careful preparation. As described later in this chapter, a formidable program of research and study was mounted by a well-qualified royal commission. There were, however, wide discrepancies between the changes the royal commission considered necessary and the form the reorganization eventually took. British two-party politics intervened, issuing in a polarization of policies in which the royal commission's recommendations, espoused by the Labour government, were killed by its Conservative successor.

This chapter is grouped with others on the reorganization of the basic units in different parts of the world. This raises the problem of whether or not there can

*Senior Lecturer, Institute of Local Government Studies, University of Birmingham and co-author of: Joyce Long and Alan Norton, *Setting up the New Authorities* (London: Charles Knight, 1972).

be said to be basic units in the British local government system. Other sections of the book cover county and metropolitan areas. Nevertheless, it seems appropriate in the British case to deal with all main types of local authority—counties, districts, metropolitan and nonmetropolitan—together. The various types of authority are interdependent, and to write about them separately would require much duplication. Also, a distinction between basic and non-basic units would be false. County and district have parallel statuses. Either they are both basic or else neither is. The description of the new system as a two-tier system can be misleading if it is seen as implying that the district tier is subordinate to the county tier or that the county tier is built on district "building blocks."

HISTORICAL BACKGROUND

The conflict of interest between types of local authority had kept to the fore problems of local government boundaries since the early part of the present century. The pattern of settlement was always well ahead of the pattern of organization. The case for radical reform had been advanced regularly since the 1920s. Clearly the human geography, pattern of life, functions of local authorities, and nature of local administration had changed so drastically since the last decades of the nineteenth century that the need for new institutions was easy to argue. Nevertheless, reorganization was a prickly matter for central government: it so obviously affected the interests of party rank and file. Central government's attempts at reaching a consensus among associations on the form reorganization should take were conspicuously unsuccessful. The issue was referred three times to commissions with independent, nonpolitical status. The 1945-49 Boundary Commission diagnosed a need for radical change, but the Labour government of the time refused to give the terms of reference and support needed to proceed with the necessary reforms. The commission dissolved, and after nine years a new commission was established to recommend piecemeal reforms, area by area. Some of its recommendations were carried through, in particular some for setting up and extending county boroughs. It failed to obtain the abolition of England's smallest county (Rutland, population 25,000) since the pressures the county interests were able to bring upon a Conservative government were too strong. More seriously, the government could not be persuaded to give the commission the powers to consider the reorganization of South Lancashire and its conurbations in the comprehensive way they felt to be necessary.

The responsible minister in the new Labour government, Richard Cross-man, accepted that the dispirited commission was unable to fulfill a satisfac-tory role and decided on its dissolution. Piecemeal, marginal solutions had proved unacceptable to two commissions. The obvious way forward was to carry out a thorough appraisal of the reforms required. Once Crossman was convinced of the need for major reform, he acted with a speed uncharacteristic of previous ministers in this area. A royal commission was appointed under the chairmanship of Lord Redcliffe-Maud with instructions to consider the structure of local government in England, outside Greater London, "and to make recommendations for authorities and boundaries, and their division, having regard to the size and character of areas in which these can be most effectively exercised and the need to sustain a viable system of local democracy." The eleven commissioners were adjured to prepare their report with all possible speed.

In 1969 the Redcliffe-Maud Commission produced the case for reform, which was accepted both by the Labour government, which held power until 1970, and the succeeding Conservative government, which found itself in a position to carry through reform. The party political division occurred not on the diagnosis but on the remedy. The royal commission's recommendations for action, although never implemented, are likely to be of at least as great an interest to the student of local government reform as the less radical pattern of reorganization finally adopted. We shall therefore describe both the commission's recommendations (which would, in general, have been implemented by the new Labour government had it won the 1970 general election) and the system that was adopted. But first we must describe the critique of the existing system developed by the commission.

REPORT OF THE REDCLIFFE-MAUD ROYAL COMMISSION

The basis of the commission's case for reform is to be found in studies prepared by its research team. A research appendix shows how the isolated nineteenth-century industrial town, which then formed a natural unit for government, had been superseded by urban areas, which often bear little resemblance to the older administrative areas and have complex relationships with the surrounding countryside. Population in the rural areas was shown to be growing faster than that in urban areas, although the growth was mainly to meet urban needs. Rural and urban populations were relating increasingly to the same resources for leisure, trade, and employment. The urban-rural dichotomy had become meaningless for planning purposes. Other studies showed the extent of the exodus of the professional and managerial classes from the urban center. Wealthier people were emigrating increasingly to so-called rural areas, thus depriving urban authorities of ratable value and of their contribution to the city government. The emigration was particularly marked among the 25-44 age group. The industrial conurbations of the Midlands and the North were shown to suffer from the main concentrations of social problems—domestic overcrowding, obsolescence of housing, and lack of basic amenities. They suffered particularly from the age of their industrial and housing stock, traffic congestion in a road network not designed for the transport problems generated by the mobility and congestion of late twentieth-century life, accompanying health problems, and a concentration of welfare problems. Local financial resources had declined as the need for social invest-ment increased. It was obvious that in so far as local authority boundaries could be widened to bring together the areas of new and affluent settlement with those of urban decay, the problem of maldistribution of financial and human resources could be partially overcome.

The commission collected a great volume of evidence from some 2,156 witnesses. Almost all the evidence accepted the need for radical change and most of it related closely to the problems of resources and needs indicated in the research studies. Typically, it made the case for more effective authorities and argued that such increased effectiveness should be sought in larger areas and stronger resources.

The commission rested its case for change, first, on the obsolete division of town and country that took no account of their interdependency and in particu-lar the division between county boroughs and counties that "builds into the system a division of interest where, in fact, there is a common interest" and made the proper planning of development and transportation impossible. It considered the division of responsibility in the counties between the county and district authorities a great weakness in view of the need for a common rational approach to problems of planning and the integration of personal social services. It found the size of most local authorities inadequate for their responsibilities. It considered the relationship between local authorities and the public unsatisfactory, largely because the public found the system too complex and difficult to understand. A more comprehensible system would, they believed, result in more accessibility, interest, awareness, and involve-ment. It found the relationship between central and local government unsatis-factory because of the great heterogeneity of local authorities. Better mutual understanding and a clearer division of function and responsibility would be possible only if local authorities were fewer and stronger in resources and in their capacity to deal with community problems. It felt the need to overcome the antagonism and division among local authorities through a new structure that would make possible a single association to look after all local authority interests and speak with one voice to central government.

The commission based its recommendations on a view of local government functions that had developed strongly in England during the previous few years, a view which attributed to local government a general responsibility for the development of the local community as opposed to a miscellany of agency functions for central departments. The purpose of local government, according to the commission,

is to provide a democratic means of focussing national attention on local problems affecting the safety, health and well-being of the people, and of discharging, in relation to these things, all the responsibilities of government which can be discharged at a level below that of the national government (para. 30); wherever local choice, local opinion and intimate knowledge of the effects of government action or inaction are important, a service is best performed by local government, however much it may have to be influenced by national decisions about the level of service to be provided and the order of priorities to be observed (para. 29).

The commission argued that the representative nature of local government is at least equal in importance to its efficiency; it is vital, in combination with Parliament, ministers, and departments, to sustain genuine national democracy (para. 28). The relationship between local and central government is fundamental to a sound system of national public policymaking. Another fundamental need is adaptiveness, the ability of local government to "adapt itself without restriction to the present unprecedented process of change in the way people live, work, move, shop and enjoy themselves" (para. 1).

The commission recommended redrawing the map of local government. The system of 79 county boroughs, 45 administrative counties, and 1,086 county districts should be replaced by 61 new main units comprehending urban and rural elements within their boundaries. Fifty-eight would have single or "unitary" authorities responsible for all main services. Three authorities centering on conurbations, however, would share the provision of services with second-level metropolitan districts. In these three metropolitan areas, planning, transportation, and major development would be at the metropolitan level, while education, personal social services, health, and housing would be at the district level. The commission put forward a series of general principles that guided it to its specific recommendations. The first was that "each local authority should be responsible for a continuous area that makes, as far as practicable, a coherent social and economic whole, matching the way of life of a mobile society and giving the authority the space it needs to assess and tackle its problems" (para. 243). Areas proposed in the evidence they received were tested for coherence by the use of journey-to-work statistics, the pattern of bus services, shopping surveys, newspaper circulation areas, and whatever other information that seemed useful. While the commission favored all-purpose authorities, it considered it to be essential that environmental services—land-use planning and the whole field of transportation—be under single control. It also argued that the "personal services"—education, personal social services, and housing—should be under a single authority.

The pattern of reorganization was largely determined by the size of authority regarded as most suitable to provide the enhanced effectiveness in planning and operation the commission sought to establish. Six research studies had been initiated to explore possible relationships between size of organization and performance. Four of these examined the relationship between size variables and output indicators. The results were negative. Predictably the available output measures were unsatisfactory, and they lacked any common denominator. Had the statistical analysis thrown up significant relationships between the size variable and the indicators, it seems doubtful that these would have supported any valid conclusions. The two remaining studies rested on the judgment of central government officials from the Department of Education and Science and the Home Office regarding a selected range of characteristics of local authorities. They indicated that the best performance for education services tended to be found in authorities with populations of over 500,000 and for children's welfare services in authorities between 350,000 and 500,000. The "least efficient" authorities had populations below 200,000. The methodology of the studies is vulnerable to criticism. Nevertheless, they reinforced a substantial weight of official evidence from central departments and local authority associations that pointed in the direction of the commission's sweeping conclusion that "the minimum size for all the main services is, desirably, a population of some 250,000" (para. 94). The commission was also of the opinion that there was a maximum size for efficiency—not much above 1 million population—at which the costs of large-scale management offset the benefits of scale. The report reinforces this argument that all-purpose authorities can be too large by suggesting that such size would mitigate against democratic control and a popular "sense of belonging" to the authority. It was this upper limit on size that justified the two-tier system for the three metropolitan areas. Metropolitan area authorities were regarded as necessary for socio-geographic reasons, but these were too large for the effective running of the personal services, which were, therefore, allocated to districts with populations generally above 250,000.

The Commission felt that there remained a need for two other types of authority. There should be regional or provincial councils (eight for the whole of England) to settle the broad economic, land-use and investment framework for the planning and development policies of operational authorities. These would not be directly elected but made up of members appointed by the local authorities of their respective areas. This recommendation foreshadowed the complex proposals of the report of the Kilbrandon Commission on the Constitution. Of more immediate interest was the recommendation for a system of small local councils "to foster the pride and interest of local communities" (para. 282). The main purpose of these councils was not administrative but to voice the opinions and wishes of the community. They therefore differed in principle from the traditional parish councils.

REACTIONS TO REDCLIFFE-MAUD

The concept of the "unitary," all-purpose authority overriding urban and rural distinctions was central to the commission's recommendations. It was also the target of some formidable critics. It was interpreted as the expansion of the county borough principle at the cost of the annihilation of the counties and the districts. The attacks on the report by the County Councils' Association and the Rural District Councils' Associations were all too predictable. It was seen as a survival battle. The Labour government, however, accepted the central recommendations with two or three important modifications: an increase in the number of metropolitan areas to five, the transfer of the education service in the metropolitan areas from district to area level, and the addition of a system of area councils within unitary authorities to bring administration closer to the community. Their program would have established the new system by 1973.

The Conservative opposition tended to favor the arguments of the counties and districts that were fighting for the alternative of the reformed two-tier system that had been rejected so decisively after lengthy examination by the commission. The Conservative shadow minister for local government, Peter Walker, consulted Conservative branches in the provinces and found bitter opposition to the unitary principle. He used the consultations as the basis for the formulation of a quite different pattern of reorganization on a two-tier basis, ready for implementation should his party win the election.

Thus opinion polarized, with the royal commission and the Labour government schemes on one side and the alternative government, the counties, and the districts on the other. The larger county boroughs naturally favored the unitary solution, but their association, the Association of Municipal Corporations, was characteristically ambivalent on the matter since the Labour plan would eliminate the smaller, non-county boroughs which formed the majority of its membership. The alignment of the urban authorities, with the Labour Party on one side and the county and the rural district authorities with the Conservative Party on the other, was, of course, traditional and was becoming more marked as party politics increased its grasp on local authorities and as the emigration of the upper social groups from the city to the county had the effect of making the cities more homogeneously working-class and reinforcing the Conservative leadership in the counties.

THE CONSERVATIVE SOLUTION

The Conservative victory in the 1970 general election determined the future of English and Welsh local government. Peter Walker, moving directly from the shadow minister role to the new senior ministerial post of secretary of state for the environment, determined to implement Conservative policies with all possible speed. A White Paper, issued in February 1971, set out proposals that were, with relatively minor changes, embodied in the Local Government Act 1972. The White Paper echoes the royal commission's report in its statement of the case for reorganization. It sought a rationalization of boundaries to bring together town and hinterland, with authorities large enough to be effective and a logical grouping of services. Where it departed from the commission was in its stress on continuity: "The theoretical advantages of radical restructuring must be weighed against the advantages of building on the existing well-established organisations." "Local Authority areas should be related to areas within which people have a common interest—through living in a recognisable community, through links of employment, shopping or social activities, or through history and tradition."

The case advanced for a two-tier system was that different services and functions require different areas. The administrative advantages of large authorities, it was argued, are required for some purposes while closeness to the community is required for others. In accordance with these arguments, the starting point for reorganization was the existing county and district structure. By means of amalgamation and some cutting and patching, existing county boundaries were modified so that, after absorbing the county boroughs, all had populations well above the 250,000 minimum laid down by the Royal Commission. Of the thirty-eight counties outside the conurbations, only four exceeded a million in population. Subsequently, the Isle of Wight, with a population of little more than 100,000, succeeded in having its special case for county status recognized, bringing the number of nonmetropolitan counties to thirty-nine. There were, however, two important innovations in the county system that accorded more closely with the royal commission's principles. Three large county boroughs based upon estuaries—Bristol, Kingston upon Hull, and Teesside—fitted badly into the plan based on existing counties. Their amalgamation with historical counties would have unbalanced the counties and done violence to the principle of common interests between urban centers and their hinterland. With much argument, three new counties were defined of a nature according to some extent with the city-region concept, the counties of Avon, Humberside, and Cleveland.

The case for the unity of the conurbations was also allowed to override county tradition. The royal commission's recommendation for three conurbation authorities for the West Midlands, Merseyside, and Greater Manchester was accepted. The boundaries of these authorities, however, were drawn rather tightly around the built-up areas so as to salvage as much as possible of the areas for surrounding traditional counties. This, of course, blatantly offended the socio-geographic arguments for unity of function and interest and raised doubts from the start about the capacity of these conurbation authorities (named metropolitan counties) to plan physical development in a rational way. Three additional metropolitan counties were planned for areas where the royal commission had found insufficient unity of interest—South Yorkshire, West Yorkshire, and Tyneside (later to be called Tyne and Wear). Inconsistently, these three included extensive rural areas and were more collections of city regions and town regions than unities in themselves. It is not surprising that the plans were criticized fiercely by the social geographers, who found in the failure to change socially irrelevant traditional boundaries and the drawing of the metropolitan boundaries the loss of a unique opportunity to match up social reality and the administrative map.

The White Paper was accompanied by proposals for metropolitan district boundaries. These preserved the biggest city areas with little change but have created some problematic patchwork-quilt authorities in a number of cases. The minimum of 250,000 population was overridden, but there was great reluctance to see these districts, which were to be responsible for education and the personal social services, drop below the 200,000 scale. It was, therefore, necessary to form new authorities by amalgamation, and in some cases more than twelve small authorities had to be joined together to create a new district of sufficient size. The practical and political problems were acute, yet these new authorities remained small in comparison with the county and big city local education and social service authorities. Despite their particular need for the ablest of administrators, they were not competitive in recruitment of staff and lacked the capacity of the larger authorities to appoint specialists.

In the case of nonmetropolitan districts, their boundaries were drawn by a statutory Boundary Commission appointed by the secretary of state. The guidelines given to the commission were that for all except sparsely populated areas, new districts should have populations of between 75,000 and 100,000; the minimum size was to be 40,000; large towns were not to be split up and so might have populations of more than 100,000; and regard was to be paid to the wishes of the inhabitants, the pattern of community life, and the effective operations of local government services. In many cases the guidelines precluded the commisson from amalgamating a town with its hinterland. There was, in fact, no time to draw boundaries that were not already on the map. It was intended that after a few years the commission, which is a permanent instrument of boundary review, would work on the reconstruction of boundaries to produce a pattern closer to socio-geographic realities. The argument of the need for closeness to the community contained the main rationale for this type of district, yet there appears little rationale for the size limits imposed and, it is tempting to ask, if there are compelling reasons of democracy for a smaller scale for housing administration and local planning, for example, why do not such reasons also apply in the metropolitan areas?

The split of functions is given in Table 22.1. The details cover Wales as well as England. Although Wales was the responsibility of a separate government department and outside the scope of the royal commission, its problems of reorganization, which had been the subject of fierce controversy and plan and counterplan for several years, were dealt with in the same legislation. The areas involve extensive amalgamations except in the case of Glamorganshire which was split most controversially into three.

It will be seen from the table that the grouping of services sought by the royal commission for the metropolitan authorities was achieved in part. The main housing function is placed separately from the personal social services, and this has perpetuated problems connected with the housing of handicapped groups. The most problematic split of functions is probably that in planning, where the districts are made responsible for most of the detail and control while the counties must ensure the effective design and implementation of strategic guidelines. Since planning functions previously had rested with the counties and county boroughs, the allocation of key powers to the new districts resulted

Table 22.1
DISTRIBUTION OF FUNCTIONS—ENGLAND AND WALES, 1974
(EXCLUDING LONDON)

Metropolitan Areas		Nonmetropolitan Areas	
Counties (6)	*Districts (36)*	*Counties (47)*	*Districts (333)*
(Pop. 1,320,000 to 2,790,000)	(Pop. 177,390 to 1,096,000)	(Pop. 109,284 to 1,426,410)	(Pop. 24,532 to 425,203)
Strategic planning and control	Local plans and most development control	Strategic planning and control	Local plans and most development control
Highways Traffic Passenger transport	Minor road maintenance	Highways Traffic Passenger transport co-ordination	Minor road maintenance Passenger transport undertakings
Land drainage Small-holdings Refuse disposal	Land drainage Refuse collection Local sewers	Land drainage Small-holdings Refuse disposal	Land drainage Refuse collection Local sewers
Limited housing powers	Housing	Limited housing powers	Housing
Town development	Town development Environmental health	Town development	Town development Environmental health
Parks, recreation, museums, arts	Parks, recreation, museums, arts	Parks, recreation, museums, arts	Parks, recreation, museums, arts
	Education Libraries Personal Social Services	Education Libraries Personal Social Services	Libraries in some cases in Wales
Fire Police Consumer protection		Fire Police Consumer protection	Consumer protection in some cases in Wales

in a multiplication in the number of planning authorities, competition between counties and districts for scarce staff, and quite new problems of coordination and control.

The fiercest reaction from the district level was on the loss of highways responsibilities. This loss and the loss of sewerage responsibilities to the new water authorities deprived them of the technical work that had been central to the interests of rural districts and county boroughs in the past. In this field and certain others the government provided in the new legislation for authorities to transfer activities to other levels by means of agency arrangements and eventually adopted a scheme whereby it acted as umpire for a limited period on agency claims by one authority on another.

Despite the fact that both the royal commission and the Conservative government sought a system under which responsibilities would be clearly allocated, it will be seen that for a number of functions powers exist concurrently at county and district levels. If coordination in planning and implementation and lack of duplication is to be achieved, the new system requires a high level of mutual understanding and cooperation between authorities. British local authorities have not been conspicuously successful in their ability to cooperate with each other in the past. Early experience of the working of the new system does not suggest that they will be more willing to cooperate in the future.

COMPOSITION OF THE NEW AUTHORITIES

So far we have been concerned predominantly with the problems of size, boundaries, and the allocation of functions. This concern reflects the emphasis in the official documents, parliamentary discussion, and public debate. It may be argued that the connections are somewhat remote between these issues of size and boundaries and the goals by which the changes were justified, such as increased effectiveness, responsiveness, and adaptability. Government can act more directly by modifying the composition of local authorities and the legal constraints on their organization. The changes of this kind incorporated in the new legislation and in accompanying orders have not radically changed the nature of the British local authority, but they are more substantial in scale and implications than the sum of previous reforms in this century.

The aldermanic system whereby a quarter of the members of each county and borough council (one-seventh in the London boroughs) had been not directly elected but chosen by the elected representatives, has been abolished. The removal of this somewhat undemocratic feature has swept away a larger proportion of the older, high-status members of councils. It was expected that pressure from the Maud Committee and others concerned with efficiency for smaller councils along with the reduction in the number of councils (excluding London) from 1,391 to 422, would cause a drastic reduction in popular representation. In the event there has been a reduction of about one-third in the number of elected representatives. The size of councils remains generally large, ranging up to over a hundred members. There are, on average, about 2,000 electors to a councillor in the nonmetropolitan districts and about 10,000 electors to a councillor in the nonmetropolitan counties.

A new system of allowances to councillors is sufficiently generous to allow some of the more heavily involved members to rely upon it for a major part of their income. Payments relate to the number of attendances on approved council business and range from two or three hundred pounds for some back-bench members to two or three thousand pounds for some chairmen. Publicity about members' earnings from this allowance has been wide, and it may be surmised to have increased the pressure on councillors to regard their work as a job rather than a hobby. Leading councillors are in an awkward halfway house between an unpaid amateur and a salaried professional role. This status appears to have an impact on officer-councillor relationships. Because of it and the pressure on resources, councillors may have become more rather than less involved in detail, as the Committee on the Management of Local Government, chaired by Redcliffe-Maud before he was ennobled, had hoped.

The Maud Committee, which reported in 1967, argued strongly for the reduction of the legislative constraints on local authority internal organization. Local authorities were required by statute to appoint certain committees and officials. These requirements were reduced in the 1972 legislation. A large number of trivial controls have been abolished, local authorities now suffer less interference on planning matters, some local powers have been clarified or expanded, the small amount an authority can spend for the benefit of its area beyond the services for which it has statutory provision has been substantially increased, and the government auditor's powers in connection with local authority expenditure have been narrowed. It is too early to appreciate the effect of these changes. They have to be seen not only in relationship to the change in the financial climate and the wrestling of central government with ways of gaining some control on public expenditure without prejudicing its policies for social investment, but also in the light of developments in local management practices.

A NEW APPROACH TO MANAGEMENT

We have already noted that a principal concern, if not the principal concern, of the originators of the reorganization was enhanced effectiveness. The recommendations of the Maud Report of 1967 and the application of corporate management concepts to local authority problems by J. D. Stewart and others in the following years, along with some experimentation with new ideas in the field, had a deep influence on a working group set up by the Department of the Environment and the Associations in 1971 to provide guidelines for organization and management in the new local authorities. The unitary concept of the royal commission was clearly influenced by a systems view of local government which emphasized the interdependency of the diverse activities of local authorities and the need to plan comprehensively for goals that could not be achieved by any one service in isolation. The ''Bains'' Working Group sought adequate means of integration for authorities to achieve corporate planning. They followed the Maud Committee's Report in recommending a limitation on the number of local authority committees and departments. Committees should relate to program areas rather than the activities of different departments. More significantly, major instruments for corporate planning were necessary in every authority: a central policy and resources committee, a chief executive without departmental responsibilities, a management team of chief officers which he would lead, and a system of interdepartmental working groups implementing tasks in a general system of corporate planning and implementation. The setting up of a personnel function was also recommended, along with a number of other ideas which have been widely influential.

These recommendations have had an immediate and direct impact on the organization of the new authorities. In many cases authorities adopted the Bains suggestions as blueprints to be followed with little modification. Space does not allow us to examine the results in detail, and it is too early to judge their success. In general it can be said that the new structures and organization have been designed to fulfill ambitious but problematical corporate objectives. They demand but cannot of themselves achieve extensive attitude change by participants at the councillor and officer level. These changes would have been much easier in a period of expansion. In a period of severely checked growth, their attainment is especially difficult.

EVALUATION: THE COSTS AND BENEFITS OF THE REORGANIZATION

The reorganization may be evaluated in terms of criteria suggested by the royal commission and in the White Paper. It has certainly failed to achieve administrative areas in many cases in which urban centers and inderdependent rural hinterlands can be treated as a unit: this objective was sacrificed for administrative convenience and respect for tradition. It has not created a system easier for the public to understand or with which they can easily identify; in fact, the dispersal of local government functions among not only new counties and districts with strange and unfamiliar names and areas but also among new health and water authorities appears to have created a more difficult set of problems for the public. Accessibility is less and involvement is less. The interests of different groups of authorities remain antagonistic and have to be reconciled at the center. Central government can still divide and rule, and the problems of coordinating central and local policymaking and planning, although perhaps simpler because of the reduction in the number of local units, still demand new solutions in terms of machinery and changes of attitude. Although the traditional identities which the Conservative White Paper sought to preserve have been maintained in most of the counties, only a minority of districts are recognizable as historical entities.

The biggest questions relate to democratic responsiveness and managerial effectiveness. The first may have increased through the effect of the reorganization in increasing the impact of party politics, since in amalgamation of party and nonparty authorities the party system almost invariably spreads to the whole. Before reorganization, 46 percent of the 1,166 local authorities for which satisfactory information is available had full party political systems. Out of 330 of the 422 new authorities, 63.7 percent have party political systems.[1] It is, of course, a controversial issue outside the scope of this chapter how far party organization enhances the democratic quality. Voting figures have not improved. With regard to effectiveness it is possible only to comment in general terms about the perceived costs and benefits of the reorganization. The changes led to a heavy strain on resources. Workloads expanded dramatically, a heavy loss of staff could not be made up economically by recruitment, and new standards and new establishments tended to be set at more generous levels. Competition among authorities for the rarer categories of staff was expensive. Staff commissions set up with an oversight on staff matters had only a marginal effect on the inflationary tendencies of such a period, concerned as they were more with protection of staff interests than with economy. Political and other interpersonal problems which occur when people find themselves grouped, willy nilly, with others from organizations with different values and attitudes exacted heavy costs in time and mental energy.

The costs are a great deal more visible than the gains at the time this is written. Unfortunately, no attempt has been made to quantify them. There is no evidence that the costs of reorganization were ever systematically considered by the royal commission or by the central government. One royal commissioner described the commission's proposals as an "unpriced menu." The Conservative menu was likewise unpriced, although its less radical nature was partly aimed at reducing the risks and uncertainties. As regards the benefits, the argument must be that these are long term.

There are two other major issues that the changes have left unresolved and that are often seen as constituting threats to the survival of the new system. The first is the means by which the extensive authority can relate to and respond to the needs and reactions of the local community. Successive governments have been conscious of the need to establish local forums for communication and possibly for administrative purposes at a local level in the urban areas, which lack a traditional pattern of parish councils. Plans for area management within large urban authorities have a closely related purpose: the scale of the new authority is too wide for dealing with some basic problems of representation and efficiency. A second issue is a representative basis for regional planning and for other functions where the regional scale has clear advantages. Existing authorities often appear to be defensive on these matters since they feel that new levels of representation would greatly increase the complexity of the existing two-level system, which already makes heavy demands on time and capacity to cooperate, and that they might even lead to the elimination of the district or county level since they would provide a means to move their existing services closer to the community or to the national level.

In retrospect, the unitary concept of the royal commission would have provided a much better stock on which to graft new developments. It could almost certainly have coped more rationally with problems of efficiency and priorities in an economic situation in which growth must be sharply contained. It is a sad fact that the carrying out of the reorganization was haunted by a sense of great opportunities missed—even among county and district staffs who, it might be thought, would have had most to lose in a system of all-purpose authorities.

NOTE

1. Figures supplied by R. A. W. Rhodes.

Britain: Scotland

*C. S. Page** **23**

Immediately prior to the 1975 reorganization, local government in Scotland was effected through 430 elected local authorities, which were widely disparate in functions and population (ranging from 300 to 945,000). The structure had ancient roots, going back to the twelfth century, but was essentially a nineteenth-century creation designed to deal with social and community problems at the turn of the century. The development of local government in Scotland paralleled, but did not follow exactly, the pattern for England and Wales. For most purposes the four major urban areas (Aberdeen, Dundee, Edinburgh, and Glasgow) were treated as separate autonomous local government units termed counties of cities (similar to the county boroughs of England and Wales). Elsewhere a two-tier system applied, comprising 33 county councils (two pairs being combined for many purposes), 197 town councils of burghs, and 196 district councils for the "landward" (nonburghal) areas of all counties but two. The burghs themselves were of two kinds, large and small—the descriptions being statutory and reflecting status and powers as well as (in general) size and population.

The electoral basis of these authorities was firm but not consistent. Some burghs were single units for electoral purposes, but the larger burghs were divided into wards, each returning three or a multiple of three councillors. Counties were divided into electoral divisions. All councillors were elected for three years. In the counties of cities and the large and small burghs, one-third of the councillors retired each year, necessitating annual elections, but in the counties and districts the whole council retired together at the end of three years. Although each county council was, for certain major purposes, operational also in the areas of the burghs within its boundary, there was no direct election of county councillors within the burghs; instead, each town council selected a number of its members to act as burgh representatives on the county council. In the district councils the membership comprised the county council-

*Formerly Senior Lecturer in Public Administration, University of Strathclyde.

lors for the county council electoral divisions in the district and district councillors elected for the electoral divisions or wards in that district.

There were also large numbers of joint committees, for example, for police and fire services, created voluntarily or otherwise under statutory powers. It was also possible for one authority to use another as its agent for certain purposes, but these powers were used very sparingly in most areas. A reorganization of the water supply service in 1968 removed this function from local authorities and replaced it (until 1975) with regional water boards made up of local authority members. There were also other joint boards.

Powers existed to permit boundary alterations as between one authority and another. Sporadic use was made of this facility, and applications normally were accompanied by deep opposition by the yielding authority. A simple procedure existed for appropriate parts of a landward area to be created as a small burgh, and this procedure was followed in a few instances. For a small burgh to be elevated to large burgh status, parliamentary authority was required and this occurred only once.

Internally, the uniform arrangement for handling the variety of services placed with each class of authorities was to set up a committee for each service and linked with separate service departments, each headed by a chief official with specialist qualifications and experience. This structure was complemented by functional committees and departments (the clerk's department, a finance committee, a finance department, and so on). Councillors were unpaid but were entitled to allowances for travelling, subsistence, and financial loss. In most cases, their work as councillors was essentially part-time.

The financial basis of local government resembled that in England and Wales, with differences reflecting the structure, functions, and traditions in Scotland and the existence of a separate legal system. The majority of the running expenses of local authorities was financed from taxation, both central and local, the proportion being higher than in England and Wales. In terms of expenditure, the significant services were education and housing (see Table 23.1). Capital investment by local authorities relied initially on loan finance for the most part, the cost of debt servicing being a critically high proportion of total local revenue expenditure. The volume of debt had risen by some 10

Table 23.1
LOCAL GOVERNMENT IN SCOTLAND: AGGREGATE REVENUE
ACCOUNT (NON-TRADING) 1972-73

Expenditure	Percent	Income	Percent
Education	39.6	Fees, rents, etc.	16.2
Housing	22.5	Taxation—	
Other services	38.1	Government grants	52.6
		Local taxation	31.2
Total	100.0		100.0

Source: Adapted from Local Financial Returns, Scotland, 1972-73 (London: Her Majesty's Stationery Office, 1973)

percent per annum since the late 1940s. The local property tax—the rates—was based upon the annual letting value of land, buildings, and so forth, beneficially occupied, and the inherent limitations of this tax, unique to local authorities, was one cause of the subventions from central government by way of grant aid.

THE ORIGINS OF REFORM

The 1975 reform of Scottish local government differed in historical origins from that in England and Wales. In particular, there was lacking the conflict between town and country which followed from the creation of the counties and county boroughs. Reform in Scotland was seldom a topic of major public concern, though by the early 1960s it had become increasingly apparent that some attention was necessary. The first postwar official document appeared in 1963, as a result of a government-sponsored review of the structure—an interesting comment on the limited amount of dissatisfaction with the structure in local government itself.

The 1963 White Paper presented several suggestions and opened them up for comment by the associations of local authorities and other interested groups.[1] The document noted that changes had occurred in the location of population and in the role local authorities were required to play and deduced that the existing structure was inadequate. The proposals were based upon a two-tier system of enlarged counties for major purposes and an amalgamation of burghs and landward areas for local services. A "First Report" on the White Paper was issued in 1964, recording the views of a working party of local authority officials.[2] The deliberations of this group took place behind closed doors, and there had been no public discussion or debate. The report revealed disagreement over the principles upon which the structure of local government should be based, and there were other matters to divide the associations of local authorities to whom the group reported. There was also strong public opposition to the secretive method adopted for analyzing and discussing the whole problem of reform, but the objections to the absence of public debate died down when it became clear that local government in Britain generally (apart from London) was thought due for thorough and independent investigation before any reforms occurred. In 1966 a Royal Commission for Scotland was set up under the chairmanship of Lord Wheatley with similar terms of reference to that for England. The commission reported in 1969 and the main substance of their report forms the basis of the 1975 reforms.[3]

In spite of the lack of widespread criticism of the existing system, the Wheatley Commission had little difficulty in detecting cogent reasons for reforming local government. They reiterated the fact that the structure had not changed (and could not change of its own volition), whereas the society served and to be served by local authorities had changed markedly since the structure was evolved. They noted that there were many small authorities and that local boundaries paid little heed to the contemporary social, economic, and operational realities. Frequently services were provided by the wrong kind of authority over the wrong size of area, interauthority friction was inherent, and organization could be duplicated. Staffs were not deployed to the best advantage, and financial resources did not match duties and powers. Moreover, local authorities relied upon (and accepted) much central direction and control; thus local government lacked significance in the public mind, and an apathetic electorate was the result.

It is difficult to imagine a more devastating survey—in marked contrast to the views (indeed, often the complacency) of many who served in voluntary or career capacity in local government and who later were often to argue strongly against any change at all. However, the commission was at pains to point out that it was the dedication and skill of those in the system that had allowed it to continue to run as well as it had. Another, albeit indirect, point made by the commission was the old-fashioned approach to management which existed and could be rectified only through concurrent structural and functional reforms.

INVESTIGATION AND RECOMMENDATIONS

The Commission's Approach

The commission began by asserting their belief in the need for local government to administer local services and retain the principles of democracy. They rejected a number of suggestions involving ad hoc organizations or the transfer of services to central government and offered four fundamental objectives of reform: first, power, to give local government a more important role in society; second, effectiveness in the exercise of functions in the interests of the people; third, local democracy, leaving decision making with an elected council directly accountable to the electorate; and, finally, local involvement. In their search for a matrix into which to fit these unexceptionable objectives, the commission surveyed the scene from two complementary viewpoints, the functions placed with local authorities and the areas over which these functions would operate. The two features combine in a local government structure.

The commisson entered into a detailed analysis of functions, though their research was less intensive than that undertaken by the commission for England. Their analysis produced six groupings, each requiring different sized areas, and these were eventually reduced to two—large-area and small-area functions. The wide-area services were seen to be strategic planning and associated functions and the protective, personal, social, and housing services. The remaining services—local planning, environmental and amenity functions, housing improvements, and libraries—were thought better suited to local provision. The analysis of areas and communities in Scotland revealed four levels—the parish, the locality, the shire, and the region. Ultimately, the shire, renamed the district, and the region were adopted, and the functions allocated between the two. A minority of the commission was in favor of using the locality as the second level, based upon placing all planning functions with the major authorities. Other possibilities, such as creating an all-Scotland authority for certain functions (for example, water) were rejected. The pattern proposed was uniform, two-tier, and superficially tidy, but its various inherent anomalies required special adjustments. It was obvious that the dramatic reduction in the number of authorities implied in the recommendations would lead to critical comment about remoteness, and an arrangement was suggested to supplement the local authorities by means of nonexecutive community councils acting as sounding boards for local opinions and channels of communication between councillor and elector. Again, although the commission attempted a neat separation of functions between region and district, some powers were to be shared (notably planning), and others, such as recreation and tourism, were to be concurrent, and in these spheres close and positive liaison between local authorities at the same and different levels would be inevitable.

The commission's recommendations extended to the future councillors and to internal structures. All councillors were to be elected directly for single-member wards or divisions and to hold office for four years, the whole council retiring together at that time. The maximum size of a council would be seventy-five, and councillors would get substantial salaries. The recommendations on internal organization and management structure built upon foundations laid down in the Maud Report[4] for England and Wales, and anticipated the Bains[5] and Paterson[6] Reports; suggestions included extensive delegation (including delegation to officials), a council "management" committee, a chief executive, and local administrative committees in the regions.

Legislation and Further Action

The Labour government went out of office in 1971, before making public its reactions to the commission's report. The White Paper[7] of the Conservative government that followed accepted in substance the recommendations and most of the detail. It was in the course of the passage of the necessary legislation that modifications, some of which were at best expedient, at worst mischievous, were made. Nonetheless, the reforms in their final statutory format took the substance of the Wheatley Report and completely changed the previous local government system. The new arrangements became effective in 1975.

The new authorities comprised fifty-three districts instead of thirty-seven (or forty-seven as in the White Paper), nine regions instead of seven (eight in the White Paper), and three islands authorities (as in the White Paper but not in the commission's recommendations). The allocation of functions followed the recommendations in the main, but there was an adjustment of the planning (and other) functions in the remoter areas, and most importantly, housing was placed with the district authorities on the English model (see Table 23.2).

Table 23.2

LOCAL GOVERNMENT FUNCTIONS IN SCOTLAND

Level	Number	Planning	Personal, Social	Housing	Protective	Environmental	Amenity
Regions Islands	9 3	Major planning, transport, water tourism	Education, social work		Fire, police, consumer, coast works		Recreation, culture
Districts Islands	53 3	Local planning, building control, tourism		Housing		Public health and sanitation	Recreation, culture

Although the commission advocated a more modern approach to management in local government and there was already a massive body of evidence and advice in this field for England and Wales, it was decided to undertake a specific report on management for the benefit of Scottish authorities, and this appeared later as the Paterson Report. It broke little new ground but analyzed in much greater detail the essential requirements for satisfactory operation of the management arrangements, as well as the theory and basic tenets of corporate management. Local authorities were offered a flexible approach through the presentation of a basic management plan with appropriate adaptations to handle the problems of large regions, small districts, and the islands authorities. The fundamental concepts were straightforward, though (as ever) differing slightly from those advocated for England and Wales in other reports.

At the elected-member level, the primary innovation was a policy and resources committee concerned with the overall view of the authority and having three subcommittees for finance, manpower, and planning and development. The principle of service committees was continued (and the education and social work committees remained a statutory requirement), but they were to work concurrently with the policy and resources committee. This committee would be linked directly with the paid staff through the new post of chief executive. This, the most senior post, would carry no departmental responsibilities (except perhaps in the smaller authorities) and would be strengthened by formal association with the director of finance, director of administration, and any director of policy planning in an "executive office." In addition, there would be the now familiar team of senior chief officials.

Implicit in such management schemes was a new role for the councillor who was seen by the commission to have two complementary tasks: first, the individual task of acting as a representative for an electorate and as a channel of communication; and, second, joining in the collective task of reaching policy decisions and monitoring their implementation. A further implication was that extensive schemes of delegation by councils to committees and by council or committees to chief officials (and by chief officials to their staffs) would be formulated and applied. The practice of internal delegation, never to the fore in the past, had to be achieved if the recommended management structures were to operate at all, let alone smoothly and to the benefit and satisfaction of the public, and if corporate management was to be more than a set of pious hopes. The moribund authorities and the new authorities overlapped for twelve months, though the latter did not become operational until the former's demise. Most of the new authorities adopted the new management structures, following (more or less) the recommendations in the Paterson Report.

A PRELIMINARY ASSESSMENT

Any pattern of local government represents a compromise involving the reconciliation of conflicting factors. The commission's task of integrating the pull toward large local authorities to fulfill the effective exercise of functions and the pull towards small authorities to meet the test of a viable system of local democracy demanded an act of judgment which as yet can be appraised only in the same terms. It is not difficult to propose other solutions to the problem facing the commission, but it is impossible to demonstrate that these alternatives (assuming that they could be translated into workable schemes) would be superior or inferior to the 1975 arrangements. Further, the whole of the new local government system in Scotland must come under scrutiny again as the plans for devolution (or whatever) to a Scottish Assembly gather force and form. Thus, no more than a tentative appraisal can be offered at this early stage.

The two most striking characteristics of the new authorities are their size—however measured—and the allocation of certain functions between the two tiers. The enlarged size of the new authorities (and it is worth recalling that even the smallest of the new authorities may still seem relatively large to local people) produces a new remoteness of the councillor from his constituency. With only one councillor (not three) for each ward, each carries full responsibility for the work of his local authority in his constituency, and particularly in the regions and notably in the massive Strathclyde region where an average population of over 24,000 persons is to be served independently by each regional councillor. This must put new strains on councillors in terms of the required time and effort to fulfill their duties, add pressure to the demand for full-time salaried councillors, and make fresh demands on the information systems and the processes of public accountability.

The commission's solution to this problem, which they foresaw, was threefold: a rationalization of the work of the councillor, greater delegation, and the creation of the community councils. The adoption of new management structures and practices has not yet been matched by universal changes in attitudes, and there is still insistence (for whatever reasons) on continuous intervention by councillors in matters that might well be thought to be administrative, operational, or even low-level routine. Full dissemination of information about policies, plans, decisions, and performance is vital if the regions are to comply with the principles of local democracy and involvement, and more must be done than fulfilment of the statutory duty of allowing press and public access to council and committee meetings and records of decisions. There are some signs of a willingness to use the media to the full, and the new nonexecutive community councils also have a role to play. Active attention to publicity and public relations will be essential.

A permanent boundary commission has been created to carry out reviews of areas and boundaries and of electoral arrangements, on a programmed basis or as required. Evidence given to the commission invited the setting up of a general local government commission with much wider powers and specifically able to receive representations that would allow Parliament to adapt the local government system from time to time, rather than wait for another overdue root and branch reform some decades way.[8] The general principle was recommended by the commission but was not accepted for legislative action.

The relationship between size and efficiency has not, as yet, been demonstrated in hard terms, and no information is available about optimum areas or populations for particular service or functions. A limited research into general administrative costs in the former authorities demonstrated that scale economies did exist, but little is known about operating efficiencies.[9] The larger authorities will automatically offer improved career prospects to the staff employed in local government and new opportunities for specialization, which would ultimately be to the benefit of the community. The reduced number of authorities lowers the number of top-level posts and flattens the shape of departmental hierarchies in the larger authorities. The immediate financial consequences of reorganization, as well as the cost of reorganization itself, cannot be forecast with any accuracy. The effect of inflation on local government expenditure and the strains caused by the fundamental nature of the reforms are bound to make any valid assessment very difficult.

The division of functions between region and district almost compels a successful search for liaison arrangements for handling the shared and concurrent functions (the islands authorities are almost completely insulated from this difficulty). To this must be added the need for internal decentralization in the large regions through a variety of subregional divisions. This two-dimensional interauthority liaison between region and district is a special, if the predominant, example of a whole range of interrelationships yet to be worked out. Many interregional and interdistrict matters at the national level will be accommodated in the new single association of local authorities, but there will be matters affecting particular contiguous regions, and others concerning a number of districts in one or a few regions. The will to operate the ''one-door'' approach to local government hinges upon a clear and constructive relationship between local authorities and between them and the reconstructed health authorities and local health councils.

An attempt at any evaluation of the liaison arrangements so far introduced or in contemplation would be premature now, but the most sensitive field lies in the links between regional social work and associated services and the district housing function. Many continue to regret that housing was placed with the districts, contrary to the commission's recommendation and presumably to strengthen the otherwise weak range of district services. The price to be paid for this decision is a fragmented activity program, and the consequences of the recommendations of the Morris Committee may be significant.[10]

From the central government viewpoint, the dramatic fall in the number of authorities simplified relationships and communcations and evened up the standard of administration and technical competence to a higher level. Attempts are being made to secure a corporate approach to local authorities by the Scottish Office, and this may be regarded as a step forward. In political terms the homogeneity of the new authorities and the creations of one association of local authorities, coupled with the increasing involvement of political parties in local affairs, must bring changes in the collective influence of local government on central government thinking and attitudes. Once again, however, the possibility of a Scottish Assembly (and its undoubted interest in local government) casts its shadow, and speculation takes the place of serious conjecture.

The reform of finance was omitted from the remit of the commission, although their report did comment on this area and limited research was undertaken.[11] Any changes will doubtless be on an all-Britain basis and independent of the achieved structural and managerial changes; though again the consequences of devolution have to be borne in mind, and many see a Scottish Assembly with revenue-raising powers as the inevitable solution to the financial strains on local government. The work of the Layfield Committee, set up to review the whole field of local government finance, extended to Scotland, and the committee gathered evidence in Scotland.[12] The major recommendations made were not accepted, and whatever action may be taken later the local financial legislation in 1975 clearly presupposed a continuance of the system of local rates on the occupation of property for some years ahead.

The situation in Scotland bears, in most respects, a marked similarity to that in England and Wales, despite the many differences in matters of detail. However, the changes made reflect the Scottish Commission's recommendations, and the resulting two-tier system is not the consequence of a political bouleversement, as occurred in England. Again, the Scottish Commission did not produce a substantial and significant minority report. The urban-rural division in Scotland, perhaps more marked in total terms than in England, has been resolved through the region-district provision, and the metropoitan areas were not seen as a specific problem calling for specific solutions. The impact of the evidence submitted to the commission by the counties of cities was quite limited, and subsequent concern has been based upon the fears of political dominance by the city district in the metropolitan-type regions or political dominance used as a weapon in attempts to break up the Strathclyde region.

Reform in Scotland occurred one year after that in England and Wales, and some of the errors made there may prove to have been avoided. On the other hand, the ripples of managerial and administrative reforms were slow to reach Scotland, and time is needed for the internal structures to be rationalized and strengthened and to settle down. The elitist nature of the strong policy committee, the management team, and ''executive office'' arrangement has already raised information and communication problems, but this is not a purely Scottish problem. The main obstacle to a stable situation lies in the uncertainties about a Scottish Assembly and the drive towards some form of separatism, seen by many opponents of the new local government as a means of making further, if incoherent, changes. Even without this, the radical nature of the reforms must delay a full appraisal for some years yet.

NOTES

1. *The Modernisation of Local Government in Scotland*, Cmnd. 2067 (London: Her Majesty's Stationery Office, 1963).

2. *Reorganisation of Local Government in Scotland: First Report* (London: HMSO, 1964).

3. Report to the Royal Commission on Local Government in Scotland (London: HMSO, 1969).

4. Committee on the Management of Local Government, *Management of Local Government—Report of the Committee* (London: HMSO, 1967).

5. *The New Local Authorities—Management and Structure* (London: HMSO, 1972).

6. *The New Scottish Local Authorities—Organisation and Management Structures* (London: HMSO, 1973).

7. *Reform of Local Government in Scotland*, Cmnd. 4583 (London: HMSO, 1971).

8. Royal Commission on Local Government in Scotland, *Written Evidence 3* (London: HMSO, 1967).

9. C. S. Page, *Administrative Costs of Local Authorities*, Research Studies no. 1, Royal Commission on Local Government in Scotland (London: HMSO, 1969).

10. A committee appointed to consider the relationships between housing and social work services and local government reorganization in Scotland; see, for example, the *Interim Report* (London: HMSO, 1974).

11. See chapter 32 of the Report of the Royal Commission and C. S. Page and E. E. Canaway, *Local Taxation*, Research Studies no. 1, Royal Commission on Local Government in Scotland (London: HMSO, 1969).

12. The Committee of Enquiry into Local Government Finance (Chairman, Frank Layfield), appointed in 1974.

Britain:
Northern Ireland

Barbara A. Carroll
*and Terrance G. Carroll**

24

For well over a decade there has been a widely experienced trend to "rational-ize" local government systems by increasing their size in order to permit a more efficient provision of services. Such reorganizations have worked well in some places and less well in others, but there is a potentially fatal flaw in the underlying philosophy of this approach. It diverts our attention from the fact that local governments are fundamentally political institutions and not ad-ministrative bodies, and it thereby creates a danger that inappropriate criteria will be employed in assessing and redesigning local government systems.

The local government system in Northern Ireland underwent such an assess-ment and reorganization between 1966 and 1973. The criteria used by the new system's architects in Ulster were those commonly employed throughout the Western world. At best the result is less helpful than it might have been; at worst it may yet prove to be tragic. The political circumstances of Northern Ireland demanded a response contrary to that dictated by economic and administrative concerns. The fact that the latter were given precedence in designing the system created in 1973 began to have important and undesirable consequences for the political lives of Ulstermen in less than five years.

BACKGROUND

The Political Circumstances of Ulster

In 1921 Great Britain recognized the independence of twenty-six Irish counties. Six northern counties remained within the United Kingdom, how-

*Barbara Carroll is with the Canada Mortgage and Housing Corporation, Govern-ment of Canada; Terrance Carroll is Assistant Professor of Politics, Brock University, St. Catharines.

ever, and a provincial government was established for Northern Ireland. A "peace, order, and good government" clause gave the new government the right to legislate on most matters that were primarily of provincial or local concern. The British government retained control over subjects normally decided at the national level in federations, and its ultimate right to exercise direct control over Northern Ireland's affairs was made explicit. In practice this power was little used before 1972, and Westminster's main source of influence was its dominant financial position. By the early 1970s over 75 percent of the Northern Ireland government's expenditures were derived from revenues directly under Westminster control.[1] In the postwar years the Northern Ireland government had foregone fiscal autonomy in return for assurances by the British government that Northern Ireland would have the necessary financial resources to supply services on a level comparable to the rest of the United Kingdom.

Throughout its history the government of Northern Ireland was controlled by the Ulster Unionist Party, which never won less than 60 percent of the seats in the legislature. Catholic parties dedicated to the unification of Ireland formed the main opposition. While complaints about gerrymandering and unfair electoral laws were frequently made by Catholics, and with some justification, it seems clear that their total exclusion from positions of authority would have been almost as certain in a completely "fair" system of the British type. Essentially the problem was one of an inability to provide any share of power to a distinct and permanent political minority.

During the 1960s a new political phenomenon appeared; a Catholic-dominated civil rights movement which demanded not the demise of the existing system but merely its reform. For the first time large numbers of Catholic Ulstermen were asking that they be given the rights enjoyed by all other British citizens rather than emphasizing their lack of allegiance to the regime. The apparent reluctance and hesitation with which the government met these demands helped to transform the situation from one typified by protest marches in the late 1960s to one dominated by guerrilla warfare in the early 1970s. Yet the fact that any concessions were made at all alienated many Protestants from the regime and led to the disintegration of the Ulster Unionist Party itself.

In March of 1972 the Parliament of Northern Ireland was suspended in the face of growing civil violence, and the British government took direct responsibility for governing the province. An attempt in 1973 to reestablish a provincial government with proportional representation of Roman Catholics and Protestants in both the assembly and the executive failed to gain sufficient support from either the Protestant community or its elected representatives to survive its first year. Similarly, an elected Constitutional Convention which sat in 1975-76 was unable to find any basis for bicommunal agreement on the structure of a new provincial government.[2]

Many Catholics had long viewed the Protestant majority as hostile and repressive, while many Protestants saw the entire Catholic minority as inherently disloyal. Neither stereotype was completely accurate, of course, but both contained some small element of truth, and the violent clashes that occurred with increasing regularity after 1968 were interpreted by both sides as providing confirmation for their view of reality. As a result most Protestants could not accept that "disloyal" Catholics should have a decisive role in governing the province, and most Catholics could not accept that their well-being should depend upon the whim and will of Protestants, as would be the case with simple majority rule.

The British government did not develop any new proposals on the future of Northern Ireland in the 1975-78 period, and there was little to indicate that this impasse might be broken in the near future. For the moment it seems that we must accept the fact that the two communities in Ulster cannot agree on a form of government for Northern Ireland as a whole. One obvious response to this dilemma would be to remove several governmental functions from the realm of constitutional politics, in which sectarian disputes color all else. If such powers were transferred to the potentially less contentious local government level, Ulstermen might be afforded at least some measure of democratic control over their society. A closer examination of the reorganized local government system will show, however, that its form precludes this otherwise sensible and potentially valuable initiative.

Social and Economic Factors

Northern Ireland has a population of about 1.5 million, with Protestants outnumbering Catholics two to one. A high rate of emigration has served to keep the size of the population remarkably stable, and a higher emigration rate among Catholics has helped maintain the religious ratio despite differences in birth rates. Belfast, the only large city in Ulster, reflects the distribution of religious groups in the total population reasonably accurately. Generally, however, Protestants form a disproportionately large majority in the more urbanized and industrialized eastern half of the province, while Roman Catholics are in the majority in the poorer, western counties.

Ulster is the least prosperous region in the United Kingdom, and on average Catholics do less well than the norm for the province. Until the end of World War II the economy of Northern Ireland was dominated by the linen and shipbuilding industries, both centered in Belfast, and by small-scale farming. In the postwar period a steady contraction of these industries and a tendency towards larger farms eliminated over 100,000 jobs in the province, while the total labor force is only half a million.[3] In 1958 the Northern Ireland government initiated a long-term program aimed at diversifying the province's economic base and reducing the chronically high unemployment rate. At the heart of this program was a "growth center" policy. Government grants and other incentives were provided to encourage the establishment of new industries in eight towns which were ostensibly chosen on the basis of their economic size, good locations, and efficient lines of communication and transportation.[4]

Despite unfavorable economic conditions throughout the British Isles, the economy of Northern Ireland expanded more quickly than that of Britain during the 1960s. Many "growth centers" and other small towns increased rapidly in size. Increasing urbanization in general and the development of the "growth centers" in particular soon began to place considerable pressure on the service and delivery capabilities of local governments, whose structures had remained virtually unchanged since the 1800s. It was this pressure that first led to a review of the local government system with a view to restructuring it, but the process of reorganization had hardly begun when it became clear that sectarian political conflicts would also have to be taken into account.

The "Old" Local Government System

Before the reorganization of 1973, the basic local government units in Northern Ireland were the six counties and the county boroughs of Belfast and Londonderry. For purposes of local administration the counties were divided into urban and rural districts, each with its own council. In 1965 there were seventy-three separate local governments in the province: six county councils, two county borough councils, ten borough (town) councils, twenty-four urban district councils (UDCs), and thirty-one rural district councils (RDCs).[5]

Significant changes in local government responsibilites had taken place between 1921 and 1966 when the comprehensive review was initiated. The general tendency was to transfer functions upward to larger or more specialized bodies; from the district level to county councils, and from the county level to the provincial legislature, or to province-wide statutory bodies created for special purposes. This trend was similar to the process that developed in Great Britain, but even more centralization took place in Ulster. By the late 1960s protective services, such as police, civil defense, and, except in Belfast, fire brigades, were provided by central statutory agencies. The Electricity Board for Northern Ireland provided this service everywhere except in Londonderry and Belfast, and the Northern Ireland Housing Trust supplemented the housing activities of local councils. The provincial government also had created boards with responsibility for general health and hospital services.[6]

Nevertheless, local councils retained control over a number of important services. Urban and rural district councils were responsible for housing, water supply, sewage, street lighting, and other minor functions. UDCs were also responsible for local public works, town planning and development, and setting local property taxation rates. All of these functions were carried out by county councils for rural areas. Borough councils provided the same services as UDCs, with the addition of certain ceremonial functions. The county councils looked after education, public health, and welfare services. In Belfast and Londonderry the county borough councils combined the responsibilities of a county council and a UDC (see Table 24.1).

A proportional representation system was being used in local government elections when the provincial administration was established, but in 1922 the

Table 24.1
**NORTHERN IRELAND: FUNCTIONAL RESPONSIBILITIES FOR
LOCAL GOVERNMENT, 1965 AND 1973**

Function	Prior to Reorganization					After Reorganization	
	County Borough Councils	County Councils	UDCs, Chartered Boroughs	RDCs	Central	District Council	Central
Health	x	x			x	x^a	x
Education	x	x					x
Welfare	x	x					x
Rating							
Setting	x	x^b	x			x	x
Collection	x	x	x				x
Public Works	x	x^b	x			x^a	
Planning and development	x	x^b	x				x
Zoning	x	x^b	x				
Libraries	x	x^b	x				x
Water, sewer, and sanitation	x		x	x		x^a	x
Street lights	x		x	x		x	
Housing	x		x	x	x		x
Fire	x^c				x		x
Police					x		x
Hospitals					x		x

Sources: Prior to reorganization—Government of Northern Ireland, *Ulster Year Book, 1971* (Belfast: Her Majesty's Stationery Office, 1971), pp. 36–38; Reorganized functions—Government of Northern Ireland, *Review Body on Local Government in Northern Ireland*, Cmd. 546 (Belfast: Her Majesty's Stationery Office, 1970), para. 74, p. 120.

^{a}District councils retained some minor responsibilities in these areas after reorganization.
^{b}These functions are performed by the county council for rural district councils only.
^{c}Belfast.

new Northern Irish government abandoned this procedure in favor of a simple majority system. Several local councils with Catholic majorities refused to recognize the new regime and indicated their allegiance to the Dublin government. As a result the Ulster minister of home affairs abolished twenty-one local governments in 1921. When these authorities were reconstituted many of the ward boundaries had been altered, switching several councils from a Catholic to a Protestant majority.

FORCES FOR CHANGE

Administrative Problems

By the late 1960s it had become apparent that the existing local government structures were illogical and inefficient. The underlying problem was one of size. Frequently the total population of a governmental division was below the minimum number required for the efficient provision of services. In addition, due to urban sprawl and the unplanned relocation effects of the government's development program, many local district boundaries had ceased to be relevant to settlement patterns. These problems contributed to a growing general inadequacy in local governments' financial resources, to disparities in the resources available to different local governments, and to disparities and general shortcomings in the level of services provided.

Of the seventy-three local governments in the late 1960s, only eight represented populations of over 50,000, while twenty-seven had fewer than 10,000 residents under their jurisdiction.[7] It has been suggested that most local government services require a minimum population of over 50,000 for efficient planning and administration, and for many functions a population counted in the hundreds of thousands would be more appropriate. For example, services such as planning, water supply, and sewage and sanitation ideally should be based upon communities of over 100,000.[8] In Northern Ireland these functions were performed by local governments which, in extreme cases, represented fewer than 2,000 people.

Because local councils lacked the financial resources required to provide adequate levels of services, they had become increasingly dependent upon grants from the provincial government and had suffered a corresponding decrease in their fiscal autonomy. The main sources of local government revenue were property taxes and grants made by the provincial legislature. In 1945 grants and equalization payments made up 40 percent of local government revenues. By 1965 the proportion had increased to over 60 percent, and conditional grants alone accounted for half of all local government revenues.[9]

The provision of publicly owned housing is a service which clearly shows the effects of these administrative and financial problems. Public housing was the responsibility of local authorities until 1945, when the Northern Ireland Housing Trust (NIHT) was established to supplement their activities. The share of housing construction controlled by public authorities expanded massively, with local councils building 38 percent of new dwellings between 1945 and 1969, and the NIHT accounting for a further 24 percent, but the records of different local authorities varied greatly.[10]

A 1971 study of housing in the province noted each of the general problems we have mentioned as specific sources of difficulties in the area of housing. It pointed out that councils in rural areas had experienced difficulties in trying to meet geographically scattered housing needs, that smaller districts had faced serious financial obstacles, and that almost a third of the province's local governments were too small to be able to hire technical and professional staff.[11] The authors of this study factor analyzed data on a variety of indicators of housing conditions in local government areas and created an index of relative housing conditions. Table 24.2 reports the scores for the local government areas in County Londonderry on this index and also indicates the number of new houses per 1,000 of population built by each councils between 1944 and

1970. Not only was there a great disparity in housing conditions between areas and a great disparity in the records of different councils, but, perhaps more surprisingly, there seems to have been no relationship between the need for improved housing in a district and the efforts of the respective local governments in this regard.

Table 24.2
NORTHERN IRELAND: HOUSING IN LONDONDERRY

Local Government Area	Index of Housing Conditions	Number of Houses Built per 1000 of Population, 1944-70
Portstewart UD	−286	1
Coleraine MB	−148	76
Limavady UD	−128	113
Londonderry UD	41	50
Coleraine RD	124	58
Magherfelt RD	197	70
Limavady RD	225	53

Source: W. D. Birrel, et al., *Housing in Northern Ireland,* Centre for Environmental Studies, University Working Paper, no. 12 (London: Centre for Environmental Studies 1971), pp. 134-35, 264.

The authors argued that a low level of cooperation typified the relationships between essentially rural districts, which included large spillover populations from urban centers, and their neighboring metropolitan areas. They suggested that councils with Protestant majorities in areas in which Roman Catholics formed a majority in the population tended to display a lack of interest in housing programs. The study concluded that it had been ''the overall structure of local government that cause[d] problems for housing policy.''[12]

None of these structural shortcomings, with their concomitant administrative problems, were unique to Northern Ireland. During the 1960s the Redcliffe-Maud Report on England and the Wheatley Report on Scotland identitified the same problems: local government systems included too many, too small areas that lacked sufficient financial resources and had inappropriate boundaries.[13]

Political Problems

During the late 1960s the civil rights movement in Ulster focused a great deal of attention upon perceived injustices in local government politics. Their campaign, and the violent conflict that grew out of it, had a decisive effect on the process of local government reorganization and upon the sorts of changes that seemed appropriate. Because of electoral gerrymandering, Roman Catholics were dramatically underrepresented on local councils, all but eleven of which had Unionist majorities. The commission, headed by Lord Cameron, that investigated the violent outbreaks of 1968 noted that, while Catholics made up 57 percent of the total adult population of seven specific areas, 60 percent of the councillors elected in those districts were Unionists.[14] That this was not simply a function of massive Catholic support for Unionists can be shown by looking at a few specific cases.

Armagh, for example, had a Nationalist council prior to 1934, when the ward boundaries were altered by the provincial government. From then on Unionists regularly won twelve of the twenty seats, despite the fact that Catholics made up 53 percent of the population.[15] Similarly, the wards in Omagh UD were altered by Order in Council in 1936. Table 24.3 shows the change that followed as Catholic districts were transferred from the South to the West Ward. The most extraordinary situation, however, was that in Londonderry, where the boundaries were changed in 1922 and again in 1936. The Cameron investigation found that almost half of the total population was lumped into one overwhelmingly Catholic ward, which elected eight councillors, while the other two wards with Protestant majorities elected twelve persons. The commission's report concluded that the attempts made to justify this situation simply "rationalized a determination to achieve and maintain Unionist elected control."[16]

Table 24.3
NORTHERN IRELAND: REDISTRIBUTION IN OMAGH, 1936

Ward	Number of Voters 1967	Councillors	
		Pre 1936	Elected 1936
North	1,089	6 Unionist	6 Unionist
South	1,182	6 Non-Unionist	6 Unionist
West	2,128	6 Non-Unionist	9 Non-Unionist

Source: D. P. Baritt and A. Booth, Orange and Green, 2nd. ed. (Brigflatts, Sedbergh, and Yorks: Northern Friends Peace Board, 1972), p. 22.

The maintenance of Unionist control seems to have been made easier by the restricted franchise employed for local government elections. Only those persons occupying dwellings, and their spouses, were entitled to vote. Subtenants, lodgers, servants, and adults living with their parents were all excluded. This eliminated about one-quarter of those entitled to vote in elections for the provincial and national legislatures, and it was felt to have weighed most heavily on the Catholic community, which is poorer and tended to have larger families. As a consequence an emotive "one man, one vote" campaign played a large part in the early days of the civil rights movement.

It was local housing policies, however, that contributed most directly to the growing political conflict. By long-standing custom, local authority housing in Northern Ireland was allocated to tenants by the elected councillor for the ward in which the dwellings were located. On an overall basis this system seems to have led to a surprisingly fair distribution of public housing. Richard Rose's major 1968 interview survey did not discover any evidence of a general pattern of discrimination in the provision of publicly owned dwellings.[17] Individual cases of discrimination did arise fairly frequently, however, and each such case was highly visible in the local community and highly emotive.

In 1968, an incident in which a needy Catholic family were passed over and a council house was allocated to the nineteen-year-old unmarried secretary of a Unionist politician sparked off a "squat-in" and protest march. This was the first occasion on which the civil rights movement employed mass demonstration techniques in the province. The publicity the march generated led to the organization of another demonstration in Londonderry in October of 1968. On this occasion fierce fighting broke out between police and protesters. Further demonstrations followed, and with increasing frequency they led to violence.[18] Attempts by the authorities to prevent and suppress such violent clashes led to further radicalization among Catholics and to more direct attacks upon the authorities.

After the Derry march the Northern Ireland Civil Rights Association issued a list of six "demands," and four of these were directed at the local government system. They demanded a universal franchise in local government elections, the redrawing of electoral boundaries by an independent commission, legislation against discrimination in employment by local authorities, and the institution of a compulsory and "fair" points system for housing allocations.[19] The complaints formed one of the many factors that contributed to an increasing polarization between religious groups in the province.

As the conflict between the two communities intensified and the British government came to play a more active role in Ulster's affairs, the provincial authorities began to give in to the protesters' demands, one by one. Because the reforms obviously were made with considerable reluctance, however, rather than helping to win the allegiance of Catholics, if anything they increased the minority's feeling of alienation from the regime. Many Protestants, on the other hand, believed that the government was wrong to make any concessions at all in the face of what they saw as illegitimate pressure. As each individual concession was made, moreover, and its specific form announced, an ever increasing number of alternatives were closed to those attempting to plan an overall reorganization. Finally, every suggested change in the local government system came to be assessed first in terms of its effects on the general power struggle between Catholics and Protestants.

THE PROCESS OF REORGANIZATION

Statement of Aims

The reorganization process was set in motion in 1966 when, in response to the administrative problems we have discussed, the minister of home affairs initiated talks with various local groups. In a Green Paper published in December of 1967, the government set out the basic philosophy and goals that were to underlie the reorganization. The intent was to "enlarge the local government base in line with the criteria of efficiency, economy and the effective representation of local aspirations."[20] The paper suggested the establishment of twelve to eighteen area councils to replace all existing units below the county level, with the eventual goal of moving completely to a one-tier system. These councils, which were to be based on the historic boroughs and towns as well as adjacent rural and urban districts, were to be given responsibility for physical and environmental services, the promotion of cultural activities, and town planning.

Before this first step towards a rational solution to economic and administrative problems could be taken any further, however, the political realities of Ulster intruded. The clash in Derry in October of 1968 was followed by demonstrations in a number of other centers. The Northern Ireland government responded by appointing a commission to replace the elected but unrepresentative council in Londonderry and by urging local authorities to institute a points system for housing allocations. A majority of Unionist backbench MPs disapproved of these reforms, and they adamantly opposed any widening of the local government franchise.[21]

In July 1969, in a further attempt to respond to the new political demands placed upon it, the government promised the establishment of an independent commission to redraw local government electoral boundaries and made the use of a points system for housing allocations compulsory. At the same time, however, the government also proposed that all of the health services provided by local authorities be transferred to the control of three to five district boards to be appointed by the minister of health and social services. This move was supported on the grounds that different types of health services were so interrelated as to preclude their division between levels of government, while many of them were so costly and so complicated that they could not be efficiently provided by local authorities.[22]

In August 1969 fierce rioting broke out between Roman Catholics and the combined forces of the police and Protestant civilians in Londonderry, Belfast, and other towns. The situation rapidly worsened to the point that the British army was sent in to restore order, and increased British political involvement followed closely. After a series of meetings between the British and Northern Irish governments, a "new" package of reforms was announced. Among the promises affecting local government were commitments:

1. To require public employers at every level to provide equality of employment opportunity
2. To establish a local government ombudsman
3. To transfer all housing functions to a new central authority
4. To assure fair representation of minorities at all elected and appointed levels of government
5. To establish an independent commission representative of minority interests to reexamine proposals for local government reorganization[23]

These promises, together with those made earlier, established to a large degree the shape the new system was to take. Two of the most onerous of local government functions, health and housing, were to be performed by bodies controlled by the provincial government, while the political aspects of local councils were to be made as open and as fair as could be ensured by law. At the same time, however, the reorganization process was in a sense returned to stage one: a new commission was to review existing proposals and make recommendations of its own. This new review body was created in December 1969, with three Protestant and three Catholic members under the chairmanship of Patrick Macrory.

THE MACRORY REPORT[24]

In its terms of reference the Macrory Committee was asked to advise the government on the most efficient distribution of local government functions, taking into account the decision to centralize public housing. Unlike the Redcliffe-Maud and Wheatley Commissions, it was not asked to take into account the need to sustain a viable system of local democracy. Indeed, there was no reference to political matters, such as boundaries or electoral systems, at all. The committee saw its function as that of a "review body" aimed primarily at reexamining previously made proposals, rather than a general local government commission that would hear all relevant evidence and then make recommendations. This view of their function was reinforced not only by their restricted terms of reference but also by the Northern Ireland goverment's refusal to allow the committee to consider the actual boundaries of the electoral districts or the voting system. In addition, both the long delay in holding the local government elections and the escalating violence and community polarization made an early report essential.

The Macrory Report was presented to the Northern Ireland Parliament in June 1970. It recommended the creation of a single-tier local government system, with twenty-six local government districts. Each of these was to be centered around a large town and was to include adjacent rural areas. Most districts were expected to have over 30,000 residents. The functions performed by these new district councils were to be greatly reduced (see Table 24.1). Virtually all of the more important local government responsibilities were to be transferred to the appropriate department of the Northern Ireland government. In addition to housing and personal health care, the report suggested that such major functions as education, libraries, planning, roads and traffic, water supply, and major sewerage systems be controlled entirely by the provincial government. To reduce the danger of inaccessibility and a lack of responsiveness to local needs which might accompany the centralization of services, the committee suggested that the various provincial departments decentralize the administration of their functions and, in some cases, even delegate administrative responsibilities to the district councils; and that district councils should have some places, although always a minority, on the departmental area boards to be established to administer regional services.

The new local councils thus were to be left with only relatively minor executive functions, such as food hygiene, refuse collection and disposal, minor sewerage systems, local parks, cemeteries, and "public conveniences." The services to be transferred to the provincial level were estimated to have cost twelve times as much as those to be left with local governments. As a result it seemed to be very easy to make the new councils much more autonomous financially than the existing ones were. The committee suggested that the Northern Ireland government set a province-wide property taxation rate to provide revenue for the centralized services, while each council would also strike a rate appropriate to its own requirements. The need for some sort of equalization grant was foreseen, but existing local governments were already raising over 80 percent of the funds spent on the services they were to be left with besides providing a smaller proportion of the revenue required for the services to be centralized.

Reaction to the Macrory Report was mixed. Among Catholics the response ranged from mild support to disinterest. Local councils were to be made more democratic but less important. Some Protestants, on the other hand, were strongly opposed to the new system. They saw it as "virtually the end of local government in Northern Ireland," meaning, one assumes, the end of unfettered Protestant control. [25] The report was accepted by the government, and an independent commissioner was appointed in the spring of 1971 to redraw electoral boundaries for the twenty-six new districts. Both because of the continuing violence and because of the magnitude of the changes being made, local government elections were postponed once again. The government hoped to hold them in the autumn of 1972, with the new system actually replacing the existing one in April 1973.

In the meantime, however, the general political situation in Ulster continued to deteriorate. In August 1971 the Northern Ireland government brought in internment without trial as a means of neutralizing suspected terrorists, and within months there were over 1,000 Catholics imprisoned under this emergency legislation. After the introduction of internment the polarization of the population was complete. Every elected Catholic representative in the province withdrew from local councils and the provincial assembly. Bombings and shootings became commonplace, with the death rate reaching one per day. In the spring of 1972 the required legislation for the new system was passed by the remaining Protestant members of the provincial assembly, but before it could be proclaimed the British government suspended the operations of the Parliament and government of Northern Ireland and took direct control over the affairs of the province. [26] The British authorities proceeded with the reorganization as planned and added a commitment to the use of proportional representation in local government elections. In May 1973, after a further delay caused by the civil strife, these elections were finally held, and the reorganized system came into being. [27]

POLITICS AND LOCAL GOVERNMENT

Recent reports on the organization of local government systems in many parts of the Western world have been remarkably consistent in both the criteria employed and the recommendations made. The general approach has been to divide services into two categories. Some services have been deemed to be essentially local because demand for them varies greatly from community to community, the "spillover" from one community to the next is minimal, and the service is of a type that may be administered reasonably efficiently within a small community. Others usually have been assigned to a higher level of government because of the importance of administrative or financial economies of scale or because of the probability of significant "spillover" from one community to another.[28]

On the basis of such a categorization, many reviews of local government during the 1960s and 1970s concluded that the existing systems should be "rationalized" by increasing the size of units and decreasing their number. Services requiring a large population base for efficient administration frequently were transferred to higher levels of government, and the financial resources of local governments were increased to permit greater local autonomy and responsibility in those spheres left under their control.

The new system in Northern Ireland fits this pattern very well. The Macrory recommendations treated the provincial government as a regional authority, which was reasonable given the size of Ulster's population and territory. Those powers commonly assigned to regional bodies in other jurisdictions were given to the provincial parliament in Northern Ireland. The new local districts were made as large as possible, while still retaining some measure of internal homogeneity. Despite the failure of the Macrory Committee to consider such matters, the political aspects of local government were fully reformed. In any circumstances other than those of Ulster everyone concerned with the reorganization might have felt justly proud of their work.

In practical terms, unfortunately, the effect of this reorganization was to democratize local government for the first time, while simultaneously removing virtually all significant powers from this level of authority. The important services were transferred to departments of the Northern Ireland government, to be watched over and controlled by the legislature. This, of course, is the level of government least amenable to reform, and five years after the local reorganization Ulstermen were still at the stage of debating proposals for complete constitutional transformation. The possibility of finding an acceptable and workable solution seems slight. In the short run this problem was minimized because Britain itself took direct responsibility for the affairs of the Northern Ireland government, but neither the people of Ulster nor the British government accepted that situation as a viable, long-term solution.

Similarly, the decision to increase the size of local districts in the interests of administrative efficiency had undesirable side effects. Local politics contributed to the general conflict in Ulster partly because of perceived injustices in the old system, and the reforms instituted should have largely solved this problem. Beyond this, however, there was the widespread distrust and antipathy between the religious communities, which created a situation in which even relations between a democratically elected majority on a council and the minority group were likely to be tense.

The group that was in the minority in a local district was likely to feel that its interests were inadequately reflected in the council's decisions, and there was a reasonable possibility that the majority groups would in fact discriminate against their minorities. The greater the religious heterogeneity in local districts, the greater the number of people affected by this problem. Despite the tendency of Ulstermen to live among their coreligionists, the physical integration of the two communities was too great for this problem to be solved entirely, but with relatively small local districts it could have been minimized by emphasizing religious homogeneity in drawing district boundaries. This is the opportunity that was lost.

Nevertheless, bicommunal cooperation has become much more common under the new system. Informal conventions have developed in several local districts that result in a sharing of top positions among Protestants and Catholics or a regular alternation in the allocation of specific positions to the various political parties regardless of religion. To a large extent, however, this relatively harmonious situation is a function of the minor nature of the responsibilities of district councils. Quite simply, there is very little to fight about. No longer do the councils control housing allocatons; no longer do they run welfare schemes; no longer do they provide health care.

Almost all of the districts do contain sizable religious minorities, however, and it seems almost certain that any attempt to alleviate the situation at the provincial level by transferring significant powers to district councils would cause the character of local politics to change yet again. Sectarian disputes might be expected to come to dominate such a system, just as they did before 1973 and as they do at the provincial level today. The districts created in 1973 are too large and religiously too heterogeneous to avoid the cleavages found in Northern Ireland as a whole if their councils were to be given responsibilities of any import.

Rather than contributing to a solution to Northern Ireland's problems, then, the reorganization of local government complicated matters by concentrating even more power at the provincial level and by making local districts more heterogeneous in religious composition. Given the circumstances of Ulster, precisely the opposite approach might well have been preferable. As long as the debate about the overall structure of government in the province was still open, both Roman Catholics and Protestants were able to accept political reforms at the local level. If, in this reformed system, the functions of local councils had been maintained or even expanded, the scope of the fundamental conflict might have been narrowed. More of the things governments do would have been handled by bodies selected by methods that were generally perceived to be "fair." The decisions councils made still would have alienated some residents, but this problem could also have been reduced in scope. If religious homogeneity rather than administrative efficiency had been the main criterion in establishing the size and boundaries of local districts, fewer people would have been continually in opposition to council decisions.

In most jurisdictions the political consequences of local government re-organization are relatively minor. Local political disputes may lead to intense electoral competition, but they are seldom important enough to result in physical clashes. Review bodies usually pay some attention to the need for representation of local interests, but administrative and financial concerns generally form the main criteria for reorganization. The ultimate standard by which a local government system should be judged is simply the degree to which it satisfies the needs of the population. In most places this is largely a matter of how efficiently desired services are administered.

In Northern Ireland, however, an even more basic need was present: the need of the people to feel that those bodies making decisions affecting their lives represented their interests. The political aspects of local government in Northern Ireland lead one in a direction almost exactly the opposite of that following from administrative concerns. Given a clear perception of the purpose of democratic governmental systems, there can be little doubt that these political concerns should have been decisive. A democratic local government system with significant powers and based upon small, religiously homogeneous districts would not have solved all of Ulster's problems. But, even if only in a small way, it could have been a start.

NOTES

1. Government of the United Kingdom, *Northern Ireland: Financial Arrangements and Legislation*, Cmnd. 4998 (London: Her Majesty's Stationery Office, 1972), paras. 16-25, p. 32.

2. See Government of the United Kingdom, *Northern Ireland Constitutional Proposals*, Cmnd. 5259 (London: Her Majesty's Stationery Office, 1973), for a description of the 1973 proposals; and Richard Rose, *Northern Ireland: Time of Choice* (Washington, D.C.: American Enterprise Institute, 1976), for an analysis of developments to early 1976.

3. Government of Northern Ireland, Ministry of Commerce, *Facts About Northern Ireland*, Mimeographed (Belfast, 1972), p. 2.

4. See Government of Northern Ireland, *Development Programme, 1970-75* (Belfast: Her Majesty's Stationery Office, 1970).

5. On the "old" local government system, see Government of Northern Ireland, *Ulster Year Book, 1971* (Belfast: Her Majesty's Stationery Office, 1971), pp. 38-42, 219-22; and R. J. Lawrence, *Government of Northern Ireland 1921-1965* (London: Oxford University Press, 1968), chaps. 6-9.

6. Lawrence, *Government*, p. 25.

7. Government of Northern Ireland, *Census of Population, 1971: Preliminary Report* (Belfast: Her Majesty's Stationery Office, 1971), pp. 10-11.

8. See George F. Break, "The Organization of Metropolitan Governments," in *Public Finance in Canada: Selected Readings*, ed. A. J. Robinson and J. Cutt (Toronto: Metheun, 1968), pp. 271-74; and D. C. Rowat, *The Canadian Municipal System* (Toronto: McClelland and Stewart, 1969), p. 138.

9. Lawrence, *Government*, p. 94.

10. W. D. Birrell et al., *Housing in Northern Ireland*, Centre for Environmental Studies, University Working Paper, no. 12 (London: Centre for Environmental Studies, 1971), p. 92.

11. Ibid., pp. 155-57.

12. Ibid., p. 155, and, more generally, pp. 133-61.

13. Government of the United Kingdom, *Report of the Royal Commission on Local Government in England*, Cmnd. 4040 (London: Her Majesty's Stationery Office, 1969) (the *Redcliffe-Maud Report*); and Government of the United Kingdom, *Report of the Royal Commission on Local Government in Scotland*, Cmnd. 4150 (London: Her Majesty's Stationery Office, 1969) (the *Wheatley Report*).

14. Government of Northern Ireland, *Disturbances in Northern Ireland*, Cmd. 532 (Belfast: Her Majesty's Stationery Office), p. 57, hereafter cited as *The Cameron Report*.

15. D. P. Barritt and A. Booth, *Orange and Green*, 2nd ed. (Brigflatts, Sedbergh, Yorks: Northern Friends Peace Board, 1972), p. 22.

16. *The Cameron Report*, para. 136.

17. Richard Rose, *Governing Without Consensus* (London: Faber, 1971), pp. 293-95.

18. *The Cameron Report*, para. 26-36.

19. Ibid., para. 189.

20. Government of Northern Ireland, *Reshaping of Local Government: Statement of Aims*, Cmd. 517 (Belfast: Her Majesty's Stationery Office, 1967), p. 3.

21. Deborah Lavin, "Politics in Ulster, 1968," *The World Today* 24, no. 12 (December 1968): 535.

22. See Government of Northern Ireland, *Reshaping of Local Government: Further Proposals*, Cmd. 530 (Belfast: Her Majesty's Stationery Office, 1969); and Government of Northern Ireland, *Green Paper on the Administrative Structures of the Health and Personal Health Services in Northern Ireland* (Belfast: Her Majesty's Stationery Office, 1969).

23. See Government of Northern Ireland, *A Record of Constructive Change*, Cmd. 558 (Belfast: Her Majesty's Stationery Office, 1971).

24. Government of Northern Ireland, *Review Body on Local Government in Northern Ireland*, Cmd. 546 (Belfast: Her Majesty's Stationery Office, 1970) (the *Macrory Report*).

25. This statement by the Unionist mayor of Belfast and reaction to the report from other sources may be found in, "Lord Mayor Lambasts Government Councils Plan," Belfast *Telegraph*, 18 December 1970.

26. The bill received Royal Assent on 23 March 1972, the day that direct rule was introduced. See Northern Ireland House of Commons, *Debates*, vol. 83 (23 March 1972), col. 1507.

27. See "Local Elections: How P. R. Worked," *Fortnight*, no. 63 (8 June 1973): 12-13.

28. See, for example, the *Redcliffe-Maud* and *Wheatley Reports*; Government of New Brunswick, *Report of the Royal Commission on Finance and Municipal Taxation* (Fredericton: Queen's Printer, 1963); and Government of Ontario, *Report of the Committee on Taxation* (Toronto: Queen's Printer, 1967).

Finland

Risto Harisalo and Pentti Rönkko*   25

The character of local government in Finland and its significance in Finnish society may be assessed from two basic standpoints: democratic values and efficiency. In the former of these contexts prime place is given to securing the possibilities of municipal self-government and participation of residents in decisions concerning the affairs of their communes. In the case of efficiency, greatest importance attaches to the provision, adequacy, and effectiveness of services.

During the last two decades the obligations of the communes have multiplied decisively with the more or less regular transfer to them of responsibility for basic services, the state retaining only the functions of norm setting, supervision, and partial coverage of costs. As the sphere of activity of the communes has expanded, more and more weight has come to be placed upon efficiency. Illustrative of the structure of municipal functions today is that about two-thirds of the running expenditure of the communes goes for health services, education, and welfare, that is, on basic public services. The proportion of the GNP accounted for by local administration rose during the period 1951-72 from 3.6 to 8.1 percent, and its part in the GNP of public administration from 46 to 58 percent. Local government thus constitutes a particularly prominent sector in the country's economy. The current difficulties in the economic situation, making a reduction in expenditure essential, have bound local administration more closely than before to the framework of overall economic policies.

The present state of local government may be analyzed from the following standpoints. In the first place, changes in the structure of Finnish society as a whole have brought an expansion and multiplication of the duties now discharged by the communes. The call for efficiency of services has also meant

*Risto Harisalo is Assistant in Municipal Politics and Economics, and Pentti Rönkko is Lecturer in Municipal Politics, Institute of Municipal Sciences, University of Tampere.

administrative changes, many of them currently under way, such as reforms in municipal administrative divisions and legislation. Also, local government is going through a period of reassessment regarding how state control should be arranged and the degree of autonomy to be left to the communes.

A NEW SYSTEM OF STATE SUBSIDIZATION

The division of activities and finances between commune and state forms a clearly defined entity. The statutes governing cost sharing comprise a system of state subsidization that controls the financial capacities of the communes. Up to about the 1940s, state subsidies were intended to subvene the functions of the communes and to increase their activity in the discharge of new tasks. Since then prime place has come to be given to the need for levelling differences among the communes and regulating their rates of taxation. Until the 1970s the economic differences among communes could be reduced by grading subsidization according to the form of commune concerned, a system which proved appropriate enough at first since differences in capacity were indeed great. However, the criterion was eventually deemed too rigid. A new system, introduced in 1969, provided for subsidization of each commune according to its respective financial status. This system involves classification of capacity, whereby the communes are divided annually into ten categories according to their relative financial standing, and special state subsidization regulations prescribing the proportion of expenditure that the state undertakes to cover for any given function in the various types of communes. For example, in the case of health and hospital facilities, state subsidization of running costs ranges between 39 and 70 percent.

This system of categorization has proved adequate to compensate for the effects of regional differentiation in the capacity of communes, but it has failed to close the gaps that existed prior to its introduction, and considerable deficiencies in it have since been acknowledged. In the first place, the legislation is inchoate and confused, and supervision of its enforcement has been too detailed and bureaucratic, concentrating far too emphatically on the technicalities of administrative accountancy. Supervision involves a great deal of work in both state and municipal administration. The state subsidies are defined as percentages of municipal expenses and not as a proportional contribution to specific undertakings, a procedure which does not make for economization and productivity on the part of the communes. Since the regulations are applicable to specific functions, the communes have most expanded their activity in fields for which state funds are available. This has distorted the structure of municipal services. Since the classification of capacity is made on an annual basis, long-term planning of activity and finance is impossible. The system in fact constitutes more of an obstacle than an aid to planning and tends automatically to increase both municipal and state expenditure.

The present system of state subsidization is based largely on an already outdated mode of accountancy whose main function is to check the legality of transactions. It contains none of the basic elements of modern accounting and financial control. Reform presumably will be achieved by the early 1980s, when the system will be simplified and clarified, state supervision reduced, and grants combined into one basic sum supplemented by special subsidies rated according to the capacity of the commune in question. Also, state supervision will cease to be a detailed check on the legal aspects of specific subsidy transactions and will seek instead to promote the objectives and the discharge of municipal functions.

MUNICIPAL PLANNING AUTHORITY

Long-term planning recently has assumed a prominent place in decision making in the communes. The planning of land utilization has constituted a statutory function for many decades. In contrast it was not until the 1960s that municipal activity came to embrace budgeting for longer terms. This is now a normal feature in the admininistration of all towns and cities and most rural communes. In the reformed municipal legislation, five-year budgeting will become a compulsory function. In addition to the planning covering all functions of the communes, a system of statutory sector planning has emerged recently to discharge their more outstanding obligations.

Planning has been recognized to be both essential and profitable as an aid in decision making. Planning methods, however, must be developed even further. Statutory planning, for example, has not been coordinated with overall activities and planning in the communes; it has tended to be bureaucratic, and it narrows the scope of self-government. Indeed, in efforts to develop the planning system the next step must be to alter its content and quality in such a way as to achieve an increase in welfare by other means than increasing staffing and subsidization.

MUNICIPAL REFORM

It was realized in Finland by the 1950s that small and economically weak communes would never be capable of discharging the new functions inevitably being imposed upon them. The municipal divisions were seen to be no longer consistent with the emerging pattern of demands. Up to the first half of this century the communes had in fact been demarcated according to the system of parishes whose requirements were entirely different from those of modern municipal administration. Hence, municipal reform began in the late 1960s.

The current municipal reform is based on legislation passed in 1967 according to which the object of reorganization was to promote an appropriate composition of communities and to improve the possibilities of both administration and finance in the communes. To achieve these aims the communes were to be formed as regional entities with sufficient economic resources and an even distribution of types of settlement and modes of livelihood. The reform sought to create communes maximally capable of sustaining economic, social, and cultural development within and around their administrative areas. It is mainly the smaller communes that are affected, but in certain cases readjustment is necessary even of communes that might otherwise be in themselves sufficient. The reform involves either the combining of communes or a revision of boundaries to conform with functional structure or again the formation of units of common activity, wherein collaborating communes nevertheless retain independent status.

Planning of the reform has sought to take into account local opinion, the bonds of tradition, and patterns of cooperation already established among communes. The original objective was a system of division giving a population of about 8,000 per commune or cooperating group by 1980, with a few communities of under 4,000 residents remaining as independent entities. However, the goals have not been achieved in all cases. Nevertheless the reform, when complete, would reduce the total number of municipalities considerably. While there were 464 in 1979, the eventual figure would be 311.

Implementation of the reform has proved extremely difficult. Plans have been ready for some years but not executed. One of the chief problems politically is whether to make the combination of communes compulsory or leave it to the respective communities to contract. The rural communes, which are particularly affected by annexation, have in most cases opposed such measures, chiefly on the grounds that these mergers would be detrimental to the possibility of their populations exerting any influence on their affairs. On the other hand, a variety of reforms in administration, particularly in the establishment of the basic school and public health systems, which require a population of 8,000-15,000, have tended to promote acceptance of the reform. Smaller communes have been obliged to arrange these facilities in collaboration with others, and the tasks have become the responsibility of larger entities formed on the basis of regional planning.

Revision of Municipal Legislation

The Municipal Law of 1948 constitutes the basic legislation governing the general pattern and functioning of local administration. In general it has proved satisfactory, providing a necessary basis and framework for the control and development of municipal affairs and economies. However, the numerous emendations made in it and the need for further development ultimately involved an overall revision, which was approved by Parliament on 10 December 1976. In the new legislation the central principles are uniformity of legislation for all municipalities, confirmation of local authority, improvement of the position of residents and of their representation and participation in government, together with a reduction in the degree of state control.

The following are some of the outstanding changes effected. The former division into rural municipalities, towns, and cities has been abandoned. The legislation is now applied to all of them uniformly, and they are all categorized as communes, except that towns and cities established before 1977 are classed as cities. Thus, of the 464 communes in 1979, 84 were classed as cities.

The communes may now support party political activity in their areas on the principle of equality and may take responsibility for various measures connected with municipal elections, for improving the function of various executive groups in the administration, for arranging training for representatives, and for meeting certain costs involved in local political activity. On the other hand, direct subsidization of the parties does not fall within the scope of the commune. The age of eligibility for the vote and for election is now eighteen years. Consent to stand for election must be obtained from an envisaged candidate, and representatives must be remunerated for any loss of income incurred in the discharge of municipal duties. Also, the number of members of the municipal councils has been increased by about a fifth, ranging between seventeen and eighty-five, according to the size of the commune.

In order to improve the opportunities of residents to influence the affairs of their commune, it is now possible to set up a system of district councils to deal with the special needs of various sections of the communes. Such subcouncils would within certain limits bear responsibility for the management of their areas. The establishment of such subsidiary bodies is a matter for each commune to decide. It would entail a subcouncil with a membership of between eleven and twenty-five elected by direct ballot in conjunction with municipal polling. Such a system would in fact function as a transitional solution to the reform of the communes, opening up a possibility for originally small municipalities to retain a degree of autonomy in larger units. The significance of the subcouncil would depend upon the residents of the district in question seriously regarding this body as a means of influence and participation. Since 1976 only one city has set up subcouncils.

According to the new law the municipal council is chaired by an elected councillor for a two-year period. The old practice of having the council chaired by the appointed city or municipal director for an unspecified period of time diverges from the system of local government in most other countries, where this function is entrusted to a representative. The old law in Finland gave particular significance to the director of a municipality in all decision making. This was considered desirable in order to safeguard continuity and reconcile divergent views. The system in large measure fulfilled expectations, and directors generally acquired a position of confidence in their localities. However, the general politicization of local government has forced a change in the system and has put the headship of the commune in the hands of the politicians.

REFORM OF STATE ADMINISTRATION AT THE LOCAL LEVEL

The system of local state administration is also to be renewed in the near future. According to preliminary proposals, the object of the reform is to gather the present diversity of functions into one entity, a local government office. This system would be based on area divisions comprising 10,000-15,000 inhabitants.

Since the present network of state administration at the local level is extremely diverse and inconsistent, a great deal of further investigation will be necessary before any actual reform can be undertaken. Particular problems here are the question of area demarcation, coordination of the functions of various authorities and organizations, and the possibility of establishing democratic representative organs for local state administration. In view of the already advanced development and established traditions of municipal administration, it is natural that as far as possible the management of local affairs should be under municipal auspices.

Sweden

Lars Strömberg*

26

Since the war great changes have taken place in both the content and structure of Swedish local administration. In this development, two partly conflicting trends can be discerned. First, the tasks of local government have been extended, especially by national government decisions. Examples are two school reforms and several reforms in the field of social welfare. The basic self-governing units—the communes—have been made responsible for implementing these instead of local state administration. Second, these changes have been made in accordance with the idea that all citizens, irrespective of which part of the country they live in, shall enjoy "equal service."

While the administration of the school reforms and of a number of social reforms has been placed in the hands of the communes, it has also been felt that if these reforms are to be carried through in a uniform manner local administration must be made more efficient. This belief has led to two major reforms in geographical apportionment within twenty-five years. The number of communes has been reduced from 2,500 in the early 1950s to 277 in 1979. At the same time a uniform communal structure has been introduced throughout the country, replacing the earlier distribution into towns, boroughs, and rural districts.

JURISDICTION AT VARIOUS ADMINISTRATIVE LEVELS

In Sweden, as in many homogeneous states, administration is a three-tier affair; the *central* level, geographically comprehending the country; the *re-*

*Professor of Public Administration, Aalborg University Center, Denmark; Assistant Professor, Institute of Political Science, University of Gothenburg, Sweden; formerly Research Fellow with the Swedish Local Government Research Group; and author of several books and articles on local government and politics. This essay is based on a longer one prepared by the author for an international conference on local government sponsored by the Polish Academy of Sciences (Warsaw, 1974).

gional level, usually comprising a county (*län*) or a region of comparable size, with a population averaging (median value) 267,000 inhabitants; and the *local* level, often geographically identical with a commune, and containing on an average 16,000 inhabitants. Though there are other ways of dividing up the administrative system, these are comparatively insignificant in the present context.

Figure 26.1 presents a survey of Sweden's public administration. In it we distinguish, on the one hand, the three levels of geographical administrative distribution and, on the other, the extent to which the various levels are politically rooted in direct elections or constitute elements in a hierarchic administrative system. At the local level the commune, the county council, and the state are all active. At the regional level some activities are subject to the county council, and some to the county boards and other state regional administrative organs. The distribution of competence as to state, county council, and commune is rather complex, not least because both county council and commune are subject to state guidance and controls which, in some respects, are most comprehensive. Two main types of tasks are enjoined upon both county councils and communal councils. There are those decided at the national level which are mandatory, the so-called specially regulated sector. Within this sector most of the educational and social systems, town planning, and building activities are the duty of the communal councils, while the county councils are responsible for most of the public health system, especially hospital administration. The county councils and, more particularly, the communes are involved in a great variety of activities which they are free to undertake according to the Local Government Act. Under this act they are at liberty to engage in such activities of public interest to the commune's inhabitants as do not fall within the province of some other organ. Examples of such activities in the communes are public transport systems, leisure activities, sports fields, swimming pools, libraries, and museums.

The postwar discussion of Sweden's local and regional administration has centered on issues related to the communes' activities and to those of the county councils and boards. The rest of this essay will touch only in passing on the regional or county level, which is the state's concern. Here we shall deal with reforms that have concerned the communes. In another essay Gunnar Wallin will deal with the regional level.

POST-WAR REFORMS OF COMMUNAL APPORTIONMENT

In Sweden, local self-government in its modern form dates from 1862. In that year the communes were adapted to a division of the whole country, which had grown up spontaneously over the centuries, into parishes (*landskommuner*), boroughs (*köpingar*), and towns (*städer*). Before long, however, this apportionment gave rise to problems, above all in connection with the large-scale population movement resulting from extensive industrialization. The

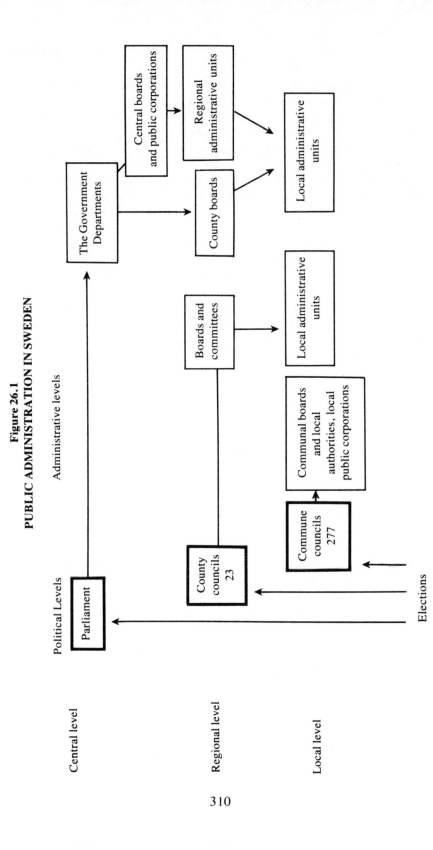

Figure 26.1
PUBLIC ADMINISTRATION IN SWEDEN

population of the rural communes fell, while there was a sharp rise in the population of the urban areas (see Table 26.1).

Table 26.1
SWEDEN: PERCENTAGE DISTRIBUTION OF POPULATION AMONG VARIOUS TYPES OF ADMINISTRATIVE UNITS, 1860-1970.

Unit	1860	1900	1920	1950	1970
Town	11.3	21.5	29.5	46.8	58.9
Borough	0.0	3.6	5.1	8.3	8.9
Rural (parish) commune	88.7	74.9	65.4	44.9	32.2
Total	100	100	100	100	100

The depopulation of the countryside and the changes in age structure that ensued led to unfavorable economic development, notably for the rural parish communes. Beginning in the early 1920s, a sharp deterioration occurred in the smaller rural communes' tax base; at the same time communal tasks in various fields became more numerous, leading to a sharp rise in communal expenditure. The small rural communes found it increasingly difficult to provide their inhabitants with a reasonable level of communal service.

Prior to 1952, three main ways of solving these problems were applied: either certain tasks were transferred to the state or the county council, or the state made grants-in-aid, or else communes were obliged to collaborate. By the early 1940s, however, it had become obvious that these solutions were inadequate. More radical measures were necessary. For this reason the government in 1943 set up a special commission to inquire into the whole question. This commission proposed that rural communes be merged into larger population units in order to achieve more "efficient" communal administration. Large communes, in the commission's view, provided a better tax base, and larger economic resources made possible a more thoroughly planned administration. It was pointed out that small communes were utterly unable to provide certain types of service. Therefore, it was necessary to merge rural communes into larger units if a total nationalization of local administration was to be avoided and local self-government maintained.

In 1946, on the basis of the commission's proposals the national authorities decided, in principle, to reapportion the communes. This decision meant that by such a merger a rural commune normally would contain 3,000 inhabitants. A minimum of 2,000 inhabitants was set as a lower limit. In 1950, after four years of preparatory work and consultations with representatives of the communes, the government decided on a reapportionment of the primary communes. This came into force in 1952. For the most part the reform only affected the rural communes. As a result of the reform the number of communes fell from 2,498 in 1951, to 1,037 in 1952. The mean population of the rural communes rose sharply, from about 1,500 to rather more than 4,100. At the same time the tax base per commune more than doubled.

Shortly after 1952 it became clear that the hopes placed in this reform had not been realized. In the postwar years urbanization had accelerated. Even when the reform came into force, commune structure had already changed greatly in comparison with what it had been in the early 1940s. More and more people were leaving the countryside, and the populations of smaller urban areas were beginning to stagnate or dwindle. One of the reform's shortcomings was becoming more and more obvious. Since the rural communes usually did not constitute regions that cohered industrially or geographically with thriving urban areas, progressive urbanization would lead to new problems for the smaller communes. Parallel with this development, the communes in the early 1950s had more extensive tasks enjoined upon them. A new reform of the elementary school placed increased demands on all communes.

Thus, for several reasons, the communal apportionment question again came to the forefront. In 1959 the minister of the interior appointed a new commission to gather information to investigate whether a new reapportionment of the communes was justified. This commission analyzed the population changes of the 1950s and the development of communal finances. It also made a prognosis of population development up to 1975. It found that in 1960 the goal of the earlier reform—a population base of 3,000 inhabitants per commune—had not been met by just over 36 percent of all communes, and that by 1975 the equivalent share would be just over 40 percent. The commission also assessed the most satisfactory population base for a commune's most important administration tasks. It was found that the pupil base for the new elementary school would need a population of between 6,500 and 8,500 for economic and administrative reasons. For an efficient social welfare system it was thought that the minimum desirable population base would be 5,000-6,000 inhabitants. With a population of this size, communes should be able to solve the problems of old age homes in a satisfactory manner. Further, the social welfare boards should be able to afford to employ specially trained staff. In other communal fields, too, the commission was of the view that larger communes were necessary. The joint planning of various activities also called for such a solution.

With a large number of communes having too slender a base for the most important branches of their activities, there were strong reasons for an urgent review of the apportionment system, notably in view of developments in education. If the commune structure were not altered, 85 percent of Swedish communes would have to collaborate in communal federations if they were to introduce the uppermost stage of the elementary school. Even if the commission did not feel it could stipulate a size norm for a new apportionment into primary communes, owing to the various demands on population base for various communal administrative fields, it did stipulate a minimum population of 8,000 by 1975. In order to prevent, for the future, population developments from giving rise to small communes, the new apportionment, in its view, ought to be based on geographically and economically coherent regions. The new communes should be built up around thriving urban areas which would provide natural centers for their surrounding districts. The commission divided up the entire country, experimentally, into such spontaneous regions (''blocks''), usually consisting of several communes. The principles behind this experiment later were to provide the basis for the effectual apportionment of Sweden into so-called block communes. The commission suggested that during a transitional period these blocks should function as voluntary cooperative regions of primary communes. To take charge of collaboration within the blocks, the communes comprising it should obligatorily set up collaboration boards. These boards were to prepare the merger into block communes and, during the transitional period, occupy themselves with such other planning matters as were of common interest, for example, in education, housing, and old age homes.

In 1961, in accordance with the commission's proposals, the government suggested a revision of the communal apportionment system. This bill was largely in accordance with the experts' proposals. But the collaboration boards, in the government's view, should be voluntary. The bill proposed that they should be utilized by the state authorities as consultative organs, notably in such investment questions as might be important to all communes within any one block and that great weight should be attached to their views. This gave the government an important instrument with which it could guide developments in the direction of a merger. Parliament adopted the government's proposals but laid even greater stress on the voluntarist principle. Further, Parliament believed that the regional principle would need adjustments, notably in respect to the 8,000 population minimum, if new communes that would be too widespread geographically or lack the necessary conditions for a natural community of interests were to be avoided. It was also enacted that each county should have a plan, to be approved by the government, for its distribution into block communes. Proposals for such a plan should be drawn up by the county boards after consultation with representatives of the communes.

In Parliament the reform was carried through by the Social Democrats, the Communists, and a majority of the Liberal party, while the representatives of the Conservatives and Centre party (at this time largely a farmer's party) opposed it. Their opposition was chiefly aimed at the principles underlying the reform, the question of guarantees for the voluntarist principle, and the alternative between an apportionment reform and other measures that could solve the small communes' problems but had been rejected in the bill, for instance, a change in jurisdiction, increased cooperation between primary communes, or greater state grants. After the block plans had been passed, in 1963-64, the government tried in various ways to hasten the mergers. Those communes which had already joined up could apply for extra tax-equalization grants. Another instrument for influencing cooperation within the blocks and for hastening the mergers was the government's distribution of funds for the localization of industry and funds for new housing construction in the blocks' central towns.

By the end of 1968, however, the government had come to the conclusion that the rate at which block communes were being formed was altogether too slow. Therefore it worked out two alternative proposals for changes in the Apportionment Act, both designed to hasten the reform. These proposals were sent out for comment to more than 1,000 organizations, most of them communes. The comments that came in showed still strong opposition to legislation to force through the reform. Of the total 848 communes, all of which were given an opportunity to express their views, 394 were of the opinion that some legislation measures were needed, while 386 communes rejected, more or less firmly, any mandatory legislation whatsoever. However, a very large share of the other organizations consulted were in favor of such legislation, and in 1969 the state authorities decided that the remaining mergers must be carried out by 1 January 1974, at the latest. This, with only a few exceptions, is what has in fact occurred.

As a result of the reform, commune structure changed radically. The number of communes fell to 277, and the average population of the block communes increased to 16,300 inhabitants. However, already 29 blocks fall below the minimum fixed by the commission—8,000 inhabitants. The most crucial effect of the reform has been that the structural differences between urban and rural communes, formerly so great, are on the way to being abrogated. The great majority of block communes will comprise large areas of countryside.

STRUCTURE OF LOCAL GOVERNMENT

As a result of the reforms in communal apportionment there is now a uniform system of local government organization, irrespective of commune type and of the historical distinctions between the tasks and organizational structure of towns, boroughs, and rural communes. Since 1977 all communes are identically structured. In all communes the highest decision-making organ is the council (*kommunfullmäktige*), which is elected by direct elections every third year. The council has at least thirty-one and at most sixty-one councillors, depending on commune size. The council decides on all planning questions and fixes the commune's budget.

A commune's central administrative and executive organ is the communal board (*kommunstyrelse*), which is elected by the council. Election to this board may be—and in the great majority of communes is—proportional. This gives the communal board the character of a coalition government, representing all political parties in the council. Its most important task is to direct the administration, take such initiatives as are requisite, and supervise the activities of other boards, themselves also appointed by the council. The communal board is responsible for economic administration and planning and has the task of preparing all matters to be decided upon by the council. Even if the communal board cannot interfere directly in the administrative activities of the various local boards and authorities, this duty of preparing all matters for the council together with the system of permanent coalition government gives it a great deal of power over communal decisions. Crucial is the board's position when it comes to proposing a budget. Here its most important task is to coordinate the demands of other communal boards and authorities and to present budget proposals.

Besides the communal boards, all communes have a great number of other boards of local authorities (*nämnder*) and other organs responsible for various administrative tasks. They can be of two main types: those the commune is obliged to set up, under special legislation, and facultative organs. Organizational structure varies widely from one commune to the next, according to size and urbanization. In a city like Gothenburg, with more than 400,000 inhabitants, there are about sixty communal boards and authorities: in a little rural commune with only about 10,000 inhabitants there are usually between fifteen and twenty, most of them mandatory. Even if the reapportionment reforms and the decrease in the number of communes from 2,500 to 277 meant that the number of laymen in the local administration was reduced, local self-government in Sweden still is characterized by the vast number of ordinary citizens engaged in local administration. Today about 45,000 persons out of a population of 8 million are elected to various positions in communal councils and boards.

THE COMMUNES AS DECENTRALIZED ADMINISTRATIVE UNITS AND AS AUTONOMOUS POLITICAL UNITS

Status of Communes in the Administration

In the mid-nineteenth century local self-government by communes was regarded as a means of achieving a decentralized and inexpensive administrative apparatus, on the one hand, and, on the other, of enabling the communes' inhabitants to participate in decision making and thus influence the forms taken by their own administration. It is obvious, however, that while the commune has grown in importance as a decentralized administrative unit largely subordinate to the state authorities, it has become weaker as an organizational unit administered by laymen. The latter circumstance is connected with two phenomena. Particularly since the war, the state's control of communal activities has grown, and communes have come to be regarded more and more as integrated elements within the national administrative apparatus. At the same time the communes' tasks have become more burdensome. Together with the apportionment reforms, this has led to a bureaucratization of communal administration and to a great growth in the number of local civil servants.

This leads us on to a discussion of the communes, both in their role of administrative units subject to state controls, and as autonomous units governed by laymen.

The Communes and the State

The state controls the communes in their way of organizing local activities and in determining the content of those activities. The Local Government Act fixes the communes' organization (their apportionment), the whole concept of what a commune is, their membership, their fields of jurisdiction, and the working methods employed in their decision making, as well as their administrative and executive organs. Local government legislation also regulates the forms for the communes' economic administration and fiscal rights. The communes are competent in two fields: facultative administration, in which a commune is free to design its own activities, and specially regulated administration, in which a commune's tasks are in greater or lesser detail fixed by various laws and regulations.

The state's control of the material contents of a commune's activities mainly takes three forms:

1. *Mandatory regulations*, contained within some law or state regulation
2. The commune's obligation to submit certain of its decisions to *government approval*
3. The regulations governing *grants-in-aid*, mandatory only insofar as a commune desires such contributions to its economy

As a rule the purpose of the state's control over the communes has been to achieve a similar level of communal service in different types of commune in various parts of Sweden. Therefore it is common to enjoin on communes a certain minimum standard, though of course they are at liberty to do better if they can. Their specially regulated administrative tasks are so comprehensive and expensive, however, that there is little opportunity for "super-standard" or unregulated activities. Certain estimates suggest that about 70 percent of communal expenditure falls within the specially regulated field.

Since the war, local government activities have increased swiftly by state mandatory regulations, and communal expenditure in 1979 amounted to 30 percent of the GNP. Even if the state covers 28 percent of the expenditure by grants-in-aid, most of it must be locally financed by the local government tax, a proportional tax on income. So while the commune to a large extent retains its responsibility for local finance, its influence over local activities has diminished.

Communes as Autonomous Political Units

Despite the fact that the greater part of the material contents of a commune's activities is fixed by the state, a commune still enjoys liberty within the "free," unregulated sector. It is here that the commune, as a local democratic organization, can meet any special local needs. The principle of local self-government, however, also implies that a commune's inhabitants are able, via the representative system, to influence the manner in which administrative decisions are made, even in fields strongly subject to state control. This is why citizen participation in communal administration has always been regarded as a crucial value, inherent in local self-government. Since the representative system was introduced into all communes in 1954, replacing the earlier system of town meetings, and as a result of the two postwar communal reapportionment reforms, the share of the population who can participate in the decision-making process in councils, boards, and local authorities has fallen sharply. The board system, however, still affords an opportunity for a considerable part of the population to participate directly, notably in small communes. But the character of lay administration differs essentially in various types of communes.

Let us illustrate this situation with some results from the Swedish Local Government Research Group's studies of representatives and local government civil servants in a sample of thirty-six communes made in 1968, before the latest reapportionment reform was carried through. These thirty-six communes were distributed into six groups, representing communes of differing size and urbanization from small rural communes to major cities.

First, the number of representatives in different commune types. Table 26.2 reveals that the greater a commune's population and the more it lives in an urban area, the more numerous its representatives. If we look at the total number of persons engaged in communal activities, Table 26.2 shows that the number of representatives is often essentially greater than the number of civil servants. This is particularly marked in the small rural commune, where representatives outnumber civil servants by ten to one (size class I, density class C); in the major cities (size class III, density class A), the civil servants outnumber the representatives by two to one.

However, with rising commune size the corps of civil servants rises a great deal more swiftly than does the corps of representatives. From Table 26.2, where the number of civil servants per 1,000 inhabitants has been calculated, a very strong "bureaucratization" is seen to accompany a rise in commune size. While in the little rural commune (size class I, density class C) there are upwards of three civil servants per 1,000, in major cities (size class III, density class A) the ratio is about three times as great. This is probably primarily a function of the increased complexity of a society with greater density and commune size. In comparison with small rural communes, for instance, the large and densely populated ones are involved in many tasks that cannot be executed without employing experts.

A more realistic assessment of the importance of lay administration is obtained by comparing the work done by representatives and by civil servants. A councillor in a small, thinly populated rural commune puts in an average of 70-80 hours' work a year on communal matters, whereas a councillor in a

Table 26.2
SWEDEN: REPRESENTATIVES AND CIVIL SERVANTS IN A SAMPLE OF COMMUNES

a. Average number of representatives in various types of commune

Density Class	Size Class		
	I	*II*	*III*
A	104	153	222
B	101	148	
C	92		

b. Average number of civil servants in various types of commune

Density Class	Size Class		
	I	*II*	*III*
A	18	111	532
B	13	73	
C	8		

c. Average number of civil servants per 1,000 inh. in various types of commune

Density Class	Size Class		
	I	*II*	*III*
A	4.3	7.3	8.6
B	3.2	5.9	
C	2.7		

d. Average number of full-time civil servants per "full-time working" councillor in various types of commune

Density Class	Size Class		
	I	*II*	*III*
A	7	28	60
B	5	18	
C	4		

Source: Swedish Local Government Research Group; mail questionnaire with councillors, 1968, and data on the civil servants in the communes.

Notes: Density classes
A over 90 percent in built-up areas
B 30-90 percent   ''   ''
C less than 30 percent   ''   ''

Size classes
I less than 8,000 inhabitants
II 8,000-30,000   ''   ''
III over 30,000   ''   ''

major city puts in on an average two or three times as many hours. Even so, and despite the fact that the representatives are more numerous in large communes than they are in small, the amount of time worked by representatives is small compared with the civil servants. In Table 26.2 an attempt is made to calculate the average number of full-time servants per "full-time" working councillor in various types of commune. In small rural communes there are four civil servants per "full-time" working councillor. In towns with more than 30,000 inhabitants, the ratio is sixty civil servants per "full-time" councillor: and in a large city like Gothenburg it is 200 to 1. It should be observed that Table 26.2 only shows the work done by councillors. In all communes there are board members who are not councillors, but their work is usually much less than the councillors'.

To sum up, one can say that though the number of representatives is large, the civil service administration is of special significance in the larger communes. In turn, the lay administration has quite a different character in large communes from what it has in small ones. In the latter, laymen carry out a considerable amount of the day-to-day administrative work, at the same time making the political decisions. As the size of commune rises the character of the work changes. In larger communes laymen are chiefly occupied with purely political functions and do less purely administrative work. In this respect the block commune reform has quite obviously changed the nature of local government. Lay administration in the traditional sense of laymen directly participating in administrative work will become less important in the future. Even if there is a certain amount of opportunity for direct citizen participation in small communes, most citizens participate only indirectly, through council elections and activities within parties and organizations.

PERSPECTIVES ON THE FUTURE DEVELOPMENT OF LOCAL GOVERNMENT

In recent years the Swedish discussion on local government through communes has come to concentrate on one question: how can citizens be given the possibility to participate more intensively in the communal decision-making process? As a result of the apportionment reforms, communes have grown steadily larger; and this in turn has led to a sharp drop in the number of communal representatives and to a rise in the numbers of local civil servants. It is estimated that as a result of the apportionment reforms some 100,000 communal representatives lost their positions. This means not only that the numbers of persons directly engaged in communal activities have fallen sharply but also that a citizen's chances of making personal contact with persons who in one way or another are involved in communal decision-making processes have been greatly reduced. Some results from the Swedish Local Government Research Group's studies also indicate that the larger communes that resulted from the reapportionments constitute a social environment that unfavorably affects citizen activity in parties and organizations. In the large urban areas, especially, such activity, measured in numbers of citizens who in some way are actively trying to influence local politics, is very small.

It is probable that as a result of the reforms the goal of achieving a relatively uniform service in communes in different parts of Sweden and of achieving a more technically efficient communal administration has been realized. But obviously it has been achieved at the expense of reducing the citizen's ability to influence communal decision-making processes, even if, in large cities, such activity probably always has been low. Despite the fact that the party system seems on the whole to channel crucial opinion within the electorate, new local organizations or activist groups outside the parties have been formed in recent years, above all in the large towns, and this can perhaps be seen as a sign of the party system's inability to absorb and channel the electorate's opinions, above all in matters affecting environmental and town planning.

In view of these phenomena, much of the public discussion of these matters in Sweden in the 1960s and 1970s has come to concentrate on the question of how to change the communal organizational structure in such a way as to give the average citizen a better chance of actively influencing decisions. Already several measures have been taken to counteract these negative consequences of the apportionment reforms and of an ever more complicated local society. Concrete instances of such measures have been an increase in the number of councillors in the communes and the introduction of an alternate system in 1971. In that year communes were also given the right to support the activities of local party organizations economically. Further, the communes have been allowed to arrange advisory referenda.

Other examples are the experimental work currently being done with advisory neighborhood councils (*kommundelsrad*) in several Swedish communes. An alternative measure which has also been discussed has been a further extension of the system of boards to comprise such smaller communal administrative units as individual schools, old age homes, and hospitals. These would then be run by committees consisting of employees and clients and elected by the council. The introduction of advisory neighborhood councils as well as an extension of the board system was suggested in 1975 by a royal commission on local government. This commission also suggested that trade unions whose members are directly employed by the commune should have representation on boards and local authorities. A bill based on the commission's suggestions was proposed to the Parliament in the spring of 1979.

West Germany: North-Rhine Westphalia

Günther Doeker*

27

In North-Rhine Westphalia in recent years few subjects have attracted more attention than territorial reorganization. Already academics, especially jurists and social scientists, and local and state politicians have written extensively about local, territorial, and administrative reorganization and its political dimension. This flood of literature seems likely to continue because two potentially contradictory issues are under debate: first, the demand by single-purpose movements (*Bürgerinitiativen*) to participate in administrative decision making, especially in cases where the social interests of citizens are directly involved in terms of "who gets what, when, and how," and, second, the demand for more effective bureaucratic management in distributing social and financial resources.

Nearly all of these studies on territorial reorganization are cast in the traditional mold that has characterized German writing on administrative problems. They focus on the machinery and statutory powers of local government in terms of legal analysis, explaining the formal provisions regulating various aspects of local and regional government. Very few writers have attempted to analyze policy outputs or the decision-making process or to discuss the distributive aspects of government in terms of the question posed in the title of Harold Lasswell's book, *Who Gets What, When and How*? This shifts the focus of research from the question of who governs to the equally important question of who benefits.[1] Studies of existing structures of local governments in Germany also reflect to some extent the bias of those consultants and practitioners who have found it more acceptable to improve technical services or planning structures than to analyze the conflicting interests of cities and regions so that formulas can be prescribed to resolve such conflict.

An analysis of the present structure of territorial government in North-Rhine Westphalia, taking into account recent reorganization, has not yet been at-

*Professor of Political Science, Free University of Berlin.

tempted. The purpose here is to examine the reformed structures and policies in terms of basic theoretical and policy assumptions. Broadly, it is an attempt to evaluate the organization of intra-state government and policy for urban and regional communities, to identify major elements and administrative factors that have determined the reorganized structures, and to offer some general hypotheses in major problem areas.

A word of caution should be added here. In attempting to translate German legal and political terminology it seems almost impossible to find analogous English terms. Nevertheless, the attempt has been made. I hope that the terms I have used will not confuse English readers.

TERRITORIAL REORGANIZATION

Causes

Local and urban government in North-Rhine Westphalia dates back to the seventeenth century, when the kingdom of Prussia incorporated territories now part of the state (*Land*) of North-Rhine Westphalia. Although there has since been a great population increase in that region, no reorganization of local government had ever taken place. Before the reform about 1,900 communities had fewer than 5,000 inhabitants, a population considered to be barely adequate to provide reasonable local community services; 1,000 communities had fewer than 1,000 inhabitants, and 566 had fewer than 500. In 1969 the smallest community had three (all female).[2]

In almost 80 percent of all communities in North-Rhine Westphalia there was a serious lack of municipal institutions capable of providing the level of services demanded in modern society. It had become obvious that it was impossible to run modern, diversified, and efficient municipal business on narrow population and financial bases. Until 1967, when the first laws concerning reorganization were passed by the parliament of the state, the system of urban government was distinguished by three broad types of local government: local municipalities (*Gemeinden*), including smaller townships, villages, and towns; counties (*Kreise*); and metropolitan areas (*Kreisfreie Städte*). Most of these municipalities had fewer than 10,000 inhabitants. The territorial structure caused extensive farming around these towns and created a gap between rural and municipal areas in terms of services such as schools and other social facilities. On the other hand, the center of community life in towns lost its attraction for industries, and they moved out into rural areas in order to profit from cheaper land and more convenient transportation. Thus, living was separated from working. The resulting increase in traffic left local municipalities with almost insurmountable problems.

The situation was similar in the second category of local government, the counties. According to German law counties are federations of constituent local municipalities. These counties were too small in area to provide adequate social services. In addition, the structural weakness of administration in the municipalities left the counties to administer social services, which should have been provided by these constituent members of the county. The third category of local and urban government is the city or metropolitan area. In North-Rhine Westphalia thirty-seven of these city governments existed, with a population of below 250,000 in twenty-five of them. In most cases the cities were expanding into rural areas since the territory was insufficient for housing and other services, but the cities left it to surrounding rural areas to provide all necessary facilities. In addition much of the urban population moved to rural areas, leaving the center of cities depopulated and their governments without necessary financial resources in terms of taxes, and so on. These developments were most conspicuous in the so-called Ruhrgebiet, the industrial center of Germany, with a population of some 5 million. Because of decreasing coal production in the area, its cities, heavily dependent on revenues from coal and steel, started to compete for new industries to replace coal and steel. The already existing cleavage between the southern and northern parts of the area was widened by this rivalry.

All these developments contributed to the disturbances already existing in relations between metropolitan and rural communities (*Stadt-Umland-Verhältnis*). Urban communities expanded into rural communities with their own life style and consequent divergent and conflicting interests. The distinction between rural and urban local government became increasingly difficult and artificial. Pressures of economics, transportation, labor mobility, and communication blurred the distinction completely. The desire for a high quality of municipal services and the demand for equality in education were strong influences in the move toward reorganization.

Local municipalities, counties, and cities, which all had and still have even after territorial organization their own traditional local self-administration, are supervised administratively by regional governments (*Bezirksregierungen*), presided over by a regional governor (*Regierungspräsident*), appointed by the government of North-Rhine Westphalia in Düsseldorf. The regional governor is politically responsible to the government of the state and cannot be removed from office by the regional government. In fact, what is called "regional government" in North-Rhine Westphalia, implying political responsibilities of elected members of regional, representative, legislative assemblies, is indeed only a second level of state administration. Regional governments in North-Rhine Westphalia (there are five existing: Düsseldorf, Köln, Münster, Arnsberg, and Detmold) are administrative-functional bodies supervising the implementation of state decisions at local levels in some social service areas. These solely administrative bodies serve also as review boards for local administration. Citizens seeking redress from administrative action of local authorities address complaints to these regional bodies. In some other areas they decide matters not within local jurisdiction in the first instance.

Territorial reorganization in North-Rhine Westphalia was primarily a device for grouping together some smaller communities, which were no longer capable in terms of size and area of providing necessary social services. But the government was not willing to provide these new communities with functional and jurisdictional powers previously within the exclusive jurisdiction of regional governments. Nevertheless, territorial reorganization at least questioned for the first time old and long accepted boundaries between communities which in social and economic terms had already ceased to exist.

Proposals for Territorial Reorganization

On 5 October 1965, the government of North-Rhine Westphalia requested a commission of experts, consisting of civil servants from the cities and the Ministry of the Interior as well as academics, to prepare a study for reorganizing local and municipal government in the state, incorporating modern tendencies and social developments. Between 1966 and 1968 three studies were produced: part A[3] analyzed the reorganization of rural areas; part B[4] dealt with problems of areas with large and concentrated populations and with problems arising from reorganizing counties; and part C[5] discussed problems arising from administering the new local and municipal governments, particularly in view of the ten existing regional governments in North-Rhine Westphalia and two larger-area special-purpose bodies (*Landschaftsverband Rheinland und Westfalen-Lippe*).

Part A recommended for rural areas the so-called nearby services community (*Nahversorgungsgemeinde.*) This concept is based on two factors: first, the new township or municipality should have a minimum of 5,000 and a maximum of 8,000 people; second, all service facilities should be concentrated in such a way that all people in that area should be able to reach all institutional and organizational services within thirty minutes from their home by public transport. In several areas, municipalities should be created with at least a minimum of 30,000 population, each providing services for both large and small towns in its particular area (so-called middle centers, *Mittelzentrum*). Both small and middle centers (type A and type B models) should be administered by one council, with a single budget and administration. In areas with a heavy concentration of population, only type B municipalities, middle centers providing their own social and other services, should be organized, so that traffic and transportation could be managed more easily.

For the reorganization of county government, the commission recommended in part B the establishment of larger area units. The counties should have a population of at least 200,000, with a maximum of 450-500,000. In addition, they should be organized according to economically sound areas corresponding to the development plan set up by the government of North-Rhine Westphalia. These new counties should use both type A and type B municipalities, as recommended in part A of the commission's report. For city government the study did not spell out far-reaching recommendations. It did suggest cities should be organized in terms of a population of 150-200,000, surrounded by and interconnected with type B municipalities. But an area should be decentralized rather than dominated by cities within easy reach of type B municipalities. Part C of the commission's report brought forward recommendations for administering the new regional system. The report recommended reducing the existing two larger-area special-purpose bodies by one in order to complement the existing regional administrative units. In addition, broad functional powers should be transferred to the new regional government bodies.

After publication of the commission's report and hearings by most local authorities and municipalities involved, the Government of North-Rhine Westphalia, a coalition of Social Democrats (SPD) and Free Democrats (FDP), decided to reorganize local and municipal government according to parts A and B. As far as the Ruhr District (*Ruhrgebiet*) was concerned, further studies were requested in order to make proper recommendations for solving the problems involved. No action was taken concerning part C of the commission's report, since the two parties were unable to agree on proper steps and recommendations implementing the principles underlying the report. Government reorganization and creation of new administrative units had to be postponed until the reorganization of municipalities and counties had taken place. Both parties also agreed to postpone any functional reorganization until territorial reorganization had been implemented. These far-reaching decisions by the government were supported by the opposition party in the state parliament, the Christian Democrats (CDU). Therefore, the reform was carried out by broad majorities. Such a broad political consensus was necessary, since the coalition government had only a small majority in the House and since the reform implied reorganizing structures, institutions, and territorial areas which had existed for some two hundred years.

In fact, the reform would have been almost a revolutionary step in terms of making local and municipal government more efficient if the government had implemented all the commission's recommendations. However, the attempt to reorganize local and municipal as well as regional government in North-Rhine Westphalia was only half-hearted. The report of the commission had recommended reorganization on three levels—territorial, functional and administrative-political—in order to achieve the greatest efficiency in providing better social services for all areas. But the government's decision to proceed solely with territorial reforms reduced the reorganization to geographical problems, which did not contribute to solving the structural and functional weaknesses of the existing local and municipal governments. Nevertheless, the minister of the interior of North-Rhine Westphalia did proceed in 1967 to implement the recommendations with respect to territorial reforms.

IMPLEMENTATION OF TERRITORIAL REORGANIZATION

Phase One

The implementation of the recommendations in part A of the commission's report was organized in two phases, phase 1, 1967-70[6] and phase 2, 1970-75.[7]

During phase 1 the implementation of territorial reorganization was predominantly introduced in those areas characterized by fragmented and superfluous local governments. Local governments concerned were asked to prepare for territorial amalgamation and to propose consolidation of various areas.[8] These proposals were then submitted to the Ministry of the Interior. It is important to note that the government, and the state administration especially, took care to reduce political tensions and often resistance to territorial reorganization. The principle of "freedom of choice" with reference to consolidation and amalgamation was carefully observed. The Ministry of the Interior established simultaneously three working groups of three and four civil servants, including in each an expert from the State Chancery, the state planning authority. These working groups were charged with analyzing all proposals made by local and municipal governments as to whether these proposals conformed to cabinet decisions and to recommendations of parts A and B of the commission's report. During the process of approving proposals by local and municipal governments, the working groups conducted intensive discussions in all 2,300 municipalities affected by the reform. Alternative proposals were introduced into the discussions and incorporated into draft proposals for territorial reorganization. Thus, these working groups became focal instruments for fostering reform ideas and concepts in all communities.

After considering all of these discussions and the alternatives proposed by their communities, the working groups prepared a final draft of the laws providing for territorial reorganization.[9] The draft was submitted to the Ministry for the Interior, discussed by a parliamentary committee, and finally formed into a law regulating territorial reorganization, taking into account the various "life styles" of these communities concerned. The procedure to prepare appropriate drafts for territorial reorganization was employed in all cases where such a territorial reform was envisaged.

During phase 1, forty-seven laws regulating territorial reorganization were passed by the legislature, so by 1970, 50 percent of the then existing local and municipal communities had been amalgamated and consolidated, and the number of communities had been reduced by half. The most imporant law regulating territorial reorganization was the law concerning the area surrounding Bonn, the federal capital of the Federal Republic of Germany. It was the first law to try to combine a reform of existing local government with a reform of county government.[10] In three cases metropolitan governments with fewer than 150,000 population were amalgamated with larger counties.

By 1969 the government and the administration had recognized that territorial reform limited primarily to smaller communities and excluding a reorganization of county and metropolitan government did not suffice. Amalgamation and consolidation of smaller local governments took place so rapidly that the proper functioning of county government was seriously questioned. The government of North-Rhine Westphalia therefore decided to introduce phase 2 in connection with what has been called the Program for North-Rhine

Westphalia 1975. Phase 2 combined the reorganization of smaller communities with that of county and metropolitan areas. The reform plan was supposed to be finalized by 1975, the year in which the parliamentary period ended and before elections in North-Rhine Westphalia were scheduled.

Phase 2

The reorganization program initiating phase 2 began with hearings, consultations, and discussions by the ministry's working groups. It was decided to initiate the first reorganization plans for the areas around Aachen and Bielefeld. Although the process of consultation took longer than anticipated, laws reorganizing these areas were passed on 1 January 1972 and 1 January 1973, respectively. The statutes passed made it possible to reduce the number of local communities to 950; administrative authorities (*Ämter*) were reduced to ninety-seven, and counties to forty-eight.[11]

Preparation and implementation of both laws initiating phase 2 of the reorganization plan led to new experiences and methods concerning territorial reorganization. These experiences revealed a much broader spectrum of factors which had to be taken into account. In fact, plan B differed somewhat from the practical preparation and implementation of phase 2. Nevertheless, the concept of reorganization recommended in plan B proved to be realistic in terms of finding proper and appropriate boundaries between newly organized local communities and counties before questions of functional divisions of services were to be discussed.

Furthermore, experience showed that problems of finding proper perspectives regarding city-area relations (*Stadt-Umland-Problem*) had to be viewed from various aspects and not necessarily as indicated in plan B. So-called solitary cities (*Solitärstädte*), that is, those without an environment (*Umland*) and a hinterland (*Hinterland*), faced different problems and showed more varied developmental perspectives than metropolitan cities as they exist in the Ruhr. In addition, the concept of organizing local communities around a center also proved valid for reorganizing counties; this was a concept that plan B did not emphasize particularly. Also, the basic question as to whether metropolitan cities and areas should be surrounded by hinterland counties (*Umlandkreise*) or sectoral counties (*Sektoralkreise*) led to the conclusion to look for specific solutions appropriate to the county or city in question.

No uniform solution seemed possible, although plan B had favored the establishment of hinterland counties. For instance, metropolitan cities like Bonn and Aachen became surrounded by hinterland counties, while Bielefeld, Münster, and Hamm received sectoral counties. It became obvious that unitary planning for all territorial consolidation was not suited to various areas if existing needs and expectations, in terms of traffic, boundaries, economics, and schooling, were to be met. The government therefore made it clear that each area should adopt only such plans for reorganization as suited the particular area and its special needs. An overall solution forcing local communities to accept the recommendations proposed in plans A and B was rejected, although the recommendations were not rejected in principle, particularly since the report also favored variations to suit the social and economic needs of particular areas.[12] Thus the government could easily argue that all territorial reorganization plans had to follow only general guidelines as stipulated in the commission's report. The constitutional court of North-Rhine Westphalia decided accordingly and held that the commission's report was not binding. Local communities, therefore, are not entitled to take recourse to the principle of equality as far as territorial organization is concerned.[13]

The government faced even more difficulties when territorial reorganization plans were proposed for the Ruhr Region.[14] The principles laid down in plans A and B of the commission's report indicated that the system proposed for local government in county areas was not adaptable to the metropolitan areas of the Ruhr. The Ministry of the Interior therefore developed a suitable system of territorial reorganization. It became known as the linked-city model (*Städteverbandsmodell*).[15] The principle was, after some territorial amalgamation, to link and regroup most of the metropolitan areas in the Ruhr into four greater metropolitan areas, each with more than 1 million inhabitants. These new metropolitan areas were to be governed by special-purpose bodies, which were especially responsible for planning, building and other communal services. Seven existing county governments would then become obsolete. However, the model developed by the ministry was not approved by the state parliament. There is reason to believe that this was because too many local governments controlled by Social Democrats would have been excluded from the decision-making process. Instead, the government decided to adopt the same system as adopted in other areas in accordance with plans A and B of the commission's report. The rejection of the linked-city model led to the establishment of the territorial organizations according to plan B. New towns with about 200,000 population were created. These would not have existed according to the ministry's proposal.

The Ruhr experience indicates that reorganization of communal structures molded in traditional politics must overcome political and practical as well as constitutional obstacles before any serious reform can be undertaken. It also shows that the creation of a Ruhr metropolitan area with some 6 million population would not solve structural weaknesses and social needs, since the problem was one of local and urban government and not of regional or larger metropolitan government. The "roof" seemed to be stretched too far to cover particular local needs and interests. Experience also indicates that metropolitan areas best serve social and economic needs when these areas have a population of some 200,000. Economically, in terms of administration and services, this population size seems to be the most appropriate.

The law concerning reorganization of the Ruhr Region, passed on 8 May 1974, finally brought the breakthrough for territorial reorganization in North-Rhine Westphalia. Indeed, no other law concerning territorial reorganization was so disputed and discussed in public—so much so that, in accordance with the North-Rhine Westphalia constitution, a referendum was called to defeat the reorganization. A single-purpose movement which started in Wattenscheid, a town in the Ruhr affected by these new plans, did not agree with plans mapped out for Wattenscheid.[16] Its aim was to include a provision in the local government act for North-Rhine Westphalia that in cases where boundaries of communities were to be changed by the state government a referendum had to be held in those communities affected when one-third of the members of a local council or 3 percent of the population requested it. In addition, the so-called citizens against reorganization wanted to maintain the existing city structure in the Ruhr and were inclined to adopt the reorganization plan already refused as unrealistic by the Ministry of the Interior. According to Article 68 of the Constitution of North-Rhine Westphalia, the initiative for a referendum needed at least one-fifth of all citizens eligible for voting in state elections, a total of about 2.4 million voters. The initiative received the signatures necessary for implementing the referendum. In February 1974, 720,000 voters, only 6.02 percent of the total voters, signed the petition to adopt the proposals worked out by "citizens against reorganization." Although in some areas there was great resistance to reorganization, the "citizens against reorganization" were unsuccessful in rural areas and in metropolitan cities. Their support came almost entirely from small, local communities, which were in the past— and would have been in the future due to the lack of financial resources— unable to provide necessary social and other services for their citizens.

After passing the law concerning reorganization of the Ruhr, the state legislature subsequently passed laws for reorganizing the areas Münster/ Hamm, Niederrhein, Mönchengladbach/Düsseldorf/Wuppertal, Köln and Sauerland/Paderborn, after appropriate hearings in these communities. The final law was passed 26 November 1974, thus concluding the reorganization of local and urban government in North-Rhine Westphalia.[17]

UNSOLVED PROBLEMS

Territorial reorganization was not necessarily satisfactory to all local and urban communities. In some cases the government would have preferred to accommodate larger areas, as in Ostwestfalen, Sauerland and Paderborn. Counties like Höxter and Olpe, with populations of under 150,000, probably will soon question their existence, since both will be unable to provide enough financial substance to meet all their social needs. Also, the "inter-city" established in the Ruhr might well become subject to changes in the forseeable future.

Even more difficult is the problem faced by metropolitan cities, which have been separated from the counties in which they are located. By amalgamations and annexations of all of the municipalities in the organized parts of the state, the cities will be completely removed from the county system of government.

In the meantime all retain their local autonomy, but only as territorial units within enlarged municipalities, with a high degree of local authority subject only to the normal supervision and control of the state and regional government. The relationship between metropolitan areas and counties (*Stadt-Umland*) is still experimental, since an appropriate solution for these problems is not at hand. On the other hand, territorial solutions in the form of solitary cities have apparently been suitable for Bonn, Aachen, Bielefeld, Münster and Hamm.

Territorial reorganization in North-Rhine Westphalia has shown the extreme difficulty of finding a structure whereby efficient and effective government is combined with the right of a community to conduct its own local affairs. At the moment it seems that reorganization of municipal government has become greatly overextended at the cost of people's participation in the political decision-making process. Furthermore, the restructuring of territorial areas did not imply reassigning functions to new communities in terms of proper and adequate financing and revenue sharing or the establishment of planning and development agencies, nor were the problems of relationship between city areas and counties fully solved. In terms of innovation, the territorial reform in North-Rhine Westphalia has nevertheless indicated that, in comparison with other federal states, such a reform is feasible only when all participants agree to dispose of existing boundaries, to structure reorganization from top to bottom, and to include metropolitan areas within the framework of reorganization. A functional and administrative reform still awaits detailed discussions and model development before it can become efficient and effective for both citizens and administrators.

Recognizing the dangers in the removal of citizens' participation from the decision-making process, the government introduced a law calling for the establishment of "districts" in metropolitan and county areas and regions.[18] The law provided for the election of representatives to district councils within larger areas. These councils were given some administrative powers over the management of various local affairs, such as road maintenance, garbage services, water supply, and some minor activities not wanted by the larger area councils. It remains to be seen whether these district councils will bring citizens' participation within the framework of local decision processes.

The geographical reorganization has produced one fundamental tendency: the dispersion of responsibility to the extent that no local body is now in a position to act as coordinator and priority setter for local government as a whole, unless one assumes that the reorganization was intended to allow the state to play this role. The district councils appear to be what might be called quasi-subordinate because of the overwhelming legal authority of the state government. It is too early, nevertheless, to judge the results of the reorganization in terms of "Who gets what, when and where?" Only the proposed functional and administrative reform will give the final answer to this question.

NOTES

1. See K. Newton and L. J. Sharpe, ''Output Studies in Britain: An Appraisal and some Proposals for Future Research'' (Paper delivered at the London Sessions on Urban Politics and Policies of the European Consortium for Political Research, 1975), pp. 2 ff.

2. See Köstering and Bünemann, *Die Gemeinden und Kreise nach der kommunalen Gebietsreform in Nordrhein-Westfalen* (Düsseldorf, 1975), p. 2.

3. Die Neugliederung der Gemeinden in den ländlichen Zonen vom 22.11.1966.

4. Die Neugliederung der Städte und Gemeinden in den Ballungszonen und die Reform der Kreise vom 9.4.1968.

5. Die staatliche und regionale Neugliederung des Landes Nordrhein-Westfalen vom 8.4.1968.

6. See Köstering and Bünemann, *Die Gemeinden und Kreise*, p. 6.

7. Compare *Nordrhein-Westfalen Plan* (Nordrhein-Westfalen, Düsseldorf: Ministry of Interior, 1975), p. 144.

8. See Köstering, *Methoden der Verwaltungsreform, Staats-und Kommunalverwaltung* (1971), pp. 85, 125 ff.

9. Compare Vorschlag des Innenministeriums zur Neugliederung des Ruhrgebiets vom 25 September 1972, pp. 295 ff.

10. See Köstering and Bünemann, *Die Gemeinden und Kreise*, p. 8.

11. ''Vorschlag des Innenministeriums zur Neugliederung des Ruhrgebiets'' vom 25 September 1972, pp. 295 ff.

12. See Köstering and Bünemann, *Die Gemeinden und Kreise*, p. 9.

13. Decision of the Verfassungsgerichtshof von Nordrhein-Westfalen vom 4 August 1972, VGH 11/71.

14. Compare Landtags-Drucksache 7/2800 vom 10 July 1973 (Ruhrgebietsgesetz).

15. See ''Vorschlag,'' pp. 1 ff.

16. See ''Der 3 Weg—Volksbegehren—Aktion Bürgerwille, November 1973; see also ''Vorschlag des Innenministeriums'' vom 25 September 1975, p. 322.

17. See Köstering and Bünemann, *Die Gemeinden und Kreise*, p. 11.

18. See Loebell and Henrichs, *Die neue Bezirksverfassung der Städte und Gemeinden in Nordrhein-Westfalen*, 2. Aufl., 1975, pp. 1 ff.

West Germany: A Survey

Frido Wagener*

28

In recent years the Federal Republic of Germany has been confronted with the problems resulting from the fragmentation of the basic units of local government, the local authorities (*Gemeinden*). Their number, in a country with about 60 million inhabitants, amounted to 24,509 in 1959, and even by the end of the 1960s the number had decreased only slightly, to 24,282 basic units in 1968. Needless to say, the large number of local authorities with consequently little power and less financial means had not been efficient enough to cope with the increased demands of the public and the rapid tempo of change in an industrial society. One only has to think of environment protection and urbanization, with its connected problems of health services, social assistance, transport, water purification, and air pollution control, not forgetting the radical changes in schools and sociocultural amenities. All these services had to be carried out within the traditional local authority structures dating from the last century.

In the second half of the 1960s, the shortcomings inevitably resulting from this situation led to a growing determination among politicians to initiate and carry through alterations and adjustments in the Federal Republic's administrative units.

*Professor of Applied Administrative Science, Post-Graduate School for Administrative Sciences at Speyer, and Honorary Professor at the University of Heidelberg; former full-time professional deputy to a local authority association. Author of *Die Städte im Landkreis* [The Towns in the County] (Göttingen: Schwartz, 1955); *Neubau der Verwaltung* [Rebuilding of the Administration], 2nd ed. (Berlin: Duncker & Humbolt, 1974); "Reform kleiner Gemeinden in Europa" [Reform of Small Local Authorities in Europe], *Verwaltungsarchiv* 62 (April 1971): 97-113; and "New Developments in Municipal Reform in Germany," *Planning and Administration* 3, no. 2 (Autumn 1976). This essay is based on a longer one prepared by the author for an international conference on local government sponsored by the Polish Academy of Sciences (Warsaw, 1974).

THE GERMAN ADMINISTRATIVE AND FINANCIAL SYSTEM

In order to understand the problems and results of the local authorities' reorganization, one first needs to know the structure of the administrative and financial systems. The basic structure of the administrative system is defined by the constitutional allocation of governmental powers as the following five levels (with numbers as of 1 January 1978):

1. 1 federation
2. 11 states (*Länder*)
3. 25 state administrative districts (*Regierungsbezirke*) and 14 regional administrations (*Regionalverbände*)
4. 235 counties (*Kreise*) and 89 noncounty towns (*Kreisfreie Städte*)
5. 3,261 local authorities

The federation, states, counties, noncounty towns, and local authorities constitute spatial administrative structures with corporate status and directly elected executive organs. They are organized as political subdivisions, whereas the state administrative districts are only dependent subunits of the six largest states. Although the regional administrations, counties, and noncounty towns fall into the category of local government, the subject of this essay will be only the fifth level, the local authorities.

It is important to know the following facts about the German financial system. About 39 percent of the total expenditure of the public budgets is spent by the federal government, about 37 percent by the state governments, and about 24 percent by the local authorities and counties. More than 80 percent of the expenses of the federal government are financed by taxes. The expenses of the states are only financed to about 65 percent by taxes, whereas some 15 percent is covered by special purpose grants from the federal government. The local authorities and counties only finance 33 percent of their expenses by taxes. A further 29 percent is financed by general grants of the states and 17 percent by specific grants of the federal and state governments. The remaining 21 percent is covered by fees, charges towards the cost of a local government service, and income from the commercial activities of the local authorities (electricity, gas, properties, lands, forests, bill posting). Of the total tax income, 85 percent (especially income tax, sales tax, and trade tax) is distributed in fixed percentages to the federal and state governments and the local authorities (revenue sharing).

TERRITORIAL REORGANIZATION

Basic Facts

The most significant change in the local government of the Federal Republic of Germany is the reorganization of local territorial units. The growing determination among politicians to initiate territorial reorganization was due to several characteristic trends related both to the socioeconomic foundations of public administration and to the function of public administration itself. These trends have changed the surroundings of administration and the administration itself and can be summarized as follows:

First, *shrinking distances*. The use of the automobile and telephone by the public at large makes it much easier to establish quick and individual connections between the administration and the citizens and vice versa. At present one automobile and one telephone connection are owned by every second or third inhabitant. The distance between administration and citizen today plays, and in the future will continue to play, a diminishing role.

Second, *equivalent infrastructure in rural areas*. The decline of agriculture, the ever growing size of the tertiary sector, and the spread of trade and industry into rural areas make it necessary to provide them with an infrastructure equivalent to that offered in urban areas.

Third, *larger populations required to carry out administrative functions more efficiently*. To make full and effective use of the service facilities provided by local authorities, expanding catchment areas with a greater number of inhabitants are required. The complexity and mechanization of service facilities presuppose that the number of people who are to benefit by them is sufficiently large. Only then is a proper level of mechanization and automation attainable, compelled by a mounting pressure of modernization upon public authorities.

Fourth, *new administrative aids*. There is an increasing use in modern administration of electric typewriters, duplicating equipment, automobiles, automatic accounting machines, calculators, and electronic data processing equipment. However, these are economical only in administrative units to which large and specialized fields of activity are assigned.

Fifth, *specialized personnel*. Public administration today leans heavily upon the skills of the expert. A growing army of highly trained staff is needed to perform functions in areas such as planning, servicing, and control. Very small local authorities and towns are not in a position to enlist the services of such specialists in sufficient number and quality because of insufficient financial resources and because specialists would not find work suited to their capabilities.

Sixth, *need of intensive planning*. Social and industrial changes in the past have brought with them the need of increased planning of functions and expenditure. Small administrative units tend towards isolated planning. They cannot permanently employ qualified planning groups. It is only in larger units that conflicting interests can be harmonized while planning the use of spatial and financial resources and the timing of investments.

Objectives

In line with the trends that have evolved during the last few decades in traffic, trade, and industry and in the development and sprawl of residential areas, the optimum size of populations looked after by organizational and administrative units has grown enormously. The effect attained through technical administrative aids tends in the same direction. Obviously, the large-scale economic enterprise in the private sector is followed by the large-scale administration. The decisive factors are now administrative success and a high degree of efficiency in public administration.

Current reforms of territorial units no longer have as their primary goal a cut in administrative expenses. The rising need of public services has resulted in a noticeable shift in reform objectives. The reform plans of previous decades time and again indicated as their main purpose a saving in personnel and costs. Sometimes the key target was the reduction of the volume of public services. In present-day reforms cost saving considerations at best play a minor role. The chief emphasis in the territorial reorganization is on a much more extended provision of infrastructure, while attempts are made simultaneously to prevent the number and cost of personnel from rising out of proportion.

Recent History

In order to get the larger areas required for town and country planning, interauthority cooperation as well as planning associations had been recommended for years. However, opinions were increasingly voiced that demanded a fundamental coincidence of planning areas and administrative areas. Centralized territorial division in rural areas not only should be the basis of interauthority cooperation in planning associations, but, likewise, the central local unit including its neighborhood was regarded as the ideal area comprising a unitary local authority (*Einheitsgemeinde*).

In 1968 it was assumed in Lower Saxony, in North-Rhine Westphalia, Rhineland-Palatinate, and Schleswig-Holstein that the lowest-level local units with a full-time staff should have minimum populations of 5,000, 7,500, or 8,000. No citizen should have to travel more than seven, eight, or ten kilometers to reach his administrative unit. In Hesse 1,500 inhabitants were thought sufficient. In Bavaria and Baden-Wuerttemberg the intention was for the time being to get along on adjustment measures, such as abolition of midget local authorities (*Zwerggemeinden*) and exclaves, promotion of voluntary amalgamations, creation of administrative communities (*Verwaltungsgemeinschaften*), municipal federations (*Verbandsgemeinden*), and similar auxiliary facilities, but without fixing minimum numbers of inhabitants. In 1968 there was a clear lagging behind both in argumentation and in intensity of the will to change by the southern states, in contrast to their northern counterparts. It was only in the north that the transfer of town and country planning to enlarged administrative units ("planning autonomy" of the local authorities) was requested.

Today the south German states no longer lag behind in territorial reorganization, although their approach was different. In Bavaria and Baden-Wuerttemberg the reform was designed to take place "from above." The number of counties and noncounty towns was substantially reduced throughout the states. The local authorities belonging to counties (*kreisangehörige Gemeinden*) were to merge on a voluntary basis. In contrast, a reform "from below" was practiced in North-Rhine Westphalia. As a first step, reform measures in local government were carried out county by county. Lower Saxony and Hesse proceeded in a similar way. Since 1970, in what are called reorganization areas, the territorial reform of counties and noncounty towns has been taking place together with that of the local authorities belonging to counties in North-Rhine Westphalia. In Schleswig-Holstein and in Rhineland-Palatinate it was the county reform that was first carried out. This was immediately followed by a new division of the multiple communities (*Aemter*) and the creation of municipal federations. In Saarland, counties and local authorities were reorganized at the same time. In Rhineland-Palatinate, Hesse, and North-Rhine Westphalia the number of state administrative districts was reduced by amalgamations.

The Present Situation

In giving a survey of the territorial reforms in the Federal Republic of Germany, a distinction must be made between the reorganization of local authorities in general and of rural local authorities in particular, as well as the reorganization of counties, towns and their surrounding areas, and the territories of the states. This essay discusses only the reform of the basic units of local government.

LOCAL GOVERNMENT REFORM. In Baden-Wuerttemberg the number of local authorities since the beginning of the reform has been reduced from 3,379 (as of 1 January 1968) to 1,101 (1 January 1978). From 1975 onward 458 local administrative units with populations of more than 8,000 have been constituted below the level of counties. In areas with a low population density, these local units consist of 371 administrative communities, whose member communities as a rule have a minimum of 2,000 inhabitants.

In Bavaria voluntary amalgamations have caused the number of local authorities to fall from 7,073 to 4,387 between 1 January 1969 and 1 January 1973. The final target, set for 1 May 1978, was a further reduction to 2,027. A population of 5,000 is viewed as the minimum size of the 740 unitary communities (*Einheitsgemeinden*). Each of them should be able to employ a full-time staff of civil servants. Instead of amalgamation into unitary local authorities, administrative communities are also permissible. Members should generally have not less than 1,000 inhabitants. The 393 administrative communities are to be not just a transitory stage, but a permanent form of organization suited to the needs of rural areas.

In Hesse the model plans published by the state government since 1969 have released a chain of voluntary and statutory combinations. The number of local authorities thus fell from 2,690 in 1967 to 416 on 1 January 1978.

In Lower Saxony, which on 30 June 1972 had a number of local authorities as large as 3,987, the first ten laws relating to local authority reforms came into force on 1 July 1972. The reform was completed on 1 March 1974, with 1,017 local authorities belonging to counties. Of these, 415 lowest-level administrative units employing full-time personnel (273 unitary communities and 142 collective communities [*Samtgemeinden*]) have survived.

In North-Rhine Westphalia, forty-seven laws were promulgated in implementing a first territorial reorganization program between 1967 and 1970, whereby the number of local authorities was reduced from 2,297 to 1,276. The multiple communities were entirely replaced by unitary communities. The second reorganization program completed the local government reform in 1974. Today, North-Rhine Westphalia had 373 unitary communities belonging to counties (*kreisangehörige Einheitsgemeinden*), but none of the multiple communities remain.

In Rhineland-Palatinate the institution of the municipal federation was introduced to take care of the activities beyond the general effectiveness and administrative efficiency of smaller local authorities. Before the beginning of the reform there were 2,893 local authorities belonging to counties. Upon the coming into force of fourteen reorganization laws, the number of local authorities with a full-time administrative staff went down to 201. This includes 164 municipal federations with an average population of over 10,000 and 3 local authorities and towns independent of municipal federations (*verbandsfreie Gemeinden und Städte*). The 2,271 small local authorities that continue to exist within the municipal federations are partly of midget size, counting but a few hundred heads.

In Saarland the territorial reform of local government was started by the "preparatory law" of 17 December 1970. The decided purpose was to amalgamate the existing local authorities to form a group of substantially larger unitary communities. The law adopted on 19 December 1973 reduced the number of local authorities from 344 to 50 unitary communities, while at the same time scrapping 42 multiple communities.

In Schleswig-Holstein reorganization was started in 1966 at the level of the multiple communities, reducing their number from 216 to 122 and increasing their populations to an average of 7,000. Amalgamations of local authorities, mainly voluntary, resulted in a reduction of their number from 1,374 to 1,126 between 1969 and 1 January 1976. Of these, 1,028 are local authorities belonging to 121 multiple communities (*amtsangehörige Gemeinden*).

To sum up, the territorial reform of basic local government units in the Federal Republic of Germany is completed. Governed by essentially identical principles, this reform has led to a drastic reduction in the number of basic administrative units (from more than 24,500 to less than 3,300). Particularly striking is the strong tendency to set up unitary communities. But the reorganization also produced new forms of organization in rural areas, such as the municipal federations in Rhineland-Palatinate and the administrative communities in Bavaria and Baden-Wuerttemberg.

FORMS OF REORGANIZATION IN RURAL AREAS. The rough outline given above of the reform measures undertaken in the Federal Republic shows that the time is over for the small, independent rural local authority, which had its affairs handled on an honorary basis. The trend is obviously towards larger administrative units. Two forms of local government administration in rural areas are conspicuous: the federative amalgamation of several small local authorities to constitute a closely knit local government association, whereby two levels of rural local government are created (a multiple community, collective community, municipal federation or administrative community); and the large rural local authority (unitary community) comprising several settlements (villages, hamlets, scattered settlements) with a one-tier administration. In the latter case, local interests may be looked after by a local council (*Ortschaftsrat*) or a chairman of the local council (*Ortschaftsvorsteher*), this, however, being no indication of an independent administrative level.

In states with firmly rooted settlement units, which as villages and small towns have for a long time had their own local government (Baden-Wuerttemberg, Bavaria), the tendency is towards uniting the smaller local authorities on a federative basis. In some of the states with existing federations of small local authorities (Lower Saxony, Rhineland-Palatinate, Schleswig-Holstein), the attempt is being made to concentrate functions in the local government association. In other states with existing federations of small local authorities (North-Rhine Westphalia, Saarland), a daring step is being taken to form large local authorities.

Even though the long-run tendency is predominantly in favor of the large rural local authority, both the two-tier administration and one-tier large authorities have their specific advantages and disadvantages. The two-tier federation of small local authorities is equivalent to a concentration of administrative authority, but it has the advantage of keeping local decision making intact. The small local authorities retain their own separate budget and financial equalization takes place on a limited scale. The populations of small local authorities still have their mayor (*Buergermeister*) as the man of their confidence, always near at hand and promptly attending to the minor business of making out certificates, posting public notices, issuing instructions to carry out local work, and so forth. All technical administrative aids may be utilized to increase the degree of internal administrative efficiency, for the higher tier is organized as an "office-sharing pool" servicing all smaller local authorities. One disadvantage is that planning and service functions (external administration) can be shifted only in part to the higher level, as otherwise no activities would be left to the small local authorities (lower level) for which they themselves are responsible.

Compared with the two-tier structure, one-tier unitary local authorities in rural areas provide opportunities to find more consistent, clear-cut solutions. There is only one administration with a uniform budget, one council, and one administrative executive. Financial equalization among the villages is perfect. Similarly, from the administrative viewpoint the unitary local authority is generally the most economical solution because the effect of rationalization obtaining in large, specialized offices makes itself fully felt. The local authority carries out all planning tasks and discharges all service functions. The advantages of sufficient administrative potential, internal and external, are obvious for local authorities with populations over 5,000 to 10,000. This solution, however, has the disadvantage that the awareness of common interests, which has not entirely disappeared in small settlement units, cannot be put to full use for the purpose of self-government in the unitary local authority. A partial remedy might be local councils and chairmen of local councils.

EVALUATION OF REORGANIZATION

Looking back on the results of the local government reform achieved so far, one notes various advantages and disadvantages. On the positive side, areas and populations within the local government units at the various levels have been adjusted. As the number of basic units is now substantially reduced, the proportion of counties to local authorities (span of control) has likewise changed from 1:60 to 1:20. The minimum population of the lowest local government unit with a full-time staff of civil servants is on the order of 8,000. Local authorities belonging to counties and basic units of local government that survived the territorial reform have the right functional size to take care of their infrastructure and are the foundation of a five-tier structure of the administrative system at large. Now that the territorial reform is completed and the main levels of public administration are spatially structured to ensure optimum sizes of populations in regard to the scope of functions assigned to them, these local government units are also relatively well-defined planning areas. They roughly coincide with the boundaries of the central system of local divisions and permit the planning of a sufficient bundle of public services and other activities.

The most serious disadvantages of the territorial reform are a deranged sense of social membership in the citizenry, both locally and regionally, lower density of mandates in the constituencies, and longer distances between the citizen and the administrative authorities. These can be remedied only in part by setting up auxiliary administrative units (consulting days), by appointing local councils, creating town districts (*Stadtbezirke*), or increasing the number of seats on local councils.

FUTURE DEVELOPMENTS

In almost all states of the Federal Republic of Germany local government reform had been completed by the beginning of 1975. In Bavaria, however, the reform was not complete until the end of 1978. This tardiness was due to the fact that local government reform is not a subject that the federal government is competent to discuss; hence every state had to find its own solution. Besides, Bavaria had more than 7,000 small local authorities before the beginning of the reform, by far the greatest portion of all the states in the country. Therefore Bavaria's reform measures in local government had to be the most severe, and the Bavarian more than any other state government had to cope with the public's mistrust of amalgamation.

In the Federal Republic generally, it is intended that the territorial reform should be followed by a functional reform, that is, a redistribution of responsibilities among the various levels of administration, mainly through the delegation of powers from the higher to the lower levels. The main objective is to bring government closer to the public and increase the general effectiveness and administrative efficiency. Thus, for example, in Baden-Wuerttemberg the local authorities are now responsible for issuing passports, building law, licenses in trade law, exemption of taxes on the acquisition of real property, and so forth. Before the functional reform, these were functions of the lower state authorities.

Now that the reform has been completed in all states, public administration, which was originally designed to maintain law and order but which in the course of time has been forced more and more to render public services, is in a better position to accept its challenge and provide each citizen in town and country with equal chances for the fulfillment of his personality. Also, industry expects the government to promote increased growth in economic productivity by reorganizing infrastructures. Territorial administrative units must be brought into line with economic and social regions in order to be able to harmonize the various organizational measures. Moreover, economic, technical and social developments have resulted in an increased range and specialization of public tasks. Owing to their volume and "repetitiveness," these can only be dealt with rationally by using modern technology. Such administrative aids, however, can be used more economically in larger administrative units. At the same time these are also better suited to the necessary specialization, which has become inevitable as administrative business has become more complicated. For a long time administrative structures lagged behind social developments. It is now hoped that these structures will prove themselves adequate to meet future requirements.

EASTERN EUROPE

USSR
YUGOSLAVIA
SOCIALIST COUNTRIES OF
CENTRAL AND SOUTHEASTERN
EUROPE

USSR:
The Urban Units

Jerry F. Hough *

29

Soviet urban government is not susceptible to easy generalization, for there are enormous variations in the size of communities that are given the status of "city." In 1974, 71 of the USSR's 1,999 "cities" had fewer than 3,000 inhabitants, while 11 contained more than 1 million persons. The soviets and party organs of the two largest republic capitals—Moscow and Kiev—are administratively independent of the provincial institutions and are supervised directly by the republic, but the small towns are not even independent of the local county and have no party organizations.[1] The analysis of this chapter basically refers to the 500 cities with populations over 50,000.

In many respects the political system of the significant Soviet cities has remained relatively unchanged in recent years. The Constitution continues to specify that elected soviets are the supreme legislative body at each territorial level, including that of the city. Each city soviet has some 130 deputies on the average, and it meets four times a year. The soviet in turn is to select an executive committee (*ispolkom*), normally of seven to thirteen persons, which supervises the various departments and administrative bureaus of city government. The chairman of the executive committee is the top official of the soviet and usually is described by Americans as the mayor of the city.

The Statutes of the Communist Party continue to state, however, that the soviets are to function under the direct leadership of the local party organ and that the Communists in every "elected" governmental and nongovernmental body are to form a party group that is bound to carry out the instructions of this party committee. As a result, even in formal and legal terms, we really should describe the seven-to-eleven-person bureau of the city party committee as the real city council, and the first secretary of the city party committee as the real mayor.

*Professor of Political Science, Duke University.

Indeed, the city party officials have been the "city fathers" in one sense that officials of the soviets (and of Western cities) have not even been able to approach. The city party committee can obligate any Communist within the city to take action, and hence it is in a position to issue binding directives to major plant managers, railroad administrators, college rectors, and local officials of the secret police and prosecutor's office, none of whom is administratively subordinated to the city soviet.

The ability of the city party organs to direct the activities of all agencies within the city is not hypothetical. One of the three secretaries of the city party committee specializes in industrial, construction, transportation, and general urban questions, and he has from five to ten men with engineering-managerial experience to assist him in these activities. These officials are deeply involved in industrial decision making itself, even including such detailed matters as the establishment of priorities for supplies deliveries. They not only handle individual industrial problems on an ad hoc basis, but often create special party "staffs" at major construction projects in the city to coordinate the work of the various subcontractors, suppliers, and city agencies involved.

The deep involvement of the city party first secretary himself in the supervision of industry and construction is clearly indicated in Table 29.1. Although some Westerners have seen the late Khrushchev period (the early 1960s) as a time of peculiar and abnormal party involvement in industrial decision making, the proportion of party secretaries with engineering education and managerial experience has actually increased over the last fifteen years. Perhaps because of the special problems involved in leading cities in a multinational context, the city first secretaries of other nationalities often have a more "political" background, but this too is changing.

Table 29.1

USSR: BACKGROUND OF NEWLY ELECTED FIRST SECRETARIES OF CITY PARTY COMMITTEES, CITIES OF OVER 100,000 PERSONS

Year of First Election	Percent of First Secretaries Who		
	Had an Engineering Education	Worked At Least Five Years in Industry*	Worked At Least Ten Years in Industry*
The Russian Republic and the Ukraine			
1958-64 (N=38)	79	55	26
1965-70 (N=27)	85	78	41
1971-78 (N=20)	85	85	44
Other Republics			
1958-64 (N=16)	38	31	25
1965-70 (N=15)	47	40	40
1971-78 (N=13)	69	62	31

*"Industry" is shorthand for industry, construction, transportation, and geology. In several cases, years spent in teaching technical subjects in a technical college are included as industrial experience.

LIMITS ON CITY POLITICAL OFFICIALS

While the political officials in the Soviet Union (and elsewhere in the communist world) have a unique authority over all types of decision making within the city—including many types of decision making that would be in the private sphere in other systems—a number of factors have limited the degree of their real control over the city. In the first place, of course, the city officials are located at a middle level in a centralized hierarchy. The city party committee is subordinated to the party committee at the next higher territorial level (generally, the *oblast* or region, but in the case of the smaller republics, the republic itself), and the executive committee of the city soviet is subordinated not only to the city party committee but also to the executive committee of the soviet at the next higher level. Most of the departments and administrative bureaus of the city soviet, such as education, health, and trade, are also officially placed in "dual subordination" to the corresponding department at the next higher level as well as to the city government. Other institutions, such as the industrial plants, naturally are also subject to the directives of their respective ministries.

The actual meaning of the system of dual subordination is enormously complex, for the real authority of the two supervisers varies from issue to issue. For example, the ministerial line of command seems relatively weak in matters relating to personnel selection and strong on questions associated with professional or methodological guidance. The ministerial superiors are also quite strong in the financial realm. The city governments have no major source of independent funding, and they are not appropriated a lump sum that they then may subdivide among the various local claimants. Instead, while there is a city budget and while city officials may shift funds within it to a limited extent, each department essentially seeks its funds from within its own ministerial hierarchy, thereby competing more with similar departments in other cities in the appropriations process than with other departments in its own city.

A second restriction on the real ability of city officials to control and plan the development of the city has been the regime's practice of financing a large proportion of the new housing in the city and a significant proportion of the construction of stores, utilities, roads, day-care centers, and city beautification outside the city budget. These funds flow into the city through the various ministries and departments, especially the heavy industry ministries, which seek to provide housing for their own employees and services for the area in which they live. The result has frequently been a Balkanization of Soviet cities and an imbalance in the services provided. A city may have as many as sixteen separate water systems, each administered separately, and access of citizens to housing and city services may vary with the "wealth" of their ministry. Even the more well-to-do central agencies often try to concentrate their expenditures on housing, leaving the underfinanced soviets to try (often with great delay) to provide services for the new area.

To be sure, the city officials have had some success in forcing or persuading the plant managers to divert some of the funds for ''social-cultural construction'' to city-wide needs and to coordinate these expenditures with those of other plants and the city soviet. In Zaporozhe, for example, the major industrial plants provided resources for a major new bridge and 800,000 square meters of new roads, and in Riazan they built a water filtration plant and widened the network of sidewalks and street lights. In Novosibirsk, twelve plants pooled their funds to build a 140-place kindergarten, while one large plant was induced to contract for a sewerage collection system, with other plants contributing a share of the costs.[2]

However, the relationship between the city's political organs and its major industrial plants has not been easy. Again and again, city officials complain that ''everything depends on the good wishes'' of the agencies involved and that many are far from generous.[3] If the ministries are not happy with the way their funds are being spent they can refuse to approve the plan, and local managers surely know how to suggest to their superiors the type of conditions to impose. The city officials have a few bargaining chips, and they can appeal over the heads of the ministries in Moscow, but the relationship is still unequal. Moreover, the dependence of city officials upon enterprise funds can make them very accommodating when the plants want to take some action that violates city ordinances or the city plan. William Taubman argued that, despite the great formal power of the city party committee, many Soviet cities really should be visualized as ''company towns,'' and this characterization is often quite accurate.[4]

RECENT CHANGES IN CITY GOVERNMENT

In all respects indicated thus far—the formal structure of the party and soviet organs and the relationship between them, the expansion of the ''political arena'' to cover many spheres of action that would be in the ''private sector'' in the West, the financing of much of city housing and city services construction through the industrial ministries, and the political strength of the heavy industrial plants in city decision making—Soviet urban government retains many of the same features that it has had for forty years. Nevertheless, it would be wrong to see the Soviet urban scene as frozen or petrified. Despite the images embodied in much Western scholarship on the Soviet Union, urban government is not a uniform phenomenon across the country which changes only in well-defined ways in response to precise central decrees. In reality, there are many experiments and variations in practice in different cities, and as these innovations spread in response to governmental and other pressures, important (if incremental) changes can occur over time in the way that city government functions and in the power that it exercises.

One such change, for example, has been the rising level of education among the personnel who staff local government. Since the late 1930s, the managers of significant heavy industry plants have been graduate engineers—a highly elite type of education in the Soviet Union—and this was often also true of the key party officials in the most important cities. However, the educational level of city officials as a whole lagged seriously. Separate statistics are not available on city party officials, but among city, county, and borough party secretaries taken together, only 18 percent had a college degree in 1952. During the next two decades, this figure increased rapidly, reaching 68 percent in 1961, 89 percent in 1966, and 97 percent in 1972.[5] The change is so pervasive that it must have occurred across all categories of secretaries, including the city secretaries.

The educational level of city soviet officials has not been as high as that of party officials, but it too has been rising steadily. In 1973, 68 percent of the chairmen of city executive committees had a college education as compared with 49 percent in 1965, while for members of the executive committee as a whole this figure increased from 44 percent in 1963 to 57 percent in 1973.[6] (Twenty-five percent of the executive committee members were workers and collective farmers—without doubt, almost exclusively workers—and since these members seldom have higher education, the figures for the more ''professional'' members of the executive committee are considerably higher.) It is difficult to believe that this change in the type of person serving as a city official has not affected officials' actual role, if for no reason than its psychological impact both upon the regional officials and the local industrial managers.

A second development of considerable relevance for the role of the city political officials has been the steady growth in the size of the urban sector and in the degree of industrial development in the country. Both in tsarist Russia and the Soviet Union, the central government has had the authority to change regional (state) boundaries at will, and, in practice, the regions have been created around the country's large cities, with these cities then serving as the regional capitals. Unlike the United States, where separate cities can function as the political, industrial, and intellectual centers of a state (for example, Lansing, Detroit, and Ann Arbor in Michigan), the Soviet regional capital traditionally has been the regional center in all these senses, and for a long time real urban life was very largely the life of the provincial capital. Thus, in 1939, 57 of the 110 cities in the Russian Republic with over 50,000 population were regional capitals, and they contained 57 percent of the republic's urban population—84 percent of the population in cities with over 50,000 persons in them.

Two political consequences flowed from this concentration of industry and urban population in the regional capitals. In the first place, the regional party organs have had responsibility for all aspects of the life of the region, and those regional officials who specialized in questions of industrial development and urban life inevitably found most of their attention focused on the capital city. The result had to be a serious reduction in the real independence of the city officials in these cities, that is, a high proportion of the major cities of the country. In the second place, most of the other cities were so small that they often were dominated by a single industrial plant, and in these cities the dependence of city officials upon the plant manager inevitably was very great.

With the passage of time, however, the officials in the major cities have gained considerably more breathing room. By 1 January 1977, the number of cities in the Russian republic with a population in excess of 50,000 persons rose to 283, and now only 25 percent of such cities were regional capitals. As a result, the regional officials supervising industrial areas have far less reason and opportunity to concentrate their attention on the capital city. Moreover, as all cities have grown in size and their industry has become more diversified, the dependence of city government upon any one plant inevitably declines. The drawing together of funds from a series of plants into a coordinated city project obviously becomes much more of a real possibility when there are a series of plants with which to deal.

A third change in the position of the city political officials has been a number of cautious and tentative steps by the central leadership towards strengthening the city's control over the development of the city. Over the last two decades, no issue has been raised more insistently in the governmental newspaper *Izvestiia*, in the magazine of the Presidium of the Supreme Soviet *Sovety deputatov trudiashchikhsia*, or in articles and books written by scholars working on local government, than the need to place all expenditures on city housing, utilities, and services under the control of the city government. The most vigorous complaint has been that the major industrial plants—and especially the industrial ministries in Moscow which control their purse strings— have little interest in an equitable distribution of services in the cities or the development of coordinated city plans.

Despite the persistence of the complaints about industrial domination and mistreatment of the city,[7] there are indications that significant, although gradual, changes are occurring in this respect. Except in a few isolated cases (such as in the financing of bus routes to new factories), the city authorities cannot obligate the plants—and especially their ministries—to make truly major expenditures for city needs, but the leadership increasingly has leaned in the direction of encouraging such allocations. In the slow and ambivalent reduction in the priority given to heavy industry and the values of industrial growth at all cost, the city officials have been among the beneficiaries.

THE GROWING ROLE OF CITY OFFICIALS

The changes in the relationship of the city authorities and the industrial managers have been gradual, but they have been occurring. Prior to the mid-1950s, the city soviets received only 10 percent of the funds allocated for housing construction in their cities. The remaining 90 percent came through the various ministries and departments, which apparently disposed of it with little thought to the overall needs of city development. (Soviet officials themselves have referred to this period as one in which the important industrial enterprises were at the center of "fiefdoms" within the city.)[8]

In the Khrushchev era some attempt was made to correct this situation. In the first place, the amount of money routed into city housing construction directly through the city soviet was increased substantially, reaching approximately 50 percent in the Russian republic by 1969.[9] In the second place, on 31 July 1957, in the wake of the decision to abolish the industrial ministries and create the regional economic councils (*sovnarkhoz*), the Central Committee and Council of Ministers passed a decision to assign to the executive committee of the local soviets "the responsibility of client (*zakazchik*) for housing, cultural-social services, and communal services done on a contract basis in the city."[10]

The "single client" (*edinyi zakazchik*) system does not give the city total control over housing and its distribution. If the city soviet (usually its capital construction administration) serves as the "single client," the governmental agencies and private cooperative societies with funds for housing construction assign them to the city soviet. The soviet then contracts with the appropriate construction trust or trusts for the construction of the number of apartment houses for which there are sufficient funds, and, when these are completed, it distributes the houses or apartments to the agencies or cooperatives in proportion to the funds originally contributed. (The agency or cooperative has the right to distribute the apartments to its individual employees or members.)

Certain advantages of the single client system are readily apparent. In the first place, since many of the smaller enterprises and departments do not have sufficient funds for the construction of an entire apartment house in a single year, the construction process can become very prolonged if they contract for an apartment house on their own. When the annual funds run out, the project may stand imcomplete for months until the following year's appropriation permits the resumption of work. It may take years for such a building to be finished. The pooling of resources is an obvious solution for this problem, for a small enterprise may receive any fraction of the apartments in a particular building, depending on the size of the funds at its disposal. In the second place, the single client system permits a more integrated development for the city. Housing construction can be concentrated where the city officials think best in light of the city plan, and it can be more easily coordinated with the provision of city services.

Despite the decree's promise that the single client system would be introduced in 1958, it began to be introduced on a gradual and piecemeal basis. Although practice varied from city to city (undoubtedly, the energy and values of the local city officials played an important part here), there was a tendency for the units with relatively small funds to reassign them to the city soviet and for the larger units to resist. (If an enterprise had funds for more than one building and had good connections with a construction firm oriented to heavy industry, it had very slight incentive to pool its resources.) There was also a tendency, quite probably stemming from different degrees of clout in the center, for the very largest cities to be able to force recalcitrant enterprises to participate and the smaller cities to be less able to do so. Thus, Moscow finally seems to have completed the transfer to a single client system by 1967, but there are still towns that have not even begun the process.[11]

In 1971 the Central Committee issued yet another decision about the ''further improvement in the work of district and city soviets,'' and the Presidium of the Supreme Soviet issued a decree specifying the ''basic rights and obligations of the city and borough soviets.''[12] The former was a typical Central Committee decision of recent years in that it ratified trends already in evidence instead of initiating a new one and in that it was not altogether consistent in its points. (For example, it asserted that ''the soviets still insufficiently coordinate the work of enterprises and organizations of different departmental subordination in the realm of housing-communal coordination, the building of social culture and services structures, and the production of consumers' goods,'' while it condemned those soviets who ''in violation of existing legislation obligate enterprises, economic organizations, and collective farms to bear large gratuitous expenses for local needs.'')

Nevertheless, the Central Committee (no doubt, really the Politburo of the Central Committee) did reaffirm the single client system, and it went considerably further in calling for city soviet coordination of other types of enterprise expenses on cultural-social items. As indicated above, this was by no means a new activity for the local political officials, but the Central Committee decision ''proposes'' that they engage in it ''more actively.'' The accompanying decree of the Presidium of the Supreme Soviet formalized this proposal by including it among the rights and duties of the city soviet:

[The city soviet] decides, with the agreement of the enterprises, institutions, and organizations located within the city, questions about the joint use of their funds allocated for housing, communal, road, cultural-services, education, health, trade, and public eating construction, and also in necessary cases about the pooling of such funds.

In addition, the 1971 Presidium of the Supreme Soviet decree also for the first time formally required the city soviet to compile an annual city-wide plan for all such construction and for the operation of all such services. (In the past, the soviet drafted such a plan only for the funds it itself expended.)

The city soviet . . . examines the drafts of the plans of enterprises, institutions, and organizations of higher-standing subordination located on the territory of the city, in particular, those concerning the development of housing and the communal economy, the construction of roads, social-cultural and services structures, the production of consumers' goods and local construction materials, beautification, trade, public eating, education, health, culture, and other questions connected with services for the population; in necessary cases it introduces its suggestions to the appropriate higher-standing organs; it confirms summary planned indicators on these questions and includes them in the plan for developing the urban economy and social-cultural construction in the city.

In addition to these decisions, the leadership also decided to conduct an experiment in the city of Orel on an extension of the single client system. In this experiment, not only were all social-cultural funds assigned to the executive committee of the soviet by the city's enterprises, but planning was extended beyond the normal one-year time span so that continuity would not be threatened by failure of any of the ministries to provide funds after the beginning of some year. After a few years the experiment was declared a success, and the Central Committee passed a decision calling for the widespread adoption of this system. But, as in its 1971 decisions, the leadership set no deadlines, and the introduction of the Orel system will be gradual at best.

Since the passing of the 1971 decrees, as some of the quotations in the early pages of this essay indicate, the movement toward comprehensive city planning and the use of the single client system has been slow. In particular, the compilation of a meaningful overall plan for housing and city services has proved to be extremely difficult. The ministries themselves do not give their final confirmation to enterprise plans until January, February, or sometimes even March of the planned year, and, consequently, the soviet has not been able to put together its summary plan until even later. At times, it does not even go through with what it considers a formal exercise. Perhaps the Orel experiment will turn out to be a viable solution to this problem, but this is still for the future to determine.

Of course, if the expenditures for key projects are agreed upon in advance, they can be included in the individual plans of the enterprises even if there is no comprehensive city plan, and, in fact, the pooling of resources and/or the use of the city soviet as the single client are based upon such a procedure. Indeed, it is even possible—and in a number of cities this has occurred—to establish a ''directors' council'' of the important plant managers in the city so that these men will have a setting in which, under the guidance of city officials, they can discuss joint action and come to some agreement about a division of labor and of funds.

The question is whether the amount of joint construction is actually increasing. Certainly the 1971 decree did specify that the agreement of the enterprise is necessary for the diversion of funds to city needs or for the pooling of resources, and, in the case of major expenditures, agreement of the enterprise also means the agreement of the ministry. There are complaints that difficulties can and do arise at all stages of the coordinating process: a plant and its ministry can categorically object to a joint project, a ministry can veto city items that a plant is willing to include in its plan, a ministry of another department can refuse to pay for any of the utilities or services that will be required by its new construction project, one of two plants (usually the biggest ones) can refuse to join other enterprises in using the soviet as a single client, a ministry can decide to put its apartment houses in an area planned for other uses and employ its power to force through its will, or a plant or ministry can simply fail to fulfill an agreement about expenditures of funds that it has already made.

And, of course, there are also complaints that, whatever the final outcome in individual attempts at coordination, the whole process takes far too much time and effort. [13]

To judge whether these complaints are the type that invariably appear when things are getting better or whether they indicate that little has changed, we really need summary expenditure data on the amount of joint construction. Nevertheless, the facts remain that the Politburo has gone on record approving greater coordination and cooperation in the housing-serving realm in the city and that the top city officials are now men (and occasionally women) with much more impressive education and experience. It seems reasonable to conclude that, for psychological reasons if nothing else, the position of the city authorities in relation to the ministerial officials must have strengthened. The ministry is not the final word if higher authorities are willing to override it.

Although we do not have sufficient evidence to permit a well-documented statement about the precise degree of change in the position of the city political officials, there is one piece of evidence that is very suggestive. The regional party first secretaries are important officials in the Soviet system (51 percent of the voting members of the 1976 Party Central Committee were or had been first secretary of a republican central committee or regional party committee, as were 67 percent of the twenty-one full and candidate members of the Party Politburo in 1979), and they are drawn from local officials with a wide range of backgrounds. The more rural areas usually have a first secretary with party and/or governmental experience in agricultural supervision, while the more industrialized regions usually have a party leader with urban experience. In the past, however, even the first secretaries with urban experience often had not occupied the post of city party first secretary in their rise upward. As Table 29.2 indicates, this situation has changed substantially in the last fifteen years. At least in the Russian republic and the Ukraine, the first secretaryship of a city committee has almost become a necessary step to the top in an urbanized

Table 29.2
USSR: PROPORTION OF NEWLY ELECTED RSFSR AND UKRAINIAN REGIONAL FIRST SECRETARIES WHO HAD BEEN CITY PARTY FIRST SECRETARIES, 1957-79

Year Elected	New Regional First Secretaries Who Had Been City First Secretaries	
	Regions With At Least 50% Urban Population[a]	*Regions With Under 50% Urban Population*[b]
1957-62[b]	15 of 45 (33%)	7 of 48 (15%)
1965-70[b]	11 of 25 (44%)	2 of 24 (8%)
1971-79	17 of 23 (74%)	6 of 25 (24%)

[a]The 1957-62 figures are based in the urban population figures in the 1959 census, while those on the 1965-79 period are based on the urban population figures of the 1970 census. The analysis is limited to the Russian Republic and the Ukraine, because the other republics have relatively few regions with 50 percent urban population.

[b]Data are not included on 1963-64 because the regional party committees were split into urban and agricultural units, and the first secretaries at that time were not comparable. A man first elected in 1963-64 who retained his post after the reunification of the party organs in 1965 is included in the 1965-70 figures.

region. This fact must reflect a belief on the part of the national leadership that the post of "mayor" now has sufficient challenge and sufficient opportunity for independent judgment that it prepares its occupant for higher political position much better than it did in the past. This must be a strong indicator of increasing authority of city political leaders and of city political institutions.

NOTES

1. For a discussion of the complexities of the definition and subordination of the small cities, see Jerry F. Hough and Merle Fainsod, *How the Soviet Union Is Governed* (Cambridge: Harvard University Press, 1979), pp. 483-84.

2. *Izvestiia*, 2 February 1974, 28 February 1974, 3 April 1974, 6 March 1976.

3. Ibid., 14 March 1976.

4. William Taubman, *Governing Soviet Cities* (New York: Praeger, 1973).

5. N. A. Petrovichev, ed., *Partiinoe stroitel'stvo*, 3rd ed. (Moscow: Politizdat, 1972), p. 274.

6. G. V. Barabashev, *Raionnyi, gorodskoi sovet na sovremennom etape* (Moscow: Iuridicheskaia literatura, 1975), p. 93; B. N. Gabrichidze, *Gorodskie sovety deputatov trudiashchikhsia* (Moscow: Iuridicheskaia literatura, 1968), p. 184.

7. See, for example, *Sovety deputatov trudiashchikhsia*, no. 1 (January 1976): 39; *Sovetskoe gosudarstvo i pravo*, no. 1 (January 1976): 23-31.

8. Robert J. Osborn, *Soviet Social Policies* (Homewood, Ill.: Dorsey Press, 1970), p. 223.

9. Ibid.

10. The decision can be found in a number of sources, including *KPSS o rabote sovetov, Sbornik dokumentov* (Moscow: Gospolitizdat, 1959), pp. 492-508. The quotation is from article 7, p. 498.

11. See *Izvestiia*, 1 April 1976. A good discussion of the problems encountered by cities as they tried to implement the 1957 decision can be found in Taubman, *Governing Soviet Cities*, for example, pp. 28-32, 83-96, 104-07.

12. The Central Committee decision was printed in *Pravda*, 14 March 1971, while the decree of the Presidium of the Supreme Soviet is in *Vedomosti Verkhovnogo Soveta SSSR*, no. 12, 1971, article 133.

13. Articles describing such problems can be found in *Izvestiia*, 6 August 1975, 13 August 1975, 27 August 1975, 6 March 1976, 14 March 1976; *Sovety deputatov trudiashchikhsia*, no. 2 (February 1974): 86.

Yugoslavia

*Željko Pavić**

30

The system of local government in Yugoslavia was completely reorganized under the federal Constitution of 1974. Because this essay was first written while the new constitutional system was still in its initial stages, it has emphasized the new constitutional and legal provisions for local government rather than current practices.

In the Yugoslav system of local government the commune is, according to the federal Constitution and the subsequent constitutions of the republics of 1974, "a self-managing community and the basic sociopolitical community based on the power and self-management of the working class and all working people." Under the term "sociopolitical community" are included all territorial units: communes, republics, autonomous provinces, federation, and, in some republics and provinces, urban and regional communities.

The Constitution establishes a presumption of competence in favor of the commune: That is, all the functions of power and management of social affairs are exercised in the commune except those exercised under the Constitution in the broader sociopolitical communities. Such a local unit has to be large enough to be capable of performing all its duties. Therefore the amalgamation of small communes has been a constant process in Yugoslav local government, and the number of communes has been reduced to approximately 500.[1]

Within each commune so-called local communities are obligatorily established. Residents of these communities decide on questions of local significance in various fields, for instance, housing, communal activities, education, child care, and consumer protection. The local community, as a self-managing territorial community of people living together in one or several villages or in individual sectors of a city, has its own bodies, resources, and charters passed by its residents. The charter of each commune lays down the method and procedure for creating local communities. According to the 1974 Constitution,

*Assistant in the Faculty of Law, University of Zagreb; co-author of *Samoupravljanje* [Self-management] (Zagreb, 1974).

local communities play an imporant role in the newly established delegation system for the communal assemblies.

The powers of central government over local government can be classified into four categories: local affairs, local elements of central affairs, affairs of special interest to the republic, and inspection activities. Regarding local affairs, the relationship between central and local government is based on mutual exchange of proposals for the organization and implementation of services, or for the improvement of the work of administrative agencies. In the second category, the local elements of central affairs, the agencies of the republic may ask for reports, information and data from local agencies. In cases when local agencies have failed to perform some of their functions, the republic agency itself has the right to perform these functions. It can initiate a procedure before the constitutional court to determine the legality of acts by a local agency, point out to the communal assembly or to its executive council presumed breaches of the law by local agencies, or initiate procedures to determine the responsibility of local administrative heads. Regarding the third category, the organs of the republic are empowered to issue binding instructions to local agencies in the affairs of special interest to the republic (in addition to powers granted in the second category). Under inspection activities, the inspectorates of central government are granted the power of unconditional delegation over local inspectorates, and they are empowered to take any matter out of local hands. Central inspectors may join local inspectors in all inspecting activities.

RECENT CHANGES

The recent constitutional changes in local government will be discussed in three parts: the structure of the communal assembly, the new type of executive body, and the urban and regional communities.

The Communal Assembly

The new structure of the communal assembly is based on three elements: workers in basic organizations of associated labor and in all other forms of associated labor, in state agencies, and in other working organizations not constituted as organizations of associated labor; workers and other citizens in local communities; and workers and other citizens organized in sociopolitical organizations (the League of Communists, the Socialist Alliance of the Working People, the Federation of Trade Unions, the Youth League, the War Veterans Federation). Therefore, the communal assembly is composed of three chambers—the chamber of associated labor, the chamber of local communities, and the sociopolitical chamber.

The 1974 Constitution established a specific system for the election of delegates to the communal assembly. Members of basic organizations of associated labor and other working communities first elect the members of

delegations by secret ballot. Candidates for members of delegations are proposed by the workers in these organizations according to the procedure for
nomination laid down by the Socialist Alliance of the Working People.
Delegations then elect from their members the delegates to the chamber of
associated labor. The same method is used for the chamber of local communities which is formed by delegates elected by delegations of working people and
citizens in the local communities. On the other hand, the function of the
delegations in sociopolitical organizations is performed by their elected bodies
specified by their bylaws or other decisions, and citizens elect the delegates to
the sociopolitical chamber by direct vote. The number of delegates to a
communal assembly is established by the communal charter. The term of
delegates to all chambers of the communal assembly (and the term of delegations) is four years. A delegate or member of a delegation may be elected for
only two consecutive terms. Also, a delegate, each member of a delegation,
and the delegation as a whole may be recalled before the end of their four-year
term by a procedure similar to that of their election. They all have the right to
resign. Moreoever, the director of a working organization or any other worker
who performs managerial functions may not be nominated as a member in a
delegation of a basic organization of associated labor. An assembly delegate
may not be a judge or an official elected by the assembly or nominated by the
executive council.

The delegates act in assembly in conformity with the basic views expressed
by their self-managing organizations and communities and the delegations and
sociopolitical organizations that delegated them. They are responsible to their
delegations and voters for their activities as delegates and must keep them
informed about the work of the assembly and their own work in the assembly.
The chambers decide on questions within the competence of the assembly
independently on an equal footing with each other or at joint sessions of all
assembly chambers. The assemblies of the self-managing communities of
interest[2] for education, science, culture, health, and social welfare decide on
an equal footing with the responsible chamber of the communal assembly on
problems within their competence. This power of co-decision can be extended
by the Constitution and charters of the sociopolitical communities to the
assemblies of other communities of interest. The constitutions of all republics
have provided for the creation of a presidency of the communal assembly. This
body acts in case of an immediate danger of war or in a state of war, when the
competent assembly chamber cannot meet regularly. It decides on questions
within the competence of a particular chamber, but it is obliged to submit all
such decisions for approval by the assembly at its next session.

The Executive Body

THE EXECUTIVE COUNCIL. Committees, the former executive organs, became
increasingly inadequate instruments for the coordination of affairs at the local
level. The Constitution of 1974 reorganized the executive system, creating the

executive council as the collective executive body of the communal assembly. The federal Constitution, as well as the constitutions of republics, describes very briefly the position and structure of this body. The executive council is responsible to the communal assembly for the state of the commune, the implementation of policy, the enforcement of regulations and other enactments of the communal assembly, and the coordination of the work of administrative agencies. The president and members of the executive council are elected by the communal assembly for a four-year term. The president may be reelected for only one more consecutive term; the other members of the executive council may be elected for three consecutive terms. The communal assembly establishes the number of members on the council by its charter or decision, usually from five to fifteen members.

The structure of the executive council in Yugoslav communes is not uniform. Three systems are used: an executive council composed of heads of administrative agencies, an executive council composed of holders of public and political office who are not heads of administrative agencies, and an executive council composed of both heads of administrative agencies and public and political officials. The third system is the most common. As an example we may take the 932 members of executive councils in the communes of the Socialist Republic of Croatia in 1974. About 35 percent were heads of administrative agencies and about 65 percent were public and political functionaries. This proportion was, of course, different in each particular commune. In some, only the president of the council was a public or political functionary and all other members were heads of administrative agencies. On the other hand, in some communes all the members of the executive council were public or political functionaries.

The procedure for the election of executive councils also varies. In most cases the president, elected by the communal assembly, proposes the candidates for the council. In this way he can influence the composition of the council he is presiding over. The same method is used for the election of federal and republic executive councils. In certain communes the president and other members of the executive council are elected by the communal assembly on the basis of a list of candidates drawn up by the communal conference of the Socialist Alliance. A delegate to the communal assembly cannot be a member of the executive council of the same commune.

THE DIRECTOR OF ADMINISTRATIVE AGENCIES. Several years ago the function of the director of administrative agencies, who coordinated these agencies and other organizations implementing affairs of special interest to the commune, was separated from the function of the assembly secretary. The assembly secretary was the head of separately organized services performing the professional work and preparing drafts of decisions on behalf of the communal assembly (for example, the budget service and teams of experts in specific fields such as urban planning and education). Thus, the communal assembly became isolated, to a certain extent, from the undesirable influence of administrative agencies. With the introduction of executive councils, which ensure the coordination of administrative agencies, the function of the director of administrative agencies became obsolete. In practice, the communes have abolished this office, ceding the coordination of administration to the executive council. The council either collectively implements this coordination or authorizes one of its members to act as coordinator.

Urban and Regional Communities

The communes in the largest urban areas are associated in so-called urban communities. In these areas the urban communes have entrusted to the urban community certain rights and duties in their common interest. The urban community's charter lays down the powers and functions of the community, its common agencies and resources, and the channels through which citizens can influence its activity. The charter is passed by the community assembly in agreement with all associated communal assemblies. Republics may transfer specific affairs falling within their competence to urban communities. Five such urban communities have been created, all in capitals of republics— Ljubljana, Sarajevo, Skopje, Zagreb, and Belgrade, which is the capital of both the federation and one of the republics.

Regional communities are ordinarily to be the form of communal cooperation. In Croatia such communities are an obligatory form of communal cooperation. The Constitution of Bosnia and Herzegovina provides that the republic statute may make it obligatory for communes to associate in regional communities. In two republics, Croatia and Serbia, and in the Autonomous Province of Vojvodina these communities are created on the basis of a social compact[3] among several communes or between communes and a republic. If the communes and the republic do not reach agreement and the compact is not concluded, the regional community is established by the statute of the republic (for example, in Croatia, where every commune must be associated either in a regional or in an urban community).

The functions of regional communities include such matters as adopting regional and social plans, ensuring economic and social development of the associated communes, performing some tasks concerning national defense, security, and self-protection, setting up common agencies, organizations, and services, passing regulations and other enactments, and implementing affairs transferred from a republic. The urban and regional communities have their own assemblies, executive councils, and other agencies. An urban community can be one of the associated members of a regional community.

CONCLUSION

The Constitution of 1974 has significantly changed Yugoslav local government. Until recently, the communal assembly consisted of the communal chamber, a classic political chamber of general competence, and the chamber of working communities, whose members were elected by workers employed in economic and noneconomic organizations. In the larger communes there were three chambers of working communities—the economic chamber, the chamber of education and culture, and the chamber of social security and health protection. Since 1974 the communal assembly has become an assembly of delegates and is no longer the classic representative body. The new assembly system is designed to coordinate the various interests of people as expressed through basic organizations of associated labor, local communities, communes, self-managing communities of interest, and sociopolitical organizations. The communal assembly is an important basis for constituting the assemblies of broader sociopolitical communities—urban and regional communities, provinces, and republics—because their delegates are elected by communal assemblies. Moreover, the self-managing communities of interest, authorized to decide together and on equal footing with the competent assembly chambers, can now exercise a significant influence over the decision-making process in the assemblies.

The former executive bodies, the committees, were composed of members elected by the communal assembly from its representatives, members elected by the communal assembly from among citizens, and members delegated directly by working and other organizations in the territory of the commune. The committees were created in different fields—economy, finance, culture, health protection, interior affairs, and so on. In relation to the communal administration they mainly exercised control functions, and the heads of administrative agencies could not be members of the committees. These bodies were so widely separated and so specialized that in the course of time they were unable to coordinate and control effectively the numerous administrative agencies. The newly established executive councils should improve the coordination and efficiency of local administration. The federal and republic constitutions of 1974 have given only a basic frame for their organization and activities so that the communes have applied very different solutions according to their individual circumstances.

The five cities divided into several communes are special urban communities in which a two-tier system of government has been established. The urban community covers services of importance to the whole urban agglomeration, while the urban communes are responsible for all other affairs of immediate significance for local residents. The establishment of urban communities is only the first step toward solving the problems of urban government. Certainly, it will be necessary to give greater consideration to such complex problems as the government of big cities in Yugoslavia because these cities have been seriously affected by the present-day process of rapid urbanization. The problems of big cities and their government are among the most urgent and important tasks of Yugoslav local government.

When districts as second-tier units were abolished in the period 1957-67, there was no other platform for the efficient cooperation of communes. It is true that the communes, especially the smaller and underdeveloped ones, were encouraged to cooperate with one another voluntarily by pooling their resources and forming joint administrative agencies, organizations, and services for affairs of common interest, but this cooperation did not develop satisfactorily. The new regional communities, created either by social compact or by statute of the republic, are expected to solve this problem by serving as a basis for more intensive intercommunal cooperation. The introduction of urban and regional communities probably means the reestablishment of two type of local units—urban and non-urban—as before 1955—as well as the reintroduction of two levels in local government.

NOTES

1. Exactly 512 communes in 1977, after the division of the cities of Skopje and Zagreb into urban communes.

2. Self-managing communities of interest are institutions through which workers in economic organizations exchange labor and resources with people employed in non-economic organizations. This is a way of direct financing of organizations in the field of public services. Communities of interest are formed in such spheres as education, culture, science, health and welfare, housing construction, power production, water management, and transport.

3. A social compact is a compact concluded between organizations of associated labour, self-managing communities of interest, chambers of economy, government agencies, trade unions, and other sociopolitical organizations. They regulate basic socioeconomic relations and other relations of broader common interest. These compacts are binding on the parties that have concluded or acceded to them. All parties are considered equal in concluding them.

Socialist Countries of Central and Southeastern Europe

Barbara Zawadzka and Sylvester Zawadzki* 31

This chapter deals with local government in Bulgaria, Czechoslovakia, the German Democratic Republic, Hungary, Poland, and Romania. It will not be concerned with the USSR or Yugoslavia, which have been dealt with in earlier chapters. Also, it will not include Albania, owing to the inaccessibility of documentary materials.

In each of the six countries covered in this chapter, local representative organs, known as councils, are elected by the population in general elections; these organs hold the key position in the system of local government. Though they carry different names in different countries, they play the role of local organs of state authority and are called upon to settle local affairs. The many features that the systems in the six countries in question share permit us to discuss a model of their systems jointly. These features are as follows:

First, the sociopolitical system in the six countries has a common historical origin, having been established as a result of revolutionary changes carried out in these countries in the final stage of World War II as a result of the struggle for national and social liberation.

Second, the socialist socioeconomic system is common to these countries and is in a similar stage of development in all of them. Having built the

*Dr. Zawadzka and Professor Zawadzki are members of the Institute of Legal Sciences, Polish Academy of Sciences, Warsaw. Dr. Zawadska is chairperson of the Institute's Research group on Local Government, and Professor Zawadzki is corresponding member of the Polish Academy of Sciences. He was editor of the *Polish Round Table Yearbook 1976-77* (Warsaw: Polish Association of Political Sciences, 1977), which contained papers from a Warsaw conference on local government in many countries. He was also editor of a book in English on local government in Poland: *People's Councils in Poland in the Light of Empirical Research* (Warsaw: Institute of Legal Sciences, 1973), and author of the essay on Warsaw in W. A. Robson and D. E. Regan, eds., *Great Cities of the World*, 3rd ed. (London: Allen and Unwin, 1972).

foundations of socialism, these countries are now building an advanced socialist society. This means that they are being gradually transformed from states ruled by the dictatorship of their proletariats into general national states. This transformation in turn is tied to the development of democratic forms of participation by citizens in the settlement of the affairs of state on every rung of administration.

Third, the leading role played by communist and workers' parties, whether in conditions of a mono-party system (Hungary and Romania) or in a system of allied parties (Poland, the German Democratic Republic, Czechoslovakia, and Bulgaria), is a characteristic feature of the political structure in these states.

Fourth, the six countries in question have common basic principles on which their systems are founded: the principle of supremacy of the working people of towns and villages and the principle of representation, which assumes that the people exercise sovereign authority through their representatives, elected to representative organs in general, equal, direct, and secret ballot.[1]

Fifth, a characteristic feature of the organization of political authority common to all socialist states and specified in their constitutions is that this organization is not based on a single central representative organ but on a multi-rung system of representative organs composed—in addition to the supreme organ—of representative organs elected in every unit of the country's administrative division.

The concept of a "pyramid of councils," with parliament as the supreme organ in the multi-level system of representation, differs substantially from concepts that distinguish between local government and state authority as well as from concepts that consider local government a form of decentralized administration, as part and parcel of executive authority.[2] As elected representative organs, councils by nature and method of constituting them are homogeneous with the supreme representative organs, namely parliaments (which carry different names in different socialist countries).

STRUCTURE OF THE REPRESENTATIVE SYSTEM

A country's administrative division carries essential significance for the multi-level system of representation; it determines the system's structure. In principle, there are two types of administrative division in the countries in question, namely a tri- and dual-level system of division. The tri-level system comprises the commune, *poviat* (district), and *voivodship* (region) level; towns belong to one of the three levels, depending on their size. At present, the tri-level system exists in Czechoslovakia,[3] the German Democratic Republic, and Hungary.[4] The dual-level system comprises rural communes and towns as basic administrative units and *voivodships* (regions) as units of a higher level. This system exists in Bulgaria, Poland, and Romania.

Observation of changes occurring in the administrative division of socialist states will disclose two tendencies: the first is to enlarge the basic rural units, namely communes; the second tendency, in a sense tied to the first, is a transition from the tri-level to the dual-level system. The dual-level system at present in existence in Bulgaria, Poland, and Romania, was introduced in the 1960s and 1970s.[5] In every case, reform of the administrative division entailed enlargement of the size of communes and diminishment of their number, with a simultaneous increase in the number of *voivodships* (regions). In Bulgaria, 867 communes were formed out of the 1,833 that existed prior to the reform, and the number of regions was increased from fourteen to thirty. In Poland, the reform reduced the number of communes from 4,672 to 2,365, whereas the number of *voivodships* was increased from seventeen to forty-nine.

In countries where the tri-level system of administrative division was maintained, the tendency also exists to increase the size of communes by various organizational and juridical methods. In the German Democratic Republic, for example, where the traditionally small commune, often comprising only a single village, has been preserved, agglomerations of communes are being formed that carry out certain tasks in common.[6] In Hungary, three types of communes exist. In addition to the "ordinary" or standard communes, there are also large communes and suburban communes, which differ in their competences.[7]

The evolution of the system of administrative division in the countries under discussion is continuing. In Poland, the number of communes is continuing to diminish. By 1 January 1977, eighteen months after the reform, their number had diminished by over three hundred, to 2,068. In the German Democratic Republic, the number of commune agglomerations is increasing. Gradual changes are also being introduced in Hungary. The intention behind these changes is to make communes not only units of administrative division but also socioeconomic units endowed with the means and resources essential to assure satisfaction of the economic, social, and cultural needs of the local population.

NATURE OF THE COUNCILS

Principles common to all socialist countries determine the position of councils as representative organs in the system of local authorities. These principles originate from the basic principles determining the position of councils in the system of organs of state authority. It is clear from decisions specified in the constitutions of all the countries in question that councils, as representative organs, hold a supreme position in the system of local organs and that a plenary session of a council is the sole body competent to make decisions on the most important local questions.

The uniform nature of the multi-level representative system means that the inner organization of local representative organs, their method of operating, and their relationship to corresponding administrative organs, to some extent resembles parliamentary organization, procedure, and practice. In particular, this finds expression in the session system, according to which local representative organs operate; the great significance of subsidiary organs of an advisory and supervisory nature, in the form of standing committees; and the obligation carried by councillors, whose position is similar to that of members of Parliament, to keep in constant touch with the electorate.

Council Sessions

Sessions of the council are the basic organizational form of activity conducted by local representative organs. Laws endeavor to make sure that the basic problems of the population of the given area are reviewed at council sessions and that the minimum number of annual council sessions is sufficient to cope with such matters.[8] Among the basic questions relative to the local population reviewed at council sessions, mention should be made of the following: resolutions determining five-year and annual plans of socioeconomic development, the budget, bylaws which comprise universally binding regulations, and resolutions that comprise directives regarding the functioning of local organs of administration, in order to achieve a more efficient satisfaction of the population's needs and requirements (for example, as regards education, health service, transport and communications, and communal economy).

Council sessions play an essential role not only in giving direction to the activity of local organs of administration but also as regards supervision over the work of administrative organs. Here, special significance is attached to council debates on annual reports submitted by the council's executive-administrative organ on fulfillment of the socioeconomic plan and budget; periodic reports on the activity conducted by the executive-administrative organ between council sessions; and reports of, information on, and assessment of the functioning of specific administrative departments. Interpellations addressed by councillors to local administrative organs and also to directors of institutions and establishments managed by these organs are an important means of supervision over local administration. Laws exist in all socialist states which envisage a special accelerated procedure for replies to councillors' interpellations.

Councils constitute their organs at plenary sessions: the executive-administrative organ,[9] standing committees, and other organs. In Bulgaria, for example,[10] judges are elected at council sessions; in Poland, people's assessors. The principle of openness of council sessions, in accordance with which the public is informed of the dates of sessions and their agenda, thus enabling citizens to attend sessions, is an important factor consolidating ties between the council and the local population.

Standing Committees

Standing committees are the council's subsidiary organs, assuring continuity of work between council sessions. These committees are an important factor in the structure of local representative organs in all the countries in question. Their principal functions are to supervise, advise, and initiate. They are formed to deal with specific sectors of management. Thus there are plan and budget committees, trade and services, culture and education, health, public law and order committees, and so on. In some countries (for instance, the German Democratic Republic and Poland), the law permits and even encourages socially active citizens who are not council members to be elected to standing committees. The model of the standing committee as a subsidiary organ of the council and exercising mainly supervisory, advisory, and initiating functions is typical for the countries in question. The position of these committees in Czechoslovakia, however, shows certain differences due to a different definition of the nature of councils in that country's legislation.[11]

Council committees can assemble more frequently than the council itself, have the possibility to penetrate deeper into local affairs within the scope of their competence, and entertain more frequent contacts with socially active local citizens. Consequently, they give concrete shape to the role of socialist representation as a form of implementing the people's sovereignty: they express the needs and opinions of local society and those of the local organ of state authority.

Council Members

It follows from the principle of socialist representation that the people's representatives elected to representative organs of every level, hence both members of local councils and members of Parliament, are bound to act in the interest of the people and in the interest of their electorate, to give expression to their needs and interests, and at the same time to coordinate the general national interest with local interests. Representatives are obligated by law to keep in constant touch with their electorate, to present regular reports on their activity and the activity of the council, to review the electorate's suggestions and demands, and, if the council in plenary session finds them correct, realistic, and socially justified, to supervise their implementation. The purpose of keeping in close touch with the electorate is, on the one hand, to assure that representatives have a good knowledge of the needs and opinions of their electorate, and, on the other, to give the electorate an opportunity to supervise and assess the activity of their representatives. All socialist constitutions specify the right of the electorate to revoke the mandate of a deputy who loses their confidence. This is spelled out in electoral laws by a procedure for the recall of representatives.

This model of representation is common to all socialist states. Differences exist not so much in the juridical model as in the sphere of specific political and organizational solutions adopted. Forms of contact between representatives and their electorate also differ in different countries. In Bulgaria, for example, the National Front plays an essential role in organizing such contacts. In the German Democratic Republic, great importance is attached to contacts between councillors and the workers' team in factories. This applies to great enterprises in particular, where many councillors are often employed.[12] In Poland, the local self-government of inhabitants of towns and villages plays an intermediary role in such contacts. Councillors submit a report on their activity to the local electorate once or twice a year (depending on the juridical regulations existing in the given country), hear the people's suggestions and demands, usually on matters of local importance (though occasionally also on questions of general social significance), and see that they are implemented. Experiences in different countries tend to prove that such ties are more lively and effective in single-member constituencies.

In the countries in question, cases of the electorate using their right to recall occur only sporadically. This does not mean, however, that this right is dispensable. Its significance does not consist of its frequent application but of the fact that the knowledge of its existence makes representatives observe the wishes of their electorate, who may apply their rights in situations when other measures are to no avail.

The Executive Committee

Repeated mention has been made of the councils' executive committees. The executive committee is a collective executive-administrative body elected by the council from among its members for the duration of the council's term of office, subordinate to the council and responsible to it. At the same time, the executive committee is the superior organ of the local administration, and its chairman is head of this administration (in towns and communes of the German Democratic Republic, he carries the traditional title of "burgomaster"). This organ owes it origin to the need to assure continuity to the work of the local representative organ, which is composed of elected deputies who, at the same time, have their professional work, and in particular to assure continuity to the administrative work, and to the need to entrust increasingly complicated administrative work to professionals. As a rule, the chairman of the executive committee and his deputies carry out their functions professionally with remuneration.

The executive committee is an organ which combines the function of organizing the council's work with that of conveying directives contained in the council's resolutions to the professional administrative apparatus. Thus it will be seen that the executive committee is an organ endowed with a dual nature: organizer of the council's work,[13] and superior organ of the local administrative apparatus. Consistent with its dual nature, the executive committee is dually subordinate: to the council (horizontal subordination), and to the superior administrative organ (the executive committee at a higher level, the Council of Ministers, vertical subordination). The executive committee's subordination to the council guarantees that it fulfills its obligation to submit regular reports to the council on fulfillment of the plan and budget. These are annual reports as a rule, and on the council's demand there may be additional reports on fulfillment of the council's specific resolutions. Vertical subordination safeguards the efficient functioning of higher-level supervision.

The mutual relationship between the two aspects of the executive committee's work assumes a different shape in different countries, partly due to differences in the composition of the executive committee. In the German Democratic Republic, for example, heads of local professional administrative organs, who in fact are councillors, are members of the executive committee. Persons who have no professional function in the council or its apparatus are admitted to membership of the executive committee in the smallest localities only. The proportion between professional and social members of the executive committee differs in different countries, and these differences are not without significance. As a rule, however, in practice the administrative element is dominant in the activity of executive committees. This dominance exerts a definite influence on the activity of the council, whose work the executive committee organizes. In practice, the executive committee often underrates the importance of the local representative organ showing an active attitude.

Awareness of the weak points of the executive committee as an institution established by the system was one of the reasons why this model was abandoned in Poland between 1972 and 1975. At present in Poland the function of the local administrative organ, which is also the council's executive and managing organ, rests in the hands of the headman (in communes and small towns), president (in larger towns and cities), or *voivoda* (administrative head of a *voivodship*).[14] He is the head of the local professional administrative apparatus and is appointed by the higher-level executive organ for an unspecified period of time, following consultation with the council concerned.[15] He remains subordinate to the council, however, primarily as its executive and managing organ. In this capacity, he implements the council's resolutions and submits reports on their execution. He remains subordinate to the council in all his work, since the principle of supremacy of the elected representative organ over the administrative organ is absolutely binding in Poland. Consequently, the headman (president or *voivoda*), like the executive committee in other countries, submits regular reports to the council on fulfillment of the plans and budget and on all his activity as the local administrative organ.

This new model of local administrative organ permitted the administrative function to be separated from that of organizer of the council's work. At present, this latter function is fulfilled in Poland by the presidium of the people's council, an organ of social composition. This organ is composed of chairmen of the standing committees; councillors' party clubs recommend leaders of local organizations of political parties to the positions of chairman and deputy chairmen of the council's presidium.[16] This solution helps to consolidate implementation of the principle of the supremacy of councils over local administration. The presidium of the people's council existing in Poland has no corresponding equivalent in other socialist countries. The specific characteristic of the solution adopted in Romania is that, in practice, the function of secretary of the local party organization is combined with that of chairman of the executive committee.[17]

THE ACTIVITIES OF LOCAL AUTHORITIES

Social ownership of the basic means of production, which constitutes the basis of centrally planned socioeconomic development, provides foundations for shaping councils not merely as subjects of the political system but also as subjects of the socioeconomic system in socialist countries. The most recent socialist constitutions, introduced in the 1960s and 1970s, formulate the guiding role of councils in the economic, social, and cultural spheres of life in a far more concrete and at the same time more complex manner. For example, article 46 of the Constitution of the Polish People's Republic, as amended in 1976, specifies: "People's councils guide the overall socioeconomic and cultural development in their respective areas of responsibility, exercise influence over all administrative and economic units in their areas, inspire and coordinate their activities, and exercise supervision over them." Article 89 of the Czechoslovak Constitution specifies the duty of councils to assure progress in various domains of social life and to provide general planned guidance in their respective areas of responsibility. Other socialist constitutions contain similar formulations.

A measure of the rank and standing enjoyed by local organs of authority and administration is their participation in the state budget, which amounts to between one-fifth and one-third of the total budget. Differences are closely tied with the system of planning and management in different countries, with periods of increasing centralization or decentralization, and with the varied scope of local powers.[18] In the course of historical development, the division of competences between councils of different levels is subject to change, which finds reflection in the proportion of the budget allocated to different rungs of the councils system.

The influence exercised by local authorities on the complex socioeconomic development of their respective areas of responsibility takes the following forms:

First, drafting and voting plans of socioeconomic development and budgets and supervising their implementation. Local plans and budgets are drafted on the strength of central indices and must conform with the national plan of socioeconomic development and the state budget voted by Parliament. The present trend in all socialist states is to raise the rank of local plans. This trend is reflected in the extension of the local planning horizon from one year to five years, in the fact that tasks of organs not subordinate to councils are included in local plans (thus consolidating the complex nature of planning), in raising the rank of local development planning, and in the transition of some countries to a five-year period of local financial planning (Hungary and Czechoslovakia).

Second, direct management of the local economy. Important differences exist in this respect among different socialist countries. As a rule, such sectors as agriculture, petty industry (based on local raw materials and working for local needs), handicrafts and services to the population, communal economy, retail trade, primary, secondary, and vocational education, health service, social assistance, culture, sport, and tourism belong to the sphere of the local economy. As a rule, these sectors are in the councils' competence, which means that councils plan their development and determine the organizational forms of their activity. Direct guidance over this sphere of activity is exercised on behalf of councils by executive managing organs which decide on the opening of new enterprises, appoint their managers, and so forth. A characteristic trend in the sphere known as the local economy is the tendency to reduce its scope; it is being increasingly included in the sphere of central management, whereas at the same time decentralization is proceeding in the sociocultural sector.

Third, in addition to management of the local economy, coordinating the activity of organs and institutions not subordinate to councils is also within their competence. The purpose of their coordinating function is to harmonize local interests with the general national interest. By reason of the coordinating rights held by councils, state enterprises controlled on the central plan level are obligated to agree with the local authority on localization of investments, coordinate their employment policy with this authority, and participate in the development of the communal economy and of the social and cultural infrastructure in towns. The coordinating activity conducted by local organs results in agreements which find reflection very often in freely concluded contracts. In certain cases, local administrative organs are entitled to make decisions that impose specific obligations on nonsubordinate organs, for example the preservation of the environment.

Fourth, councils have the possibility of settling local matters autonomously by way of social initiatives. This method finds expression, for instance, in voluntary social undertakings that serve to satisfy the needs and requirements of the local population.

Fifth, supervisory rights are enjoyed by councils over all organs, both subordinate and nonsubordinate, that operate within their area of responsibility. Councils exercise their supervisory function through their standing committees and also by coordinating all forms of social supervisory activity (conducted by trade unions, social organizations, and organs of citizens' local participation). With this end in view, in 1978 committees of social supervision were formed in Poland, attached to people's councils. Their coordinating and supervisory rights will gain increasing importance.

This list does not exhaust the activities in which local authorities engage, especially since there are differences among the socialist countries surveyed here. For instance, of considerable significance in some countries are agreements concluded between councils for the purpose of settling specific questions.

THE AUTONOMY OF LOCAL AUTHORITIES

We come now to a highly important subject, the degree of autonomy enjoyed by local organs of authority and administration. This subject is closely connected with the principles of the system of democratic centralism, which is intended to assure uniform state guidance in fundamental matters of general national significance and to provide broad opportunities for the development of local initiative and activity. The doctrine of socialist constitutionalism indicates that a specific degree of both decentralization and autonomy is an indispensable condition of implementing the principle of democratic central-ism. This found reflection in the previously mentioned definition of councils as not merely local organs of authority but as organs of local self-government.[19] Conformity with principles does not exclude differences on the optimal degree of decentralization and autonomy of local organs, however.

Some constitutions lay special emphasis on the autonomy of councils in guiding socioeconomic progress in their area of responsibility and provide guarantees protecting this autonomy. For example, article 43, paragraph 1, of the Hungarian Constitution, which specifies the functions of councils, stresses on three occasions that councils exercise a given function "autonomously." With the purpose of guaranteeing the autonomy of councils, the Hungarian Constitution specifies the competences of different local organs—councils, executive committees, and local administrative organs—as well as the condi-tions under which these competences may be transferred. The Hungarian Constitution also attaches great importance to the question of safeguarding the financial foundation of the council's autonomy: the National Assembly deter-mines the sources of the councils' income and the amount of state subsidies for five-year periods.

The Czechoslovak Constitution rules that "councils dispose of material and financial resources essential to assure execution of tasks specified in the plan, which they use as responsible administrators of their areas" (article 90, paragraph 2). The law on councils develops this decision. As in the Hungarian Constitution, this law states that local councils conduct their activity autonomously, guided only by laws and other generally binding juridical regulations" (paragraph 38).

In the German Democratic Republic, the law on local councils protects their autonomy, specifying the powers vested exclusively in local representative organs (paragraph 7). These powers include establishing plans of develop-ment, town and country planning, establishing local plans and budgets, and making decisions on adhesion to the commune collectives and on changes in the borders of administrative divisions.

These statutory guarantees of the autonomy of councils in settling the affairs of their respective areas of responsibility, particularly as regards planning and finance, give concrete shape to the concept of councils outlined in socialist constitutions—as real representatives of their area of responsibility and as organs disposing of resources indispensable for autonomous settlement of local affairs.

The questions discussed above are closely connected with the system of supervision over local organs of authority and administration. As a rule, supervision is exercised separately on the level of organs of state authority and on the level of administrative organs. Consequently, supervision is exercised on a dual or even treble level. On the level of organs of state authority, supreme supervision is exercised by parliaments or their presidia (as mentioned above, Czechoslovakia is an exception in this respect), and by people's councils of a higher level. This means that a higher-level administrative organ does not have the right to annul resolutions of a people's council of lower level; it may only suspend their execution. A council's resolution may only be annulled by a higher-level council, and only if the resolution infringes the provisions of law or is contrary to the fundamental line of state policy.

As regards councils' executive managing organs, supervision rests with the Council of Ministers (government) and executive managing organs of a higher level. The supervision of councils is similar to juridical supervision, whereas the supervision of executive managing organs contains many elements of directory supervision. Supervision over departments headed by ministers is of an even more directory and detailed nature. In Hungary, this level of supervision was abolished in order to restrict the tendency toward excessive centralism, whereas in Poland it was limited to establishing merely the general principles of implementation of ministerial tasks.

The nature and method of exercising supervision over local organs of state authority and administration is of fundamental signficance from the point of view of uniformity of state policy on matters of general national importance and also for assuring the specific degree of autonomy to local organs that is essential to the development of social initiative, the improvement of the standard of management, and the consolidation of the system of self-government.

CONCLUSIONS

In the light of experiences to date, it may be affirmed that the system of local authorities in socialist states has displayed many positive sides. Foremost among them are the following:

First, the system gives citizens broad possibilities to exercise an influence on the settlement of local matters as well as general national affairs. This influence is not limited to electing representative organs. Citizens can exercise a direct influence on decisions made by these organs if they obligate their representatives to follow a specific line of action and subsequently supervise their activity. Citizens may also participate in the work of standing committees and in organs of social self-government of different kinds, as well as in advisory bodies attached to organs of local administration.

Second, the system permits the general national interest to be harmonized with local interests by combining uniformity essential on a national scale with the specific characteristics of different units of the country's administrative division and promotes development of social initiative from below.

Third, it enables coordination (at plenary sessions and in the work of standing committees) of the political and social factor with the professional factor, with professional knowledge essential to optimal decision making.

Thus the system provides essential conditions for establishing a correct order of priority of aims and for selection of the most effective ways and means of attaining them.

On the strength of empirical studies of the system of local authorities, studies which have been most extensively developed in Poland,[20] it may be said that the model of local authority presented here is not taken full advantage of, for both objective and subjective reasons, for attaining envisaged aims. Consequently, various activities have been undertaken to assure more complete implementation of the model outlined in regulations established by law and also to assure its further improvement, particularly from the point of view of the needs and requirements of an advanced socialist society.

Among the principal directions taken by this activity, mention must be made of the following:

First, there is action aimed at raising further still the rank and standing of people's councils as representative organs, such as reinforcing the role of councils' plenary sessions and that of their standing committees, and strengthening the position of councillors. This entails increasing the role of councils in the decision-making process as well as reinforcement of their supervisory function in the struggle against bureaucratic distortions.

Second, in connection with the trend to consolidate the councils' role as organs of self-government, efforts are being made to develop and consolidate their direct ties with society, also to develop their ties with various forms of workers' self-government in the state enterprises, with tenants' self-government in towns and villages, and with social organizations and various forms of citizen participation.

Third, increasingly great attention is being given to the financial foundations of the councils' autonomy, to legal guarantees of their autonomy, and to the development of their coordinating role. This will enable councils to assure the complex development of their respective areas of responsibility and to increase their social initiative.

Fourth, and last, increasing attention is being shown to improvement of the methods of functioning of organs of local administration. This trend is reflected in measures aimed at improving the organizational structure of local administration, raising the professional qualifications of administrative personnel, improving the quality of rules and regulations of law (through the elimination of superfluous regulations), and consolidating the efficiency and legality of activity conducted by organs of local administration. Measures taken in Hungary, Romania, and Bulgaria include the introduction of court supervision over the legality of administrative decisions, and in Czechoslovakia and the German Democratic Republic, the introduction of such supervision in respect of certain specific matters; a marked tendency exists in Poland to adopt a similar solution.

The directions of activity specified above testify to a marked trend to develop and consolidate democratic methods of procedure, and to increase and improve the effectiveness of the system of local authority established in the socialist states of Central and Southeastern Europe.

NOTES

1. Indirect elections to regional councils in Hungary are the only exceptions. Nevertheless, these councils are also constituted by way of election, and in practice, in accordance with political directives, approximately 80 percent of their members are councillors of local councils elected in direct general elections.

2. S. Zawadzki, "The Concept of Local Democracy in a Socialist State on the Basis of Experience in Poland," *Politiikka*, no. 1 (1977).

3. Only in the Czech Republic, not in the whole state. A dual-level administrative division exists in the Slovak Republic.

4. In Hungary, no councils exist at the intermediary level, namely the district, only local administrative organs. Where conditions permit, the district is being eliminated as a unit of administrative division and rung of administration, communes and their local organs being subordinated to the authorities of neighboring towns. For the time being, however, a tri-level administrative division prevails in most of the country.

5. In Bulgaria, this reform was introduced somewhat earlier, in 1959; in Romania, in 1965; and in Poland, 1975.

6. H. Melzer and W. Weichelt, "Main Tendencies in the Development of the Local Organs of State Power in German Democratic Republic," in *Polish Round Table Yearbook 1976-1977*, no. 7 (Wroclaw-Warsaw-Cracow-Gdansk: Polish Association of Political Sciences, 1977).

7. O. Bihari and J. Halász, "Development Trends of Local Councils in the Hungarian People's Republic," in *Polish Round Table*; O. Bihari, "Problems of Self-Government in the Councils of Hungary," *Acta Iuridica Academiae Scientiarum Hungaricae*, nos. 3-4 (1974).

8. In Poland and Hungary, the law on people's councils rules that at least four sessions must be held annually. In some countries, the number of obligatory sessions depends on the council's level; in Bulgaria, for example, regional councils must hold a session once every three months, and commune councils once a month; in the German Democratic Republic, regional councils must assemble at least four times a year and all other councils at least once every two months.

9. The only exception is Poland, where, since the reform of 1972-75, councils' executive managing organs are constituted according to a different procedure (to be discussed later).

10. Regarding the system of local authorities in Bulgaria, see B. Spasov, *La Bulgarie* (Paris: Librairie générale de droit et de jurisprudence, 1973); D. Dokov, "Sozialistische Vertretung und Demokratie," in *Socialismus und Demokratie* (Berlin: Staatsverlag der DDR, 1977); Y. Radev, *Principes de la constitution bulgare de 1971* (Sofia: Sofia-presse, 1974).

11. Regarding the system of local authorities in Czechoslovakia, see J. Grospic, A. Sojka, and K. Svoboda, "Characteristic Features and Tendencies of Development of Local Organs of State Power and Administration in Czechoslovakia," in *Polish Round Table*.

12. W. Sternkopf, *Der Abgeordnete der örlichen Volksvertregung* (Berlin: Staatsverlag der DDR, 1974); W. Bernet, *Der Kreistags-abgeordnete* (Berlin: Staatsverlag der DDR, 1975).

13. A few exceptions to this principle, strictly controlled by regulations, exist in some countries (Romania, the German Democratic Republic, and Poland prior to the reform).

14. S. Zawadzki, ''The Reform of Local Government in the Polish People's Republic in the Years 1972-1975,'' in *Polish Round Table*.

15. Councils may submit motions to the higher-level administrative organ requesting recall of the headman, president, or *voivoda*.

16. This last is not settled by rules of law but results from the implementation of political directives issued by the Polish United Workers Party.

17. I. Vintu, ''Une période nouvelle au cours du développement de la démocratie socialiste en Roumanie. L'accroisement du rôle des conseils populaires,'' *Revue Roumaine de Sciences Sociales*, no. 2 (1976); I. Benditer and E. Pipernea, ''Die Vervollkonnung des Systems der obersten Organe in der sozialistischen Republic Rumäniens,'' *Ost-Europa-Recht*, no. 1 (1976).

18. In Poland, the budget of people's councils may provide some illustration of changes which have occurred in this respect. In 1951, this budget totalled 12.4 percent of the national budget; in 1960, 26.3 percent; in 1970, 26.7 percent; in 1974, 30.8 percent; and in 1978, 18.6 percent of the overall national budget.

19. The Polish Constitution (article 43, paragraph 1) and the Bulgarian Constitution (article 110) specify that councils are local organs of state authority and basic organs of social self-government. This definition applies to councils of every type and level.

20. Since 1965, these studies have been conducted by the Polish Academy of Sciences' Institute of State and Law. The results were published in *Probelmy Rad Narodowych* [Problems of People's Councils], of which forty-two volumes had been published up to 1978, and also several monographs.

PART IV

The Basic Units in Developing Countries

Introduction

As in the developed countries of the world, in recent years there has been much reorganization of local government in the developing countries. The essays in this part have been grouped into sections by continent or region because general characteristics and problems of local government are common to the countries in particular areas of the world. These sections begin with essays on one or two important countries where significant reorganizations have occurred and then conclude with a comparative essay on the whole or rest of the continent or region. Thus, the section on Africa has essays on Ghana and Nigeria and then survey essays on the developing countries that were former British and French colonies, respectively. Similarly, the section on Asia has essays on India and China and a comparative essay on other countries in Asia. The section on Latin America has an essay on Brazil and a survey essay on Latin America, while the section on the Middle East contains essays on Egypt, Turkey, and the fertile crescent countries.

Because the developing countries are spread around the world and have different histories and widely varying conditions, it is difficult to generalize regarding the nature of their reorganizations. Common to many of them, especially in former British and French colonies, has been the adoption or inheritance of decentralized structures of local government. There has been much questioning of whether these structures suit the peculiar conditions of developing countries. As pointed out particularly in the essay on Anglophone Africa and in the survey essays on Asia and the Middle East, the need for national integration, planning, and economic development has demanded greater centralization. This need frequently has resulted in the restructuring or creation of a regional or provincial level of government which, though some or all members of its councils are elected, is firmly under central political and bureaucratic control. It amounts in practice to a deconcentration of the central administration rather than a relatively autonomous level of government.

AFRICA

GHANA
NIGERIA
ANGLOPHONE AFRICA
FRANCOPHONE AFRICA

Ghana

*William Tordoff**

32

When Ghana's Convention People's Party (CPP) first assumed office in 1951, it took over institutions inherited from the British. This legacy included provincial and district administration, revolving around civil servants, a native administration system centered on the chiefs, and an embryonic representative local government system in the main towns. Impatient for change, Nkrumah's government lost no time in introducing major local government reforms, for which the way had been paved by the Reports of the Watson Commission of 1948 and the all-African Coussey Committee of 1949.[1] Under the Local Government Ordinance (1951) local and urban councils were set up by statutory instrument as basic units to provide local services, such as primary education, sanitation, and markets. Two-thirds of the council members were popularly elected, while one-third of the membership was reserved for representatives appointed by the traditional authorities; the provision for traditional representation was abolished in 1959. District councils were also established, members being elected from the lower authorities, upon which the district councils were financially dependent. They constituted a second tier and undertook large-scale projects, provided major services such as road maintenance and medicare, and maintained law and order.

These new authorities superseded the former native authorities and operated alongside city and municipal councils, for which separate provision was made in the Municipal Councils Ordinance of 1953. Various amendments to the original legislation were made between 1951 and 1961, and these were incorporated into the Local Government Act of 1961, the latter being a consolidating measure relating to local government in general.[2] It continued to apply until February 1966, when President Nkrumah's government was re-

*Professor of Government, University of Manchester. The author wishes to thank Professor D. K. Greenstreet of the School of Administration, University of Ghana, for his assistance in revising this essay (originally written in 1975).

moved by the military. The demise of representative local government at that time was not a matter of deep regret, since its record, over a period of fourteen years, had been disappointing. The government constantly juggled the number and size of the councils, particularly in the period after June 1957, when the Greenwood Report found that there were not only too many small, ineffective units but also that the "two-tier" system of district councils and local and urban councils had not proved successful.[3]

Before independence the working of many councils was disrupted by inter-party rivalry—intense in the Brong areas of Ashanti where the CPP was pitted against the National Liberation Movement—and by traditional disputes, such as that between Dormaa and Wamfie in Western Ashanti.[4] Councils were subjected to considerable political interference at the hands of local CPP officials and, following independence, by district commissioners. Like the regional commissioners above them, the latter were political appointees after independence; however, an administrative framework of regional secretaries and government agents (subsequently senior executive officers) in the districts was retained. Though a number of commissioners were removed for corruption or incompetence,[5] so long as a commissioner enjoyed the confidence of his regional commissioner and, above all, of the president himself, there was little that the minister responsible for local government could do to curb his excesses. Nevertheless, the responsible ministry (often the Ministry of Justice) persevered with the experiment in representative local government. The difficulties facing it were immense. Many councils were inefficient and even corrupt, and, in view of the sharp distinction made between central government and local government institutions, the latter, with inferior salary scales and poorer promotion prospects, could not attract staff to match the quality of those entering the civil service. In these circumstances, supervision of the local authorities was barely adequate, despite sound institutional devices, such as the local government inspectorate system established after independence.[6]

Moreover, in the period up to February 1966, local authorities were heavily dependent on the central government for both development finance and technical assistance. Departments and agencies of the central government operated in a wide variety of fields, including education, medicine, and agriculture. To maintain separate central and local government structures in the rural areas entailed a considerable waste of human and material resources through unnecessary duplication and overlap between the various agencies involved. Though the district commissioner was responsible for coordinating the efforts of these agencies, departmental officers of the central government worked vertically out of the district to regional and national headquarters and were given little discretion to act on their own authority. Horizontal coordination between departments was therefore weak, and unnecessary delay, as well as frustration, occurred as matters vitally affecting the locality were referred to the parent ministries in Accra.

TRANSITION: 1966-74

As far as local government is concerned, the period 1966-74 can be regarded as transitional, filling the gap between the discredited system under Nkrumah and the new structure, heralded with the publication of the Mills-Odoi Report of 1967,[7] but only instituted from 1974 onwards. In March 1966, one month after the coup, the ruling National Liberation Council (NLC) set up in each region a regional committee of administration, consisting of the two most senior members of the army and police in the region, together with a senior civil servant. Regional committees were to maintain law and order, exercise overall control of government activity in the regions and inform the government of the needs of the people. In what was claimed to be a further measure of decentralization, a broad-based but nonpolitical regional planning committee was established in each region in October 1967. A regional management committee followed in June 1969, with the regional chief executive—the civil servant who was secretary to the regional committee of adminstration—as chairman and the regional heads of government departments as members. The chief executives were to consult the committees "on all matters of substance affecting administrative or programme management in the region."[8]

The NLC amalgamated a large number of the former (161) administrative districts to give a new total of forty-seven.[9] Each district was placed under the control of a district committee of administration, comprised of one police officer and one civil servant, and was made responsible for maintaining law and order and for coordinating the work of the government departments in the district. Each district included within its boundaries a number of local authorities, for which local management committees were responsible.[10] As before, they were overdependent on government subsidies and often failed to provide basic amenities, such as public lavatories, out of the rates they collected.[11] Town and village development committees, chaired by chiefs and sub-chiefs, were established at the lowest level of administration.

Despite its initial popularity, the NLC lacked a firm base of legitimacy and therefore turned for support and advice to the civil service, its "most important corporate ally,"[12] and the chiefs, as well as professional, business, and other elite groups. The Mills-Odoi Commission of Enquiry, established in April 1967, found that the machinery of government was characterized by "excessive centralisation of authority and resources in Accra" and "an almost completely ineffective local government system" based on nonviable units. It recommended radical decentralizaton and the creation of a single, unified public service, which would absorb the existing local government service. Government, it said, should be regarded as "a single operation wherever and by whom carried out."[13]

The NLC accepted the main recommendations of the Mills-Odoi Commission and took account of them, as well as the proposals of the Siriboe Commission,[14] in making changes in the structure of local administration between 1967 and 1969; it was recognized that full implementation would be a lengthy process. The principle of decentralization was endorsed by the Constituent Assembly which sat in Accra in the first half of 1969 to adopt a new constitution for the Second Republic. The Constitution, which came into force on 1 October 1969, made provision for the establishment of regional councils (to be planning and coordinating bodies) as well as district and local councils. Though the principle of local participation was conceded at all levels, regional heads of ministries were to be ex officio (nonvoting) regional council members in what, overall, was a bureaucrat-dominated structure. In a clear concession to the chiefly interest, the Constitution provided that while two-thirds of the members of a district council should be elected, one-third should be chosen by the traditional authorities. Local councils also were to include traditional members. Functions were defined only broadly in the Constitution itself (Chapter 16: Chieftaincy and Local Government), and Parliament was left to fill in the details, particularly in relation to the district, which was to be the fundamental local government unit, and the local councils.[15]

After considerable delay, Dr. Busia's Progress Party government introduced the Local Administration Bill (1971), which offered "something more than local administration by civil servants, but a good deal less than local government by elected councils."[16] However, elections to the new local councils, scheduled for April 1972, had not been held before the military again assumed power. Political parties were once more proscribed and, pending the introduction of a new structure, the arrangements for local administration under the National Redemption Council (NRC) were similar to those which had obtained in the first period of military rule. Subject to overall policy direction by the central Ministry of Local Government, effective control was vested in the regional and district administration, though—as befitted a government whose populist style was reminiscent of Nkrumah and the CPP—there was some limited opportunity for popular participation through, for example, town and village development committees.

THE NEW STRUCTURE

The new local government system, which is being introduced by the military government under the Local Government Act (1971), as amended by NRC Decrees 138 (1972) and 258 (1974), is based substantially on the Mills-Odoi principle that central ministries and departments shall deal with broader issues of national policy and planning, leaving local affairs to be managed at the local level. When finally established, it will be an integrated structure comprising four tiers: regional councils, district councils, area, municipal, urban, and local councils, and town and village development committees.

Sixty-two district councils (instead of the fifty-eight originally proposed) have been established on a nonelective basis. They are deliberative and consultative bodies, with their functions limited to taxation, legislation, policy formulation, and the periodic assessment of the performance of the district chief executive and the professional staff; however, the councils have no say in personnel matters.[17] The area of a council's jurisdiction coincides with that of the administrative district, though the areas vary widely in the size of the population each contains, as do the councils in the size of their membership. Two-thirds of council members are government nominees, while one-third represent the traditional authorities. With only a few exceptions, government departments operating at the local level have become in effect divisions of the council, responsible for the relevant function of the council in which a department specializes.

The civil servants in these departments have been assigned to the district council and made responsible to the district chief executive, who is the administrative head of the council; however, for purposes of technical guidance, transfers, training, promotions, and postings, they will retain membership in their parent ministries and departments. The district chief executive works through the executive committee, the council's policy-making body; there is also a district education committee and a district planning committee, a bureaucrat-dominated body responsible for drawing up and seeing to the implementation of regionally approved development programs.[18] Though responsible to the regional administrative officer and through him to the regional commissioner, the district chief executive represents the head of state, as well as the Ministry of Local Government, at district level—he flies the flag and occupies what everybody calls "the DC's office." Officially, his relationship to the district council chairman should be "the same as exists between the Managing Director of a business organisation and the Chairman of the Board of Directors of the firm." In fact, district chief executives other than city managers also served as council chairmen until February 1977, when chairmanship elections were held, as a result of which a number of chief executives were confirmed as chairmen, other councils electing one of their own members as chairman. There is thus a real danger that district chief executives will be drawn into the political arena.[19]

Former local government employees have been formally absorbed into the civil service at a level commensurate with their qualifications and experience. The central government now pays the salaries and wages of all employees of the district council and, on the recommendation of a local government grants-in-aid commission, awards grants to supplement the revenues the councils can raise locally through taxation and medium-scale commercial, agricultural, and industrial ventures. (Larger-scale ventures are the responsibility of regional development corporations, established in 1973 by NRC Decree No. 140). Under the new structure, the district council therefore has ceased "to have a separate identity from Central Government institutions operating at the District level, the two institutions being fused into one through a process of institutional integration and manpower absorption."[20]

To supplement the district councils, the government is also pledged to establish 243 local, 19 urban, 4 municipal, and 6 area councils both to support the development programs of the district councils and to identify, organize, and coordinate community projects. However, except for the six area councils established for the Accra City Council in August 1977, these councils—unlike the former local councils—will have no real powers of their own but will perform such functions as are delegated to them by the district councils. To facilitate the transition from the old system of local government to the new, the councils were not to be brought into being until twelve months after the other councils had been established; however, only the six area councils in Accra district existed early in 1978. As far as practicable, the (predominantly rural) areas of the local councils will coincide with the jurisdictional areas of traditional authorities. The councils will be composed of traditional rulers and government-appointed members. The latter will mainly be representatives of the various town and village development committees which, except in some parts of the northern and upper regions, have been established throughout the country on a nonelective basis by district chief executives. The intention is that they should provide facilities and services at the grass-roots level and help collect revenue for the district council, which is the sole rating authority.[21]

At the other end of the scale, nine regional councils, one for each region, are projected and will undertake regional coordination and planning; they will be heavily dependent on the central government for funds. A regional council will be composed of two members elected by each district council within the region and two representatives from the regional house of chiefs for the particular area, with the regional administrative officer and other departmental heads as ex officio members, subject to the proviso that in no circumstances shall the latter exceed one-half of the total council membership. The chairman will be appointed by the central government. As agent of the latter, the council will be responsible for the supervision and management of national programs within the region. Through its regional planning committee, it will also coordinate the development programs of the districts to ensure that they conform with the approved regional plan, and it will make recommendations to the central government for funding the programs. Future annual estimates will be prepared district by district rather than departmentally. Until the new regional councils come into being, these functions are being performed by the existing regional organizations, headed by the regional commissioners; as Akuoko-Frimpong points out, this is an unsatisfactory but necessary arrangement.[22]

At the national level, the Ministries of Finance and Economic Planning will examine critically the competing claims of the regional councils in order to determine what grants should be made. They will be advised by the Ministry of Local Government, which will serve as a central coordinating body; it is already responsible for all matters of policy relating to district councils as a whole, including their size, scope, powers, and functions. With respect to certain policy issues, regional organizations will deal directly with the appropriate ministry or department, and they and the regional councils will deal with the head of state on matters of policy relating to general administration, peace and security, and in emergency situations.[23]

In explaining the most important difference between the old local government system and the new system which was about to be introduced, the principal secretary, Ministry of Local Government, wrote in 1974:

As against the present system under which responsibility at the local level is dispersed among a multiplicity of agencies and institutions without any clear definition of function or limitation of authority, there will be only one unit of administration at the local level, all other agencies will be fused into this one unit and this one unit will be vested with their responsibilities and functions.[24]

He also stated that the civil service, in response to its additional responsibilities at the local level, should "increasingly transform itself from a predominantly regulatory and controlling body into a dynamic instrument for social and economic change."[25] Under the impact of these reforms it was anticipated that the confusion and duplication of the past would be eliminated, manpower utilized more efficiently, the incidence of tension and conflict between administrative officers and the chairman and members of council reduced, financial performance improved, and better services offered to the people, resulting in a significant increase in overall development.[26]

These hopes may prove illusory. As J. K. Nsarkoh points out, a four-tier system of local administration may prove too elaborate for a country covering an area of only 92,000 square miles with a population of some 10 million. Problems also may arise from the "double allegiance" of ministerial and departmental officers working in the district—to the district chief executive for day-to-day administration and to their parent ministry or department for technical guidance.[27] Moreover, it is by no means certain that conflict between councillors and the district chief executives will be reduced if the government, despairing of effectively supervising the local authorities from outside, persists in putting chief executives inside the council machine. Finally, Henry Akuoko-Frimpong points to a number of particular problems which give cause for concern. District councils are still heavily dependent on the basic and property rates, and, even though the central government has assumed responsibility for paying the salaries and wages of council staff, they do not have adequate sources of revenue. Some councils are also operating well below their staff establishment; Accra City Council, for example, needs several more engineers, medical officers, and architects. Again, heads of decentralized ministries and departments have often been unwilling to cooperate with the Ministry of Local Government, which acts unofficially as a super-ministry, and there have been calls for its replacement by a central coordinating agency with more political and administrative weight. The ministry itself has suffered from the high turnover of the commissioners (ministers) in charge—there have been at least five commissioners since 1974. Moreover, some traditional rulers and their traditional councils have been lukewarm in support of the new district councils and have pressed for further restructuring of the machinery of government at both district and regional levels.[28]

CONCLUSIONS

The recent local government reforms amount to an exercise in the deconcentration of administrative authority rather than in political devolution, though elements of both deconcentration and devolution remain, as they do in most systems of public administration.[29] They signal a departure from the principle of representative local govenment, without reducing the reality of central control. It is above all the bureaucracy that has gained through the new structure; like the Kenya government, the Supreme Military Council (formerly the NRC) regards the administration as the main agent of development.[30] The result is a system of government that resembles the French model of administration more closely than English-style local government. What Ridley and Blondel said of France might, *mutatis mutandis*, be applied to Ghana today. Central control of local government, they wrote,

follows from the unity of the state. Clearly, the central government is the higher organ: in modified form, the principle of hierarchic subordination still applies...Local authorities...are branches of the state, just as the central government, and indeed public corporations, are branches of the state. They are responsible in their sphere for the organisation of those state functions (public services) which are local in character.[31]

The officials of the various organs, both at the central and local level, together form the administration of the country.[32] The district chief executive in Ghana is a prefect-like figure.[33] He is but the "new priest writ large," the modern prototype of the "old presbyter"—the colonial district commissioner.[34] Or perhaps one should say, more accurately, that such would be his role if the reforms, as envisaged in 1974, were fully implemented.

Popular participation in government will not necessarily decrease sharply under the new structure, even though members of the district councils (and the regional councils to follow) have not been elected at the polls. If decisions are made by civil servants at regional and district levels instead of being referred by ministerial representatives to their parent ministries in Accra, there will be more inducement than previously for individuals and groups to exert pressure locally. It is probable, too, that nongovernmental decision making will be "a significant element in the allocation of resources at the local level."[35] This certainly has happened in the past—no one was more aware than Nkrumah's ministers of the yawning gap at all levels of government between the political structure and political process—and could happen again, perhaps because of the dominant role played in a particular issue by a local institution or individual, such as a chief, or because of the distortion of the decision-making process by bureaucratic incompetence and corruption.

One question is whether the military government has found ''the proper balance between a system of quasi-autonomous elected council . . .and straight-forward administration by agencies of Government.''[36] The provision that district council seats shall be filled by government nominees and traditional representatives is not likely to be accepted by political parties operating under a successor civilian regime. The proof of the pudding will be in the eating, but unfortunately the new structure is taking such a long time to establish that the regional, district, and other councils will have little, and in some cases no, opportunity to prove themselves, ''before the politicians return.'' On the other hand, the old record will not be hard to beat: the former local authorities incurred the bulk of their expenditure on general administration and other recurrent items, and development expenditure as a percentage of total expenditure amounted to only 6.7 in 1970-71, 7.7 in 1971-72, and 7.3 in 1972-73.[37] It is to be hoped that the new structure, perhaps modified to incorporate the elective principle, is thoroughly tested over a number of years before it is scrapped or radically revised.

This in turn, however, leads to a further question: whether the new local government structure will in fact be fully established on the lines envisaged in 1974. The long delay in setting up regional, municipal, urban, and local councils, is not due solely to the military government's concern to devise a new form of constitutional government, preparatory to the restoration of civilian rule, and the consequent shift in emphasis from local to national reform. It also results from a lack of political commitment to the new structure. The bureaucrats, too, seem to be ''dragging their feet'' in implementing administrative change: those at the center evidently are reluctant to accept any diminution in their decision-making powers, while regional officials show signs of wanting to retain control over their own field officers.[38] There is scant prospect at present of district chief executives exercising ''full financial control of all departments operating at the local level.''[39]

Proponents of representative local government in Africa may see the recent reforms in Ghana as retrogressive. They will perhaps argue that the experiment in Ghana has failed because it was never given ''a real chance,'' pointing with some justification to the frequent '''metamorphoses' in area and functions'' before the 1966 coup.[40] But the record after 1966, when local authorities had a more stable existence, is not much better, as is shown by the auditor-general's report covering the period 1967-69.[41] Moreover, evidence from other parts of Commonwealth Africa casts grave doubts on the suitability of English-style local government in conditions where the government, be it civilian or military, often rests on a narrow base of legitimacy and is engaged in such a constant struggle for survival that it will not risk conferring extensive autonomy on local representative bodies.

Sadly, the record of failure is more striking than the record of success. Representative local authorities have been suspended in Sierra Leone, having been ''chronically sick'' for several years,[42] and the retention of district commissioners seems essential if any services are to work in the provinces. English-type local government has also disappeared in Tanzania, where changes remarkably similar to those in Ghana have taken place since 1972: district development councils, each serviced by a district development director, have taken the place of the former local authorities, and local government staff have been absorbed within the civil service. Moreover, the immediate effects are much the same—the increase in power of the bureaucrats in local affairs has taken place at the expense of popular participation.[43] The Southern States of Nigeria suffered for twenty years from "the stagnation and corruption in local government" until, in 1970, the Southeast (now Cross River) State blazed a new trail by abolishing English-type local authorities in favor of a new kind of "development administration" revolving around divisional development councils and area development committees, with implementation resting with the divisional agencies of government.[44] In Zambia, rural local authorities have minimal functions—they do not deal, for example, with primary education—and hardly justify the substantial amounts of public money spent on them.[45] It is noteworthy that the Simmance Report recommended in 1972 that the local government and civil service staffs in Zambia be merged,[46] a recommendation so far successfully resisted by the Ministry of Local Government, while two years earlier a Local Government Study Group in Botswana had suggested that the establishment of a single, integrated public service be considered.[47]

To quote instances of failure and difficulty in working carbon copies of English local government in Commonwealth Africa,[48] however, is not to argue against incorporating the principle of representation in African local government. It is to be noted that the military government of Nigeria, Africa's most populous state, has taken steps since September 1975 to constitute "within the entire federation, 'a third tier of government,' in the form of local councils endowed with powers and finances of their own and accountable to local electorates."[49] The absence of any provision to elect local authority members in Ghana will prove a weakness if its effect is to entrench (though this, of course, could result from an election, too) a local elite which, in alliance with the bureaucracy, can block egalitarian and other policies prejudicial to its own interest. All that is being argued here is that Ghana's radical departure from English-style local government is fully warranted by the facts.[50] Changes in structure may occur over the next few years and elements of the previous status quo may be restored. What is likely to persist and prove of lasting value is the creation of a single, unified public service. In opting for such a service, Ghana has followed the lead shown by Tanzania; other countries in Commonwealth Africa may follow suit. Thus, though Nigeria has not adopted this solution, it was reported in 1971 that a unified local government service had been created in each of Nigeria's Southern States, with local government staff placed on a basis of equality with civil servants.[51] All of this suggests the emergence of something new and significant in what we should probably now call "local administration" in Commonwealth Africa—a much closer fusion between central government and local government than has obtained in the past.[52]

NOTES

1. *Report of the Commission of Enquiry into Disturbances in the Gold Coast, 1948* (Chairman, Mr. Aiken Watson) (London: Col. no. 231, 1948); *Gold Coast: Report to his Excellency the Governor by the Committee on Constitutional Reform, 1949* (Chairman, Mr. Justice J. H. Coussey) (London: Col. no. 248, 1949).

2. J. K. Nsarkoh, *Local Government in Ghana* (Accra: Ghana Universities Press, 1964).

3. *Report of the Commissioner for Local Government Enquiries, June 1957* (Accra: Government Printer, 1957), pp. 1-39. Mr. A. F. Greenwood, permanent secretary, Ministry of Local Government, was the sole commissioner.

4. William Tordoff, "The Brong-Ahafo Region," *The Economic Bulletin* (Legon) 3, no. 5 (May 1959): 5, 9.

5. See Robert Pinkney, *Ghana under Military Rule, 1966-1969* (London: Methuen, 1972), pp. 90-94.

6. See A. F. Greenwood, "Ten Years of Local Government in Ghana," *Journal of Local Administration Overseas* (London) 1, no. 1 (January 1962); and Nsarkoh, *Local Government in Ghana*, pp. 292-99.

7. *Report of the Commission on the Structure and Remuneration of the Public Services in Ghana, 1967* (Chairman, Mr. Justice G. C. Mills-Odoi) (Accra-Tema: State Publishing Corporation [Printing Division], 1967).

8. See Pinkney, *Ghana under Military Rule*, pp. 100-05.

9. The CPP government frequently changed the number of districts into which the country was divided for administrative purposes. The figure 161 is given in Ibid., p. 102.

10. Ibid., pp. 102-03.

11. *Report of the Auditor-General on the Accounts of Ghana. First Report for 1971: Local Authorities and Educational Institutions 1967-68/1968-69* (Accra, 1971), quoted in "Probing Ghana's Councils," *West Africa* (London) (25 June 1971): 717.

12. Robert Dowse, "Military and Police Rule," in *Politicians and Soldiers in Ghana*, ed. Dennis Austin and Robin Luckham (London: Cass, 1975), p. 21.

13. Mills-Odoi Report, pp. 3-4.

14. *Report of the Commission of Enquiry into Electoral and Local Government Reform*, part 3 (Chairman, Mr. Justice J. B. Siriboe) (Accra: Government Printer, 1968). The commission accepted most of the fundamental recommendations of the Mills-Odoi Commission but suggested some changes (such as the introduction of a local government grants commission) and made thoughtful and practical proposals of its own. Both reports are discussed by D. K. Greenstreet, "Trends in Decentralisation in Ghana," *Quarterly Journal of Administration* (Ife) 5 (October 1970-July 1971): 167-82.

15. Greenstreet, "Trends," pp. 179-80.

16. "Ghana's Local Government Framework," *West Africa* (30 January -5 February 1971): 130.

17. "The New Local Government Set-up," mimeograph (Accra: Ministry of Local Government, n.d.), p. 18; H. Akuoko-Frimpong, "Problems of Local Administration in Ghana Today," in *A Revival of Local Government and Administration?* Collected Seminar Papers no. 23 (London: Institute of Commonwealth Studies, University of London, January-May 1978), pp. 20-21. See also J. K. Nsarkoh, "Ghana's New Machinery for Local Government," *Greenhill Journal of Administration* (Legon) 1, no. 3 (October-December 1974); "Our New Local Administration Machinery," *Working Paper Series*, vol. 76-6 (Legon: School of Administration, University of Ghana, September 1976); and "Election of Chairmen of District Councils in Ghana— February, 1977," *Working Papers Series*, vol. 77-2 (Legon: School of Administration, University of Ghana, March 1977).

18. Nsarkoh, "Our New Local Administration Machinery," pp. 8, 18, 20-21; Akuoko-Frimpong, "Problems of Local Administration," pp. 20-21.

19. "The New Local Government Set-up," p. 16; Nsarkoh, "Election of Chairmen of District Councils," and Akuoko-Frimpong, "Problems of Local Administration," p. 21.

20. "The New Local Government Set-up," p. 5.

21. C. T. Oddoye, "The New Local Government System," *Civil Service Journal* (Accra) (1974): 13; Nsarkoh, "Our New Local Administration Machinery," pp. 6, 28 (notes 12-15); and Akuoko-Frimpong, who gives the number of municipal, urban, and local councils to be established as 267: "Problems of Local Administration," pp.21-22.

22. Oddoye, "New Local Government"; Nsarkoh, "Our New Local Administration Machinery,"; Akuoko-Frimpong, "Problems of Local Administration," pp. 19-20, 24-25.

23. Oddoye, "New Local Government," pp. 13-14.

24. Ibid., p. 14.

25. Ibid., p. 12.

26. Ibid., p. 14.

27. Nsarkoh, "Our New Local Administration Machinery," pp. 2, 12, 18.

28. Akuoko-Frimpong, "Problems of Local Adminstration," pp. 24-27.

29. Ronald Wraith, *Local Administration in West Africa*, 2nd ed. (London: George Allen & Unwin, 1972), p. 177, quoted in Akuoko-Frimpong, "Problems of Local Administration," p. 23.

30. Cherry Gertzel, *The Politics of Independent Kenya* (London: Heinemann, 1970), p. 30; and "The Provincial Administration in Kenya," *Journal of Commonwealth Political Studies* (Leicester) 4, no. 3 (November 1966).

31. F. Ridley and J. Blondel, *Public Administration in France* (London: Routledge & Kegan Paul, 1964), p. 87.

32. Ibid., p. 86.

33. Greenstreet shifts the analogy. For him, it is the regional administrative officer (to whom the district chief executive is responsible) who is the counterpart of the prefect. He likens the district chief executive to the "manager" in the Republic of Ireland. "Trends in Decentralisation in Ghana," p. 182. Akuoko-Frimpong maintains that the internal structure of the district council resembles in certain respects the

council-manager plan of the United States: "Problems of Local Administration," p. 19.

34. "Matchet's Diary," *West Africa* (8 September 1975): 1045.

35. This was the conclusion reached by Joel Samoff through detailed studies of three key issues—primary education, liquor licensing, and jobs—in Moshi, Tanzania. *Tanzania: Local Politics and the Structure of Power* (Madison: University of Wisconsin Press, 1974), p. 85 and *passim*.

36. "Ghana's Local Government Framework," *West Africa* (30 January-5 February 1971): 131.

37. Oddoye, "New Local Government," p. 12.

38. Akuoko-Frimpong, "Problems of Local Administration," pp. 23-24.

39. "The New Local Government Set-up," quoted in Akuoko-Frimpong, ibid., p. 25.

40. "Probing Ghana's Councils," *West Africa* (25 June 1971): 717.

41. *Report of the Auditor-General . . . 1967-68/1968-69.*

42. "Sierra Leone's Chronic Sickness," *West Africa* (23-29 January 1971): 97-98. See also Christopher Clapham's excellent study: *Liberia and Sierra Leone: An Essay in Comparative Politics* (London: Cambridge University Press, 1976).

43. See Julius K. Nyerere, *Decentralization* (Dar es Salaam: Government Printer, 1972), pp. 1-12; and James R. Finucane, *Rural Development and Bureaucracy in Tanzania: The Case of Mwanza Region* (Uppsala: Scandinavian Institute of African Studies, 1974).

44. "Local Government in West Africa: 4, Nigeria's Southern States," *West Africa* (20-26 February 1971): 214.

45. William Tordoff, "Local Government in Zambia," in *Local Government in Southern Africa*, ed. W. B. Vosloo, D. A. Kotze, and W. J. O. Jeppe (Pretoria: Academica, 1974), ch. 10; and "Local Administration in Zambia," in *A Revival of Local Government and Administration?*, Collected Seminar Papers no. 23, pp. 31-43.

46. *Report of the Working Party Appointed to Review the System of Decentralised Administration* (Chairman: Mr. A. J. F. Simmance) (Lusaka: Cabinet Office, May 1972), pp. 103-04. Initially, the proposal was limited to the staff of district councils, to be established by amalgamating the former rural and township councils within each district.

47. *Report of the Local Government Study Group*, mimeograph, confidential (Gaborone: 1970). A presidential commission is now reviewing the structure of local government in Botswana, where (predominantly) elected district councils have a better record of performance than in most English-speaking African states.

48. See the statement made by a special correspondent, concluding his survey of local government in Sierra Leone, Ghana, and Nigeria: "It is now clear that carbon copies of English local government do not work in Commonwealth West Africa." "Local Government in West Africa: 6, A Look at the Future," *West Africa* (6-12 March 1971): 275.

49. Keith Panter-Brick, "The Reform of Local Government in Nigeria," in *A Revival of Local Government and Administration?*, Collected Seminar Papers no. 23, p. 1.

50. The special correspondent referred to in note 48 above attributed the breakdown of local government in Ghana, as well as in Sierre Leone and Nigeria, to the corruption

of elected councillors, shortage of resources and trained staff, and the difficulty of finding the optimum size of local government units. "Local Government in West Africa: 6, A Look at the Future," pp. 275-76.

51. Equality was first achieved in the Western State (Circular No. 1 of 1971, dated 6 January 1971, and back-dated to 1 April 1969), and was subsequently adopted by the other states. "Nigeria's Southern States," p. 213. However, further changes have been made in accordance with the *Guidelines for Local Government Reform*, issued by the Federal Military Government in 1976. Each state in Nigeria has now established a local government service board, which is mainly responsible, on behalf of the local authorities, for recruiting, posting, and disciplining the more senior staff. As a temporary measure—until adequate substitutes have been trained—most of the senior positions are held by middle-ranging administrative officers on secondment from state governments. Panter-Brick, "The Reform of Local Government," pp. 5-6.

52. See "A Look at the Future," p. 275.

Nigeria

*John B. Idode**

33

The history of local government in Nigeria has been a turbulent one. In the colonial situation, the colonizers found willing allies in the traditional rulers around whom they built systems of native authorities based on the principle of "indirect rule."[1] Although "indirect rule" proved successful in Northern Nigeria, it was an unwelcome imposition in the southern part of the country, where it met with bitter opposition.[2] Following the rise of the post-1945 nationalist movement, an English type of three-tier local government was established in Eastern Nigeria in 1950. The Western Region introduced a similar system in 1952. Northern Nigeria followed suit in 1954.

Since independence in 1960, local governments in Nigeria have undergone a series of changes. These changes include the removal of functions from the local governments to the state bureaucracies, complete elimination of the powers and status of the local governments and the deconcentration of the state bureaucracies to the local areas, and brief flirtations with modified versions of the American city-manager plan and the French prefectoral system in several parts of the country. Thus, prior to 1976, there was a proliferation of local government reforms in Nigeria. It was only in 1976 that the federal government took the initiative and reintroduced a modified version of the English pattern of local government on a nationwide basis in Nigeria. In this essay, we will outline the basic provisions of the 1976 reform, examine what is old and new in them, and attempt an assessment of the new local government system.

*A Nigerian official who has been concerned with local government. He worked as Administrative Officer in the civil service of Bendel State from 1970 to 1975, and recently completed his Ph.D. in Political Science at Carleton University with a thesis on "Bureaucracy's Role in Rural Development in Nigeria: The Experience of Bendel State" (1979).

THE REFORM OF 1976

Provisions of the Reform

In July 1976 the government of the Federal Republic of Nigeria issued a set of guidelines[3] for the reform of local government in the country. The broad guidelines, within which each state government could make minor modifications to suit its own peculiar environment, came into force in December 1976. The structural reorganizations brought about by the reform are far-reaching. While centralization was the general tendency in all the nineteen states of Nigeria until 1976, decentralization was the cardinal tone of the 1976 reform. The reform finally abolished the "provincial," "divisional," or "development" administration systems under which state field administrative officers ran local administration in many parts of Nigeria.[4] Under the reform, all the statutory functions of local government in Nigeria were concentrated in multipurpose single-tier institutions called "local governments." The local governments became the only level of government, below the state level, recognized by the federal government. But where appropriate, specified functions could be delegated by the local governments to subordinate councils to which financial allocations can be made from the local government budget. The new local governments were given a large degree of autonomy in the making of their budgets and the execution of their numerous functions.[5] Local governments, according to the guidelines, serve populations of between 150,000 and 800,000.[6] However, there is no hard and fast rule about the population of a local government area, as long as the population does not exceed the stipulated range. In Bendel State, for example, the average population of a local government area is 200,000. The local governments should be sufficiently large and economically viable to be able to plan and execute development projects.

Members of the local governments are directly or indirectly (according to the wish of the state government) elected on a no-party basis. Some members of the local government council are, however, appointed by the military governor. Council members are elected for a three-year term, which may be renewed. The chairman of a local government council is either appointed by the military governor, from a list of three councillors selected by the members, or a council elects a chairman from its own membership. Such election is subject to ratification by the military governor. Traditional rulers (emirs, obas or chiefs) may be ceremonial presidents of local government councils.

Generally, all local governments are advised to minimize the number of committees and to have two standing committees, finance and general purpose, and education. But local governments may operate a few other committees. The political control of the local administration by a council is exercised through a number of supervisory councillors (not more than four), each of whom is chairman of a small committee concerned with the political direction of a group of departments or a single department such as education. These chairmen are political heads of the departments of the local government and are automatically members of the Finance and General Purpose Committee. This committee is responsible for the day-to-day policy matters of the local government and is, in effect, the "cabinet" of the local government council. Supervisory councillors may give orders to administrative/professional heads of departments on policy matters, but may not interfere in the internal management of the departments.[7]

The chief executive of the local government is the Secretary to the Local Government (SLG) and is appointed by the state government and not the local government. For purposes of appointment to all senior positions in the local governments, each state has set up a Local Government Service Board. This board serves the local governments as the Civil Service Commission serves the civil service. The SLG and other senior staff of the local government are members of the Unified Local Government Service (ULGS). Appointment, promotion, transfer and discipline of all senior staff in the local government are the responsibilities of the board. A state government may decide to allow the board to delegate its responsibilities to the SLG or to retain such responsibilities in the board, which must consult with the local governments in exercising these responsibilities. The SLG is responsible for the day-to-day running of the affairs of the local government.[8] To assist him in the execution of council's policies are departmental heads of the local government who are also senior officers belonging to the ULGS.

In the area of local government financing, the reform made provision for a steady source of revenue to enable the new local governments to carry out their much-increased functions. In 1976 the federal government allocated ₦100 million (about $160 million) for distribution to the local governments in the whole country.[9] State governments were also directed to pay 10 percent of their recurrent revenue to the local governments. These sources of funding from the senior levels of government later became a permanent aspect of the new local government system.[10] In addition to these revenue avenues, local governments are also expected to use their internal sources of property rating, community tax, liquor licensing, bicycle fees, miscellaneous fees and loans.[11]

Similarities with Previous Reforms

We should now examine how the new reform resembles or differs from previous reforms in the Nigerian local government system. The new reform resembles the local government reforms in Nigeria in the 1950s in three ways. First, the idea of the "supervisory councillor," which is the cornerstone of the new system, is not new in Nigeria. Since the early reform of the Nigerian local government system in the 1950s, the "portfolio councillor" has been popular in the local government system of Northern Nigeria. In the large emirates of the north (Kano Emirate for example), large departments like Education, Works and Health were under the political control of a "portfolio councillor." It has been stated that in the Northern Region, the local government system was so efficient in the provision of essential services that even if the regional (now state) governnment collapsed, the local governments were capable of running vital services in the region.[12] The local government system in these emirates was built around the "portfolio councillor" and the "departmental head" as an administrative professional.

Second, the allocation of functions to the new local governments remains the same. The early reforms of local government in Nigeria during the period 1950-54 devolved extensive functions to the local governments. These functions included the maintenance of law and order, rural development schemes, public roads and bridges, health, water supply, housing and agriculture.[13] After independence in 1960, most of these functions were removed gradually from the local governments and vested in federal and state ministries, public boards and corporations. For example, in the Midwest Region (later Bendel State), local government police forces were disbanded in 1964 and their personnel handed over to the Nigerian Police. Local government police forces in other regions were also abolished. In 1966 public water undertakings owned by the local governments in the Midwest Region were handed over to the Water Board. In 1968 state and local school boards (under the state government) were created and took over the administration of schools from the local governments. Forestry, agriculture, town and country planning, and hospital administration were handed over to state government bodies between 1969 and 1972.[14] The dilution of the prestige and powers of local governments in respect to the new state bureaucracies became a common feature of the post-military period until 1976. In almost all the states in the federation, the reforms in local administraton had marked a shift of powers, manpower and financial resources, from the local authorities to the state ministries. Under the 1976 reform, most of the powers and functions which had hitherto been taken away from the local governments were restored.[15]

Third, the committee system in the local government council is not an innovative idea. In many parts of Nigeria, the committee system was widely used until 1966 when the military's intervention in politics resulted in the large-scale dissolution of local government councils, and "committees of management" or "sole administrators" were appointed to run the councils.[16] In Northern Nigeria, the portfolio councillors and the chairman of the local government council formed the cabinet of the local government. Under the new arrangement, the supervisory councillors and the chairman of the local government, members of the Finance and General Purpose Committee, function as the cabinet of the local government council.

Innovations of the Reform

Let us now turn to the innovations introduced by the reform. The first impressive new element in the 1976 reform is the intervention of the federal government in local government matters. Before the reform, the state governments were fond of changing their local government system at will. No national guidelines or directives were followed. Under Nigeria's federal system, local government is a state and not a federal responsibility. Thus, we have seen in the earlier part of this paper how the three regions of Nigeria promulgated different ordinances in the 1950s to establish their own local government systems.

After the creation of twelve states in 1967, a similar pattern of nonuniformity in local government continued. In 1972 the Western State (Now Ogun, Oyo and Ondo states) reformed its own local government system by adopting a modified version of the American city-manager plan, introducing a one-tier system, removing the traditional rulers (chiefs and obas) from local government affairs, and directing that 40 percent of local revenue raised annually should be used for local development efforts. In the Midwest State, local governments were abolished in 1974 when the state government promulgated the Development Administration Edict. The edict introduced a two-tier structure of Development Councils and Development Committees in what it called the "development administration system."[17] The new system resulted in the deconcentration of state ministries to the field and the appointment of a civil servant (Resident) as the head of the entire government operation in each administration division. Members of the development councils and development committees were selected by the state government. In 1972 the East Central State (now Imo and Anambra states) introduced a two-tier prefectoral system tailored on the French model. Under what it called "divisional administration," direct control of the system by the state cabinet and the military governor was exercised through state-appointed divisional officers. In the South Eastern State (now Cross River State), the new system of field administration was directly controlled by the Ministry of Development Administration, while only advisory and tax collecting roles were assigned to the traditional authorities. In the Rivers State, the government also centralized the functions of local administration under the state ministry. In the northern states, the local government reform of 1972 renamed the "Native Authorities" as "Local Authorities," watered down the position and powers of the emir in the local government, and increased the role of the new state bureaucracies. An end to the creation of diverse local administrative systems in Nigeria was achieved in 1976 when the federal government introduced a fairly uniform system of local government for the whole country.

In addition to the introduction of a fairly uniform local government structure, the 1976 reform brought the federal government into the direct financing of the local governments. The state and federal governments were required, under the new arrangements, to pay statutory grants to the local governments. Prior to 1976, attempts to convince the federal government to pay grants to local governments in order to minimize their financial problems did not yield any dividends.[18] But as a part of the new reform, as we have noted, the federal government allocated ₦100 million (about $160 million) for distribution to the new local government during the 1976-77 financial year. In the 1977-78 fiscal year, the federal government decided that 5 percent of retained federal revenue was to be allocated as statutory payments to the local governments. The state governments were also required to allocate 10 percent of their recurrent revenue to the local government as grants. The money from both federal and state sources was to be shared on the basis of 25 percent equally and 75 percent according to population. During the 1977-78 financial year, the nineteen local governments in Bendel State received a total of nearly N30 million (about $50 million) from both federal and state sources. If this new method of making statutory allocations to the local governments is strictly followed, the local governments will be assured of a sound financial base necessary for the planning and the execution of development projects.

Apart from the emergence of the federal government as a financier of the new local governments, another innovation of the reform is the acceptance of local government as a meaningful third level of government in Nigeria. We have seen that, in the past, local government areas were created at will and their councils established and dissolved as the state government wished. The functions performed by the local governments depended on the wish of the state governments. The 1976 reform set the approximate size of a local government area, as well as the functions to be performed by the local government. More importantly, the reform has made provision for the powers, human resources and financial base to enable the local governments to discharge their duties. To prevent the state governments from fragmenting or eliminating the local governments, the new Nigerian Constitution, which came into effect in October 1979, includes provisions to safeguard the position of the local governments as a third level of government in the federation. However, the state governments will continue to draw up guidelines for the local governments to follow in the discharge of their duties and will supervise the activities of the local governments. Federal grants to the local governments will continue to be paid to the state governments, which are required to add their own allocations and distribute the funds to all the local governments in their areas of jurisdiction. By these arrangements local governments are given a large degree of autonomy in the discharge of their functions, but they are not completely independent of the state governments.

Another innovation worthy of comment is the exclusion of party politics from local government elections. It is true that party politics played a major role in the creation of economically unviable local government units and escalated the rate of corruption in local government administration in many parts of Nigeria between 1960 and 1966.[19] But party politics at the local level also provided a training ground for political aspirants at the state and federal levels of government. Although the exclusion of party politics from local government elections has worked well in countries like Canada, it is difficult to see, given Nigeria's historical development, how the next civilian government will be able to keep local governments free from partisan politics. It should also be mentioned that the provision for indirect elections to the local goverments in some parts of the country undermines the supposed democratic intentions of the reform. In order to give the people the opportunity to elect one of themselves to represent their local interest, direct elections based on universal suffrage should be adopted in all the local governments in the country.

APPRAISAL OF THE NEW SYSTEM

An evaluation of the new local governments, in the light of their performance since December 1976, is now appropriate. While some progress has been made, problems abound in the operation of the new system. In the first place, the difficulty of drawing a line between policy and administration at the local level has become a source of friction. There have been numerous clashes between political functionaries (chairmen and supervisory councillors) and the chief executive (secretary to the local government).[20] The political functionaries, who are full-time appointees, tend to interfere too often in the running of the local governments. For example, a supervisory councillor for works in one of the nineteen local governments in Bendel State was reported to have fired a road laborer without the knowledge of the chief executive. Yet, the councillors were given no control over staff persons under the new system. Perhaps the education of the local politicians about the provisions of the new reform and the limit of their policy-making role would help to improve *esprit de corps* in the local governments.

Both the federal and state governments are already taking action to educate both the politicians and officials of the new local governments. The federal government has commissioned two institutions—the Institute of Administration at Ahmadu Bello University, Zaria, and the Department of Public Administration at the University of Ife—to organize and conduct a series of administrative and management training programs for the senior officers of all the local governments in Nigeria. A total of 173 participants, mainly secretaries to the local governments, were expected to attend the Ife seminar and workshop. The subjects treated during the training period included leadership role, internal organization of the local government, financial management and mobilization of citizens for local development. It was expected that after a period of two years, all the secretaries of the local governments would have attended the training courses along with some of their senior assistants. The training of the junior officials of the local governments is conducted by the state ministries of local government in their respective local government training schools.

The education of the local government politicians is undertaken through a number of conferences organized at the state level. Representatives of the local politicians also attend the local government conferences at the national level. But, in 1978 the Nigerian Institute of Management (NIM) expanded its training programs to include chairmen, supervisory councillors and secretaries of the local governments. A two-week course, which was the first in the series, took place at Kano in February 1978. The subjects taught were organization for dynamic action, process of effective leadership and motivation, and communication and control.[21] In addition to education and training, it is also necessary to reexamine the issue whether there are enough policy-making functions to demand the appointment of full-time chairmen and supervisory councillors in the present stage of development of the local governments.[22]

Another problem facing the new local governments is the untimely and inadequate release of allocated funds. It is not enough to vote funds for distribution to local governments. It is equally important that budgeted funds should be released promptly and regularly if budgetary promises are to be translated into results. But, unfortunately, reports show that in the first two years of their existence, the local governments did not receive prompt and regular payment of grants from the federal and state governments.[23] For example, out of the ₦12 million allocated to local governments by the Sokoto State government for the 1977-78 fiscal year, only ₦8 million was distributed, while only ₦7 million was paid out of the ₦18 million expected from the federal government.[24] In Benue State, some local governments warned that many development projects already started were likely to be stopped because of shortage of funds.[25] Local governments should not depend too heavily on the senior levels of government for funds, if they are to develop and expand an adequate range of local services. They should also seek to maximize their own independent sources of revenue, which now include property rating, community tax, and tenement rating. In order to broaden the independent financial base of the local governments, the 1977 National Conference on Local Government held at the University of Ife recommended that vehicle licenses and cattle taxes collected in rural areas should be turned over to the local governments. Other problems identified in the local governments are shortage of qualified technical manpower, and corrupt practices.[26]

On the positive side, the new local governments have successfully executed a large number of development projects, such as motor parks, markets, feeder roads, bridges and culverts, health and maternity centers, classrooms, water supply and purchase of road equipment. It is true that in the large emirates of the former Northern Region of Nigeria, native authorities had been able to provide such services. But in the southern part of the country, where local governments were highly fragmented, their ability to provide these services after the 1976 reform marked a notable improvement in local government and administration.

The involvement of local governments in the planning and implementation of development plans is another area in which the new system has begun to show some impact. In the past there had been much talk about the integration of local government plans in the state and national development plans, but practically no action had been taken towards the realization of this goal. For example, at the 1964 National Conference of Local Government held at the Insititute of Administraton, Ahmadu Bello University, Zaria, a number of recommendations were made to the governments of the Federal Republic of

Nigeria on how to involve the local governments in national development planning and execution. But the recommendations were not implemented. In 1977, a National Conference on Local Government recommended that each local government in Nigeria should establish a small planning unit to identify and appraise projects for the developments of the local government to be integrated in the State Development Plan. In addition, each Ministry of Local Government was advised to establish an Economic Planning and Research Unit to link the development plans of all the local governments in a state with those of the state government and also to provide assistance and advice to the Economic Planning Units of the local governments. Working on the basis of guidelines issued by the Ministries of Local Government, the local governments in the country submitted plans for 1978-80 for incorporation into the 1975-80 development plans of the various states. A collection of the development plans of the nineteen state governments and that of the federal government is published as the National Development Plan. Through the framework described above, the local governments will be involved in future development plans. In fact, as early as April 1979, the local governments had begun to submit proposals for inclusion in the 1980-85 development plan.

CONCLUSION

We have seen in this paper that since the local government ordinances were promulgated in Nigeria in the early 1950s, changes in local government have been numerous and far-reaching. Most of the systems experimented with have not proved successful. It is hoped that the few innovations introduced by the 1976 reform will be the beginning of a change for the better. There was, however, a degree of uncertainty as civilians prepared to take over the reins of government from the military in October 1979. One wonders whether the new rulers will once again dismantle the present system and set up new ones.

Nigeria's new local government reform, with its insistence on decentralization, appears to be inconsistent with the general trend in Africa. African countries, since the decade of independence in the 1960s, have generally adopted centralization in their local government systems. The basic characteristics of the centralization measures include a combination of representatives and officials in council membership; staff and funds belong to the central government and are allocated to the areas for local disposal; and the field administrator reemerges at the core of local authority either as chairman or as chief executive. Decision making over the resources available to government has been concentrated in the hands of a national executive. The justifications for these centralization tendencies include the argument that public finance and trained manpower are in short supply when compared with the task that the state is to undertake, and so their allocation is deliberately concentrated in a single organization at the national capital. Moreover, a "socialist" ideology and the fear of regional cleavages often lend force to the centralization movement, and insecurity within the bureaucracy drives field officials to refer all major decisions to their headquarters.[27]

But the questions which remain to be answered at this stage of Nigeria's decentralization measures are: Will the experiment be successful? Or will it fail like previous local administration reforms in Nigeria and many other African countries? If the experiment proves to be successful, will this success reverse the present centralization trend in African countries? These are moot questions and only time will supply the answers.

NOTES

1. Indirect rule was introduced by Lord Lugard in 1919. Under the system, the traditional ruler was the titular head of the native authority. But the real powers to maintain law and order, collect and spend taxes, and run the administration rested with the divisional officer, who was the direct representative of the colonial administration. See A.H.M. Kirk-Greene, ed., *Principles of Native Administration in Nigeria* (London: Oxford University Press, 1965).

2. In Eastern Nigeria where there were no traditional rulers, but democratic village assemblies, indirect rule failed woefully. The Aba Riots of 1929, in which market women reacted against the appointment of "red cap chiefs" and the imposition of taxes, are indicative of the failure. In Western Nigeria, indirect rule was a partial success because the "obas" (traditional rulers) were widely accepted as the rightful rulers. But with the arrival of Western education, nationalist agitators rose to challenge the obas' right to represent the people in the colonial government.

3. Federal Republic of Nigeria, *Guidelines for Local Government Reform* (Kaduna, Nigeria: Government Printer, 1976).

4. See *West Africa*, no. 3087 (30 June 1976): 1242.

5. *Guidelines*, p. 3.

6. Ibid.

7. Ibid., p. 9.

8. For details of the full functions of the SLG in one Nigerian state, see "Local Government Edict, 1976," published as *Bendel State of Nigeria Extraordinary Gazette*, vol. 13, no. 59 (13 December, 1976), Part B, sec. 87.

9. *West Africa*, no. 3087 (30 June 1976): 1242. See also *Guidelines*, p. 14.

10. The new constitution came into effect in October 1979, but the financial arrangement discussed in this essay was already operative.

11. *Guidelines*, pp. 13-14.

12. See B. C. Smith, "Field Administration and Political Change: The Case of Northern Nigeria," *Administrative Science Quarterly* 17 (1972): 99-109.

13. For example, see Western Region of Nigeria, *Local Government Law, 1957* (Ibadan, Nigeria: Government Printer, 1958), Cap. 68.

14. The transfer of functions from local governments to state and federal departments is well documented by Murtala Ahmed, "The Effect of the Transfer of Functions from Local Government Authorities to Federal and State Governments" (Student Paper, D.P.A. Course XII 1974/75, University of Ife, Institute of Administration, 1975); and J. E. U. Oyemike, "Financial Relationship between the State Government and Local Government in the Midwestern State" (Student Paper, H.D.L.G.F.A., 1973/74, University of Ife, Institute of Administration, 1974).

15. One old function which was not reinstated in 1976 was the operation of a local government police force.

16. Ronald Wraith, *Local Administration in West Africa* (London: Allen and Unwin, 1972).

17. Government of the Midwestern State of Nigeria, *White Paper on Development Administration* (Benin City, Nigeria: Government Printer, 1974).

18. See University of Ife, *The Future of Local Government in Nigeria* (Ile-Ife: University of Ife Press, 1969).

19. For details of the impact of party politics on local government affairs in one Nigerian state, see Olu Fadahunsi, "The Politics of Local Administration in Western Nigeria, 1958-68," *Quarterly Journal of Administration* 11, nos. 1 and 2 (1977): 97-113.

20. An elucidation of the problems and prospects of the new local governments is presented in John B. Idode, "The New Local Government System in Nigeria: A Preliminary Assessment of Performance, Problems and Prospects" (Paper prepared for the Department of Public Administration, Faculty of Administration, University of Ife, May 1978).

21. *Business Times* (Lagos), 21 February 1978.

22. Some of the local political functionaries earn annual salaries of over ₦6,000 (US $9,600), excluding various allowances. The salaries and allowances may be a drain on the scarce local government funds.

23. Many of the local government chairmen interviewed across the country on this matter were disappointed over the manner of paying grants to the new local governments. See *Daily Times* (Lagos), 28 January 1978.

24. *Daily Times* (Lagos), 16 February 1978.

25. Ibid.

26. For an example of proved corrupt practices, see Mr. Justice Obi's *Report on the Judicial Inquiry into the Oredo Local Government* (Benin City, Nigeria: Government Printer, 1978).

27. See Philip Mawhood and Ken Davey, "Anglophone Africa," and V. Subramaniam, "Developing Countries," in this volume.

Anglophone Africa

Philip Mawhood and Ken Davey*

34

Apparent diversity and an underlying consistency characterize the local government patterns of Anglophone Africa. It is difficult to make general statements about the formal structures without inserting numerous exceptions, but underlying trends prevail over the whole area.[1] Every country except Ethiopia and Liberia has a common administrative inheritance from the British, but present-day structures of administration do not necessarily conform to colonial models. At one point the inheritance has been accepted, at another rejected, and most countries have engaged in new thinking since independence day to modify old institutions or create new ones in response to changing political demands.

Until the 1950s, rural areas were controlled by generalist administrators belonging to the central government and assisted by a growing number of technical officials and a hierarchy of chiefs, headmen, and revenue collectors. In countries where "indirect rule" was at its strongest, the chiefs in conjunction with representative councils raised enough revenue to finance a range of local services and capital works but remained under the ultimate supervision of the district commissioner or district officer.

The colonial secretary's dispatch of February 1947 heralded reforms which continued throughout the 1950s, progressively introducing principles of local government drawn from the British domestic model. There were five of these principles:

*Both authors are members of the Development Administration Group in the Institute of Local Government Studies, University of Birmingham, England, and served as administrators in Africa before moving into university teaching and research. They have published extensively on local government and administration in developing countries. Ken Davey is currently acting leader of the group, and Philip Mawhood until recently was seconded as Professor of Local Government at Ahmadu Bello University, Zaria, Nigeria.

1. Local authorities should be institutionally separate from central government and assume responsibility for a significant range of local services (primary education, clinics and preventive health services, community development, and secondary roads being the most common).
2. These authorities should have their own funds and budgets and should raise a substantial part of their revenue through local direct taxation.
3. Local authorities should employ their own qualified staff, who could be seconded from the civil service where necessary in the early stages.
4. The authorities would be governed internally by councils, predominantly composed of populary elected members.
5. Government administrators would withdraw from an executive to an advisory inspectorial role in relation to local government.

STRUCTURAL CHANGES SINCE INDEPENDENCE

By the mid-1970s these five principles were widely in retreat, at least in rural areas. In the towns local government has generally continued with structures based on the earlier models, modified in relatively minor respects. In one-party states the councillors are often selected through party machinery rather than open public elections. The mayor or chairman may be a party office holder, appointed ex officio, where he is not actually a government administrator. Supervision over the budgets and legislation of the urban councils is usually closer than in colonial times; however, the councils continue to employ their own staff and raise directly a large part of the revenue they need for administering local services.

It is in the rural areas that the change has been most evident. A number of the larger countries—notably the Sudan, Tanzania, and Ghana (and some of the Nigerian states before the reforms of 1976-77)—have made structural reforms of their rural local government that amount to creating a new type of institution. [2] The representative body is a mixture of locally elected councillors and central government nominees (often, but not always, government officials). Distinctions between central and local revenues are blurred, with the use of a single treasury office at the local level, or abolished altogether. The higher executive staff are central civil servants, and the functions of the local body usually include all the main developmental services: agricultural extension, animal husbandry work, primary education, rural medical services, district roads, water supplies, forestry, land control, and development planning. There is a tendency for the local authority to be given the power to coordinate all departments of the field administration as well and thus to become the sole, multipurpose representative of the central authorities.

Despite this consistency among several countries with very different ideologies, it has to be said that no general move towards the new type can be identified. Countries with smaller populations, such as Sierra Leone, Gambia, Malawi, and Botswana, continue to operate local authorities of the earlier separate kind, exercising a full range of functions, in rural as in urban areas. In Malawi and Gambia the generalist administator is ex officio chairman of the district council, while in Botswana he is an official councillor only. In the northern states of Nigeria, the chairmanship generally falls to a traditional emir in a local authority and to a generalist administrator or other government appointee at the level of area councils.

Several countries are at a stage which must be regarded as transitional. There is first the common reaction among the new rulers after a military coup of dissolving all local councils and substituting government officers, either individually or collectively as "management committees." This phase was brief in Ghana and Nigeria, but in Uganda it has lasted throughout the Amin regime. Secondly there are the countries where (as in Zambia) rural local government was always weak or where (as in Kenya) it reached a condition of near breakdown, largely because government withheld the resources local authorities needed to respond to the demands it made upon them. Here the response has been to keep the local councils in being but to withdraw from them the major functions of primary education, clinics, and road works. A network of government-dominated development committees is set up in parallel to the local authorities, but (in contrast to Tanzania) their coordinating role is not reinforced by any formal authority over individual services. Their functions are to draw up local plans and supervise their execution rather than to control the whole of government activity in the area.

To assess all these changes properly one must discard the welter of sweeping value judgments with which they are normally discussed. Governments are accused of centralizing to satisfy their craving for omnipotence; councils, conversely, are said to be characterized by various combinations of corruption, bankruptcy, and political extremism. Majority party groups exclude their opponents from council and committee seats; ministers pack public enterprise boards with their protégés. Councillors vote themselves excessive allowances; national elites manipulate tax, tariff, price control, and import licensing structures to entrench their economic privileges. The same appetites and pressures apply at both levels. The real question is not whether the actors, central or local government, political or bureaucratic, have behaved well or badly, but how far the institutions themselves have encurged them to do so.

Local Autonomy and Its Effects

Compared with the preceding situation, the reforms of the 1950s stressed the "separateness" of local authorities from central government. While this stress was acceptable in the colonial situation, its effects since the coming of independence have been unfortunate. This can be seen by examining the five principles presented above in their practical application.

First, local authorities were to be separate legal entities with functions distinct from those of other public agencies at local level. This gave full rein to the natural tendency of parallel institutions to develop mutual antipathies—to strengthen their internal cohesion by rivalry with others. It also presupposed that some functions were suitable for local political management and others were not. This proved an oversimplification. Local authority responsibilities, on the one hand, often suffered from the reluctance of councillors to impose communal discipline—impartial taxation, regular dipping of livestock, and the repayment of credit, to mention only a few examples.(Contrary to popular myth, the arts of control become more important as development progresses.) Central government, on the other hand, often abandoned its former habit of discussing its own local operations with councils on the ground that these were not "local government responsibilities." Local interests continued to penetrate government decisions through the network of political or personal relationships, but these favored the interests of those who possessed "pull" at the center; wider communal interests were deprived of access to the open forum of debate in the councils. Finally, the division of functions among local authorities, government departments, statutory boards, and the cooperative movement hampered the evolution of an integrated approach to rural development.

Second, local authorities were to have independent accounts and budgets, partly financed by direct taxation. This principle was justified by two considerations. The first was the "development-from-below" theory that local communities should choose how big a tax burden they would bear in the interests of development; they would be more willing to contribute if they could see the money spent locally on programs that were to their liking. The second was the desire of national treasuries to meet some of the financial pressures of independence by reducing their commitments from central revenue sources. This policy frequently proved the Achilles' heel of local government in Africa. Governments normally retained the more lucrative, elastic, and collectable revenue sources, leaving local authorities dependent on forms of mass personal or property taxation with low ceilings, revenues which are administratively and politically difficult to exploit in countries where the vast majority of people are poor, self-employed, and dispersed in rural areas. Augmenting grants from the center rarely took comprehensive account of the real expenditure needs (including the implications of government's own policies over wage and price levels or the expansion of local services) or of the real potential for direct taxation. The supposed freedom of councils to suit their tax rates to their ambitions was largely dissipated by the narrowness of grant formulas and the growth of their fixed commitments on devolved services like primary education. Transferring central commitments to local government often meant that the government was able to spend its marginal revenue on less developmental items such as embassies and war surplus aircraft, so that vital local services simply lacked their appropriate share of overall national resources.

The third principle was the separation of central and local government staffing, which often duplicated the strain on scarce financial and manpower resources. Even when emoluments are competitive, only the largest local authorities can offer the same career prospects as central government or public enterprise in a period of rapid "localization." Most unfortunate perhaps was the way that central civil servants lost a sense of identity with local authorities in the areas where they worked. Seeing themselves as the modernizing elite, bureaucrats often equated "local government" with conservative and parochial interests—anti-national and anti-progressive—which were to be regarded contemptuously or patronizingly.

The dominance of the elected member also distinguished local government from those other public agencies whose political direction was diffused through a large bureaucracy over long distances. The resulting difference in managerial style was obvious. There are strong and legitimate differences in approach between local bureaucrats and politicians. They are seen, as Colin Leys has pointed out, in the attitude to the development process, which planners regard as a long-term national strategy but which councillors regard as a competition for the jobs, contracts, and amenities offering localized and immediate benefits for the lucky winner.[3] There are also the tensions between professionals anxious to preserve high standards of services and politicians who wish to spread the services as widely as possible. There is confusion over the divide between policy and implementation, which becomes hazier than ever when the smallest decisions can change the way of life of a village or an individual. One effect of applying British local government principles in Africa has been to institutionalize these conflicts of approach, turning dialogue into confrontation between central and local government or between councillors who "decide" and officers who merely "advise."

The final principle concerned the withdrawal of the government administrator from active mangement of a local authority's affairs. It symbolized a new, stylized role for central government as the purely external watchdog of integrity and efficiency. Systems analysts argue that all organizations need external pressure to keep them intent on output rather than self-maintenance; for administrators in Africa this proposition brings to mind many former battles with local authorities over unnecessary expenditure on allowances, entertainment, secretaries, and the like at the expense of direct public service. Control of this kind is necessary rather than inimical to the health of local government.

When the administrator was "on the inside" of a local authority he could influence its behavior because he had advance warning of potential irregularities with the councillors and to some extent he championed their interests with central government; moreover, the council's effectiveness reflected on his own. All these conditions changed with the separation of the field administration from local government. Local authorities began to feel the lack of someone to defend their interests with other agencies that affected them closely; external control became remote and delayed, and audit, for example, frequently fell years behind. Moreover, governments often failed to exhibit the impartiality and rectitude implicit in their role. Controls were exercised to favor one local faction with influence at the center over another which held the majority in the council. Disengagement from local government could even make the central government behave irresponsibly, imposing decisions on local authorities which would not have been taken if it had had to face the consequences itself. One government in a single year reduced local authority tax rates. abolished local authority medical charges, and increased local authority teachers' salaries without any adjustment of the grants it paid.

It would be inaccurate to indicate a universal failure of the British model in tropical Africa. There have been times and places where local government systems have worked extremely well. But where strong intergrity of purpose is lacking on the part of central or local government personnel, there are powerful seeds of dissension and decay in the system, particularly in its emphasis on the separate identity of local authorities.

Centralized Structures Provide No Alternative

Yet the need for decentralization remains. Experience makes it clear that the local agencies of government can rarely be effective without discretion over the use of resources such as money and staff. (A complete rural development program in one Kenyan division collapsed because a central ministry withheld authority for spending £20 until the planting rains were over.) Rural works programs—the use of development funds on large numbers of small, locally initiated and managed schemes—can be more productive than large centrally run projects. The pursuit of such goals as coordination and participation is as much a matter of procedure as of structure, and nationally derived policies are only nominally implemented if they fail to evoke local understanding and support. There are also the analogous findings of research into industrial management, that rigidly hierarchical systems do not operate effectively in the conditions of change and uncertainty charteristic of development administration.

So the new patterns are being tried, and typically they reverse the principles of the 1950s model. Council membership combines representatives and officials; their powers of oversight extend to most governmental functions at the local level (the usual exceptions being "national"facilities, such as trunk roads, research stations, justice, and security); staff and funds belong to central government and are allocated to the area for local disposal, normally after some degree of bargaining; and the field administrator is once again at the core of the local authority, either as chairman or as chief executive.

These new patterns clearly overcome some of the superficial failings of the old. But they must also be seen with unease as part of the centralizing trend in government activities which is characteristic of the whole period since independence day. Decision making over the resources available to government has been concentrated as much as possible in the hands of a national executive. Public finance and trained manpower are seen to be in short supply relative to the tasks the state is to undertake; so their allocation is deliberately concentrated in a single organization at the national capital. A "socialist" ideology and the fear of regional cleavages often lend force to the movement, and insecurity within the bureaucracy drives field officials to refer all major decisions to their headquarters.

So far the material results of increased central direction have been poor in terms of the social and economic development governments are seeking. So far as rural sector statistics can be extracted, the aggregate picture is often one of near stagnation. The rural sector of the economy is typically associated with a peasant society relying on a mixture of subsistence and cash-crop production. Here and there small groups of farmers have become suddenly richer through adopting a new crop, but the great mass see little or no improvement in their living standards. An increased provision of schools and medical services can be observed in some areas but without any decisive change in the direction of economic and social development for the rural population as a whole. The larger towns and industrial areas are sharply distinguished by a different social and economic pattern in which the educated elite and skilled workers are dominant. Most of the new wealth produced is directed here (though a little of it trickles back to the rural areas through extended-family networks) , and it is hardly surprising that the larger cities are growing at an explosive rate.

FORMAL CONCENTRATION AND INFORMAL DISPERSION OF POWER

The simple imposition of a more centralized pattern in the processes of government has, in fact, failed to produce developmental effects for the rural people who still form the great bulk of the population. Yet increased development is said to be the main reason for introducing closer supervision and tighter central control. The explanation may be found by looking at the divergence between the formal organization of governments and their real power to influence events. This gap probably has been widening in recent years.

As the countries of tropical Africa moved from the colonial to the post-colonial situation they underwent a number of changes. First, local political forces became more powerful in proportion to central ones. The colonial government, especially in the rural areas which contained most of the population, had exercised a power clearly based at the capital and mediated by "deconcentrated" officials. The national rulers, by contrast, had built up support in those areas mainly through public meetings addressed by local leaders. The radio had not been freely available to them, and newspapers exercised only a marginal impact outside the towns. At independence, therefore, the new rulers needed to rely upon a population mobilized under many local groups and individuals; the national party label and doctrines were acknowledged, but there was a strong local bias to popular understanding of political matters.

Second, the central power could no longer offer the backing, in the last resort, of overwhelming force to its representatives in the regions and districts. The distant threat of battalions which could be moved in from other dependencies, or even from the metropolitan country, should not be underestimated as an influence in the most tranquil of administrative situations. The confidence it gave to a colonial official often enabled him to overcome minor resistances long before any thought of active coercion arose. With independence this factor was removed. Military support from the former colonial power could still be called in, but only by accepting a loss of face and declaring a national crisis (as President Nyerere did in Tanzania after the army mutinies of 1964). For the most part, the new governments' actions had to be limited to those which could find positive consent within the nation.

Third, the center's linkages with local institutions through its own local representatives had become weaker in several ways. Expatriate officials of the colonial period formed a culturally distinct group whose ultimate allegiance to London and Paris it was unnecessary to question. They were almost invariably middle-class, university-educated, and the products of a common administrative training in Europe. From the time of independence onward their role in local administration was progressively taken over by other political actors— whether bureaucrats or party men—whose cohesion among themselves and with the central leadership was much reduced by comparison. Their cultural background was more heterogeneous than that of the colonial administrators, and there was a wide variation in the education and administrative training they had received. It was less easy to make them accountable for their actions to the central rulers.

It is important to note that all these factors contributed to a shift in real power away from the center and towards the localities. The only environmental factor working in the opposite direction was the increase, at the moment of independence, in popular support for the national leadership and its ruling party. This is a quantity not easily measured but it was certainly less than the rhetoric of mass national mobilization assumed. A handicap from which some of the leaders suffered was the limited resistance they had encountered before assuming power as the new governments. Small resistance meant that the "national struggle" was often largely mythical, and the consequence was small popular mobilization to the national unit. Thus the security of the central rulers was less after independence than in colonial times, and their relations with local political institutions could no longer be conducted along the old lines.

The rulers' response was to seek means of building up their own influence through new and old political instruments alike. The party could be used to bring in support from the general public direct, and the administration had its inherited legitimacy to contribute, provided that its loyalties could be assured. But fresh political resources had been generated during the period of nationalist agitation, and stronger measures of formal centralization, through party and administration, were not enough to bring these resources fully under control. At the same time the general political situation had become more fluid, and new prizes lay open to competition for those who were building their careers. The central rulers sought to obtain economic growth and national integration without antagonizing too many of the established interests. These circumstances favored experiments with new institutions rather than attempts to make the existing ones work better. The result was a proliferation of organizations (community development, cooperatives, village development committees, and others) which competed with local government as the rulers' prime means of influencing peasant life. Even where the success of these organizations in achieving development goals was very limited, they diverted finance and skilled staff away from the local authorities and so contributed to their decline. However, they seldom had responsibility for taking major spending decisions; consequently an increasing share of public revenues was being transferred in this period from "decentralised" authorities to central or "deconcentrated" agencies of government.

A similar centralizing drift was taking place within the deconcentrated system, as more of the important decisions were referred to central departments and political leaders in the national capital. For the local authorities, such autonomy as had been achieved began to be undermined. The powerful corps of generalist field officials, upon whom they had depended for guidance, had lost its more senior members. Financial demands on the authorities grew steadily, as we have said, with wage inflation and the higher standard of services expected, but their revenue in taxes and subventions was never allowed to keep pace with the demands.

We have then a formal picture of centralization in the decision-making machinery of government. But when we consider the impact of this change upon the real world, the picture takes on an unreal quality. As Zolberg[4] and others have pointed out, there are in these countries two separate allocating systems, the traditional and the modern. Structures of authority set up for "modern" purposes have no necessary impact upon the traditional system at all, yet it is through the latter system that peasant communities can most effectively be influenced. The "cognitive map" of the 80 or 90 percent of the population who live on the land is largely made up of traditional cultural traits, and local interests bulk in it. It is one thing for a peasant to vote for a leader who claims to represent African socialism but quite another for him personally to give up cultivating his fields for private profit and devote himself to communal production. Similarly, economic and social modernization are accepted so long as the measures needed do not depart too far from perceived peasant interests. Beyond this point consent is no longer given, and cooperation with the modernizers breaks down. Many studies have shown that African peasants are highly rational in applying their own perceptions of what is desirable: if the rural sector has not changed in the direction the rulers wish, it may be because the rulers have not offered acceptable rewards for change.

THE PROBLEM OF EFFECTIVE DECENTRALIZATION

The question that remains about the new local organizations in Africa is this: Can they provide the bargaining machinery needed for regulating differences between the center and the localities? They will not do so if all the real discretion over programs is reserved to decision makers who are dependent upon the national government, and there is no reason to suppose that the organizations themselves will escape from the universal tendency of power to drift toward the center. A locally elected representative inevitably is handicapped in understanding or influencing "modern" allocations; his influence can perhaps be reinforced, but only if the government is determined that it shall be.

The British colonial model of local government succeeded best in places where the local authorities not only handled relatively large resources but were also supervised by a strong field administration committed to making local decision making happen. The object must still be in some way to create a balance between local autonomy and central supervision, but guaranteeing the former is manifestly the harder task.

It is unlikely that local decentralized bodies will be effective, under African conditions, unless the government itself accepts decentralization as an important aim of its organization—ranking equally with such aims as civil service efficiency and the impartial administration of justice. This brings us back to the issue of conflict between the demands of local autonomy and the competing claims of government departments, public corporations, political interest groups, and individual politicians: the local authority may often need protection against these. Within its own organization, technical officers are influenced through their vertical links with individual ministries and boards; if the local unit is weak, these influences may prevent it from developing any corporate approach to local problems. The essential building blocks for such a local authority must therefore be

1. A central department to represent and, when necessary, defend it, in addition to serving as the channel of communication with the national government
2. Supports provided to uphold the efficiency of the local executive, including sympathetic routine guidance as well as the finance to pay those qualified staff who are not centrally employed
3. Suitable electoral structures and training to ensure that the local decision makers are competent and broadly representative of all groups
4. Substantial revenues and substantial discretion in the spending of them, though here the interpretation of "substantial" has to depend very much upon local circumstances

The new "mixed" structures of local government or administration which have been described still need to prove themselves in the countries where they are being tried. Their advantage is that, with the field administrator at the core of the local body, government can more easily trust it to handle large public resources and carry wider responsibilities. The question remains whether the essence of decentralization will have been preserved. Will the new bodies as such be able to exercise any real discretion over the choice of programs and locations? Will the elected representatives be able to exercise much influence, compared to that of the bureaucrats and party functionaries? Or will the pressures of political reality turn this into another form of ''deconcentrated'' decision making, behind a front of democratic consultation?

NOTES

1. This essay is partially based on material that appeared in Davey's ''The Changing Pattern of Local Government: From Mackenzie to McKinsey,'' *World Development* 2, no. 2 (February 1974): 71-73, and based on Mawhood's ''Negotiating from Weakness: the Search for a Model of Local Government in Countries of the Third World,'' *Planning and Administration* 1, no. 1 (Winter 1974): 17-32.

2. There is no uformity in names or formal descriptions of these institutions, which are superficially rather dissimilar. Tanzania sees them as a total break with the earlier forms of local government, and calls them (regional or district) development committees. The key units in Ghana (district councils) and in the Sudan (people's executive councils) are regarded as democratic local government in a strengthened form, taking over control of the field administration as well as playing their more traditional role as a service institution.

3. C. Leys, *Politicians and Policies* (Nairobi: East African Publishing House, 1967), p. 51.

4. A. Zolberg, *Creating Political Order* (Chicago: Rand McNally, 1966).

Francophone Africa

Michael A. Cohen *

35

Local government in post-independence francophone Africa has continued to be deeply rooted in French local government theory and practice. Despite African accession to national independence and the evolution of new forms of former colonial relationships, local government is based on fundamental principles of French administrative law and organization.[1] Urban government has been structured according to the French law of 1884, providing for communes with mayors, municipal councils, and specific revenue and expenditure powers. Pre-independence communal structure has remained essentially intact despite many changes in the size, character, and problems of urban areas. The specific application of French municipal law to the colonies in the post-World War II period came through the Loi-Cadre and municipal reform in 1955-56. These laws permitted the establishment of communes of different types, according to population size and potential tax base. The 1955 law actually mentioned specific towns throughout "Afrique Occidentale Française" which would be given communal status. This process and the interesting political circumstances surrounding the changes in jurisdictional status have been described in several studies of this period and do not deserve renewed attention.[2] The failure of this colonial system to adapt to new urban conditions since 1960, and its gradual transformation as a result of institutional changes beyond its control has not, however, received the attention it deserves.

This essay will focus on four processes which have reshaped urban local government in francophone West Africa:

1. The spatial growth of urban areas beyond previous jurisdictional boundaries
2. The growth of overlapping forms of area administration over urban affairs

*Urban Projects Department, World Bank. These are the author's personal opinions and do not in any way reflect the views of the Bank, or conclusions reached by Mr. Cohen in his capacity with the Bank.

3. The transfer of public sector responsibilities to the private sector, particularly in the provision of urban services
4. The continued adoption of urban administrative innovations developed in France

Each of these processes has helped to give a new face to municipalities in francophone Africa. They have, in a sense, become more important than the organizational structures and administrative procedures left behind by colonial rule. As such, they point to the need for a reform of formal institutions in order to better meet the needs of the people living in their areas of jurisdiction.

THE SPATIAL GROWTH OF URBAN AREAS

All of the major cities and most of the secondary urban centers in the states of the former Afrique Occidentale Française have doubled if not tripled their demographic size since the administrative reforms of 1955-56.[3] This demographic growth, at rates from 3 to 10 percent per year, has transformed cities like Abidjan from 125,000 in 1955 to 1 million in 1975. Even Ouagadougou, a small city in a rural country, has grown at roughly 7 percent per year since 1960. Table 35.1 presents a brief survey of these data for a sample of cities.

Table 35.1
FRANCOPHONE AFRICA: GROWTH OF URBAN CENTERS, 1960-70

City	Percentage Rate of Urban Growth 1960-70	1970 (000's)	Slums and Squatter Settlements as Percentage of City Population
Dakar	6.0	650	60 (1971)
Abidjan	11.5	550	60 (1964)
Ouagadougou	7.0	105	70 (1966)
Douala	4.1	250	80 (1970)
Yaounde	6.8	165	90 (1970)
Lome	8.2	148	75 (1970)

Source: U.N., *World Housing Survey* (January 1974).

Demographic growth has been coupled with spatial growth which has quickly led to large peripheral settlements on the borders of these towns. Pikine, a squatter settlement started in 1952 outside Dakar, now has more than 200,000 inhabitants. Abobo-Gare, on the northern edge of Abidjan, has grown from 15,000 in 1970 to 180,000 in 1975. Pikine is the second largest urban center in Senegal, after Dakar, while Abobo-Gare is the third largest urban settlement, after Abidjan and Bouake, in the Ivory Coast. This spatial growth has counterparts in most cities in Africa. With compound urban growth rates higher than anywhere else in the developing world, African cities have been faced with problems of expanding and diversifying their institutional structures to meet increased needs of varying types.

The origins of this areal growth must be understood if administrative reforms to meet changed conditions are to be formulated. Three factors have stimulated peripheral urban growth rather than increased densification in city centers: demolition of squatter settlements in the city center; attraction of lower land prices on the periphery; and lack of effective urban policy concerning land use and densification.

The demolition of squatter settlements by municipal and national authorities as an effort to "maintain standards" and the modern appearance of large cities has been a major pressure on urban residents to locate their households on sites beyond municipal jurisdiction and/or interest.[4] By moving far from central city areas, low-income households can find land that does not interest local authorities where they can build dwelling units of any type or standard. This move is often very expensive in terms of increased daily transportation costs but it allows some residential security. A second factor is the attraction of low prices for land purchases, or, in many cases, no cost at all for squatting on unclaimed land. Cheap land is a welcome alternative to rapidly increasing land prices in most African cities. The lack of any effective land-use policy by urban authorities is a third factor leading to a so-called *habitat spontane* (spontaneous housing), defined as housing built between Friday night and Monday morning, on the urban periphery. Governments have not focused sufficient attention on the need to densify residential neighborhoods and to mix residential with commercial and industrial uses. While *cadastres*, land registry systems, have been established in Abidjan and Ouagadougou, they are not managed by the municipality but rather by the Ministry of Finance. Land policy questions usually come under the Ministry of Construction and Town Planning and/or the Ministry of Public Works.

Taken together, the forces leading to urban sprawl in francophone African cities require substantial policy initiative by local governments if they are to be brought under control. Policy reforms concerning squatter removal, residential land use, and land price controls could lead to a slowing down of the process of spatial growth. This would have several advantages for local governments, including reduced capital costs for infrastructure in new areas, such as roads, water supply, sewerage, and transport. These policy changes, then, could reduce urban sprawl and, after some redrawing of jurisdictional boundaries, reduce the need to continue redrawing municipal boundaries every few years.

THE OVERLAP OF URBAN AREAL ADMINISTRATION

An important part of the process of local government in francophone Africa, as in France, is the overlapping responsibilities of urban authorities and larger prefectoral units. The existence of *préfectures* and *sous-préfectures*, which are supposed to coordinate all national government activity within given jurisdictions, limits the control of urban authorities over policies and programs affecting local areas.[5] This system institutionalizes conflict between two lines of administration and, given the relative scarcity of local versus national financial resources, leads to the subordination of local authorities to nationally appointed *préfets* and *sous-préfets*. This problem has been resolved in some secondary urban centers in the Ivory Coast with the appointment of *préfets* as mayors, or *préfet-maire*. This combination of two roles, with supposedly divergent interests, in a single individual reflects the submission of the local responsibility to the national administration.[6] It is no accident that, under this system, municipal elections would have been meaningless and, in fact, were not held from 1956 to 1976. This twenty-year period saw the decline and eventual disappearance of local municipal councils.[7]

This situation is particularly interesting in view of the fact that, under French municipal law, both the administrator of the *commune*, whether elected or appointed, and the *préfet* or *sous-préfet* are under the responsibility of the Ministry of Interior. The former is supposed to represent local interests, while the latter represents national interests at the local level. How these roles differ in particular policy areas and how divergent positions are reconciled within the Ministry of Interior depend on personalities and political bargains within individual countries. While the mayor of Abidjan is a powerful figure within the single political party, the Parti Démocratique de la Côte d'Ivoire, and has therefore been able to maintain the upper hand in relation to the *préfet* of Abidjan in affairs within the city limits, the mayor of Dakar appears less powerful than the governor of Cap Vert, the peninsula on which Dakar is located. In the latter case, the governor, not the mayor, is responsible for demolishing squatter housing and relocating the residents. While overall policy towards squatter removal is decided at the national level in all the francophone countries, it is nonetheless indicative of the level of authority that intervenes in neighborhood problems.

As suggested below, administrative incursions into the jurisdiction of communes has quickened through administrative innovations borrowed from France, such as a regional planning unit (Délégation à l'Aménagement du Territoire et à l'Action Régionale-DATAR), interministerial commissions, and municipal districts, as in Paris. These added to the prefectoral system will further diminish the responsibility of local government.

TRANSFER OF RESPONSIBILITIES TO THE PRIVATE SECTOR

The weakness of urban government is illustrated most dramatically by the declining quantity and quality of urban services provided by the public sector. In some cities, the communes have experienced periods when absolute total revenue declined for several years, despite continuous population growth. This occurred in Abidjan from 1965 to 1970.[8] Financial constraints coupled with decreasing control over local affairs, given the incursions of national administrative institutions, led to a situation in which municipalities decided they no longer could provide public services on economic terms and these services might be carried out more effectively by private enterprise. This has led to a general pattern whereby garbage collection, water supply, bus transport, and sewage processing have been turned over to private companies. The two major reasons for this situation, financial constraints and growing demand for services, deserve detailed attention.

On the financial side, the *communes* are severely limited in their revenue-generating powers. All decisions must be approved by the Ministry of Interior. While the cities have increased their potential tax base rather substantially, particularly through new industrial and commercial areas, as well as an almost doubling or tripling of residential units since independence, most of these properties have been exempted from property taxes. Commercial and industrial enterprises, often financed by foreign capital, benefit from investment codes which include long-term exemptions, sometimes for twenty years. Nevertheless, they utilize urban infrastructure and services for which they do not pay their share of the cost. Many residential properties exist beyond the old communal boundaries, and their owners are thus able to evade taxes. They, too, benefit from urban infrastructure and services, which they receive at minimal cost. Those properties and enterprises legally obligated to pay taxes to the municipalities often simply do not pay, knowing that municipal tax collection efforts are too ineffectual and disorganized to catch up with them. In Abidjan, only an estimated 55 percent of all assessed property taxes is collected annually. This situation was recognized by President Houphouet-Boigny in 1974, when he called together civil servants and warned them that failure to pay the taxes could lead to their replacement within the administration.

At the level of individual services, it was also apparent that municipalities were not managing and pricing services in an economically sustainable manner. Growing deficits, service breakdowns, and citizen complaints eventually forced public authorities to actively seek other solutions. This became particularly crucial as demand grew rapidly. Demand for water for household consumption grew at least as fast as population. This was often coupled with faster rates for commercial and industrial use.

Several examples of the tranfer of services to the private sector illustrate this pattern. They also, however, show that other serious problems have resulted from this consequence of the decline of municipal government. In Dakar, Senegal, the bus company was placed under the responsibility of the Renault Automobile Company of France. Bus service improved noticeably in the Cap Vert region, although it was accompanied by a fare increase. Reportedly, as the price for taking on the company, Renault also asked the government for the abolition of the *cars rapides*, or mini-bus fleet, which transports a large proportion of the population at prices significantly less than the public, privately run bus company. This request was turned down after pressure from the city population which justifiably wanted to continue *cars rapides* service.

Another example has been the improvement in garbage collection and urban sanitation as a result of a French firm taking responsibility for this service in several major francophone African cities. While a labor-intensive service, the application of a cost-effective approach to the problem, motivated by private profit, has led to obvious improvements in the cleanliness of urban areas. Water supply has also increasingly become the responsibility of *sociétés d'Etat*, or state-owned corporations, which have developed pricing policies that have kept the corporaton financially solvent. Though legally public sector enterprises, these *sociétés d'Etat* have used private sector methods to improve service for particular client populations.

While upper- and middle-income groups have hailed these improvements in urban service provision, it should be noted that the pricing policies of these private sector firms have tended to neglect the needs of low-income groups. The result is that service through these firms is concentrated in areas of effective demand, that is, where households are willing to pay high prices for high quality service. Households unable to afford these costs are simply excluded. They are forced to turn to the mercy of other private providers of these services, such as private water venders or the *cars rapides*. While the high degree of competition in the latter case keeps costs down, this is not so in water supply, where private venders charge at least five times more for a given quantity of water than the *société d'Etat*.

ADOPTION OF INNOVATIONS FROM FRANCE

A fourth factor affecting the transformation of urban government in francophone Africa has been the adoption of three innovations in the past ten years: establishment of regional and spatial planning authorities, creation of metropolitan districts, and use of interministerial commissions to coordinate urban development efforts.

The appearance of regional and spatial development planning units within francophone African goverments followed several years after the creation of the Délégation à l'Aménagement du Territoire et à l'Action Régionale (DATAR) in France. The introduction of a spatial planning unit within the Ministries of Planning has created opportunities for coordination among sectoral ministries, such as Town Planning, Public Works, or Interior. Whether these units will be able to use their enlightened social and analytic approaches to change the content of policy will be answered in several years. It is apparent, however, that DATAR has changed the terminology used in the Ivory Coast five-year development plan, that regional planning philosophy is being applied in Upper Volta in the rural development efforts of the *Organismes Régionaux de Développement* (ORDs), and that local jurisdictions in several countries are beginning to be considered within a macro-spatial and administrative framework. In the Ivory Coast, DATAR, within the Ministry of Planning, is responsible for the supervision of the preparation of the Abidjan Master Plan.

A second far-reaching administrative innovation is discussion of the creation of a district for the metropolitan Abidjan area, along the lines of the District of Paris. This administrative form is the umbrella under which neighborhoods are given communal status, including some local taxing and expenditure powers. In 1975, a working commission of the PDCI, the political party, was examining the advantages of creating such a district, with a centralized investment budget and a decentralized recurrent budget. This proposal faced complicated public finance problems, which remain to be resolved.

A third innovation has been the use of interministerial commissions to coordinate urban development policy and planning. In 1966, a *Commission Interministériel pour le Développement de la Région d'Abidjan* (CIDRA) was created to review the programs of different ministries in the capital. In Upper Volta, the *Conseil National de l'Urbanisme*, headed by the minister of public works, transport and urban planning, reviews all technical studies of urban centers and must approve all policy measures affecting physical planning. Decisions of the *conseil* are then passed on to the cabinet of the government of Upper Volta, presided over by the president, General Sangoule Lamizana, who personally approves them. While this level of detailed involvement by the president of the country in spatial plans and engineering studies is only possible in a small country, it does demonstrate the administrative incursions into the jurisdicton of local authorities.

DIRECTIONS FOR THE FUTURE

While there has not been a formal reorganization of urban government in francophone West Africa since 1955-56, the four processes discussed above have changed the range of authority and process of urban administration. Rapid urban growth coupled with administrative incursions into areas formerly under municipal jurisdiction have reduced the importance of urban government in managing urban areas. While the scale and diversity of urban problems have grown, formal government institutions have not adapted to new conditions. Current proposals for a metropolitan district in Abidjan, the fastest growing city in this region, reflect the perception that some drastic administrative reforms will be necessary if local government is to be able to provide the range of services necessary for a large city. Other centers, such as Ouagadougou, Lome, and larger secondary towns, such as Bouake in the Ivory Coast and Bobo-Dioulasso in Upper Volta, should first use their existing structures more efficiently before large-scale reforms are contemplated. They are not yet pressed by demographic and spatial growth to the same degree as Dakar or Abidjan.

This brief survey of the pattern of urban government in francophone Africa suggests that variables outside the formal local government structure often have greater impact on the process of local administration than do internal factors. The colonial framework for urban government has not been directly adapted to new conditions; the result is a loss of authority and jurisdiction to other institutions which are in the process of filling the gap in municipally provided services and administration. Whether existing social and economic conditions, particularly in terms of the need for urban services, will become so difficult as to make local government reform urgent obviously will depend on the continuing growth of these towns and cities. In the long run, however, it is clear that new efforts will be necessary to resurrect a viable, effective system of urban government to meet future needs.

NOTES

1. See, for example, Pierre Lampue, "Le régime municipal dans les Etats africains francophones," *Revue juridique et politique* 22, no. 2 (April-June 1968): 463-72.

2. See L. Gray Cowan, *Local Government in West Africa* (New York: Columbia University Press, 1958); and M. J. Campbell, T. G. Brierly, and L. F. Blitz, *The Structure of Local Government in West Africa* (The Hague: Nijhoff, 1965).

3. This process has been reviewed in detail in *La Croissance Urbaine en Afrique Noire et à Madagascar* (Paris: Centre National de la Recherche Scientifique, 1972).

4. See Michael A. Cohen, *Urban Policy and Political Conflict in Africa: A Study of the Ivory Coast* (Chicago: University of Chicago Press, 1974). For a general treatment of this problem, see John F. C. Turner, "Housing Priorities, Settlement Patterns and Urban Development in Modernizing Countries," *Journal of the American Institute of Planners* 34 (November 1968).

5. See Brian Chapman, *Introduction to French Local Government* (London: Allen and Unwin, 1953).

6. See Michael A. Cohen, "The Myth of the Expanding Center: Politics in the Ivory Coast," *Journal of Modern African Studies* 11, no. 2 (June 1973): 227-46.

7. C. Hoguie, "Structure et organisation communales en Côte d'Ivoire," *Revue juridique et politique* 22, no. 2 (April-June 1968): 371-78.

8. Cohen, *Urban Policy and Political Conflict in Africa*.

ASIA

India

*B. S. Khanna and S. Bhatnagar**   **36**

With the end of British rule in South Asia in the latter half of the 1940s, there emerged several new sovereign states, namely India, Pakistan, Burma, and Sri Lanka. The two Himalayan kingdoms of Nepal and Bhutan, which had long been under British hegemony, also reclaimed their independence from the foreign influence. In the 1970s, another sovereign state, Bangla Desh, was born as a result of a revolt by the eastern wing of Pakistan. The dawn of independence ushered into all these countries an era of hope and expectation. Besides introducing significant constitutional and political changes, the new regimes of these countries made attempts at development planning with a view to bringing about radical changes in the socioeconomic pattern of their populations. These changes and the modernization process intimately affected, among other institutions, local government. In this essay, we shall be concerned with an account of the local government system of that country of the region which has the largest and most diverse population and which possesses comparatively a more stable and democratic political system and a long record of extensive development planning.

India is a vast country, having an area of 3,287,782 km² (seventh in the world) and a population of a little over 600 million (second in the world), as per 1978 estimates, a population distinctive for the sociocultural diversity among its people. Four out of every five Indians live in villages that number as many as 575,936.[1] The pace of urbanization has been increasing very quickly, and, as a result, the number of towns and cities has gone up to 2,643, of which 148 have a population of over 100,000 and 9 over 1 million each. There are representative local government institutions in both the rural and urban areas

*B. S. Khanna is Professor of Public Administration, Panjab University. He has published a monograph, *Village Institutions in Punjab*, and also contributed papers on local government to several professional journals. S. Bhatnagar is a Reader in Political Science in the same university. He has published two books, *Panchayati Raj in Kangra District* and *Rural Local Government in India,* and has contributed papers on problems of local government and allied subjects to various national and international journals.

which, in the former case, are commonly called the *panchayati raj* institutions and, in the latter, the municipalities; the metropolitan cities have municipal corporations. The representative local government is based upon legislation passed by each of the twenty-two states and nine union territories, which together form the Indian Union. Besides enacting legislation, these state governments and union territory administrations provide financial and administrative assistance to these bodies and also exercise an overall control over them in regard to their day-to-day working. The union government has also assumed the role of coordinating and assisting the state governments in the organization and management of the local government in their respective areas. As a result, the local government patterns in the various states are more similar than different.

Broadly, the local government system of the country is of a dual nature. Besides the representative local government organization, there is the district administration in every district into which a state is divided. The district administration comprises the field agencies of the various departments of the state government which perform most of the regulatory and developmental as well as quite a few of the civil functions. A high-ranking, multifunctional administrator (called either the collector or the deputy commissioner) has overall responsibility for coordinating and directing the district administration. In most of the states, he also has been vested by the state government with the general responsibility for the oversight of the representative local government organizations as well and can intervene when he finds irregularities and malpractices taking place within any of these organizations. In recent years, a growing effort has been made to increase the functions, authority, and autonomy of the representative local government organizations as part and parcel of the process of decentralization in a developing democratic system.

DEVELOPMENT OF LOCAL GOVERNMENT

India has a long tradition of local government. It existed in ancient and medieval times and was mostly rural and traditional in character.[2] It enjoyed considerable autonomy in the management of local affairs and disputes. When the British started extending and consolidating their political power during the nineteenth century, they built up an increasingly centralized administrative system which proved inimical to the vigorous functioning of the village *panchayats*, with the result that they gradually ceased to exist in the length and breadth of the country. After some time an attempt was made to set up in a few selected towns, mostly inhabited by the British merchants and administrators (besides, of course, the local people) some sort of local organization beside the usual district administration. Thus, a municipal corporation was established at Madras in 1688, followed by that of Calcutta and then Bombay. It was Lord Mayo, the governor-general, who took the initiative for a policy statement by the central government in the form of a resolution in 1870, stressing the need for setting up local bodies to take care of local affairs of both towns and villages. In 1882 a more definite policy statement was made by the central government during the tenure of Lord Ripon as governor-general. But the pace of the organization of local bodies was very slow, and the bodies created were by no means representative in character. They were comprised mostly of nominated members and covered only a few places in this vast land. The Royal Commission on Decentralization in its report (1909) expressed dissatisfaction with the progress and recommended a more vigorous policy of decentralization, aiming among other things at the speeding up of the process of establishing local bodies (*panchayats*) in the numerous villages of the country. On the eve of the first momentous constitutional reforms, the government of India passed a resolution in 1918 stressing the significance of a numerical expansion as well as a democratization of the organizational structure and an increase in the functions of these local bodies. It also underlined the need for a relaxation of the control of the provincial governments over these bodies.

Under the new constitutional set-up, introduced by the Constitutional Act of 1919, the portfolio concerning the local bodies became for the first time the responsibility of the Indian ministers in the provincial governments. This development led to the adoption of several measures toward the areal extension, administrative improvement, and democratization of the local bodies. A number of commissions and inquiry committees, appointed by the government in one context or another, strongly recommended further decentralization of power, democratization of the local bodies, and extension of their coverage.

In spite of the greater stress on the significance of local bodies (municipalities, *panchayats*, and district boards) and the adoption of various measures to develop them, their working was only a qualified success. These bodies did, however, stimulate civic consciousness and people's participation. But many of them suffered from shortcomings and maladies of various types. These were due to four main factors: structural and financial inadequacy; too much rigidly and the punitive nature of the provincial government's control; the poor quality of the leaders elected to these institutions; and the government's indifference toward the problems and betterment of these bodies. No wonder, then, that a depressing picture was painted by a few keen observers of the working of local bodies in 1947, when one political chapter in the history of the country was closing and a new one was being opened.[3]

In independent India (since August 1947), several significant developments have taken place in the field of local government. Because of the increased importance of the local bodies in the new constitutional and political set-up of the country, we would prefer to call them, from now on, representative local governments.

The developments in this field have been generated mainly by two factors: constitutional and political changes and socioeconomic developments. Since the nation had adopted a democratic constitutional system, it was appropriate that all political institutions, formal as well as nonformal, be molded in the larger democratic frame of the country. Keeping in view this necessity, as also the constitutional obligations as laid down in Article 40 of the Constitution (that state governments would make efforts to organize village *panchayats*), made many a state government attempt to pass legislation toward the democratizaton of the organizational structure and the decentralization of more and more functions and powers to the representative local governments. The adoption of development planning in the early 1950s and the consequent socioeconomic changes further accelerated the development of these institutions.

Various committees appointed from time to time by the union and state governments, and also by the periodic conferences of the state ministers, have continuously applied themselves to the problems of rural and urban local governments, and made numerous recommendations for the reorganization and administrative improvement of the local administrative set-up. The five-year plans have also referred to the increasing developmental role and the consequent need to reorganize local governments. We may briefly review the findings and recommendations of some of the important probes conducted over the years in this field.

The Local Finance Enquiry Committee (1950) recommended ways and means to augment the financial resources of local governments so as to enable them to perform their increasing mandatory and optional functions more adequately. A few years later a critical examination of rural local governments was made by a high-powered committee (called the Balwahtrai Mehta Team) appointed by the Planning Commisson to suggest the role that these governments should play in the comprehensive rural development program (termed the Community Development Programme, CDP) which has been under way since 1952. The committee recommended in 1957 that institutionalized participation of the people was very desirable in the effective implementation of this program and for broadening the base of development in the country. The committee recommended substantial decentralization of powers from the state governments to the local rural government, which was to be restructured for this purpose. This was commonly called democratic decentralization and aimed at a major reorganization of the whole set-up of the rural sector of local government.

The reorganized rural local government was named (by the late prime minister, Jawaharlal Nehru) as *panchayati raj*. It was to comprise three interlinked levels: *panchayats* at the village level, *panchayat samiti* at the block level (a block comprised a rural population of about 60,000), and the *zila parishad* at the district level. Besides civil functions, the interlinked bodies were also to perform an increasing number of development functions relating to agriculture, animal husbandry, rural infrastructure, and rural social services. The main responsibility, authority, and resources were to be placed in the hands of the middle-level tier, the *panchayat samiti*. While the *panchayat* was to be elected directly on the basis of adult franchise by the whole village population, the other two bodies were to be constituted indirectly by means of election from among the members of the immediately lower bodies. A few categories of members were to be included in all these bodies from certain sections of the rural population. The *panchayat samiti* and the *zila parishad* were required to constitute committees for the efficient conduct of their business. A new segment of administration to be called development administration was to be built up to serve as the administrative arm of these local bodies.

The state governments started reorganizing their rural local government mainly on the basis of the recommendations of this committee, though some of them brought in variations to suit their distinctive needs. Moreover, they were now expected to play the role of guide, and provide financial assistance to the *panchayati raj* institutions in terms of the challenging rural development program to be entrusted to them.

Several problems arose in regard to the working of the new system of *panchayati raj*: inadequate finances, inefficient officials, tensions between officials and elected representatives, strong political pulls and pressures, rivalries between the state leadership and the local leadership, widening corruption both among the decision makers and the officials, and the inadequate caliber of many elected representatives. To study these problems, several committees were appointed from time to time by the union and state governments. The successive five-year plans also gave serious thought to this important area of national development. Once again, there took place a wide national debate on whether the task of rural development should be entrusted to these bodies or to the district administration. A high-powered committee (Ashoka Mehta Committee) recently was set up by the union government and submitted its report in 1978. The failings of the system notwithstanding, the committee reaffirmed its faith in decentralization as a part of the democratization process in the country and suggested not only decentralization of functions to *panchayati raj* but also its restructuring and reorientation with a view to substantially improving its politico-administrative capabilities. The union and state governments have yet to decide upon follow-up action.

As regards urban local government, it has also been undergoing several changes. These have been based upon suggestions and recommendations flowing from four main sources:

1. Committees appointed by several state governments to study specific or general municipal problems and suggest ways and means to tackle them
2. A committee termed the Rural-Urban Relationship Commitee, set up by the union government in 1963 not only to review the relationship between municipal government and *panchayati raj* but also to suggest ways and means to more efficient and effective performance of functions (which were to be increased) by the municipal governments

3. Conferences of state ministers and administrators as well as mayors, organized by the union government with the objective of pooling, coordinating, and crystallizing ideas on municipal government
4. Five-year plans, which began to lay emphasis (especially from the 1960s onward) on development policies regarding urban planning and land use

Some follow-up action has been taken by the state governments under the general guidance and with the financial assistance of the union government. Fresh legislation and suitable administrative measures have been adopted for the reorganization and reorientation of municipal government. But the steps taken as yet fall far short of the challenging needs of the growing towns, cities, and metropolitan areas.

RURAL LOCAL GOVERNMENT

Structures and Functions

Looking at the structures and functions of the *panchayati raj*, which had been adopted in fifteen out of twenty-two states and four out of nine union territories by 1978, we find several variations. In ten states and two union territories there was a three-tier *panchayati raj*, while in five states and two union territories, there was a two-tier system. Among the latter five states, four did not have a *zila parishad* and one (Tamil Nadu) had a development council in place of a *zila parishad*.

There were also differences regarding decentralization of functions, powers, and resources from the state government to *panchayati raj*. Maharashtra and Gujrat belonged to one end of the continuum with very substantial decentralization; Rajasthan and Andhra were somewhere in the middle; whereas all other states fell at one point or the other of the scale. On the whole, decentralization was limited even initially, and later on some of the developmental functions, powers, and resources were actually withdrawn from the *panchayati raj* institutions by the state governments concerned.

A third aspect of the organizational structure of *panchayati raj* is the distribution of these functions, powers, and resources among the three or two tiers of the system, as the case may be.[4] There were three main models in this connection. In Maharashtra, most of the decentralized functions and powers were concentrated in the hands of the *zila parishad* and some were given to the *panchayats*, while the *panchayat samiti* was to act as the agent of the *zila parishad* for developmental programs and projects. In Gujrat, the functions and powers were shared by all the three institutions (*zila parishad*, *panchayat samiti*, and *panchayat*), with the *zila parishad* having some edge over the other two. Rajasthan provided the model as suggested by the Balwantrai Mehta Team, the main concentration of decentralized function and power being in the *panchyat samiti*, with the *zila parishad* playing only an advisory and coordinating role. The *panchayats* were given several functions but were to work under the overall supervision of the *panchayat samiti*.

The Maharashtra model provided for a direct election by all the adult voters of the villages both for the *zila parishad* and the village *panchayat*. The *panchayat samiti*, however, had been accorded the status of an area committee of the *zila parishad*, consisting of only those members of the *zila parishad* who represented *samiti* areas concerned. In Gujrat, the *zila parishad* consisted of both the directly elected members and the presidents of the *panchayat samitis*, the latter sitting in their ex officio capacity. Here too the *panchayats* were directly elected. In Tajashthan, there were direct elections only for the *panchayats*, while both higher tiers drew their membership from the ranks of the presidents of the immediately lower-level bodies, thus providing for an organic linkage among all three tiers of the system.

Other states provided for the composition of the *panchayati raj* institutions as a variation of these three models. There also existed almost everywhere provisions for the cooption of the women and socially backward sections of the village society and for the nomination of the representatives of such functional organizations as rural cooperatives and marketing societies. Besides, the members of the state legislatures (MLAs) and national parliament (MPs) were also associated with the *panchayati raj* institutions in one way or the other in almost every state, so as to provide some linkages between the local leadership and the higher-level political leadership.

In most of the states, the development administration was put only partially under the control of the *panchayati raj*. The state governments retained a good deal of control over the administration and allowed the *panchayati raj* institutions to make a limited use of the existing administrative set-up. Only in Maharashtra and Gujrat, most of the departments concerned with various sectors of rural development had been transferred to the administrative control of the *panchayati raj* in a significant way.

Political parties were not allowed to function in the *panchayati raj* institutions, though only by convention and not by law. This implies that these institutions were treated more as administrative agencies rather than as political entities. This political vacuum was not conducive to vitality. The Ashoka Mehta Committee did not approve of this self-imposed denial to participate in local affairs by various political parties of the country and, instead, strongly favored their active participation in all programs of a local nature.

In all the states concerned, except Tamil Nadu, there was a provision for the setting up of a *gram sabha*, or village council comprising all the adults of the village. This body was to meet periodically not only to elect members (even the presidents in some states) of the village *panchayats* but also to exercise a scrutiny of the budget and the program of activities to be undertaken by the *panchayats*. In actual practice, however, these village councils did not meet or transact any significant business in most of the states.[5]

Performance

The performance of the *panchayati raj* institutions needs to be reviewed from three angles: political, social, and economic. While taking on overall view of their functioning during the 1960s and 1970s, we must not forget that their performance has tended to be very uneven on account of the different sociopolitical enviroment in various states as well as differing attitudes of state governments toward these institutions. Where the environment has been less hostile or depressing, the state governments have shown genuine interest in nurturing them right from their inception; and where the organizational structure of these institutions has been appropriately designed to attract leaders of good caliber, their performance has tended to be satisfactory and in some respects even commendable. This has been the situation in Maharashtra and Gujrat. In Karnataka, Tamil Nadu, Andhra Pradesh, and Kerala, the performance has been partially satisfactory. Elsewhere, the position has been less satisfactory. We shall briefly review here the achievements and weaknesses of the *panchayati raj* institutions in the country as a whole, based on the research findings of social researchers and inquiries made by various committees and study teams set up from time to time by the union and state governments.

Politically, *panchayati raj* constributed, both functionally and dysfunctionally, to the overall democratic development of the country. The *panchayati raj* institutions opened for the rural people vast avenues for participation in the twin process of decision making and decision implementation in such vital fields of their welfare as relate to their all-round development. This broadened the base of a developing democratic system, and provided a valuable opportunity for the emergence of political leadership from among the rural people. At the same time, it stimulated political consciousness and awareness among many sections of the rural population who had tended to be politically apathetic in the past. This has contributed to the diversification and articulation of people's demands. It has also tended to bridge the wide gap between the bureaucracy and the people, thereby contributing to the processes of development programs or project implementation. Again, it has led to the emergence in many places of a new institutional leadership which is comparatively younger in age, change-oriented, and more dynamic than the traditional leadership in the old rural local government.[6]

At the same time, *panchayati raj* has aggravated political factionalism, corruption, partisanship, and ineptitude in decision making on the part of the bureaucracy in particular. There have been many cases of abuse of powers by the political elite within the institutions for selfish or factional gains. Also, elections have led to malpractice, occasional use of violent means, and intergroup tension. Too much political interference in administration has diluted the efficiency and impartiality of the local administration. Administrative corruption has thus been aggravated.

The new leadership, though progressive in outlook, has tended to be deficient in national outlook, with the result that they have not been able to bring about a synthesis between the local and national loyalties; thus parochial tendencies have been quite active in many parts of the country. Further, the new leadership has not been able to do much for the uplift of their brethren for obvious reasons, even though a golden opportunity has been afforded to them.

Socially, the village people have come to pass through what may be described as the stage of social fermentation.[7] A tremendous degree of social consciousness seems to have been generated all over the country, and, as a result, the older gap between various caste and class groups has tended to become narrower, though in some places caste rivalries have even been aggravated. This is perhaps due to the fact that all hitherto suppressed social tensions have not only come to the surface, but in certain cases have become quite sharp. Those sections of society which earlier were suppressed socially, economically, and politically became conscious of their suppression, no longer seem to be content with their lot, and wish to claim their due share of power at all levels of the society. Most of the present-day social tensions are thus the outcome of the new wave of social consciousness that is sweeping the countryside of India.

Economically, the *panchayati raj* institutions have been given very restricted developmental powers except in Maharashtra and Gujrat. Some states (like Punjab and Haryana) never gave them these functions and others (like Andhra Pradesh and Rajasthan) withdrew them after some time on grounds of their inefficient performance. In recent years, a large number of complex client-oriented and area-oriented rural programs has been formulated and implemented under the Fourth and Fifth Five-Year plans. But with the exception of Maharashtra and Gujart, nowhere have the *panchayati raj* institutions been associated with their execution, much less with their formulation. This indicates the distrust on the part of the higher-level political and bureaucratic leadership toward the *panchayati raj* institutions, resulting partly from the past record of the poor performance of these institutions and partly from the jealousies that the latter nourish toward them. On the whole, then, the impact of the *panchayati raj* institutions on economic development of the rural masses has been rather insignificant. But indirectly these institutions have stimulated the rural people to cultivate a developmental psyche and thereby boost the rate of economic development of rural areas.

It has been pointed out by critical observers of the rural development scenario that the story of the ups and downs of the *panchayati raj* can be divided into three parts—the phase of ascendency (1959-64), the phase of stagnation (1964-67), and the phase of decline (1967-77).[8] Several factors can be identified as contributing to this decline. First, there seemed to be an inadequate conceptual understanding of its status and role. Some treated it as an administrative agency, others as a grass-root democratic entity. In most of the states the objectives of these institutions as "fountainheads of democracy" have not been clearly spelled out. This not only led to confusion regarding their role but also permitted the state governments to continue treating them in the same old manner (as their administrative agencies and appendages of the district administration). The result was that there occurred a crisis of expectations as well as uncertainty on the part of the newly elected *panchayati raj* leaders.

Second, the pattern of distribution of functions and powers among the various tiers of the *panchayati raj* as also the pattern of their election resulted in structural inadequacies. Instead of making the district level *zila parishad* the kingpin of the organizational set-up, most of the states created the *panchayat samiti* and accorded to it the central status. At the same time, efforts were not made to develop a strong and efficient administrative set-up at the *samiti* level. Poor administrative infrastructure coupled with poor political leadership rendered the whole scheme ineffective. On the other hand, *panchayati raj* institutions in Maharashtra gave a comparatively much better account of themselves both as democratic and as developmental units, largely because the *zila parishad* had in that scheme been assigned the key role and because efforts had also been made to strengthen its administrative apparatus.[9]

Moreover, elections to the *panchayati raj* institutions were not held in most of the states for a long time. In certain cases, these were delayed for over ten years. The hesitation on the part of the state government to hold elections on schedule, on account of political distrust and jealousy on the part of the state-level political leadership, generated power intoxication in some of the local leaders or an attitude of helpless dependence on state leaders.

Third, the rural poor could not be expected to find an adequate representation on *panchayati raj* institutions by open election contests. They needed to be given a reservation of seats in proportion to their population at least till they came to be socially and economically at par with the comparatively affluent classes and the rural rich.

Fourth, keeping the political parties completely out of the *panchayati raj*, even in a formal sense, did not provide democratic motivation and developmental direction to the new leaders. Nor did it strengthen political cohesion or promote the sense of accountability among the leaders for the decisions and actions that they were required to take from time to time. They were also deprived of the opportunity for orientation and subsequent reorientation for the responsibilities and tasks to which most of them were strangers.

Fifth, the bureaucracy did not pull its weight properly in the implementation process. There were frequent tensions between the bureaucracy and the *panchayati raj* leaders on account of their confused perception of roles and of the need for cooperative functioning. Moreover, the tendency of the local bureaucracy to look toward the district administration and the state-level administrative heads for promotion, transfers, perquisites, and the protection of their interests further weakened their loyalty and orientation to *panchayati raj* institutions.

Among the environmental factors, mention may be made here of only two such factors. First, the state governments miserably lacked both the interest and will to properly nurture and strengthen the *panchayati raj* institutions. Instead of adopting a constructive, helpful, and remedial attitude, they mostly preferred to make use of the deterrent measures whenever they came across any lapse on the part of the *panchayati raj* institutions. This policy dwarfed the development of these institutions. It has been very aptly remarked by a highly knowledgeable inquiry committee that "the lukewarm attitude of the political elite at higher levels towards the strengthening of the democratic process at grassroots was generally the crux of the matter."[10]

The second environmental factor was the existence of gross social and economic disparities and low social ethics among the people of the country-side. Unless meaningful steps are taken to redistribute lands, provide to the rural poor financial assistance to improve their economic lot, spread literacy and education on a mass scale, tremendously extend the coverage of the mass media, and the like, the socioeconomic environment will continue to create obstacles in the path of the *panchayati raj*. While the *panchayati raj* would tend to influence the socioeconomic environment as it gained momentum, the improvement of this environment by means of the steps suggested above would influence the working of the *panchayati raj* in a vigorous and meaningful manner.

PROPOSALS FOR REORGANIZATION

The *panchayati raj*, as established on the lines suggested by the Balwantrai Mehta Committee, needed to be reviewed comprehensively with a view to eradicating such weaknesses as have crept into it, so that it may be able to face the challenge of rural development, which over the years has become stronger in intensity, wider in scale, and more complex in nature. A high-powered committee under the chairmanship of a distinguished leader (once a union minister and also the vice chairman of the national planning commission), Ashoka Mehta, was set up in December 1977 and submitted its report in August 1978. The governing perspective of the report, according to the committee, had been the functional imperative of adequate decentralization for effective development. With this perspective in mind, the committee made a number of general suggestions in regard to the reformulation of "structures, functions and the utilisation of financial, administrative and human resources of *panchayati raj* institutions" so that these institutions can develop the capability for the proper management of rural development programs. The committee in making these suggestions claimed no more than to "indicate the spectrum of possibilities while the state governments would have to work out the actual details keeping in view their changing requirements.''[11] The state governments, however, were asked not to forget to link "institutions of democratic decentralization with socially motivated economic development."

The main features of the reorganization of *panchayati raj* as suggested by the commitee may be summed as follows. First, there is to be progressive decentralization of developmental functions and powers from the state government to *panchayati raj* institutions. The pace and scope of decentralization may vary from one state to the other and from time to time depending upon the environmental factors and the vitality acquired by the institutions concerned.

Second, the key institution to which the powers, functions, and resources are to be progressively decentralized is to be the district-level *zila parishad*, which can have more political and administrative competence. The structure of the *zila parishad* would have to be reorganized in three main ways. First, its council would have to draw its membership partly by direct election, partly by indirect election of ex officio entry, and partly by means of cooption and nomination of certain categories of people. In other words, while fresh blood is to come in by direct election, linkages are to be established with the lower tiers (*panchayat samitis* or *mandal panchayats*, as the case may be) through some of their office bearers who would hold office in their ex officio capacity. Besides, representation is also to be given on the *zila parishad* council to large municipalities, district-level cooperatives, women, and those persons with a special interest in rural development. Again, the *zila parishad* is to set up functional committees to manage the functional programs—agricultural, industrial, educational, social welfare, family welfare, and public works. While the overall control would rest with the *zila parishad* council, these committees would concern themselves with the implementation aspect of these functions.

Third, while the *zila parishad* would have a chief executive officer, to be drawn from the Indian Administrative Service, who would be the overall administrative head of the *zila parishad*, the administrative control of the functional committees would be the responsibility of the district-level head of the department concerned (with which the committee would deal). He would also act as the secretary of the committee.

Fourth, below the district level there would be the *panchayat samiti*, but only in those states where it already exists. In the course of time, these are to be replaced by *mandal panchayats*, which are to be set up straightaway in those states in which there are no *panchayat samitis* at present. A *mandal panchayat* is to be constituted for an area that is much smaller than the *panchayat samiti* but definitely larger than that of a village *panchayat*. The *mandal panchayat* is to perform not only the municipal and maintenance functions but to activate the rural people as well as undertake the implementation of developmental projects to be entrusted to it by the *zila parishad*. A *mandal panchayat* is to be constituted by means of a direct election. A section of its members, however, is to consist of representatives of the farmers' service societies, women, and others.

Below the *mandal panchayat* there is to be the village-level committee, which would consist of the members elected from the village concerned to the *mandal panchayat* and the *zila parishad* and also of representatives of the rural poor, that is, small marginal farmers. The village committee is to perform functions allocated to it by the *mandal panchayat*. There is to be no *gram sabha* (village council), and thus this body is to be abolished wherever it exists. A fifth feature is that special measures are to be taken to enable the weaker sections of the rural people to participate in decision making as well as receive a fair share in the benefits flowing from developmental plans and projects. One measure proposed by the committee is that seats may be reserved for scheduled castes and tribes both in the *zila parishad* and the *mandal panchayat* in proportion to their population. Another measure is to be a committee of social justice to safeguard the interests of the weaker sections. In addition, the committee suggests that the expenditure to be incurred on the programs earmarked for the welfare of the scheduled castes and tribes be conducted by an independent body.

Sixth, the political parties are to be allowed to contest elections to *zila parishad* as also to the other tiers of the *panchayati raj*. They should also take an active part in decision making at all levels. Their participation would promote the functioning of the *panchayati raj* institutions. It would also help mobilize people's cooperation. The quality of leadership might also improve.

Seventh, with a view to forging effective coordination in development planning between the rural and urban areas, representation has been provided to the municipalities both at the *zila parishad* and *mandal panchayat* levels. This is an important recommendation in view of the increasing interdependence of the people of the two areas.

Finally, in order to improve the caliber of leadership at the level of the *panchayati raj*, to arouse political consciousness among the people and, further, to give development orientation to the administrative personnel of these institutions, the committee has recommended a massive program of education and training to both the leaders and the civil servants working in these institutions. It has also recommended revision and rationalizaton of rules and procedures of administration in the *panchayati raj* institutions in order to reduce delays, wastage, and graft.

The proposals of the committee regarding the reorganization and revamping of *panchayati raj* were discussed recently by the National Development Council (the highest decision-making body of the nation with regard to states' administration). Both the state chief ministers and the union government agreed that there was an imperative need to provide substantial opportunity for the people to participate in rural development by decentralization of more functions and powers to the *panchayati raj* institutions. But the council rejected two of the important recommendations. One related to the progressive replacement of the three-tier system of *panchayati raj* by a two tier-system, the *zila parishad* and the *mandal panchayats*. It was felt that every village, big or small, must retain its *panchayat*, which the people have become used to over the years. The second related to the role of political parties. It was felt that the *panchayati raj* institutions, being primarily treated as the development agencies, should not be encumbered with competitive party politics.

The state governments have yet to take the follow-up action in regard to the reorganization of *panchayati raj* in the light of the decisions of the National Development Council.

Our own view is that any reorganization scheme should consider the following four points:

1. Decentralization of functions and powers to *panchayati raj* institutions should be genuine, sincere, and well regulated.
2. State governments should have the political will and constructive attitude for guiding, motivating, and helping the *panchayati raj* institutions to grow in vitality, strength, and maturity.
3. There is a need to cut down political rivalries between the *panchayati raj* leadership and state-level leadership by political linkages through political parties, which should be allowed to contest elections to *zila parishad* as much as to state legislatures and other public offices.
4. Due care should be taken to streamline and reorient the administrative side of the *panchayati raj* institutions in the interest of efficiency and effectiveness of planned development.

MUNICIPAL GOVERNMENT

As mentioned earlier, the pace of urbanization has been increasing in recent decades, and this has resulted not only in the increase of population of the existing cities and towns but also in the creation of new towns. Obviously, the number of urban local bodies has been on the increase. We shall, however, concern ourselves here with the two important categories of such bodies (municipalities and municipal corporations) that are democratic in character and ordinarily exist in towns and cities, while the other categories—notified area committees and town area committees—are only partially democratic, are fewer in number, and exist only in very small towns.

Since the dawn of independence, there has been more than a ten-fold increase in the number of municipal corporations (from three in 1947 to forty-one in 1979). This increase has been due to the elevation in status of a number of towns from municipalities to municipal corporations. Similarly, the municipalities, which have been graded into three categories, have also shown an upward trend with regard to both their number and their area. In 1979, their number stood at 1,404. Municipal corporations, compared with the municipalities, possess larger powers that have been decentralized to them by the state governments. Even among the municipalities, powers have been variously distributed, depending upon the class of the municipalities, class one having the largest number of powers and class four the smallest.

Besides having a larger area and population and also larger revenue, a municipal corporation has a more clear-cut functional division between its deliberative and executive wings than has been the case in the municipalities. By law, powers and functions have been allocated separately to three organs: a directly elected council, exercising powers in regard to policy formulation, approval of major programs and budgetary proposals, prescription of rules and regulations, and exercising an oversight on the working of the other two organs; a standing committee elected by the council and having the responsibility for formulating various civic programs within the framework of the general policy of the corporation, for budgetary proposals and for exercising general supervision over program implementation; and a commissioner, who is generally appointed by the state government on a tenure basis from among the members of the higher career civil services and has the responsibility for day-to-day administration. The powers of appointment and approval of contracts as well as that of incurring expenditure have been allocated among the three organs, the council having been given the largest share. The effective working of the corporation depends not only upon the capability and integrity of each organ but also upon their mutual relationship.

In recent years there has been a trend in several states to restructure the municipalities (especially the larger ones) with a view to bringing about a similar separation of powers and functions between the deliberative and executive wings. Two main factors have been responsible for this trend. First, it was expected that this separation would considerably cut down political pulls and pressures on the municipal administration. Second, it was further felt that if political interference were reduced, administrative capability would increase and strategies of action would be decided by comparatively more competent persons without being hamstrung by expediency-ridden politicians.

Another structural change has been to initiate the move to set up functional committees in those municipal institutions where they did not exist earlier. Thus, the committee system is beginning to function increasingly to take care of program formulation and implementation in specific functional fields, such as education and health. The standing committee is expected to provide coordination among the committees while the council provides policy direction. Here there is a trend parallel to the one in *panchayati raj* institutions, where committees have been used increasingly.

In municipal corporations there is provision for internal decentralization of functions and powers so as to bring the municipal administration nearer to the people, thereby helping to eliminate the sense of alienation they develop toward the municipal authorities. This decentralization has been only administrative in character. The Hyderabad municipal corporation, for instance, has set up local area officers. Similarly, the Delhi corporation has constituted zonal offices. There is thus a trend, though embryonic, toward a two-tier municipal administration.

Another significant change in some of the states has been the formation of state-wide cadres of the higher (and in some cases even the middle-level) categories of municipal personnel for the purpose of promoting better administrative capability and integrity. In some states there are unified cadres (common pools for the municipalities in a state) and in others integrated cadres (common pools for state departments and municipalities). Moreover, there is now common recruitment, which is generally done through state public service commissions, for higher and middle-level personnel. [12]

Another recent development in the field of personnel management has been the setting up of regional training institutes to provide basic education and refresher courses for the municipal personnel. The union and state governments have collaborated in setting up these institutes in universities in certain cases and as autonomous entities in others. At present there are such institutes in Delhi, Bombay, Hyderabad, Lucknow, and Calcutta. [13] The governments want to increase the number of these institutes because the existing arrangements are inadequate, keeping in view the large number of municipal institutions in the country.

As regards the functions of the municipalities, they are of two types: mandatory and optional. In some states there has been a tendency on the part of the government to take over some of the municipal functions on the plea that these were being managed inefficiently and inadequately. Thus elementary and secondary education as well as health services have already been taken over by the state governments in Punjab, Haryana, and Himachal Pradesh. [14]

Similarly, various aspects of urban development have been engaging the attention of the planners and leaders of the country. In recent years the union government has promoted urban development programs, some independently and some in collaboration with the state governments concerned. In the 1960s, the union government gave grants to the state governments to prepare city development as well as regional development plans for various cities, and in the 1970s this function was left to the exclusive care of the state governments. In addition, a number of programs of slum clearance, environmental improvement of slum areas, sewerage, development of metropolitan cities and areas of national importance, and community development programs were initiated by the union government with the help of the state governments. [15] The Fifth Five-Year Plan spelled out a few objectives of urban development, which in turn necessitated the formulation of a land-use policy, revision of legal enactments relating to urban development activity, mobilization of resources from within and without the country, and improvement of local planning development organization. On the whole, there is a tendency on the part of the state governments to bypass the municipal authorities in regard to urban planning and also in some cases of specific civic service improvement.

Some of the new planning organizations set up or enlarged were improvement trusts, metropolitan development authorities, and urban and town development authorities. This obviously raises the question of whether special bodies should be entities within a municipal government or should be outside its orbit. The first alternative may mean better integration but poor personnel competence, while the second alternative can pose the problem of inadequate coordination, with its injurious consequences. It should not, however, be difficult to design organizational arrangements that combine autonomy and integrated municipal government. Similarly, special functional agencies have been set up on a semi-autonomous basis in large cities to manage some of the municipal utilities and major services. This has tended to weaken municipal government, though it has improved the efficiency of management of the utilities and service in many cases.[16]

The relationship between state government and municipal government has undergone a change in recent years. With a view to carrying out their promotional and controlling roles more vigorously, most of the state governments have enlarged their state-level departments of local government and renamed them departments of rural development and local government. Moreover, these departments have set up directorates to take care of the operational and routine matters relating to local governments. In some states, the directorates have further constituted inspectorates to deal with the problems of local government on the spot. The union government has been providing increasing coordination, policy guidance, and financial assistance to the state governments in regard to various types of urban developmental needs.

The control of the state governments over municipal government has never been constructive or supportive, and at times it has been obstructive.[17] Hence there is a need to restructure this relationship on more healthy lines. An experienced administrator has aptly suggested the following measures in this behalf:

1. Replacement of the present organizational jungle by a new system to ensure proper development and maintenance of local government services and to ensure rectification of malpractices and inefficiencies
2. Clear-cut demarcation of limits of state control and assurance that these limits are not transgressed because of political and bureaucratic aggressions
3. Spelling out of the limits of autonomous action by municipal government

In spite of the structural and functional changes and improvements, the performance of municipal government has, by and large, tended to be discouraging in most of the towns and cities. This has been commented upon by many observers, administrators, public men, and scholars as well as by various inquiry committees and study teams of the government. Here are the comments of one distinguished scholar.

The corporation and municipalities are, by and large, centres of inefficiency, corruption and political nepotism. Most of them are bankrupt and cannot in any way tackle the big problems in the field of housing, transport, environmental pollution, etc. Besides, they do not have adequate legal powers and the administrative machinery to implement a modern master plan. In short, the municipalities are not geared to urban planning as understood today, but merely perform municipal functions as understood in the nineteenth century. They have neither the financial viability nor the legal backing to confront urban problems except in limited spheres such as zoning and land use planning.[18]

To sum up, the record of the municipal institutions in most cases has been far from satisfactory. The result is urban decline and decay. Clear thinking, comprehensive strategies, mobilization of resources, reorganization of municipal bodies, more effective functional coordination and even integration between various organizations concerned with urban development—all these are needed more than ever in view of the challenging problems of growing urbanization in India.

PERSPECTIVE

Ever since attaining the status of a sovereign state, India has been striving hard to build up a democratic political system and devise a suitable administrative structure capable of coping effectively with the problems of the socio-economic development of her fast-expanding population. In the ongoing, highly complex political process at work in this context, it is being widely realized that decentralization has an ever increasing role to play. Important political circles are, therefore, ardently advocating that a fresh look be given to the centralization-decentralization continuum and that local government, which is one very important (if not the most important) institutional form of politico-administrative decentralization, be comprehensively reorganized so that it may be able to play its role more effectively.

The problems of local government need to be studied more in the context of the situation to develop in the years to come than that of the current state of affairs. One big challenge the future will bring is the rapid expansion of the country's population, already the second largest in the world. A second important problem is the rising expectations and aspirations of the people in general and of the hitherto socially and politically neglected sections, who are being socialized to new values. Both these factors will impinge upon the availability of the civil amenities to the people. Also to be considered, however, are the environmental problems of water and air pollution and the ruthless exploitation of natural resources. Local governments can undertake heavier and newer responsiblities if we plan their politico-administrative development and take appropriate measures to bring this about according to a time schedule. The major measures we propose are as follows:

First, the dichotomy in our thinking about local government should be given up. We need to treat both urban and rural sectors of local government as two intertwined parts of a bigger whole—representative local government, as a third level of the total political system (the other two being the national and the state governments). The Rural-Urban Relationship Committee has pointed out the need for coordination between the two. Already municipalities are represented in rural councils of the higher level in the states of Gujrat, Uttar Pradesh, Orissa, and Madya Pradesh, but much more coordination and in some cases integraton needs to be effected. Our planning for rural development and urban development, in the context of the fast-expanding size of the cities and towns, has been too segmented. We need to cross not only the boundary of a village or a town but to be more meaningful our planning in the future has to cut across the boundaries of many villages and towns. Thus, instead of the disjointed system of rural and urban planning, we shall have to develop the concept of area and regional planning for some of the utilities (transport, for instance) and services (education, for instance).

Second, political parties should be allowed to participate in the working of the local government in order to ensure effective political accountability for policies and standards of performance. Moreover, political parties need to do some thinking on local government and the problems thereof. Reasonable political competition among parties can result in the institutional invigoration of local government.

Third, a cooperative type of federal system is emerging in the country as a result of continuous adjustment of relationships between the union and state governments. Though local government, unlike the union and state governments, has no constitutional status, still it needs to be made an active partner of the federal system. This is possible only if the existing relationship between the state and local governments, based as it is on an authority-subordination concept, is radically transformed into one of cooperation and mutual understanding in which the state government plays the role of a senior and helpful partner.

Fourth, human and financial resources should be developed rationally. The political elite and the administrative personnel in local government need to be thoroughly reoriented so that they are adequately equipped both psychologically and functionally to perform their respective roles more efficiently, honestly, and effectively. While proper political recruitment of the elite would need the attention of the political parties, administrative recruitment would have to be improved considerably so that merit alone is taken as the main selection criterion. Similarly, financial resources need a big and appropriate augmentation if local government is to undertake its responsibilities in a more satisfactory manner. Conventional thinking about local finance and financial management would have to yield place to a new scientific thinking so that financial resources facilitate rather than constrain the functioning of local government.

Last, the management in local government is outdated, dilatory, wasteful, and corrupt. It needs to be rationalized, modernized, and revitalized by the adoption of the concepts and techniques of modern management. This calls for a thorough overhauling of the institutions of local government and of the existing rules and procedures of work.

In fact, the whole local government set-up of a vast, highly diverse and socially complex country like India needs continuous thinking based on appropriate research so that it is renewed and revitalized periodically. Thus, it will be constantly geared up to undertake expanding, heavier, and more sophisticated responsibilities in a more meaningful and vigorous manner.

NOTES

1. For details about the land, its people, and its socioeconomic and political institutions, see *India Reference Annual, 1978* (New Delhi: Government of India, Publications Division, 1978); and for greater details refer to the *Gazetteer of Indian Union*, vols. 1-4 (New Delhi: Government of India, Publications Division, 1978).

2. For a detailed description of the local government system of ancient India, see Radha Kumud Mookerji, *Local Government in Ancient India* (Delhi: Motilal Banarsisas, 1958); and also H. D. Malaviya, *Village Panchayats in India* (New Delhi: All India Congress Committee, 1956).

3. For a detailed account of the development of local government during British rule, see Hugh Tinker, *Foundations of Local Self Government in India, Pakistan and Burma* (London: Athlone Press, 1954): and also S. Bhatnagar, *Panchayati Raj in Kangra District* (New Delhi: Orient Longman, 1974).

4. See Henry Maddick, *Panchayati Raj: A Study of Rural Local Government in India* (London: Longman, 1970); and also S. Bhatnagar, *Rural Local Government in India* (New Delhi: Light and Life, 1978).

5. Refer to the *Report of the Study on the Position of Gram Sabha in Panchayati Raj Movement* (New Delhi: Government of India, 1963).

6. Refer to A. H. Somji, *Democracy and Political Change in Village India* (New Delhi: Orient Longman, 1971); and S. Bhatnagar, "Grassroot Politics in India: A Case Study of the Kangra Valley," *Asian Survey* (May 1975).

7. See Douglas Ensminger, *Rural India in Transition* (New Delhi: All-India Panchayat Parishad, 1972); and also R. N. Haldipur, "On Remodelling Panchayati Raj," *Indian Journal of Public Administration* 17 (July-September 1971).

8. *Ashoka Mehta Committee Report* (New Delhi: Government of India, 1978).

9. See *Report of the Evaluation Committee on Panchayati Raj* (Bombay: Government of Maharashtra, 1971).

10. *Ashoka Mehta Committee Report.*

11. Ibid.

12. See Sriram Maheshwari, *Local Government in India* (New Delhi: Orient Longman, 1978).

13. See A. Avasthi, ed., *Municipal Administration in India* (Agra: Lakshmi Narain Aggarwal, 1972).

14. See S. Bhatnagar, "Challenges of Urbanisation and Public Policy in India (A case for local government)," *Social Sciences Research Journal* (Chandigarh) 1, no. 1.

15. See *India Reference Annual 1978*.

16. See Mohit Bhattacharya, *Nagarlok* (New Delhi) 2, no. 4 (1970).

17. For critical assessment of the performance of the municipalities, see Avasthi, *Municipal Administration*.

18. Ashish Bose, ''India, the Urban Context,'' in *India Since Independence*, ed. S. C. Dube (New Delhi: South Asia Books, 1977).

People's Republic of China

Robert E. Bedeski*

37

Since at least the third century B.C., government in China has functioned at three levels: central, regional-provincial, and local. Throughout this long history, however, the dynamics of centrifugalism and centripetalism have produced an oscillation which one ancient author characterized as, "Unity always follows fragmentation, and disunity follows unity." In certain periods of dynastic strength, central authorities exercised hegemony, while long periods of weak centralism were marked by a regionalism reminiscent of successor states to the Holy Roman Empire. It would be safe to speculate that, based on historical precedent, no arrangement of political power can be regarded as permanent in China.

The People's Republic of China since the Great Proletarian Cultural Revolution (GPCR) (1966-69) is no exception. After several years of turmoil and purges, two identifiable persuasions emerged which have affected governmental policy and structure. The moderates (with Premier Chou En-lai as spokesman) preferred a return to some of the pre-GPCR structures and personnel. From their perspective, China had succeeded in avoiding the perils of backsliding and revisionism which the GPCR had been initiated to eliminate. Such "renegades" as Liu Shao-ch'i and Lin Piao were defeated, and now the revolution could return to the main task of constructing socialism.

The more radical persuasion (grouped around Yao Wen-yuan and Chiang Ching, the wife of Mao Tse-tung) demanded that the Cultural Revolution's "new-born things" (including the May Seventh Cadre Schools and revolutionary committees) be promoted and made part of the new state structure.

*Associate Professor of Political Science, Carleton University, Ottawa. Chairman of the Department of Political Science 1979-1980.

It is within this context that changes in local government must be examined. The future direction of political structures and relations between government and society depends, to a large degree, upon the extent to which the "new-born things" are incorporated in the state and how they affect the relations among the various levels of government and party administration.

SUBNATIONAL GOVERNMENT STRUCTURES

When the Communists came to power in 1949, they divided the country into six administrative regions comprising several provinces each. These regions were headed by military administrative commissions, which were agencies of the central government and supervised the work of provincial, municipal, and county authorities. These regional commissions exercised considerable autonomy, and at least two leaders, Kao Kang and Jao Shu-shih, were later accused of running "independent kingdoms." The regions were abolished in 1954 with the introduction of a new constitutional system based on local administration at provincial and sub-provincial levels.

The next major reform in local government came in 1958. The Central Committee of the Chinese Communist Party (CCP) adopted an ambitious program of intensive economic development known as the "Great Leap Forward." This plan called for rapid industrialization, and, to support it, further collectivization of agriculture was needed. Land reform had occurred in 1950, and during the following years government moved towards collective agriculture. In April 1958 the model commune of Weihsing (Sputnik) was established in Honan province as a result of merging a number of producers' cooperatives and consisted of approximately 43,000 people. The proclaimed purpose of establishing communes was to speed the transition to full communism by facilitating the development of industry, agriculture, and cultural and educational work. The people's commune was to be the basic unit of Chinese society and administration.

The regulations for the Weihsing commune stipulated that it was to have the same confines as the township (*chen*). The members of the township people's congress were concurrently to be the members of the commune congress. Likewise, the township people's council, the executive body, was to serve concurrently as the commune's management committee. The township head was also to serve as commune head, and his deputies were commune deputies. In effect, the communes merged the administrative and representative functions of the townships with the productive, mobilization, cultural, and educational organization of the lower levels. On 29 August 1958, the Central Committee passed organizational regulations on the commune system. These regulations suggested that communes might form federations, with the county as the unit.

THE CULTURAL REVOLUTION AND THE REVOLUTIONARY COMMITTEES

The Great Leap Forward did not achieve its ambitious goals. People's communes were also established in the cities but were not as effective as in the countryside. There followed a period of economic and political retrenchment as agricultural production faltered. More pragmatic policies, including private plots and financial incentives, attempted to raise production. Mao Tse-tung had lost some power, however, and felt that these policies indicated backsliding that seemed to characterize the post-Stalin era in the USSR. Revisionism and betrayal of the Chinese revolution became epithets hurled by Maoists at "China's Khrushchev," Liu Shao-Ch'i.

Liu replaced Mao Tse-tung in 1959 as chairman of the republic and was held responsible for the so-called revisionist policies of the post-Great Leap years. In 1965 Mao launched his attack to regain control of the Chinese revolution and oust Liu and his followers from positions of power. To fully accomplish this, however, Mao had to shatter the party apparatus, build new institutions of political power, and call on the People's Liberation Army (PLA) to assist his own forces. The turmoil that ensued is known as the Great Proletarian Cultural Revolution.

The major institutional changes began in early 1967, with the "January Revolution" in Shanghai. Maoist "revolutionary rebels" sought to seize power from the Shangai Municipal Committee and the Shanghai People's Congress. The rebel group was congratulated by the Central Committee, which was controlled by the Maoists at that time. Other rebel groups throughout the country were urged to "learn from Shanghai." Throughout 1967, supporters of Mao and Lin Piao, the minister of defense, seized local power from the "capitalist roaders," that is, followers of Liu Shao-ch'i. The theoretical journal, *Red Flag*, called for the thorough smashing of the organs seized and building new "state organs of the proletarian dictatorship."[1]

The new state organs at the local level were provisional power structures composed of a three-way alliance, including: pro-Maoist party cadres, representatives of the army, and leaders of the rebel organizations. In this distribution of power, the alliance could draw on the past expertise of the cadres to give stability at the local levels, the army as the only united force in the country, and the younger rebels who were given a share in the fruits of their victory.

A major difference between these new revolutionary committees and the system of congresses inaugurated with the 1954 Constitution was that the latter were formed at the lowest levels of society—the village and urban district. The revolutionary committees, on the other hand, were introduced at the provincial level to replace party committees and provincial congresses. Only after "preparatory" and revolutionary committees had been established in a province were the lower-level committees attempted. Another difference was that, prior to the GPCR, party and government lines of authority had been separated.

With the introduction of the revolutionary committees, party and government activities were merged. In one province, for example, it was stated that the revolutionary committee would be the leadership organ for party, government, financial, and cultural affairs in the province. Finally, the new revolutionary committees were to be provisional organs until new forms could be inaugurated and new party committees formed.

No legal regulations concerning the organization of the revolutionary committees were issued when first formed—unlike the commune movement in 1958, when the Weihsing commune was the model for the whole country. By the end of 1967, however, the organizational pattern of the committees emerged more clearly. The Peking Revolutionary Committee, for example, had ninety-seven members, of whom thirty-two were on its standing committee.[2]

Some provincial revolutionary committees had as many as 250 members. Most appeared to take over the functions of the former people's councils, and seemed to be drifting into the old patterns of rules and performance. However, factionalism within the rebel organizations and conflicts between old and new cadres made consolidation difficult. The presence of the army helped stabilize the situation in several areas. Revolutionary committees were also established in the autonomous regions. The committees were completed by September 1968, not through election but by "consultation," which was claimed to conform best to the needs of "proletarian democracy." *Red Flag* stressed that the 4,000 members of the provincial revolutionary committees were "comrades who have been steeled and tempered in the storms of revolution and selected only after repeated debates, fomentations, consultations, and checkups; they are even more compatible with the proletarian democracy than those chosen by election as practiced in the past."[3] Thus it appeared that these new structures were to be made a permanent feature of the state system.

One of the targets of the Cultural Revolution was the growing bureaucratization of party and government. The proliferation of offices and administrative personnel was not conducive to the "continuing revolution" and socialist transformation of Chinese society as envisaged by Mao Tse-tung. The new policy was "better troops and simpler administration." In 1968, the central authorities pressured the revolutionary committees to reduce support personnel. In Honan province, personnel were cut from over 200 to less than 100. Two general offices and eight working teams were consolidated into four teams.[4]

After the purge of Liu Shao-ch'i in 1968, the national leadership sought to reform administrative work and increase production. Models of working styles were identified and publicized. The spirit of sacrifice and self-sufficiency Peking sought to promote was epitomized in the example of the work at the Taching oil fields in the northeast, and Chinese farmers were urged to "learn from Tachai," a poor commune in Shansi which transformed itself into a relatively prosperous enterprise by hard work, collective effort, and the diligent application of Mao's thoughts. Revolutionary committees throughout the country were pressured to reduce paper work and decrease the number of meetings. Separation between officials and the masses was to be reduced by emphasizing face-to-face leadership. Administrative personnel were to be rotated so that at any given time one-third were to be engaged in manual labor, a third would be studying at lower levels, and the other third would be doing administrative work.

The revolutionary committees combined party and governmental functions at the provincial and local levels. After the Ninth Party Congress, however, the regime decided to rebuild the former dual structure. On 9 September 1970, the Central Committee of the CCP announced plans to prepare for the Fourth National People's Congress. The congress was to have convened in late 1968, but the radical changes at the local level made it unclear whether or not the system of people's congresses would be re-established. The party also had to be rebuilt, and by August 1971 all twenty-nine provincial-level party committees had been set up. Only by restoring party authority could Lin Piao's emerging military dictatorship be eliminated, since the military tended to dominate the revolutionary committees. Another shift took place when the content of the three-way alliance was redefined. In late 1970, the ''three-in-one'' formula no longer referred to masses, cadres, and soldiers but had shifted to indicate the combination of old, middle-aged, and young people. These changes and the gradual replacement of military administrators by civilians must have indicated to Lin Piao that his political position was eroding.

THE CURRENT SYSTEM OF LOCAL GOVERNMENT

The current political structures increasingly resemble those of the period before the Cultural Revolution. The party dominates government and administration, and many cadres and leaders who were purged have been rehabilitated and restored to their former positions. The revolutionary committees were called upon to help in rebuilding the party, but in many places they have been reluctant to give up power. During the Cultural Revolution, revolutionary committees were established somewhat indiscriminately in schools, factories, and villages. Many of these have been disbanded or merged with local party committees. According to Article 34 of the new 1978 State Constitution, ''People's congresses and revolutionary committees are established in provinces, municipalities directly under the Central Government, counties, cities, municipal districts, people's communes and towns. . . .Organs of self-government are established in autonomous regions, prefectures, and counties.''

The fate of the revolutionary committees remained a matter of debate after the Tenth Party Congress of 24-28 August 1973. Chou En-lai failed to mention them among the ''new-born things'' of the Cultural Revolution, while the new appointee to the Politburo, Wang Hung-wen, said it was necessary to give ''full play'' to the role of the revolutionary committees. Only in December 1973 were the revolutionary committees mentioned in the press among the "new-born things." The left wing of the party continued to support the committees, which have dropped PLA representatives in many areas. They continue to supervise the government bureaucracy and serve as the focus of governmental control in the provinces in a way similar to the role of the eclipsed people's council. But they do not have the same authority and leadership as during the turbulence of the Cultural Revolution. The moderates hope to return to the former system of congresses and councils, fearing perhaps that the revolutionary committees may once again compete for power at the expense of the party. At the same time, however, moderate forces prefer to avoid criticism that they are seeking to undo the gains of the Cultural Revolution.

The future status of the revolutionary committees has constitutional and structural as well as political importance for the Chinese system. One of the major tasks of the Fourth National People's Congress (13-17 January 1975) was to ratify a new state constitution, which was formally adopted on 17 January 1975. The role of the party was more explicit in the 1975 document than in the 1954 Constitution. For example, Article 21 (1954) reads: "The National People's Congress is the highest organ of state authority in the People's Republic of China." The corresponding sentence in the 1975 Constitution (Article 16) is: "The National People's Congress is the highest organ of state power *under the leadership of the Communist Party of China*" (emphasis added). Section Three of the 1975 Constitution deals with "Local People's Congresses and Local Revolutionary Committees." According to Article 22,

The local revolutionary committees at various levels are the permanent organs of the local people's congresses and at the same time the local people's governments at various levels. . . .Local revolutionary committees are responsible and accountable to the people's congress at the corresponding level and to the organ of state at the next higher level.

The next article deals with the functions of the revolutionary committees:

The local people's congresses at various levels and the local revolutionary committees elected by them ensure the execution of laws and decrees in their respective areas; lead the socialist revolution and socialist construction in their respective areas; examine and approve local economic plans, budgets and final accounts; maintain revolutionary order; and safeguard the rights of citizens.

In other words, this formula means that the revolutionary committees serve the same functions as the old people's councils under the 1954 Constitution.

Government and administration did not await constitutional ratification, and local structures found their patterns within the parameters bequeathed by the Cultural Revolution and its aftermath. The people's communes still dominate the countryside and combine political and economic administration. The Chienming commune, for example, lies 150 kilometers east of Peking in Hopei province. It has a population of 14,500 persons living in 2,600 households. Leadership is provided by the commune party committee, which consists of two senior cadres, fourteen middle-aged, and two youth cadres.[5] This commune consists of twenty-one production brigades. One of these, the Hsipu Brigade, consists of three production teams with 217 households and 1,176 persons. Administrative work is performed by the revolutionary committees at the levels of commune and production brigade. In place of the township people's congresses specified in the 1954 Constitution, there now appear "commune members' representative assemblies" in their place.

The people's commune is a large collective owned by all its members. There is collective ownership at each level of organization with the production team as the basic unit. These teams own land, animals, and small machinery and organize the labor of their members. A production team handles its income and distribution separately, bears its own losses, and keeps some of its profits. Production brigades handle larger projects, such as small irrigation works, shops for processing products, orchards, schools, and clinics. Brigades may also own larger farm machinery. Large-scale enterprise may be run by the commune. Tractor stations, hydroelectric power installations, repair shops, forests, experimental farms, middle schools, and hospitals are among the commune's economic undertakings.

According to Communist ideology, this system of organization is not permanent. The regime expects that as the proletarian dictatorship becomes more consolidated, commune members' socialist consciousness will continue to rise, and the collective economy will become stronger. Then, the poorer teams will reach the economic level of more prosperous teams and there will be greater mechanization of agriculture. As this occurs, the production brigade, and later the commune itself, will become the basic accounting unit. With this, ownership of land and capital will shift upward until the system of collective ownership will eventually be replaced by ownership of the entire people, represented by the state.

Democratic centralism continues to be the organizational principle of the commune. There are representative assemblies at the commune, brigade, and production team level elected by the respective members. Every member has one vote and is eligible to be elected. Between sessions of the assemblies, work is carried out by a permanent body—the revolutionary committee in the commune and brigade, and "leading group" in the production team. Production plans are drawn up by the revolutionary committees and leading groups, based on targets set by the state. Draft plans are discussed by the membership, then revised and put into final form. The commune members reserve a certain amount of time every week for political study. These sessions are organized by the party organizations at different levels.

The revolutionary committees are also in control of provincial and municipal governments. In 1973, Kiangsu province, with a population of about 47 million, was divided into seven large districts and seven province-level cities.

The province was further subdivided into sixty-four counties and four cities administered by the districts.[6]

The Kiangsu provincial revolutionary committee was established in March 1968, and in early 1973 had 165 members. Its standing committee had forty-eight members and was chaired by General Hsu Shih-yu, who was later transferred to Canton. Hsu was concurrently chairman of the provincial party committee. About 40 percent of the revolutionary committee personnel had served in the provincial government before the Cultural Revolution. The party provided political leadership, and the revolutionary committee handled administration and other aspects of state power. The party committee had 130 members, 9 of whom were on the standing committee of the revolutionary committee. Twenty members of the party committee were classified as military, and the majority of the nine party representatives on the standing committee of the revolutionary committee were soldiers.

Another provincial revolutionary committee in the northeast consisted of 140 members early in 1973. The membership proportions were 20 percent PLA, 60 percent revolutionary masses, and 20 percent party cadres. The standing committee had twenty-eight members, with 25 percent (and the chairman) from the PLA. The committee supervised the work of nine administrative organs: propaganda, education, planning, finance, trade, capital construction, industry, and agriculture. These organs controlled the work of the respective bureaus in the provincial government. Bureau policy for the provinces was generally made by the central bureaus in Peking.

Municipal government is organized somewhat similarly. The Shenyang Revolutionary Committee controls five urban districts, four suburban districts, and two counties, each with its own revolutionary committee. With a population of 4.2 million, its area is half urban and half rural. As in provincial government, there is considerable overlap between party and revolutionary committee staff and leadership. There are seven administrative groups under the municipal revolutionary committee. These include the offices of administration, political affairs, security, industry and communication, finance, education and culture, and planning. Each group is responsible to the municipal revolutionary committee and the party committee.

In addition to the twenty-one provinces and five autonomous regions, the major subdivisions of Chinese administration include three municipalities which are controlled directly by the central government: Peking, Shanghai, and Tientsin. Peking is divided into five urban and four rural districts. Each is divided into a number of neighborhoods and administered by a neighborhood revolutionary committee. One neighborhood, Fengsheng, contained 52,978 people in 1973.[7] When its revolutionary committee was founded during the Cultural Revolution, twenty-seven members were elected. Ten were government workers assigned to the locality, and the remainder were workers in local factories, teachers, and other neighborhood people. Following the "three-in-one" combination, the committee includes young activists, as well as middle-aged and elderly people who had previously been active in community work and leadership.

A neighborhood is further divided into residential areas, twenty-five in Fengsheng. Each consists of one to eight lanes with 400-800 households and about 2,000 people. All residential areas have a residents' committee which works under the neighborhood revolutionary committee. This is described as a "self-governing people's organization, not a unit of government." The residents' committee does the day-to-day work of serving the people and carrying out the assignments of the neighborhood revolutionary committee. The residents' committee is elected and has fifteen to twenty-five members who serve without pay. Many are retired workers or cadres. The jurisdiction of the residents' committee is further subdivided into three to six groups of 120 households each. Each group is divided into units of forty to fifty people for purposes of study and other affairs.

One of the main tasks of the neighborhood revolutionary committees is to organize the urban residents into classes for studying the works of Marx, Engels, Lenin, Stalin, and Mao Tse-tung. People are organized to discuss national and world affairs and to carry out the policies of the party and central government. The committees also establish small factories, operate nurseries and kindergartens to supplement those of the municipality, and take the lead in various cultural, educational, and health affairs of the neighborhood.

Collective leadership is emphasized at the neighborhood level, with a chairman and several vice chairmen. Ideally, they must spend much of their time with local study groups and go into the streets to learn about local conditions from the residents themselves. Each member of a neighborhood revolutionary committee is responsible for certain areas. After meetings, the members visit leaders of lane or residents' committees and explain decisions and how to implement them. Local complaints concerning public services or economic conditions are usually channelled through this grass-roots hierarchy. Health clinics have been established in the more advanced residents' committees offices.

Economic as well as political and social functions are served by the neighborhood revolutionary committees. The Fengsheng committee, for example, runs seven factories, producing springs, insulating materials, rubber products, clothing, metallurgical materials, and cardboard boxes. Most workers live within a fifteen-minute walk of the factory, a factor which undoubtedly reduces pressure on public transportation. Similar to the communes, brigades, and teams in rural areas, the factories are political divisions as well as units of production. Factories are collectively owned and receive political and ideological leadership from the neighborhood revolutionary committee. Profits from the factories go to workers' benefits and are invested in new buildings and other capital improvements. Workers receive free medical care, and nursery care for children of women workers is paid partially by the factory. The neighborhood factories complement state-run plants, and there are neighbor-hood production groups which process goods. Schoolchildren also play a part in production, with part of their curriculum devoted to work as well as study. Even the aged play a role in home workshops or in doing services such as washing, mending, and child care to relieve housewives for production.

CONCLUSIONS

Since the Great Leap Forward, the Chinese authorities have sought to create a system that fuses politics and economics. Collective ownership of productive factors, not the notions of free individuals exercising the rights of democratic citizenship, has been the guiding principle of administration. All individuals in the Chinese state are enmeshed in a web of political, economic, and social roles that reinforce the power and scope of the state. Pre-revolutionary China was weak and impoverished, and the present leadership is determined to weld its hundreds of millions into a unified source of political and economic power. To accomplish this they have sought to eliminate alternative and potentially competitive focuses of autonomous power. Religious organizations, political parties, ethnic minorities, and local governments have been domesticated so that their existence and legitimacy depends on the state.

This imperative toward centralization and unification is not new in China. During 1974, official organs led the "Criticize Confucius and Lin Piao Movement." Even in this ideological campaign the thrust toward greater centralization was evident. The attacks on Lin Piao and purges of his military followers put the army on the defensive and facilitated the transfer of power at provincial and local levels from the army to the civilians. Simultaneously, there was a rebuilding of party structures and the rehabilitation of purged leaders. The official reasons for attacks on Confucius were that Lin Piao was a "sworn follower" of the Sage and attempted to reinstate the discredited slave-owning philosophy of past ages. Whatever the merits of the charges, their explanation and embellishment resulted in sometimes esoteric historical arguments which sought to revive the Legalist school of political philosophy, a persuasion which was eclipsed for over two millennia by Confucianism.

An increasingly prominent theme in the 1974 polemic or Legalism was the expression of a single unified state under a single ruler. The emperor Ch'in Shih Huang, who unified the feudal states of China in 221 B.C., has been held up as a modernizing figure who swept away obscurantism, particularism, and other obstacles to achieving a new state of history (in the Marxist sense). The underlying moral of this revival is that *unification and centralization is a necessary prerequisite to economic development.* Chinese Communism sees history as a struggle between two opposing lines. In the time of Ch'in Shih Huang, it was a struggle between the slave-owners (represented by the thoughts of Confucius) and the feudal landowners (whose spokesman was Li

Ssu, the prime minister of Ch'in Shih Huang). At one point the struggle was expressed in a debate over the form of administration:

A big controversy centering on "whither the Ch'in Dynasty" arose after Ch'in Shi Huang had unified China. The focus of the struggle was whether to establish the prefecture and county system with centralized power or to restore the ducal states system of the slave-owning class. Its essence was a struggle between the two lines—one of which persisted in progress and unification and the other stood for restoration, retrogression and split. [8]

The second "line," incidentally, also characterized the "Lin Piao line." A debate between the "two lines" ensued, and the emperor decided on the system of prefectures and counties rather than restoring the aristocracy to power. The latter system led to "never-ending wars between different states" in the past, and so "Ch'in Shih Huang set up the first centralized feudal state with a revolutionary approach." The emperor divided the country into thirty-six prefectures, each governed by a magistrate directly under the central government. Each prefecture was divided into counties and governed by a county magistrate, with officials supervising military and legal affairs: "All major government officials in local government were appointed and removed by the emperor, and no post was hereditary. This was an important reform. National affairs were run by the emperor himself who also issued laws and decrees." [9]

The reforms of the Ch'in emperor established a system which subsequent dynasties followed and which set the stage for further economic and cultural development. Confucianists through the ages condemned the Ch'in emperor as a tyrant. The Communists agree, but they conclude that because he unified the country and repressed the slave-owning aristocracy his merits outweighed his demerits.

This raising of the stature of China's first unifier cannot be discounted as mere historical revisionism. More probably it provides a parable innocent enough on the surface but loaded with an important political message for the initiated. Moreover, the central government sees provincial governments as potential competitors and alternative bases of power. Modern political unification in China has usually been accomplished at the expense of provincial autonomy. The central government prefers to reduce all territorial units to administrative extensions of itself, particularly in light of the experiences of the Cultural Revolution, when some provincial governments exercised considerable independence from Peking.

In sum, towards the end of the third decade of Communist rule in China considerable centralization had taken place, and the foundations of local administration appeared to be settled. Informal arrangements indicated that the dual system of party and state apparatus had replaced the fusion of the Cultural Revolution, though the new Constitution of 1975 was needed to ratify this development.

Local government in the People's Republic is a vital extension of state and party power and facilitates the management of society, the economy, public security, and national defense. Modern China has achieved a degree of control over the population barely dreamed of by the strongest historical dynasties. Peking's success can be explained only in part by its organization of coercion. Efficient and honest administration at local levels recognizes the importance of public participation in making decisions. The fallibility of local elites is balanced against the emphasis on "serving the people" and encouragement of local initiatives. Despite Mao Tse-tung's continuous stress on "struggle and contradiction," the traditional Chinese ethos of harmony still finds expression in the balance between local and national priorities, and elite guidance and mass democracy. Local government, similar to other aspects of China's social and political development, tends to be a unique response to specific problems informed by a general ideological ethos which mixes Maoism with some traditional values. As such, the lessons of the Chinese experience may be limited to China herself, and then only to a particular period in her modernization.

Since the death of Mao Tse-tung on 9 September 1976, broad policy and structural changes have been initiated by the new leadership. Revolutionary committees in non-governmental units were abolished in 1978. In the new Organic Law for Local People's Congresses and Local People's Governments (adopted on 1 July 1979 by the National People's Congress), no mention is made of the revolutionary committees. Beginning in 1980, the system of local government will closely resemble that of the period of the 1950s. A major innovation will be an electoral system which specifies secret ballots at all levels. In several local elections in late 1979, it was also specified that there were to be more candidates than offices, so that a more democratic competition could emerge. These and other changes in the legal system have been justified as necessary antidotes to the confusion and disorder of the Cultural Revolution.

NOTES

1. *Red Flag*, no. 3 (1967).
2. *Communist China 1967* (Hong Kong: Union Research Institute, 1969), p. 131.
3. *Red Flag*, No. 14 (1968).
4. *Communist China 1968* (Hong Kong: Union Research Institute, 1969), 130.
5. *Peking Review* (20 December 1974): 13.
6. *Chung kung nien pao 1973* [Communist China Year Book], 2 vols. (Taipei: Institute for the Study of Chinese Communist Affairs, 1973), 1:40.
7. *China Reconstructs* (August 1973): 2.
8. *Peking Review* (13 December 1974): 13.
9. Ibid.

Other Asia

Harry J. Friedman*

38

Local governments in most of Third World Asia were never marked by any great degree of constitutional autonomy, although some were subject to occasional loosening of central government bonds and all were able to exercise varying degrees of autonomy whenever central governments failed to maintain physical control. Despite the minimal legal autonomy of the past, the trend in recent years has been toward still more centralized control.

This trend has not been merely generalized and abstract. Rather, particular types of changes have marked the movement toward tighter reins at the center. These have taken the form of new or modified economic institutions, bureaucratic structures, actions against regional ethnic groups, and even rhetorical devices.

CHANGES INVOLVING CENTRALIZATION

In the first place, national governments are striving to emphasize primarily economic change, not social or political development at the local level, in contrast with some of the earlier programs in the late 1950s and early 1960s. In that period, spokemen frequently would make public statements concerning the need for social and political "breakthroughs" in their age-old "traditional" societies. They did not deny economic problems. Instead, they stressed "prerequisites" for "progress."

As a consequence of these emphases, many countries adopted "community development" and various types of "extension" programs, ostensibly stressing social changes at the local level. Later, the same governments, assisted and sometimes prodded by Western technical assistance officials, moved to what they often saw as a "next step," the creation of formal local councils to supplement and then replace the more general and less integrated institutions begun during community development phases.

*Professor of Political Science, University of Hawaii.

The local councils approach stressed the interaction of government bureaucrats and elected local officials in the same governing bodies. While this approach evolved before long into merely another extension of the administrative arm of central governments, in their first stages these councils were intended partly to provide additional arenas for the politicization of local populaces. Indeed, for a short time, they did serve as channels for an increasing rate of demands from historically nonpoliticized villagers.

It may have been these early signs of articulation, or it may have been simply the increased national dissatisfaction with the slowness and maldistribution of economic gains that prompted central governments to downgrade the importance of the local councils approach. In most places, the bodies were never formally abolished, but in some they were "reorganized" into different patterns, and in others they were left to languish with limited financial resources and with emphasis obviously placed elsewhere.

No less apparent is the accelerating increase in bureaucratic structures, with administrative "solutions" to local problems from "the top" or center. These are intended to substitute for alleged "inefficient," or "corrupt," or "fragmented" processes that are derived from a variety of local political traditions.

This is not to say that the "bureaucratic" approach, instead of the 'political" approach, is a new or different element in local government. On the contrary, it has always been present and in modern times may always have been dominant, particularly in former colonies, that is, most Asian countries. The current tendency, however, is the apparent attitude of most central governments toward their local systems. They seem to have given up on attempts to reverse the old reliance on administration as a dominant form of governance and instead have attempted to justify a heavy reliance on bureaucracies as a "need."

Reduced Participation

In so doing, central governments have reduced the extent of political participation in national decision making. By permitting fewer forms of local political processes, by attempting to subsume more of them under an umbrella of unified bureaucratic structures, central governments administer policies *to* local levels far more than they permit themselves to be influenced *by* the variations of local institutions.

Part and parcel of this renewed emphasis on bureaucratic government at the local level is the use of government officials for most planning activities. For a brief period in the 1950s and 1960s there were attempts in a number of Asian countries to involve popular institutions deliberately in planning processes. Just as models of social and political development gave way to exclusive use of economic models, however, so has participation in planning been replaced by administrative planning.

Some additional changes in local government, growing out of increasing centralization, resemble the pattern of increased bureaucratization but are based on different reasons and take slightly different forms. These are the attempts to suspend local control of political processes when a regional group within a country is in active opposition to the political powers at the center. In such circumstances, central bureaucracies may also become predominant in a particular locale, but they are there not so much to implement a national policy as to suppress or eliminate the local power. Sometimes the military is the chief bureaucracy in use, but sometimes it supplements, or is supplemented by, a central civilian agency.

Dual Governments

Local government under these conditions sometimes becomes two different types of creatures simultaneously. On the one hand, it may be nothing more than central administrators acting ''locally'' on a short- or long-range basis, an ''official'' local government, as it were. On the other hand, there may also be a local government not recognized by the center but holding authority granted to it by limited portions of the citizenry and exercising power over, perhaps, a larger portion of the regional population. This description does not necessarily encompass only a movement in open rebellion. It may also include a focus of discontent not yet coalesced sufficiently to be recognized as a unified opposition to the ''official'' government. A continuum could be drawn expressing different versions of such a ''dual'' system, ranging from scattered ''vigilante'' groups to large-scale, organized, competing ''governments.''

Public Pronouncements

Along with these various actions limiting the autonomy of local governments in most countries of Third World Asia is a changed form of rhetoric, public pronouncements which set the tone and establish the frame of reference for policy decisions. Several ''themes'' appear to be fairly common in recent years.

One type of statement affecting local government begins with the same ideas affecting central governments in some countries: politicians are ruining the country; they're corrupt; they're getting in the way of those who are only seeking to carry out their duties; they merely talk and don't act; they're selfishly seeking gain only for themselves, and so on.

In contrast, the public rhetoric of top leaders stresses opposite qualities of appointed officials: they're trained, skillful, efficient, selfless, and so forth. Generally speaking, the positive adjectives are applied only to those at or near the top of administrative hierarchies, not those considered to be further down the line. Again, this is in keeping with the trend toward greater centralization of authority and power at increasingly higher levels.

Additionally, there seems to be an increasing attempt to convey an image of ''new'' types of government officials, with particular emphasis on a picture of those capable of combining efficiency with reliance on contemporary technology, such as computerized systems of administration, electronic communication, all-jet airlines, and short-haul helicopters. The word most often applied with pride to those who utilize these instruments is "technocrats." The implication is that technocrats are capable of operating governments in much better fashion for the good of the country than are politicians and their administrative underlings.

Most of the foregoing is, of course, applied to the changes in central government systems. The relation to local government, however, is that technocracy, with its emphasis on a combination of technology and bureaucratic efficiency, requires local levels more easily manipulated, more easily controlled, and more in line with the types of personnel presumably operating the total system at the top.

In the Philippines, Indonesia, Malaysia, and Pakistan, particularly, local governments find themselves subject to attempts to eliminate deviation and autonomy. In response, some local government leaders try to resist at least some of those attempts, and the overall picture, therefore, is one of uneven and erratic moves toward tight centralization.

CURRENT TRENDS

Substituting for active movements toward political participation in significant decision making, local governments have instead focused attention on economic institutions of various types. In most cases the specific action has been dependent on the most immediate problem pressing for attention.

Economic Institutions

One form of action has been creation of, or reemphasis on, local-level cooperatives. Both Indonesia and the Philippines, for example, have made use of this mechanism in recent years, although cooperatives have not had as long a history of effort there as in the former British colonies—India, Pakistan, and so on.

Indonesia tends to have a unique approach to the use of the institution, particularly when economic crisis provides a reason for the central government to move in vigorously on local arrangements. Such a period, for example, occurred in 1973, when rice shortages compelled the national government to enlarge its domestic procurement programs drastically. As Allan A. Samson has written about the resulting loss of autonomy from these local institutions:

The government's procurement effort was channelled through BUUD (Badan Usaha Unit Desa—Village Business Unit), originally intended as a series of autonomous rural cooperatives, but which came to be regulated by local government officials who received their orders and specified targets from higher in the national bureaucracy. It was the function of BUUD to regulate agricultural production and administer procurement targets. Theoretically 10% of the farmers' crops were to be sold to BUUD. In many areas, however, overzealous officials demanded 20% to 30%. In early June as it became apparent that sufficient rice was not being stockpiled, the government banned the inter-provincial transport of rice in an attempt to force farmers to sell to local BUUD. Many district heads even forbade district trade.[1]

In the Philippines the martial law regime of President Marcos has created the *samahang nayon*, or farmers' cooperative, which in some ways has been subject to less coercion than the Indonesian version. In this case, however, the Philippine cooperatives may be faced with a loss of local autonomy for other reasons. Cooperatives, although frequently an appealing device to political leaders seeking rural economic panaceas, are enormously complex social institutions. Their history in South Asia, even up to modern times, is a well-documented version of the difficulties they pose for their advocates.

Thailand seems to be moving in a slightly opposite direction, primarily by providing increased funds to try to *ensure* greater local government viability.[2] Making money available to rural areas is not unique, of course, in Asian countries where peasant farmers have long been among the neediest persons in the world. To use such funds for strengthening local government, however, is not common. This new policy of making a substantial sum available to sub-district (*tambon*) councils "for immediate relief of rural distress" has been accompanied by attempts at administrative and investment decentralization. The money was used for such public construction works as canals and levees to attack directly problems of rural unemployment, not unlike what the Bangkok *Post* once called "this Rooseveltian 'New Deal' welfare-type public spending."

Even Thailand, whose leaders talked of aiming for the kind of national planning processes that work "from the *tambon* upwards," just as some other countries advocated in the 1950s and 1960s, does not go all out for local autonomy. While needs of *tambon* development are actively sought and included in planning, nevertheless *national* government programs and personnel are utilized for implementation. Reliance on local institutions, or even strengthening of local institutions in order to be able to provide them later with more autonomy, is at a fairly rudimentary stage, despite apparent intentions to provide more local strength and autonomy than is the trend in other countries.

In other countries of South and Southeast Asia, too, the difference between economic and political programs at the local level is not really as significant a type of distinction as it might be. Rather, the difference lies in emphasis and timing. By way of illustration, Malaysia is one state where emphases have varied from a more equal mixture of economic and sociopolitical local development to one concerned more heavily with economic development. During the early 1960s, locally oriented programs included digging of major drainage canals, tree-replanting programs, land resettlement, road construction and repairs, as well as school and library expansions, health clinic establishments, local elections, and even assistance for religious instruction. In recent years, suspension of local elections, cessation of moves toward local councils, and the replacement of "self-help" community development projects with administered rural development programs is more characteristic of Malaysia's picture.[3]

Pakistan, too, which once experienced heavily the same sweep of local "democracy," voluntary organizations, and "grass-roots participation," that some of its neighbors did, now manages to focus attention almost solely on rural economic programs, leaving debates over political change to the national level. In fact, the provincial level of government is as "local" as political strains may be felt.

Increased Bureaucratization

Perhaps marking the trend away from local autonomy and toward greater control by the central government as much as any single factor is the increasing visibility of bureaucratic structures. Again, this is by no means a complete novelty. In this respect, too, there has been a long history. Yet, the periodic establishment of councils, assemblies, and boards throughout the region indicates there has been an equally strong desire in recent times for a variety of representative, sometimes elective, bodies.

Now, however, governments are creating new bureaucracies at the local level at a fairly rapid clip. What makes this especially significant is the nature of the bureaucratic model as a form of organization. As an "ideal type," in the classic terms of Max Weber, bureaucracies, with their rigid compartmentalization, career-oriented professionalism, sharp divisions of authority, and specialization, all packaged in the hierarchical, traditionally pyramidal form, represent the most highly suitable structures for establishing and maintaining control functions.

In Indonesia the use of bureaucracies seems to carry a touch of irony. On the one hand, demands from the top for implementation of programs, particularly agricultural ones, combined with the heavy influx of military officers in administrative positions, are requiring increasing amounts of coercion to "govern" locally. At the same time, however, experienced and trained administrative personnel are spread thinly and, as Gary E. Hansen has pointed out, are sorely in need of help, particularly at the sub-regional level.[4]

While it's true that Indonesia has not moved drastically from emphases on social development at the local level to economic change alone, as is true in some other places, nevertheless the stress on bureaucracies is still apparent. In 1974, the central government launched its second five-year plan with extensive provision for such local-level projects as primary schools, rural housing, sub-district health centers, and rural drinking water facilities.[5] Yet, little or no attention is given to revitalizing village decision-making processes, or extending the potential for autonomy in district and sub-district councils. On the contrary, politics seems destined "to take a back seat to economics."[6]

The point here is not that the mere establishment of various institutions resembling ''democracy'' will yield a viable, autonomous, local government. In fact, too much attention may be paid in Indonesia to the *appearance* of bureaucratic responsiveness to public demands, instead of *actual* responsiveness to, or even encouragement of, public demands. What would be a surer sign of local-level strength would be the establishment of conditions requiring administrators to gain the public's confidence and trust by increased responsiveness. This can be produced, perhaps, only by authentic, indigenous, local institutions of complexity and strength. [7]

In Thailand, too, there is a long history of local government as administration, implemented from the top through bureaucratic organizations originating in the central government, the common pattern in most of Third World Asia. The far-reaching changes at the center since the student revolution of 1973, however, may introduce some local government changes. Again, Thailand may be the one situation where events are moving to more autonomy and more participation, but less bureaucratization.

Furthermore, when movements toward change sweep a country, there is a tendency for change to take place even in areas where there is no direct action. Local levels are seeking outlets for demands under the encouragement of more widespread institutional participation generally, particularly in the universities. Regional universities, outside the traditional Bangkok setting, are engaging actively in direct community development projects, not merely generating specialized knowledge for use by others. These impacts on local forms of government are still in too early a stage to see just how much change eventually will take place, but when there are varieties of institutional activities under way, even the old-line bureaucracies become more active, responsive, and change-oriented. [8]

While the trends in Indonesia, Malaysia, and elsewhere are significant, increased bureaucratization of local government may be more pronounced in the Philippines than in other places. This may be true simply because past experiments with locally elected, representative institutions were familiar, far-reaching, and widespread. Any change from them would naturally appear to be magnified. On the other hand, appearance alone does not account for the total impact. The martial law regime in the Philippines is becoming increasingly bureaucratized in all respects. Continuing the trend at the local level is merely a matter of consistency.

Changes in the Philippines have taken place at all levels. First there was the establishment of a Department of Local Government and Community Development for the first time at the cabinet level. Then there was the division of the country into eleven regions, with a corresponding attempt to downgrade the importance of the provinces, probably because their governors represented competing political power. In the name of improved implementation of development programs, each region was assigned a presidential regional officer for development (PROD) to supervise all appropriate programs within the particular region. (A counterpart of PRODs has been the establishment of COPEs, coordinating officers for program execution, who are responsible for coordinating individual programs on a nationwide basis. These, however, are not local government officials.)[9]

It is at the sub-regional level—indeed, at the sub-provincial level—that the most far-reaching bureaucratization is occurring in the Philippines. The long-standing electoral process for local officials has been scrapped, and all local government officials are in the process of being appointed throughout the seventy-five provinces. Former *barrio* councils have been replaced by *barangays*, or citizens' assemblies, which are meant to reflect identity with ancient organizations in the Philippines, dating back to pre-Spanish times.

No less an authority than the secretary of the Department of Local Government and Community Development has written that the *barangays* originally were established by the martial law regime to be consultative bodies for the government's programs but are now used as implementing agencies for programs decided elsewhere.[10] This may be in tune with the central government's desire to seek successful implementation wherever possible, but it will doubtless condition the citizenry to avoid local autonomy over time.

While the secretary has contended that the establishment of the department enables rural local government to increase its bargaining power at national levels, the decrease in local policy-making power may ensure that there are no rural local interests to be represented at the national level. All interests very well could be submerged into policies made at the top. The same trend is discernible, too, in urban local government with consolidation of units in the Manila metropolitan area into one unified whole late in 1975. Nationally centralized control is assured with the appointment of Imelda Romualdez Marcos, wife of the president, as governor of the new integrated municipal government.

Anti-Regional Autonomy

If the meaning of local government is not confined merely to formal legal structures, then the relation of regional groups as local "governments" to a national picture become more evident. Actions taken by central governments against regional dissidents represent still another way in which local autonomy has been decreasing. Furthermore, much of the centrally instigated change directed at local levels is an attempt to find additional ways to integrate all aspects of a society into a common framework.

An alternative way to treat complaining and dissenting minorities would be to decide that not all elements of a society have to be totally integrated as soon as possible. It may be that insufficient attention has been paid to changing definitions of national aspirations in the contemporary world. Many societies contain groups that define the national situation differently from those who exercise central government power. These groups see themselves, frequently, as alternative governments in "local" areas, not as subordinate governments in a hierarchy. Yet, they do not necessarily favor a complete break or secession. Rather, they see advantages to both sides if they can remain within a nationally unified framework, but with as much autonomy as possible.

The "instinct" of most central governments is to try to force the "straying lambs" back into the fold. This frequently stiffens the resistance of the local minorities and drives them further away. Again, an alternative plan, almost never implemented in the area, would have central governments admit some justice in the local version of the situation and permit a minority to define some conditions for staying within the national boundaries. Such a policy could persuade the local government that there is no desire and no attempt to destroy it but rather a recognition that local minority leaders are often legitimate representatives of local interests and not "subversives."

There are numerous ways to analyze the relation of dissenting minorities to the national polity, of course, but there is a strong reason to study it in the context of "local government" changes. When all is said and done, perhaps the single most important point about local government is not the nature of structures, processes, and functions, but rather the questions of who governs and how and why and with what kind of consequences, just as these are the major questions for any kind of government.

The answers to those questions do make a difference in the nature of local government. In Pakistan, for example, the province of East Pakistan was once a local government and contained other local governments, all of them subject to pressures from the center to conform to centrally directed goals and policies. In fact, the "center" very often consisted of appropriate goals and policies for West Pakistan, rather than a total nation-state.

At the height of the conflict between the two wings, the "Six Points" proposed by East Pakistan constituted a manifesto for autonomy within the boundaries of national unity. It's true that some would regard that statement as advocating so much autonomy that the nation would no longer be regarded as such. Given the ultimate consequences, however, it would seem that in some respects Pakistan might have been better off to provide maximum autonomy if its goal was to retain East Pakistan. The establishment of Bangladesh was perhaps a sign that such an alternative is always a possibility in other countries where strong local dissenting governments may be forced to seek independence rather than merely greater autonomy.

In the Philippines, large parts of the southern island of Mindanao are governed by Muslim minorities claiming to represent cultures, social organizations, and political traditions different from the central government. They, too, contend that they do not seek independence but rather more oportunity to conduct their ways of life in a manner that they understand better than the distant "strangers" in the north. The central government is continuing to try to crush what it defines as a rebellion and apparently great amounts of force are required in the attempt, with some reports indicating that entire towns have been devastated in what is little short of an internal war.

Similar situations are not unknown in Indonesia, Thailand, and Malaysia, although the circumstances may be different in each case. The most current and prominent appears to be in Thailand, where the almost classic description of dissent fits the northeastern part of the country—lower economic levels, alternative ideologies, entry of outside national states, and so forth. Despite the changes that have taken place in other aspects of the central government's relations with local government since the student-created changes of 1973, the ways of dealing with northeastern Thailand seem to remain the same, with continuing attempts to tie the area more closely to other parts of the country.

Indonesia and Malaysia went through periods of wrestling with centrifugal pulls at earlier dates, in each case utilizing strong military and police action to counteract minority movements. In both cases, the center prevailed and continues to, but whether the central government's problems are "solved" in some ultimate sense is hardly likely. Centrifugal pressures continue in both countries and the use of force from above to maintain governmental processes seems almost to become a permanent feature of the political landscape.

Changes in Rhetoric

The remaining aspect of the changing trend in local government may not be the most powerful, but it may be the most indicative of the kind of trend involved. It consists of the explanations and rationalizations used to describe and justify government actions. The new rhetoric consists of arguments both against past conditions and favoring new arrangements.

Some of the emphasis has been on blaming politicians and political parties for past failures in attempts at modernization and economic development. At the local government level this has taken the form of criticizing parties for politicizing local traditions, presumably "purer" in their original forms. Pakistan, Malaysia, and the Philippines have put particular stress on this form of policy statements. Other rhetorical changes, such as in Indonesia, have tended to downgrade the more obvious types of ideological devices, not necessarily eliminating ideology, as R. William Liddle has pointed out, but rather foregoing its more "frantic" features.[11]

What is favored, rhetorically, can be surmised from the other types of activities in the new local government trends. Public statements tend to favor such ideas as "efficiency" and "technocracy." Too much emphasis on politics not only interferes with wise decision making, so these opinions say, but also interferes with the smooth execution of plans formulated by experts. As indicated earlier in this chapter, too, "technocrats" are considered to be the wave of the future for solving problems. In the Philippines, where the term is used most frequently and widely, technocracy is considered to be the application of modern, scientifically based technical knowledge, an impossible process, it is contended, when politics is given free rein to deal with public policymaking.

On the local government scene, an example of technocracy is the use of special coordinating officials, designated by the kind of acronyms (PRODs and COPEs) that imply "systems" at work, not merely individual bureaucrats. In turn, they are assisted, presumably, by technology in the necessary "feedback" for information processing and "corrected" policy decisions. A computerized feedback system called "Monitoring of Vital Economic Reforms" (MOVER) is supposedly part of the technocracy which is an "improvement" over older, political forms of local government decision making. The chief danger, it seems, in relying on technocratic manifestations of government is that it may be relying too heavily on an appearance of scientific solution rather than a demonstrated scientific solution. The result could very well be shutting off needed criticism on the grounds that "science knows best," without actually utilizing scientific feedback as needed.

CONCLUSION

There is a risk in seeking to identify changing trends in local government across too many national boundaries, even in a common region. The fact is there are continuing variations among those compared and a considerable amount of imprecision exists in statements purporting to make widely applicable generalizations. This risk is magnified when an attempt is made to project the trends into the future. Too many elements obviously interact to make general statements of trends outdated in even a near future. It is difficult enough to project such trends for one country, let alone many.

Still, observers seem to agree generally on the direction of changes outlined here. Increased centralization and decreased local autonomy, increased bureaucratization and decreased political participation—all have been noted by others for more than one local political system. Continuation of this trend could deny, perhaps permanently, to local populations the opportunity to live under strong, viable, experimental, local governments.

NOTES

1. Allan A. Samson, "Indonesia 1973: A Climate of Concern," *Asian Survey* 14 (February 1974): 161-62.

2. Bangkok *Post*, 5 April 1975.

3. Marvin L. Rogers, "The Politicization of Malay Villagers: National Integration or Disintegration?" *Comparative Politics* 7 (January 1975).

4. Gary E. Hansen, "Indonesia 1974: A Momentous Year," *Asian Survey* 15 (February 1975): 155; and *The Politics and Administration of Rural Development in*

Indonesia: The Case of Agriculture (Berkeley: Center for South and Southeast Asia Studies, University of California, 1973), pp. 131-35.

5. Hansen, "Indonesia 1974," p. 155.

6. Ibid., p. 156.

7. Donald K. Emmerson, "Bureaucratic Alienation in Indonesia: The Director-General's Dilemma," in *Political Participation in Modern Indonesia*, ed. R. William Liddle (New Haven: Yale University Southeast Asia Studies, 1973), especially pp. 101-06.

8. For comparisons of districts involving different rates of change, see Clark D. Neher, *The Dynamics of Politics and Administration in Rural Thailand* (Athens: Ohio University Center for International Studies, 1974), especially pp. 27-31.

9. Alejandro Melchor, "The *Do Tank* Machinery of the Government," *The Fookien Times Yearbook 1973* (New York: International Publications Services, 1974), pp. 185-88.

10. José A. Roño, "Contributions of Local Government to Rural Economic Development," *The Fookien Times Yearbook 1973*.

11. R. William Liddle, "Modernizing Indonesian Politics," in Liddle, ed., *Political Participation in Modern Indonesia*, pp. 177-200.

LATIN
AMERICA

BRAZIL
OTHER COUNTRIES

Brazil

*Diogo Lordello de Mello**

39

Brazil is a federal country composed of twenty-two states, a federal capital district, and three federal territories. All states and territories are divided into municipalities, of which there were 3,972 in 1978. A municipality comprises both the rural areas and the urban communities within its boundaries. The seat of a municipality is called a city, regardless of its size, and the seat of a district, which is an administrative subdivision of a municipality, is called a village. There are, therefore, only three levels of government in Brazil: federal, state, and municipal.

HISTORICAL BACKGROUND

After the revolution of 1930, a new constitution was adopted that began a trend, that continues today, of reducing the powers of the states in favor of the central government and the municipalities. The 1934 Constitution made the municipalities more autonomous by calling for the election of the mayor and not only of the council, as was the case before in many states; by reserving certain taxes to the municipalities, thus making a tripartite division of taxation; and by making the municipalities free to organize and run their services and to spend their revenues.

The 1934 Constitution was soon superseded by the 1937 *coup d'état*, which put Brazil under the Vargas dictatorship. All elective offices were suppressed, including the municipal ones, and a highly centralized system of government was established. Yet, the municipalities retained their newly acquired tax powers, and the central government extended to them its effort to modernize

*Director, Instituto Brasileiro de Administração Municipal, Rio de Janeiro; formerly Mayor of Brasìlia, 1961. This essay is based on the author's longer "Municipal Reform in Brazil Since 1946," a paper submitted to the Public Administration Division of the United Nations in 1972 for its Working Group on Major Efforts on Municipal Reform in the Last 25 Years.

the administrative machinery. This prepared them for greater responsibilities in the years to come.

The Municipal Reform of 1946

With the overthrow of the dictatorship in 1945, municipal autonomy was again included in 1946 among the basic principles of the constitution, which again meant that the federal government could intervene in the states in order to maintain or restore that autonomy. A second objective of the 1946 reform, the amplification of municipal tax powers, was important in the sense that municipalities were given absolute discretion in levying, collecting, and utilizing the taxes reserved to them. A major change from the 1934 Constitution was the transfer of the tax on industries and professions entirely to the municipalities (the previous system was a fifty-fifty share with the states). The third and last objective of the reform was the most important as far as the typical Brazilian municipality was concerned. A system of shared taxes was set up according to which the municipalities were to participate in certain federal taxes and in the proceeds of state revenues.

A main reason for this tax-sharing system, besides strengthening municipal finances in general, was to pump federal money into the economy of the country's backward regions. Although the share of each municipality appeared small when 10 percent of the federal income tax was divided by the large number of municipalities in existence, it represented a bounty to the poor municipalities, which thereby received what was soon called their "minimum wage." For almost half of them, their income tax share was their most important source of income; for many it was their only significant income. Furthermore, when multiplied by the large number of municipalities of a state, this revenue became a substantial injection of money into the state economy. Some states soon found out that they could channel more federal funds by multiplying their municipalities.

Appraisal of the 1946 Reform

The prevailing concept of local autonomy meant that no supervision was to be exercised over the local governments by the higher levels. Thus, legal equality of the local governments with regard to the state and the federal government was the natural outcome. Also, the 1946 reform did not depart from the long tradition of treating all municipalities on equal terms, regardless of differences in their actual capabilities to exercise the powers granted them. This symmetry has been pointed out by many students of Brazilian institutions as an absurd and undesirable feature of the Brazilian local government system. Indeed, it was a pity that concentration on other considerations led the 1946 reformers to overlook this matter entirely. The list of municipal functions was so broad that even the smallest municipalities had concurrent powers with the states and the federal government in providing local services. Since the financial resources put at the disposal of the municipalities did not equal these theoretical powers, the devolution became senseless in many cases. Besides, by allowing concurrent municipal, state, and even federal action in a same functional area, the system made it extremely difficult to determine responsibility for a certain function.

Since municipal powers with respect to the two other levels of government were defined in the Constitution itself, the Supreme Court was soon called upon to decide on several questions arising from the tripartite division of powers relating to municipal taxation. Its decisions in taxation matters involving the municipalities had far-reaching consequences in broadening the scope of certain taxes and therefore strengthening municipal finances. As to the position of the municipalities before the states and the central government, the reiterated view of the court has been that the municipalities enjoyed complete administrative or hierarchical autonomy: mayors and councils were not subordinate to any higher authority but owed obedience only to valid laws. Further, in order to be valid, a federal or state law touching on municipal matters has to respect municipal powers as described in the Constitution and not be against the "peculiar interest" of the municipality, as interpreted by the court.

This construction makes it clear that the validity of laws passed by the municipalities could be tested against state and federal laws, and even against the state constitutions. Indeed, in several instances, a municipal law has been declared valid against a state statute or constitution. The hierarchy of federal or state over municipal laws prevailed only in the case of concurring powers or when in conflict with express federal or state powers. In summary, had it not been for the Supreme Court, the local government system created in 1946 certainly never would have liberated itself from much of the stigma of centralization and tutelage it had inherited.

Since the power to create new municipalities was used rather liberally by most states, the number of municipalities increased from 1,668 in 1946 to 4,114 in 1964. This multiplication of municipalities had both positive and negative effects. On the positive side, in a vast country with many underdeveloped areas like Brazil, the incorporation of even poor municipalities is perhaps the easiest, most democratic, and possibly the cheapest way of bringing the presence of government to the area. Tradition has shown that, in Brazil, only the existence of a municipal government with its minimum governmental apparatus and its organized political life will make the state and federal government interested in providing services to the area. On the negative side, a few states abused their powers to create new municipalities by playing pork barrel politics—creating local offices to be manipulated by the state political bosses. Municipalities were thus created with an eye on the federal income tax shares to which they were automatically entitled. These abuses had a bad effect on the image of local government in Brazil.

Two things could have made the 1946 reform far more effective. One was a clear division of responsibilities among the three levels of government for the provision of local services; the other was a scheme for implementation, of which technical assistance should have been a major element. Because the municipalities had such extensive legal powers to provide services, the functional boundaries between the different governmental levels were often blurred. The municipalities either did not have the financial means to match these powers or had to compete with the state or federal governments to render services in the fields of education, health, agricultural development, and even public utilities. Therefore the municipal government could not really be valued as a purveyor of services. Its role became eminently political in several senses, including the fact that it was, after all, a broker between the local community and the higher levels of government in securing local services. Professor Frank Sherwood has called attention to the high importance of the political outputs of the Brazilian municipality in comparison with its service outputs.[1] This situation tends to alienate members of the municipal system, since the political outputs are scarce in terms of resources and citizen's participation. The local governments become very much an instrument to be manipulated by the higher-level politicians, with whom municipal leaders have to go along in order to secure services to the community.

The lack of an implementation scheme was perhaps more tragic. Had such a scheme been devised, many adjustments certainly would have been made as the problems emerged. Instead, every agency or institution with a part in the implementation process worked on its own, without any coordination or terms of reference but those contained in the federal constitution. Since the central government had called upon itself the task of revitalizing municipal life and institutions, it would have been perfectly consistent with this aim to develop an implementation scheme which, among other things, would have included a grants-in-aid system to stimulate the states to guide the municipalities and provide them with technical assistance.

This does not mean that the 1946 municipal reform was a failure, far from it. The reform was an extraordinary accomplishment in many respects, from the point of view of strengthening local government and of enhancing democratic institutions. The municipalities, especially the more prosperous ones, did their share in accelerating economic growth and modernization. They could have done more had it not been for those two grave omissions of the reform.

THE POST-1964 PERIOD

The grave political and economic conditions that prevailed in Brazil after the resignation of President Quadros in 1961 led to the revolutionary movement of 31 March 1964, which introduced profound changes in the political and governmental institutions of the country. Among the avowed aims of the movement were curbing inflation; restoring governmental authority; strengthening the executive branch of the government; fighting corruption; resuming the level of economic growth attained in the second half of the 1950s; administrative reform; overhauling the national tax system; and modernizing the governmental process, including speedier legislative procedures.

On the political level, the movement is characterized by a deep distrust of political activities on traditional terms, a marked reserve against the efficiency of legislative bodies, and an overly dominant concern for national security (that is, the defense of the state against subversion from both within and without). In the name of national security and of the moralizing objectives of the movement, federal powers have been greatly increased both legally and de facto, and a considerable degree of centralism has been introduced in the governmental system of the country, at the expense of state and municipal autonomy.

Several changes have been introduced with the objective of promoting accountability and controlling the utilization of public funds by the municipalities. There also has been a continuous effort to gear the municipalities to the policies of the central government for speeding up economic and social development. This has led to a certain blurring of jurisdictional boundaries in many aspects of governmental activities in such a way that it is often difficult to identify the source of decision in many actions that are apparently taken by the local governments.

At the same time, the basic aspects of the municipal system have been maintained. These include the council-mayor system of government; the tier system; the separation of powers between mayor and council; the direct election of mayors (with exceptions) and councilmen; the creation of municipalities by the states (although now subject to federally prescribed conditions); protection of municipal autonomy against state intervention in municipal affairs; administrative and fiscal autonomy (with limitations); and the former functions of the municipalities.

It is more appropriate to speak of *reforms* than of a municipal reform since 1964. Changes have been introduced piecemeal, without any systematic plan or scheme, often by trial and error, and as part of broader reforms. The only terms of reference for the changes introduced are the general aims of the revolutionary movement mentioned above.

The Tax Reform of 1966

The first and most important of the reforms bearing upon the municipalities was the tax reform of 1966, perhaps the most meaningful the country has experienced so far. Its main objective was to streamline the tax system and make it rest more on economic rather than legalistic or purely fiscal bases. In the process, however, the municipalities lost several of their taxes, among these the lucrative tax on industries and professions and the tax on transfer of real property, which went back to the states. They kept only the taxes on urban real estate and on services, but the latter has maximum rates set by federal law.

The power to levy the rural land tax was transferred to the federal government, although 80 percent of its proceeds are transferred to the municipalities. Also, a national tax code was adopted in which strict definitions have been made of the conditions for levying every tax, fee, and special assessment. To compensate the municipalities for the loss imposed on them by the tax reform, they were, given a share of 20 percent of the state sales tax. This immediately became the most important source of revenue for the prosperous municipalities.

At the same time, the system for sharing the federal taxes on income and industrial products with the municipalities was changed, first to reduce the income tax percentage to be shared from 15 to 10 percent and, second, to make the distribution depend on population instead of the grant of an equal share to each municipality, as before. Of the Municipal Participation Fund, as this revenue-sharing scheme became known, at least 50 percent was to be used for capital expenses. It was subject to strict accountability to the Federal Tribunal of Accounts, which was made its guardian and empowered to calculate the share of each municipality. The fund's money was deposited automatically in a special account in the Bank of Brazil, and it was not included in the federal budget. The theory was that the money belonged to the municipalities and did not constitute federal revenue. Payment to the municipalities was also automatic, depending only on the authorization of the tribunal, and the federal treasury had nothing to do with it. This seemed a great improvement over the previous system, for it represented a guarantee against the uncertainties that had characterized this source of revenue in the five or six years before the change was introduced. The states were also included, and a State Participation Fund was created. Distribution was on the basis of the inverse of their per capita income. Since the state capitals of the northeast suffered tremendously with the reform, this same criterion was adopted for the capitals, instead of the population basis established for the other municipalities.

The new tax system had hardly gone into effect when it was abruptly changed on 30 December 1968 to reduce from 10 to 5 the percentage of income and industrial products taxes to be shared with the municipalities and the states. So, the next day the mayors of small municipalities awoke to find their budgets for the fiscal year that was to begin on 1 January 1969, slashed by as much as 20 to 45 percent. The same decree established that the resources from the Municipal Participation Fund should be used only in the functional areas included in the strategic development plan of the federal government. Furthermore, the fund was now considered *federal* money subject to inclusion in the federal budget. Although the Bank of Brazil continued as the distributing agency and the Federal Tribunal of Accounts as its guardian, its ultimate control was transferred to the federal treasury. These moves were justified as necessary to the fight against inflation. It was argued that the sums transferred were disproportionately large to be used at the will of the local governments.

Unlike its 1946 and 1961 predecessors, the tax reform of 1966 made the municipalities greatly dependent on the federal and state governments. The municipal income that is now raised by the municipalities from their own tax sources represents only a minor proportion of their total revenue. In the underdeveloped northeast, where more than a third of Brazil's municipalities are located, the revenue from the Municipal Participation Fund and the municipal share of the state sales tax accounted in 1969 for 65 to 80 percent of municipal revenues, according to a study made by the Brazilian Institute of Municipal Administration. Similarly, in the prosperous south, the percentages oscillated between 62 and 80, except for the larger cities. A grip on their finances from above is therefore the common fate of all municipalities.

This grip was made even tighter by the strict accountability imposed on the municipal governments. As mentioned, the Federal Tribunal of Accounts must pass on all expenditures incurred with the revenues from the Municipal Participation Fund. Detailed regulations have been set forth by the tribunal, which a large number of municipalities have been unable to observe for lack of trained personnel and adequate technical assistance. Relieved of most of its duties in relation to the pre-auditing of federal expenditures by the administrative reform of 1967, the tribunal has been able to devote most of its time to the control of the Municipal Participation Fund and to the enforcement of its regulations.

The Federal Constitution of 1967

The Federal Constitution of 1967, the first passed after the movement of March 1964, as well as its amended version of late 1969, empowered the states' tribunals of accounts or similar organs to audit the municipal accounts prior to the decision of a municipal council, which cannot reject a tribunal's recommendation against the approval of the accounts except by a two-thirds vote. This practically puts an end to the previous system under which control of municipal accounts was devolved upon the municipalities by the states.

Furthermore, the present Constitution has increased from two to six the cases in which a state can intervene in the municipalities, the additional cases referring to questions of accountability, non-observance of constitutional principles related to the organization and function of municipal government, corruption, political subversion, and failure to spend on primary education at least 20 percent of municipal revenues from taxes.

The incorporation of municipalities was made subject to federal regulation, although the states maintained the prerogative of incorporation. The inability of many municipalities to render satisfactory accounts to the Federal Tribunal of Accounts is leading to a review of present requirements of incorporation, so as to make them still more strict. In the minds of some people, the viability of a municipality tends to be equated to its ability to render these accounts and make good use of the Municipal Participation Fund.

Concern for national security led to the reestablishment of the appointment of the mayors of the state capitals, municipalities considered important for national security, and those located on the frontiers of Brazil. The number is less than 150, but they account for more than a third of the total urban population of the country, since almost all major cities are state capitals.

Many reforms introduced in the federal system of government and administration were also imposed on the states and municipalities by the Constitutions of 1967 and 1969, and by special laws. The most important refer to the strengthening of the executive at the expense of the state legislatures or municipal councils; the speeding up of the legislative process; the streamlining of the budgetary process and the supremacy of the executive in budgetary matters; the establishment of strict norms of conduct for the legislative bodies and their individual members; the calling of bids; the basic principles of civil service in relation to the merit system; tenure of office and retirement; and prohibition of revenue sharing with tax collectors and inspectors, used before as an incentive to increasing tax productivity.

These reforms were inspired mainly by three factors: a deliberate effort to strengthen the executive, a distrust of traditional politics and of the efficiency of legislative bodies in general, and a concern for accountability and morality that has permeated the 1964 movement from its inception. A still stronger executive has emerged from all these reforms at the three levels of government, as its power to initiate legislation on all fiscal, financial, and budgetary matters has become practically absolute. The chief executive can request urgency for the bills of his initiative (except codes) so that they can be voted swiftly. Amendents to bills dealing with financial or budgetary matters are not accepted if they increase the total level of expenditures proposed by the executive or if they change the objectives of a given project or program. The budget proposed by the executive cannot be rejected by the legislature or council under penalty of becoming law automatically. Deficitary budgets are prohibited.

In February of 1967 a decree-law on the responsibility and accountability of mayors and councilmen was passed which defined several cases of impeachment of mayors and councilmen by the municipal councils and which made into crimes punishable by the courts a long series of offenses against the municipal patrimony and some principles of financial, budgetary, and personnel administration, as well as the violation of valid federal, state, and municipal laws. Other offenses were listed which would lead to the impeachment of the mayor or councilmen by the council.

Federal and state relations with the municipalities have experienced a marked improvement since 1964 in terms of cooperation for rendering local services. Some loan and grants-in-aid programs were initiated which have made a significant contribution to the improvement of city life in many communities, especially in relation to water supply, housing, and other urban services. Now the federal government is using its powers to lead the municipalities into upgrading primary education. A minimum wage for teachers has been set and municipal revenues earmarked for education.

The modernizing potential of all these measures is considerable, but it is checked by the low cultural level of the population in many communities of the interior and by the lack of adequate orientation and technical assistance to the local governments. Here again we face the problem of implementation, as with the 1946 reform. The Ministry of the Interior, which was created in 1964, although in command of such powerful agencies as the Superintendency for the Development of the Northeast (SUDENE) and of the Amazon (SUDAM), and the National Housing Bank (BNH), is still without an adequate organization and without cadres to cope with the task of implementing the reform. Some of the most important and interesting programs of municipal development are under the Ministry of the Interior, such as the loan programs for housing, water, sewers, and local planning. The Federal Service for Housing and Urbanism (SERFHAU), created within the ministry to run the loan programs for local planning and to function as a federal technical assistance agency to the municipalities, was abolished in 1975.

The Ministry of Planning, absorbed with other great issues of national development, was unable, initially, to give the intellectual leadership that a municipal reform requires for its conception and implementation. Its Institute for Applied Economic Research, which is a kind of brain trust of the Ministry and of the federal government, could indeed make a valuable contribution to a systematic treatment of municipal reform, but the problem does not seem to have high priority in the ministry. Yet, in 1972, a Secretariat for Articulation with the States and Municipalities (SAREM) was created within the ministry and has been gaining considerable force as the main federal agency for inter-governmental relations.

In the meantime, an interesting phenomenon occurred with the Federal Tribunal of Accounts. Although its legal authority in relation to the Municipal Participation Fund does not go beyond auditing and accounting control, the tribunal took an increasing role in establishing criteria of convenience for the utilization of the fund, thus filling a power vacuum left by the Ministries of Planning and the Interior. This trend, however, has been checked by the Ministry of Planning; otherwise, the tribunal would have become a strange, de facto kind of ''Department of Local Government'' for all Brazilian municipalities. Indeed, the loudest voice that has been heard in Brazil in recent years on municipal affairs is that of the tribunal. Surprised, even shocked by the inability of many municipalities to render correct account of the Municipal Participation Fund, the tribunal, through some of its members, even advocated some drastic reforms of municipal institutions, such as the substitution of a manager for the elected mayor and stricter requirements for the incorporation of municipalities. In the volatile institutional climate of the country in its search for economic, social, and political development, these ideas may have a pleasant ring for those who value technocracy above local democracy and may therefore result in profound changes in the municipal system in Brazil. More recently, however, other members of the tribunal are tending toward a more understanding and didactic position for the agency.

Two rather innovative provisions were introduced in the 1967 Constitution and maintained by the constitutional amendment of 1969. One says that municipal organization may vary according to local peculiarities. The other empowers the federal government to establish metropolitan regions for the performance of services of common interest to a metropolitan area.

The first of these provisions has not yet been implemented. The long tradition of symmetry in municipal organization has prevented the states, at which the first provision is directed, to understand its real meaning and thus assign functions and powers to the municipalities according to their degree of economic and cultural development or to other factors indicative of their capacity to perform functions. Several states, failing to grasp even remotely the reach of the provision, limited themselves to transcribing it word for word in their constitutions and municipal organic laws, instead of making use of it. An application of the principle has been made by the Brazilian Institute of Municipal Administration in the draft of the municipal organic law of the state of Bahia, but the legal advisor to the legislative assembly refused to accept the innovation.

Metropolitan Regions

The institutionalization of metropolitan areas, after several years of study and discussion by the interested ministries—Planning, Interior, and Justice—was finally the object of Complementary Law No. 14, of 8 June 1973, which regulated the constitutional provision for the establishment of metropolitan regions. Eight such regions were created by that law: São Paulo (in the state of São Paulo), Belo Horizonte (in Minas Gerais), Porto Alegre (Rio Grande do Sul), Recife (Pernambuco), Salvador (Bahia), Curitiba (Paraná), Belém (Pará) and Fortaleza (Ceará). Later, Complementary Law No. 20 of 1 July 1974, which joined the States of Guanabara and Rio de Janeiro into a single state (Rio de Janeiro), created the ninth metropolitan region, Rio de Janeiro.

The main points covered by Complementary Law No. 14 are:

1. The enumeration of the municipalities in each region, the number of which ranges from thirty-seven in São Paulo to two in Belém. (Rio has fourteen.)
2. The definition and composition of the governing boards of the metropolitan entity, which are (1) a deliberative council, composed of five members appointed by the state governor (one to be indicated by the mayor of the state capital and another by the mayors of the other municipalities). Later, Federal Complementary Law No. 27, of 3 November 1975, made the state governor ex officio president of the deliberative council, thus giving a very strong say to the state in metropolitan affairs; and (2) a consultative council, made up of one representative of each of the municipalities in the region and presided over by the president of the deliberative council.

3. The powers of each of the above bodies, which are (1) for the deliberative council, to promote the elaboration of the plan for the integrated development of the region, to program metropolitan services and to coordinate the execution of programs and projects of metropolitan interest, including the unification of common services, whenever feasible; and (2) for the consultative council, to advise the deliberative council, upon its request, on any matters of metropolitan interest and to present suggestions on the elaboration of regional plans and the rendering of services.

4. The definition of the services of metropolitan interest, which are: (1) integrated planning for the social and economic development of the region; (2) basic sanitation, mainly water supply, sewerage, and public cleaning; (3) metropolitan land use; (4) transportation and road system; (5) production and distribution of piped gas; (6) development of water resources and control of pollution, according to federal regulations; and (7) other services that may be added to the competence of the deliberative council by the federal law.

5. The priority of the municipalities included in the metropolitan development plan for obtaining federal and state financial support for the provision of services and the execution of public works of a metropolitan interest.

The law neither created a metropolitan government nor defined the nature of the metropolitan executive entity or agency. Indeed, it was left up to the states to determine the nature of the agency, which can take several forms, such as a quasi-governmental autonomous authority (autharchy), a public enterprise, a foundation or just a semi-independent commission. Three states—Rio Grande do Sul, Pernambuco, and Rio de Janeiro—have opted for the foundation scheme; two have chosen the public enterprise solution (Bahia and São Paulo); two, the autharchy (Ceará and Minas Gerais); and two, the commission (Pará and Paraná). Nor did the law provide for any financial source for the metropolitan regions, which do not possess taxing powers. They are, in fact, no more than administrative agencies of their respective states. Another curiosity about the law is that the social services, such as education, health, culture, and recreation, were not included among the services of common interest to the regions.

It caused a certain amount of surprise that the federal government kept itself out of the metropolitan councils, thus giving cause, initially, to the suspicion that the central government was not interested in the subject. Further developments at the federal level since the new administration took over in March 1975, and since the fusion of the former states of Guanabar and Rio de Janeiro, have changed this view considerably. In mid-1974 a National Commission for the Metropolitan Regions and Urban Policy (CNPU) was set up by the federal government (composed of representatives of four ministries and of the National Housing Bank and four nongovernmental representatives). Since then, the federal government has launched a massive plan for urban development, with emphasis on metropolitan areas, especially those of Rio de Janeiro and São Paulo.

The nine metropoitan regions operate quite differently in many aspects. Some, like Porto Alegre, São Paulo, Belo Horizonte, Recife, and Salvador, have been rather effective in preparing plans. Rio de Janeiro, on the other hand, although the newest and with few plans, has done much in implementation, under the thrust of the fusion process of the two former states.

Political relations between the state government, that is, the deliberative council and some of the metropolitan municipalities, especially the state capitals, have been uneven throughout the country, and particularly difficult in Rio de Janeiro, since the city of this name must get accustomed to the idea of having become just a municipality, with greatly reduced functions and revenue, after being a city-state (the capital moved to Brasília in 1960) and the capital of the country since 1763. Much cooperation exists, however, in Porto Alegre, which created a more or less informal metropolitan organization years before the federal government established the metropolitan regions. São Paulo has a very peculiar political problem. A state secretariat for metropolitan affairs was set up to command the metropolitan public enterprise, but this rather strange arrangement makes it difficult for the secretariat to define its role with respect to the other state secretariats, as many metropolitan functions are also statewide functions, such as education, health, transportation, recreation, and public utilities.

The actual division of functions between the metropolitan entities and their respective municipalities still remains a moot question, in spite of Complementary Law No. 14 or rather because of the simplistic way in which the law dealt with this problem.

Finance has also been a crucial issue, even for Rio de Janeiro and São Paulo, which get top priority from the federal government. A major reason is the very low level of indebtedness of state and local governments, a fact that has been aggravated by a recent Senate resolution putting very strict limits on that level and thus preventing agencies like the National Housing Bank to lend their extremely abundant funds earmarked for urban development to the state and municipal governments.

Four regions (Recife, Salvador, Rio de Janeiro, and São Paulo) have set up special funds for financing metropolitan operations and projects, but the main source for metropolitan project financing has been the federal government, either through outright grants or loans, or both.

In summarizing the muncipal reforms that have been introduced in the country since 1964, it should be pointed out, first of all, that the reform process is proceeding actively, often by trial and error, without self-defined plans and objectives, except those that constitute the guidelines of the revolutionary movement of 1964. Concern for accountability, corruption, and national security is a major ingredient of many of the reforms, so much so that, in contrast with the liberal position of 1946 and 1961, signs of a counter-reform can be detected in many of the measures adopted since 1964.

The intention to modernize is also present in many of the reforms that have been introduced or attempted, but its success is limited by the lack of adequate technical assistance to the municipalities.

Finally, one of the most interesting and positive aspects of the post-1964 reform is the federal government's conscious effort to make municipal actions fit into the broader national objectives, such as curbing inflation and implementing strategic development programs. Never before were local policies so attuned to national purposes. The recent interest of the federal government in the metropolitan areas also falls into this category, as the nine established metropolitan regions comprise the most dynamic areas of the Brazilian urban and industrial sector and more than a third of the total urban population of the country.

CONCLUSION

The two main reforms of the Brazilian municipal system since 1946 are markedly different in some of their most relevant aspects, but both reflected the prevailing *Zeitgeist* of Brazil. The first was a segment of the redemocratization process of the country that came in great part as a consequence of Brazil's participation in World War II on the side of the Allies. It was essentially liberal, with more concern for the reestablishment of local democracy and the strengthening of municipal finances than for efficiency and accountability. Its key word was autonomy.

The second reform, begun in 1964 and still going on, raises the banner of morality, efficiency, and accountability. In many respects it can be considered a counter-reform or at least a reduction of some of the gains made by municipalities in their autonomy. Its key word seems to be conformity with the tenets of the 1964 revolution.

In some respects, however, the two reforms are similar. Neither was the result of a preconceived plan or of a study of municipal problems; neither devised an implementation scheme (at least the present one has not so far); and neither has put an end to the awkward symmetry of the municipal system according to which all of the nearly 4,000 municipalities have the same basic organization, powers, and functions. Moreover, neither has made a definition of functional boundaries between the municipalities and other levels of government so as to avoid the absurd system of concurrent powers that so much impairs the functioning of the municipal governments as purveyors of services to their respective communities.

The post-1964 reform shows three very positive tendencies that may have a far greater impact on the municipal system of Brazil than the previous one. The first is a concern for the modernization of municipal government and administration. The second is the development of a rational grants-in-aid system and of municipal credit programs. The third is an effort to bring municipal action into line with national policies and objectives in the development process. A fourth dimension is the emergence of a concern for urban problems, of which the creation of the metropolitan regions is a result.

NOTE

1. *Institutionalizing the Grass Roots in Brazil: A Study in Comparative Local Government* (San Francisco: Chandler, 1967).

Latin America

Lawrence S. Graham *

40

One of the perennial themes encountered in public documents, official reports, and governmental programs in Latin America is the call for local government reorganization and greater citizen mobilization at the grass-roots level. For more than a century now governmental reformers throughout the region have seen more vital municipalities as a corrective to excessive centralization of power at the national level. Regardless of how this ideal is stated in the extensive public law literature accumulated over the last century and a half, in individual country constitutions, or in executive decrees, one is confronted continually with a quite different national reality whereby effective financial resources and decision-making authority affecting local services are concentrated in the hands of central government authorities.

Mexico is a case in point. The Constitution of 1917 states succinctly the legal doctrine of the free and autonomous municipality. Literally hundreds of theses and articles have been written on the topic, reviewing the legal principles identified with municipal autonomy. In them, once recognition is given to the discrepancy between legal theory and the practice of local government, the usual practice is to conclude with a normative restatement of the ideal of municipal sovereignty. But the reality with which one is faced consistently is that of a highly centralized state in which the necessary economic and technical resources are concentrated in a number of governmental organizations located in the nation's capital.

Rather than attempt a piecemeal review of current reorganization endeavors in each of the individual Latin American states, the intent behind this chapter is to identify more clearly from a broader, cross-national perspective the obstacles to more effective local government institutions and to greater citizen involvement at the grass-roots level in those programs affecting most directly people's daily lives. Juxtaposed against these obstacles to change will be

*Professor of Government and Associate Director, Institute of Latin American Studies, University of Texas at Austin.

reference to several recent experiments in reorganization designed to overcome present difficulties.

THE PAST RECORD

The major obstacle to effective change in local government throughout Latin America lies in the preeminence of a unitary state model derived from nineteenth-century Western Europe and the failure to confront this reality effectively. Even in those instances where federal systems exist in form (Argentina, Brazil, Venezuela, and Mexico), state structures and organization are centralist in their impact.

Only in the case of Cuba has it been possible to break fundamentally with organizational structures, financial practices, legal traditions, and political values associated with concepts of centralized state authority dating back to the Napoleonic reforms of the early 1800s. When compared with the other Latin American states, the Cuban example is especially notable, for there are few if any other cases in the Americas where a regime has had such success in mobilizing large numbers of people at the grass-roots level and in expanding their involvement in programs of the national government committed to basic change. These programs include projects for the reduction of inequities in services provided to citizens in rural and urban areas, development schemes for the creation of a more extensive national economy, and policies favoring the incorporation of the rural population into a more comprehensive political system.

Except for Cuba, then, the dominant governing mentality throughout Latin America has been and continues to be one that exalts state supremacy: the concentration of economic and political resources in the hands of national governments confined to a single decision-making center whose political, economic, and social significance overwhelms that of any other single area under its jurisdiction. The economic form taken in such instances is usually that of state capitalism, whereby the public sector assumes primary responsibility for promoting economic growth and mediating between national and international market forces. The administrative formula adhered to more often than not exalts the maintenance of a common set of central ministries designed to regulate public and private activities in each of the major sectors of the economy, concurrently with the random creation of a host of decentralized, autonomous agencies, in order to meet specific needs in stimulating economic growth and in providing new social services.

Increasingly this tradition of state supremacy, when combined with the expanded role of government in socioeconomic affairs, has led to the formation of complex and intricate governmental bureaucracies, centralized in theory but divided in practice into a series of competing public organizations and subunits, each jealous of its own prerogatives and in competition with the others for limited economic resources. As a corrective to this dispersal of

central government authority in the nation's capital, proposals to create devices for the central coordination of public policy are frequent. Today these
often take the form of elaborate schemes for mounting national planning
systems under executive authority.

More importantly, the impact of the centralization and reconcentration of
bureaucratic power in the nation's capital, no matter how dispersed its actual
application may be within individual agencies and ministerial divisions, is
such that few services can be provided at the local level that are not the function
of some field organ of a central government ministry or autonomous agency.
Thus, while the Latin American states make provision for municipal government and many have created in addition regional authorities in the form of
provincial governments, there are few instances where local authorities are
allotted sufficient responsibility to have direct impact on the lives and property
of local residents. Few prefects, governors, or mayors can deal with local
affairs effectively without first consulting with national authorities, and even
then the resources for implementing these proposals usually remain in the
hands of ministry officials.

When issues relating to systemic reform are raised, the normal sequence is to
begin with a reaffirmation of greater citizen participation in government at the
local level and to finish with a set of recommendations opting for increased
control over and more effective integration of political and administrative
activities at the apex as well as the subnational level. As a consequence, if one
traces the history of local government reorganization in the region over the
long run, one will discover in most instances that it is impossible to separate
proposals for local government reorganization from national debates over the
centralization and decentralization of authority and the elaboration of proposals for expanded schemes of regional government. The norm in the larger
states is for provisions made for local government to be tied to regional
governments of a prefectural type. Although labels usually disguise this reality
and the title of governor may well be used, as in Argentina and Mexico, such
public officials function more often as agents of the national government in the
provinces, representing an extension of the national authority structure rather
than as local representatives of autonomous political and administrative subsystems, as one will find in such countries as the United States or Australia.
Because there are few autonomous areas of action assigned to local authorities
at the provincial or municipal level throughout Latin America, most attempts
at reorganization and endeavors to give new life to local institutions atrophy
because the fiscal resources and the technical know-how necessary for the
provision of expanded governmental services remain the property of bureaucratic agencies of the national government and their local representatives.

Aside from the responsibilities of the national government for such public
services as health, sanitation, education, water control, and regulation of
private sector activities, the maintenance of law and order also follows the
same general norm. Virtually all the Latin American states establish central

governmental control over their police forces, usually within the context of dual organizational structures. Generally speaking, one will find a country police force operating in urban and rural areas which is organized, recruited, paid, and partially controlled by the army. Its name varies; in some localities it is known as the *guardia civil*; in others, the *guardia republicana*; and in still others, the *carabineros*. Then there is the state police proper, which in most cases functions not as a paramilitary organization but as a civilian one. These men generally have responsibility for maintaining public order, investigating crime, compiling records, and assisting judicial authorities in inquiries. Included within this second type of police organization often are specialized divisions for police intelligence work and counterespionage. The usual organizational structure in this latter case is pyramidical, with central control emanating from a division for police affairs in the Ministry of Interior in the capital city. In practice, activities of the state police become subjected to dual controls, one set stemming from the central office through a hierarchy of officials and a second from the local governor or prefect who oversees all such activities within a province or department.

By the time one arrives at the municipal level, the responsibilities assigned to the mayor or municipal president and his council are residual at best. These pertain specifically to the city and its environs, for example, the provision of water and electricity, garbage collection, supervision of local markets, and the regulation of city or town traffic (through the municipal police). In tax collection about the only resources left to draw upon are limited to such areas as levies on property, fees set for municipal licenses, and taxes collected on movies, sports, and cultural affairs. In instances when local elections are held, competition for local office may well lead to a lively political game which can give the outsider a feeling of municipal vitality. But once elected, the mayor and council members have limited responsibilities and a constrained capacity to attend to local necessities. To a considerable extent, the degree to which the local leadership is able to meet demands for improved services and new facilities, such as a school, a medical clinic, or a public market, comes to depend not on their own initiative and responsiveness to local needs but on the extent to which they have established linkages with regional and national authorities, political as well as administrative.

Despite these circumstances, attempts at local government reorganization are almost never linked to this wider reality in which both public services and financial resources are weighted in the direction of the national government. Two cases will suffice here as illustrations: the Brazilian experience with federalism and with municipal and state autonomy under the 1946 Constitution (1946-67) and the Peruvian experiment with reconstituting local authorities during the Belaúnde administration (1963-68).

Brazil (1946-67)

In any discussion of local government reorganization, the Brazilian case warrants special attention. Before 1968 Brazil alone in Latin America had a functioning federal system. The other instances of federalism (Argentina, Venezuela, and Mexico) constitute instances of federal constitutional theory combined with national realities of centralized state authority and power structures. Both in theory and in practice, however, not only did Brazil have a legacy of strong regional government, but also after World War II a concerted attempt was mounted by governmental reformers to strengthen local autonomy. Reacting against the centralism of the Getúlio Vargas dictatorship (1937-45), they sought to bring into existence meaningful local self-government. Accordingly, explicit provision was made in the 1946 Constitution for municipal and state government, and financial resources were assigned to each level, distinct from those of the national government.

Over a period of twenty years, municipalities burgeoned all over Brazil, and lively municipal politics came into being. In some areas local politics took the form of maintenance of traditional rural power structures in the hands of a local landlord, as was the case in many medium-size and small towns in northeastern Brazil. In others, competitive local politics emerged, as was the case increasingly of such states in the central south as Minas Gerais.

The community politics literature in Brazil, much of it published in Portuguese and made available through the *Revista Brasileira de Estudos Políticos*, reflects this experience. Yet, these studies and others published by Diogo Lordello de Mello[1] and Frank Sherwood[2] always contrast the reality of a lively local politics with awareness of the fact that local autonomy during this period bore little relation to the ability of these local governments to provide local services. Some of them (especially in the state of São Paulo) were well organized; others (particularly those in impoverished areas of the country) were quite deficient. But in all, a dual set of authority relations emerged. One set was essentially horizontal and involved local and regional politics, while a second, primarily vertical in character, depended on local authorities' ability to obtain services from the central ministries and autonomous agencies of the national government and to channel them into their communities through these organizations' field agencies. Even when tax reform during the 1960s substantially increased local government resources, this dependency of local government in Brazil on the public bureaucracy at the center for many essential municipal services and programs of importance to local residents continued.[3]

Peru (1963-68)

If the attention given to the decentralization of political power in Brazil in 1946 was at least congruent with local and regional traditions and prior experience with semi-autonomous state government, the Peruvian experiment with local government reorganization in 1963 bore little relation to national realities. Not only did the regime lack the necessary administrative resources, it had few if any of the political resources needed to make effective its commitment to more dynamic local institutions.

The central fact in Peruvian political and economic life has long been the preeminence of Lima over the countryside, to such an extent that the disparities between the capital city and the provinces have proven to be insurmountable. Belaúnde ultimately found this to be the case as did those revolutionary-minded military officers who, on displacing Belaúnde from office five years later, sought to build a new society by incorporating the rural and urban masses into the nation's political and economic life. Consequently, when local elections were held in Peru in 1963 for the first time in forty-three years, few people were prepared to deal with the extensive local government reorganization called for by the government's commitment to local autonomy and decentralization. Regardless of numerous attempts over the next five years to stimulate local initiative and build support for President Belaúnde Terry's concept of a "democratic" Peru, restrictions on finance, the concentration of administrative resources in central government agencies, and the longstanding practice of looking to Lima for the resolution of local problems made meaningful functioning of subnational units largely an impossibility.

Although individual experiences among the other Latin American republics vary greatly and the specifics of each case are indeed different, the overall impact is much the same. Few empirical studies of intergovernmental relations exist. Rarely are debates over local government reorganization linked to identifying the ramifications of state supremacy and traditions of unitary government for the creation of more dynamic municipalities. Most action, whether it is conducted independently by a national government or with the assistance of an international agency or foreign government, has been and continues to be geared to dealing with the symptoms—the absence of sufficient financial resources, the lack of technical expertise, and the failure to stimulate sufficiently local initiative—rather than with the actual causes of apathy and resignation among so many residents of provincial towns and communities.

PROGRAM INNOVATION AT THE LOCAL LEVEL

Among recent endeavors to change the character of life at the community level in urban and rural localities outside Latin America's capital cities and its poles of industrial growth, such as Monterrey in Mexico or São Paulo in Brazil, three experiments stand out as exceptions to the generalizations just made: the creation of Committees for the Defense of the Revolution in Castro's Cuba, the SINAMOS experiment in Peru, and the regional development program established by the government of the State of Mexico in Toluca, Mexico. Each has been directed at changing the conditions of life for citizens in communities outside cosmopolitan centers and in poor neighborhoods where public services are traditionally the most deficient. While none of them can be called officially programs of local government reorganization, each has had an impact at the municipal level.

Cuba

The Cuban case is obviously the most radical. It has been the most far-reaching in its ability to mobilize people at the grass-roots level and to involve them more effectively in government programs intended to improve conditions of life in rural and urban localities. Equally important has been the expansion of governmental services hitherto enjoyed almost exclusively by privileged elements in urban society to nearly all Cubans. As the Cuban Revolution has become institutionalized and the new regime has rebuilt the Cuban state in the image of a socialist republic, the instruments for grass-roots mobilization—the Committees for the Defense of the Revolution (the CDRs)—have evolved from committees intended to identify those opposed to the Revolution or excessively passive in their revolutionary commitment into action groups of local citizens concerned with a host of activities oriented to the improvement of living conditions in these groups' immediate environs. At present the CDR organizational network extends from a National Directorate, downward through provincial directorates and district organizations, to sectional and neighborhood units.

While individual instances of the CDRs in action vary from success stories where they have taken on functions related to local development to cases where over time they have lost their effectiveness as local instititutions as the Revolution has aged, they have become essential links between the national government and individual localities. Observers of the Cuban scene, such as Richard Fagen[4] and Douglas Butterworth,[5] have called attention to the effectiveness of these groups in creating a sense of community among citizens where beforehand none existed and in promoting programs directed at improving conditions of life in rural and urban areas. Since field work on these organizations and their relation to other public organizations is limited, it is difficult to assess the extent to which they have replaced earlier local government arrangements. But what is apparent is that in the transition from the older state model dominant in Cuba, from independence down to 1961, to a Latin American version of a socialist republic, a much more responsive and dynamic set of local institutions has emerged. These organizations have broken decisively with pre-revolutionary patterns whereby local institutions were essentially adminstrative in character and decisions affecting living conditions, if they were made at all, were a function of extra-community organizations.

Today the CDRs have become a model that is being examined with interest by other developing countries. In their search for grass-roots organizations capable of mobilizing citizens in large numbers to support new state arrangements, the CDRs provide a framework and suggest a strategy for stimulating local initiative and encouraging attitudes geared to community problem solving by local residents themselves. However, it is not easy for outsiders actually to evaluate the effectiveness of these mechanisms in Cuba for improving local living conditions.

One attempt at evaluating Cuban experience in this area is Butterworth's review of the general record left by the CDRs and his case study of the activities of neighborhood groups in one particular urban housing project. In this instance, neighborhood CDRs in cooperation with the sectional or zone committee responsible for that area transformed what had previously been an urban slum into an organized neighborhood with adequate housing and community services. Yet, Butterworth goes on to report, in 1966, two years after their formation and the initiation of the housing project, the CDRs in that locality had become paralyzed. What is interesting about his discussion and what sets it aside from other materials is his realistic evaluation of the CDRs as grass-roots organizations, pointing out their achievements as well as calling attention to the fact that they have not provided a facile solution to the problems presented in mobilizing and integrating residents of impoverished urban areas into the larger society.[6]

Regardless of the problems encountered in establishing continuity in such programs and in institutionalizing the CDRs as local-level organizations capable of maintaining their vitality across time, the committees for the defense of the revolution have supplied an effective means for reaching the local population, mobilizing it, establishing a network of communications, and linking local needs with national programs operating out of bureaucratic agencies of the central government. It is this set of experiences which is to be contrasted with what has become the norm of externally administered local services elsewhere in most of Latin America.

Peru

In Peru, by contrast, the military government led by General Velasco Alvarado (1968-75) sought to organize its programs for the rural and urban masses by working within the framework of existing state institutions, reordering them and creating new entities as the situation demanded. Before dealing with issues of mass mobilization, the military first undertook an administrative reorganization of the central government, readjusting and implementing recommendations formulated during the Belaúnde administration. As a consequence, earlier concepts regarding the desirability of a centralized and hierarchically ordered set of governmental offices with responsibilities for coordination and control retained considerable vitality. Included within these changes were the ''rationalization'' of executive responsibilities under the authority of the Council of Ministers (in which the professional military held all key administrative positions), a formalized council of presidential advisers called COAP (in which staff functions were clearly separated from line responsibilities), and a revitalized National Planning Office (which was intended to have sufficient power to ensure implementation of its directives).

Along with these changes, the military created a central government office with responsibility for achieving more effective popular participation in government and promoting social mobilization throughout the country: the National System in Support of Social Mobilization (SINAMOS). This organization was simply superimposed over preexisting subnational units while related programs, such as the Belaúnde Government's *Cooperación Popular*, were incorporated into its national structure. At the departmental, provincial, and district level, local authorities continued to function as delegates of the national government, and the military government reverted to the traditional practice of designating provincial and district council members by appointing civilian representatives from within their constituencies.

SINAMOS's goal was to mobilize Peruvian society as a whole in such a way that the entire population eventually would be organized and integrated into the new state that the military envisioned itself as creating. Whereas the organizational apparatus arrived at in Cuba was the consequence of revolutionary upheaval, Peruvian innovations in organizing the population at the grass-roots level reflected a strategy of anticipating revolution by creating and administering revolutionary change through state organizations designed to restructure society, while ensuring that the military would remain in firm control of the process. As an administrative agency, with its main office in Lima and regional offices providing the necessary linkage between the center and local units, SINAMOS was assigned sufficient power to intervene in the activities of other governmental organizations. Programs related to local development and the improvement of living conditions remained the responsibility of the central ministries and their field offices. But it was SINAMOS's responsibility to ensure that their administration would become congruent with the needs and aspirations of the local population affected by such programs. In terms of local government reorganization, what this represented was the creation of a device for the control and regulation of the development programs administered by central ministries at the local level through the creation of an independent set of organizations with surveillance power over the programs of bureaucratic entities and simultaneously the representation within SINAMOS of citizen groups at provincial and local levels.

In actuality these ambitious goals were never realized. Once it became clear that mass mobilization and organization would not necessarily create a citizenry compliant with the desires of a revolutionary-minded military government and instead were stimulating the formation of political groups with their own desires for autonomy, the military moved to curtail SINAMOS's activities. Eventually (after power had passed from "left-oriented" officers to more "centrist" ones led by General Morales Bermúdez in August 1975), the decision was made to disband it by the end of 1978. At the height of its influence in 1972 and 1973, when its identification with the *pueblos jóvenes* (the slum areas surrounding greater Lima) was the most positive, the immediate consequence of its actions was to reorder local governmental activities by creating alternative linkages with urban and rural groups previously outside the governmental system without abolishing existing municipal institutions. Provincial councils coinciding with city boundaries, and district councils within them, continued to function throughout this period in accord with the prefectural model of a centralized state system. Equally hierarchical in structure and concept, SINAMOS's regional and zonal offices worked to help form new citizens' groups which would be linked to the revolutionary government through system affect and provision of new public services: neighborhood organizations, youth associations, worker organizations, cooperatives, rural organizations, and professional and cultural associations.[7]

Ultimately such a schema failed for the simple reason that alternative mass organizations regulated by a "new state," dominated by the military and compliant with its wishes, proved to be unattainable. Having destroyed the political and economic power base of Peru's old elites, the military proved unable to generate sufficient support among the civilian population to create the new order it so desired. Without economic resouces to fund its programs and increasing opposition from all sides, it had no alternative by 1978 but to begin the search for an appropriate mechanism to return power to civilians and minimize further military losses.

Mexico

The third example of a new departure in local government reorganization is the program proposed by the governor of the State of Mexico in 1973 and implemented during 1974 and 1975. In this case the strategy arrived at took place in a context whereby the existing structure of national, state, and local government was accepted as given and revolutionary changes were deemed to be beyond consideration.

In Mexico the central fact which any local government reorganization attempt must confront is the primacy of the state governor. Despite whatever legal theory might have to say about autonomous municipal government, the realities of Mexican politics are such that one encounters a highly centralized national government in which local autonomy is restricted, a complex set of central government ministries and autonomous agencies that constrain effectively pressures for local autonomy, state governors whose roles are political, essentially, rather than administrative, and substantial program autonomy in the field activities of the central ministries within the individual states.[8] The initial success of the program begun in the State of Mexico was a consequence of working within the context of this reality. Rather than embark on an extensive discussion of the desirability of local autonomy, the governor mounted a program focused on the need to deal with the development problems of the state integrally through the amassing of state and local resources in a single program in which the activities of all major actors could be coordinated more effectively.

A critical part of this program was the utilization of the state university by concentrating the necessary technical expertise to effect such a program within a semi-autonomous university institute: the Instituto de Desarrollo Urbano y Regional (the Institute for Urban and Regional Development) in the state capital, Toluca. Within the institute, four programs were set up in close relationship with each other: urban and regional planning, public administration, business administration, and environmental engineering. Each was linked directly with local communities and the overall program operated in close contact with the governor's office.

Rather than deal with individual municipalities on an isolated basis, the primary thrust of this program was to present a view of the problem of local development in the state as regional in character and to insist that the revitalization of local government be dealt with through the establishment of a common set of mechanisms, bringing together mayors, council members, local administrative authorities, state officials, representatives of federal agencies within the state, and university personnel with technical expertise. By establishing a common set of programs, with the governor as the key to action, problems related to deficient municipal services, industrial development, pollution stemming from the rapid industrialization of the Valley of Mexico, and urban development were all approached on a regional basis.

Nevertheless, despite great promise, this program too has encountered difficulties: its long-term potential for restructuring local government relations has proven minimal. Linked to the personality of the incumbent governor and his ability to develop and maintain a specific set of center-region-locality relations, the ending of his *sexenio* (his six-year term of office) signalled the decline of the program and raised the queston of how to sustain its dynamism in the future.

A RESTATEMENT OF THE ISSUES

When these three programs are compared with most other attempts at local government reorganization in Latin America, the contrast is great. None of them has proven ideal in the sense that all previous difficulties have suddenly been resolved, nor can they be classified as resounding successes. But, what sets them aside from earlier endeavors and makes them worthy of consideration in planning future local government reorganizations is their recognition of the fact that ultimately it is the region—be it a federal state, department, or province—that provides the missing link. Programs intended to have an impact on localities in diverse regions of the modern state and designed to stimulate greater citizen involvement at the local level must, in short, be tied to more general strategies giving central recognition to the linkages between community, region, and nation. In formulating social and economic development programs and in building more integrated political economies within the framework of existing nation-states, more recognition must be given to the complexity of intergovernmental relations throughout Latin America. The declaration of an ideology of local government development or the provision of funds to stimulate local initiative, when isolated from national power structures and from the way political and administrative resources are allocated within the state, stand little chance of success over the long run.

Within Latin America, where centralized state authority and concentration of economic and political resources in the capital city constitute the basic reality, the time has come to cease repeating platitudes identified with local initiative and municipal autonomy. Instead, what is needed is more empirical information stating the real nature of intergovernmental power relations at the regional and local level within specific national settings. With this information in hand, nationals might then proceed to elaborate more realistic programs for local government reorganization which, by recognizing this reality, can be tied in more effectively with country-wide programs designed to achieve a particular type of modern state. Within that setting, questions concerning the mobilization of the citizenry at the grass-roots level must also be confronted. Regardless of the model a country selects for attaining its modernization goals, there comes a point at which careful and studied attention must be focused on how best to develop and maintain linkages with the rural and urban masses. In the final analysis, whether one is working within the framework of a system of interest representation that is pluralist (representative democracy), corporatist (bureaucratic-authoritarian), or monistic (authoritarian socialism), effective local government reorganization must be situated in its broader regional and national context and conceptualized above all in linkage terms.

NOTES

1. Diogo Lordello de Mello, *Problemas Institucionais do Município* [Institutional Problems of the Municipality] (Rio de Janeiro: Instituto Brasileiro de Administração Municipal, 1968) and *Organização do Município* [Municipal Organization] (Rio de Janeiro: Fundação Getúlio Vargas, 1965).

2. Frank P. Sherwood, *Institutionalizing the Grass Roots in Brazil: A Study in Comparative Local Government* (San Francisco: Chandler, 1967).

3. Gilbert B. Siegel, "Brazil: Diffusion and Centralization of Power," in *Development Administration in Latin America*, ed. Clarence E. Thurber and Lawrence S. Graham (Durham, N.C.: Duke University Press, 1973), pp. 321-81.

4. Richard R. Fagen, *The Transformation of Political Culture in Cuba* (Stanford, Ca.: Stanford University Press, 1969), especially pp. 69-103.

5. Douglas Butterworth, "Grass-Roots Political Organization in Cuba: A Case of the Committees for the Defense of the Revolution," in *Latin American Urban Research*, vol. 4 (*Anthropological Perspectives on Latin American Urbanization*), ed. Wayne A. Cornelius and Felicity M. Trueblood (Beverly Hills, Ca.: Sage, 1974), pp. 183-203.

6. Butterwoth, "Grass-Roots Political Organization," pp. 189-201.

7. Details regarding the organization of SINAMOS are to be found in Henry A. Dietz, "Bureaucratic Demand-Making and Clientelistic Participation in Peru," in *Authoritarianism and Corporatism in Latin America*, ed. James M. Malloy (Pittsburgh, Pa.: University of Pittsburgh Press, 1977), pp. 413-58. Alfred Stepan's *The State and Society: Peru in Comparative Perspective* (Princeton, N.J.: Princeton University Press, 1978) contains a good, general assessment of Peru's military regime.

8. For an analysis of intergovernmental relations in Mexico from the perspective of state and local government, see Lawrence S. Graham, *Mexican State Government: A Prefectural System in Action* (Austin: Institute of Public Affairs, The University of Texas, 1971).

MIDDLE EAST

EGYPT AND IRAN
TURKEY
FERTILE CRESCENT COUNTRIES

Egypt and Iran

Ann T. Schulz*

41

In central Iran, a district governor finished his tour of Gachsar village. The day was warm. He drank the orange soda offered to him by the secretary of the cooperative society. Several villagers stood around him, themselves not drinking. Perhaps that evening, some thousand miles away in Egypt, Subra el-Gedida's mayor preempted the town ambulance. He needed an official car to greet a visitor. Both mayor and governor are national officials; privilege accompanies national authority.[1]

In Egypt and in Iran, national regime politics shape the structure and process of local government. When late Egyptian President Nasser took power in 1954, as head of the new republican government, he began to restructure local government along the lines of an evolving single-party regime. President Sadat disassembled that structure in the 1971 "correction of the revolution." In Iran, Mohammad Reza Shah Pahlavi was initiating changes in local government during the same time period that were to symbolize popular participation without relinquishing the court's control over critical local issues. The local institutions that will succeed those created by the Shah are likely to be stronger. The differences among the several systems of local government illustrate the dependency of local government upon national politics.

During the 1960s and 1970s, local government underwent many changes in both countries. Despite the very real differences between local government in republican Egypt and monarchical Iran, both confronted similar changes in trying to promote regime security. Most of the local government reorganizations were designed to consolidate the power of national elites over provincial politicians, who earlier had been arbiters in the political process as influential landowners and merchants. In their efforts to consolidate power, both leaders brought new national bureaucracies to localities and created formal institutions of popular government that were expected to undermine traditional networks of influence operating at the local level.

*Research Associate Professor, Department of Government, Clark University, Worcester, Massachusetts.

At the very time that the popular institutions were being established, national elites were intervening increasingly in local politics. This sequence of events posed an apparent contradiction to administrative theory which often relies upon unidimensional concepts like centralization to describe the relationship between central and local governments.[2] In practice, the formal decentralization of authority to local governments has, more often than not, been accompanied by the centralization of effective political power. This certainly has been the case in Egypt and Iran, where newly formed popular councils have had little more than an ombudsman's influence, while traditional provincial elites have seen their political influence eroded by national bureaucracies.

Regime security and economic growth together provide the basis for national intervention in local politics. For example, the Shah's plans to make the city of Isfahan into Iran's military aerospace center would not have materialized had the decision been left to the political process to resolve. Isfahan was an agricultural center and a textile manufacturing city with an active bazaar and religious community. The influx of foreign laborers and technicians, the deterioration of the bazaar in competition with modern businesses, and the jarring impact of the new activities on farming in the region were the object of intense criticism by many native Isfahanis. The Shah's controversial militarization programs were not subjected to local debate and approval.

The historical role of provincial cities as agricultural and commerical centers can still be seen in the way that provinces are governed, despite the impact of contemporary national regime politics.[3] In the past, city and country were integrated within provinces (in Egypt, governorates) for purposes of governance. The independent corporate character of modern city government has developed only slowly.

The authority of provincial governors today continues to reflect the historically close relationship between cities and their surrounding rural areas. Contemporary provincial governors exercise as much influence in city affairs as do mayors and municipality officials.[4] Egypt's local government law no. 124, promulgated in 1960, acknowledged this tradition by granting provincial status to the country's four largest cities, formally administered by governors. In Iran, the offices of governor and mayor are formally distinct, but in the larger cities there is considerable competition between the two over their respective influence in municipal politics.[5]

The majority of Egyptians and Iranians live in rural areas. Because of the numbers of persons they serve, rural local government effectiveness is particularly important. At the same time, the high rate of urban migration that both countries have experienced in recent years and the threat of political instability that accompanies the migration means that municipal officials have a prior claim on public resources. City officials are under tremendous pressure to improve the quality of urban services to respond to the expanding population. Provincial executives, especially the governors, are critical intermediaries between these local officials who have competing interests.

So that provincial executives would be encouraged to mediate local conflicts, both the Egyptian and the Iranian regimes tried to increase the discretionary authority of provincial governors over provincial budgets and planning operations. But the central ministries still operated largely outside the sphere of the governor's office and closely guarded their own bureaucratic interests.

In effect, local government reorganization in Egypt and Iran has bureaucratized local politics and centralized political control over local affairs, while acknowledging the legitimacy of popular government at the local level by establishing elected councils. Figure 41.1 below shows the framework within which these changes were effected.

Figure 41.1
EGYPT AND IRAN: LOCAL GOVERNMENT UNITS

EGYPT

Region (24)[a]

governor executive council people's council
party secretary and executive bureau
ministry offices
|

Urban Municipality (134) (*markaz*)

mayor executive council people's council
party leadership group and executive committee
ministry offices
|

Rural Municipality (997)

mayor executive council people's council
cooperative board combined service unit

IRAN

Province (23)[b](*Ostan*)

governor-general council party committee
ministry offices
|

Township (151) (*shahrestan*)

governor council party committee

council **Municipality**   **District (459)**
  mayor party committee governor administrative council
  service authorities   ministry offices
  | |

Local Municipality[c]   **Village Group (1,543)**
local mayor   mayor
               |

             Village
      headman council party committee
         cooperative board

[a]UAR, Ministry of National Guidance. *The Yearbook, 1966* (Cairo). Figures in parentheses refer to numbers of the unit designated.

[b]Iran, Plan and Budget Organization—UNDP, *An Administrative Framework for Regional Planning* (Tehran, September 1974).

[c]In 1975, only one city, Isfahan, was divided into local municipalities.

BASIC UNITS OF GOVERNMENT

Grass Roots

For centuries, the village has been the basic unit of government in rural areas. Landholding and agricultural production patterns determined village governmental practices. The village was not a corporate unit. Village affairs were managed by village headmen, who customarily were representatives of the local landholder, and by informal councils of village elders.

Village government changed with land redistribution. Egypt's new republican government initiated land reform when it took power in 1952 as a preliminary step toward the local government reforms that came in 1960.[6] Iran's major land reform program was promulgated in 1962; succeeding reforms in local government came five years later.

With land reform under way, both regimes reorganized rural government by establishing formally elected village councils and village executives, by bringing cooperative organizations to the villages, and by grouping villages into larger administrative units. The basic purposes of the reorganization were to replace the landowner with central bureaucratic officials, to organize social services in a more uniform manner, and to promote local acceptance of the regimes' fiscal requirements and substantive policies through the intervention of local councils.

The new governmental institutions in rural areas included the cooperative society, the popular councils, political party units, and, in Egypt, the combined service center. In both countries, all these local agencies are supervised by national ministries. The cooperatives' authority is not always coterminous with the boundaries of a village, but often the same people are found to be holding office in both the council and the cooperative simultaneously.

One of the major problems confronting rural development planners in Egypt and Iran has been the small size of many villages and their lack of correspondence with agricultural production areas. In response to this problem, reorganization in Egypt stressed flexibility in delineating the jurisdiction of agencies. In 1960, the smaller Egyptian villages were grouped together into rural municipalities, for which popular and executive councils perform general governmental functions. The jurisdiction of Egyptian cooperative societies, on the other hand, included portions of the populations of several villages if the landholding and farming patterns lent themselves to such an arrangement.

In Iran, a village cluster (*dehestan*) was created in 1937, but it did not take on any administrative or political significance. In the mid-1970s, under Minister of Agriculture Mansour Rouhani, villages in particularly productive regions were singled out for development and people were encouraged to migrate to them from poorer areas. Rouhani's ideas were extremely unpopular, and he was removed from office in 1977, before the program had any effect on the administrative structure in rural Iran.

The distinction between urban and rural municipalities in Egypt is made on the basis of economic activity within the population center. Those towns in which there is commercial or industrial activity are accorded urban status. According to Iran's local government laws, a population center of 5,000 or more persons automatically becomes a municipality. One difference between city and village government in both countries is the complexity of the governing framework authorized by law—including the number of committees to be established by the popular councils and the division of functons within the mayor's office. Another distinction between city and village government is the status and influence of local executives. In both Egypt and Iran, the mayorality of a large city is a prestigious position and the post is reserved for individuals who have some influence in national political circles.[7] In Iran, for example, army generals often were seconded to be the mayors in the larger or politically sensitive cities.

In Iran, urban officials also have much more fiscal authority than do rural headman. Until 1977, villages were authorized to impose only one tax, 2 percent of agricultural income. Even that was given up when it became too costly to collect in contrast to the readily available oil revenues. Municipality officials, though, supervise a complex tax structure, with taxes levied on business as well as on individuals. Municipal officials in Iran also have more legal responsibilities than do village officials. The administration of an Iranian city is more realistically compared to that of a rural county or district than with villages.

District and Township

In rural Iran, the district (*bakhsh*) is the most important unit of government for villagers. Most ministries have officials posted in the districts who implement ministry programs there and who serve on the district governor's district advisory council (*shorā-ye bakhsh*). There is no popular elected council at the district level.

Above the district, Iran's urban centers and rural districts are grouped together in townships (*shahrestān*), a new designation for a traditional governmental unit, the *farmāndāri* or governorate. In 1970 legislation, a directly elected township council was established and shares authority with the township governor. Township officials, particularly the councils, have assumed little of the power that was authorized to them in that legislation. In practice, district and municipal officials usually pass over the township agencies, going directly to the provincial governor or ministry directors with requests and for their approval of local decisions.

The same statute created councils at the provincial (*ostān*) level to approve budgetary decisions made by the governors. The provincial councillors were elected indirectly from the township councils. They were beginning to participate in implementing regional development projects at the time that the Shah's government was overthrown in early 1979.

POPULAR COUNCILS

Composition

Until 1971, the composition of local popular councils was strikingly different in the two countries. The Egyptian councils were constituted in such a manner that local government was more consolidated than it was in Iran. According to the 1960 local government law of Egypt, local councils were to consist of (1) a majority of Arab Socialist Union party representatives (first elected, then appointed from that base by the district party secretary); (2) persons nominated by the minister of local administration; and (3) (ex officio) ministry representatives. The councils were, in practice, dominated by the ex officio members. In 1971, under President Sadat's regime, the council system was restructured and an executive council and a popular council were created at the rural, urban, and regional levels. The popular councils were made up in part of persons elected by local party members and the remainder elected from the central people's council of the party. Ministry representatives served on the more powerful executive council.

The 1907 Fundamental Law of Iran (the Constitution) provided for the formation of provincial councils. Legislation in the years following authorized the establishment of administrative and popular local councils. However, most of this early legislation was not implemented or implemented only erratically throughout Iran. In 1967, enabling legislation detailed electoral procedures and formal powers for what became the first comprehensive system of village and city councils. Both types of councils were composed entirely of elected representatives, although the elections were neither open nor democratic.

The differences in council structure reflect the different models from which the council systems were drawn. The laws formulating Iran's council system emphasized symbolic popular participation while little was done to bring together local officials and national bureaucrats serving at the local level. Those of Egypt, in the words of the 1962 National Charter, emphasized "popularity and progressiveness." The mixed councils illustrated the significance that Nasser increasingly had placed upon creating new configuratons of power at the local level that would be able to effect change on behalf of the national regime without the necessity of continuous intervention by national officials.

In Iran, the distinction between local councils and national bureaucrats was diminished by working committees on which councillors and bureaucrats served jointly, but the Shah was not as interested as Nasser in building stable political alliances at the local level to support his rule. Aside from the internal security apparatus (important in Egyptian politics as well), the regime's provincial support was to rest more upon spreading the oil revenues around than on political consolidation and compromise.

Bureaucratic Control

Popular councils in both countries were subject to the control of central ministries and, in that way, were regarded by constituents and councillors alike as creatures of the national regime. Iran's Ministry of Interior was charged with supervising municipal councils and provided mayoral candidates to them from a national pool. Village councils were placed within the jurisdiction of the Ministry of Urban Development and Housing. The ministries supervised local fiscal operations and the selection of local executive officers.

In Egypt all popular councils were subject to supervision by the Ministry of Local Administration until 1971, when the ministry was abolished and replaced by a Ministerial Committee for Local Administration. The hierarchical delegation of authority made the executive councils of rural municipalities immediately responsible to the urban executive council in that district and the urban council, to the governorate.

Relations between the elected local councils and their executive agents vary. The Egyptian rural municipal councils replaced the village headman. Municipal councils were empowered to elect mayors, or council chairmen, until 1965. In that year, authority to make appointments was granted jointly to the governor, provincial director of municipal councils, and the provincial official of the Arab Socialist Union party.

In Iran, the village council serves alongside the headmen who is appointed by the township governor. City councils have the formal authority to elect and dismiss mayors, although in actuality the Ministry of Interior, the governor, and the prime minister are more influential in making the selection. The main difference between Egypt and Iran is that Egyptian law authorized outside intervention in the selection of mayors, while it was informal in Iran. The distinction between the law and practice in Iran effectively undermined the legitimacy of the councils in their members' eyes and in those of their constituents.

Functions

The authority of local officials is extensive. Both Egyptian and Iranian local officials have authority over local roads, slaughterhouses, parks, and general sanitation and public health procedures. In addition to these responsibilities, Egyptian officials are authorized to establish, equip, and administer schools, hospitals, water works, gas and electric systems, post offices, markets, and cemeteries. The Egyptian councils also may run local transport systems and supervise labor employment projects. In both countries, local officials also are charged with promoting local industry.

The major responsibility of Iranian municipalities that is not covered in Egyptian legislation to the same extent is that of zoning and city planning. City plans, drawn up by national agencies, are enforced by the municipality. This was one of the most controversial activities, because issuing or withholding building permits was an effective political weapon.

The way in which local councils exercise their authority comes under careful scrutiny by the central government in both countries. In Egypt, this became official when the authority of the popular councils was shifted to the local executive councils, made up of local representatives of national ministries. In both countries, local councils act more as supervisory and grievance committees than as policy-making bodies, despite their legislated mandates. In neither country do local officials have authority over police or the courts. They are virtually unable to enforce their own regulations.

Fiscal Authority

The principal source of local government revenue in both countries is the property tax. Under the 1960 Egyptian local government law, property tax revenues were divided between local authorities and a national fund, from which revenues were redistributed among the regions, according to need. In the 1971 law, localities fared still better. Property tax revenues were to be divided within the regions, with one-fourth going to the regional government and three-fourths to the municipal and village governments.

In addition, regional governments draw revenue from a share of national customs taxes and taxes on movable property. The regions may in turn allocate a portion of these revenues to the municipal and village governments. There are also local taxes on vehicles and on business licenses, grants-in-aid from the central government, loans, and returns from public enterprises such as utilities. A major portion of local revenues accrues from the grants-in-aid.

In 1971, the sources and levels of local taxing authority were expanded in other ways. Specific authorization was granted to localities to tax entertainment facilities and the lottery. Governors were authorized to impose excess taxes up to 10 percent of the building property tax and 8 percent of the land tax and to contract bank loans up to 10 percent of the regional budget on their own initiative.

Local municipal revenues in Iran come from a combination of local property taxes, municipal service receipts, loans, local shares of national taxes, and grant-in-aid. In 1971, the property tax (*no sazi*) came under the control of municipal elites. Since then, it has become the major source of tax revenue for most cities—supplementing local shares of national customs and sugar taxes, which legally are required to be redistributed among the provinces according to population, and from there to the localities. In addition, municipalities are authorized to impose taxes upon specific commercial establishments (movie houses, bars, beauty shops) and users' taxes on slaughterhouses, electricity, water, and natural gas. Grants-in-aid can be arranged through the provincial governor's office. Finally, cities can acquire bank loans, which are underwritten by the Plan and Budget Organization.

In both countries the implementation of tax laws is shared by local and national officials. In addition, local budgetary expenditures are supervised by higher authorities. In Iran, for example, there are uniform city budget regulations that stipulate the percentage of municipal expenditures that must be allocated to each program area. In Egypt, regional budgets were forwarded along with local budgets to the Ministry of Local Administration. The minister, in consultation with the governor, could amend any of them, adding items required by law or removing expenditures deemed nonessential. According to the local government laws in Iran, the provincial governor may intervene in the municipal budget process only if the locality has approved a deficit budget. Subsequent to the governor's intervention, the revised budget returns to the council for approval.

POLITICAL PARTIES AND LOCAL POLITICS

Contrary to the trend toward nonpartisan local government in the United States, in Egypt and Iran political parties were expected to increase their role in local government. The "top-down" organization of political parties in the two countries and the fact that both were essentially single-party states made the local units of the parties somewhat different from their counterparts in competitive party systems. In particular, local party leaders could not depend upon their contributions to the party to ensure their political futures. While the Egyptian Arab Socialist Union (ASU), founded in 1961, was at the height of its influence in national politics in the late 1960s under Ali Sabry's tutelage, local party leaders were in a very weak position, easily removed from office. In Iran, the dominant Iran Novin Party had no significant influence in local elections. Its successor, the Rastakhiz Party (1975-78) had just begun to organize local branches when the monarchy was overthrown.

Earlier in this century, political parties had local influence through the individual patrons with whom they were identified. During Egypt's parliamentary period under the monarchy (1923-52) political parties competed in national politics by organizing voters through the power of particular local landholding families.[8] By 1960, eight years after the military coup overthrew the monarchy, Nasser's regime was secure enough to take on these traditional political patrons and replace them with a centrally controlled political organization. This approach to local politics continued until President Sadat disassembled the Arab Socialist Union's organization in the early years of his presidency.

Iran had a similar experience with competitive party politics during the period of parliamentary ascendancy from 1941-53. Local patrons gave party names to the group that supported them. The exceptions were a few parties that were identified with an ideological stance (the communist parties, radical nationalist and separatist parties, and religious groups). But, in general, party politics at the local level was informal and personal.

Structure

The ASU's grass-roots original leadership was called the committee of twenty, a group elected by village party members. In 1965, the committee's functions were taken over by a "local leadership group" and a youth organization. The leadership group consisted of local party activists and government administrators, selected by the regional party secretary. Similarly, the secretaries of the ASU district and regional levels were appointed by national party officials. The structure of relationships among the ASU, the local councils, and bureaucrats serving at the local level was very much like local government in the Soviet Union, although the ASU was far weaker than the Communist party.

In his reorganization of local government in 1971, President Sadat began to assert his own authority over the party organization by giving the ASU central people's council direct representation on local councils. The members of the central council were elected by the rank and file of the party, so party leaders lost even the minimal power they had enjoyed over the party organization. President Sadat also purged anti-government party leaders from local party units. There was no doubt that, between president and party, the president came first.

The constitution of Iran's new Rastakhiz party was announced in May 1975. The Rastakhiz never did gain a position of influence in Iranian politics like the ASU had in Egypt, but its constitution indicated the importance that was to be placed upon grass-roots politics and the need for political action on behalf of the regime at that level. According to the constitution, the basic party unit was to be the local chapter, which in turn would have constituted the village or town council. A party council was to have been convened at each level of government.

The Iran Novin party, predecessor of Rastakhiz, had no impact on local politics other than to discourage political participation among those who resented the facade of democratic party politics that Iran Novin represented. The ASU's place in local government had been authorized by national legislation and was encouraged by President Nasser's use of the party as a vehicle for rewarding and punishing politicians. At the height of the ASU's influence, the dividing line between party and council was indistinct. The Iranian parties did not have that formal support. Nor did the Shah give them informal encouragement. Local politics was not so consolidated in Iran. The regime's tendency to ignore the need for political organization—built upon a foundation of political compromise—at the local level in Iran had fairly predictable consequences. The political vacuum at the local level became apparent when the Shah's regime fell. As the 1978 revolution progressed, local governments were the first to collapse. Revolutionary groups seized power in Mashhad, Qom, and in sections of Teheran and Shiraz, while Prime Minister Bakhtiar's caretaker government still held authority over the national government.

LOCAL DEVELOPMENT AGENCIES

The fragility of local government institutions in Iran had little to do with substantive policy issues. Local councils and party committees had little influence over public policy and most of their constituents realized that. The Shah, like Egyptian President Nasser, based his appeals for popular support in large part upon the regime's ability to improve public services at the local level, and as a result he retained his control over policymaking. Most public services provided locally were managed by national ministries and special service agencies, not local politicians.

Still, the bureaucrats serving at the local level were unable to avoid conflicts over whether they were to be politically responsive to local interests or to national directives. The root of this dilemma was in the economic changes that had occurred during the 1950s and 1960s and had contributed to growing inequalities among the regions. In Egypt, regional planning had been dominated by the national bureaucracy and had produced large-scale development projects, like the Tahrir reclamation project, which had bureaucratic support even though they widened the gaps among regions. In Iran, regional investment decisions had been guided by a national alliance among public and private sector elites that had been advocating an "unbalanced growth" model, singling out specific regions as development "poles."

By the 1970s, the underdevelopment of some regions had stimulated modest governmental efforts to decentralize regional development planning and the operations of some of the ministries. One of the effects that decentralization had, whether intended or not, was to make provincial (regional) officials accountable for the shortcomings of regional development plans and to substitute a largely symbolic participation in planning for planning performance.

In 1975, Egyptian planners proposed that regional economic boundaries be redrawn to correspond more closely to existing administrative regions. Regional governors already had been authorized to take more responsibility for regional development.[9] In Iran, in 1975, provincial offices of the Plan and Budget Organization were set up and made responsible for implementing specific regional projects like school construction, rural health centers, and handicraft industries.

In both countries, the response of regime elites to regional inequalities, which were in large measure a consequence of their own planning decisions, was to adopt community-wide welfare programs. It was this kind of program that regional and local officials were allowed a share of administering, not the major regional investment programs. For example, in Egypt, rural agencies, called combined units were organized in 1960. The combined units served collections of villages; they were never assumed to be instruments of local authority. The purpose of these units was to coordinate the rural development activities of medical, social service, and education officials. Control over the units has been a bureaucratic pawn. In 1960, the Ministry of Local Affairs took over the units from the Ministry of Social Affairs. Three years later, the Ministry of Social Affairs again gained control over them.

Other reforms in local government built upon traditional institutions as a basis for extending bureaucratic authority. This was the case with agricultural cooperatives. Historically Iranian and Egyptian farmers had cooperated on their own initiative in making collective decisions governing the use of land and water. In some areas, joint land ownership (*musha'*) also was common. What the governments' cooperative systems added was control over the agricultural sector by national bureaucratic elites rather than private landowners. In both countries, agricultural cooperatives were established following the initiation of land reform. The chief functions of the cooperatives were to serve as a channel for agricultural credit, supervise tax collection, and regulate food and cash crop markets.

Until Egypt's 1960 local government reorganization, membership in cooperatives was voluntary. After 1960, farmers within the jurisdiction of "reform cooperatives" were required to join them. Taking an active role in the cooperatives lent prestige to the position of local landowners; so, many were willing to join without being forced to do so.[10] The composition of these cooperatives came to resemble that of the local councils, with middle-class landowning farmers dominating their operations. At the same time, the cooperatives were part of the bureaucratic regime. They were supervised by the Agricultural Credit Bank, which was in a position to allocate funds for agricultural development according to national planners' priorities, which were not necessarily those of local farmers and particularly not those of the small farmers and farm laborers.

In Iran, agricultural cooperatives were authorized in 1955, and extended along with land redistributon throughout the 1960s. If farmers wanted to receive land under the redistribution program, they were required to become members of a cooperative. But by 1978, agricultural planners were so convinced of the failure of the cooperative system that it was about to be scrapped, and the Ministry of Land Reform and Rural Cooperation had been absorbed into the Ministry of Agriculture and Natural Resources. The reasons for the cooperatives' failure were several. First, much of the investment in agriculture (which had, in any event, taken second place to military and industrial development) was in agribusiness and farm corporations. Second, the intervention of the national bureaucracy and of national regime priorities into the cooperative movement had made farmers reluctant to participate fully in the local societies.

In cities, too, critical public policy issues are under the jurisdiction of national agencies or of centrally controlled local agencies. For example, both the Egyptian and Iranian regimes rely on municipal authorities for providing basic public services such as water, sewerage, electricity, and transportation. These authorities have incorporated governing boards at the municipal level. But in Egypt the authorities are accountable to the local executive councils (local representatives of national bureaucracies), and in Iran the governing boards are subject to the supervision of specific ministries. In neither country do local elected councils have any influence over the local public service authorities.

During the time period under discussion, Iran had begun an experiment with elected local councils to oversee the operations of specific ministries at the local level. Local health councils, set up in 1965, consisted almost entirely of health professionals, with the exception of the mayor and the chairman of the municipal council, who were charged with the supervision of medical facilities and personnel. Education councils, organized in 1969, were made up of elected members, municipal administrators (serving as ex officio members) and representatives from designated local educational institutions.

The education councils functioned in an advisory capacity, theoretically, to the Ministry of Education. They were granted budgetary review authority and the authority to set local salaries for employees of the ministry. But their authority was largely illusory. Members of the councils were appointed, not elected. Furthermore, even Ministry of Education bureaucrats serving at the local level had little or no authority to deviate from centrally planned budgets and administrative regulations; so there were few local decisions for the councils to oversee.

The councils' creation illustrated the regime's sensitivity to its dominance in virtually every aspect of public policy. Again, however, as in the case of the popular councils and local party units, local participation in policymaking was symbolic, not substantive. In that context, the proliferation of local, government institutions during the late 1960s and 1970s only served to fragment local authority still further.

CONCLUSIONS

The dominance of the national regimes in the operations of local government and in public policymaking at the local level is a function of the newness of local government as well as of the colonization of local politics by national regimes. Local government organization in the Middle East is a recent phenomenon. In some countries, local government did not exist in any formal sense prior to World War II. In April 1975, for example, Saudi Arabia's King Khalid planned to open administrative centers in that country's eleven provinces, a first step toward deconcentrating national bureaucratic authority. In Jordan, the national Ministry for Municipal and Rural Affairs was promoting the establishment of separate administrative agencies for municipalities.

The simultaneous elaboration of local government and of the consolidation of national regimes presents a picture of equivocation in national policy toward local government. Reports on local government in Egypt, Tunisia, Morocco, Jordan, Iran, and Pakistan all indicate that local authorities have many responsibilities but little power.[11] The primary impediments to responsible local government in each case appear to have been the failure of national regimes to concede to local officials any significant fiscal authority or authority over significant personnel decisions.

The severe limitations on local participation in policymaking has not necessarily affected the quality or quantity of public services. In fact, national intervention in local government was critical to the expansion of public services in rural areas. The economic and political power of large landholders was rarely exercised on behalf of expanding public services beyond the most rudimentary of agricultural supports. The creation of rural local government institutions was part of a profound shift in the distribution of power away from the largest landowners to the national bureaucratic elite. In the short run, at least, improved public services in many localities accompanied that change.

In the larger cities, however, change readily occurred without the deliberate intervention of national elites. Urbanization spontaneously created new policy issues and new elite structures. Local government in the cities is more complex and has received far more attention from administrative reform groups. Municipal reorganization during the 1960s and 1970s included enlarging the tax base available to municipal governments, establishing public service authorities, and developing personnel training programs for muncipal officials.

The several important problems with municipal government that remain stem from the continued perception of the city as an administrative center for surrounding regions as it is reflected in the power of regional governors over city politics and from the fragility of the national regimes, which makes regime elites extremely reluctant to see any consolidation of power in city politics.

The emphasis laid upon increasing governors' powers with respect to the national government in both Egypt and Iran needs to be accompanied by the similar expansion of municipal executives' powers so that each issue does not need to be transmitted up the hierarchy for decision. This is particularly true of Iran where large cities are governed jointly, in effect, by a governor and a mayor. The greater complexity of large cities increases the costs of fragmented authority and of limitations upon autonomous local taxing authority.

In terms of the balance between national regime priorities and the need for consolidating power at the local level the reorganization measures comprised in Egypt's 1971 laws were retrogressive. The unique opportunities for formal consultation and coordination of administrative and "popular" perspectives that had been built into the decision-making structure at each level of government prior to that time were an innovative contribution to local government in Nasser's reformist, republican regime.

The contradictions between local popular council government and highly centralized national regimes can make a mockery of both and contribute to creating a political vacuum at the local level. The beginnings of local government in the modern Middle East illustrate the apolitical qualities that grass-roots government characteristically has had in the Third World. Iran, under the Shah's rule, was particularly striking in this respect. The proliferation of local councils, committees, and agencies effectively inhibited the consolidation of power at the local level.

NOTES

1. Iliya F. Harik, *The Political Mobilization of Peasants, A Study of an Egyptian Community*, Studies in Development, no. 8 (Bloomington: Indiana University Press, 1974).

2. James Fesler, "Approaches to the Understanding of Decentralization," *Journal of Politics* 27 (August 1965): 536-66, describes the complexities of decentralization.

3. Paul English, *City and Village in Iran* (Madison: University of Wisconsin Press, 1966); Ira M. Lapidus, ed., *Middle Eastern Cities* (Berkeley: University of California Press, 1969).

4. See Jamil Jreisat, "Provincial Administration in Jordan: A Study of Institution Building" (Ph.D. diss., University of Pittsburgh, 1968), for references to the same phenomenon in Jordan.

5. Frank Sherwood, "Cities in Iran: Notes on Their Problems and Governance," mimeographed (Los Angeles: University of Southern California, School of Public Administration, 1961).

6. Robert Daniel Springborg, "The Ties that Bind: Political Association and Policymaking in Egypt" (Ph.D. diss., Stanford University, May 1974), p. 96.

7. Ibid.,p. 101.

8. Harik, *The Political Mobilization of Peasants*.

9. James Heaphey, "The Organization of Egypt: The Inadequacies of a Non-Political Model for Nation-Building," *World Politics* 18 (January 1966): 177-93.

10. Springborg, "The Ties that Bind," p. 124.

11. Douglas E. Ashford, *National Development and Local Reform* (Princeton: Princeton University Press, 1967); Jreisat, "Provincial Administration in Jordan"; Ann Schulz, "The Politics of Municipal Administration in Isfahan, Iran," *Journal of Adminstration Overseas* (October 1975): 228-39; and Heaphey, "The Organization of Egypt."

Turkey

Douglas E. Ashford *

42

Though Turkey remains in many ways an agricultural society, it is industrializing rapidly. About 70 percent of the population is still in the villages, provincial centers, and towns, and this population still has decisive power in elections. Nonetheless, of the roughly 1.2 million jobs created from 1963 to 1967, only 200,000 were in agriculture. In the first plan period (1962-67), agriculture provided less than a third of the expected increase in employment, and services about half the expected increase, but industry surpassed its target.[1] Development is placing the new incentives and opportunities in the cities. From 1963 to 1972 agriculture's share of the GNP decreased from 41 to 28 percent, while industry increased from 17 to nearly 23 percent. The rates of growth in the industrial, service, transport, and housing sectors are all more than double that of agriculture.[2]

There is no doubt that the cities will grow rapidly in importance, the expectation being that by the late 1970s about half the population will be in urban centers.[3] One of the most serious questions facing Turkey is whether the country possesses the political and administrative capacity to make this transformation in an orderly and efficient manner. A main theme of this essay, therefore, is the impact of rapid urbanization on Turkish local government.

MUNICIPAL GOVERNMENT

Municipal government in Turkey is based on the same principles as provincial and village government. Indeed, were size alone used as an indicator, it would appear that many municipalities are extremely rural and probably more closely linked to rural society than to industrial society. There were 1,571 municipalities in 1972, of which 1,090 were under 5,000 persons.[4] On the other hand, the province of Marmara, was 47 percent urban in 1965, while the Black Sea Region was 14 percent urban in 1965. All 61 provincial head-

*Professor of Government, Cornell University, Ithaca.

quarters are classified as municipalities, 554 of the 572 sub-province centers are municipalities, and 332 of the 887 districts are municipalities. This leaves 618 municipalities not linked directly to the provincial administration system.[5] Very little research has been done on how governors, *kaymakams* (sub-governors), and other officials relate to the municipal governments where the two systems overlap. Such knowledge would be useful in understanding how the central administrative system and the more autonomous towns and cities manage, or fail to manage, to cooperate. The popular predominance of the municipality system is clear from total figures: of the 36 million persons in Turkey, roughly 17 million, or 49 percent of the population, come under the municipal government and administration.[6]

The overall pattern of migration to cities is known, though it has not been worked into Turkish development plans. Since 1950 the three largest cities, Istanbul, Ankara, and Izmir, have accounted for two-thirds or more of internal provincial migration, Istanbul alone accounting for nearly half.[7] Special urban authorities are being discussed, and Istanbul has begun to organize a metropolitan authority to overcome the highly divided structure of local administration in that region. Other provincial and municipal administrations are more concerned with migration falling outside the major urban centers. This migration is not negligible, being nearly 200,000 persons in 1950 and 1955, and over 300,000 in 1960. Geray also provides a regional breakdown of urbanization that helps reveal the diverse nature of the administrative problem. Using the 10,000-and-over cut-off, Marmara was 43 percent urban in 1960; Southern Anatolia, Aegean, and Inner Anatolia 25-30 percent urban; while the South Eastern, Eastern Anatolian, and Black Sea regions were 10-15 percent urban.

The Municipalities Law was passed in 1930, and has not been changed significantly since that time. Under the law, a village or town can apply for municipal status if it has a population of 2,000 or more. Petitions to become municipalities are filtered through a number of agencies of government, starting with governors and continuing to the Council of State and the president. By achieving municipal status a community qualifies for additional grants-in-aid and funds from the Bank of the Provinces, considerably increasing its access to loans and grants. Though no careful study has been done, it is generally recognized that political pressures, often through parties, are important in having municipal status granted by the central administration. Over the past ten years from twenty to sixty new municipalities have been created each year,[8] but this cannot be due entirely to party pressures. From 1970 to 1972, a period of coalition government under martial law constraints, 204 municipalities were added, the largest number in any single year since 1960. No doubt much of the pressure also comes from the severe multiplication of urban problems as a result of the urbanization pressures described above. Within the Turkish system elevation to municipal status is the sole alternative to provide a measure of local autonomy in seeking solutions to local problems. No detailed analysis of the additions has been made, much less the justifications, but Soysal notes that "almost all" of the municipalities added were below 20,000 persons, while the ratio of population living in larger municipalities has increased.[9]

Like the provincial and village laws, the Municipal Law carefully enumerates the obligations of the municipality under the general aim "to regulate and meet the civilized and common needs of the urban population, to provide for their health, safety and welfare and to prevent the deterioration of the urban discipline." The main compulsory duties are to control public places (bars, coffee houses, hotels, cinemas); to cooperate with central government in preventative disease measures; to manage burials; to ensure sanitation in slaughterhouses and restaurants; to provide public transport, building inspection, fire protection, and street cleaning; and to prepare plans for expansion and investment for at least five years in the future. Where annual revenues exceed 50,000 lira, obligations increase to include construction of slaughterhouses and wholesale markets; where revenues reach 200,000 lira, orphanages, maternity hospitals, day nurseries, and other facilities become obligatory. At the luxurious level of 500,000 lira, stadiums and race tracks are required. The wholly unrealistic nature of the law has long been recognized, and in 1973 legislation was pending to revise the Municipal Law.

Each municipality has a mayor, municipal council, and municipal committee. The members of the council are elected for four years by direct vote and under proportional representation by party. Voters must be literate, resident for six months, twenty-five years of age or more, and under no obligation to the government (have done military service, do not hold a municipal contract, and so on). The 1963 law on Elections also provides that civil servants running for office must first resign their posts, nor can a candidate for the council hold any other elected post at the village, provincial, or national level. This is an intriguing departure from the basically French character of Turkish local government, and in practice it eliminates one of the important political links between lower levels of government and the center that operates in the French system. Unlike the provincial council, ministerial approval is not required for all decisions of the municipal council. Some decisions, such as budget and finance (municipalities can issue bonds), require provincial authorization; some go to the Council of State (loans for over twenty-five years); some issues, such as boundary disputes, may be decided by the Council of Ministers. It is not a strict *ultra vires* requirement, for acts of the municipality not explicitly qualified by law are legitimate unless challenged in the courts by the "tutelary" authorities, meaning in most cases the Ministry of the Interior.[10]

The municipal council elects its own municipal committee, which also includes the appointed heads of municipal services. It oversees the daily workings of the mayor and the possibility of deadlock is forestalled by giving the mayor the right to bring such issues before the highest local representative of the central government, in most cases the governor. Until the electoral reform of 1963, the mayors were elected by the councils, but now they are elected directly for four years. Rather more than the governors, whose dependence on the center is quite clear, the position of the mayors is more demanding and potentially more conflictive. Increasingly, the mayorality has become a position of acknowledged influence and probably is the most fully politicized post below the national legislature. A survey done in 1964 indicates that compared with those occupying administrative positions in provinces and villages, the municipalities, as one might expect, have more highly educated personnel. Of the mayors in 1964, 55 percent had only primary education, but 22 percent had secondary education and 23 percent lycée or university education.[11] In 1972, only 11 percent of the mayors had less than primary education, 60 percent primary school education, and 29 percent lycée or university.[12] Thus, the increase in the number of municipalities in the late 1960s seems to have added a number of less-educated mayors, no doubt in the smaller towns and cities.

Interest in municipal elections appears to have diminished between the 1963 and 1968 contests, though the overall level compares favorably with local elections in many industrial nations. Sixty-nine percent of the eligible voters went to the polls in 1963, and 59 percent in 1968. The results for most recent municipal elections for the two major parties are given in Table 42.1. The results confirm the often recognized loss of support of the Peoples' party in municipal politics, though the total figures tell nothing about the relation of these losses to the rural-urban continuum. Nor do the figures tell whether the growing influence of the Justice party in urban politics can be attributed to its more liberal, business orientation, though this would be consistent with the results. The overall trend should be qualified with Ozbudun's analysis of national voting on a different urban-rural breakdown. Despite the Justice party's rural traditions, it did better in cities than in the countryside in all three national elections in the 1960s. Nonetheless, it did lose urban support across the country except in the East Central region. The People's party made small gains in all the more developed regions, except in the three eastern regions and the South Central region, where both urban and rural support declined.[13] The comparison indicates that the national loss of strength of the Justice party has not been reflected proportionately in municipal elections. The reasons for this difference in the voters' perception of national and local representation deserve more careful analysis than is possible here.

MUNICIPAL FINANCE

All municipalities have the same revenue sources as defined by law. These include a share of national and provincial taxes, involving income, customs, and excise taxes, which are much larger than funds shared by provinces and villages; direct taxes, including income from levies, licenses, and fines; and income from municipal utilities. In 1962, roughly a fourth of municipal revenues came from national and provincial taxes, nearly half from municipal

Table 42.1

TURKEY: MAYORALTY AND COUNCIL ELECTIONS, 1963 AND 1968

Election	Number of Votes (thousands)		Percentage of Votes		Number of Mayors or Council		Percentage of Mayors or Council	
	1963	1968	1963	1968	1963	1968	1963	1968
Mayor								
Justice Party	1,366	1,510	45	47	505	603	48	56
People's Party	1,062	996	35	31	335	292	33	24
Council								
Justice Party	1,357	1,403	47	50	7,469	9,957	47	52
People's Party	1,039	1,501	36	37	6,485	6,575	41	34

Source: Mahalli Idarelerimiz Ile Ilquili Bazi Gerel ve Sayisal Biliger [General and Statistical Information on Local Administration] (Ankara: Ministry of the Interior, 1972), p. 54.

levies, fees and fines, and about a fifth from public utility profits.[14] The total income of the municipalities for 1962 was over 900 million lira and nearly 3 billion lira in 1972, slightly more than triple the earlier figure. Compared to provincial and village budgets, the municipalities in 1972 were spending about three times as much as the provinces and about six times as much as villages. To provide a rough comparison, Table 42.2 has been devised to compare overall finances at the two levels in the Turkish system.

Table 42.2
TURKEY: AMOUNTS AND PERCENTAGES OF CURRENT, DEVELOPMENT, AND TRANSFER FUNDS FOR PROVINCES AND MUNICIPALITIES IN 1972 (MILLIONS OF TURKISH LIRA)

	Total	Current	Development	Transfer
Provinces	928	533 (57%)	214 (23%)	181 (20%)
Municipalities	4,300	2,410 (58%)	1,144 (27%)	46 (1%)

Source: *Mahalli Idarelerimiz Ile Ilquili Bazi Gerel ve Sayisal Biliger* [General and Statistical Information on Local Administration] (Ankara: Ministry of the Interior, 1972), pp. 23, 62.

As the table indicates, municipalities have fared well in acquiring a share of developmental funds. The budgeted figure does not include loans from the Provincial Bank of over a billion lira.[15] The municipalities have benefited from their degree of autonomy and had accumulated large deficits, which have also multiplied their income more than is possible for provinces. In 1965, the government decided that municipal finances were in such irreparable condition that, like the state economic enterprises, the municipalities had their debts deleted and transferred to the treasury.[16] There is a certain irony in this debt consolidation, for in effect it has permitted the municipalities to benefit from deficit financing, while the Ministry of Finance has on the whole held the line against deficit financing for the government and the more directly controlled provinces.

Only 80 percent of nationally collected taxes shared with municipalities are distributed. Their balance is held by the Ministry of the Interior in the Municipal Fund and used to finance long-term loans without interest for municipalities under 50,000 persons for the improvement of local services, such as water, sewerage, and electrification. Thus, there is some redistribution of income within the municipality system, though the use of the fund has sometimes produced partisan political controversy and generates considerable lobbying by mayors of any political persuasion in the Ministry of the Interior. In most countries, property taxes provide the major share of local income, but in Turkey they amount to only 2-4 percent.[17] Property taxes are collected under the new Fiscal Law by the Ministry of Finance, previously by the provincial administration and Ministry of the Interior. The municipalities receive a fourth of the property tax back, so the total amount raised, at least under the old tax assessments, was minimal. To a remarkable extent, then, the local government system has been energetically fostering development over the past decade with no effective means of taxing the expanding property base except as it may be reflected in individual incomes.

MUNICIPAL STAFF

Municipalities come under national civil service requirements, a condition that municipalities have tried unsuccessfully to revise. This means that the increased incomes and benefits passed on to the civil servants under the reforms of the 1960s has placed a large burden on local government but, of course, has also protected municipalities against the loss of personnel to better paid jobs at the center. From 1961-67 the total number of municipal employees increased from 37,263 to 45,432.[18] As a proportion of all state employees the municipal system, unlike the provincial system, diminished slightly in relative importance, accounting for 15 percent of all state employees in 1961 and 13 percent in 1967. However, the most rapid increase in municipalities came after 1967 so that more recent figures might show that municipal personnel have actually remained about the same proportion of all state employees. For the period available, municipalities were adding employees much more slowly than the government as a whole, making a 22 percent increase over the six years while the total increased 30 percent.

The 1963 census helps in understanding the quality and utilization of municipal personnel.[19] Like the provincial figure, the census records a larger number than the personnel account, 45,131, as compared to 39,908 for 1963. Very likely the frequent practice of part-time and extraordinarily paid employees accounts for the survey arriving at a higher number than the official budgets. As might be expected, muncipalities have been able to employ significantly better educated people than the provincial administration, a differential in the working of the two systems that must enhance the development of the more urban centers. The census showed 11 percent of the employees illiterate, 17 percent literate only, 47 percent with primary education, and 5 percent with "middle school" education. Nearly 2,000 had a lycée education and 1,685 a university education, as compared with 500 and 141, respectively, for provincial administration. Some rough idea can be had of their impact on more rural areas by examining their location among types of municipalities. Nearly 30,000 of the 45,000 employees were in provincial centers, all of which are classified as municipalities, and about 15,000 or only a third of these personnel work in district, sub-district, or village-level municipalities. Compared to the provincial administration, municipal administration seems somewhat less competitive. Over 5,000, or about a third, of the 16,283 civil servants in provincial government entered through competitive examination; in the municipalities, despite the higher educational level, about 13,000, or 29 percent, entered by competitive exam. Personnel expenditures account for 36 percent of municipalities' total expenditure, and 64 percent of current expenditure.[20]

CONCLUSION

Geray has pionted out that the smaller municipalities have greater need for governmental support, for most are in transition between being a village and becoming a town.[21] Much the same conclusion would be made in reasoning about the relation between agricultural products and light industry. Consumption is fairly well organized, and the surrounding regions have in most cases reached a high level of commercial agriculture so that farmers are able to utilize urban services and meet urban demands. The situation is much different in the 1,090 municipalities under 5,000 persons, which are in many ways advanced villages, or possible communities that have exercised their political influence more successfully to acquire the advantages of municipal status. Another 217 municipalities fall between 5,000 and 10,000 persons.

The Geray case study points out that where small communities become municipalities, budgets usually double from their village level, nearly all the increase being absorbed by the central government. In the communities he studied, 70 percent of the budget came from the center. In addition, the improvement loans from the Provincial Bank have gone almost entirely to municipalities, and the Ministry of the Interior has its own long-term, interest-free loan fund to help smaller municipalities. All these facts underscore both the need as well as the capabilities for assisting and coordinating change in growing communities. Under the present system, however, neither needs or resources seem to be brought to bear on local problems in terms of these structural difficulties. Though the Turkish government has made several efforts to develop a more integrated approach to urban development, change in the cities seems to depend heavily on the politicians and the private economic sector.

NOTES

1. Turkey, State Planning Organization, *Second Five-Year Plan* (Ankara: State Planning Organization, 1967), p. 142.

2. Turkey, State Planning Organization, *Summary Third Plan* (Ankara: State Planning Organization, 1972), pp. 4, 6.

3. Ibid., p. 54.

4. *Mahalli Idarelerimiz Ile Ilquili Bazi Gerel ve Sayisal Biliger* [General and Statistical Information on Local Administration] (Ankara: Ministry of the Interior, 1972), pp. 9, 49.

5. Ibid., p. 47.

6. Ibid., p. 6.

7. Cevat Geray, "Urbanization in Turkey," in CENTO Symposium, *The Role of Local Government in National Development* (Ankara: CENTO, 1965), p. 127.

8. *Mahalli*, p. 48.

9. Mumtaz Soysal, *Local Government in Turkey*, (Ankara: Institute of Public Administration, 1967), p. 23.

10. Soysal, *Local Government in Turkey*, p. 26.

11. Ruşen Keleş and Cevat Geray, *Turk Belediye Baskanlari* [Turkish Mayors] (Ankara: Turkish Municipalities Association, 1964), p. 17.

12. *Mahalli*, p. 58.

13. Ergun Ozbudun, "Political Participation in Turkey" (unpublished manuscript), especially chapter 5, "Urban-Rural Differences in Political Participation."

14. Soysal, *Local Government in Turkey*, p. 28.

15. *Mahalli*, p. 72.

16. Soysal, *Local Government in Turkey*, p. 29.

17. Estimates taken from Soysal, *Local Government in Turkey*, p. 29; and Walter F. Weiker, *Decentralizing Government in Modernizing Nations: Growth Potential of Turkish Provincial Cities* (Beverly Hills, Ca.: Sage, 1972), p. 23.

18. *Kamu Personeli Kadro Istatistikleri* [State Personnel Account, 1961-1967] (Ankara: State Institute of Statistics, 1969), p. 7.

19. *Deylet Personel Sayimi: Ozel Idareler ve Belediveler [State Personnel Census: Provincial Governments and Municipalities]* (Ankara: State Institute of Statistics, 1964).

20. *Mahalli*, p. 79.

21. Cevat Geray, "Basic Problems of Small Municipalities in Turkey: A Case Study," *Siyasal Bilgiler Farultesi Dergisi [Political Science Faculty Quarterly]* 23, no. 2 (June 1968); 117-35.

The Fertile Crescent Countries

*Jamil E. Jreisat**

43

The fertile crescent countries of Iraq, Jordan, Lebanon, and Syria have been the scene of intensive efforts to reorganize local government. For the past thirty years, the national governments of these countries have sought to make their local governments more democratic, efficient, and responsive to goals of national development. These four Arab states traditionally have had similar forms of local government due to common traditions and experiences. The effects of the long Ottoman rule over Arab society are still discernible in local adminstration; the French administrative influence even more so, even in countries with a history of British colonial interference, such as Iraq and Jordan.[1]

THE TRADITIONAL SYSTEMS

The province (*muhafazah*) is the largest and most important unit of local government. Under it, there is a district (*qada*) headed by a chief (*qaimmaqam*). Iraq, Jordan, and Syria (but not Lebanon) have subdistricts (*nahiyah*) headed by a director (*mudeer*). The lowest level consists of cities and villages, each with an elected head and council.[2] The province is headed by a governor (*muhafez*), who is appointed by the minister of interior, as are the heads of districts and subdistricts. The governor is an agent of the central government, and the district heads report to it through him. The province may have several districts and subdistricts, determined mainly by size and population.

Central public services of health care, security, finance, public works, and so on are administered in the province directly by the national ministries and departments. The governor coordinates the field offices and engages in certain

*Professor of Political Science, University of South Florida.

supervisory powers over the central staff. Central governments traditionally have used the local authorities as extensions of their apparatus and as a means of enforcing their will. Consequently, under the colonial system (especially the Ottoman) local authorities were centers of tax collection, conscription, and maintaining order. The highly centralized French administrative model served well the objectives and policies of Ottoman rule (and the subsequent French and British mandates) in the four Arab countries. The advancement of the local people was incidental, as local authorities were tied to the needs and interests of outsiders.[3]

The elimination of Ottoman rule in World War I did not mean independence for the Arab countries; they saw themselves forced into a new colonial relationship with the French in Syria and Lebanon and the British in Iraq, Jordan, and Palestine. The new colonial powers, preoccupied with keeping their territories tranquil and secure, found the centralized pattern of local administration convenient. Public participation or national development took a back seat to organizational effectiveness whenever administrative changes were made. With the attainment of independence came far-reaching changes through legislative codes and official decrees. The new systems became concerned with development, participation, and welfare. Structures were altered to make implementation of the new goals and policies easier.

REORGANIZATION EFFORTS

In Iraq, local authorities operated for many years under the ever-present shadow of the central government. The government maintained tight control by appointing local administrators, subsidizing local budgets, and reserving for itself the power of approving important local decisions. The central government earlier had created the province council, with members both appointed and elected, to enhance the powers of the province. Other national efforts followed, attempting to activate local units and permit them greater discretion in managing local affairs.

Of all reorganization plans in Iraq, none was so profound as the 1974 Law of Self-Governing for the Kurdistan Region.[4] This law established a region larger and more authoritative than the province for all areas in the northern part of the country with a majority of the population from Kurdish ethnic background. The region is a self-governing unit within the republic, and the Kurdish language is recognized as official along with Arabic. Many aspects of the law are unique to Iraq. It recognizes the national rights of minorities and formalizes the means to exercise them. It provides for an elected legislative council and spells out its responsibility for the economic, social, and cultural affairs of the citizens. The council also approves regional developmental planning (within the requirements of the central planning process) and the means for its implementation.

The law also establishes an executive council for the region, consisting of a chairman, a deputy, and other members of equal number to that of the central administrative units in the provinces within the region. The president of the republic names a member of the legislative council chairman of the executive council. The executive council operates as long as it enjoys the formal vote of confidence of the legislative council. The central government maintains a direct relationship with the region. Its national ministries supervise their field offices in the local units. The police force answers to the Ministry of Interior. Under certain conditions, the president can dissolve the legislative council and order new elections. A national judicial body resolves conflicts between local and central jurisdictions and passes on the constitutionality of administrative decisions.

In Jordan, local participation in developmental programs became a national value, and the relationship between central and local authorities was restructured to encourage it. First a 1965 ordinance recognizes the province administration as a legal person. In this ordinance the governor is recognized as the head of public administration and the senior government official in the province, in addition to previously held powers as an agent of the central government. Second, earlier codes provided for some representation of local citizens, but not until the creation of an advisory council in 1965 was there a mechanism to carry out such activity. The advisory council, as the representative of local interest, participates in the formulation of local policies. Third, the ordinance makes the governor and his administration responsible for fostering socioeconomic progress. The advisory council, representing the public, and the executive council, representing the heads of field line agencies, help the governor in the implementation of the new objectives and policies.

Before the current civil war, Lebanon had been trying since 1959 to decentralize province administration. Policies were aimed at increasing the authority of the governor to decide regional matters without prior review from the capital. Field offices, except for justice and defense, were granted greater decision-making powers. The promulgated goals were to enhance the role of province administration in area development and provide greater efficiency and effectiveness.

Syria launched its campaign to change the structure and reformulate the functions of its provinces before many of the other Arab countries. The 1957 Code of Administrative Organization provides for greater powers for the governor, a province council to assist him, and an emphasis on developmental and welfare values. Three-fourths of the members of the province council are elected by province voters.

After the Ba'th party came to power in the mid-1960s, a new law replaced the 1957 code. The ideology and values behind the proposed changes were new to the Arab world. The expressed party policy was to tranform the society—politically, economically, and culturally—into a system devoid of exploitation where authority resided in the "masses of the people." The party established "people's councils" at all levels of local authority, with most of the members elected. Each council has an executive council, with two-thirds of its members elected from within the people's council and the remaining third appointed from within the membership or from the population at large. Finally, the province has a separate budget and power to levy taxes and fees for services, in addition to receiving grants and loans from the central government.

ANALYSIS AND EVALUATION

The reorganization attempts of the four Arab countries are expressions of three mutually influenced, explicitly stated objectives—decentralization, participation, and development. Codes, directives, and official pronouncements strengthening the province and its governor and increasing citizen participation in local affairs reflected these objectives and created the means to implement them. Responsibility for a whole range of developmental programs, including the areas of administration, education, communication, and culture, was transferred to the local units. It is important, albeit axiomatic, to state that formal policy statements do not necessarily provide a true guide to understanding real government objectives.[5] Furthermore, officials may codify and promulgate policies, but this does not automatically ensure their implementation.

The reorganizations in the Arab states may be analyzed on two levels. One is the question of organization and adminstrative processes; the other is the issue of nation building and citizen relationships to political structures. Leemans articulates this distinction:

A decentralization policy thus clearly represents an amalgam of objectives which can be widely different in nature but which by and large can be characterized as being ideological or utilitarian. The former are based on a political ideology, or more generally, on a philosophical concept of man and society. Utilitarian objectives aim first and foremost at achieving certain results.[6]

In Lebanon, traditional patterns of interaction between local and central authorities have not been seriously altered. Central control persists over virtually all proposed public expenditures. Transfer of power between political structures is inhibited because the balance of political powers among rival sectarian leaders and communities is so sensitive. The Lebanese confessional system left its impact on interaction between citizens and administration, and deep-rooted public attitudes and customs toward governmental offices influence administrative performance. Officials are regarded as representing religious constituencies rather than as persons responsible for specialized activities falling within the authority of their offices. Such particularistic patterns of interaction have survived all efforts of change.[7]

National efforts to reorganize local authorities in Jordan were not much more successful. Only minor changes in traditional norms and processes were made, and the gap between conception and application of administrative reform is clearly discernible. For example, governors were given more responsibility and greater workloads, but the central ministries reserved the right to approve local decisions. The Council of Ministers may call back transferred powers at will. There were problems in the implementation of the provision of the 1965 code that allowed the provinces to formulate their own budgets. The scarcity of economic resources reinforced already rigid central control over the disbursement of funds. Also, many central ministries were reluctant to implement the decision to decentralize because they questioned the administrative capability and technical competence of the local administrators.

In Syria and Iraq, the controlling Ba'th Party is committed to social reform, economic development, and improving the quality of life for the society's poor. Central planning has been utilized as a major instrument to direct developmental efforts and to mobilize human and material resources toward such established goals. Such measures extended the scope and intensity of national powers over all aspects of societal life, consequently counterbalancing the efforts to decentralize and encourage local participation in the decision-making processes.

The necessity for strict political loyalty in Syria and Iraq has also interfered with local control of local affairs. Both national governments have adopted new policies that drastically depart from the status quo, and the leadership is wary of opposition from traditional forces, foreign intrusion through local groups, and conflicts within the ruling party itself. Thus, central interference in local affairs is frequent.

In summary, reorganization efforts in the fertile crescent countries were aimed at improving the overall structure of local government and administration to accomplish the adopted policies and objectives. There is evidence, however, that impediments to such reforms have not been overcome. Local governments in these countries face the same sorts of problems that most local systems of the developed world face to some degree: inadequate finances, lack of qualified people to staff agencies and serve on councils, and entrenched local interests that resist change. In addition, the governments are acting on the simplistic theory that promises the attainment of administrative and developmental change by using legalistic means to alter governmental structures and functions.

But the examination of the concepts and the processes of reorganization of local authorities in these Arab states reveals other peculiar problems. Implementation of the reorganization scheme in Jordan would mean drastic alteration of some of the basic values and premises of the traditional political structure. Decentralization and popular participation in local public policy-making would dilute central powers and create competing local forces. Faced with such a development, the national rulers tenaciously guard their traditional prerogatives and political powers.

Lebanon faces a problem similar to that of Jordan. The implementation of proposed changes could undermine the sensitive balance of sectarian representation in the system. Religious groups, conservative political parties, and landowners with large holdings suspect all attempts to change political or administrative processes. Representation of traditional confessionalism is always accorded more importance than administrative efficiency or universal democratic norms.

In Syria and Iraq, there is no wavering of purpose or hesitancy of action. Political ideology is clearly defined by the party in power. Commitment to socioeconomic advancement is also pronounced. The immense economic control by nationalist-socialist political regimes, however, strengthened the hands of central authorities in a direction opposite to that of the proposed values for local reorganization. The strong centripetal force generated by national planning is further enhanced by considerations of political loyalty and national security under conditions of questionable political consensus.

Iraq faces a unique problem posed by its dealing with ethnic and linguistic groups, particularly the Kurdish community. This issue has been a serious threat to national unity, erupting in several periods of armed resistance by the Kurds, who have disguised their quest for independence in appeals for autonomy. The central authority, trying to preserve the unity of the country, reacted militarily. The cycle of violence was terminated by the compromise that was reached and legislated in the Law of Self-Governing for the Kurdistan Region, 1974, as discussed above. The law exemplified the positive attitude of the central government toward creating homogeneous local units in defined areas of socio-anthropological and linguistic cohesion. Judgments on the reorganization introduced in 1974 should be based not on the promulgated principles but on the success of enforcement. The actual interaction between the central and regional authorities will determine the degree of decentralization and representation and accomplishments in the developmental field.

Finally, one of the most relevant and least understood problems of administrative change in the Arab world is the attitude of the citizenry. It is difficult to break away from a sense of subordination and submission to higher offices after years of colonial rule and authoritarian governments. This is true even when the top leadership is genuinely willing to allow greater autonomy, local participation, local initiative, and less central authoritarianism.

THE URBAN ISSUE

The problems of urbanization in the Arab world have not been sufficiently examined and analyzed, and accurate and recent data are often unavailable. Nevertheless, certain significant aspects of urban life in the countries of the fertile crescent that affect the administrative process within city government are pointed out.

First, the Arab world has experienced accelerated growth since World War I. In fifty years, city populations doubled. (Most Western societies took two centuries to reach that proportion of growth.) Of today's developing regions, the Arab world is second only to Latin America in urbanization. Figures for the early 1970s reveal that the percentage of people living in cities of 20,000 or more was 30 in the Arab world (currently estimated at 35), 35 in Latin America, 17 in Asia, and 10 in Africa.[8]

Second, urban growth in the four Arab states has been lopsided. In each country, one or two cities have experienced spectacular growth and concentration of industrial production, services, culture, transportation, and so forth. The most drastic expansion has occurred in the captial cities of each country. Table 43.1 indicates the percentage of urban population and the single-city dominance in these countries.

Table 43.1
URBANIZATION IN THE FERTILE CRESCENT COUNTRIES

Country	Total Population (millions)	Urban	Capital and Population (millions)	Capital's Per-cent of Urban Population	Capital's Per-cent of Total Population
Iraq	12	35%	Baghdad (2)	48%	17%
Jordan	1.7[a]	60%	Amman (0.75)	62%	44%
Lebanon	3	60%	Beirut (1)[b]	55%	33%
Syria	7	45%	Damascus (1)	32%	14%

Source: Tabulated from H. S. Haddad and B. K. Nijim, eds., *The Arab World: A Handbook* (Wilmette, Ill.: Medina Press, 1978).

[a]Without the occupied West Bank
[b]Adjusted figure.

The rapid growth of urbanization has been caused by both natural increases in population and migration to the cities from the rural areas. Social scientists distinguish between "urbanization," representing quanitative increase in popualtion, and "urbanism," denoting a certain quality of city life. Urbanism "is reserved by sociologists for qualitative change in people's outlook, behavioral patterns, and the organizational networks which they create and participate in."[9] The growth was not always accompanied by changes in life style, impersonal relations, universalism, and a modern outlook.

The growth of the cities expanded their boundaries dramatically.[10] For example, Amman increased in area from 45 square kilometers in 1956 to 110 in 1971, or twelve times its size in 1948.[11] The reasons for this growth are those that caused similar increases in Beirut, Damascus, and Baghdad: concentration of economic activities, government departments, and services; low productivity in the agricultural areas; availability of social, cultural, and recreational services, and so forth. A unique factor in the growth of this city, however, is the mass exodus from the West Bank of the Jordan River by the Palestinian people caused by the Israeli occupation of their lands. The excessive, rapid growth of Amman and the other Arab capitals led to complex social, cultural, administrative, and health problems. The demand for drinking water increased to a point that exceeded available supply. Problems of housing, roads, traffic, and unemployment drained the meager financial resources of the municipality.

The boundaries of the province and the municipality are identical in Beirut, and the governor of the province is also mayor of the city. In the other capitals—Amman, Damascus, and Baghdad—the mayor is not a provincial governor, and, like mayors of other cities, he reports directly to the Ministry of Local Government. Municipal councils are usually elected, but they are generally subservient to the will of the mayor. As in other units of local government, and for similar reasons, extreme centralization is the main characteristic of central-municipal relations in the four states.[12]

The problems of municipal and village councils in Jordan and the policies developed to cope with them are typical of, if not identical with, what is happening in the other Arab states. Therefore, a closer look at the Jordanian scene provides sufficient representation of the current situation in the four countries.

The National Planning Council in Jordan has pinpointed the following major problems:

1. Increased migration from rural areas to the city;
2. Meager financial resources;
3. Lack of citizen participation in local development programs;
4. Inadequacy of criteria measuring the performance of local government;
5. Absence of overall planning for projects in villages and towns;
6. No clear definition of the responsibilities and powers of central government bodies involved in village and municipal affairs; and
7. Shortage of technical and administrative personnel.[13]

The organizational and policy measures proposed by the National Planning Council to deal with these problems in the three year plan (1973-75) contain these recommendations:

1. Formulation and adoption of a master plan to observe demographic aspects and population distribution with an eye toward reducing population pressure on the big cities, especially the capital
2. Adoption of a master plan for villages and towns based on the requirements of the comprehensive regional plan
3. Provisions for incentives to divert economic activity into rural areas and create employment opportunities there
4. Enactment of legislative measures ensuring a clear definiton of responsibilities and powers of central offices dealing with municipal and village councils
5. Providing municipal and village councils with greater financial resources by offering them easy-term domestic and foreign loans, tax levies on beneficiaries of new projects, and private contributions
6. Promoting citizen participation in community development.

The ultimate goal of such policies is to activate municipal and village councils to share more in the efforts of national development and upgrade their capabilities to provide public services. The creation of a separate Ministry of

Municipal and Rural Affairs in 1965 and a Municipal and Village Loan Fund in 1966 constituted a major organizational change to meet these ends. These bodies provide technical skills and help finance municipal and village projects. Almost all of Jordan's municipal councils have been instrumental in implementing projects such as building roads and providing electricity and water.

In conclusion, the governments of Jordan, Lebanon, Iraq, and Syria have demonstrated dynamic and innovative capabilities to reorganize their traditional local authorities to serve new values and goals. It is premature to render final or conclusive evaluation of some of the changes, because many are at the initial stage of implementation, as in Iraq. Other organization efforts have proved less successful than anticipated. The hope for these systems, however, may prove to be in the continuity of the process of adaptation, its comprehensiveness, and the readiness of the systems to accept change, rather than in specific and concrete results.

It should be emphasized here that some of the problems facing local authorities in the fertile crescent countries can be solved more easily than others. Programs of action can be designed to increase citizen involvement in governmental operations, improve administrative performance in specific public services, reduce local financial dependency on the central purse, adopt higher technologies in carrying out public programs, and so forth. The real challenge to these systems, however, is in resolving the conflict created by competing tendencies within national policies. On one side, there is an increasing central regulation of economic and social life, particularly in Syria and Iraq, resulting from greater emphasis on central planning and national development, in addition to the constant efforts to preserve political control over local jurisdictions. On the other, changes are made to enhance local initiatives and to generate greater local participation in governmental decisions. The balancing of such opposite influence requires political and economic decisions of the highest order.

NOTES

1. Jamil E. Jreisat, "Administrative Change of Local Authorities: Lessons from Four Arab Countries," *Journal of Comparative Administration* (August 1970): 163.

2. Ibid., p. 162; and Harold Alderfer, *Local Government in Developing Countries*, (New York: McGraw-Hill, 1964), p. 49.

3. Jreisat, "Administrative Change," p. 165.

4. *Al-Jumhuriyah* (daily Arabic paper in Iraq), 12 March 1974.

5. A. F. Leemans, *Changing Patterns of Local Government* (The Hague: International Union of Local Authorities, 1970), p. 17.

6. Ibid., p. 17.

7. Cf. E. R. Crow, "Confessionalism, Public Administration, and Efficiency," in *Politics in Lebanon*, ed. L. Binder (New York: John Wiley, 1966), pp. 174, 175.

8. Saad E. M. Ibrahim, "Over-Urbanization and Under-Urbanization: The Case of the Arab World," *International Journal of Middle East Studies* (January 1975): 33.

9. Ibid., p. 38.

10. L. W. Jones, "Rapid Population Growth in Baghdad and Amman," *The Middle East Journal* (Spring 1969): 209.

11. Government of Jordan, National Planning Council, *Three Year Development Plan, 1973-1975* (Amman: National Planning Council, 1972), p. 292.

12. Alderfer, *Local Government*, p. 49.

13. Jordan, *Three Year Development Plan*, pp. 292-99.

PART V

Conclusion:
Trends and
Problems

Introduction

The essays in Part 5 discuss general trends in metropolitan and regional reorganization and the restructuring of local government in developed and developing countries and are based mainly on the essays in the corresponding parts of this volume.

Thus, the essay by Victor Jones and Patrick O'Donnell discusses the growing problem of governing metropolitan areas and the various arrangements that have been tried in an effort to solve this problem. The authors note that by 1970 nearly a quarter of the world's population lived in urban concentrations with a population of more than 100,000. They stress the complexity of metropolitan reorganization, the fact that it must be continuous, and the relevance of central-local relations. They also point out the advantages of a metropolitan government, though there are difficulties in measuring its success. They conclude that, while circumstances vary, in many cases a second tier of metropolitan government would seem to be the best solution. Although it cannot cure all the ills of metropolitan areas, it can be part of the cure.

In his essay on regions, Fred Bruhns develops the interesting view that the creation or reform of regional or county government is really a reform of central-local relations. He argues that the objectives to be served by such a level of government differ according to whether a country's overall system of government is centralized or decentralized. Some nations may be in need of decentralizing central powers to such a level of government as to obtain more local participation, while others may be in need of centralizing local powers to such a level as to integrate the fragmentation resulting from excessive decentralization. He then classifies eight of the countries where a regional or county level of government has been recently created, reformed, or proposed, according to their degree of centralization. Thus, he puts Belgium, France, and Italy in the category of high centralization, and Australia and Canada in the category of high local fragmentation, with Ireland, the Netherlands, and Norway about midway on the scale. This enables him to arrive at enlightening comparative conclusions regarding the reform strategies used by the governments of these countries and the responsiveness of these strategies to problems or needs.

The essay on developed countries by R. A. W. Rhodes is broad in scope. It begins with a thought-provoking criticism of existing approaches to the comparative study of local government. He analyzes the compendious, case-study, problem focus, community power, output, and structuralist approaches to comparative study and finds them all unsatisfactory because they do not recognize the overriding importance of intergovernmental dependence. He argues that central-local relations must be the starting point for cross-national comparisons and proposes an approach requiring a comparison of the relative degrees of autonomy of the various local units. He then uses this approach to analyze the reforms dealt with in Part 3 by asking several questions: Why was reform proposed? What criteria were used for the new units? What were the consequences of reform? What was the relationship between the forces promoting reform and the type of reform adopted, in terms of whether it emphasized more efficient service or greater participation? This enables him to make some stimulating comparative comments on the nature of the reorganizations adopted in recent years by the developed Western democracies.

Professor Subramaniam's essay on the developing countries similarly stresses the need to consider the degree of autonomy enjoyed by local government. Using the former British and French colonies as his main illustrations, he argues that most scholars have ignored the historical causes that have promoted centralization and weakened local government in developing countries. Despite the British tradition of decentralization through local government, British rule in the colonies created a pattern of centralization and "unleashed a rival tendency toward centralization on the part of educated Africans and Asians," with the result that the ruling elite in former British colonies "praise decentralization and practice centralization." Similarly, French rule produced a French pattern of centralism that was absorbed by the native political elite. Added to these influences have been the centralizing forces in the postwar period of modern technology and rapid economic development. The result has been weak local government. Professor Subramaniam also argues that because of the need for greater centralization in the developing countries, it is unfair to compare them unfavorably with Britain, the United States, or Western Europe, where strong local government developed under special conditions. He concludes that "local government in developing countries has been judged too long by the artificial standards derived from exclusive developments in nineteenth and twentieth century Britain . . . United States, and the free cities of Europe."

In my concluding essay I identify what seem to be the main trends and problems connected with the restructuring of local government throughout the world. Two universal trends observed are worldwide urbanism and industrialism, both of which are centralizing forces demanding larger units of government for the sake of efficiency. To prevent a shift of powers and functions from local to central government, many countries have consolidated and enlarged their local governments. But this has created a new problem of remoteness from the citizens, despite increasing demands for citizen participation in government. I then consider the two-tier system of local government as a potential solution to the growing conflict between the objectives of efficiency and participation and discuss the main criteria for determining whether a country or state needs a second tier of local government. Finally, I explore the crucial questions of the autonomy and strength of local government and argue that the key issue is local government's share in the total of governmental decision making within a country. One must consider not only a local government's freedom to make its own decisions about important matters but also the ability of local governments to influence decisions at a higher level of government. I conclude that the central question regarding any reorganization of local government is whether it has a centralizing or decentralizing effect. It is significant that the authors of all the concluding overview essays lay great stress on this question.

Metropolitan Areas

Victor Jones and Patrick O'Donnell * **44**

The growth and prolific increase of the world's major metropolitan areas has taken place almost entirely in recent times. Few cities of over 1 million inhabitants existed at the beginning of the twentieth century. Between 1900 and 1951, the number of metropolitan areas with a population of over a million increased from twenty to ninety-five. Metropolitan areas flourished during the exceptionally prosperous decades of the 1950s and 1960s. By 1970 the number of cities of over a million had increased to 155. There has been a proliferation not only of large cities but also of middle-sized urban centers. In the mid-1950s, International and Urban Research at the University of California at Berkeley estimated that there were 720 metropolitan areas with populations over 100,000. There were another 326 cities which, though not classified as metropolitan areas, had 100,000 inhabitants. By 1965, the number of urban centers of over 100,000 or more inhabitants had risen from its mid-1950s level of 1,046 to 1,400. By 1970, 864 million people, or 23.8 percent of the world's population, were living in urban areas with 100,000 or more inhabitants.[1]

THE PROBLEM OF METROPOLITAN ORGANIZATION

"The adequate organization of modern metropolitan areas is," as Charles Merriam said in 1942, "one of the great unsolved problems of modern politics."[2] In only a few of the 340 metropolitan areas of over a half-million inhabitants (cities alone or cities and surrounding built-up areas) or even among the 155 aggregations of over a million inhabitants have there been major efforts to reorganize local government to meet the need for subnational governance of those matters that spill over local boundaries.

In some instances, the local jurisdiction may be so "over-bounded" that the unsolved problems are not multi-jurisdictional. Rome, for instance, includes

*Professor Emeritus, and Research Assistant, respectively, Department of Political Science and Institute of Governmental Studies, University of California, Berkeley.

most of the built-up area of the Italian capital of 2.5 million people, while in the Milan region in the north of Italy, where communes are small, the communes exhibit all the interjurisdictional problems commonly attributed to metropolitan areas.

Frequently, the interjurisdictional significance of local problems is not recognized, or, if recognized, it has a lower claim upon the attention of rulers or influential people than such problems as economic development, national integration, and political instability. In every nation, it is necessary to secure at least formal action by a senior government in order to bring about metropolitan reorganization. If political leaders and government officials do not recognize the problem, or if they consider it to be relatively unimportant or are fearful of antagonizing local or national interests, of if they look upon the proposed reforms as politically unfeasible or philosophically undesirable, local governments in metropolitan areas will not be reorganized.

The constraints of inertia based on tradition, organizational immobility and the long lead time necessary for putting together changes acceptable to diverse interests must be recognized. Americans frequently blame their constitutional system of federalism and separation of powers for the difficulties of reorganizing local governments, and some look with envy on parliamentary systems where metropolitan governments have been "easily" established, as in Toronto, elsewhere in Ontario, and in Winnipeg, or in London and the rest of Great Britain. The long years of preparation are overlooked in the excitement of relatively instantaneous ministerial and cabinet decision, relatively short parliamentary debate, and the near certainty of parliamentary approval. In Toronto's case, action was preceded by almost a decade of public discussion and official consideration of problems arising from rapid suburban growth. As Plunkett notes in his essay, another decade elapsed before the Ontario government moved to reorganize local government outside Toronto.

Expectations need not be lowered in recognizing that many years, frequently decades, will intervene between the perception of metropolitan problems and reorganization of local government. For example, at least forty-two years intervened between the establishment of the Ullswater Commission in 1921 and the passage of the London Government Act of 1963. Another ten years elapsed before local government in the other large metropolitan areas was reorganized, as part of the general reorganization of local government throughout the remainder of England, Wales and Scotland.[3]

This does not mean that there is no reorganization at all preceding, or even in the absence of, a basic restructuring of local government. However unsatisfactory it may be to some people, highly complex cities and metropolises do persist without formal reorganization of their governments. This is possible because of informal and formal arrangements and understandings among local governments and between them and central government agencies, or ad hoc regional arrangements. Frequently, the most pressing interjurisdictional problems are assigned to special statutory authorities, resulting in what Henry

Mayo calls government by *ad hockery*. Special-purpose metropolitan agencies are not confined to the United States or to other English-speaking countries.

Intergovernmental Relations as Metropolitan Governance

More significant is the widespread use of associations of local governments.[4] Although most authors in this volume describe such associations in pejorative terms, as half-way structures, as defensive leagues, or nongovernments, their widespread appearance suggests that they represent the essence of metropolitan governance: namely, the structure of relationships among governmental and other organized actors with interests in completing or preventing activities with interjurisdictional impacts. They should also serve to remind us that local governments are tough organizations in most countries surveyed in this volume. It is not impossible to reorganize them or even to replace them as has been done in many countries surveyed in this book, but they have been able everywhere to delay reorganization for decades, affect its terms, and, in some instances, notably the United States, prevent it. Even after as thorough a reorganization as that of Greater London in 1963, we see the emergence of more or less voluntary associations of local government as instruments of consensus formation, cooperative services, and the common management of some relationship with the Greater London Council and the ministries. Even before the reorganization of 1963, there was the Metropolitan Boroughs' Standing Joint Committee going back to 1912. The Standing Conference on London and South East Regional Planning was created in 1962 to deal with an even larger region of intergovernmental relationships.

The essays in this book indicate that central governments are increasing their involvement in the governance of metropolitan areas. It is unlikely that this trend has run its course. In fact, it is likely to be accentuated with the continued increase in the proportion of a country's population living in metropolitan areas, with increased concern over land use and environmental quality, and with national and even international management of trade-offs between economic stability and development. Therefore, intergovernmental relations will be at the center of metropolitan governance even if all local governments in a metropolitan area are consolidated into a single unitary metropolitan government. Furthermore, inter-local relationships will continue in all imaginable situations except those of complete consolidation, such as Winnipeg.

The essays in this book also indicate that little attention has been paid in metropolitan reorganizations to the structure of intergovernmental relationships. The Herbert Commission on Local Government in Greater London was not instructed to consider central-local relations. Axworthy asserts that the government of Manitoba in its regional legislation for Winnipeg failed to address the problems of intergovernmental relations. Even in federal systems, where responsibility for local governments presumably is vested at the state or provincial level, national governments are increasingly concerned with the "adequate organization" of local government in metropolitan areas. Axworthy, in fact, maintains that "the Winnipeg case also shows that a shift of attention from local government to provincial and federal governments might be a more productive strategy in gaining solutions to urban problems."[5]

However, in most, if not all, countries, it is as impossible to ignore the role of some kind of local authority in metropolitan governance as it is to overlook the direct and indirect involvement of central governments. If local government, in Axworthy's words, is not to be an "overrated activity," questions of jurisdictional competence, administrative efficiency, financial and other types of equity, representativeness, accountability, and participation must be addressed by local and central officials and by other concerned parties.

Metropolitan Reorganization Never Final

As a final comment on Merriam's statement, we must recognize that what he called an "adequate organization of modern metropolitan areas" will always be a "great unsolved problem." This does not imply that reorganization is not desirable and, in many instances, necessary. Without reorganization, other necessary steps to solve urban problems will be difficult or impossible. Reorganization, however, is only a new framework of interpersonal and interorganizational relationships. As obvious as the statement may be, it should be remembered that reorganization will be productive of the values sought by the reorganizers only if people and organizations act positively and intelligently within the new system of constraints and freedoms provided by the reorganization to deal with substantive problems. Furthermore, there are likely to be unanticipated consequences of any action at any time, and this likelihood is compounded when the action is as systemic and comprehensive as the reorganization of local government in a large, complex metropolis. A further complication arises from the fact that other events in the metropolis, its periphery, the nation, or even the world affect the operation of a reorganized government. These matters concern us in two ways: first, they make it exceedingly difficult to evaluate the performance of a reorganized governmental system, and, second, they ensure that the process of change is never ending. In this sense, Merriam's goal of an "adequate organization of modern metropolitan areas" will never be realized.

The provincial government of Ontario presents a rare example of frequent and thorough reexamination of local government reorganization. Metropolitan Toronto was created in 1954. Basic changes were made by the legislature only fourteen years later, following an extensive and thorough review by a royal commission. Less than a decade after the 1967 reorganization, the entire system was again under review by another royal commission headed by a former provincial premier, John Robarts. Between 1967 and 1974, ten other regional governments and one district government were established outside of Toronto.[6] Already the government has authorized an independent review of the older regional governments. In most societies, it is assumed that once a reorganization has been made, no serious effort will be undertaken for generations to disturb the network of understandings and expectations that grow up within and around it. Yet, some people would consider the reforms of the past to be the obstacles of today. A prime example is New York City, which was created at the turn of the century in a truly magnificent metropolitan reorganization.

New York City is also a prime example of a metropolitan government whose territory was too restricted at the time of reorganization. Since then, the metropolis has spread into twenty-five counties in three states. Likewise, the territory under the Greater London Council is only a segment of the larger metropolitan region of South East England. Restricted boundaries which are politically feasible will always fall short of the growing metropolis until the dynamics of population growth change to a steady or declining state.

We have reviewed briefly the principal reasons why modern metropolitan areas are not adequately organized. Even so, there have been significant and basic transformations of local governments into metropolitan and regional governments since World War II: Tokyo, Toronto, London and other British conurbations, Paris and other French regions, Stockholm, Winnipeg, Miami-Dade County, Jacksonville, Nashville, and Indianapolis, Manila, Rio de Janeiro, São Paulo and six others in Brazil. We would also include a much larger number of reorganizations by means of councils or associations of governments whose organizational metamorphosis is not yet clear: Vancouver, Minneapolis-St. Paul, Atlanta, Portland (Oregon), French intercommunal syndicates, joint committees and advisory councils in Australia, the Swiss association of communes, the *pre-gewesten* of the Netherlands, Frankfurt and other West German regions, Dublin, and several hundred nonstatutory councils of governments in the United States.

OBJECTIVES OF METROPOLITAN REORGANIZATION

The agglomeration of large numbers of people in metropolitan centers has placed considerable pressure on governmental institutions at all levels but especially at the local level. During the past several decades, the expanding populations of big cities have created a demand for many services. The millions of people who live in the metropolitan areas around major cities have come to expect decent housing, workable means of transportation, efficient water systems, modern sewage treatment facilities, adequate police and fire protection, and reasonably livable environments.

In addition to the demand for new services and regulations and the more satisfactory delivery of old services, there has been increasing concern in the past decade and a half about the ability of large governments to respond to more local interests, open up the governing process to citizen participation, and deal on a humane scale with individuals. These two concerns have simultaneously motivated efforts of different groups within the same metropolis to reorganize its government. Neither group has recognized the impossibility of achieving a combination of both values when pushing unrestrictedly for the maximization of any one value. However, there have been those—many of them in positions of leadership and decision making—who recognize the difficulties of reconciling the two values but have attempted to do so.[7]

Except in a few places, most of which have been discussed in this book, traditional forms of local government inherited from the pre-metropolitan era, and often from the pre-urban era, still serve as the prevailing institutions for the management of public affairs in the massive urban agglomerations of today. Nonetheless, the pressures to bring governmental institutions into line with metropolitan needs and local desires have been considerable. As a result, numerous modifications have taken place in the operations of public authorities in metropolitan areas.

In discussions of metropolitan reorganization there is frequent confusion over the exact meaning of the term ''metropolitan.'' One ought to distinguish between two distinct meanings of the word. First, a ''metropolis'' in the older sense of the term refers to a major center of urban activities, a place where large numbers of people are concentrated and important economic, political, and cultural activities take place. Second, there has more recently come into vogue the term ''metropolitan area,'' which is generally understood to mean ''a city with its suburbs.'' Corresponding to these two different meanings of ''metropolitan,'' two distinct classes of metropolitan ''problems'' can be identified. One group consists of all the difficulties characteristic of large urban centers: rapid growth, traffic congestion, air pollution, crime, inadequate housing, and so forth. A second group results specifically from the fragmentation of metropolitan areas into central cities and suburbs. Metropolitan reorganization efforts generally attempt to solve both some of the longstanding problems characteristic of all metropolitan areas and some of the more specific problems attributable to urban fragmentation. However, the problems arising from urban fragmentation especially have stimulated efforts at metropolitan reorganization.

Metropolitan reorganization is often promoted because it can help ''rationalize'' outdated structures of local government. Several different types of rationalization can be identified. The first may be called ''efficiency rationalization.'' New organizations operating on a metropoitan-wide level, it is claimed, can provide services more efficiently than the existing public authorities. The belief that integration is capable of producing greater economy and efficiency in government lay behind many of the early proposals for metropolitan reorganization. Also, recent advocates of metropolitan reorganization in many nations have been arguing that, unlike existing local public authorities, metropolitan governments are able to take advantage of economies of scale, avoid the duplication of services, and coordinate public resources on an area-wide basis. Although the argument for metropolitan government based on efficiency may have to be modified in the light of concrete evidence,[8] the desire to achieve ''efficiency rationalization'' still provides an important justification for many metropolitan reorganization efforts.

A second form of rationalization, which metropolitan reorganization aims to achieve, can be characterized as "equity rationalization." Different forms of metropolitan areas have widely varying tax bases and resources. Also, various parts of metropolitan areas frequently provide very different levels of public services. Central cities and suburbs especially are likely to suffer from substantial differences in their capacities to finance and deliver services. In the opinion of many reformers, regional integration provides a way for cities to match capacity with need. Through the consolidation of cities and their suburbs, it may be possible to equalize the burden of taxes and the levels of basic services throughout metropolitan areas.[9]

A third form of rationalization that occasionally motivates metropolitan reorganization is "administrative rationalization." In many metropolitan areas today, a bewildering array of local governments, special districts, and other public agencies are found. The New York Metropolitan Area, with its more that 1,400 "governments," is perhaps the classic case, but many other major cities suffer from a similar profusion of public authorities. The reforms of the Paris Region provide a clear-cut example of metropolitan reorganization undertaken for the purpose of "administrative rationalization." This district contains seven departments and 1,305 communes. It is placed under the authority of the Prefect of the Paris Region. As Robson and Reagan conclude, "the net effect of these reforms is to impose a powerful, centrally controlled superstructure over the departments and communes, to rationalize the prefectural organization, and to leave untouched the obsolete system of communes.[10]

Besides permitting the rationalization of public authorities along one or more of the lines just mentioned, metropolitan reorganization may serve a variety of other purposes. For instance, metropolitan reorganization is occasionally embarked upon because cities want to deal with entirely new, area-wide problems. Thus, the concern with air and water pollution and, more broadly, with the environment has prompted many cities in the past few years to create new agencies with metropolitan-wide responsibilities. Also, the desire to extend traditional public services (such as transportation and public housing) has sometimes served as an impetus to form metropolitan-wide organizations. Stockholm's efforts to solve its housing shortage through city-suburban cooperation have brought into being an entire metropolitan government, the Greater County Council.[11]

Metropolitan reorganization can be undertaken to encourage economic development. One of the chief reasons for the establishment of the Quebec Urban Community has been to encourage economic development.[12] The creation of Greater Manila has been regarded by Philippine leaders as a cornerstone of their plans for national economic development.

Metropolitan reorganization can be undertaken for political as well as economic reasons.[13] The importance of political considerations is fairly obvious in the case of cities with competitive party systems. The consolidation of a core city with its suburbs often draws new voting population within the jurisdiction of the central city. If a political party in the central city stands to gain considerable electoral support as a result of regional integration, it may be inclined to back measures for metropolitan reorganization. (Conversely, of course, a political party in the core city may vehemently oppose integration if such a move threatens to undermine its electoral position.) There are other political reasons besides electoral advantage for introducing metropolitan reorganization. Most notably, in recent years many national and provincial governments have found it desirable to promote metropolitan reorganization as part of the overall effort to enhance their ability to plan and control urban development.

In addition to the purposes of metropolitan reorganization already discussed, one final set of objectives should be mentioned. Large cities are generally associated with a reduction in citizen participation; and, in the long run, political apathy threatens the legitimacy of government. As a result, many of the recent proposals for metropolitan reorganization have placed a strong emphasis on fostering citizen participation. In general, citizen participation can take two forms: indirect participation, through elected representatives, and direct participation, through active citizen involvement in urban affairs. At various times in the past few decades, both of these forms of participation have emerged as important goals of metropolitan reformers. The creation and operation of the Winnipeg Unicity is especially relevant to this point. Specific provision was made for structural features ''designed to give local citizens close contact and access to city decision makers.'' Axworthy believes that they have not been successful.[14]

In sum, metropolitan reorganization has been undertaken for a variety of reasons: to achieve efficiency, equity, or administrative rationalization; to provide new services or extend traditional ones; to encourage economic development; to gain electoral advantage or increase political control; and to promote citizen participation. Actual efforts at reorganization have been undertaken for one or more of these reasons; and in practice it is probable that all major changes in the structure of metropolitan institutions have been ''overdetermined,'' that is, the result of a piling up of sufficient reasons to make a major break with the status quo possible.

FORMS OF METROPOLITAN REORGANIZATION

Unitary government for metropolitan areas has been achieved by various means, involving annexation of nonmunicipal territory or the amalgamation of governmental units.[15] The formation of Winnipeg's Unicity in 1972, after an initial experiment with two-tier metropolitan government, is described in Lloyd Axworthy's essay in this book.

The formation of unitary metropolitan governments is severely constrained by several factors. Above all, existing units of local government are likely to oppose amalgamation into large metropolitan governments. Political resistance to annexation, especially on the part of well-established suburban governments, frequently has been successful.[16] Even in places where annexation has been undertaken, often the central cities have not been able to bring enough of the fringe area under their jurisdiction to establish truly metropolitan-wide authorities. In general, the opportunity to establish unitary governments by annexation or amalgamation would appear to be restricted to certain kinds of cities, namely, those metropolitan areas where expansionary central cities heavily dominate the weaker, unincorporated suburban communities on their fringes, those areas where the metropolitan area is small in size, or those areas where the process of metropolitan reorganization is already considerably advanced.

Recently, two-tier metropolitan governments have shown greater promise than unitary governments. Their creation may involve the replacement of the existing institutions of local government by a new set with a multipurpose, area-wide metropolitan authority and a number of smaller units of government for local purposes. London, of course, has been the classic example of a two-tier metropolitan government, which was retained in the 1963 reorganization. More commonly, two-tier metropolitan governments have been established by superimposing a multipurpose metropolitan authority on top of existing local governments. (However, during the process of metropolitan reorganization, the sub-metropolitan units have often been consolidated or otherwise modified.) Two-tier governments of this kind are becoming fairly common in Canada. Plunkett points out that this is in effect a modification of the county. A few but important upper-tier county governments are developing in the United States, notably in Los Angeles, California, and Dade County, Florida.

The major advantage of two-tier metropolitan governments is that regional functions can be assigned the upper tier while still relying upon local governments to perform services that may more effectively or responsibly be delivered at the sub-metropolitan level. Another advantage of two tiers is that they are often more feasible politically than unitary schemes for metropolitan integration. Since plans for two-tier governments have generally allowed the existing sub-metropolitan units of government to survive, they have been opposed less vigorously by local officials than schemes for unitary governments. Finally, two-tier systems of metropolitan government have permitted the traditional forms of local representation and citizen participation to survive.

The difficulties with two-tier systems are closely related to their advantages. Since such systems have entailed the distribution of responsibilities between two different levels of government, they have raised the problem of which functions are "metropolitan" in scope and which are "local." Although almost everyone has agreed that certain kinds of comprehensive planning should be in the hands of metropolitan authorities, many government responsibilities and services (police, health, education, and so on) do not belong clearly at either level. The political and economic stakes involved in deciding which level of government should be in charge of a given task, such as the control over land use, have sometimes been very high. Another problem with two-tier systems has been that, because functions and powers are split between the two levels, such systems have sometimes proved to be incapable of developing basic policies, which many people consider to be needed in metropolitan areas. A final, closely related difficulty has been that the traditional mechanisms for representation that have been retained in two-tier systems have continued to inhibit political participation among certain groups which have usually been excluded, notably minorities and the poor. Winnipeg shows, however, that even a unitary system, with special provisions for participation, may not result in open governance.

Both of the general approaches to metropolitan reorganization examined so far—unitary and two-tier metropolitan governments—involve a significant rupture with the tradition of local autonomy and independence; and both of these approaches entail important new multipurpose authorities with metropolitan-wide powers and responsibilities.

A third approach to metropolitan reorganization, which has proven to be more acceptable to existing local governments, consists of establishing loose confederations of local goverments. One obvious advantage of such cooperative confederations is the lack of strong political opposition, as long as no effort is made to convert them into regional governments. Associations of governments have provided an institutional framework for local governments to meet with one another and work out difficulties, and they have furnished mechanisms for coordinating area-wide programs. But, on the negative side, cooperative confederations have revealed several shortcomings. Since these confederations have been made up of well-established local governments, they have not shown much interest in changing the status quo. Furthermore, even when associations of governments have formulated innovative policies, they have lacked the power to implement them. In other words, because of their localistic and voluntary character, associations of governments have often proved incapable of meeting the pressing needs of major urban areas.

Joseph Zimmerman, in this volume and elsewhere, refers to the use of associations or councils of governments as "the ecumenical approach."[17] He goes on to dismiss them as "suffering all the disadvantages of the United Nations," since they are not actual governments. But this is too cavalier a dismissal, since in many parts of the world there would, in the absence of the ecumenical approach, be no regional organization of any kind. Associations or councils of governments in one form or another, with varying degrees of authority and effectiveness, are to be found in too many parts of the world for them to be dismissed as an idiosyncratic American aberration. After all "ecumenical" is an honorable term, signifying the principles or practice of promoting cooperation or better understanding among different organizations. It is also a synonym for "worldwide" and serves to remind us of the ubiquity of intergovernmental relationships in metropolitan governance and of the organizational toughness of local governments.

In sum, there are a variety of ways in which metropolitan areas have been reorganized. All of these ways have their disadvantages as well as their advantages. In light of powerful impediments to the formation of unitary governments and the limited utility of loose confederations, two-tier metropolitan government appears as a welcome alternative. The current popularity of two-tier governments assuredly reflects their suitability to the conditions in many large metropolitan areas. Thus, even though they too have their shortcomings, two-tier governments offer a hopeful course for future metropolitan reorganization.

PERFORMANCE OF METROPOLITAN GOVERNMENTS

It is difficult to measure the performance of metropolitan governments.[18] Most of them are so new that it is impossible to give a comprehensive, balanced evaluation of their strengths and limits. Second, it is difficult to obtain "hard" data on their performance. One can, of course, look at metropolitan authorities' budgets, and one can conduct surveys to determine whether citizens are satisfied or dissatisfied with their new metropolitan governments. Yet, evaluating government performance is complex, multidimensional and elusive; and it depends to a great extent on the criteria of evaluation selected by the investigator. A third difficulty in evaluating metropolitan governments is that it generally is not possible to compare their current performance with their performance in earlier, pre-metropolitan periods. For one thing, external circumstances have changed; and, for another, metropolitan governments typically perform new services (for instance, water and air pollution control or planning) which had never before been undertaken. Fourth, evaluating the performance of governments in reorganized metropolitan areas by measuring them against those in unreorganized areas involves tricky—and, in certain respects, insoluble—questions of comparability. Fifth, it is very difficult to distinguish variations in government performance that are specifically due to reorganization from variations attributable to more general causes, such as inflation.

Despite these constraints, the question must still be posed: how well have metropolitan governments succeeded, relative to more traditional forms of local government, in dealing with general urban problems? At this point it is simply too early to say. For those seeking encouragement, innumerable examples of successes on the part of metropolitan governments could be cited. But examples of failures are also plentiful, and, ultimately, examples do not constitute proofs. Only after metropolitan governments have been in operation for a decade or more and their performance can be systematically compared with that of more traditionally organized cities, will there be an adequate basis to decide if area-wide authorities possess special capabilities for solving deep-seated urban problems. At present, logic and intuition rather than facts are still our principal guides.

As far as efficiency and economy are concerned, the actual performance of metropolitan governments appears to have been mixed. The operations of some newly established metropolitan authorities have been quite disappointing. For instance, the initial performance of Winnipeg's Unicity has led Axworthy to say that ''the new arrangements have in some ways made the old system look like a veritable model of efficiency.'' Hopes that metropolitan governments would soon realize considerable savings do not seem to have been fulfilled. There have been substantial initial costs involved in setting up regional authorities, and these initial costs often have made the first few years of metropolitan governments quite expensive. The costs of many of the services taken over by metropolitan governments have been increasing very rapidly; and, contrary to some people's assumptions, metropolitan authorities have not always been able to realize economies of scale. Such economies are not automatic; rather, they must be exploited. In addition, there also exist diseconomies of scale. While certain services may be best handled on a metropolitan basis, others may be performed more inexpensively by sub-metropolitan units.

A second goal of metropolitan reformers has been to achieve greater equity within metropolitan areas. Metropolitan fragmentation occasionally has permitted enormous disparities to develop among various urban sub-communities, not only in burdens of taxation but also in levels of service. Moreover, an area-wide strategy, it has been argued, is essential to overcoming urban poverty, racial segregation, and, specifically, problems relating to substandard housing. The United States is certainly not the only country where the employment of a metropolitan approach to urban problems has been motivated by considerations of equity. In Great Britain, London's metropolitan reforms have had the effect of distributing that city's resources more evenly. Although metropolitan governments have had some successes such as this, they have also had some failures in their efforts to equalize services, spread costs, and overcome social problems.

Among the principal reasons for the creation of metropolitan governments, and also of more limited area-wide authorities, has been the demand for new area-wide public services. In the past several years, regional authorities (usually in collaboration with national or state governments) have made important contributions to improving the quality of water and air in metropolitan areas. Pollution remains a serious problem in most metropolitan areas around the world; but in this key area regional authorities already have begun to demonstrate their superiority.

In addition to performing hitherto neglected tasks, regional authorities have helped extend traditional urban services, such as transportation and public housing. The creation or extension of mass transit sytems has occurred in Tokyo, Stockholm, Winnipeg, and elsewhere. Almost invariably, the development of mass transit has been the responsibility of regional authorities, generally aided by state and national governments.

Some new metropolitan governments have deliberately sought to stimulate indirect citizen participation through a system of more effective electoral representation by preserving traditional (sub-metropolitan) units of government. The retention of traditional forms of representation has been a prominent feature of metropolitan reorganization schemes not only in England but also in Canada, Sweden, Switzerland, and the United States. The preservation of local units of government probably has provided an outlet for popular participation that would otherwise be lacking. But, on the whole, as sub-metropolitan governments have lost many of their historic powers and functions to higher authorities (including metropolitan governments), they seem to have declined as meaningful arenas for political participation. Sensing that the crucial decisions affecting urban areas are being made increasingly at higher levels, citizens are losing interest in the ''sandbox'' of local politics. Meanwhile, the new metropolitan authorities being set up have not yet become the focus of substantial political interest or organization except in a few cases.

CONCLUSIONS

At the beginning of this essay it was said that the adequate organization of metropolitan areas has long been an unsolved problem. However, the past few decades have witnessed important new developments in the area of metropolitan reorganization. First, although metropolitan governments have not been as efficient as was hoped, there are many reasons besides efficiency for supporting a metropolitan approach to urban problems. Second, the past few decades have shown that it is not necessary to decide between Balkanized local government on the one hand or comprehensive unitary government on the other. Clearly, it is now possible to choose from among a fairly wide range of types of metropolitan governments. The various two-tier (and even three-tier) metropolitan governments that have appeared recently seem to offer an especially promising set of models for non-reorganized metropolitan areas to consider. Finally, the innovators in the field of metropolitan reorganization have gained considerable day-to-day experience. This detailed, practical experience has much to teach those cities just embarking upon reforms.

At the present time, despite the continuing adoption of reorganization schemes by many cities, integrated forms of metropolitan government are the exception rather than the rule. Most cities throughout the world have merely modified their traditional forms of local government instead of instituting basic changes. That is to say, rather than forming regional authorities, they have employed limited, piecemeal methods to deal with area-wide problems. Despite considerable criticism by reformers, the gradual modification of traditional local government and the proliferation of ad hoc authorities continue to be the most common responses to the problems raised by metropolitan growth.

Of course, the past few decades have provided some discouraging lessons. Metropolitan reorganization is still experimental. It is not yet possible to gauge for sure the impact of structured reforms in metropolitan government upon the political, economic, or social affairs of cities. Also, so far metropolitan governments have not been very successful in directly involving the urban population in the governance of large cities. Last, it is becoming clear that metropolitan reorganization alone cannot eliminate the most serious, underlying problems that plague metropolitan areas. More basic political and economic processes ultimately will decide the fate of modern cities. Yet, even if metropolitan reorganization is by itself no panacea for the ills that afflict contemporary urban societies, it is part of the cure.

NOTES

1. Kingsley Davis, *World Urbanization, 1950-1970*, Vol. 2: *Analysis of Trends, Relationships and Developments* (Berkeley: University of California, 1972), p. 9; Richard L. Forstall and Victor Jones, "Selected Demographic, Economic and Governmental Aspects of the Contemporary Metropolis" in *Metropolitan Problems*, ed. Simon R. Miles (Toronto: Methuen, 1970); United Nations, *Demographic Yearbook: 1974* (New York: United Nations, 1974), Table 8.

2. Foreword to Victor Jones, *Metropolitan Government* (Chicago: University of Chicago Press, 1942), p. ix.

3. For similar temporal lapses, see Chapters 2, 4-8, 16 of this volume.

4. See Chapters 4-9, 11-13, 16 of this volume. For London, see also Gerald Rhodes, ed., *The New Government of London* (London: Weidenfeld, 1972), pp. 184, 198, 306, 332-41, 446-48.

5. Chapter 3.

6. Chapter 1.

7. Both the Herbert Commission's report on local government in Greater London (1960) and the Redcliffe-Maud Commission's report on local government in the remainder of England and Wales (1969) are remarkable for extended discussion of the "health of local government." See the discussion in chapter 22 of this volume, and in Gerald Rhodes, ed., *The Government of London: the Struggle for Reform* (London: London School of Economics and Political Science, 1970); and Rhodes, ed., *The New Government of London*; also Frank Smallwood, *Greater London* (Indianapolis: Bobbs-Merrill, 1965).

8. See Elinor Ostrom, "Metropolitan Reforms: Propositions Derived from Two Traditions," *Social Science Quarterly* 53 (December 1972): 474-93.

9. But see this volume, chapter 1; and Albert Rose, *Governing Metropolitan Toronto* (Berkeley: University of California Press, 1972), pp. 176-84.

10. W. A. Robson and D. E. Regan, eds., *Great Cities of the World* (London: Allen and Unwin, 1971), p. 27.

11. This volume, chapter 15; see also Thomas J. Anton, *Governing Greater Stockholm* (Berkeley: University of California Press, 1975), pp. 55-59, 87-91, 120-21.

12. Chapter 2, this volume.

13. Chapters 3-5, 11, 22, this volume.

14. Chapter 3, this volume.

15. A comprehensive examination of the need for metropolitan reorganization in the United States and of various approaches to reorganization may be found in U.S. Advisory Commission on Intergovernmental Relations, *Substate Regionalism and the Federal System*, 5 vols. (Washington, D.C.: U.S. Government Printing Office, 1973-74). Volume 1 deals with special districts, councils of governments, and other regional councils; Volume 2 consists of case studies; Voume 3 deals with unitary and two-tier schemes; Volume 4 with the allocation of functions between area-wide and local governments; Volume 5 consists of Canadian case studies. See also Kent Mathewson, ed. *The Regionalist Papers* (Detroit: Metropolitan Fund, 1974).

16. Chapter 4, this volume.

17. See especially Joseph Zimmerman, "Metropolitan Ecumenism: the Road to the Promised Land," *Journal of Urban Law* 44 (Spring 1967): 454 ff.

18. The most comprehensive attempt to evaluate the performance of a reorganized metropolitan government has been that of the London Study Group. See Rhodes, ed., *The New Government of London*.

Regions

Fred C. Bruhns*

45

There are several reasons for the utility of analyzing similarities and differences in strategies by which countries reorganize their regional or county governments. Such reorganizations almost always involve substantial reforms in a nation's intergovernmental relationships, between national (central) and local levels of government. These relationships are significant and play a dynamic, even crucial role in shaping the entire governmental system of any country, regardless of its political, ideological, or economic classification as liberal-democratic, Marxist, capitalist, or socialist.

In turn, regional, provincial, county, and district governments, being intermediate levels of governance, play important roles in intergovernmental relations as negotiators between central and local interests and as potentially large contributors to effective conflict management and mediation. Finally, the effort to reorganize and reform existing patterns of intergovernmental relations appears to be responsive to a perceived need whose urgency is felt almost universally. This need is evidenced by the large number of countries that, during the last decade or two, have actively engaged in proposing, enacting, or implementing substantial reforms in intermediate-level governance.

Empirical data concerning these reforms are now becoming available from an ever increasing number of countries whose national systems of government frequently differ strikingly. However, the pace with which these data are being collected, translated, cross-nationally compared, and analyzed by an international community of scholars is, as yet, painfully slow. What are the reasons for this neglect? We do not believe that these reforms lack in significance or fail to attract scholarly interest. Could it be that the paucity and obsoleteness of the conceptual framework at our disposal comprise a more convincing reason? Specifically, does the generality and vagueness of concepts such as centralization, decentralization, and deconcentration, which are currently used to inter-

*Associate Professor of Public Administration at the Graduate School of Public and International Affairs, University of Pittsburgh.

pret changes in intergovernmental relations, cause extraordinary difficulties when attempting to understand and compare these reforms? For the reasons that follow, we are inclined to give much weight to this argument.

Even a cursory cross-national examination of intergovernmental reform efforts reveals that the basic motivations for these efforts appear, broadly speaking, to be quite similar in most countries. The main goal is professed to be a dual one, requiring what seem to be almost contradictory strategies: on the one hand, to obtain more participation or involvement in governmental decision making from the population at large and especially from local levels of government and, on the other, to reduce excessive fragmentation in the articulation of local interests and to consolidate the latter so as to obtain a usable input into and integration with national decision making. If both parts of the goal are to be pursued simultaneously—and often they must—strategies will have to be devised to include centralization as well as decentralization measures and both encourage and discourage local participation in decision making, though not necessarily at the same governmental levels, places, or time. Nevertheless, what we have here is a difficult paradox.

That the paradox exists and that the difficult task of dealing with it assumes a particular urgency today can be explained historically. In the not-too-distant past, when government at all levels was not yet service-oriented and its task was more or less limited to maintaining law and order and collecting governmental revenues, relatively few relationships existed between national and local levels of government. The few services that the national government did provide, such as roads, railways, mail services, and other basic items of infrastructure, usually were managed by the national government's own deconcentrated officials. Whatever local government existed was left to fend for itself, with little or no aid to be expected from central levels, and thus was even less able to provide services than national government.

The advent of modern technology and what has been called the "revolution of rising expectations" profoundly changed these feeble central-local relationships. Everywhere national governments recognized that modern technology permitted them increasingly to control and plan economic and social development, facilitating their nation-building task. On the other hand, citizens everywhere demanded a larger and fairer share of the fruits of economic growth, with heavily increased expectations of what government should provide in terms of economic and social services. Finally, both national governments and citizens realized that national development, with the efforts, risks, and sacrifices always needed for long-term public investments, had to be a shared goal, requiring active participation and a high degree of cooperation from a motivated citizenry. Thus, there was an ever widening recognition that developmental objectives could not be reached without a national government motivating its local governments by offering them an equitable partnership and devolving to them some of its decision-making power and resources. With this recognition translated into action, however, and local governments becoming more powerful, the Pandora's box of local fragmentation opened, and steps to consolidate local interests and integrate them with national interests became imperative.

Through a comparison of national efforts in the reorganization of regional or county governance, we hope to gain some insight into how various countries cope with the pressing contemporary need for changing their central-local relationships in order to obtain a closer, more effective partnership in the pursuit of national development. Regional, country, and other intermediary governmental arrangements can play a crucial role in these efforts. A model for such comparisons, in order to be useful, must focus on the problems of contemporary intergovernmental relations. More specifically, its centerpiece ought to consist of variable clusters directly related to the simultaneous but opposite problems of high centralization and high local fragmentation which we have identified. Thus, the proportional relationship between these two main problems would be an essential indicator for reform needs and reform achievements in any country. Whether a nation is in greater need of decentralizing (to obtain more local participation) rather than of integrating the fragmentation of already existing local politics and participation (centralizing) is, we believe, a key question to be asked in this type of comparison.

As a first step, therefore, we have chosen from the reports on regional reorganization in Part 2 seven countries and the Canadian province of British Columbia and have classified them into three groups, according to the balance between their major pre-reform needs and problems in regard to centralization and decentralization. We have come to the conclusion that in three of the eight cases—Belgium, France, and Italy—the problem of high centralization appears to overshadow greatly the problem of high local fragmentation. In Australia and British Columbia, on the other hand, the problem of high local fragmentation seems to overshadow that of high centralization. In the remaining three countries, Ireland, the Netherlands, and Norway, these twin but opposite problems appear to be fairly equal in size or importance, that is, in a state of approximate balance. Assuming that our classification is correct, these three country groups (each with a different constellation of reform problems or needs) can be compared meaningfully with regard to their reform strategies and the responsiveness of these strategies to reform problems or needs.

Before proceeding with this, however, a few methodological remarks are in order, though space limitations prevent us from justifying in detail our classification. The terms "centralization" and "local fragmentation" were applied to governmental decision making. Since the latter concept, however, is quite vast, we distinguished in "governmental decision making" political, economic, sociocultural, and administrative arenas. Though somewhat artificial due to their close interrelationship, the distinction assists in obtaining useful indicators for both local fragmentation and centralization, as well as a better estimate of the total balance between the two with which a country has to cope. Factors such as a unitary or federal system of government, historical experience, traditions of central control and hierarchical patterns in administration, traditions of local autonomy, territorial subdivisions, political party systems, types of economic planning and control, and existing ethnic or other socio-cultural cleavages were then considered in each country's four arenas of governmental decision making in order to classify countries into one of the three groups.

RESPONSIVENESS OF REFORM STRATEGIES TO NEEDS

When examining reform strategies in our first group of countries where high centralization is the main problem, some prominent characteristics not salient in the strategies of the other two groups appear to be present. We find in France, Italy, and Belgium that the national government, recognizing, almost reluctantly, that there is no other way to obtain the essential cooperation of lower levels of government than to share power with them, attempts to plan and control the decentralization, which is the priority need, tightly and in advance. The establishment of regions and of some form of intermediate-level, general-purpose governance, which is close enough to the center for control and sufficiently remote from local levels not to be unduly subject to centrifugal forces of local fragmentation, is chosen by them as a suitable instrument. In spite of substantial resistance shown by some central government officials, mostly those affiliated with functionally specific ministries, there is no con-vincing evidence that the national government as a whole is unwilling to decentralize, but the level of governance to which power is devolved down-wards is only the next lower one on the hierarchical ladder. If the next lower level is too far removed from the central government, as is the case with the *département* in France and the province in Belgium, the reform creates a new legal level of governance closer to the national government, in this case, the region.

The reform steps used to implement this limited but genuine decentraliza-tion are given a legal foundation on the highest level which may indicate firmness and steadiness in purpose as well as a cautious, controlled, and gradual approach. Thus, a series of constitutional revisions in Belgium recent-ly created three types of regions and regional councils (language, cultural, and socioeconomic) as well as the establishment of regional development com-panies; economic decentralization was enacted by the national parliament. The Fifth French Republic, avoiding constitutional amendments, has enacted since 1958, through its National Assembly (parliament), various laws designed to result in a devolution of decision-making power to a lower—though not much lower—level of governance. The regional reform law of July 1972, which legally gave birth to twenty-two regions as "public establishments" and endowed each of them with two regional assemblies with fairly well-defined powers and responsibilities, has been the present culmination of this process. In Italy, where regions and regional consciousness have a much older tradition and are, therefore, somewhat less "artificial" governmental constructs than in Belgium and France, regional governance and institutions were already foreseen in Italy's post-World War II Constitution of 1 January 1948. However, it took some twenty-four years before the national parliament and the government in Rome promulgated the necessary laws and decrees to give to all the regions listed in the Constitution operational reality.

In summary, the intergovernmental reforms in the three unitary nations discussed here appear to present the following common characteristics: First, the national government has demonstrated a clear willingness to decentralize, but only gradually and under carefully controlled conditions to be spelled out by the Constitution or national legislation, less by national government decrees. Second, devolution or delegation or some central-level power has been directed not to the many lower units of local government but to a limited number of regional units—thirteen in Belgium (counting all types of regions), twenty-two in France, and twenty in Italy—in order to facilitate the cautious, gradual, controlled approach taken by the reform. These regional units constitute the highest level below central governance, and regions were newly created where they did not exist previously. Third, regional governance is designed as all-purpose, general, and multifunctional governance; it is not limited to only one or a few specific governmental functions. Whatever decentralization occurs is mostly areal, not functional decentralization, with power being devolved to certain spatial subdivisions of the national territory. Fourth, resistance to these reform strategies appears to originate primarily from parts of the central government itself, mostly from the functionally specialized ministries in the national capital, which fear a decrease in their power of controlling the adequacy of performance in their specific functional tasks and frequently claim that subnational, all-purpose governance lacks the technical expertise needed for decentralized decision making. Fifth and last, low-level local government (mayors, town councils, and so on) and the general population are often ignorant or indifferent with respect to this type of reform, through some may show more active resistance through publicly criticizing the national government's efforts to decentralize as being wholly insufficient. Some also may attack regional governance, especially where it did not exist previously, as being unresponsive to the needs of their communities or other small local units and as constituting an additional screen or barrier to the communication channel through which articulations of local interest are transmitted to the national government, which is still, in their eyes, the supreme decision maker. In terms of imagery, the popular name given to the national government's regional decentralization efforts in France expresses, perhaps, the typical feeling of local leaders and interested common citizens in all countries that have enacted this type of reform. The term is "deparisinization"—a lessening of the governmental weight and power of Paris, the national capital, which is perceived as a needed first step toward decentralization but not yet as something that has arrived at lower levels, satisfying local aspirations for increased autonomy.

Though our sample of countries is very small and probably not too representative, differences in the five characteristics summarized above can be recognized when one examines intergovernmental reforms in Australia and British Columbia, which we classified as cases where the problem of high local fragmentation clearly overshadows that of high centralization. In regard to the first two characteristics, instead of a clear intent to bring about decentralization, as gradual and limited as that may be, we find that the central governments in Australia and British Columbia are much more ambiguous in their motivations for reform. Australia is reported to have been committed to a system of regional governance only as an experiment to be tried out in the commonwealth territories, not in the six states, and only when the Labour party was in power. Even under those conditions, the commitment seems to have been half-hearted and was faced with strong opposition in the commonwealth parliament and by a majority of state governments which did not pass any basic regional legislation. Moreover, a non-Labour party coalition has returned to power at the national level and with it has come a more conditional and selective approach to regional decentralization. The new coalition might devolve functions and resources to new forms of regional governance only where local authorities have amalgamated sufficiently to reach specified minimum population sizes and are capable of shouldering regional responsibilities and taking the needed initiatives.

For British Columbia, the report indicates that the major motivation for regional governance is a disbelief on the part of the provincial government's Department of Municipal Affairs (DMA) that "existing local government structures were capable of taking care of the myriad problems which would come with future population growth and urbanization," though it also indicates than an extension of central control by the DMA to meet these problems is considered undesirable. Regional governance became anchored here in law (through amendments to the Municipal Act) in 1965, and the regional legislation first permitted a local authority unit (for instance, a municipality), being a member of a region, to "opt out" of a particular regional function and thus not to contribute to the cost of performing that function. Twenty-eight regional districts thus were formed between 1965 and 1968.

Though the regionalization laws later were tightened in respect to regional functions which had to be assumed, the author of the report comes to the conclusion that, by the end of the first decade of regional governance, "no major functions had been transferred from municipalities to the regional districts, and regional government generally had not impinged upon the operation of the municipalities." Regionalization, which the central (provincial) government had intended primarily as a measure for consolidating the fragmentation of local and parochial interests thus had not had much success, especially in regard to a regional planning function which the DMA had hoped to establish but which only a few regions had adopted. However, since regional rather than local authorities would now be given the major role in handling "any functions new to local authorities, such as air pollution control and noise abatement, and also arranging financial assistance for urban and local affairs expected to come from Canada's federal government," the author anticipates ''a slow accretion of regional functions affecting municipalities.'' Thus, while reasons for the reforms are different, and motivations and approaches mixed and more ambiguous and half-hearted than with the first group of countries we examined, some form of regional governance is an essential reform feature in Australia and British Columbia also.

In regard to the rest of the reform characteristics we summarized for Belgium, France, and Italy, even sharper differences are found. As the reports show quite clearly, regional governance in Australia and British Columbia is conceived of and designed primarily as a functional arrangement rather than the spatial, areally based subdivision of general, all-purpose government found in our first group of countries. For dividing the whole country into parts for the purpose of good government, functional re-division is preferred and emphasized over areal re-division as a principle of organization in Australia's and British Columbia's intergovernmental reforms. Speculation on the reasons for this emphasis is not possible here. It may well be worthwhile, however, to explore elsewhere the hypothesis that emphasizing a re-division of functions rather than areal re-division may be the more suitable reform strategy for solving problems of high local fragmentation, while the reverse may be true for coping with problems of high centralization.

Resistance to the regional reform in Australia and British Columbia does not come primarily from the governmental level superior to the region, as it did in the first group of countries, but mostly from below, at lower local levels, which resent regionalization as a centralizing measure impinging on their rights and privileges. Finally, the low-level local government's image of the reform is different. Australia's and British Columbia's municipalities or rural communities have some degree of local autonomy to defend. They are, therefore, more likely to feel affected and even threatened by a shift of central government power to regional levels (which may lead, in turn, to a more direct control over them) than the communities in our first group of countries which had little autonomy to defend and thus were likely to welcome mildly or be indifferent to decentralization measures, which did not affect them directly.

Coming to our third group of countries, the unitary states of Ireland, the Netherlands, and Norway, where problems of high centralization roughly balance those of high local fragmentation, we find that no clear pattern in terms of the five variables used for the first two groups of countries can be established. Applying them to the third group would produce a picture too ambiguous and contradictory to permit a clear distinction of this group of countries from the previous two. This is not unduly surprising when one considers that a fairly even balance between the two major but opposite reform needs exists in the third group, as compared with the strong (though different) states of imbalance present in the first two groups. The essays appear to reveal, however, at least one reform characteristic common only to the third group of countries. It is most clearly expressed in the report on the Dutch reforms where one reads that ''administrative reform . . . wavers between two poles,'' functionally effective administrative centralization and territorial decentralization.

This "wavering," for which we find examples also in the reports on Ireland and, less clearly, on Norway, seems to indicate that intergovernmental reform patterns in these countries frequently shift gears from efforts at decentralization to those at centralization and back.

In the Netherlands, reform efforts to obtain some form of regionalization through voluntary intermunicipal cooperation, which left the power of municipalities and provincial governments, being "sacrosanct," intact, were followed by proposals to combine the existing eleven provinces into five or six units. This, in turn, was recently succeeded by a scheme to substitute twenty-six "mini-provinces" or regions for the eleven provinces, while municipalities would be amalgamated to achieve a minimum population of 10,000 for each. None of these reform plans was implemented successfully; the constant shift in direction—the latest being a shift in emphasis from voluntary cooperation on the local level to devolution of power from the central to provincial levels—created much confusion, however.

In Ireland, this shift of direction in reform efforts can be observed also. The Fiánna Fail government's reorganization proposals of 1971, the first comprehensive review of the local government system since 1898, advocated amalgamation through the abolition of many statutory urban district councils and all statutory town commissions, with their functions to be transferred to the county councils. This was repudiated in 1974 by the new Fine Gael Labour government, which states that it "rejected the plans by the previous administration to abolish small local authorities and further centralize the local government system," adding that "urban areas presently without a statutory local authority have been invited to consider establishing one."

In Norway, the two major reforms that established county councils elected by direct, popular vote and with their own administrative staff, quite separate from existing municipal councils with their local staff, were legislated only in 1974-75; they are too recent to show a shift of direction in reform efforts. The author of the Norwegian report, however, when speculating about the consequences of these reforms, shows many substantial crosscurrents and contradictory forces at work. The reader may well ask whether the new administrative structure he foresees, "a kind of democratic feudalism" in which local government "is based upon a hierarchical system where no decision is made on a level higher than necessary, and where democratic control is an active element on all levels," will be obtainable without further reform efforts, some of which will constitute a shift in direction from previous efforts.

Since the reports on countries in our third group do not provide us with an abundance of information, we may be permitted to add data on a country not discussed in this section of the book but belonging also to the category of countries in which the need for decentralization roughly equals the need for consolidation of local fragmentation. This is Poland, which provides an excellent example for continuous policy shifts in her reforms. Here, the number of territorial units on the lowest (community) level, each provided with an authority structure in the form of a local "Peoples Council," increased by some 250 percent between 1947 and 1958, reaching a total of more than 9,000. It then decreased to 2,750 between 1958 and 1974. In 1950, the local councils assumed responsibilities as local organs of the national administration, and up to the 1970s their executive power, especially that of their "presidia," seemed to increase steadily. The reforms of 1972-73, however, transferred their function as local organs of the national administration to individual administrators appointed by higher levels; the councils retained only a general supervisory role in formulating local policy and monitoring its implementation. Thus it is clear that reform trends toward decentralizing power to the local communities were at least partially reversed by trends toward consolidating local fragmentation and re-centralizing power on higher levels.

Another basic policy change, the significance of which still needs clarification, occurred in 1975, affecting the territorial units on the district (*poviat*) and province (*voivodship*) level whose number and position in the administrative hierarchy had remained fairly constant during reforms occurring between 1947 and 1974. The number of units on the provincial, that is, the highest subnational level more than doubled (from twenty-two to forty-nine), while the more than 400 district units were abolished.

What are the reasons for these constant shifts in reform policies, the apparent lack of continuity in pursuing reform goals, and the administrative "wavering" between functional centralization and areal decentralization measures which seem to characterize intergovernmental reforms in the four countries just discussed? To us, it appears plausible to view these shifts and changes in policy as a response to the need to cope with the problems of high centralization and high local fragmentation sequentially whenever these two opposite problems are of fairly equal size. Under these conditions, we believe, a national government can ill afford to attack both problems simultaneously and define reform policies for the long term. Doing so would require the adoption of policies and administrative measures too contradictory and too subject to political dissent to be implemented in practice. Here our paradox applies: a government would be paralyzed if it had to pull with equal strength and at the same time in opposite directions. A feasible alternative in this situation is to attack, pragmatically, one of the two equally important problems after the other, taking into account feedback and results before deciding when to shift gears from efforts of decentralization to those of centralization and back. This, we hypothesize, is the pattern for reform strategies which nations in our third group of countries are obliged to follow.

In conclusion, we would like to state that we are woefully aware of the inadequacy of our sample as well as the limited number of variables it was possible to examine in this comparison. What we did, however, increased our confidence in the utility of a model which attempts, for the purpose of comparing reforms in intergovernmental relationships, to focus on the process of balancing opposing forces affecting these relationships.

Developed Countries

R. A. W. Rhodes*

46

The reform of local government has been one of the major growth industries of the past decade. Throughout Western Europe and North America the boundaries, structure, functions, and finance of local government have been reviewed, revised, reformed and even revisited. Though there are case studies of the reform of individual local government systems,[1] comparative studies of these reforms are conspicuous only by their absence.[2] A short essay cannot even hope to repair this omission. But by adopting an explicitly comparative perspective it may be possible to raise questions about the reform of local government that are obscured by the focus on individual countries. As a first step, let us review the existing methods of comparison and then turn to examine the case studies of reorganization in developed countries.[3]

THE COMPARATIVE STUDY OF LOCAL GOVERNMENT

The comparative study of local government, in its widest sense, has not existed and does not exist. Rather, this field of study has existed in three restricted forms: the compendious, the case study, and the problem focus. The compendious approach to comparative local government takes a feature such as structure or finance and marshalls all the available information on that subject. The case-study approach takes either a specific country or a specific function in a country and describes it in detail, often with passing reference to other countries. The problem focus approach takes a specific problem associated with local government, such as urbanization, and compares the various ways in which the problem is tackled. Local government may play a prominent or a subsidiary role in such studies depending upon which unit of government is most active.

*Lecturer in Government, University of Essex; co-author (with C. Hull) of *Intergovernmental Relations in the European Community* (Farnborough, Hants, 1977); editor of *Training in the Civil Service* (London, 1977).

The Compendious Approach

The virtues and defects of the compendious approach can be seen in S. Humes and E. Martin, *The Structure of Local Government: A Comparative Survey of 81 Countries* (The Hague: International Union of Local Authorities, 1969). The virtues of the book lie in the massive amount of information drawn together into one volume that compares the various systems by dividing them into four continental groupings. Within each of these groupings, there is a division on cultural grounds. For example, Europe is divided into the South (France), the North (West Germany), the East (USSR), and finally Great Britain and Ireland. The division on geographical criteria is largely a heuristic device which facilitates the arrangement of the information. The division on cultural grounds, however, is of greater interest. In particular, Robert Alford has argued that an examination of cultural variations will enable valid comparisons to be made.[4] An analysis of variations in political cultures raises important questions about the relationship between national and local governments. For example, it has been argued that France's "fragmented political culture" underlies the emphasis on hierarchic control in the administration of local affairs.[5]

Unfortunately, the concept of national political culture is not used in an explanatory manner by Humes and Martin. Rather, they are simply concerned to group their data. As a result, no attempt is made to explain variations either between or within cultural groupings. Thus the USSR and Yugoslavia are grouped together when perhaps the most interesting question concerns less the similarities between the countries and more the reasons for their divergence—a divergence accomplished by Yugoslavia under less than favorable circumstances. This limitation is explicitly recognized by the authors: "Little, if any, attempt has been made to evaluate whether these systems do, in fact, function as laid down by the law, nor is the social-ecological setting in which government operates thoroughly defined."[6] To this extent, therefore, the authors disarm criticism and prompt gratitude for the compendious task they have performed.

Reflections on the limitations of their work, however, cannot cease with this disavowal. The question of how to define local government is not simply an exercise in semantics. Substantive problems are involved. By concentrating on legal provisions, Humes and Martin do not determine whether the local structures are local *government* or local *administration*. Such a question can be answered only by looking at the actual workings of the structure and asking what the relationship is between national and local governments. In other words, the autonomy of local structures is assumed rather than ascertained with the result that doubts can be cast on the supposition that they are comparing the same thing in every instance.

A. H. Marshall has suggested that local government has three essential characteristics: "operation in a restricted geographical area within a nation or state; local election or selection; and the enjoyment of a measure of *autonomy* including the power of taxation."[7] On the other hand, Humes and Martin define local government as: "infra-sovereign geographical units contained within a sovereign state or a quasi-sovereign province state."[8] As such, local government is said to have the following characteristics: a defined area, a population, a continuing organization, the authority to undertake and the power to carry out public activities, the ability to sue and be sued and to enter into contracts, to collect revenues and to determine a budget.[9] But ostensibly local government characteristics can be found in other administrative agencies. For example, the French *arrondissement* (outside Paris) is surely better viewed as an administrative division of the national government denoting that area administered by a sub-prefect than as a unit of local government.[10] The basic point is that the notion of local government invokes the concept of some degree of autonomy and comparisons of degrees of autonomy cannot be made by reference to legal texts. One key variable is the relationship of a particular local institution to the national political system. It may or may not be autonomous. The nature of the relationship is a question to be answered and not asserted solely on the basis of legal prescriptions. Unless it is answered, there are no grounds for supposing that local government is the common unit of comparison. The comparison could equally well be between local government on the one hand and any deconcentrated unit on the other.[11]

The critical comments on the work of Humes and Martin are less a criticism of their particular book, however, than of the whole field of comparative local government. Generally, it is too readily assumed that local government is an independent feature of the national political system and as such comparative work can ignore the national setting. Alternatively, it is assumed that local government is wholly a creature of its national government and any local comparisons must await the creation of satisfactory theories of comparison at the national level. As Daland has pointed out:

Urban governments stand in a relationship to their national government (and the urban system to the national system) such that both produce significant impacts on the other. Perhaps unfortunately, however, scholars and others tend to view urban government either from the point of view of the national impacts on the local system or the reverse—the impacts of the local systems on the nation.[12]

In other words, there does not appear to be a prima facie case for the assumption of either independence or dependence. Rather, attention should focus on the interdependence of the two levels of government. There is no evidence that local government is wholly conditioned by the national setting, just as there is very little information on the comparative degrees of autonomy of local government within their national structure.

There is, of course, an indicator of autonomy—the proportion of local income raised by the local unit—and the few existing comparative studies of local autonomy utilize it extensively.[13] The argument states that the greater the proportion of total income raised by the local unit, the more convincing the presumption of autonomy. There are problems with this kind of analysis. For example, in France, the communes derive on average 15.5 percent of their current income from central government, and yet the prefectoral system exercises tight control.[14] In Japan, local authorities raise 64.8 percent of their revenue from direct taxation, and they are subject to enormously detailed control.[15] As Davey has pointed out, this indicator of autonomy is far too crude. He suggests

For it [local autonomy] to be genuine, a wide measure of governmental operation in the field must be devolved on local authorities; they must have sufficient resources, particularly of finance, to meet their responsibilities as they think fit; they must have extensive freedom to do what they choose in the way they choose.[16]

This approach is commendable for a number of reasons. First, it recognizes that autonomy is meaningless if there are few functions for local authorities to carry out. Second, his emphasis on resources leads to a recognition of the importance of elasticity of income as distinct from source of income. Independent sources of income eroded by inflation are of limited utility. Third, his discussion of discretion shows that independence of income in a context of tight central control does not give local autonomy. Davey's argument makes it quite clear that local government is subject to a system of regulation and that any discussion of autonomy must recognize the complex of factors involved.

The Case-Study Approach

The case-study approach to comparative local government suffers from the same limitation as the compendious approach: it is not truly comparative. In so saying, I am not implying that the approach is without value. Clearly, detailed studies are important prerequisites of comparative work. Unfortunately, however, many case studies are either splendid in their isolation—that is, the research is noncumulative even for one country—or are drawn from a number of countries but cannot be compared systematically. Moreover, the number of case studies is still somewhat limited.[17] Some of the strengths and weaknesses of the case-study approach can be illustrated by examining A. H. Marshall, *Local Government Abroad* (London: HMSO, 1967) and M. Kesselman, *The Ambiguous Consensus: A Study of Local Government in France* (New York: Alfred A. Knopf, 1967).

In reaching its conclusions on the management of British local government, the Maud Committee commissioned a number of case studies of local government abroad. Dr. A. H. Marshall undertook the investigation for the committee and studied the United States, Canada, Ireland, the Netherlands, Sweden, and West Germany. The study is eminently unsatisfactory as a comparative exercise, and the terms of reference under which the material was collected ensured that it should be so. The research was designed to meet the needs of the committee and not the requirements of a comparative study. Consequently, the experiences of a wide range of countries was required. To collect information on and compare six countries on the basis of brief visits made over a period of eighteen months was a virtually impossible research design. It is not surprising to find, therefore, that information cannot be compared systematically, that many aspects of local government are ignored altogether, and that the studies of individual countries do not consider the interaction of national and local government.

Nonetheless, the Maud Committee felt justified in making unfavorable comparisons with England on the basis of this research. This was, to say the least, unfortunate:

What sort of impression would a distinguished foreigner get if he were to pay a visit of one or two months to England and was shown around by a group of local authority association officers and chief officers of some local authorities—with "scarcely a minute lost." He might even get an unfavourable impression of his own country as compared with Britain if he knew the details of its local government system.[18]

There could be no better illustration of the dangers of the case-study approach. Even if the studies of the individual countries have merit—and in this case they do—the temptation to unwarranted generalization is great even though there are no clear criteria for comparison.

Kesselman's study of French local government, on the other hand, illustrates the benefits that can be derived from the case-study approach. He examined a characteristic style of French local politics, which is termed "local consensus." The study proceeds in three stages. First, he examines local electoral behavior, concluding that it is characterized by the search for consensus within the communes. Second, he examines the role of the mayor, suggesting that he is crucial to the maintenance of consensus. Finally, he examines the relationships between national and local government, and it is this aspect of his study that is particularly relevant here. Kesselman argues that the communes' perceptions of the state are crucial for understanding the formation and maintenance of consensus: "The image is a martial one; the state will have to be vanquished or, probably more accurately, manipulated before the commune can get what it wants."[19] In the face of perceived difficulties in obtaining state approval for local projects, it is important for the commune to present one face to the national government and for the mayor, who will negotiate for that project, to preserve that unity.

The fascinating aspect of Professsor Kesselman's study lies in his description of the complex interrelationships between the national and local government. Not only do state attitudes condition local behavior but national political institutions—the National Assembly—are entwined in the complex of relations.[20] Moreover, later studies suggest that, if anything, Kesselman has understated the complexity and extent of the interpenetration.[21] Clearly, however, Kesselman's study lends strong support to the contention that central-local relations are of prime importance for the comparative study of local government.

Although the case-study approach can have distinct virtues, its chief problem centers on the random nature of the information. The studies do not add on to one another thereby building up a systematic body of knowledge. Rather, one has interesting splinters from a collage whose true worth is concealed because the pieces are not glued into a picture frame. It is this simple fact that underlies the assertion that the case-study approach is not comparative. Some studies, such as that of Professor Kesselman, illustrate the importance of themes central to comparative local government. Others, such as the Maud investigations, indulge in passing reference as the basis of comparison, with inaccurate results. Yet others use a case study of another country to provide idiosyncratic and stimulating insights into facets of their own system.[22] In spite of these virtues, however, the limitations of a case-study approach should not be ignored. Comparative studies must provide systematic and, on a more idealistic plane, cumulative knowledge. In many respects, this is beyond the case-study approach.

The Problem Focus Approach

The problem focus approach avoids a number of the difficulties discussed so far primarily because it does not adopt local government as its focus. Consequently, the particular problem of defining local government to ensure that like is compared with like is side-stepped. The approach is well illustrated by A. H. Walsh, *The Urban Challenge to Government* (New York: Praeger, 1969). This study is based on case studies of thirteen urban areas. Each case study followed a common research design, explored a common problem, and formed the basis for the summary, analytical volume. By focusing on the problems of urban areas, the question of defining local government is avoided. Attention is focused on the government-administrative machinery found within the urban area irrespective of whether that machinery is designated local government or a deconcentrated unit of central government. This focus means that the relationship between national and local government is not assumed to be one of either dependence of independence. Rather, the nature of the relationship becomes an important question for the research to answer. Significantly, Walsh's answer to the question is that the relations vary considerably:

Autonomous local government has been described as having "its own capabilities to receive messages from the environment, to process those demands, and to direct its outputs towards the functions it seeks to fulfill." In the cities reviewed here, local government rarely has such capabilities to process major developmental demands.[23]

Instead, one has a situation in which the "decision making processes consist in the interaction of the several levels of government."[24] She criticizes the fallacy whereby "decentralization is viewed as a singular process rather than a multi-dimensional set of relationships."[25]

Research findings of this kind make it imperative to clarify concepts such as local government by examining variations in local autonomy and the nature of the relationship between the various levels of government. It is possible that such analysis will reveal that a substantial degree of local autonomy can exist only in very specific circumstances.[26] It is perhaps time to recognize that the comparative study of local government is but a part of a different, wider field of study, that of decentralization.

Added point is given to this remark, by noting the limitations of a problem focus approach. The term "urban area" is not without its difficulties. As Williams has pointed out, "The disparate nature of urban studies adds up to an eclectically assembled heap of disorganised observations."[27] Two main ways of conceptualizing urbanism have been employed—one describing it as a way of life, the other stressing its spatial nature—with little agreement between them over concepts. To abandon the attempt to define local government, therefore, is not to gain in conceptual clarity. It is merely to substitute a different set of ambiguities and difficulties. A problem focus can raise important issues but it is not without problems of its own.

THE STUDY OF COMPARATIVE URBAN POLITICS

This brief discussion of the various approaches to the study of comparative local government has ignored the fact that comparative studies of various, more limited aspects of local government have been undertaken under different labels, local politics, urban politics, and community power being some of the more prevalent. Irrespective of the particular label—and I propose to use the term comparative urban politics—work on these topics is directly relevant to the field of comparative local government. The question arises, therefore, of the problems of comparative research in the sub-area of comparative urban politics.

I have already touched upon one of the problems, the definition of "urban," but there are others. As Elkin has pointed out, the governmental patterns within urban areas are so varied that it is not clear what they have in common.[28] It is not possible to resolve this problem by focusing on the government of the central city.[29] As a result, it becomes necessary to look at the various approaches used by researchers to assess their utility in comparative analysis. Although it is a somewhat oversimplified scheme, I have classified these approaches into three main groups—community power, output, and structuralist approaches to urban politics.

Community Power Studies

The American literature in this area is too well known to warrant repetition here.[30] It is perhaps less widely known that in recent years there has been a growing concern to explore the extent to which such studies can be applied to other countries, especially Western Europe.[31] Without going over the well-worn ground of the methodological difficulties and conceptual confusions of the original community power studies, it is worth noting the problems of this approach in a cross-national context. To begin with there is the notion of "community," one scarcely amenable to easy definition when restricted to relatively small areas within one country. When it is extended to large urban areas on a cross-national basis, the problem of definition becomes even more intractable. However, this is not the major problem. As with the more traditional literature on comparative local government, there is the difficulty, to use Elkin's term, of the "openness" of urban politics.[32] The politics of urban areas are not insulated either from the influence of other units of government or from the influence of national economic, social, and political factors. Yet the community power literature through its focus on the community tends to isolate the unit under study from such external influences. As Clark has pointed out, the concern with central-local relations in the study of urban politics is recent, and there are "few coherent theories and little precise empirical work in this area."[33] The common assumption that the local community is a closed system has limited, therefore, the applicability of the community power approach to the cross-national study of urban politics.

There is at least one other limitation, "where to begin. In a country where little previous work on local politics and community decision making has been completed, what kinds of information are most productively studied?"[34] One of the consequences of this lack of information is that the comparative study of urban politics is only rarely comparative.[35] For the most part, research has been single-country case studies, although some of it has been comparative within that country.[36] In other words, the community power approach, in spite of its paraphernalia of modern social science and its concern about the generality of concepts, has almost exactly the same defects as the more traditional comparative studies of local government: it has ignored intergovernmental relations, and it is case study oriented.

Output Studies

Output studies or explorations of variations in the patterns of policies (or, more accurately, expenditures) of subnational units of government has been a burgeoning field of late.[37] The model used is basically a simple systems (input, black box, output) model. Apart from the obvious criticisms about the level of generality of systems theory, there are other important limitations from the standpoint of comparative research. Although ostensibly an open systems approach, the environment or input side of the model has been very crudely conceived. It tends to be limited to demographic and economic variables. Consequently, the impact of other units of government is not considered. It will come as little surprise to the reader, therefore, to learn that such studies face the problem of defining a common unit of comparison. As Fried notes for his study of Swiss, Italian, and German cities, "There are important differences among the three countries—differences which make it more fruitful, at least at this early stage, to emphasise intra- rather than international comparison."[38]

In the absence of a definition of "cities" that takes account of differences in the law, structure, finance, and autonomy of local units of government in the three countries, one can only agree with Professor Fried. This is not to argue that the output model is inherently incapable of providing the theoretical base for cross-national studies. I am simply pointing out that its ability to provide such a base remains undemonstrated and that, as before, future developments must incorporate intergovernmental relations.

The Structuralists

To this point, I have been considering approaches to the comparative study of urban politics which have been heavily dominated by American political science. Theirs is not the only intellectual influence in the field. Following the Althusserian interpretation of Marx, a number of European scholars have developed a distinctive neo-Marxist or structuralist interpretation of urban politics.[39] To date, little of this research is available in English, although its influence is beginning to be felt. This is the wrong place to provide a summary of this intellectual strand, but two points should be noted.

First, there is considerable emphasis on the spatial or locational aspect of urban areas and its relationship to the allocation of social and economic resources.[40] Apart from raising the key question of who gets what, this approach attempts to specify precisely the nature of the objects under study, namely, urban politics and urban sociology. In other words, from a comparative standpoint, this approach does not evade the problem of the comparability of the unit of analysis but confronts it directly.

Second, the structuralist approach lays considerable emphasis on the impact of national economic and political factors on urban politics, even if the various writers disagree about the relative importance of these two sets of factors. Again, the approach focuses on an issue which is central to the comparative study of local politics. However, this theoretical potential has not been translated into actual comparative research.

I am aware that this brief review of comparative urban politics has not done justice to the various schools of thought. But if my discussion has been brief, it has had a precise and narrow focus. I have attempted to show that, although both the more traditional studies of comparative local government and the comparative study of urban politics may differ in their methods and objects of study, nonetheless they share two problems: the definition of comparable units of analysis and the analysis of the interdependence of local and national government.

A PROPOSED APPROACH

In Keith Henderson's words, those studying comparative local government are "charting new terrain."[41] In view of the importance of the interdependence of the two levels of government as the starting point for comparing local government, I now propose to sketch ways and means by which this interdependence may be studied.

As a first step, each local authority should be viewed as an organization embedded in a complex network of relationships with other organizations in its environment. In order to perform its activities, it will have to work with other local authorities, the field agencies of central and state government, and the departments of state and national governments. Each of these organizations will have its own set of activities and responsibilities which are probably legally specified. In order to carry out its specific activities and legal responsibilities, an organization will have to exchange resources with the other organizations in its network. Moreover, each organization will have different valuations of the overlapping activities. Some will accord an activity a high priority, others will consider it peripheral to their main activities. Such differences in the priorities or goals of an organization will determine which resources it needs and the organizations with which it will interact. Variations in goals and in the need for resources generate the use of strategies to manage the interdependencies within the network of organizations.[42]

A brief example may serve to clarify the above concepts. Assume that a local authority wishes to take action to alleviate the incidence of homelessness in its area and that it has the legal competence to so act. Further assume that a different type of local authority is legally responsible for the provision of housing—until recently this was the situation prevailing in England outside the conurbations. In other words, for the problem of homelessness, the local authority will find it is not operating in a vacuum. Its responsibilities and those of the other local authorities overlap. Such an overlap can pose severe problems. For example, the authority may increase its expenditure on homeless families only to find that it has made no impact on the problem because the housing authority next door has increased the number of evictions for rent arrears among tenants of municipal housing, knowing that such families would be taken care of by the neighboring authority. Consequently, it becomes important for the first authority to develop a strategy for managing the conflict of aims with its neighbor.

What kind of strategies can be used to manage these interdependencies? At least six possible strategies can be identified:

1. Coalition—the organization joins with other organizations.
2. Co-optation—the organization incorporates the organization(s) on which it is dependent into its own decision-making structure.
3. Bargaining—the organization bargains with the organization(s) on which it is dependent.
4. Penetration—the organization penetrates the organization(s) on which it is dependent. Penetration is the opposite of co-optation.
5. Socialization of conflict—the organization involves previously uninvolved organizations in its conflict in an attempt to change the balance of forces.

6. Setting up or making use of a supra-organization—the organization shifts the arena of decision to another organization of which it and the other organizations are members.[43]

Given that there is a range of possible strategies, what factors influence the choice of a particular strategy? I suggest that the range and type of resources available to the organization will influence the choice of strategy. Included among the resources available to central departments and local governments are:

1. Constitutional-legal resources—the greater the range of functions devolved to local government the wider the range of strategies open to local government and the less the dependence on central government.
2. Financial resources—the greater the quantity and elasticity of financial resources available to local government the wider the range of strategies open to it and the less the dependence on central government.
3. Political resources—the more local political structures are formalized and express local distinctiveness and the greater the involvement of local political leaders in national political structures, the wider the range of strategies open to local government and the less the dependence on central government.
4. Professional resources—the greater the extent to which local officials (as distinct from elected representatives) are professionalized and the greater the extent to which those professions are locally rather than nationally organized, the wider the range of strategies open to that local authority and the less the dependence of local authorities on central government.
5. Hierarchical resources—the less the degree of supervision exercised by central departments, the greater the opportunities for local authorities to employ strategies and the less the degree of dependence of local authorities on central government.

Of the available strategies, the greater the resources available to a local government the greater the possibility that the strategy adopted will be that of bargaining, whereas coalitions are attractive to organizations with limited resources. Quite clearly these suggestions do not exhaust the list of possibilities, and this view of intergovernmental relations as interorganizational dependencies could be developed much more fully. But, in spite of the brevity with which I have outlined this view of interoganizational dependencies, it should now be possible to see the contrast with the more common models of central-local relations.

There is a tendency for these models to stress partnership or agency views of the relationship. In the first, the local authority is an independent unit of government with its own rights and responsibilities. In the latter, local government has a hierarchic relationship to central government, administering nationally determined services. The model put forward here, however, points to the variety of relationships between the two levels of government. Moreover, it does not specify by definition what form the interdependencies should take. For example, local authorities may penetrate or be penetrated by central govenment. The nature of the relationship is a question to be answered, not a definitional product of a certain view of what local government ought to be.

Apart from emphasizing the importance of studying the variety of relationships between organizations, the above approach has a number of advantages for cross-national studies of local government. It becomes feasible to accept each country's legal-constitutional definition of local government. But, and it is a very important but, the approach then requires that the local units be compared to ascertain the extent of their dependence on other organizations. In other words, the legal definition can be used because the approach requires that the relative degrees of autonomy (dependence) of the various units be compared.

It could be argued that British local authorities have considerably more discretion to raise and spend their own revenue than French local authorities (the financial dimension), but that French local authorities have more influence over national policymaking as it affects their area (the political dimension). Dependence/independence can be examined along a number of dimensions. By assuming that a local authority occupies a network of relationships, requiring that this network be described, analyzing variations in goals and resources, and analyzing the relationship between available resources and the strategies for regulating interdependencies, the above approach facilitates an analysis of the central-local relationship along a variety of dimensions.[44]

THE REFORM OF LOCAL GOVERNMENT

In studying the reform of local government, all the issues raised in the previous section are crucially important. Before discussing the similarities and differences in the reforms of local government in developed countries, it is important to determine what is being compared. Even more importantly, the phrase ''the reform of local government'' raises the central issue of an alteration in central-local relations or the areal distribution of powers.[45] To reform local government is to reform the structure, functions, and finance of local authorities. Such changes inevitably raise the question of the relations between central and local government—who does what? If the functions are being reviewed, who is to carry them out? Does local government get an increase or a decrease in its range of responsibilities? If it loses functions, are there compensatory gains along other dimensions? What are the views on the nature of interorganizational relations implicit or explicit in the reallocation of functions? The redistribution of functions is not, therefore, simply a technical exercise. It is fundamental to the structure of government authority within a country. Moreover, in analyzing these changes it is not simply a question of what is done under the general heading of local government reform but, more importantly, why was it done to what kind of governmental unit with what consequences for interorganizational relations? The comparability of the units of analysis and the nature of intergovernmental relations are, given the arguments of this paper, central to any discussion of local government reform.

Before directly confronting these issues, however, I propose to try to identify the major common features of local government reform in Western Europe and North America by examining why the reforms took place, the criteria used to demarcate the new units of local government, and the consequences of reform.

Why did reform take place? The answer to this question is relatively easy. There is almost a "conventional wisdom" on the need for reform. The arguments are that there are large numbers of small authorities; that the resultant limited financial resources and expertise led to wide disparities in service provision between urban and rural areas and an inability of authorities to respond to the increasing tempo of socioeconomic change; that the process of urbanization had made a nonsense of local government boundaries; that the split between urban and rural areas frustrated, in the face of urban spillover, any attempted planning; and that urban problems require planning at a metropolitan-wide or regional level. Less commonly, there was concern to decrease local governments' dependence on central government monies (as in the United Kingdom) and to improve the opportunities for and effectiveness of citizen participation (as in Sweden). The overwhelming impression to be gained from these essays on local government reform, however, is that the efficacy of service provision was the dominant reason for undertaking reform.

What criteria were used for the new units? To answer this question, I can do no better than quote from Barbara and Terrance Carroll's essay in this volume:

Recent reports on the organization of local government systems in many parts of the western world have been remarkably consistent in . . .the criteria which have been employed. . . .The general approach has been to divide services into two categories. Some services have been deemed to be essentially local because demand for them varies greatly from community to community, because the "spillover" from one community to the next is minimal, and because the service is of a type which may be reasonably efficiently administered within a small community. Others have usually been assigned to a higher level of government because of the importance of administrative or financial economies of scale, or because of the probability of significant "spillover" from one community to another.

In brief, the key criteria have been to minimize spillover and maximize economies of scale.

What were the consequences of reform? As before, there are remarkable uniformities among the various local government reforms. There has been a process of rationalization characterized by a reduction in the total number of units and an increase in the size of individual units. To a lesser extent there has been a tendency for the range of functions performed by local government to be reduced and, even if not reduced, reallocated among the various types of local authority.

Two *caveats* to these generalizations must be noted. First, the comprehensive nature of the reforms varies. In some countries, the reforms have been undertaken on a step-by-step or gradual basis (West Germany) whereas in others the system has been reformed in one fell swoop (England). Second, in some countries the reduction in the range of local government functions has been accompanied by a decrease in the range of controls over the remaining functions.

To this point, the discussion of the reform of local government has emphasized the nature of the changes in terms of structure and functions, but there is another point of similarity, namely, that the reform of local government led to a decrease in the opportunities for citizen participation. The essay on Canada talks of "a crisis of representation." The essay on Sweden talks of reform being achieved "at the expense of reducing the citizen's ability to influence communal decision-making processes." In North-Rhine Westphalia reform was "at the cost of people's participation in the political decision-making process." In England one of the "biggest questions" relates to "democratic responsiveness" and the problem of how the authority "can relate to and respond to the needs and reactions of the local community." As before, the conclusion that emerges is that there is enormous uniformity in the consequences of local government reform across the several countries.

In a number of respects this is a singular, if not amazing, state of affairs. Why, given the variety of local government systems, is there such uniformity? The beginning of an answer to this question is suggested in the essay on the reorganization reports in New Brunswick and Nova Scotia:

Neither report approached the subject of municipal reorganization from a systematic theoetical perspective of the democratic purposes and value of local government. Both commissions approached the subject from the perspective of provision of services, with a shared concern that the services be provided in the most economic and efficient manner possible.

In the remainder of this essay, I provide an alternative interpretation of the reform of local government, an interpretation which does not approach the subject "from the perspective of provision of services."

An Alternative Interpretation

The key question to ask about local government reform is: How has reform altered the existing areal distribution of power?[46] And, for comparative study, the key question is: What was the relative degree of dependence of local authorities on other organizations, both before and after reorganization? By focusing on these two questions, it should be possible to compare like with like. It should be possible, for example, to determine if Danish local government was more dependent on other organizations than English local government before it was reformed, how much this relationship was changed by reform, and the relative degrees of dependence of local authorities in the two countries following reorganization. Nor should it be forgotten that there are a variety of strategies for managing the interdependencies inherent in a network.

Thus, even if English local government lost functions when reformed (the constitutional-legal dimension), it may have gained in its ability to penetrate national politics and influence policymaking affecting local authorities (the political dimension). Dependence is a multidimensional phenomenon. In analyzing the effects of reorganization, due recognition must be accorded this fact.

From this perspective, it should be clear that many of the similarities between local government reforms in the several countries are, if not superficial, at least of secondary importance. Considering the reasons for introducing reforms, it should be clear that any diagnosis of the defects of local government that does not explicitly confront the nature of intergovernmental relations has avoided the major issue. In order to understand local government reform, therefore, it is necessary to ask why the issue was avoided. Why was reform conceived in terms of the better provision of services? The short answer to the question would be that central government was not prepared to contemplate a major debate of the existing areal distribution of powers because of the difficulty of building a consensus on this issue. Focusing on the provision of services collapses the discussion of means and ends, of why local government and why this distribution of power, into a focus on short-term problems of inefficiency and inadequate financial resources and expertise. To borrow a phrase suggested to me by Professor Douglas Ashford, local government reform conceived in this way is a ''non-policy'' because it has been designed to avoid the basic policy issue. As a non-policy, as a discussion of local service provision, it is far easier to build a consensus on how and why to reform local government.

This line of analysis suggests some reflections on the form and consequences of local government reform. The ability of central government to determine the shape and direction of reform presumably will be influenced by the strength of local government. The greater the penetration of central government by local government and the greater the bargaining resources of local government, the less the ability of central government to undertake comprehensive reform. For example, it could be argued that the French government's inability to reform local government results from the influence of local political elites at the national level, whereas reform in England was undertaken because local authorities have not significantly penetrated the national political system. To what extent, therefore, is the gradual introduction of reforms an indicator of the relatively greater independence of a local government system when compared with a system where comprehensive reform was the order of the day?

Another interesting hypothesis centers on the extent to which the areas of local authorities correspond to ethnic, religious, class, or other cleavages. To the extent that socio-economic-political divisions are institutionalized in local government, the greater the problems of building a consensus on a desirable areal distribution of powers with a consequent reticence on the part of the central government to alter the existing areal distribution of powers and a preference for gradualism.

The way in which the problem of local government reform was defined also suggests why reform has had one specific consequence, namely, decreased opportunities for citizen participation. Given that local government reform was defined as a non-policy, the issue of participation could not be raised without raising the specter of a debate on the distribution of power. It is scarcely surprising, therefore, that reform did nothing to enhance citizen participation. Quite simply, this item was excluded from the political agenda.

Thus, the degree of dependence of local authorities on other organizations can be seen to influence the way in which the issue of reform is posed: whether in terms of provision of services or the areal distribution of power; the relative emphasis in reform proposals on efficiency and citizen participation; and the manner in which the reforms are introduced—comprehensively or gradually.

Unfortunately, it is only possible to point to hypothetical differences between the several countries in their reforms of local government. In order to compare effectively the reform of local government, there must be a common unit of comparison. In addition, any comparison must encompass an analysis of the resources available to local government and their relationship to the various strategies available for managing the interdependencies between organizations. Such an analysis must recognize that different strategies based on different resources could be equally effective in managing the interdependencies. There is no easy way to compare the autonomy of local authorities, but no cross-national explanation of local government reform—its gestation, form, and consequences—is possible without an analysis of variations in that autonomy. Exploring variations in interorganizational dependence provides the basis for such an analysis.[47]

NOTES

1. See R. A. W. Rhodes, "European Local Government: A Bibliographical Essay," *Local Government Studies* 1 (October 1971): 49-61.

2. The major exception is A. F. Leemans, *Changing Patterns of Local Government* (The Hague: International Union of Local Authorities, 1971).

3. This essay deals mainly with the developed Western countries. The essays on Eastern Europe were not available when it was written.

4. R. R. Alford, "The Comparative Study of Urban Politics," in *Urban Research and Policy Planning*, ed. L. F. Schnore and H. Fagin (Beverly Hills, Ca.: Sage, 1967), pp. 263-302; and R. R. Alford, "Explanatory Variables in the Comparative Study of Urban Politics and Administration," in *Comparative Urban Research*, ed. R. T. Daland (Beverly Hills, Ca.: Sage, 1969), pp. 272-324.

5. See N. Wahl, "France," in *Patterns of Government*, ed. S. H. Beer and A. B. Ulam, 2nd ed. (New York: Random House, 1962), pp. 275-305; and G. A. Almond and S. Verba, *The Civic Culture* (Princeton, N.J.: Princeton University Press, 1963), p. 28.

6. S. Humes and E. Martin, *The Structure of Local Government: A Comparative Survey of 81 Countries* (The Hague: International Union of Local Authorities, 1969), p. 23.

7. A. H. Marshall, *Local Government in the Modern World* (London: Athlone Press, 1965), p. 5 (my emphasis).

8. Humes and Martin, *Structure of Local Government*, p. 27.

9. Ibid., pp. 27-28.

10. Ibid., Exhibit 1, p. 28.

11. My distinction between devolution and deconcentration follows H. Maddick, *Democracy, Decentralisation and Development* (London: Asia Publishing House, 1963), p. 23.

12. R. T. Daland, "Comparative Perspectives of Urban Systems," in Daland, ed., *Comparative Urban Research*, p. 36.

13. See, for example, A. H. Marshall, *Local Government Finance* (The Hague: International Union of Local Authorities, 1969); and F. P. Sherwood, "Devolution as a Problem of Organisation Strategy," in Daland, ed., *Comparative Urban Research*, pp. 60-87.

14. G. Levillain, "Local Government Finance in France" (Report prepared for the XIXth World Congress of Local Authorities, Vienna, 16-21 June 1969).

15. Marshall, *Local Government*, p. 325.

16. K. J. Davey, "Local Autonomy and Independent Revenues," *Public Administration* 49 (1971): 45.

17. For a number of references, see Rhodes, "European Local Government," pp. 53-54, 58-61.

18. J. Stanyer, "The Maud Committee Report," in *Local Government in England 1958-1969*, ed. H. V. Wiseman (London: Routledge and Kegan Paul, 1970), pp. 64-65.

19. M. Kesselman, *The Ambiguous Consensus* (New York: Alfred A. Knopf, 1967), p. 77.

20. Ibid., pp. 79-90.

21. See, for example, Jean-Claude Thoenig, *State Bureaucracies and Local Government in France* (Berkeley: Department of Political Science, University of California, 1975); and Jean-Pierre Worms, "Le Préfet et ses notables," *Sociologie du Travail* 8 (1966): 249-75.

22. See, for example, I. B. Rees, *Government by Community* (London: Knight, 1971).

23. A. H. Walsh, *The Urban Challenge to Government* (New York: Praeger, 1969), p. 179. Walsh is quoting Sherwood, "Devolution," p. 69.

24. Ibid., p. 153.

25. Ibid., p. 179.

26. Ibid., pp. 179-80.

27. O. P. Williams, *Metropolitan Political Analysis* (New York: Free Press, 1971), p. x.

28. S. L. Elkin, "Comparative Urban Politics and Interorganisational Behaviour," in *Essays on the Study of Urban Politics*, ed. K. Young (London: Macmillan, 1975), pp. 158-59.

29. For an extended discussion of this point, see Daland, ed., *Comparative Urban Research*, and Willams, *Metropolitan Political Analysis*.

30. For a bibliography, see C. M. Bonjean, T. N. Clark, and R. L. Lineberry, eds., *Community Politics* (New York: Free Press, 1971); and for an extensive selection of articles, see M. Aiken and P. E. Mott, eds., *The Structure of Community Power* (New York: Random House, 1970).

31. See, for example, T. N. Clark, ed., *Comparative Community Politics* (New York: Halsted Press, 1974).

32. Elkin, "Comparative Urban Politics," pp. 160-62.

33. T. N. Clark, "Community Autonomy in the National System," in Clark, ed., *Comparative Community Politics*, pp. 21-22.

34. T. N. Clark, "Preface," in Clark, ed., *Comparative Community Politics*, p. 11.

35. Eight of the articles in the Clark reader are specific to one country, five are discussions of the problems and prospects of comparative research, and only one reports comparative research. Moreover, this last study, while reporting data on three countries, only compares the "cities" *within* each country, not between countries. An interesting exception to this comment is P. Jacobs and J. Toscano, eds., *The Integration of Political Communities* (Philadelphia: Lippincott, 1964).

36. See, for example, Clark, ed., *Comparative Community Politics*, chs. 5, 6, 9, 10.

37. See, for example, T. R. Dye, *Politics, Economics and the Public: Policy Outcomes in the American States* (Chicago: Rand McNally, 1969); R. I. Hofferbert, *The Study of Public Policy* (New York: Bobbs, Merrill, 1974); R. Lineberry and I. Sharkansky, *Urban Politics and Policy* (New York: Harper & Row, 1971); and I. Sharkansky, ed., *Policy Analysis in Political Science* (Chicago: Markham, 1970).

38. R. C. Fried, "Politics, Economics and Federation: Aspects of Urban Government in Austria, Germany and Switzerland," in Clark, ed., *Comparative Community Politics*, p. 315.

39. See C. G. Pickvance, "On a Materialist Critique of Urban Sociology," *Sociological Review* 22 (1974): 203-20; C. G. Pickvance, ed., *Urban Sociology: Critical Essays* (London: Tavistock, 1976); and D. Harvey, *Social Justice and the City* (London: Arnold, 1973).

40. For a non-structuralist approach which similarly emphasizes the relationship between location and the allocation of resources, see Williams, *Metropolitan Political Analysis*.

41. K. M. Henderson, "Charting a New Terrain: Comparative Local Administration," *Public Administration Review* 27 (1967): 142-47.

42. Earlier studies which have focused on intergovernmental relations include D. Ashford, "Theories of Local Government: Some Comparative Considerations," *Comparative Political Studies* 8 (April 1975): 90-107; Elkin, "Comparative Urban Politics"; J. K. Friend, J. M. Power, and C. J. L. Yewlett, *Public Planning: The Intercorporate Dimension* (London: Tavistock, 1974); D. Schon, *Beyond the Stable State* (London: Temple Smith, 1971); Sherwood, "Devolution"; Thoenig, *State Bureaucracies*.

43. Elkin, "Comparative Urban Politics," p. 175.

44. The reader interested in pursuing this line of thought can consult J. D. Thompson, *Organizations in Action* (New York: McGraw-Hill, 1967).

45. The phrase is taken from A. Maass, ed., *Area and Power* (Glencoe, Ill.: Free Press, 1959).

46. For an analysis of local government reform in England from this standpoint, see R. A. W. Rhodes, ''Local Government Reorganisation: Three Questions,'' *Social and Economic Administration* 8 (1974): 6-21.

47. This paper was prepared early in 1976 and only minor changes have been made prior to publication. Since this paper was written, I have developed the approach in considerably more detail. See R. A. W. Rhodes, *Future Research into Central-Local Relations in Britain: A Framework for Analysis* (London: Social Science Research Council, 1979). Although the two papers complement each other, the current version represents an early statement of the interorganizational framework and the interested reader should turn to the later paper for a more adequate statement.

Developing Countries

V. Subramaniam *

47

Students of local government in developing countries talk euphemistically about its ups and downs, regret its late development and the obstacles in its path, but are not keen to explore the historical reasons that have weakened it right at its birth and thereafter.[1] This tendency goes further in the Afro-Asian commonwealth countries, where much centralization of decision making hides under the holy name of decentralization. This paper will examine those factors during the period of colonialism that led to its being bypassed by the nationalist movement in each country and another set of factors that have weakened it in practice while glorifying it nominally—after independence. But before going into this, we need to say a few words about its development before the beginnings of British or French colonial rule.

Orientalists know all about the thriving institutions of village self-government in India before British rule, and the anthropologists can tell us a lot about the African genius for small-group democracy in their villages and tribal councils, but the average Western political scientist is not usually as much aware of either as he is of the "introduction" of local government by the British. A brief reference to these is necessary to emphasize the fact that local government was neither new nor foreign and to direct our attention to other socio-historical reasons for its weakness.

Unlike the Chinese imperial bureaucracy, the administrative systems of the Indian and Southeast Asian empires built up an extremely vigorous system of village self-government involving practically all administrative activities, including the collection of royal revenue.[2] The peak of glory was reached in

*Professor of Political Science, Carleton University, Ottawa; author of numerous articles in academic journals and of *Social Background of India's Administrators* (New Delhi: Ministry of Information and Broadcasting, 1971), *The Managerial Class of India* (New Delhi: All India Management Association, 1971), and *Transplanted Indo-British Administration* (New Delhi: Ashish, 1977).

South India and Sri Lanka during the medieval period as attested by thousands upon thousands of temple and rock inscriptions and copper plates. In particular, the village of Uttaramerur recorded all the changes in its constitution and all its administrative activities for over four hundred years continuously in rock inscriptions. In North India, village self-government suffered a decline with the rise of the Delhi Sultanate and later, under the heavy centralization of the Moghul Empire.[3] As a reaction, villages tended to become self-sufficient at a low level. But in both North and South India, village self-government lost its vigor and vitality during the anarchy of the eighteenth century. It was capable of revival under suitable conditions, but the introduction of local self-government under British rule did not provide them.

In Africa, tribes like the Ibo were well known for their strong tradition of village and tribal democracy.[4] Even in the case of tribes under chiefs, most routine matters were settled by the village and tribal council of elders. While the pattern of tribal and village self-government varied widely, there was no need for teaching Africans the elements of local self-government. Here again, the occasion for its introduction under British rule was not the most propitious.

To put it briefly, both in Africa and Asia, British rule first created its own pattern of administrative centralization and consequently unleashed a rival tendency towards centralization on the part of educated Africans and Asians. After both centralizing tendencies had entrenched themselves, it tried to introduce local self-government exactly at that stage when it would be suspected and ignored by the centralized nationalist movements. These hindering factors might have weakened after the attainment of independence by these countries, but the new drive towards economic development has placed the ruling elite of these countries in an ambivalent position. On the one hand, they need all the local initiative and, on the other, much local subservience to central allocation of resources; consequently they praise decentralization and practice centralization.

FORMER BRITISH ASIA

The nature of the British conquest of India from Lord Wellesley to Lord Dalhousie worked towards centralization of power with all the means of modern communication, and Britain's success in crushing the 1857 rebellion largely confirmed this tendency. British Indian advocates of some decentralization had been reduced to a small minority and the "Government of India" was one and unitary.[5] The pillars of this unitary rule were the district collectors whose powers were unified and concentrated fairly early in the history of British rule in India. The main argument for concentrating executive, judicial, and all other powers in their hands was generally straight and simple, namely, that a united front must be presented to the ruled.[6] Though the British made a lot of fuss about "trusting the man on the spot," this was not decentralization but simple deconcentration of administrative authority to the "local men," and it worked in the interests of centralized authority because of the great similarity of their background and breeding. The district collector or his equivalent was the common denominator of all British administration in the empire, and he dominated or debilitated all other institutions.

Centralized British administration also generated an educated middle class, first in India and later in Ceylon, Malaysia, Africa, and the Caribbean, and this class acquired certain centralizing and "uniformatizing" tendencies everywhere, tendencies which became pronounced in the nationalist movement later.[7] Thus in India, Macaulay's introduction of Western education created an educated Indian class first in Bengal and soon after in Madras and Bombay with a general emerging all-India outlook. By 1886, this class had already organized the Indian National Congress to fight for various political and administrative demands. It was well after all this that some form of limited local self-government was granted by the well-meaning Liberal party viceroy, Lord Ripon. While it was well received by the moderate nationalist movement, attention had already been diverted to more serious issues, and within the next decade the organized nationalist movement was already fighting against the partition of Bengal and propagating the Swadeshi movement. Simultaneously, more hot-blooded youths had started a terrorist movement. In fact, the enthusiasm for Ripon's local self-government was extremely short lived; it had come too late. Moreover, the grant of local self-government was restricted by the supervision of the district collector.

More radical developments in this century pushed all concern with local self-government into the background for the nationalist movement, which was almost totally concerned with organizing the movement on an all-India basis and fighting for full independence without accepting partial grants. On both these counts, local government was bypassed either as too local or a halfway house. The top leaders of the Indian National Congress were chairmen or mayors of local councils, and the Congress as an organization fought local elections during the late 1920s and 1930s, but all this was looked upon as tactical and incidental. Indeed, the Congress after 1920 under Mahatma Gandhi and his colleagues considered any acceptance of a localized or halfway arrangement a self-defeating diversion.[8] During the first half of this century, local government was thus condemned to inattention by the leading nationalist organization to the mercies of others who would not matter much in independent India. To sum up, a centralizing British rule produced a centralizing nationalist movement which brushed aside belated grants and reforms of local government—all with the inevitability of Greek tragedy.

It was not till the Balwant Rai Mehta Report of 1950 in independent India that some genuine enthusiasm arose for local self-government at all levels.[9] But the factors that brought this about also contained the seeds of its debilitation. The national extension scheme started by official initiative soon after India's independence did not generate much popular enthusiasm for village improvement, and the Mehta Committee recommended that the only way to create local initiative and participation in economic growth was local self-government at various levels and integrated into a system. The report was implemented in most states, and *panchayati raj* has come to stay as a permanent feature of the Indian political system.[10] Much research has been conducted on it, and in general it has been judged a qualified success. Most researchers have attributed its shortcomings (apart from lack of revenue) to the dominance of the upper castes and to "official interference."

The latter highlights the implicit rivalry between the two motivating forces of local government in India and indeed all developing countries: namely, local participation in the governmental process for its own sake and local initiative and participation to promote economic growth as patterned by the central government of the country. The latter motivation tends to dominate not only because the central government (or the state government in India) gives grants making up the major part of a local body's budget but also because it provides skill and supervision through its officers. To remind the reader of the obvious, local government has not replaced the apparatus of district administration anywhere as yet but has only supplemented it. The district collector has no formal powers over the local bodies, but he is still an important source of influence. Thus in India the technical staff, starting with the block development officer, is still under the control of the state government and the district collector. In short, local government, while successful in its own way, is integrated into the overall centralized system of district administration. In India the new system of *zila parishads* (district assemblies) may in due course replace this with a self-contained local government system, but these *parishads* have been installed only recently and only in a few states.

FORMER BRITISH AND FRENCH AFRICA

The African story bears broad resemblances to the Indian. It is shorter but the same interplay of centralizing British rule with centralizing nationalist movement repeats itself, with similar consequences. British colonial administration started seriously early in this century in Africa with the policy of indirect rule, a policy supported explicitly by reasons of economy, simplicity, and social evolution, and implicitly by a strong British feeling against an educated middle class. This feeling had been conceived against the rebellious Indian middle class and nurtured in Africa against the growing Creole-educated class. As a result, indirect rule was not only supportive of the traditional elite of emirs and chiefs but directed *against* an emerging African middle class all over British Africa. Elsewhere I have elaborated how, by the turn of the nineteenth century, the British in India were dead set against the educated middle class, which challenged them on the political front with agitation and on the commercial and other fronts with competition.[11] They tried in every way to undermine it and to prop up the traditional elite of maharajahs and zamindars, but they failed miserably. Hence, they were determined not to repeat "this mistake" in Africa and turned directly to the traditional elite for collaboration through their policy of indirect rule.

In the early years, indirect rule killed traditional local government among the Ibos and buttressed the chief against traditional controls like his council all over Africa. The effort to induct educated Africans into this council came too late in the 1930s, when they had already turned away from this to organize a nationalist movement in West Africa. In East and Central Africa, the movement started later—as education too spread later—but the gap between the nationalist movement and indirect rule widened there, too. The Creech-Jones memorandum on local government in 1947 and its subsequent implementation came too late to attract the best men among the educated, who by then had concentrated on national issues through the nationalist movement.[12]

In all this, the same logic operated as in India. British administration centralized power through the district secretary or commissioner, and the nationalist movements, too, had to be organized on a countrywide basis to present a united front to this centralized administration. Western education had created a class with this countrywide orientation and also with suspicion of British offers of "local" self-government, just as in India.

Independence came to the African colonies in quick succession in the late 1950s and early 1960s. The nationalist movements in most cases had time only to organize a united front against colonial rule, without going far in the direction of national integration. This they set out to do soon after independence through the political party and through a politicized civil service as well as by whatever other means came in handy. In this deep commitment to national integration against divisive tribal and regional loyalties and then to economic growth, local government could survive only on the condition that it aided the integration and growth.

The compromise solution practiced all over English-speaking Africa is to control local government by strict legislation and through the new politicized structure of district administration. The head of the district is usually a political appointee often in charge of the party organization, too, and more powerful than a former district collector. The elected local government body is tolerated only to the extent to which it can work along with the district administration toward integration (by not pressing local demands too far) and economic growth (by cooperating with the appropriate government committees). The district development committee, found all over Africa, is the main composite body of politicians, officials, and local government members, where the latter are tamed into subordinate cooperation.[13]

The verbal emphasis on decentralization in Anglophone African countries is based partly on semantic confusion and partly on hypocrisy. The central authorities need quick action in the regions and want to delegate decisions to *appointed* civil servants and party officials. They refer to this as "decentralization," which has nothing to do with power to elected local-government bodies. Also, there is a pendulum-like movement of giving local governments some power and withdrawing it when they perform well below expectations. In short, African leadership's advocacy of decentralization need not be confused with any commitment to more local self-government.

Developments in French Africa were simpler. The British had to invent the all-purpose, all-powerful district administrator for the colonies, for he had no counterpart back home. The French needed only to replicate their own prefectoral system in the colonies and create the commandant of the circle in the image of the *préfet* of the *département* in France. The French genius for centralization had a freer hand in French Africa, known as *France d'outre-mer*, with several colonies bound together into the two large units of French West Africa and French Equatorial Africa. There was no suggestion of local government except for French citizens in a few cities till 1956, when the famous Loi-Cadre created a territorial assembly for each colony (now called territory) and also made provision for local government on the French model, that is, local government strictly and firmly controlled by the district prefect Even this provision was not fully availed of by every "territory," and when they became free in the 1958-60 period, there was no positive urge to create a strong local government system nor any hesitation, as on the part of centralized nationalist movements in Anglophone African countries, but only sheer apathy. The result was replication of French local government with the elected *maire* automatically being subordinated to the prefect. Sometimes even this was not seriously attempted, as in the Ivory Coast where a detailed local government act was passed with much trumpet and fanfare only to be shelved.[14]

Francophone African disinterest in local government flows from a concatenation of causes different from those operative in India and Anglophone Africa, where a centralized nationalist movement arising in response to centralized colonial administration considered local government an unimportant diversion both before and after independence. There was practically no nationalist movement in French Africa before World War II. The French policy of assimilation and association had virtually absorbed, either into colonial administration or into the professions in France, most of the educated Africans who might have formed the nucleus of the nationalist movement. After World War II, the African elite was drafted into French politics in Paris before they came back to Africa to organize their own nationalist parties. Their centralist tendencies were not conceived as retaliatory safeguards *against* a centralizing colonial administration but rather as necessary replications of French centralism itself. The French African political elite absorbed and adopted it almost unconsciously, in three successive stages, as part of the French civilization they admired.

As educated African *évolués* and *assimilés*, they wanted full control of the existing centralized colonial administration minus the hated *Indigénat* and rarely voiced the cry of decentralization. As members of the French Parliament in the next stage of decolonization, they learned more about French centralized administration, while a few, such as Houphouet-Boigny and Senghor, learned more about political control of it as cabinet ministers and ministers of state. The third and last stage of decolonization reinforced these centralizing tendencies in complementary ways.

In the earlier stage of participation in the French Parliament, French Africa had replicated the French multi-party system and multi-trade union systems, but they got tired of its imitative ineffectiveness. In Paris, they learned to present a reasonably united African front to win their points through bargaining within the French multi-party system, and in their own countries they had to shape cohesive territorial parties instead of branches or replicas of French parties to win elections, as soon as it became clear in 1956, according to the Loi-Cadre, that political power was being transferred more to individual colonies than to a French African federation. To these two factors were added the influence of De Gaulle's personality and Gaullist philosophy, both of which favored centralization emotionally, even while he himself worked towards decentralization—unsuccessfully. French African political thinking had thus been moving steadily toward centralization for several decades, and the difficulty of integrating and governing a newly independent African country was just the final immediate reason for the political elite in each country to choose a one-party state with weak, cosmetic, local government institutions.

In effect, Anglophone and Francophone African countries have arrived at the same arrangement of a centralized one-party state with weak local government, though by somewhat different routes and with rather different explanations. While the Anglophone countries use the rhetoric of decentralization to draw a veil over the reality of centralization (shaped by recent historical factors), the Francophones have less need to be hypocritical as they consciously follow French centralism, reinforcing it with their own recent experiences. Indeed, they have built an elaborate mystique over *"le parti unique"*—and keep things balanced in the field by promoting a studied rivalry between the political party branch chief and the administrative prefect.

In concluding this comparative account we may repeat that British colonial rule in general has tended to galvanize the elite of the colonies into a centralized nationalist movement with at best a tolerant view of decentralized local government, while French colonialism led to the same result by another route. Even where decentralization was a religious creed with such a great nationalist leader as Mahatma Gandhi, it had very little influence on the course of the freedom movement. It was centralized with his own blessing well before independence, and after independence, the "practical" leaders who took over entertained some decentralization in the form of widespread local government or *panchayati raj*, but only as an instrument of centrally directed development plans.

TECHNOLOGY AND ECONOMICS

We should now add a few brief remarks about the centralizing effect of technology and economics on developing countries. Technology contributed to centralization of decision making in three complementary ways. By conquering distance through better and quicker communication, the traditional basis of local decision making was undermined, and centralization was promoted by a central pool of information. Planned division of work, coordination, distribution networks and automation, and other such organizational devices of industrial society promoted oligarchy in the decision process, and various tools of information processing topped by the computer reinforced centralized decision making. These three effects of technology, first felt in developed countries, were soon transferred to developing countries through their educated middle classes and through the universalizing and uniformatizing trends of technology.

Second, all developing countries were committed not only to economic development in general but were initially bent on "catching up" with the developed countries in terms of industrialization, import substitution, and planning. All this led to the central control of scarce resources both in the interests of efficient exploitation and against regional appropriation of them and possible separatist tendencies. The Katangan separatist movement based on local copper resources and Biafran separatism based to some extent on oil resources were extreme instances of the latter. But the potential existed in all developing countries and so arose the compulsive central control of resources which was consequentially allied with central planning.

Fear of regional separatism has since been cut down to size gradually but has been replaced by the enveloping fear of international capital and international market forces. The "development decade" of the 1960s proved a disappointment essentially because most developing countries lost out in the world market in regard to the prices of their primary products and most of them lost all control of capital investment in their economies either to large private banks or international monetary institutions. The 1970s have proved even worse. This experience has promoted an emotional (and perhaps irrational) climate of centralization on the one hand and a loud demand for a new international economic order on the other. To sum it all up, universal technology, centralized planning, and international economic forces together have created a somewhat irrational pro-centralization climate of opinion in developing countries.

The exception that highlights the rule is India after the Emergency, during which there developed a certain degree of tight centralization by the Union government. Not unnaturally, the Janata party, which defeated that government in the 1977 elections, adopted the battle cry of decentralization which was interpreted soon after to mean more attention and power to the rural agricultural sector. An inquiry commission on *panchayat raj* (village local government) made recommendations in favor of reforms as well as more powers. On the economic front much was said about more investment in the agricultural sector to balance earlier overinvestment in the industrial sector. In the final outcome, these declarations about decentralization were all overshadowed by the growth of state or regional separatism. In the northwest and northeast the chief ministers of Kashmir and West Bengal voiced a demand for more powers to the states, while the chief ministers of the four southern states (Andhra, Pradesh, Tamilnadu, Karnataka, and Kerala) conferred and expressed similar demands as well as strong opposition to the imposition of Hindi and to the request of Prime Minister Desai not to hold such a conference. It is quite apparent that the enthusiasm for decentralization has abated at the center in view of its identification with state and regional separatism.

COMPARISONS AND REFLECTIONS

The foregoing account identifies a major continuing trend towards centralization in most developing countries based on the two factors of their colonial experience and post-colonial economic compulsions, including the urge for centralized planning control of resources. This overall trend is more crucial in explaining the comparative weakness of local government than the various local and immediate factors discussed by Mawhood and Davey in their chapter. I will go further and argue that the trend is not altogether regrettable because the exaggerated regret expressed by some enthusiastic students of local government arises mainly from unfair and misleading comparisons with three isolated historical cases of the evolution of strong local government in Britain, the United States, and Western European cities. In these three cases some exceptional historical circumstances encouraged the development of decentralization and preserved it against centralizing tendencies later.

In the case of Britain, the crucial period for the British political and administrative systems was the golden age of the landed aristocracy and gentry from the Glorious Revolution (1688) to about the 1870s, when British local government took on its basic shape. Well before the Glorious Revolution, Britain had established national unity and identity and had controlled feudal separatism, so that the enlightened landed aristocrats and gentry who took over in 1688 could build their own ethic of the gentleman-amateur. This began to influence all areas of activity in Britain, particularly politics and administration, in the period after 1870 when administrative reforms took place. As a result, the generalist administrator, governed by the gentleman-amateur ethic, took over central administration, and the voluntary services of the country squire were replaced with elected county councils together with the committee system, which best suited the peer-group ethic of the landed gentry. The implicit assumption of this arrangement was that central administration would not expand too much out of London into hundreds of branch offices but would delegate administration of much central legislation to local government bodies, and this assumption has been borne out by developments in this century. What made for strong local government bodies was the country squire tradition which the landed aristocrats in Parliament wanted to preserve and extend, and what made for its survival in an age of increasing administrative work was the implicit assumption that wherever possible central administration should delegate to local government.

Neither of these conditions was met in Western Europe nor in the colonies. The absolute monarchs of France and Prussia had to ensure national unity and strength through a centralized bureaucracy about the same time that the British landed aristocrats were building up their gentleman-amateur ethic and laying the foundations of decentralized local government and generalist administration. A similar compulsion as in eighteenth century France and Prussia towards nation building has led developing countries before and after their independence toward centralized administration and economic planning and at best instrumental local government.

The vigor of European city government is a residue of the early period of feudal weakness when powerful commercial and craft interests secured the ''freedom'' and self-government of several prosperous cities. The orientation of the commercial and craft elites of these cities had something in common with the peer-group ethic of the British landed aristocrats, and the elites were allowed to survive, as weak kings needed them against rebellious nobles and strong kings needed them for financial reasons. Similarly, the relative strength of local government in the United States may be traced to successive historical factors. The early Puritan settlers passionately believed in the community of the elect and nurtured strong local government, and the federal constitution later left much to local initiative. Over and above this were the powerful American urge to form all sorts of associations, which Tocqueville noticed and recorded, and the exploration of the West, which also promoted local organization. All of these positive tendencies might have been weakened considerably in this century by the advances of technology and industry and the large-scale mobility of Americans from state to state. But just about that time, U.S. politics developed the two-party system based on two umbrella-like parties harboring, affiliating, and encouraging all types of functional and local organizations for better articulation of interests. Local governments thus got a new lease of legitimacy and vitality as local interest groups. None of these developments was possible in the colonies and newly independent countries.

To sum up, local government in developing countries has been judged too long by the artificial standards derived from exceptional developments in nineteenth and twentieth-century Britain, Puritan New England, the expanding United States, and the free cities of Europe. It is time that its ''limited'' development in the new nations is set against the similar history of Western Europe, particularly France, and against the historical compulsions of colonialism, nationalism, and economic development.

NOTES

1. For example, even in this book, the only article to examine such reasons, namely, Philip Mawhood and Ken Davey, "Anglophone Africa," does not go beyond the immediate and recent causes. Works on local government in developing countries, such as Hugh Tinker, *Foundations of Local Self-Government in India, Pakistan and Burma* (New York: Praeger, 1968), pay only minimal attention to this point.

2. There are several standard works on village self-government in South India during the Chola period: K. A. Nilakanta Sastri, *The Colas*, 2d ed. (Madras: University of Madras, 1975), contains a summary of this material and ample cross-references. For Ceylon, see E. R. Leach, "Hydraulic Society in Ceylon," *Past and Present* (London) (Spring 1969), which contrasts Chinese bureaucracy with the Indian system of using self-governing villages in imperial administration.

3. K. M. Panikkar, *A Survey of Indian History* (Bombay: National Information and Publications, 1947), pp. 241-42. Panikkar attributes the anarchy in North India in the eighteenth century, following the decline of the Moghul Empire, to its centralization policies under Akbar. Earlier, this had reduced local initiative to the lowest level.

4. The misunderstanding of Ibo democracy by the British is discussed in detail in A. E. Afigbo, *The Warrant Chiefs*, Ibadan History Series (London: Longmans, 1972).

5. The unitary nature of the government of India is stressed in several standard works on Indian administration, for example, Ramsay Macdonald, *The Government of India* (London: Swathmore, 1919); C. P. Ilbert, *The Government of India* (Oxford: Clarendon, 1898); and M. Ruthnaswamy, *Some Influences that Made the British Administrative System in India* (London: Luzac, 1939).

6. This idea is repeated in several memos of British governors-general and administrators. A good summary of such views is to be found in *The Report of the Indian Statutory Commission*, Cmd. 3369 (London: HMSO, 1930) 1, paras. 307, 315-22; and Macdonald, *The Government of India*, pp. 95-98.

7. I have elaborated my general theory of the "derivative middle class" in several conference papers, for example, "The Role of the Middle Class in Developing Countries" (East African Universities Social Science Conference, Dar-es-Salaam, December 1970); "The Professional Middle Classes and Post-Colonial Societies—A Soothing Socio-historical Explanation of Ethnic Imbalances" (East African Universities Social Science Conference, Kampala, December 1971).

8. V. Subramaniam, "The Evolution of Minister-Civil Servant Relations in India," *Journal of Commonwealth Political Studies*, 1, no. 3 (1961).

9. The Balwant Mehta Study Team Report, vol. 1, is reviewed in M. V. Mathur and Iqbal Narain, eds., *Panchayati Raj, Planning and Democracy* (London: Asia Publishing House, 1969), pp. 79-94.

10. For a summary of recent researches, see the special issue of the *Indian Journal of Public Administration* no. 3 (1965), on "The Collector in the 1960's," and Iqbal Narain et al., *Panchayati Raj Administration* (New Delhi: Indian Institute of Public Administration, 1970).

11. V. Subramaniam, "Indirect Rule and the Indian Middle Class," in *India and Africa*, ed. Ali Mazrui. The article is also included in my book, *Transplanted Indo-British Administration*.

12. N. U. Akpan, *Epitaph to Indirect Rule* (London: Cass, 1967) recaptures the feeing of dissatisfaction with "indirect rule" on the part of the educated African class.

But this dissatisfaction had also led them to build up a country-wide nationalist movement and become lukewarm to the grant of local self-government.

13. The district development committee consists usually of (a) members of the elected local government body, (b) local party chiefs, (c) senior administrative and technical officers of the district, and (d) the district governor or secretary. For a descriptive account of these committees in Tanzania, see Henry Bienen, *Tanzania, Party Transformation and Economic Development* (Princeton: Princeton University Press, 1967), pp. 322-33; in Kenya, Göran Hydén et al., *Development Administration, The Kenyan Experience* (Oxford: Oxford University Press, 1970), pp. 196-99; in Zambia, see William Tordoff, "Provincial and District Government in Zambia," *Journal of Administration Overseas* (London), part 2 (1969).

14. See Martin Staniland, "Local Government in the Ivory Coast," *Journal of Administration Overseas*, parts 1, 2 (1970).

Concluding Remarks

Donald C. Rowat

48

In a conclusion that must necessarily be brief, one cannot hope to discuss all of the common trends and problems of local government around the world. I will therefore only focus on what appear to me to be the most important problems and on possible solutions to them. I will then discuss the difficult problem of comparing the strength of local government in different countries.

TRENDS AND PROBLEMS

Two universal trends that have had an impact on local government everywhere in the world are the growth of urbanism and of industrialism. Since World War II, these trends have affected both developed and developing countries at an accelerating pace. The result has been to crowd more and more people into urban centers and to turn a larger and larger proportion of the working population into earners of wages or salaries.

The rapidly rising urban population has had serious results for local government. One of the most far-reaching results has been a remarkable increase in the average population of urban municipalities and, by the same token, in the distance between the citizen and his local government. Another consequence has been the development of huge metropolitan areas in most countries and of fragmented local government within these areas. As the Jones-O'Donnell essay shows, the typical way of meeting the problem of rapidly growing population in the suburbs had been for the central city to try to annex them by expanding its boundaries. But this solution has failed, largely because the suburban municipalities have opposed their own demise through annexation and have been strong enough politically to prevent it. Consequently, a wide variety of cooperative arrangements and ad hoc bodies have had to be created to handle problems and provide services on a wider-than-local basis. The result has been complexity and confusion for the local voters, who do not know where to fix responsibility for the solution of metropolitan problems.

The growth of industry is closely connected with that of cities. It results in a growing integration of a nation's economy and in problems that must be dealt with on a nation-wide rather than local basis. Thus, differentials in wealth increase, and, for the sake of equity, it must be taxed and redistributed by the central government. Also, there arises a need to provide social and other services at an acceptable minimum standard across a nation. In other words, there is a general trend toward centralization in order to gain greater uniformity, equity, and efficiency. In many countries it has become painfully evident that units of local government created for an agricultural economy are too small and financially weak to provide an acceptable level of great variety of local services that the public demands in the modern industrial state. To prevent these services from being taken over by central governments, to stem the tide of centralization, and to keep local government strong, an obvious solution is to consolidate the units of local government into larger units. In many countries of Eastern and Western Europe, such as Poland, Denmark, Great Britain, and Sweden, the number of the basic units of local government at the lowest level has been drastically reduced in recent years through such consolidation.

In the face of the increasing remoteness of local government caused by cities' rapidly expanding populations, a more recent trend has been a growing recognition of the need to keep local government close to the people and to preserve and enhance their participation in the political process. It is also being realized that the consolidation of local governments into larger units makes the problem of remoteness even more serious. In large metropolitan areas where the central city has been allowed to annex the suburbs the problem of remoteness has become particularly serious. In such an area there may be only one local government for a million or more citizens. To call such a government "local" seems ridiculous.

A problem that affects developing countries in particular is the implication of the aims of national integration and development for the strength of local government. The need for national integration does not admit much decentralization of power to local government, and national economic planning requires strong direction from the central government in formulating and implementing national plans. As Professor Subramaniam has shown, the developing countries inherited a colonial tradition of weak local government, and the aims of national integration and development have favored a continuation of this weakness. Often developing nations adopted the forms of Western local self-government but not its substance. Despite the claimed need for citizen participation to achieve rapid economic development, in practice this has meant only participation in implementing national plans, not making local decisions about local matters.

THE TWO-TIER SOLUTION

While the impact of urbanism and industrialism is to require larger units of local government for greater efficiency, economy, and equity, the need for citizen participation calls for small units, with governments that are close to the citizens. These conflicting objectives are to a large extent reconciled in a two-tier system of local government, that is, one that provides a second level of government which administers services requiring large areas for efficient administration and equitable finance. The basic units at the lowest level then can be left unconsolidated so as to keep them small and their local governments close to the citizens. Frequently the councils of the second-tier units are elected directly so as to provide direct participation by citizens on this level of local government as well as on the lower level.

A second tier of local government seems to be particularly appropriate for large metropolitan areas. In such areas there is a need to provide many services on an area-wide basis, yet a consolidation of all local governments in the area would create a single local government too remote from the citizens. Long-standing examples of two-tier systems for metropolitan areas are found in London, England, and Toronto, Canada. Experience demonstrates, however, that such systems do not keep local government close to the citizens if the units at the lower level have large populations. Yet it is typical for the core city of a metropolitan area to have a very large population. One solution would be to carve up the core city into several units of local government and to keep the suburban units similarly small. An alternative to the two-tier system is a unitary government covering a whole metropolitan area but with the area divided into numerous districts having elected consultative or advisory councils, as in Winnipeg. The experience of some Eastern European countries with local citizen participation is also well worth studying. In Warsaw, for instance, numerous elected "block" councils have been created to look after minor social and cultural affairs related to daily life in apartment blocks. However, local councils that are only consultative or only administer minor matters are not real governments like those in the lower tier of a two-tier system.

The two-tier solution can also be applied to a system of local government across a whole province, state, or country. A number of countries already have a second tier of local government, often called county government. But in some cases the county governments are weak, as in the province of Ontario, where they do not even include the cities. In these cases it is a question of reorganizing and strengthening the second tier. In several other cases as Part 2 reveals, an entirely new second level of local government has been created or proposed.

In considering the structural reorganization of local government, the main alternatives appear to be either a drastic consolidation and reduction in the number of basic units or the creation of a second tier of government for regions. In the latter alternative, the basic units are left untouched except for raising wider-than-local functions to the second-tier level and perhaps consolidating a few of the smallest and least efficient basic units. For countries contemplating reorganization, it is important to consider which alternative is preferable under what conditions. Let us therefore review some of the main considerations that must be taken into account in trying to decide whether there is a need for regional government.

Obvious criteria are the country's total size and population. If the size or population is so great that a consolidation of the basic units would create units so big or with such large populations that the local governments are remote from the citizens, than a second tier of local government would appear to be needed. Another obvious consideration is whether the country has a unitary or federal system of government. If the country already has state or provincial governments then clearly the need for a second level of local government is much less. However, this again depends upon the size and total population of the country and its states. Among the federations of the world, it is typical for the states to vary tremendously in size and population so that there may be a need for a second tier of local government in the larger states but not in the smaller ones, where the state government can perform the functions that would ordinarily be performed by the second tier. In Canada, for instance, the provinces vary in population from over 8 million in Ontario to only about 115,000 in Prince Edward Island. The latter has such a small population that local governments have been considered unnecessary in the rural areas. Instead, the provincial government provides local-government services to the rural population. Because the populations of New Brunswick and Newfoundland are also relatively small, a second tier of local government is not needed in these provinces either. However, I have concluded that a second tier would be desirable for all of the other provinces in Canada.[1]

Other criteria to be taken into account are:

1. Whether within a country there are already clearly defined regions which need political expression through regional governments
2. Whether the number of local governments is too great for their effective supervision by government at a higher level
3. Whether the average population of the local governments is too small for them to finance and administer services efficiently
4. Whether there is a need to prevent or promote centralization

Let us briefly examine each of these criteria.[2]

Within a country there may be clearly defined historic regions that have no corresponding governments to express the community of interest of their populations. If such regions already exist, the case for a second tier of local government to encompass them would appear to be strong. A serious problem in attempting to apply this criterion, however, is that the existing political system may prevent the expression of such "other-based" interests—interests based on geographic boundaries other than those of the existing political units. Professor J. E. Hodgetts has suggested that in Canada the parliamentary system of government may have had this effect at both levels of government.[3] The strictness of party discipline may have prevented the adequate expression of other-based interests through the existing party system. An example at the federal level is the break-away political parties based on the prairie region. At the provincial level, the strictness of party discipline in Ontario may be preventing the expression of strong interests based on the Northern Ontario region. The existing political system, then, may obscure regionally-based communities of interest.

This raises serious research problems: How do we know when or where strong regional communities of interest exist? What are their geographic limits? Is the community of interest based mainly on economic interests or on a strong, subjective *feeling* of community? How strong must this feeling be to warrant a regional unit of government? One can see that the concept of community of interest is almost impossible to apply operationally. Another complicating point is that over a period of time a political unit will create its own community of interest, the nation being the most obvious example. The national government reinforces the concept of the nation and the feeling of nationalism. Similarly in a federal system the provincial boundaries mark out and create communities of interest within those boundaries. So, although one can provide for an existing community of interest by creating a political unit for it, one can also create a community of interest by creating a political unit. The latter type of community feeling is no less genuine. Hence the prior existence of regional communities of interest is not a necessary condition for the creation of regional governments.

Indeed, where countries are historically divided into clear-cut regions, the regional communities of interest in some of them may be so strong as to constitute divisive forces in the country if they are given expression through regional governments. If so, this would be a strong political argument against regional government. Such an argument can be used with reference to some of the regions in Italy. Another example, but at a different level, is the state governments in Yugoslavia. A main reason for the great autonomy given to the local governments in Yugoslavia may have been the desire to strengthen them as a countervailing force against the state governments, thus weakening the latter and preventing them from fragmenting the country.

Even where a country is not clearly divided into regions based on historic cultural, ethnic, or linguistic differences, some economic geographers believe that it is possible to divide a country into political regions by basing them on spheres of influence of large urban centers. It is clearly true that economic, social, and cultural influences spread out in concentric circles from urban centers. These economic geographers believe, then, that the way to define regions is to find the limits of the "waves" of influence by drawing boundaries along the lines where the waves from different urban centers collide. However, there are two serious difficulties with this easy analogy. Urban centers vary greatly in size, so that strong waves from a large city may override weaker waves from a smaller one, and one cannot find lines where the waves collide. Also, urban centers send out a great many waves of different kinds and intensity. These travel different distances and meet the corresponding waves from other urban centers at different points. Hence, it becomes impossible to draw a *single* line around an urban center's area of influence, and one is left with a complex overlay of regions representing the boundaries of influence of different economic, social, and cultural forces. The difficulty is that real social and economic life is a complex continuum of interrelationships. We must therefore conclude that, except possibly for metropolitan areas, there is little prospect of finding within a country a single set of regions that represent a natural bunching of econonic, social, and cultural interests. However, once a set of political regions has been decided upon (that is, their general number and size), the work of economic geographers may be valuable in deciding the precise boundaries by trying, so far as possible, to group together the various economic, social, and cultural spheres of influence of large urban centers.

Regarding the second criterion listed above, the number of basic units of local government may be so great that it is impossible for the senior government to control, supervise, or even deal with them effectively. The literature on public administration recommends a narrow ''span of control,'' i.e., that a superior officer or unit should have to deal with only a few inferior officers or units. However, many countries, and even provinces and states within federations, have hundreds of local governments with which the superior government must try to deal. Thus, Saskatchewan, with a population of only about a million, has over 800 local governments. It is interesting that most of the world's federations have a small number of states with which the central government must deal, and none has more than fifty. We may conclude that in any country or state where the number of basic units of local government is very large, and even after consolidation would still be large, say more than a hundred, the case for regional government is strong. The superior government would than have to communicate with and supervise only a small number of regional governments, which in turn would each have to keep in touch with only a small number of the basic units below them.

The third criterion indicates that the average population of a country's municipalities may be too small, so small that most of them cannot raise enough money through taxation to provide local services of an acceptable standard and cannot afford to hire skilled personnel or take advantage of the economies of large-scale operation. I have estimated the minimum population for the efficient operation of a multipurpose unit of local government at about 50,000.[4] But if the basic units are consolidated to create an average population of this size, they become too remote from the citizens. The advantage of a second tier is that it permits the lower-level units to remain small and hence close to the citizens.

Large grants from the senior government to existing small units may be considered as an alternative to reorganization. They would raise the overall standard of local services and permit some hiring of more skilled personnel, especially if the grants were made on an equalization basis so that the smallest units got the most help. Thus, such grants would lower considerably the average minimum population necessary for efficient local-government operation, but they still would not give the advantages of large-scale operation and would perpetuate the existence of small inefficient units. Moreover, if the grants became too large, this would result in central control of local government because, as experience has shown, the temptation for a senior government to attach conditions to its grants cannot be resisted. For these reasons, massive grants are not an acceptable alternative to consolidation or the creation of regional government, and regional governments, too, should have revenues that are not mainly in the form of grants.

As for the fourth criterion, there is considerable controversy over whether regional government promotes or prevents centralization. Some people, concentrating on the relationship between the basic units and the regional governments, argue that their creation represents a centralization of local functions and powers. Other people, focusing on the relationship between the central and regional governments, regard their creation as a move in the direction of decentralization because they can take on functions formerly performed by the central government and because they make it unnecessary for the central government to take over local functions for reasons of efficiency. Professor Bruhns has argued in his survey essay that regional government may represent a move toward either centralization or decentralization, depending on whether the political system of a country is too decentralized or too centralized to begin with. Certainly where the political system of a country is too centralized or where the creation of regional governments would prevent the central government from taking further functions from local government, the case for regional governments would appear to be strong.

Unfortunately, the social sciences have not yet developed methods by which the criteria discussed above can be applied precisely or balanced against one another to determine their relative importance. Hence, the question of whether a tier of regional governments is needed in a country, and in particular their size and number, is still very much a matter of political judgment.

THE STRENGTH OF LOCAL GOVERNMENT

As we have noted, often developing countries have reorganized local government so as to retain the structures and forms of autonomous self-government but not its substance, and local government has remained weak. Hence, a crucial question to ask about a reorganization of local structures is its overall effect on the strength of local government. As R. A. W. Rhodes has argued in his essay, the central-local relationship is crucial to the comparative study of local government because it determines the power and even the very nature of local government. Before much progress can be made in comparative studies, a way must be found to measure or at least estimate the relative power of local government in the overall political system of a country. Since the process of decision making is central to the exercise of power in any political system, one must therefore study the role of local government in this process. One must ask, What share does local government have in the total of all governmental decision making in a country? In this connection, one must also ask to what extent local governments are able to influence decisions made by senior governments, either state or central. A full analysis of the strength of local government must take both of these questions into account.[5]

Local Government's Share of Decision Making

Regarding local government's share of all decision making, one must consider not only the legal and financial power formally granted to the municipalities but also their freedom to make their own decisions in practice. As R.A.W. Rhodes shows, they may appear to have great financial power in the sense that they raise nearly all of their own revenues, yet they may be closely controlled in other ways by the central government.

Among the formal provisions, key ones are whether the principles of locally elected councils and local autonomy are embedded in a country's constitution, and whether in the constitution or national law the municipalities have been granted a broad range of decision-making power. For instance, they may have been granted control over their own local constitution or form of government, as with the grant of "home rule" in the constitutions of some U.S. states, or they may have been granted a general and permissive power to make bylaws. Another key criterion is how much power the municipalities have been given to raise their own revenues through taxation. Other important considerations are whether the central government must approve bylaws or budgets and whether there is a central control or supervision over local staff or administration. For instance, the central government may appoint the local chief executive or other administrative officers or have to approve their appointment or qualifications. On the political side, one must look at the political party links between the upper and lower levels and the extent to which central power is exercised over local government through the party system.

A problem in trying to determine the true strength of a system of local government is that its independence and freedom may be constrained in many subtle ways by legal and financial provisions or political practices the importance of which is difficult to judge. For instance, there may be shared taxes over which the municipalities have no control or central grants requiring the municipalities to meet certain standards as a condition of receiving the grants. A further problem in making comparisons is that local governments may possess alternative types of strength; they may have considerable independence from the central government but provide very few services, or they may provide a very wide range of services the administration of which, however, is supervised by the central government. The local governments of the United States and Canada seem to fit more into the first category, while those in many European countries fit more into the second. The difficulty is to determine whether the total share of decision-making power exercised by local government is greater in the former case than in the latter.

Local Government's Influence

Regarding the second question posed above—local government's influence on decision making at a higher level—the considerations become more subtle and their importance more difficult to judge. For instance, just as the political party system may provide an opportunity for a senior government to influence local governments, the reverse is also true. In a particular country or party situation it may be difficult to discover in which direction the predominant influence flows. Structural aspects of local government that seem to be important to our question are whether the executive is plural or singular (an executive committee or a mayor) and whether the executive is chosen by the council or is elected directly. If the chief executive is a directly elected mayor, as in most of Canada and the United States, he is likely to have more political power and exert more influence on the senior government. For instance, a main reason that the governments of Ontario and Quebec have rejected the idea of directly elected executive heads of their metropolitan governments has been the fear that such "super mayors" in Toronto and Montreal would rival the provincial prime ministers in power and importance. Also relevant are whether national political parties participate in local elections, whether local councillors can serve concurrently in legislatures, whether the political party in power at the local level is different from that at the higher level, and whether local executive committees represent a single political party or are coalitions.

Several other factors no doubt affect the ability of local government to influence the higher level. One is the strength of the national associations of local governments and their officers. Another is whether a second tier of local government has been created. This would be likely to strengthen local government in dealing with the senior government, though the latter might also find it easier to supervise the local level. Another consideration is a central government's practice of secrecy or openness in consulting interest groups on matters of policy. Local governments may or may not be consulted by a central government before it makes decisions on matters that concern them. The traditions of different countries appear to vary considerably in this respect. The provincial governments in Canada, for instance, often decide policies and introduce legislation affecting local governments without consulting them first. Thus, a few years ago, the prime minister of Ontario announced without consulting the city governments that they must install an entirely new type of public transit, overhead monorails. In Switzerland, on the other hand, the federal government instituted a formal procedure of prior consultation with interest groups and lower governments in 1947, and this procedure has been widely adopted among the cantons.

In a federal system of government, the ability of local governments to influence decision making at the federal level also becomes relevant. For instance, one must note whether there is a national association of local governments and, if so, examine its ability to influence federal policy. One must also note whether there is any tri-level machinery, such as the United States Commission on Intergovernmental Relations, through which representatives from local government may exert an influence at the higher levels.

The emphasis placed on central-local relations by the other final essays and my own observations lead me to conclude that the most significant aspect of any reorganization of local government is its effect on the strength of local government. One must examine the matter from the viewpoint of both aspects discussed above, local government's freedom to make its own decisions about important matters and its ability to influence higher-level decisions. One must also take into account a great many factors affecting these aspects. A fundamental and overriding consideration, however, is whether a country has an authoritarian regime. If so, then regardless of how extensive the powers of the reorganized local governments may be in formal law, their actual freedom to make their own decisions and their influence on decisions at a higher level are not likely to be very great.

NOTES

1. See my *The Canadian Municipal System: Essays on the Improvement of Local Government* (Toronto: McClelland & Stewart, 1969), part 6, esp. pp. 155-60.

2. These four criteria are examined at greater length in ibid, pp. 151-60.

3. J. E. Hodgetts, "Regional Interests and Policy in a Federal Structure," *Canadian Journal of Economics and Political Science* 32 (February 1966): 1-14.

4. Rowat, *Canadian Municipal System*, p. 157.

5. For a fuller discussion of these questions, see my "Role of Canada's Urban Municipalities in Governmental Decison-Making," *Studies in Comparative Local Government* 8, no. 1 (Summer 1974): 43-49.

Bibliography of Comparative Materials

This bibliography contains only comparative materials that deal with local government in two or more countries. The literature on individual countries is so vast that it would have been impossible to include materials on all of the countries dealt with in this volume. Since genuinely comparative literature is relatively scarce, it is believed that most of the comparative studies done in recent years are contained in this bibliography, which is organized under three heads: bibliographies, books and documents, and articles and papers. References to single chapters in books are included with articles and papers. As an aid to students, brief annotations have been added to the listings in many cases. I should like to thank William G. Fitzpatrick, a post-graduate student at Carleton University, for his help in extending and updating my bibliography.

BIBLIOGRAPHIES

Booth, David Allin. *Council-Manager Government 1940-64: An Annotated Bibliography*. Chicago: International City Managers' Association, 1965.

Hanna, W. J., and Hanna, W. L. *Politics in Black Africa: A Selected Bibliography of Periodical Literature*. East Lansing: Michigan State University, 1964. Articles on urbanization and local government.

International Union of Local Authorities. *Metropolis*. The Hague: Martinus Nijhoff, 1961. Nearly 1,000 entries; North America excluded.

International Union of Local Authorities. *Metropolis: A Selected Bibliography on Metropolitan Areas*. The Hague: IULA, 1968.

Mahayni, Riad G. *Urbanization In The Middle East: A Bibliography*. Public Administration Series Bibliography, no. P-23. Monticello, Ill.: Vance Bibliographies, July 1978.

Rhodes, R. A. W. "European Local Government: A Bibliographical Essay," *Local Government Studies* (October 1974).

Wallace, R. H., ed. *International Bibliography and Reference Guide on Urban Affairs*. Ramsey, N.J.: Ramsey Corporation, 1966. Index of authors, titles, and cities; 500 references, 1823-1966; brief annotations on books.

BOOKS AND DOCUMENTS

Akpan, N. U. *Epitaph to Indirect Rule: A Discourse on Local Government in Africa*. London: Cass, 1967.

Alderfer, H. F. *Local Government In Developing Countries*. New York: McGraw-Hill, 1964.

Anderson, W., ed. *Local Government in Europe*. New York: Appleton, 1939. Includes France, Germany, Italy, U.K., USSR., and central-local relations.

Ashley, Percy. *Local and Central Government: A Comparative Study of England, France, Prussia and the United States*. London: J. Murray, 1906.

Bureau of Municipal Research. *Reference Handbook on Metropolitan Areas*. Toronto: Bureau of Municipal Research, 1967.

Campbell, M. J.; Brierly, T. G.; Blitz, L. F. *The Structure of Local Government in West Africa*. The Hague: Nijhoff, 1965.

Canada, Parliament, Special Joint Committee of the Senate and the House of Commons on the Constitution of Canada. *Minutes of Proceedings*, no. 39. Ottawa: Queen's Printer, 1971. Federal-urban relations in Canada, the United States, and Australia.

Clark, T. N., ed. *Comparative Community Politics*. New York: Halsted Press, 1974. Includes Austria, Germany, Switzerland.

Cornelius, A., and Trueblood, Felicity, eds. *Latin American Urban Research*. Beverly Hills, Ca.: Sage, 1974. Latin American urbanization.

Cornelius, Wayne A., and Kemper, Robert V., eds. *Metropolitan Latin America: The Challenge and the Response*. Beverly Hills, Ca.: Sage, 1978. Mexico City, Lima, Caracas, Rio de Janeiro.

Cowan, L. G. *Local Government in West Africa*. New York: Columbia University Press, 1958.

Daland, R. T., ed. *Comparative Urban Research*. Beverly Hills, Ca.: Sage, 1969. Methodology of comparison.

Dye, Thomas R., ed. *Comparative Research in Community Politics*. Proceedings of the Conference on Comparative Research in Community Politics. Athens, Georgia: University of Georgia, 1966. See especially the essay by O. Williams, "A Framework for Metropolitan Political Analysis," pp. 41-56.

European Conference of Local Authorities. *Yearbook*. Strasbourg, ECLA, 1964.

Gutkind, E. A. *The International History of City Development*. 8 vols. New York: Free Press, 1964-72.

Hall, P. *The World Cities*. 2nd ed. London: Weidenfeld, 1977.

Hambleton, Robert. *Policy Planning and Local Government*. London: Hutchinson, 1978. Compares New York, Boston, Stockport, U.K., Liverpool.

Hammond, B. E. *The Political Institutions of the Ancient Greeks*. London: Clay and Sons, 1895. Compares Greek city-states with European local government.

Harris, G. M. *Comparative Local Government*. London: Hutchinson, 1949.

Haus, Wolfgang, and Krebsbach, August, eds. *Local Government Laws in Europe*. Stuttgart: Kohlhammer, 1967.

Hauser, Phillip M., and Schnore, Leo F. *The Study of Urbanization*. New York: Wiley, 1965.

Heidenheimer, Arnold J., ed. *Political Corruption: Readings in Comparative Analysis*. New York: Holt, Rinehart & Winston, 1970. Local governments of Western Europe included in comparison.

Hicks, Ursula K. *Development from Below: Local Government and Finance in Developing Countries of the Commonwealth*. Oxford: Clarendon, 1961.

Horan, James F. *Experiments in Metropolitan Government*. New York: Praeger, 1978.

Humes, Samuel, and Martin, Eileen. *The Structure of Local Government: A Comparative Survey of 81 Countries*. The Hague: International Union of Local Authorities, 1969.

Hunter, G. *The New Societies of Tropical Africa*. London: Oxford University Press, 1962. Compares national and local structures.

International City Manager's Association. *The Municipal Yearbook*. Chicago: ICMA, annual. Statistical data on U. S. and Canadian cities.

International Union of Local Authorities. *Local Government in the 20th Century: Proceedings of the Jubilee Congress, Brussels, 1963*, and *The Development of Local Government in the Past Fifty Years* (35 national reports). The Hague: Nijhoff, 1963.

International Urban Research, *The World's Metropolitan Areas*. Berkeley: University of California Press, 1959.

Jacob, Philip E., ed. *Values and the Active Community*. New York: Free Press, 1971.

Kantor, Harry. *Patterns of Politics and Political Systems in Latin America*. Chicago: Rand McNally, 1969. Includes a brief description of the local government system in each Latin American state.

Lagroye, Jacques, and Wright, Vincent, eds. *Local Government in Britain and France* (London: Allen and Unwin, 1979).

Lapidus, Ira M., ed. *Middle Eastern Cities*. Berkeley: University of California Press, 1969.

Leemans, A. F. *Changing Patterns of Local Government*. The Hague: International Union of Local Authorities, 1970.

Mackenzie, W. J. M., ed. *The Government of Great Cities*. Manchester: University of Manchester Press, 1952. Pamphlet, 13 pp.

Maddick, Henry, *Democracy, Decentralization and Development*. London: Asia House, 1963.

Marshall, A. H., *Local Government in the Modern World*. London: Athlone Press, 1965.

Mumford, Lewis, *The City in History*. New York: Harcourt, 1961. Especially chapters 16-18.

Robson, W. A., and Regan, D. E., eds., *Great Cities of the World: Their Government, Politics and Planning*. 3rd ed. London: Allen and Unwin, 1972. Essays on twenty-seven cities in two volumes; comparative Introduction.

Rodwin, Lloyd. *Nations and Cities: A Comparison of Strategies for Urban Growth*. Don Mills, Ontario: Nelson, 1970. Compares Venezuela, Turkey, U.K., France, the United States.

Rowat, D. C., ed. *The Government of Federal Capitals*. Toronto: University of Toronto Press, 1972. Essays on seventeen capitals, with a comparative conclusion by the editor.

Royal Institute of Public Administration. *Development of Local Government in the Colonies*. London: RIPA, 1955. A Conference at Cambridge, 22 August-2 September 1955. See especially appendix on various countries—British Guiana, Java, Kenya, Uganda, and others.

Tarrow, Sidney. *Partisanship and Political Exchange in French and Italian Local Politics*. London: Sage, 1974. Mayors and party affiliation in France and Italy.

Tarrow, Sidney, and Katzenstein, Peter. *Territorial Politics in Industrial Nations*. New York: Praeger, 1978.

Tinker, Hugh. *The Foundations of Local Self-Government in India, Pakistan and Burma*. London: Athlone, 1954.

Toynbee, Arnold. *Cities on the Move*. Toronto: Oxford, 1970.

United Nations. Department of Economic and Social Affairs. *Planning of Metropolitan Areas and New Towns*. New York: United Nations, 1967.

———. Division of Public Administration. *Decentralization for National and Local Development*. New York: United Nations, 1962. Distinguishes four types of local government.

———. Economic and Social Council. *Report on Cities*. New York: United Nations, 1969.

Walsh, Annmarie H. *The Urban Challenge to Government: An International Comparison of 13 Cities*. New York: Praeger, 1969.

Warren, R. O. *Government in Metropolitan Regions: A Reappraisal of Fractionated Political Organization*. Davis: University of California Press, 1966.

Wraith, Ronald. *Local Administration in West Africa*. 2nd ed. London: Allen and Unwin, 1972.

———. *Local Government in West Africa*. London: Allen and Unwin, 1964. Nigeria, Ghana, and Sierra Leone.

Zink, Harold. *Rural Local Government in Sweden, Italy and India: A Comparative Study*. London: Stevens, 1957.

ARTICLES AND PAPERS

Adeniyi, E. O. "The Institutional Framework for Planning and Managing Urban Settlements in the Developing Countries of Africa." *Planning and Administration* 1 (1975): 71.

Ashford, Douglas E. "French Pragmatism and British Idealism: Financial Aspects of Local Reorganization." *Comparative Political Studies* 2 (July 1978): 231-54.

———. "Parties and Participation in British Local Government and Some American Parallels." *Urban Affairs Quarterly* 2 (September 1975): 58-81.

Banfield, E. C. "The Political Implications of Metropolitan Growth." *Daedalus* 90 (Winter 1960): 61-68. Metropolitan government in two contrasting systems, U.K. and United States.

Befu, H. "The Political Relations of the Village to the State." *World Politics* 19 (1967): 601-20. Examines primitive, classical, and modern villages.

Brierly, T. G. "The Evolution of Local Administration in French-Speaking West Africa." *Journal of Local Administration Overseas* 5, no. 1 (January 1966): 56-71.

Bruhns, Fred C., "Recent Regional Approaches to Local Government Reforms: A Comparison Between France and the United States." Paper prepared for the International Conference on the Current Trends in Local Power and Authority in the Contemporary World, Warsaw, September 1974.

Chapman, Brian. *The Profession of Government*. London: Allen and Unwin, 1959. Regional and local government in Europe, pp. 65-73.

Corry, J. A. *Elements of Democratic Government*. 4th ed. New York: Oxford University Press, 1964. Chapter on local government in United States, U.K., and France.

Dreyfus, Simone. "Capital Cities: A Jurist's View." *Local Government Throughout the World* 5 (December 1962): 59-61.

Fowler, Edmund P., and Lineberry, Robert. "The Comparative Analyis of Urban Policy: Canada and the United States." In *People and Politics in Urban Society*, edited by Harlan H. Hahn, pp. 345-68. Beverly Hills, Ca.: Sage, 1972.

Hsueh, S. S. "Local Government and National Development in Southeast Asia." *International Social Science Journal* 21 (January 1969): 45-55.

Ihrahim, Saad E. M. "Over-Urbanization and Under-Urbanization: The Case of the Arab World." *International Journal of Middle East Studies* (January 1975).

International Political Science Association. Research Committee on Comparative Local Politics. *Papers Given at World Congress*. Ottawa: I.P.S.A., 1970, 1973, 1976.

Jreisat, Jamil E. "Administrative Change of Local Authorities: Lessons from Four Arab Countries." *Journal of Comparative Administration* (August 1970): 163.

Keating, Gerald. "Local Government Finance Reform in the United Kingdom: Its Potential Impact on the United States." *Governmental Finance* (Fall 1978): 37-39.

Lambrechts, W. "Regionalization and Administration: Effects and Prospects." *International Review of Administrative Sciences* 34, no. 3 (1973): vi-viii. Summary of article in French on Belgium, France, Italy, the Netherlands, and developing countries.

Mawhood, P. "Negotiating from Weakness: The Search for a Model of Local Government in Countries of the Third World." *Planning and Administration* 5, no. 1 (1971): 17-32.

Meyer, Poul. *Administrative Organization*. London: Stevens, 1957. Chapter 16 compares local governments in Europe.

Miller, D. C. "Decision-Making Cliques in Community Power Structure: A Comparative Study of an American and an English City." *American Journal of Sociology* 64 (November 1958): 299-310.

Nolting, O. F. "Europe's Manager Plan." *National Civic Review* 48 (March 1959). In Finland, Germany, Norway, Sweden, and Ireland.

Rahman, A. T. R. "Theories of Administrative and Political Development and Rural Institutions in India and Pakistan." *Journal of Administration Overseas* 8 (October 1969): 243-56.

Robson, W. A. "Metropolitan Government: Problems and Solutions." *Canadian Public Administration* 9 (March 1966): 45-54.

Rokkan, Stein. "Cities, States, Nations: A Dimensional Model for the Study of Contrasts in Development." In *Building States and Nations*, edited by S.N. Eisenstadt and S. Rokkan. Beverly Hills, Ca.: Sage, 1973.

Rowat, D. C. "The Government of Federal Capitals." *Indian Administration and Management Review* 2, no. 3 (July-September 1970): 38-47.

―――. "The Problem of Governing Federal Capitals." *International Review of Administrative Sciences* 36, no. 4 (1970): 347-55.

―――. "The Role of Canada's Urban Municipalities in Governmental Decision-Making." *Studies in Comparative Local Government* 8, no. 1 (Summer 1974): 43-49.

Suski, Julian G. "Municipal Government in Europe and Canada: A Comparative Study." *Canadian Public Administration* (September 1965). Compares Canada with U.K., France, Netherlands, Denmark, and Switzerland.

Uppendahl, Herbert. "Check upon Administration in Germany and England—A Comparative View of the Ombudsman." *Local Government Studies* 4, no. 3 (July 1978). How individual rights are protected from local government administrative actions.

Index

About the Editor

DONALD C. ROWAT, professor of Political Science at Carleton University in Ottawa, Canada, has written or edited more than fifteen books and reports on local government and public administration. Fifty-one scholars from around the world joined Professor Rowat in contributing essays to the *Handbook*.